Contents

Table of Contents

Editor's Note

These are exciting times for rail travelers and it's an exciting time for me, too. Houghton Mifflin has entrusted me this year to carry on the work of *Eurail Guide* creators' Marvin and Barbara Saltzman. Big shoes to fill!

I've not had the pleasure of meeting the Saltzmans, but unbeknownst to them, they played a major role when it came to my travels, and later, my decision to become a travel writer and editor. Whether I was off to Europe, Canada, Mexico or roaming around the United States, the Saltzman's guide was always nearby, and I could always rely on their personal tips for off-the-beaten-track rail rides, fascinating museums and travel advice that you'd never find in a general-subject guidebook.

My initiation into the world of trains began in 1970, when a high school chum persuaded me to join her and her cousin on a wild train ride to Mexico City from the dusty California border town of Mexicali. I haven't stopped riding the rails since. In 1993, I signed on as editor of *The International Railway Traveler*, the newsletter of the Society of International Railway Travelers, and have spread the word about the joys of rail travel to whomever will listen. I feel very fortunate that I can bring the magic of rail travel to the Saltzman's loyal followers and, hopefully, to new generations of rail-travel enthusiasts.

The Saltzman's concept of keeping things simple is a good one, so you won't see sweeping changes to the guide. What we *have* done is add some items to help put you on track to your rail adventure a little faster. At the beginning of each chapter or country, we've added a section with information about each country, from tourist office phone numbers, E-mail addresses and Web sites, to currency information. Another area gives an overview of the country's railway. We've expanded the section for disabled travelers, too, providing additional resources and tips. Look for more information about transportation systems in major cities to help you find your way around town, after you arrive. And for Internet surfers, there's a list of cool—and sometimes hard-to-find—Web sites just for rail enthusiasts. There's all this and much more in the 1998 edition of the guide.

We're always interested in hearing from you, with your latest "finds," whether it's a fantastic train ride or a bargain of a hotel near a train station. If we can verify the information, we'll put it in next year's edition, along with your name. If there's anything we can do to improve the guide, please don't hesitate to send your comments and suggestions. You can write to me at P.O. Box 3747, San Diego, CA 92163, or send E-mail to irt.trs@worldnet.att.net. I'd be delighted to hear from you.

Gena Holle,
Editor

Acknowledgments

Since that first slim edition of *The Eurail Guide* appeared in 1971, train travel the world over has continually improved and flourished. So has *The Eurail Guide*. For this, the third edition, devoted solely to train travel in European destinations, there are many to thank.

This book could not have been made possible were it not for its parents, Marvin and Barbara Saltzman. They conceived of the idea and their creativity and love for the project will remain in its pages for many editions to come.

We are also grateful to the many railways, tourist commissions and travel agencies for providing us information, including extraordinary assistance from Steve Forsyth, Forsyth Travel Library; Rail Europe's Cece Drummond, Andy Lazarus, Chris Lazarus and Rose Morgan of A.J. Lazarus Associates, Rail Europe's marketing representatives; Pat Titley of BritRail Travel International; Lynne Bobak and S. Chloe Winiesdorffer of DER Travel Services; Mary Anne Reynolds at Amtrak; and Owen Hardy, President of the Society of International Rail Travelers.

Many thanks are also in order to Georgia Govern, Ann Flaherty, Karla Von Huben and Beverly Horton, who spent countless hours gathering information, verifying phone numbers and addresses and updating schedules. Much appreciation to Steve Sebree, Moonlight Graphic Works, for the fantastic new maps, and to computer guru Dharmaja Acterman, of Aspiration Computer Training, who helped this diehard PC user move into the world of Macintosh without too much trauma. And finally (but hardly last!) thanks to my husband, V.J. Cucchiara, for helping keep this "train on the track," with your extraordinary patience and encouragement.

The other important members of *The Eurail Guide* family are the scores of readers who have written us over the years telling of their train travel experiences. Comments about your train journeys are always welcome and appreciated.

Gena Holle,
Editor

Eurail and Train Travel Guide to Europe

Using the Eurail and Train Travel Guide

For those of you new to the guide, welcome to the 3rd edition! And to old friends, welcome back! You'll be pleased to see that like all good train systems, we continue to modernize, update and expand. Notice our new title, *Eurail and Train Travel Guide to Europe*. The name change recognizes all the Eurailpass countries as well as those that don't accept the passes.

The *Eurail and Train Travel Guide to Europe* is the most complete train guide on the market. And right up to press time, our rail experts are revising and updating so you will have the latest information to plan your trip. We've made every effort to provide prices for 1998, but sometimes those prices arrive too late for our publishing deadline. As always, the guide has been carefully designed to help train-travelers plan and budget their rail travels, move swiftly from city to city and capture both the pleasures and efficiency of rail travel in Europe. Keep in mind the following key features. They'll help you get the most out of the *Eurail and Train Travel Guide to Europe*.

• Check and double-check departure and arrival times The *Eurail and Train Travel Guide* offers you hundreds of precise timetables and schedules—in fact, the most complete, compact selection of schedules available to individuals. Train schedules have been selected to serve as model itineraries. Although all times listed here are accurate, according to the published *Thomas Cook* schedules (the number appearing at the front of each schedule refers to the *Thomas Cook Timetable* number), precise times in all countries are subject to change and modification without notice. Additionally, new trains and supplementary and seasonal trains are added and deleted all the time. This is normal and standard. In fact, train schedules undergo minor changes in Europe every three months. Always check and double-check the departure and arrival times listed here and in all timetables. Most likely, changes will be slight and have little or no effect on the excursions described in this guide. However, a few minutes here and there might make the difference between a swift connection and a wasted afternoon.

• Prices Although the prices for train tickets and passes listed here were verified and accurate at printing, don't take them for gospel. All prices are subject to change. Expect increases of two percent to five percent in a given year. And, certain trains require supplementary fares; these, too, are subject to change.   Note: Prices in this book are in U.S. dollars and other European currencies based on October 1997 exchange rates. To calculate prices in other currencies, consult current exchange rates. Note that the rate listed in the daily newspaper is the rate between banks. The rate you will get is usually at least five percent lower.

• **The 24-hour clock** International train schedules are almost always quoted according to the 24-hour clock, and thus the *Eurail and Train Travel Guide* maintains this practice. You might not be used to seeing 6 P.M. written as 18:00 or midnight as 24:00. Between midnight and 1:00 A.M. time is depicted as 00:01 to 00:59. This might seem like the military, but it's standard fare around the world and good to get used to.

• **Travel days and dates** Unless designated otherwise, all schedules shown in this guide indicate daily departures. Likewise, schedules featured here are based on the prime travel season of late May to late September. That is when most guide users plan to travel. It's true that schedules tend to change slightly during the off-season and thus, as with the timetables, checking and rechecking schedules is highly recommended.

   A note on certain schedules: British timetables differ from the Continental pattern. Summer timetables for British rail service begin on the first Monday of May. Changes occur on various dates, first in October and then again in January. Unless designated otherwise, the departure and arrival times given in this book are for the summer tourist season and apply to trips that will be made from late May to late September. In most cases these schedules change only slightly during September-May.

   In most European countries, a summer timetable goes into effect on the last Sunday of May or the first Sunday of June, and remains in effect until and including the last Saturday in September. Winter schedules usually start on the Sunday following the last Saturday of September and run until and including the Saturday preceding the last Sunday of May of the following year.

• **Frequency** Highly traveled routes and lines between major cities are served by frequent train service. It is therefore not necessary in these cases to list all times of all trains. Train options from Paris to Lyon or London to Manchester are just too numerous to list. When the word "frequent" is noted, you can count on a minimum of one train every hour in the period indicated.

• **Order of excursions listed** In the guide you will find numerous suggestions of preselected round-trip excursions or circle trips originating from key locations or base cities. The order these round-trip excursions are listed is as follows:

(1) One-day excursions from a base city to an interesting destination, including practical travel information and information on what to see and do there. The schedules for one-day, round-trip excursions, however, do not always reflect all the departure times from either the base city or the destination city. Only those departure times involved in making a one-day round trip are shown. On particular routes, there are frequently later departure times from the base city and earlier departure times from the destination city than those shown, although these clearly would not be applicable to the one-day, round-trip excursions.

(2) Scenic train rides, many of which can be made as a one-day round trip or circle-trip.

(3) International rail service (trips to adjoining countries).

• **Stations** It is important to remember that many cities have more than one train station. In such cases, the name of the applicable train station is indicated (in parentheses) after the name of the city. In Austria, Germany, and Switzerland, train stations often do not have names, in which case the station is always indicated by the generic "Hauptbahnhof."

• **Before Leaving** Before traveling, find out if the countries you plan to visit offer low-price train passes. And when those countries do provide train passes, make sure to inquire before leaving home if the passes must be purchased in your country of origin or in the country you will be visiting. There's nothing worse than a great deal you can't cash in on.

• **Reader Response** Information concerning international travel is constantly changing. The editors of the *Eurail and Train Travel Guide to Europe* wholeheartedly welcome correspondence from readers who have suggestions, tips, and pertinent information that can be verified and incorporated into the next annually revised edition. Thank you in advance for helping fellow rail travelers. Address all your letters to: Houghton Mifflin, *Eurail and Train Travel Guide to Europe,* c/o Marnie Cochran, 222 Berkeley Street, Boston, MA 02116

CHAPTER 1

Appreciating the Pleasures of Train Travel

Why Take the Train?

Since that first slim edition (96 pages) of the *Eurail Guide* appeared in 1971, train travel, especially in Europe, has continually improved and flourished. The 36 Trans-Europ Express trains that were in service in 1980 have since been replaced by a fleet of faster and more frequent EuroCity trains. Some 350 of those futuristic high-profile ultra-speed TGV trains (train à grande vitesse) now grace many European tracks and soon they will be joined by new double-deck TGVs. It's no wonder TGVs are considered ultra-fast. Their average operating speed ranges between 186 mph and 220 mph, although on a test run in 1990, a TGV won a world speed record when the speedometer hit 320.2 mph.

This is an exciting time for train travel. Europe continues to add new services like the Paris-Brussels-Amsterdam TGV, dubbed *Thalys*. Another newcomer, *Artesia,* is a TGV-Pendolino combination of daylight runs operating between France and Italy. Look for more inter-European TGV lines to debut soon. Schedule-cutting *Euromed* trains were introduced on Spain's Barcelona-Valencia-Alicante corridor, and Italy's own *Eurostar Italia* and new deluxe hotel trains whooshed their way on to the rail scene this last year.

Trains are really giving the airlines a run for their money these days, too, especially in Europe. The Channel Tunnel, linking France with Britain, is a good example. It's had its share of financial setbacks, and then there was the devastating tunnel fire in 1996, involving a car-carrying Le Shuttle train. Still, travelers continue to flock to Eurostar, the passenger rail service offering convenient downtown-to-downtown London-Paris and London-Brussels schedules through the Channel Tunnel. In three hours you can be in Paris, while the London-Brussels trip clocks in at three hours fifteen minutes. By train and ferry, these trips used to take seven hours and five hours, respectively. For flyers, add in the time getting to and from airports, which are usually way out in the suburbs, and Eurostar wins, hands down. And that doesn't even take into consideration how comfortable the train is, with its roomy seats and ample leg room. Eurostar's 18-car trains can carry up to 794 passengers, the equivalent of two jumbo jets, but they hardly feel like a cramped, noisy airplane cabin. First-class passengers can sit back and enjoy a gourmet meal at their comfy, wide seats. And standard class seats on Eurostar are a delight; no elbow-in-the-side-of-your-seatmate action here. On the train, you can mosey on down to one of the two bar cars for some socializing. Or, if you have kids, escort them to the special play area—try to find one of those on a plane!

Since November 1994, when Eurostar began operating its spiffy cream and yellow trains at speeds of up to 186 mph, airlines have found these routes are no longer the cash cows of pre-Eurostar days. Some carriers have experienced declines in revenue of over 20 percent in the London-Paris market alone. As a result, the airlines have had to rethink their position on budget fares. Airfares within Europe have always been outlandishly expensive. Now low-fare airlines are starting to crop up around Europe, and some airlines are even seeking arrangements with railways for air-rail deals, which will only serve to benefit travelers. A perfect example of the "if you can't beat 'em, join 'em" attitude, is the Virgin Group, headed up by Virgin Atlantic Airways maven, Richard Branson. His company owns a percentage of London and Continental Railways Ltd., which in April 1996, began operating Eurostars in Britain under the banner Eurostar (UK). And Branson's Virgin Group is also busy buying up rail franchises that went on the auction block because of British Rail's breakup.

Train travel in the 1990s is a long way from the clunky way backpackers roughed it in the late sixties and early seventies (for those who relish roughing it a little, though, there are still plenty of opportunities in countries that haven't quite reached Europe's high train travel standards).

For more than a quarter of a century the editors of the *Eurail Guide* have claimed that the most economical, safest, most convenient, interesting, and pleasant way to travel and really see the world is by train. Although it's doubtful you need convincing, consider the following:

• When traveling by train, departures are rarely delayed by weather, as often happens with air or automobile travel.

• When traveling by train, departures and arrivals are in the center of cities, not in far-off suburbs, saving travelers lots of time, effort and expense. In fact, in Europe and Japan, many high-speed trains actually get you from a hotel in one city to a hotel in another city faster than by airplane when the distance is 250-350 miles.

• The cost of the least expensive, non-air-conditioned, standard transmission compact car in Europe, traveling 350 miles per day, can easily come to more than $100 per day, once you add rental fees, gas and tolls.

Picking up a car at the airport will add more to the rental bill because of airport surcharges. While the surcharges are reasonable at many airports, airports in Austria, Belgium, Italy, Luxembourg, Switzerland and the UK charge from 10 percent to 13 percent of the rental rate. Other countries charge flat fees, from $10 in France to a whopping $25 the Netherlands.

Car rental rates listed below were based on quotations from U.S.-based car rental companies. Rates quoted are for the summer of 1997 (the rental companies wouldn't predict 1998 prices) and show ranges for subcompact and automatic models rented for one week, picked up and dropped off in the same country, with unlimited kilometers and usually no air conditioning. In many countries subcompact cars are economy models like Ford Escorts or Fiestas and VW Golfs. Collision-damage-waiver (CDW) insurance is not included in these rates; it can range from a few dollars a day to $20 or more in some countries.

Austria: Subcompact $168-$233, automatic $246-$460, including 21.2-percent tax
Britain: Subcompact $113-$236, automatic $182-$329, including 17.5-percent tax
Denmark: Subcompact $236-$415, automatic $476-$1,193, including 25-percent tax
Finland: Subcompact $388-$575, automatic $499-$1,756, including 22-percent tax
France: Subcompact $186-$215, automatic $264-$572, including 20.6-percent tax
Germany: Subcompact $97-$160, automatic $190-$285, including 15-percent tax
Ireland: Subcompact $173-$340, automatic $218-$$742, including 12.5-percent tax
Israel: Subcompact $119-$427, automatic $298-$553 (no tax)
Italy: Subcompact $214-$350, automatic $401-$800 including 19-percent tax
Norway: Subcompact $273-$357, automatic $533-$777, including 23-percent tax
Poland: Subcompact $244-$491, automatic $941-$1,049, including 22-percent tax
Sweden: Subcompact $254-$455, automatic $545-$736, including 25-percent tax
Turkey: Subcompact $266-$467, including 15-percent tax; automatics weren't available, but mid-sized standard models ranged from $378-$634

Gas prices, regular unleaded, per gallon (based on car rental agency figures and *Travel Weekly* data)

Austria: $3.80	Netherlands: $4.39
Britain: $3.50	Norway: $4.54
Belgium: $4:20	Italy: $4.39
Finland: $4	Ireland: $4.24
France: $4.22	Spain: $3.50
Germany: $3.86	Sweden: $4.31

Hotels in major cities rarely include parking in their rates; expect to pay between $10-$20 per day. And, if you're driving the toll roads of Austria, France, Greece, Italy, the Netherlands, Norway, Portugal or Spain, add another $5-$25 per day in tolls to your budget. Some superhighways have extra fees. Say you're renting a car in France, but want to drive it into Switzerland. Be prepared to fork over a $27 fee for a sticker to use the Swiss superhighway. Get caught without the sticker and you'll face a hefty fine, unless you ask the rental company in France to give you a sticker, which they may or may not agree to do.

In 1997, gas prices and car rental prices were slightly lower than in 1996 and rail fares rose slightly. Here are a couple of driving versus rail comparisons: For two people traveling together and renting a car in France for a week, each would pay $179, including operating expenses. Buying second-class rail tickets for a week's worth of rail travel totaled $190 per person. Two people renting a car in Italy for 14 days would dish out $489 a piece, including operating expenses, while the per-person price of a 15-day Eurail Saverpass, requiring two or more people traveling together, would be just $228.

Then, of course, there's the fatigue of driving, the exasperation of congested traffic, insane holiday patterns in many European countries, and the increasing nuisance and health risk of intense diesel fumes on major European roadways.

Now consider the train.

One can travel on high-speed, air-conditioned trains with any of nearly 200 bargain European train passes, for $14-35 per day. For example, a first class Eurailpass for 15 consecutive days is about $36 per day, while a Eurail Saverpass for 15 consecutive days, and requiring at least two and up to five people traveling together, comes out to $30.50 per day. And if you'll be away a while and plan marathon train-riding, a three-month unlimited-travel first-class Eurailpass checks-in at $17 per day. Some individual country passes are real deals, like the Hungarian Flexipass allowing 10 days of travel in one month for $80; that's only $8 per day. The passes all represent fantastic bargains in comparison to car rental or air travel, as do also the many European national and regional train passes listed throughout chapters 6 and 7.

By train, you reach thousands of interesting destinations that aren't accessible by air. Let's not talk about the worries, frustrations, and delays of socked-in airports, lengthy check-in requirements and baggage waits. Or, if driving, unexpected flat tires, the trauma of unfamiliar and congested arteries of foreign cities, strange traffic laws. Or of the many other problems, expenses, and inconveniences connected with airplane and auto travel. Let's focus on trains.

Whether in London or Berlin, you will find food, information on local tours, assistance in obtaining lodging, money exchange, waiting rooms where you can relax, shoe repair kiosks and more, at the principal rail stations. There is also the local flavor.

If you plan your itineraries well, you will see an array of visual delights that airplane passengers never see: indescribable seashores, vineyards tinted with afternoon sunlight, castles that have been straddling hilltops for centuries, raging rivers, breathtaking waterfalls, Alpine summits, remote villages founded before Christ, fjords, forests, lovely orchards and pastures—a feast of colorful scenes to enjoy long after the trip ends. You can take pictures or shoot video footage without having to pull over or take your eye from the road. You can meet strangers native to the country you're in or passengers also on their way somewhere new to you. You're free to read, to write, to drink, to flirt (this depends on your situation), to sleep, to daydream, to take a walk.

On a train you experience the sublime sensation of freedom, never losing your connection to the landscape around you, yet are detached from the trappings of daily life outside. You're a spectator and a participant all at once, and even at high speeds you come to understand another country through its changing terrain, land formations and distances between places. Traveling by train can elevate the act of travel from a banal transportation experience to a poetic event—all without sacrificing practicality!

As you approach your destination, you can feel the charge of excitement as people around you prepare their belongings and the train begins to brake. The new cityscape comes into focus and you feel energized, maybe even rested and refreshed. Perhaps you've even had time to shave or put on your makeup. A cup of local espresso or a glass of beer may await you at the end of the platform.

You say good-bye, maybe exchange addresses with those Amsterdam businessmen, students from Oslo or that Greek army officer, Croatian geologist, Uruguayan cardiologist, North Dakota farmer and his Chinese-Canadian wife, Emily, who gave you a bunch of Italian grapes, the family from Brazil with the twins, a Russian woman living in Frankfurt, the professor of French from Boston who knows your dentist. You get the picture. Your sense of the world and its people has grown overnight and you're glad to be alive. Welcome to train travel!

If you simply must get your hands on a steering wheel while traveling, ask your travel agent or any of the rail pass suppliers listed in the guide about rail passes that combine a few days of driving with a few days of railing.

CHAPTER 2

Rail Pass Nuts and Bolts

Since 1959, that famous train travel bargain called the Eurailpass has been offered by Western European rail companies throughout the world, revolutionizing the scope of low-budget travel. Eurailpasses made their mark during the sixties and seventies when Europe's trains instantly became accessible to young North American backpackers; 39 years later the Eurailpass is still going strong.

Today, there are over 20 variations of the Eurailpass and nearly 180 different multinational, national and regional rail pass options to wade through. In this chapter we'll discuss passes in general and the different Eurailpasses and spinoffs like Europasses and Saverpasses.

Sorting Out Rail Pass and Ticketing Options

Decisions. Decisions. With all the passes on the market—it seems new one's appear on the scene almost every day—you're probably wondering how you'll ever make sense of them all. You're probably asking: should I buy an unlimited pass good for travel on any day within a particular validity period or one that's valid for a handful of days within a certain period of time? A rail/drive pass? A rail/air pass? Or, should I buy individual tickets instead of a rail pass? It's a lot to absorb, but the information in this chapter will guide you through the rail pass maze and enable you to decide which pass, if any, will best meet your needs.

Start by asking yourself some questions. How much time do you want to spend riding the rails? Do you plan to cover a lot of miles by train? Will you take daily train trips from a base city to explore the region? Or will you use the train to get from point-A-to-point-B, then stick close to a base city and maybe explore by public transit or car?

If you decide to do lots of riding or take daily rail excursions, consider buying an unlimited pass. An unlimited pass offers flexibility. You don't have to spend your trip counting rail days or worrying that you'll come up short at the end of your pass validity period if you decide to ride an extra train or two. Often spur-of-the-moment rides turn out to be the best, like when the locals tell you to hop this train or that to the next city for a must-see flea market or an absolutely divine restaurant serving up heavenly dishes prepared under the watchful eye of the family matriarch. With an unlimited pass, you won't be frittering away precious vacation time waiting in line to buy tickets. Now that many major European stations have installed automated ticketing centers, you can get your own seat reservations on the spot, if you have a credit card. And, yes, most machines do have instructions in English!

If you won't be doing much exploring by train, a more flexible pass with less travel days, say, any ten rail days within a two-month validity period, might be the way to go. Another option for travelers with limited time are rail/drive and rail/air passes.

Other passes offer deals to two or more people traveling together, or to groups, seniors, and students. Sometimes you can pick up a good deal on a pass for travel during the off-season. And if you've got access to the World Wide Web, look for sales there. Web addresses are included in this book, where applicable.

To figure out which is best for you, a pass or separate tickets, pull out the trusty atlas and map out a rough draft of your itinerary. Calculate about how many miles you think you'll travel per day, and how many days you plan to take train trips. Say you and a friend plan to travel together to visit five major cities in France, Italy and Switzerland. You'll probably cover about 1,100 train miles. The cheapest pass for that trip would be a five-day/two-month Europass companion pass for $261 per person, first class. To break even, you'd have to travel 694 miles, so here the pass is the better buy. If your mileage estimates come within around 90 percent of the break-even mileage for a particular pass, then it's probably worth buying. If it's less than 90 percent, you might be better off with individual tickets. Remember, though, that passes often have extras and discounts associated with them that you won't find with individual tickets.

On the other hand, if you're headed to Spain for two weeks and plan to take no more than five day trips from Madrid to destinations like Toledo or Avila, or about 750 miles total, then you'd be better off with point-to-point tickets. To break even with a five-day Spanish Flexipass, priced at $260 per person, you'd have to travel 1,666 miles.

Europe's Multinational, National and Regional Passes

• **Multinational Passes** Eurailpass, Europass, Benelux, Scanrail, European East Pass, and Balkan Flexipass are multinational rail passes because with them, you can travel in more than one country.

The Eurailpass and Saverpass, offering unlimited travel on any or all days for the duration of the pass, entitle riders to train travel in the following 17 countries: Austria, Belgium, Denmark, Finland, France, Germany, Greece, Holland, Hungary, Republic of Ireland, Italy, Luxembourg, Norway, Portugal, Spain, Sweden, and Switzerland. In addition, Eurailpasses are honored on those trains running to and from the airports of the following cities: Amsterdam, Barcelona, Bilbao, Dusseldorf, Geneva, Frankfurt, Malaga, Paris, Pisa, Vienna, and Zurich. Passholders also receive reduced fares on many bus and boat lines in Eurailpass countries. Adult Eurailpasses are sold only for first-class travel, and youth Eurailpasses are only for second class. The Eurail Flexipass and Eurail Saver Flexipass (two or more traveling together) is also valid in the above 17 countries. A rail/drive option is available, as well.

The Europass, a Eurailpass spinoff, is also a multinational pass. It offers travel in France, Germany, Italy, Spain and Switzerland, with optional zones, Austria/Hungary, Benelux, Greece and Portugal. You can purchase travel for any five days within a two-month period in one zone or up to four zones; extra travel days are available for purchase.

Variations of the Europass include a rail/drive option, a companion-pass, where two people travel together and a youth pass. Europass is a good choice for travelers who want to focus on a particular region, say, Germany, Austria and Switzerland or Austria and Hungary, but don't plan to do a whole lot of riding.

Also under the multinational banner is the Benelux Tourail Pass, covering travel in Belgium, Netherlands and Luxembourg and the Scanrail Pass, taking in Denmark, Finland, Norway and Sweden. The European East Pass opens the door to the Czech Republic, Hungary, Poland and Slovakia. Explore Bulgaria, Greece, Macedonia, Montenegro, Romania, Serbia and Turkey, with a newcomer, the Balkan Flexipass. Passes like these are often better buys over the Eurailpass because travel is centered on a limited area.

• **National Passes** National rail passes good for travel within one country are often cheaper then multinational passes, especially if you're willing to travel second class. If you plan to concentrate on just one country, this type of pass will probably save you some money over a regular or flexible Eurailpass. There are some pros and cons to these passes. Eurailpasses offer lots of extras and bonuses, but national passes are limited. There are exceptions, though, like the Swiss Pass. It offers something Eurailpass doesn't: free or discounted travel on private railways like the *Glacier Express, William Tell Express* and *Bernina Express.* Before signing up, always ask the reservation agent or retailer about what bonuses or extras are associated with a pass.

Passes that fall into this category are the Austrian Railpass, the various British passes such as BritRail Pass, BritRail + Eurostar, Freedom of Scotland Travelpass, Bulgarian Flexipass, Czech Flexipass, Finnrail Pass, France Railpass, German Railpass, Greek Flexipass, Hungarian Flexipass, Irish Explorer, Ireland's Emerald Card and Irish Rover, Italian Railcard, Holland Railpass, Norway Railpass, Polrail Pass, Portuguese Railpass, Romanian Pass, Spain Flexipass, Sweden Railpass and Swiss Pass. These passes offer a variety of options, from rail/drive combinations to senior, youth and companion fares.

• **Regional Passes** This type of pass usually covers a specific area within a country or a round trip from a country's border crossing or international airport to one destination inside the country. This pass is handy when your main pass isn't valid in the country issuing the border pass; use your primary pass to get to the border, then the regional pass from the border into the other country.

Some examples of regional passes include the BritRail Southeast Pass for unlimited travel in southeast England, Prague Excursion Pass, covering travel from any Czech border crossing to Prague and return and the Copenhagen Sightseeing Pass. The Copenhagen pass is valid only for Europass or German Railpass holders; it's good for travel from any German or Danish border crossing to Copenhagen and return.

Eurailpass and BritRail Rules and Pointers

Over 100,000 miles of European train travel is available to those in possession of a pass. Rest assured that despite the main options open to train-travelers over the age of twenty-six–first—class tickets, Eurailpasses, BritRail passes, national/regional passes, and second-class tickets—train travel with one or more of the Eurailpasses or BritRail passes, is the most economical and interesting way of experiencing international travel. But there are lots of distinctions, nuances, and tips you need to know to maximize the impact and enjoyment of your journey.

• **Refunds** Since rail passes are neither refundable nor replaceable, consider purchasing one of the following plans offered by suppliers that will cover lost or stolen passes.

Rail Europe's Pass Protection Plan is applicable for all rail passes issued through Rail Europe including all Eurail Passes, Eurail Drive, Europasses, Europass Drive and all national and regional Rail and Rail'N Drive passes.

The Plan will compensate you for the unused portion of your lost or stolen rail pass and is available for US $10 (CAN $12) per person/pass.

To qualify for reimbursement, just purchase a replacement rail pass or rail ticket and complete your rail travel. You must also file a police report. A flyer that explains the program is included with each pass purchase.

Reimbursement is based on the unused value of the pass. The Plan does not cover Eurostar, Thalys or point-to-point tickets, reservations, couchettes or sleepers.

DER Travel Services' Lost Rail Pass Refund Program is a similar plan that will refund 100 percent of the unused portion of a pass or rail pass/drive program if a loss or theft occurs while traveling in Europe, if the pass was purchased through DER Travel. DER's plan costs $10 per pass and it must be purchased the same time as the pass. If a loss or theft occurs, you are required to file a police report within 24 hours, then, within 30 days of returning home, send a notarized written report with the official police report and replacement ticket receipts to DER Travel Services.

For travelers to Britain, BritRail Travel offers a program call Pass Protection that will refund 100 percent of the unused portion of a lost or stolen pass Classic or Flexipasses. In 1997, BritRail charged $10 per pass for the coverage. The protection must be purchased within 14 days after the pass was issued or the day prior to departure for Europe. The loss or theft must be reported to the police within 24 hours of the incident, and upon return home, within 30 days a notarized written report and police report must be submitted to BritRail to obtain the refund.

• **Validity** All Eurailpasses become valid on the first day they are used, after first having been recorded at the ticket office of the station from where the first journey began. You must start to use your Eurailpass within six months after the date of purchase. Thus, a purchase on February 1 requires a first use before August 1. Longer delays invalidate the pass. It's a good idea to protect yourself from having your pass rendered partially or wholly invalid because the validity dates were entered incorrectly. The Eurailpass must be validated at the station ticket office. Do this before you ever set a foot aboard a train, or risk paying a fine. Allow enough time to wait in line, and make sure you have your passport with you or the pass can't be validated. Once you're at the window, the clerk writes on the pass both the first and last day it can be used. Before he does this, though, write a note with what you believe are the validity dates, show it to him, and ask him if he agrees with those dates. Only when he says your dates are correct, or explains why they are not, should you hand over the pass and let him enter the dates. Once the clerk has written validity dates on the face of your Eurailpass, those dates cannot be changed, because any alteration of the dates invalidates the pass. Whatever you do, don't attempt to validate the pass yourself. You're only flirting with trouble here. If your handiwork is discovered, the pass will be voided and confiscated, and you could end up paying a fine to the railway.

Flexible pass holders have an additional procedure to follow, besides that for validating their pass. Before you use your pass for the day, don't forget to write in the date in ink in the appropriate box on the pass. A word of caution. It's not a good idea to wait until you get on the train to fill in the date information. If the conductor comes along and catches you at this, he could confiscate your pass and levy a fine for not having a ticket.

For flexible-type passes, a rail travel day is considered from midnight to midnight. For example, if travel starts after 7 P.M. (19:00), you'd write in the next day's date in the box.

Since proof-of-purchase stubs are a thing of the past, it's a good idea to make two photocopies of your pass. Take one with you and leave one at home.

• **Savings** The standard Eurailpass and BritRail Pass offer users unlimited travel, meaning precisely that: You can literally travel 24 hours a day for the entire period of validity. Countless travelers have used three and four times the price of their pass in train travel, saving hundreds of dollars from what their itinerary would have cost had they used ordinary tickets. The bargain does not end there. Tickets for the high-speed (EC), Inter-City (IC), Thalys and super-speed "TGV" trains cost more than an ordinary slower train on the same route, with supplementary charges ranging from around $5 to over $18, thus boosting the cost of regular tickets by as much as 25 percent. Happily, Eurailpasses include unlimited use of EC, IC and TGV trains without having to pay anything extra, except, maybe, a small fee for a seat reservation, which is required on certain trains, like TGVs.

When you compare the price of a pass to point-to-point tickets, often point-to-point tickets may appear, on the surface, less expensive. But consider this, the unlimited travel Eurailpass is more than simply a ticket to ride the train. Passholders get all kinds of bonuses like free passage on selected ships and ferries, buses and tourist railways. An unlimited travel pass also gives you the freedom to pick up and go at the drop of a hat. Don't like the city you'd planned to spend a few days in? Hop the next train out of town. You don't have to hoard travel days, or pass-up that "you must go" day-tripper recommended by a local.

On the other hand, not all Eurailpasses or BritRail passes are wholly economical. Some European itineraries are less expensive when you purchase regular train tickets or one or a combination of national and regional rail passes, described elsewhere in this guide (see France Railpass, German Flexipass, Benelux Tourrail, etc.). The only way to find out if a Eurailpass or one of the numerous other passes will save you money is to compare their price with the total prices of tickets for particular itineraries.

Savings Tip: Buy your pass at the end of December to hedge against any price increases in the new year. The only catch is that rule that you have to use the pass within six months of purchase. This is an excellent plan, though, for off-season spring travel, or, if you buy a three-month pass, it'll take you through the summer months, at last year's prices.

• **Classes** Most train systems have first and second-class cars. If you have hesitations about second-class space in Europe, don't. Seats are completely acceptable, especially on trains in Austria, Belgium, Denmark, Finland, France, Germany, Holland, the Irish Republic, Luxembourg, Norway, Sweden, and Switzerland.

Although first-class is more comfortable and less crowded, it is of course more expensive. If you are considering traveling in the often crowded second-class, compute second-class fares at two-thirds of the first-class fares shown. This will give you the approximate price of a second-class ticket. While second-class is usually more crowded than first-class, often the disadvantage of having to stand because all the seats are occupied can be simply overcome by arriving early at the rail station. In Europe, first-class cars (and the first-class portion of mixed-class cars) are often marked by a yellow line running above the windows on the outside of the train. Note: Although second-class tickets cost 66 percent of first-class tickets, the cost of a typical second-class itinerary is often more expensive than when traveling first-class with a Eurailpass!

• **Reservations** Many EC, IC, and TGV trains require reservations, as well as payment of a supplement. Often the price of the reservation is included in the supplement and the cost of the supplement is covered by the pass. However, Eurailpass travelers must still pay the small fee of usually $3-$8 for each seat reservation. Reservations can usually be made up to two months in advance. Other trains that require reservations include the Italian Pendolino, Eurostar Italia and all long-distance trains in Spain.

• **Time savings** Eurailpasses and BritRail Passes add precious time to a travel schedule, in that travelers in possession of most passes no longer need to stand in a ticket-selling line. Delays in line of up to 30 minutes are not uncommon. And don't forget, if you buy an individual ticket in some countries, like France, Italy and Netherlands, you must validate the ticket in a machine on the platform before boarding the train. In some Eastern European countries, foreign nationals can't even buy a rail ticket for international travel at the railway station. Instead they must go to the local tourist office, where long waits in long lines is the norm. Frequently, foreign nationals are asked to pay for tickets using Western currency. These little tasks are time-wasters that can be eliminated when you purchase a rail pass.

With or without a pass, if reserved seats are required or desired, it is necessary to allocate time for the separate seat reservation line when you have not made reservations before starting your trip. For more information about reservations see Chapter 3.

• **Itineraries** With the 100,000-plus available miles of track on the Continent and Britain, you've got a wellspring of rail-riding choices. In the guide, we've listed nearly 1,000 train trips in Britain and throughout the 17 Eurailpass countries, for passholders. Because of the many rail travel options available in Britain and on the Continent, there's a special section called the Route Chart, to help you plan your trip. You'll find it in Appendix A. The first step in using the Route Chart is to list your itinerary destinations. If you're thinking about buying a Eurail pass, it is advisable to schedule any part of your trip that is not in the 17 Eurailpass countries (such as England, Yugoslavia, etc.) either before or after the days you are touring the countries in which your Eurailpass is valid. The same advice applies if you're thinking about buying a BritRail Pass. This way, you'll avoid consuming Eurailpass or BritRail Pass days and thus can buy the shortest and least expensive pass necessary. Next, consult the Route Chart and note the first-class fare for each leg of your trip that can be covered by Eurailpass or BritRail Pass.

Route Chart

Thanks to the unique and essential Route Chart, found in Appendix A, scheduling your train travel, matching your trips with validity periods of the available train passes, computing all ticket prices, and, perhaps most importantly, determining the most advantageous Eurailpass, BritRail Pass, national pass, or series of ordinary tickets to purchase has been made easy and accurate. The Route Chart is accurate enough to help you decide whether you want to make a particular trip in one day or break it up into two, or more, shorter trips. With the Route Chart you can quickly discover the least expensive way to complete your itinerary, and, if using one of the passes, how to coordinate timetables. Essentially you become your own, personalized travel agent!

How to Use the Route Chart

The travel time figures noted between two cities represent the longest or shortest possible time for each trip. Night trains often show longer running times than day trains. Many night-trains in Europe deliberately slow down or stop mid-journey, so as not to arrive at major cities at an impractical, early time. Additionally there may be two or more trains running during the day, one of which is a fast express that makes the trip in less time than what is indicated on the Route

Chart. So, take into consideration that the guide deliberately errs only on the long side. Despite this, the time shown in the Route Chart, as a rule, is rarely more than 10 percent greater than the fastest time between two cities.

Eurailpass, BritRail Pass and Miscellaneous European Pass Prices

Because Britain is a major player in European rail travel and because it's possible, by the time you read this, that Rail Europe and BritRail Travel International have joined forces to sell each other's passes, we've decided to include, after Eurailpass details, the prices for standard BritRail Passes and applicable variations like the BritRail +Ireland Pass. Other passes for Britain can still be found in the chapter on Britain. This section is followed by an overview of miscellaneous European passes such as InterRail Cards and EuroTrain tickets.

Prices quoted in this guide are based on current exchange rates and information and thus are subject to modification. Individual country pass prices are shown in their respective currencies or U.S. dollars and also are subject to modification. In the country chapters, you'll be advised if you have to purchase that country's pass before leaving the States or after arriving at your destination.

Most sources for Eurailpasses and ordinary tickets sold by individual European countries charge a non-refundable $10-$15 handling-fee or issuing-fee. Some fees are per order, some per pass. Some travel agencies may also charge a handling fee. Be aware.

The Passes

····· Eurailpass

Commentary: Depending on your itinerary, the least expensive formula can be buying a combination of Eurailpass and ordinary train tickets. For example, when traveling by train in excess of the 21-day period with the $280 ($186 second class) Frankfurt-Copenhagen ride scheduled for the last day, you'll save $20-$114 (depending the class of travel) by buying a one-month Eurailpass for $864 (instead of $698 + $280 = $978 for first class, or $698 + 186 = $884, second class). On the other hand, if you're traveling the Geneva-Zurich route on the twenty-second day, you'd be better off with a 21-day Eurailpass and point-to-point tickets for Geneva-Zurich ($698 + $115 = 813 first class, $698 + $71 = $769 second class). In this case buying a one-month pass would cost you money, between $51-$95. Calculate carefully before purchasing. All prices listed are subject to change and may vary slightly between companies like Rail Europe and DER Travel Services.

Prices are per person for 1998, unless noted otherwise.

- First-class, consecutive days:
  $538 for 15 days
  $698 for 21 days
  $864 for 1 month
  $1,224 for 2 months
  $1,512 for 3 months

Children between the ages of four and eleven pay half the adult fare. Children under four travel free.

••••• Eurail Flexipass

Terms are the same as Eurailpass; offers non-consecutive first-class travel days within a two-month period.

$634 for any 10 days within a 2-month period
$836 for any 15 days within a 2-month period

Children between the ages of four and eleven pay half the adult fare, Children under four travel free.

••••• Eurail Saverpass

This pass for unlimited first-class travel allows two-to-five people to travel together year-round with the same privileges as the consecutive-days Eurailpass described above.

$458 for 15 consecutive days
$594 for 21 consecutive days
$734 for 1-month
$1040 for 2 months
$1286 for 3 months

Children between the ages of four and eleven pay half the adult fare. Children under four travel free. Children count toward the minimum group number.

••••• Eurail Saver Flexipass

Valid for first class travel. This flexible pass offers year-round savings for two-to-five people traveling together.

10 days in 2 months $540
15 days in 2 months $710

Children between the ages of four and eleven pay half the adult fare. Under four, free.

••••• **Eurail Youthpass**

This pass is for unlimited second-class train travel in the same 17 countries that honor the first-class Eurailpass. The Youthpass is available to individuals under twenty-six and although it offers only second-class travel, price-wise it could prove a better deal for young travelers on a budget. Eurail Youthpass buyers must prove they are under twenty-six on the first day they use the pass.

15 consecutive days	$376
21 consecutive days	$489
1 month	$605
2 months	$857
3 months	$1059

••••• **Eurail Youth Flexipass**

This pass is also valid for second-class travel. Like the Eurail Youthpass, it is available only to passengers who are under twenty-six on the first date of travel.

10 days in 2 months	$444
15 days in 3 months	$585

••••• **EurailDrive Pass**

Same privileges as the Eurailpass. Features four days of unlimited first-class train travel plus three days of a Hertz or Avis rental car with unlimited mileage, tax, basic liability insurance, and drop-off (providing that drop-off is within the same country as that in which the car is rented) within two months. Purchase up to five additional rail days plus additional car days. Hertz cars are not available in Norway, Finland or Greece.

Car Categories	2 Adults* 1st Class	1 Adult 1st Class	Add'l Day Car
Economy (A)	$350	$435	$58
Compact (B)	$380	$495	$78
Intermediate (C)	$395	$525	$88
Add'l Rail Days (5 max.)	$55	$55	

* Prices are per person based on two people traveling together. Third and fourth person sharing the car pay $268 per person. Children 4-11 pay $134.

••••• **Europass**

A flexible pass for unlimited first-class train travel in five countries: France, Germany, Italy, Spain and Switzerland. Extend your travels by adding extra rail days or any of these associate countries: Austria & Hungary, Benelux (Belgium & Netherlands & Luxembourg), Greece, Portugal.

Travel agencies outside Europe sell Europasses worldwide, along with Rail Europe and DER Travel Services. See listing "Where to Buy Passes" for additional sources.

	2 Adults*	Adults
Any 5 days in 2 months	$261	$326
with 1 associate country	$309	$386
with 2 associate countries	$333	$416
with 3 associate countries	$349	$436
with 4 associate countries	$357	$446
Extra rail day	$ 33.50	$ 42

*Per-person, based on two people traveling together; 40 percent companion-discount included. Children between the ages of four and eleven pay half the adult fare, under four, free.

•••••Euro Youthpass

This pass is limited to those who are under age twenty-six on their first date of travel. It offers unlimited second-class train travel with the same conditions as the Europass.

Any 5 days in 2 months	$216
with 1 associate country	$261
with 2 associate countries	$286
with 3 associate countries	$301
with 4 associate countries	$309
Extra rail day	$ 29

•••••Europass Drive

This pass lets you alternate the train, for longer distances, with an Avis or Hertz rental-car for side trips. Train travel available for first class only. This pass is offers three rail days with two car days within a two-month period. You can buy up to seven additional rail days plus additional car days. Category A is not available in Italy, and in Switzerland, Avis doesn't offer automatic transmissions.

Car Categories	2 Adults* 1st Class	1 Adult 1st Class	Add'l Day Car
Economy (A)	$265	$315	$55
Compact (B)	$280	$355	$75
Intermediate (C)	$290	$370	$85
Compact Automatic (D/E)	$310	$415	$105
Add'l Rail Days (5 max.)	$42	$42	

* Prices are per person based on two people traveling together. Third and fourth person sharing the car pay $210 per person. Children 4-11 pay $105.

Europass Bonuses

In addition to the regular rail routes, the following European transportation routes and services are included in the Europass:

France: the scenic Digne-Nice-Digne train route.

Germany: steamers operated by KD German Rhine Line (Cologne-Mainz-Cologne), and on the Mosel and Cochem Rivers. Also on the Mannheim-Nuremberg "Castle Road" and the Frankfurt/M-Fussen "Romantic Road" guided bus tours.

Switzerland: regular steamer service on the Rhine River (Schaffhausen-Kreuzliner-Schaffhausen), Aere River (Biel-Solothurn-Biel), and on the lakes of Biel, Brienz, Geneva, Lucerne, Murten, Neuchatel, Thun, and Zurich.

Eurailpass Bonuses

In addition to unlimited train travel, the Eurailpasses include numerous free bonuses or reduced prices for boat trips, buses and private railways. Many of these bonuses are not listed in the Eurailpass brochure, such as discounts on several Norwegian fjord boats and Swiss cable cars. It is always a good idea to show your Eurailpass before purchasing any bus, boat, cable car or train ticket in Europe. You have nothing to lose, and sometimes you'll be pleased to profit by an unexpected perk. In many cases, rides that are not covered completely with a Eurailpass will, however, include a discount. Use of a free transportation bonus such as a ferry trip does, however, require the use of a travel day. The only exception is travel on the Wasa or Silja Line (Sweden). There is no reason to miss out on these. Here are the readily known discounts available to Eurailpass holders:

Austria
• Two track railways: (1) Puchberg am Schneeberg-Hochschneeberg and (2) St. Wolfgang-Schafbergspitze.
• Steamers on Lake Wolfgang.
• 50% Reduction on Lake Constance, Linz-Passau-Linz, and Vienna-Budapest ships.

Belgium
• 35% reduction on the Ostend-Ramsgate ferry operated by Régie belge des Transports Maritimes.

Denmark
Ferry crossings: Århus-Kalundborg, Knudshoved-Halskov, Nyborg-Korsør, Fynshav-Bøjden and Rødby-Faerge-Puttgarden (Germany). Ferry crossings operated by the Danish and Swedish State Railways between Helsingør and Helsingborg (Sweden).
• 25% off Flyvebådne hydrofoils between Copenhagen and Malmo.

• 50% off on Stena Line ferries between Frederikshavn and Göteborg.
• 30% reduction on Color Line between Hirtshals Kristiansand.
• 20% off Scandinavian Seaways line between Esbjerg and Harwich, Far Oer Islands and between Copenhagen and Oslo.
• 50% reduction on Hjørring-Hirtshals private railroad.

Finland
• Free passage on day sailings in both directions of the Silja Line Vaasa-Umeå (Sweden) and Vaasa-Sundsvall (Sweden).
• 50% reduction on the Helsinki-Travemunde (Germany) ferry.
• Free rides on buses which operate on occasion as train substitutes.
• Group and student rates apply to for the ferry crossing between Helsinki and Travemünde on the Finnjet if booked one week prior to departure. Adults receive 50% discounts off full fare for sleep-in compartments or in Budget or Tourist I S classes.

France
Eurailpasses are valid on Irish ferries between Cherbourg/Le Havre and Rosslare/ Cork. Port taxes are extra and payable in local currency. Advanced reservations required for cabin accommodations. Reservations required in July and August for all classes of accommodation.
• Nice-Digne or v.v. on Chemins de Fer de la Provence trains.
• 30% off regular fare to foot-passengers on P&O European Ferries between Calais and Dover (England).
• 30% percent reduction on regular fares for the ferry between Le Havre/Cherbourg and Portsmouth (England).

Germany
• Free sightseeing cruises on the Rhine, between Cologne and Mainz, and on the Mosel, between Koblenz and Cochem. (Eurail Youthpass holders pay an extra charge on express-steamers. Everyone pays an extra charge on hydrofoils.)
• Two ferry crossings: Puttgarden-Rodby Faerge (Denmark) and Sassnitz-Trelleborg (Sweden). Sassnitz is the most direct gateway from Berlin to Stockholm or Oslo, with both day and night trains operating on these routes. Steamers operated by the KD German Rhine Line making regular runs on the Rhine between Cologne and Mainz, and on the Mosel between Koblenz and Cochem. This does not include the ships making cruises of several days between Basel and Rotterdam or between Trier and Koblenz. There's an extra charge for hydrofoils.
• Europabus lines: 189 Burgenstrasse (Castle Road) only from May until September, between Mannheim-Heidelberg-Heilbronn-Rothenburg ob der Tauber-Ansbach-Nuremberg. 190 Romantische Strasse (Romantic Road) only from April until October, between Frankfurt-Rothenburg ob ter Tauber-Fussen.
• 50% off regular fare for Travemünde-Trelleborg (Sweden) ferry crossing on the TT Line.

• Group and student rates apply to the Finnjet ferry crossing between Travemünde and Helsinki.

• 50% off the full fare on TR Line ferries crossing between Rostock and Trelleborg.

• 50% discount on steamer service on Lake Constance between Romanshorn and Friedrichshafen and between Rorschach and Lindau. Steamer day trips between Passau and Linz by Wurm and Köck.

• Eurail Youthpass holders can take 40% off on the round-trip bus fare between Braunschweig and Berlin operated by Bayern

• 25% reduction on two mountain railroads: Garmisch-Zugspitze (Schneeferner-haus) mountain railroad and selected cable cars in the summit area. Plus a reduced fare on the Freiburg (Breisgau)-Schauinsland rack railway.

Greece

• The ferry crossing from Patras to Brindisi (see note under "Italy" Chapter 6). Only Hellenic Mediterranean Line or Adriatica di Navagazione Line honor passes.

Italy

• The ferry crossing from Brindisi to Patras (see notes under "Italy" Chapter 6). Only Hellenic Mediterranean Line or Adriatica di Navagazione Line honor passes. Warning: It's imperative to read notes under the Italy section before planning your itinerary! Don't let yourself be diverted to other ships at the Patras or Brindisi rail stations away from the Hellenic Mediterranean Line or Adriatica di Navagazione Line (the only ferries that honor Eurailpasses). Others make the voyage but charge large fees. Numerous cases have been cited of passengers deceived into believing these ships accept Eurailpasses. Steep charges were extorted after it was too late for passengers to leave departed ferries and return to the correct docks. The two proper lines charge pass holders $15 between June 10 and September 30. Reservations ($3 each) are advisable when using Eurailpass.

• Passes are valid for ferry crossings between Civitavecchia to Golfo Aranci (Sardinia) and Villa S. Giovanni to Messina (Sicily).

Ireland

• Eurailpasses are valid on Irish ferries between Rosslare/Cork and Cherbourg/Le Havre. Port taxes are extra and payable in local currency. Advanced reservations required for cabin accommodations. Reservations required in July and August for all classes of accommodation.

• Bus Eireann offers passholders a discount on its 3-day Rover ticket. It's valid on Bus Eireann Expressway and Provincial Services in the Republic of Ireland and on bus Eireann City Services in Cork, Limerick, Galway and Waterford. The reduced fare is IR£25. The ticket is valid for three days' travel within eight.

Spain

• 20% reduction on ferry crossings operated by Trasmediterranea between Barcelona and Palma de Mallorca and Valencia and Palma de Mallorca.

Sweden
• Three free boat trips: Helsingborg-Helsingor (Denmark). Trelleborg-Sassnitz (Germany). Helsingborg-Helsingør (Denmark) operated by the Swedish and Danish State Railways; Trelleborg-Sassnitz (Germany); and, Umeå-Vaasa (Finland) and Sundsvall-Vaasa on the Silja Line.
• 25% off Flyvebådne Company hydrofoils between Malmö and Copenhagen.
• 50% off regular fares for crossings on TT Line's Trelleborg-Travemünde ferries.
• 50% off regular fares for crossings on TR Line's Trelleborg-Rostock ferries.
• 50% off on Stena Line ferries between Göteborg-Frederickshaven (Denmark).
• 50 % reduction on the Inlands Banan between Mora and Gällivare.

Switzerland
• Lake boats on the Biel, Brienz, Geneva, Lucerne, Murten, Neuchatel, Thun, and Zurich lakes.
• River boats on the Rhine (Schaffhausen-Kreuzlingen) and Aare (Biel-Solothurn) rivers.
• 50% reduction on Lake Constance boats between Romanshorn-Friedrichshafen and Rorschach-Lindau.
• 35% reduction on the Alpnachstad-Mt. Pilatus funicular and the Kriens-Mt. Pilatus cable car.
• 35% reduction on the entrance fee to Lucerne's Transport Museum, the largest of its kind in Europe.
• 35% reduction on steamer service on Lake Constance between Rorschach and Romanshorn.
• 50% reduction on Bürgenstock funicular.
• 25% discount on the Jungfrau Region Railways.

Besides free transportation, passholders are entitled to discounts on hotels, car rentals and more. Hilton International will take between $30-$40 off the published full-price room rate at many locations. Hertz Europe discounts standard car rental rates by 30 percent. Look for 25 to 35 percent discounts, too, on Channel Tunnel Eurostar trains. First-class Eurostar fare discounts are also accessible to Eurail Youthpass holders.

Eurostar Channel Tunnel Tickets
In late 1994, the French, British and Belgian Railways received approval from the Intergovernmental Safety Commission to begin operation of trains through the Channel Tunnel. This service linked Paris to London in three hours and Brussels to London in three hours and 15 minutes. Since the inaugural trip, millions of passengers have used Eurostar between London-Paris and London-Brussels.

Eurostar links the three capitals with 16 daily departures between London and Paris and seven daily departures between London and Brussels. Plans are in the works to start daylight Eurostar service between the European mainland and Glasgow, Edinburgh, Manchester and Birmingham.

Eurostar prices change frequently and new services are constantly being introduced such as the summer 1997 package to Disneyland Paris, complete with Disney characters roaming the trains!

These one-way full-fare rates for adults were in effect as of late-September, 1997, on the London-Brussels and London-Paris routes.

First Class $139-$199 (includes a meal at your seat)

Second Class $75-$139

Each Eurostar has two buffet cars for standard class passengers. There are also special fares for 26 and younger, Eurail passholders, and group rates.

Two new classes of service were introduced in 1997, First Premium and Second Plus.

Premium Plus is available daily on the London/Ashford/Paris route, and is a cut above regular first class service. Passengers ride in a dedicated coach, receive higher levels of attention and a wider variety of meal and beverage selections than in regular first class. This service also offers an airline ticket exchange with British Midland, taxi transfers in London or Paris, 10-minute check-in (instead of 20 minutes) and access to Eurostar lounges. The price at press time was $293 one way.

Second Plus is available weekdays on the London/Ashford/Paris/Brussels and London/Ashford/Calais/Lille routes. One or two cars, depending on demand, will be dedicated to Second Plus travelers. Second Plus passengers receive complimentary newspapers and are served first by the food trolley. The one-way fare at press time was $159 between London and Brussels and London and Paris; London-to-Lille was $135.

Tickets are available in Britain, Belgium or France. Rail Europe and BritRail Travel have joined forces to create Eurostar USA. Now you can buy both Rail Europe and BritRail products through one number. In the U.S. and Canada call 800-EUROSTAR.

Sometimes promotional fares are offered through Rail Europe's Web site: http://www.raileurope.com.

Le Shuttle through the Channel Tunnel

Rail/drive passengers can use Le Shuttle, the car-carrying trains that run through the Channel Tunnel, to travel between Britain and the Continent. Just show up with your car at either entry point, Folkestone in Britain or Calais in France. Or make an advance reservation. Prices vary, depending on the type of ticket you buy. There's a five-day round-trip ticket, economy round trip and single tickets. There's also a premium service called Club Class, which includes priority boarding, access to a special lounge before boarding and a meal aboard the shuttle. Once ticket formalities are taken care of, you drive your car on to a double-deck rail car for the 35-minute trip (night services take 45 minutes). Le Shuttle even has a special service for cyclists that runs several times per day. Bikes are carried on a trailer, while cyclists make the trip in comfortable minibus. Hertz offers car rental deals that include the tunnel tariff. For instance, in September 1997 a 10-day economy rental picking up in downtown Paris and dropping off in downtown London was $383, including the Chunnel ticket.

In 1997, round-trip fares ranged from £149 for nighttime travel to £199 for peak-hour travel. There also were five-day round-trip tickets from £89 for nighttime travel to £129 for peak-hour travel.

Call these numbers for Le Shuttle info/reservations:

> France: 03 21 00 61 00
> Netherlands: 020/ 420 33 33
> UK: 0990 35 35 35

Le Shuttle has an official Web site at: http://www.le-shuttle.com/car/lesuk/uk_frame.htm. Or log on to the unofficial site at: http://mercurio.iet.unipi.it/eurostar/LeShuttle.html.

BRITAIN'S TRAIN PASSES

BritRail Classic Pass The BritRail Pass, the United Kingdom's version of the Eurailpass (which does *not* cover Britain), provides unlimited first- or standard-class rail travel in England, Scotland and Wales. Senior fares are for travelers 60 years and over; youth fares are limited to those ages 16 to under 25 and is for standard-class space. New to this year's rail guide is a section in the Route Chart that provides sample fares and travel times between London and cities throughout Britain. The 1998 prices are:

	8 days	*15 days*	*22 days*	*1 month*
Adult				
First Class	$375	$575	$740	$860
Standard Class	$259	$395	$510	$590
Senior				
First Class	$318	$489	$630	$730
Youth				
Standard Class	$205	$318	$410	$475

These passes do not cover travel in the Republic of Ireland or in Northern Ireland (*which is covered by BritRail Pass +Ireland, discussed later*) and *they cannot be purchased in Britain.* They can be purchased worldwide through the offices of BritRail Travel International, its representatives, and travel agencies outside Britain. Validate these passes at the rail station's "Travel Centre" before starting your first trip with them. The rail official will mark your pass with that day's date and the appropriate expiration date.

It is a good idea to protect yourself from having your pass rendered partly or wholly invalid because the validity dates were entered incorrectly.

Before the rail official writes on the pass the first and last day it can be used, you should write a note with what you believe are the correct validity dates, show it to the seller, and ask if he or she agrees with those dates. Only when the official says your dates are correct, or explains why they are not, should you have the dates entered on your pass.

(Be sure to follow the European custom of showing the day of the month first, followed by the number of the month. In Europe, July 8 is 8/7. If you wanted to take a train to Edinburgh, leaving London at 2:00 P.M. on July 8, your note for a reservation would read: "Edinburgh 14:00 8/7.")

BritRail Flexipass   Valid for one month. (For "Youth," the 15-day pass can be used within two months.) Same conditions and purchase locations as BritRail Pass. The 1998 prices are:

	4 days	8 days	15 days/1 mo.	15 days/2 mo.
Adult				
First Class	$315	$459	$699	-
Standard Class	$219	$315	$480	-
Senior				
First Class	$269	$390	$590	-
Youth				
Standard Class	$175	$253	-	$385

BritRail Party Passes   New for 1998 are Party Passes, which allow groups of three or four to travel together at substantial savings over the regular pass or flexipass. You must always travel together, though, to get the savings.

BritRail Classic Party Pass

| | *First Class* | | *Standard Class* | |
Adult	*Groups of 3 per person*	*Groups of 4 per person*	*Groups of 3 per person*	*Groups of 4 per person*
8 days	$313	$281	$216	$194
15 days	$479	$431	$329	$286
22 days	$617	$555	$425	$383
1 month	$717	$645	$492	$443
Senior				
8 days	$266	$239	-	-
15 days	$408	$367	-	-
22 days	$525	$473	-	-
1 month	$608	$548	-	-
Youth				
8 days	-	-	$171	$154
15 days	-	-	$265	$239
22 days	-	-	$342	$308
1 month	-	-	$396	$356

BritRail Flexi Party Pass

| | *First Class* | | *Standard Class* | |
Adult	*Groups of 3 per person*	*Groups of 4 per person*	*Groups of 3 per person*	*Groups of 4 per person*
4 days in 1 mo.	$263	$236	$183	$164
8 days in 1 mo.	$383	$344	$263	$236
15 days in 1 mo.	$563	$524	$400	$360
Senior				
4 days in 1 mo.	$224	$202	-	-
8 days in 1 mo.	$325	$293	-	-
15 days 1 month	$492	$443	-	-
Youth				
4 days in 1 mo.	-	-	$148	$131
8 days in 1 mo.	-	-	$211	$190
15 days in 2 mo.	-	-	$321	$289

BritRail Pass 'N Drive Provides two options, both within one month. Either three days of BritRail Flexipass plus three days of an Avis car rental, or six days of BritRail Flexipass plus seven days of car rental. Minimum age for rental is 25. Rates listed are for one driver, additional drivers subject to additional charge.

Manual Transmission		3 day rail/ 3 day car Adult	Senior	6 day rail/ 7 day car Adult	Senior
A Economy	Standard	$325	-	$634	-
	First	$393	$360	$740	$689
C Compact	Standard	$372	-	$746	-
	First	$440	$407	$852	$801
D Intermediate	Standard	$416	-	$848	-
	First	$484	$451	$954	$903

Automatic Transmission		3 day rail/ 3 day car Adult	Senior	6 day rail/ 7 day car Adult	Senior
F Intermediate	Standard	$496	-	$1035	-
	First	$564	$531	$1141	$1090
G Full Size	Standard	$576	-	$1221	-
	First	$644	$611	$1327	$1276
Additional Adult	Standard	$153	-	$234	-
Rail Supplement	First	$221	$188	$340	$289

BritRail Pass + Ireland Unlimited train travel in England, Scotland, Wales, Northern Ireland and the Republic of Ireland. Also round trip Stena Line ferry passage between Holyhead and Dun Laoghaire or Dublin, Fishguard and Rosslare or Stranraer and Belfast by ship, HSS or Stena Lynx Catamaran. Bring along one child (5-15) per adult pass for free; children 5-15 half price, under five, free. The 1998 adult prices are:

First Class	5 days/1 month	$473	10 days/1 month	$698
Standard Class	5 days/1 month	$359	10 days/1 month	$511

BritRail Family Pass Buy one adult or senior pass and one accompanying child (5-15) gets a pass of the same type and duration, free. Additional children purchase the appropriate pass at half off the adult pass price. Children under five ride free. The Family Pass is available with BritRail Classic Pass, BritRail Flexipass, BritRail Senior Pass, BritRail Pass + Car, BritRail Pass + Ireland.

BritRail + Eurostar 1998 information was unavailable at press time. Check with BritRail Travel or Rail Europe. In 1997, travelers could combine a first- or standard-class BritRail Flexipass with a standard class Eurostar trip through the Channel Tunnel. The pass was valid for travel around Britain for either four or eight days out of a three-month period. Eurostar reservations had to be made before departure. A Eurostar ticket voucher was issued and then exchanged for the ticket. Children's discounts weren't available in 1997. Prices listed here are from 1997.

	One-way Eurostar		Round-trip Eurostar	
	First Cl.	Standard Cl.	First Cl.	Standard Cl.
4 days in 3 months	$422	$262	$557	$319
8 days in 3 months	$553	$354	$693	$413

Where to Purchase Eurailpasses and BritRail Passes

Many travel agents are equipped to sell most Eurailpasses and BritRail Passes, however, the following sources specialize in train passes and offer them directly to the public. Unless noted, these companies accept major credit cards.

BritRail Travel International
1500 Broadway
New York, NY 10036
Tel.   (888) 274-8724 (toll-free)
Tel.   (212) 575-2667
Web: http://www.britrail.com/us/ushome.htm
Passes sold: BritRail Passes, Eurostar tickets

CIT (Italian State Railways)
6033 W. Century Blvd., Suite 980
Los Angeles, CA 90045
Tel.   (800) CIT-RAIL
            (310) 338-8616
Fax   (310) 670-4269
Hours: 09:00-17:30 PST
Passes sold: Eurail, BritRail, Germany, Italy

CIT (Italian State Railways)
342 Madison Ave., Suite 207
New York, NY 10173
Tel.   (800) 223-7987
            (212) 697-2100
Fax   (212) 697-1394
Hours: 09:00-17:30 EST

CIT (Italian State Railways)
1150 City Cousillors Street, Suite 207
Montreal, Quebec (H3A 2E6)
Canada
Tel.   (800) 361-7799 (within Canada)
            (514) 845-9101
Fax   (514) 845-9137
Hours: 09:00-17:00

CIT (Italian State Railways)
80 Tiverton Court, #401
Marktown, Ont. Canada L3R OG4
Tel.   (800) 387-0711
            (905) 415-1060
Fax   (905) 415-1063
Hours: 09:00-17:00

DER Travel Services
German Rail, Inc.
9501 West Devon Avenue, Suite 400
Rosemont, IL 60018
Tel.   (800) 782-2424 (passes)
Tel.   (800) 337-8724 (pt-to-pt tickets)
Tel.   (800) 860-9944 (brochures only)
Fax   (800) 282-7474
Hours: 07:30-19:30 CST Mon-Fri
Web: http://dertravel.com
Passes sold: Eurail, Balkan, Benelux, Scanrail, Austria, Britain, Denmark, Germany, Greece, Italy, Netherlands, Norway, Prague, Spain, Sweden

DER Travel Services
904 The East Mall
Etobicoke, Ontario M9B 6K2
Canada
Tel.   (416) 695-1211
Fax   (416) 695-1210
Hours: 09:00-18:00

Forsyth Travel Library, Inc.
1750 East 131st Street
P.O. Box 480800, Dept. E
Kansas City, MO 64148
Tel.   (800) 367-7984
         (816) 942-9050
Fax   (816) 942-6969
E-mail: forsyth@gvi.net
Web: http://www.forsyth.com
Hours: 09:00-17:00 Mon-Sat
Passes sold: Eurail, various country passes, Italian Kilometric Tickets, BritRail
passes, sleeper space on British trains and point-to-point tickets in Europe.

Rail Europe
500 Mamaroneck Avenue,
Suite #314 (correspondence only)
Harrison, NY 10528
Tel.   (800) 4-EURAIL (438-7245) (U.S.)
Fax   (800) 432-1329
Tel.   (800) 361-RAIL (361-7245) (Canada)
Web   http://www.raileurope.com.
Hours: 07:00-19:00 MST
Passes sold: Eurail, Balken, Benelux, European East, Scanrail, Austria, Bulgaria,
Czech Republic, Finland, France, Germany, Hungary, Italy, Norway, Portugal,
Romania, Spain, Sweden, Switzerland

Rail Pass Express
2737 Sawbury Boulevard
Columbus, OH 43235
Tel.   (800) 722-7151
         (614) 889-9100

Fax   (614) 764-0711
Passes sold: Eurail, Balkan, Benelux, Scanrail, Austria, Britain, Denmark, Germany, Greece, Italy, Netherlands, Norway, Spain, Sweden

Rick Steves' Europe Through the Back Door
120 Fourth Avenue N.
P.O. Box 20009
Edmonds, WA 98020-9509
Tel.   (206) 771-8303
Fax   (206) 771-0833
Passes sold: Eurail, BritRail, Austria, Benelux, Czech Republic, France, Germany, Hungary, Italy, Norway, Portugal, ScanRail. Spain, Sweden, Switzerland

Scantours
Tel.   (800) 223-7226
          (310) 636-4656
Fax   (310) 390-0493
Passes sold: Eurail, Balken, Benelux, European East, Scanrail, Austria, Bulgaria, Czech Republic, Finland, France, Germany, Hungary, Italy, Norway, Portugal, Romania, Spain, Sweden, Switzerland; does not accept charge cards.

Elsewhere in the World
AUSTRALIA: CIT-Australia Pty. Ltd.; Concorde International Travel; Thomas Cook Pty. Ltd.; Rail Plus
EGYPT: Thomas Cook Overseas Ltd.
HONG KONG: Hong Kong Student Travel Ltd.; Schenker Travel, Thomas Cook Overseas Ltd.
INDIA: Travel Corporation India Ltd.
INDONESIA: Pantravel Travel & Tourism Service
ISRAEL : European World Representatives
JAPAN: Japan Travel Bureau; Ohshu Express Ltd.; Recruit From A Inc.; Travel Plaza International Inc.
KOREA: Seoul Travel Service, Ltd.
MALAYSIA: Boustead Travel Services Sdn. Bhd.
NEW ZEALAND: Atlantic and Pacific Travel International, Ltd.; Thomas Cook Holidays
PAKISTAN: American Express International Banking Corp.
PHILIPPINES: PCI Travel Corporation; Thomas Cook Inc.
SAUDI ARABIA: Alrajhi Wings for Travel and Tourism; Orient Travel & Tours
SINGAPORE: American Express Travel Service; Thomas Cook Travel Services

SOUTH AFRICA: World Travel Agency Ltd.
SRI LANKA: Aitken Spence Travels Ltd.
TAIWAN: American Express International Ltd.; Federal Transportation Ltd.
THAILAND: DITS Travel (Diethelm International Transport Services, Ltd.)
UNITED ARAB EMIRATES: Thomas Cook A.L. Rostamani (Pvt) Ltd.

Other Passes, Discounts and Information

Besides the Eurailpass and Eurail Youthpass, there are other ways to save money when traveling in Europe by train: special discount tickets, coupons, and special passes, issued independently by various countries. Details on these other passes appear in this guide under the individual country listings, and most must be purchased in the respective country. Also within each country chapter, are listings for tourist offices and agents who represent European railways. Often, tickets and special passes can be purchased through these offices.

Since regulations on discount tickets change frequently, it is suggested that you contact the office nearest you for information before leaving for Europe.

The passes below are geared to seniors and travelers under the age of twenty-six. They must be purchased overseas.

Miscellaneous European Passes

••••• Rail Europ Senior (Senior Citizen Pass)

This senior-citizen pass offers senior citizens (age 60 and older) a 30 percent discount on first- or second-class train tickets. Purchasers must buy a national senior pass from one of the issuing countries. That pass becomes a Rail Europ Senior Card. The pass is only sold to persons who can prove that they are permanent residents of one of the participating countries: Austria, Belgium, Croatia Serbie Slovenia, Czech Republic, Denmark, Finland, France, Germany, Great Britain, Greece, Holland, Hungary, Republic of Ireland, Italy, Luxembourg, Norway, Portugal, Slovakia, Spain, Sweden, and Switzerland. Valid for one year, these passes are sold at main rail stations of the issuing countries.

Use of Rail Europ Senior is limited by each of the participating countries. In France this pass is called the Carte Vermeil Plein Temps. In 1997, it cost FF279 and allowed as much as a 50 percent discount on French trains (for "Blue Period" travel). The Italian version of the card sold for L33000 in 1997, and offered a 30 percent discount for travel in 24 countries. Only a few seats are allocated to holders of Carte Vermeil on TGV trains, other high-speed trains, and EuroCity trains. Remember, the limitations (including times and days of use) on use of Rail Europ Senior can be significantly different in each of the participating countries.

····· Inter Rail Cards

The famous Inter Rail Card offers unlimited, second-class train travel, but can be purchased only in Europe and Morocco, and is valid only for persons under twenty-six years old who can prove that they have resided at least six months in the issuing country. The bearer can travel half fare in the issuing country and free on the railways of the other countries purchased. This is very advantageous to young travelers already residing or studying in Europe.

The validity period begins on the first day the card is used, and that day must be within two months after the card is purchased. The card also includes discounts on ships (Irish Sea, Spain-Morocco, France-Corsica, Italy-Greece), as well as on selected Swiss private railways.

The Inter Rail Card is sold at most rail stations in the following 28 countries (see "The Zones" below) and must be paid for in the currency of the country that issues it.

The price is more or less the same in the 28 participating countries, but does experience some fluctuation according to exchange

The prices listed here in British pounds are from late 1997.

One-zone pass	15 days of unlimited travel	£189
Two-zone pass	1 month of unlimited travel	£224
Three-zone pass	1 month of unlimited travel	£249
Global seven-zone pass	1 month of unlimited travel	£279

The Zones

Zone 1:	Great Britain, Northern Ireland, the Irish Republic
Zone 2:	Finland, Norway, Sweden
Zone 3:	Austria, Denmark, Germany, Switzerland
Zone 4:	Bulgaria, Croatia, the Czech Republic, Hungary, Poland, Romania, Slovakia
Zone 5:	Belgium, France, The Netherlands, Luxembourg
Zone 6:	Morocco, Portugal, Spain
Zone 7:	Greece, Italy, Slovenia, the European part of Turkey, and the Brindisi-Patras-Brindisi ferry

····EuroTrain Tickets

These tickets are discounted up to 40 percent on train and ship passage to over 2,000 destinations in all of Eastern and Western Europe (22 countries), including Turkey and Morocco, for anyone under twenty-six years old on the first day of travel, regardless of residence. A ticket is valid for two months and allows as many stopovers as desired.

Available in the U.K. from Eurotrain, Dept. E-93, 52 Grosvenor Gardens, London SW1W 0AG. In France, an equivalent discount service is called B.I.G.E.

Eurotrain also offers a series of Explorer Passes that cover different groupings of European cities. The following prices were valid in late 1997.

Dutch Explorer: London-Amsterdam-Brussels-Brugge-London £75

Spanish Explorer: London-Paris-Toulouse-Biarritz-San Sebastian-Madrid-Barcelona-Lyon-Paris-London £215

Riviera Explorer: London-Paris-Pisa-Rome-Florence-Basel-Luxembourg-Brussels-London £210

Venetian Explorer: London-Amsterdam-Cologne-Munich-Innsbruck-Verona-Milan-Lyon-Paris-London £220

Rome Explorer: London-Paris-Pisa-Rome-Florence-Lucerne-Strasburg-Luxembourg-Brussels-London £205

Eastern Explorer: London-Amsterdam-Berlin-Prague-Budapest-Vienna-Zurich-Brussels-London £240

From U.S. dial (011 44 171) 730 3402; in Britain and Europe dial 0171 730 3402.

Student, Teacher (or Faculty) and Youth Discount Cards

• International Student Identity Card (ISIC)

This well-recognized card (more than a million issued every year) is an international passport to low-cost travel for students over the age of twelve. Bearers of the ISI card are entitled to discounts on rail, air, bus, and ferry travel, as well as entrance fees to museums, theaters, cinemas, and other places of interest in approximately 90 countries.

Cards issued in the U.S. carry basic accident/sickness insurance, which includes emergency evacuation insurance coverage outside the 50 United States and District of Columbia up to $25,000 and features a 24-hour, toll-free ISIC Help Line. The toll-free number helps students replace lost traveler's checks or passports, or locate English-speaking doctors and lawyers.

Although there is no maximum age limit for the card itself, some transportation companies (airlines, steamships, etc.) and other vendors have imposed their own age restrictions for the use of this card. If you're over thirty, some companies, movie houses, etc., don't like the idea of your profiting from student status. Try to insist.

Upon buying the card, students also receive the International Student Identity Handbook, which lists worldwide discounts and benefits. Even if a student discount is not posted, holders of the card should always ask about a discount before payin full price.

Developed and regulated by the International Student Travel Confederation, the card carries the owner's full name, birth date, citizenship, school name, and photo. The official U.S. sponsor of the card is CIEE (Council on International Educational Exchange). The card is available from CIEE's Council Travel offices nationwide as well as from hundreds of university and college campus offices.

The 1998 card is valid September 1, 1997 through December 31, 1998 and costs $20. Applications must also include a passport-size photo (with name printed on back) and proof of current student status (copy of transcript, letter from registrar, or copy of bill showing payment of enrollment fees). For insurance purposes, applicants must provide the name, address, and telephone number of beneficiaries.

• International Teacher Identity Card

Full-time faculty members at accredited institutions can enjoy the same discounts, insurance coverage and validity periods as ISIC cardholders, with the ITIC card.

Requirements for obtaining the card are the similar, too, such as providing a passport-size photo and proof of teacher status. The card costs $20. Certain airlines may impose age restrictions for discounted airfare, however.

• Go 25: International Youth Travel Card

This card is not limited to students and is available to anyone regardless of nationality who is at least twelve but not over twenty-five at the time of purchase. Proof of age may be a passport (or photocopy of the data page from a passport), copy of a driver's license, or copy of a birth certificate. The benefits include significantly reduced fares on regularly scheduled airlines between the U.S. and Europe, Asia and Latin America, and also from Europe to Africa, Asia, and the Middle East.

The Go-25 Card also offers holders advantages concerning in-hospital health care and accident insurance while traveling outside the U.S. The card affords users access to the aid provided by the Traveler's Assistance Centers in case of medical, legal, and financial emergencies while abroad. Lastly, it provides certain discounts on transportation, tours, accommodations, restaurants, museums, theaters, cultural attractions, and historic sites.

The card includes the same $25,000 insurance coverage as the other two cards. It's valid for one year from time of purchase and costs $20.

To Apply for Both Cards

For information about CIEE's educational programs and for a copy of "Student Travels," a free magazine covering traveling, studying and working abroad, and descriptions of CIEE's products and services, call (888) COUNCIL (268-6245). For travel information, or a copy of "Student Travels," call (800) 2-COUNCIL.

Council also has a Web site: http://www.ciee.org/travel/index.htm

CHAPTER 3

How to Plan a Rail Itinerary

Every successful train trip contains three essential dimensions: the amount of time you have, the interesting destinations you choose, and the scenic routes you decide to take.

Organizing Your Trip

When your schedule and budget permit, it is recommended that the minimum length of a train trip through Europe should be 23 days, including arrival and departure days.

Once you've arrived at your destination, don't plan lots of activities for your first day, other than getting settled into your hotel and recharging your batteries after the long and fatiguing journey—especially if you've traveled from North America's West Coast. Very few people are immune to the effects of transiting many time zones and the temporary hindrance of jet lag. The time they arrive at their destination, say frequent travelers, figures into just how much they're affected by jet lag. Most seem to agree that late afternoon arrival is best. They get to their hotel, have a light dinner, take a short walk, then hit the rack for a good night's sleep. By the next morning, they say, they're in sync with the local time. For morning arrivals, suggest the road warriors, it won't hurt to take a nap. Don't sleep the day away, though, otherwise you'll be up all night! Everybody has their own technique for lessening the ravages of jet lag. If you're new to international travel, your best bet is to kick back the first day and put off any major activities, if possible. That leaves only 20 active days for sightseeing, however, which isn't really that much time if you plan on visiting numerous European countries.

Most travel writers recommend staying a minimum of two or three nights in most cities you visit, with only occasional one-nighters mixed in the itinerary. This, of course, depends a lot on you. You may opt for five nights in Paris and only two in Munich, or three in Vienna but one in Budapest. Even the sturdiest traveler, though, develops a psychosis when spending too many consecutive nights in different hotel rooms. Besides, if you travel mostly by day, as is suggested to see the country-side and meet and converse with fellow passengers, you will arrive in a city late in the day. And if you leave the next morning, you are certainly not going to see much in that city.

But on a two-night basis you can cover 10-11 different cities during your 21 full days in Europe. Reducing a trip to 14 days means reducing the number of cities to five or six. If 14 days is your limit, the 15-day Eurailpass and some fast footwork will still let you have a happy tour while covering a great deal of the continent. All this depends on your time restrictions.

Choosing Destinations

After deciding the length of time you have to tour, the next step in itinerary planning is to pick the places you want to visit, and most people usually have more cities in mind than time, energy and distance will allow. Unless you are indifferent to 15-hour journeys that bring you into a destination late at night, knowing the travel time between each point on your itinerary is essential. The timetables in this book give you that information on nearly 1,500 different rail trips and thousands of schedule combinations.

The common sense approach is to consult a map with a mileage scale and visualize what is practical and what is not while composing a list of places to see. Part of this narrowing-down process depends on what interests you the most. List destinations in order of your priority. Could you really spend three weeks in Europe and not visit the Sistine Chapel? Would your Aunt Olga forgive you if you passed up that invitation at her cousin's farm in Bergen? You decide. Obviously, if, for example, seeing the great art masterpieces is a priority, you'd want to select Paris and Florence over Avignon and Naples. If your interest is Alpine scenery, you are going to concentrate on Bern and Salzburg, not Barcelona and Copenhagen.

Selecting Routes

At this point, you have determined how many days you will be in Europe, where you want to go, and what's feasible in that time. You should now consider the most rewarding routes and the use of special trains.

The journey from Paris to Marseilles, for example, can be made on any one of a dozen ordinary slower, and often more scenic trains instead of the high-speed TGV. If you'd like to stop for lunch in Dijon, don't take the TGV. However, if you'd like to get to Marseilles by noon and be on the beach by 2 P.M. (or 14:00!), you better opt for the faster train. A traveler has the same sort of choice of railway routes all over the world; the fastest train is not necessarily the most interesting, and yet the commonplace, slow-train may be a real waste of time—or be an extraordinary experience. Be aware that there are choices, and then evaluate them.

Reservations—Train and Hotel

Train Reservations

Since 1989, it has become increasingly easy to make train reservations before arriving in Europe. Most travel agencies now sell tickets and can make both your seat and sleeper reservations. This does not mean that you must have seat reservations: they are required only on selected trains. However, anyone traveling on main routes during peak tourist months without reserved space will probably make the trip standing in the aisle and being brushed up against every 30 seconds by passengers ambling along the corridor. Keep in mind that Europeans can, and do, reserve train seats up to two months in advance. Don't be alarmed to see a very ordinary train from Bordeaux to Tours on an October Monday morning completely sold-out.

Reservation clerks in many (especially smaller) European cities speak little or no English, although most train stations have multilingual information stands staffed with friendly workers. Writing out your request in clear and simple terms can save you much time in communicating and help insure against getting a less-than-perfect reservation. You should note on paper your destination, time and day of departure, and any other preferences. Be sure to follow the European custom of showing the day of the month first, followed by the number of the month. July 8 is "8/7." And use the 24-hour clock! If you wanted to take a train to Milan, leaving at 1:50 p.m. on July 8, your note should read "Milan -13:50- 8/7."

Eating and Seating

If you decide to dine at your seat or in your train compartment rather than in the restaurant car, you might want to request a window seat when making your train reservations. On most European trains–other than TGVs–these are the only seats that have a full, fold-out table. In some compartments, the seats next to the sliding door also have a fold-out table. Other seats have airplane-style meal trays. Moreover, window seats, especially in train cars with six-seat compartments, afford you a better view of the scenery.

Smoking or non-smoking?

Another variation in seat reservations is that on nearly all European trains you can reserve seats in compartments where smoking is either prohibited or permitted. Depending on your preference, this can make a great deal of difference in either enjoying or detesting your trip. In Europe, smokers can be vehement about their habit and don't always understand or care about the arguments for not smoking. Carefully selecting your reserved seat is thus your guarantee to comfort.

Picking Sides

And still another reservation option to keep in mind is the side of the train you prefer to sit on. Often there is a decided sightseeing advantage on one side and a corresponding disadvantage on the alternate side. Think of the Alps or the Mediterranean or Lake Como. Obviously if you are traveling along the Riviera, the view of the Mediterranean is possible only on the left side if you are traveling west, and on the right side when going east. After logic tells you which side of the train offers the best view, you can ask if there are any seats on that side, when you make your seat reservation.

Train Reservations: Pros and Cons

When making reservations in Europe, the reservation charge ranges from $3 to $8 per ride. Reservations for seats on Europe's greatest trains can be made as much as two months in advance, and many Europeans grab spaces on them soon after they become available to be reserved. Casual tourists may discover that a few days before they want to travel on a special train, it is completely sold-out.

While most European trains do not require reservations, many do: French TGVs, certain InterCity trains, some EuroCity trains that go between countries, overnight trains, X2000, AVE, Pendolino, Cisalpino, Thalys and Channel Tunnel Eurostars. Since these trains accept reservations two months in advance, think about reserving seats even before you arrive at your destination, if you're on a tight schedule.

Reserving Before You Leave

For holders of Eurailpasses, French train tickets, French national passes, or the national passes for most other European countries, note that if you purchased your tickets or passes from a North American office of Rail Europe, the same issuing office can make your train reservations (required and optional) for most European countries. This can be very helpful. Rail Europe charges $11 per person, per seat reservation (including cable fee), plus a single $10 service charge for shipping and handling. Two people reserving seats on three trains would have six reservations totaling $66 plus $10, for a grand total of $76.

The North American offices of Italian State Railways listed in this guide also make reservations for train trips in Italy and most (but not all) other European countries, but only when a Eurailpass has been purchased from them. Note, though, that they do not make reservations in connection with Italian passes or ordinary train tickets. The maximum number of reservations they will make is three trips per pass. Their fee is $10 per train seat, which includes all communication fees. The cost for two people reserving seats on three trains, therefore, is $60. However, two people traveling together are not permitted to reserve six trains.

Eurailpass holders who make seat reservations after arriving in Europe, are exempt from the reservation fee. This does not apply to Italy's special "Pendolino" trains, though, for which a hefty supplement ranging from $6 to $28 is charged. The supplement, however, includes a reservation fee and a meal!

If you have purchased your Eurailpass, German national pass, or tickets for German trains from one of the North American offices of DER (U.S. and Canadian offices listed in this guide), these offices will reserve any number of trains up to 10 days prior to each train's departure at a charge of $10 per person, per train, plus $8 per order for Priority Mail charges.

It is always advisable to have the office that issues you the Eurailpass to telex, fax or E-mail your reservation requests to Europe. It's faster than snail mail and you'll have a better chance of getting the seats you want.

BritRail Travel International also will make seat and sleeper reservations for clients who have purchased passes. In late 1997, the charge for seat reservations was $7 per leg per person. A first-class sleeper cost, per person, $52, a standard-class sleeper $43, beyond the price of the rail pass or point-to-point ticket. BritRail doesn't charge any additional handling fees, unless the reservation is made two weeks, or less, before departure. Then, overnight or second-day delivery charges would apply.

Reserving on the Spot: Avoiding the Lines

If, on the other hand, you wait to reserve train space just before each departure, keep in mind that at most European stations you must get in one line for a ticket and in a different line for a seat reservation. Of course, if you have a Eurailpass you eliminate having to wait in the ticket line for a long time.

As a matter of fact, you can face long waits in as many as five different lines. Part of the trick of making the most of your limited time is to avoid standing in any. The lines include information, ticket purchases, seat reservation, hotel accommodations, and baggage checkroom. There are tricks to eliminating line waiting for general information discussed in Chapter 4. Having a Eurailpass solves the ticket line wait. The solution to the hotel accommodation line is to make reservations before you leave home. The baggage check-room problem is discussed in Chapter 5.

There is another way to reduce the amount of time spent in either the ticket or seat reservation lines. These lines are far shorter Monday to Thursday than they are on the weekend. Mid-morning tends to be a better time to buy tickets or make reservations than during the lunch hours or in the early evening when it is the height of the commuter rush hours. During the mid-June to mid-September tourist season, it is often advantageous to have a hotel concierge or *pensione* owner obtain your reservations for you. Or, use a local travel agent.

In any case, be sure to make reservations in the country you will be touring as much in advance as possible, preferably upon your arrival in the city you will be continuing your tour from. Requirements for reservations vary from country to country and, within a country, from city to city. In some Italian cities, for example, reservations cannot be made less than two hours before a departure. Milan requires three hours notice. Rome requires five hours notice! Let's say that your trip consisted of a New York-Paris flight, followed by a train trip to Geneva, and a second one from Geneva-Rome. Make the Paris-Geneva reservation on your first day in Paris, and make the Geneva-Rome reservation upon arriving at the Geneva station.

Five Simple Train Reservation Tips

1. When you leave your compartment to go to the W.C. (toilet), dining car, or merely to stretch your legs, leave some object on your seat—a newspaper or hat—something to inhibit unreserved seat-grabbers from settling down in your space during your absence. While it is true that the conductor will aid you in removing an interloper, finding the conductor, explaining the problem and using his intervention is somewhat more bothersome than simply preventing the event.

2. Don't waste time trying to make a seat reservation for a train trip within Belgium, Holland, Luxembourg, or Switzerland. These countries sell seat reservations only for rides going into another country. However, finding a seat on the trains of these countries is not a problem except on peak travel days. The only time you might need a seat reservation for a trip within these countries is for tourist trains, like Switzerland's *Glacier Express*, or *Bernina Express*.

3. On a normal working day, even though the reservation clerk claims all seats on a certain train are already reserved, you can often hop aboard and find an empty seat. Many European business people, when undecided about which train they will be taking, make several reservations to cover all possibilities, and then forfeit the fee on unused reservations. This practice accounts for some unused seats being marked "reserved." If traveling without seat reservations, be careful not to waste time taking a reserved seat while the unreserved ones are filling up. Check the seat chart outside each compartment or on each seat before you sit down (some countries—Sweden and Yugoslavia—don't use reservation labels). If you're ousted by the legitimate reservation holder, you may have to stand during the rest of the ride.

4. If the required advance time for making a seat reservation has run out, seek the conductor and, in your most charming manner, tell him (or her) your destination and seek his assistance in finding you a seat. As a brand of their own, train conductors are for the most part remarkably courteous, good humored, and cooperative and many, you will observe, welcome the opportunity of using their authority constructively.

5. Never, never discard a train ticket until after your trip has been fully completed and you have left the arrival station. You will frequently ride a train for hours without being asked to show a ticket or pass. Then, after you get off the train, you could discover that you are required to show your ticket or pass at the station exit, as is true in many London subway stations. If you have thrown your ticket away, you will undoubtedly end up having to buy a second one, or pay a fine for not having one. Your best bet is to always hold onto your ticket, whether or not a conductor checks it.

Hotel Reservations

Once you've selected the main elements, namely the amount of days, the specific cities, the trains and the routes, and train reservations, you're ready to consider whether you want to reserve hotels in advance. There are pros and cons to both. In any case, all *Eurail and Train Travel Guide* recommendations are based on information recently verified by firsthand experience. The qualification "recently" is noteworthy, because the quality of hotel and restaurant services is subject to periodic fluctuations. Management changes (and quality with it) faster than annually revised editions of any guide can wholly keep up with. When possible, consult competent travel agents, travel publications, and travel information sources that have current input from recent travelers. The best information comes from people who have just been there. Sometimes you can get this sort of information through newsgroups on the Internet. The Web sites listed in Appendix B often have links to helpful newsgroups. To maximize your chances of landing great information, ask lots of questions.

How you deal with the hotel issue is really up to you. Are you the kind of person who winces at the word "surprise?" Someone who wants to know what's going on every day? Or do you like to just grab a bag and go, with no particular plan in mind?

For those who want to maximize comfort and security, this guide recommends reserving hotel accommodations well in advance, and, when possible, to reserve train seats whenever you are sure you want to be on a particular train on a certain date.

Some travelers object vehemently to such pre-planning tactics such as advanced reservations, claiming that you cannot be as footloose or carefree as you would like, linger where you have discovered unexpected attractions, or make impetuous detours or departures. There is no question that for those travelers forced to lead ordered routines, there are few activities that offer as much freedom as does train travel. The spontaneous choices you can make are vast. The feature that many people find irresistible about European trains is how easily one can, an hour after starting a ride going in one direction, abort at an approaching station and head elsewhere. If flexibility is essential and you relish venturing into the unknown, advance hotel reservations may not be important to you.

One way to maintain flexibility is to book hotels as you go, using a phone card. Before leaving home, consult your favorite guide book, or the tourist offices where you plan to travel, then make a list of prospective hotels to take with you. It's probably a good idea, too, if you're not familiar with your destination country's language, to jot down key phrases like *Do you speak English?*; *How much is a double room with toilet and shower?*; *Do you have rooms available for tomorrow night?* (or whenever you want to arrive). Most hotel proprietors, though, speak "hotel" English, so you should be okay, unless you're traveling to the boonies.

Buy the phone card after you arrive in Europe. They're available at post offices, tobacco stands and airport and railway station newsstands. When you're ready to move on, pull out the list and start dialing.

Phone cards come in different time units, and sell from about $5. For instance, a French phone card with 50 units of calling time sold for just over $8 in 1996. That should be more than enough time for a three-to-four-week trip. You'll probably have to ask someone or dial-up an English-speaking operator for the city or country dialing code for your destination city. You're probably thinking you'll be intimidated using European phones. Don't be. These days, many European phones have automated language-options, so they're easy to use.

On the other hand, if you ever have played an entire night of poker without holding one winning hand; or arrived in Copenhagen on the opening day of a World Bank Conference (no rooms within 20 miles); or traveled to Paris where the International Air Show opened on the day of your arrival, the most popular horse race on the Continent was being run the next day (no room within 30 miles), and your next stop was Dijon, where your first six choices of hotels were *complet*, even though nothing special was happening that week, you might want to rethink the advantages of advanced bookings.

From May through early October, European and non-European tourists pack all classes of hotels in leading European cities. Trade shows and business conventions pick up the slack instantly in September, October, March, and April. A hotel in Bordeaux (not Paris or Rome, mind you) responded to a request for reservations on July 13 that it was booked for the two nights needed in early October! Sometimes the difficulty of finding a room stems from a local holiday, a long weekend, a special event, or a large party that has booked all the rooms in a small region.

If you travel Europe without advance room reservations from March through October, it is wise to arrive in your destination city early in the day. Rooms that are available because of no-shows or last-minute cancellations frequently are taken before mid-afternoon. Otherwise, you can spend a lot of time room hunting.

Upon arriving without a hotel reservation, go at once to the tourist accommodations desk in the train station. For a fee of $2 to $4, a host or hostess will telephone hotels, pensions, or bed and breakfasts to find you a room that comes close to your specifications. In certain cities (Amsterdam, Bergen, Brussels, etc.), this convenient service is not offered at the station but can be found at the city tourist office, often only across the road from the rail station, but sometimes quite a distance from it.

In the peak summer touring months you'll find long lines and if, as is usually the case, your stay is brief, you'll have to devote precious visiting time to finding a room. When traveling in groups of two or more, one person should remain at the station guarding the luggage while the other or others canvass the area near the station to find a room. All over Europe, you'll find many hotels within a radius of two or three blocks from the rail station. Many non-Europeans are unaware that stations even in the smallest cities have comfortable waiting rooms with upholstered chairs. If you follow this technique, be sure to use the shelter of these waiting rooms. Don't leave luggage unattended for even a few minutes. Besides the peril of theft, Europeans are very sensitive to all potential risks of terrorism. In Paris and London train stations, the police often collect and blow-up unattended bags.

Another housing solution used successfully by many is: get out of town immediately and stay in the suburbs, don't even attempt to battle the hustle and hassle of finding a hotel room downtown in a major city. This is possible, provided that the suburb is linked by train with the city you want to tour. Just pick a town of moderate size about 30-45 minutes train travel time away from a major metropolis and head there. On the plus side, you're more likely to find an affordable room. On the down side though, the town may be less interesting or downright dull and ugly and train service may be limited at night, forcing you to forego those theater tickets or late-night bar-hopping.

Preparing for an Autumn Tour

One thing usually overlooked in European off-season itinerary planning is that after early September—and fall is outstanding for touring Europe—English-language city sightseeing tours are often discontinued as the volume of tourists decline, particularly in important but smaller cities such as Avignon, Verona, Rouen, Tours, etc. If this poses a problem for you, in that you were counting on taking these city tours, there's no reason to despair. Nearly every city in Europe, even hamlets such as the charming port of Honfleur in Normandy, has a tourist office that supplies comprehensive folders in English. These folders include fine city maps, interesting descriptions of principal attractions and suggested walking tours that allow visitors to find on their own, and at their own pace, the most worthwhile historic sites, museums, churches, palaces, and other local high spots usually available in a motor-coach sightseeing-tour.

By early September, though, many city tourist offices run out of the current brochures. To insure against this disappointment there is a precaution you can take. Early in the year, write to the cities you plan to visit and request copies of literature and tourist maps in English. This can also help you decide what to visit and how long to spend at a destination.

Within each country chapter is the address and phone number for that country's tourist office in the U.S. These offices are extremely helpful and will usually go the extra mile to help you plan your trip. When you write or call, tell them specifically what you're interested in doing or seeing. Ask, too, about discount coupons for museums, sightseeing, hotels and dining. Best of all, tourist offices don't charge a dime for a world of information.

Publications for Savvy Travelers

It is more than useful, it is necessary, to arm yourself with a varied collection of up-to-date and informative guides, maps, and books if you want to be an informed and intelligent traveler. There are literally hundreds of sources of published information, ranging from great collections of general travel guides covering entire continents to highly specialized and thematic guides covering everything from restaurants and hotels to churches, cemeteries, wines, boutiques and even Paris *arrondissements*. And then there's all those travel Web sites. You neither want to load yourself down, nor spend your whole trip with your nose in a book, but a carefully chosen selection of documentation is essential. As Alvin Toffler so poignantly documented in *Powershift*, it is information, even more so than cash, that opens doors in our contemporary world. This is equally true in the realm of individual travel, especially when it comes to destinations that are experiencing rapid change. Here are a few helpful suggestions on how to become a "savvy" traveler before venturing off.

Consumer Reports Travel Letter Consumers Union produces a highly useful 24-page monthly newsletter on travel called the *Consumer Reports Travel Letter* (CRTL), in which worldwide travel services, money saving opportunities on major travel purchases, and astute tips on avoiding travel scams and overcharges are discussed. Throughout the year, CRTL presents annual country-by-country evaluations of train passes, company-by-company comparisons of rental car rates, ratings of major airline and hotel services, and a wide variety of strategies for finding the best travel values and keeping travel costs to a minimum. CRTL was one of the first consumer travel publications to highlight discount airline tickets from consolidators and to describe and compare half-price hotel programs. Like other Consumers Union publications, CRTL remains wholly unbiased and is careful about not accepting advertising or free travel services. For its $39 annual subscription, write to: CRTL, Dept. 'E', 101 Truman Avenue, Yonkers, NY 10703, or telephone (800) 234-1970.

Society of International Railway Travelers   For $59.95 per year, join the Society and receive 12 issues of *The International Railway Traveler* newsletter, chock-full of the latest rail news and articles about train travel, from luxury to seat of the pants. Membership includes discounts on Society-operated trips and rail-travel videos and other items. Call (800) IRT-4881 for details.

Thomas Cook European Timetable   The venerable *Thomas Cook European Timetable* has been published in England consistently (under seven other titles) since 1873 with the sole interruption occurring during the war years. Its younger sibling, the *Overseas Timetable*, founded in 1981, was prompted by the increased interest in train travel outside Europe. These publications have become the bibles of reliable and comprehensive train schedules for much of the world. The *European Timetable* (covering Britain and the Continent), scheduled for monthly publication on the first day of each month, comes out with great regularity although sometimes with slight delays. The *Overseas Timetable*, which covers the rest of the world, is issued every other month, beginning in January. Summer European train schedules appear in the June, July, August and September *European Timetable* issues. The latter contains an advance Winter Supplement. Similarly, the February through May issues contain advance Summer Service Supplements.

Besides train, boat, and bus schedules, the publications, codified with an extensive array of symbols for services and other data, which are translated into ordinary language at the start of each edition, also provide information on available food services and sleeping accommodations.

The Thomas Cook publications are condensations of much more extensive national timetables published by all major countries. Inexpensive and complete national timetables can be purchased at rail stations in many countries.

Because some countries do not offer their own timetables, or run short of them, *Cook's* is valuable for carrying along on a trip as well as for studying at home while planning an itinerary. Numerous readers have reported that having a copy while touring allows them to make impromptu changes in travel plans. One flaw in Thomas Cook's system consists of its reliance at times, on individuals of varying competence in underdeveloped countries where governments have not responded to pleas for "official information."

Caution: As is stated in each edition of the *Thomas Cook European* and *Overseas Timetables*, the services shown are subject to alteration, and travelers should recheck departure times upon arriving in each station.

Both publications can be obtained in North America from Forsyth Travel Library, P.O. Box 480800, Dept. E, Kansas City, MO 64148, or by telephoning (800) 367-7984 or (816) 942-9050 Monday-Saturday 09:00-17:00. Order with Visa, MasterCard or Discover by fax, (816) 942-6969. Include card number and expiration-date. Order by E-mail: forsyth@gvi.net. Each edition sells for $27.95 plus $4.50 for Priority Mail shipping. A combined shipping for the *European Timetable* and the *Thomas Cook Rail Map of Europe* costs $38.95 plus postage. Thomas Cook's publications are also available on the World Wide Web at http://www.forsyth.com.

Besides the Cook's timetables, books and maps, Forsyth's also sells European and Australian rail passes, and can book Channel Tunnel services, European sleeping-car accommodations, point-to-point tickets and groups. Forsyth's is the official membership agency for Hostelling International (formerly American Youth Hostels).

You can also pick up the Cook's timetables in Britain at Thomas Cook offices, many book stores and rail station newsstands. If you'll be passing through Britain on your way to the Continent, it's cheaper to buy them there. The books are harder to find on the Continent. Larger cities are your best bet. Look for a Thomas Cook office or check the newsstand at major railway stations.

Eurail Timetable/Horaire Eurail/Eurail Fahrplan   The *Eurail Timetable/ Horaire Eurail/Eurail Fahrplan* contains most connections between important cities in Western Europe. It is sold at major European rail stations and is highly useful.

Horaires Lignes Affaires   Another timetable, specialized and far more condensed than *Thomas Cook's*, is free. Offered by the French National Railroads, the very useful 32-page mini-folder is called *Horaires Lignes Affaires* (*Business Route Timetable*). Containing May-September schedules, it has timetables for many trains that connect French cities with each other and with foreign countries.

Other Useful Sources

Insight Guides   In total, there are over 200 titles in the *Insight Guide* series covering destinations large and small all around the globe. *Insight Guides* introduce a traveler to a destination with history, culture, and color photography. Read them before you go for "insight" in to the culture you're about to experience or peruse after you return from your trip to remind you of the sights you've just seen.

Insight Pocket Guides   Unlike most travel guides, *Insight Pocket Guides* are designed for those on a limited schedule, who need essential information in a format that is clear, concise and easy to access. In each *Insight Pocket Guide*, travelers will find practical and specific advice on what to do and where to go without the clutter and unnecessary detail found in many planning guides. As with the *Insight Guides*, *Pocket Guides* cover destinations all over the world and have brilliant color photography.

Insight Guides and *Insight Pocket Guides* are available in most travel and trade bookstores. To order by phone in the U.S.: (800) 225-3362 or Canada: (416) 475-9126, (905) 475-9126, fax (905) 475-6747. In the U.S., fax credit card orders to (800) 634-7568. Visa, MasterCard, American Express; include account number and expiration-date.

On the Web
We've roamed the World Wide Web, tracking down the best travel and rail-oriented sites to help you plan your trip. Check out Appendix B.

CHAPTER 4

Don't Miss The Train!

Cities with More than One Train Station

After arriving three days ago from London's Victoria Station at Paris's Gare du Nord station, you've spent a few absolutely lovely days in the French City of Lights, and now it's time to say au revoir and move on. Your train for Marseilles leaves in an hour and you've properly taken the *Métro* across town, blew kisses to the Eiffel Tower, and have returned in blissful innocence to the same station where you first arrived. You look up at the board of departures and gasp; there are no trains to Marseilles! "Impossible," you whelp, you've paid for secure reservations. You rush to the information window ready to scream or sue somebody. There is a line—a woman with lots of gold jewelry, a French poodle in each arm, and a cigarette dangling from her lips, is inquiring about the car-train to Bezier over the Toussaint long-weekend. There are now only ten minutes before your supposed departure time and you are jumping out of your skin. Finally you reach the front of the line only to learn from a SNCF clerk who keeps saying in his accented English, "Too bad, too bad," that Paris has six major train stations, and you needed to be at the Gare de Lyon, not the Gare du Nord, and now there's no time to make the departure. "Too bad." You'll lose the TGV reservation fee and, worse, the next TGV gets you to Marseilles too late to attend the Prince concert you reserved tickets for on your Amex card, and that cute hotel that you'd reserved four months earlier promised to hold the room only until 6 P.M. And tomorrow you need time to visit the museum before catching the train to Genoa. Everything is going wrong. Panic. Sniffle.

This cruel dramatization is just a friendly reminder that major cities in countries around the world from France to China to India have more than one major train station. Determine beforehand whether your departure or transfer city has more than one station. If so, make sure, if you are changing trains to continue to your destination, that the train departs from the station you are at. Ask at the information booth upon arrival or simply consult the *Thomas Cook European* or *Overseas Timetable*. Don't rely on getting that information an hour or so before your departure from someone such as your hotel clerk or a taxi or bus driver. If you're making a transfer, be certain that there is adequate time to get from one station to the other.

Here is a handy reference chart listing the 70 European cities with more than one rail station. Cities outside Europe with multiple stations are listed in their respective chapters.

Antwerp	Dublin	Lodz	Prague
Athens	Dunkerque	London	Ramsgate
Barcelona	Essen	Lyon	Rome
Basel	Exeter	Madrid	Rotterdam
Belfast	Folkestone	Malmo	San Sebastian
Belgrade	Geneva	Manchester	Seville
Berlin	Genoa	Marseilles	Southampton
Bilbao	Glasgow	Milan	Stockholm
Boulogne	Halsingborg	Moscow	Tilbury
Brussels	Hamburg	Munich	Tours
Bucharest	Harwich	Naples	Turin
Budapest	Hendaye	Newhaven	Venice
Calais	Irun	Oporto	Vienna
Casablanca	Le Havre	Orleans	Warsaw
Cologne	Leningrad	Oslo	Weymouth
Como	Liege	Paris	Wiesbaden
Copenhagen	Lisbon	Portsmouth	Zurich
Dover	Liverpool		

A Handy Vocabulary Chart for the Word "Train Station"

estacion	(Spain)
statione	(Italy)
Bahnhof	(Austria, Germany, and Switzerland)
la gare	(France)
Train station	(U.K. and Ireland)
Gare	(Belgium and Luxembourg)
Järnvägstation	(Sweden)
togstation (s-tog)	(Danish)

Finding Your Train

When you get to the train station, it's a good idea to check the schedule board for your train's departure track and to see whether the train will leave on time. Usually, when you walk in the door, there's a large electronic arrival and departure board with schedules flipping and whirring, as trains come and go. On the platform are stationary schedule boards; departures are generally printed on yellow paper, arrivals on white. These schedules on the platform provide information about the train's consist and station stops en-route to its final destination.

Often, especially for long-distance and night-trains another glass-encased board, usually called Composition of Trains, shows the train in miniature, right down to the locomotive and the direction the train is headed. In France, look for boards lettered "Composition des Trains" or "Placement des Voitures," in Italy, "Composizione Principali Treni." But don't worry too much about the name, just look, usually on the platform closest to the station, for the little trains encased in glass. The boards are similar throughout Europe. Each car's location on the board coincides with numbers painted on the platform or on signs hanging above the platform. You'll find your car number on the ticket, if you've made a reservation. Match it up with the one on the display then head to that spot on the platform; it'll save a mad dash up and down the platform looking for your car.

Once in a blue moon, though, the train won't stop at its designated track, as your editor found out a couple of years ago in Italy. We were headed to the towns of the Cinque Terre, from Sestri Levante, along the Gulf of Genoa. We'd arrived at the station a little early and decided to head over to the posted track. Well, for some reason at the last minute, the train was diverted to another track. Not understanding much Italian, and engrossed in our books instead of what was going on around us, we probably missed any announcement made, so of course, we missed the train! Most likely, others on the platform scurried to the other track to catch the train. The lesson here is to pay attention to everything going on around you. Even without knowing Italian, we probably could have avoided missing the train if we'd paid attention. Fortunately, trains on this route were frequent, but next time we might not be so lucky.

Finding Your Train Car: Train Splitting

How can one fail to admire the superhuman efficiency of Europe's vast international rail systems? Thousands of trains daily transport millions of people while achieving a dependability factor that is nearly perfect. An important part of this remarkable capacity is the technique of avoiding unnecessary duplication of personnel and equipment by switching cars, splitting trains, and calibrating transfer times between connections to a bare minimum.

There are a few simple things to remember when boarding your train. Before you leave the central hall of the station, ask if the car in which you will be starting your journey is going all the way to your destination. Often it is scheduled to be switched to another train or will at a particular city break from the rest of the train and join a piece of another train heading to a completely different destination. If this is the case, you must know at what point you must transfer from this train to another train en route to your destination or switch to another car on the initial train you've boarded. It's easier than it sounds.

If your car is to be switched to another train, note the name of the city where the switching will occur, the time it will take place, and the name of the stop just prior to the switching point. When you are on the correct track, and you are ready to board your train, your last step is to mount the correct car. Where a train originally consists of cars that are eventually going to different destinations, each car is clearly marked with the name of the city where it originated and the name of the city where it will terminate. Frequently, the sign will also designate some of the key cities where it makes stops. For example,

VENEZIA

Bologna — Firenze

ROMA

This sign shows that this train car originated in Venezia, makes stops at Bologna and Firenze, and terminates in Roma. If you're not versed in one or more foreign languages, you might find the names of certain cities to be less than obvious to you. Your mind will quickly learn to make the simple deduction, that Venezia is Venice, Firenze is Florence, and Roma, of course, is Rome. It's a little trickier when, for example, you're boarding a French train headed for Prague via Germany, or an Italian train heading to France. Did you know that Paris in Italian is Parigi or that Antwerp is the Flemish name for Anvers, or that the German city of Aachen is Aix-la-Chapelle in French?

Next to the fold-out steps that lead up into the train car you'll always see either the number "1" or "2" written on the side of the car or flashed on a digital panel, designating first-class or second-class seats. You may find a first-class car coupled to a second-class car, and both are marked with the same origin-destination sign. Or, a single car may be marked "1" at one end and "2" at the other end, indicating that one half is first-class and the other half is second-class. Although train cars are numbered, the order often gets shuffled. Generally, the first-class cars are found closest to the station hall and thus require less of a walk for the higher paying customers.

If you decide to sit in another car that will not be going all the way to your destination, what you must be careful about is that a car change or splitting doesn't occur while you are several cars away from your seat (and from your baggage, which usually is stowed either in your compartment or at the end of your car). You don't want to end up going in a direction that is not in your plans, and you certainly don't want to chug off to Luxembourg while your suitcases head to Munich or Vienna!

One U.S. Army colonel traveling with his family reported such an experience: while off to grab a sandwich in the bar car, the train split. "I got about as far as what had been the middle of the train…and there was no more train! I was heading off towards an unknown direction, without my family, at approximately 80 mph with all of our money but without my passport or train-ticket." The brave soldier who'd gone involuntarily AWOL finally circled back and met up with his worried wife and kids in Metz, "practically in a pool of tears."

Moral: Don't stray from your car while the train is stopped in a station. When traveling as a family or small group, each person should carry his or her own money, passport, and ticket or train-pass.

Train Changing: The Connection Time

Frequently you will find that you cannot take a train directly to some point, and will need to change trains at a designated city. In many cases the connections are very convenient, so that you change from one train to another with only a short waiting period at the transfer station. For example, there is no direct train from Zurich to the popular location of Locarno, but the Zurich-Milan train arrives in Bellinzona at 12:33, and a train for Locarno departs Bellinzona just five minutes later at 12:38. This is completely normal and should not create too much stress. The track for the Bellinzona-Locarno train is next to the track on which you arrive from Zurich, making this an effortless change. Even if the Zurich-Milan train is running a few minutes late–you will be amazed how rarely trains in Western Europe are even slightly off-schedule–your walk from one train to the other on this connection is about ten feet, and for short delays the second train, or local train, will wait for the first train, or principal train.

On the other hand, international trains from Eastern countries (Turkey, Greece, etc.) usually arrive late due to delays at border-crossings. In these cases, and in the case of a short transfer time in large city stations, the problem is the distance between tracks. Be ready to step off the first train when it pulls into the transfer station. You may find you are arriving on Track #2 and departing from Track #21, a considerable distance and invariably involving first descending into the underground walkway that connects all tracks, and then climbing up the steps leading to your departure track. This transfer problem is compounded if your first train arrives late and the second train is an express train that cannot detain its scheduled departure time.

Normally your first train will arrive on schedule and you have more than enough time to make the change. However, it is best to ask the conductor aboard the first train how far your arrival track will be from your departure track. You might have to make a mad dash for it. Sometimes you'll have to jump on the closest car of a train that is just about to pull out and then weave your way through the corridors a half a mile until you finally make it to your reserved seat or at least to a car that is heading to your destination. Such intense situations make for exciting stories, but do tend to be rather stressful.

One American expatriate from Boston writes about a harrowing experience worth sharing with other train travelers. Several years ago, he dropped off his wife and four-year-old son one Sunday in front of the Frankfurt main station, 30 minutes in advance of their train departure to Berlin, and then went off to return their car rental only to find that the Sunday drop-off point was two kilometers away. Unable to find a ride back or hail a taxi, he was forced to frantically hitchhike back to the station, and finally ran searching madly for the right track, noticing on the large clock overhead that it was exactly the time of departure!

The right track eluded him and he rushed over to the train board and gleaned the schedule. Track 17. Off he dashed to the far end of the station only to spot that the Berlin train was already pulling out of *Gleis* 17! Warning bells were cautioning to keep away from the moving train. Sprinting behind and then alongside the last car in a scene reminiscent of the war film "Von Ryan's Express," he began slapping wildly at the glass panel of the already shut train door and screaming out of desperation in his broken German, "Mein Kind, mein Kind ist im Zug," (My child is on the train!). Adrenaline pumped, and, miraculously, the massive Bundesbahn locomotive, already halfway out of the station screeched to a halt. It was the first time in history that a tourist had ever stopped a passenger train in Germany; and the conductor, red with anger and ready to slap the obstructive traveler with a stiff fine, collared the man demanding that he quickly board the train and "produce the child." That is what he did, saving himself from prosecution and finally joining his family on the trip to Berlin.

Know your track number!

A Handy Vocabulary Chart for the Word "Track"

Anden	(Spain)
Binario	(Italy)
Gleis	(Austria, Germany, and Switzerland)
Perron	(Denmark)
Quai	(France)
Spår	(Sweden)
Spor	(Holland and Belgium)
Spor	(Norway)
Track	(U.K. and Ireland)
Voie	(Belgium and Luxembourg)

Most train stops in Europe are efficiently very brief: two or three minutes. Where a stop is fairly generous, say 20 minutes or more, it is often because some car on the train is being switched to another train and possibly also to another station. You may be seated facing forward when you pull into a station and depart riding backwards!

Unwary passengers are apt to get out of the train at a stop and wander away discovering too late that their train has left without them! When you have the urge to stretch your legs, get some fresh air, and check out the trackside attractions, try not to venture away more than a few feet away from the door of the train car. That way, if your car is being switched or the stop is shorter than you anticipated, you can jump back aboard.

CHAPTER 5

Valuable Train and Travel Tips

Pre-Trip Checklist

• It is always wise to make photocopies of your airline ticket, rail pass, the identification page of your passport, your driver's license, and the credit cards you take with you. Leave one set of photocopies at home and take another set with you, storing it in a separate place from the originals.

• Leave a list of the serial numbers of your traveler's checks at home. Take a copy of that list on your trip, but keep the list separate from the checks. As you cash each check, tally the ones that remain unredeemed. This way you can spot if there is anything missing.

• If you wear glasses or contact lenses, pack an extra set. If there are any particular medicines you need, bring along an ample supply as well as a copy of prescriptions and generic names of those drugs. Keep these in your carry-on luggage. Leave medicines in their original labeled containers so as not to complicate customs processing. If any medications contain narcotics, carry a letter from your physician attesting to your need to take them. Leave a copy of your medical and dental records with a relative or friend.

• Include a tag or label with your name and address inside each piece of luggage, and lock your bags.

• Arrange to have a friend, neighbor or professional service (make sure they're bonded) look after your pets and/or property while you are away. It'll save you from having to tell too many people, like the post office or paper delivery person, that you'll be away for a while. If you have an answering machine and plan to leave it on while away, whatever you do, don't state on your outgoing message that you're off on vacation and will be back on such and such a date. Believe it or not, people do this, and more than a few of these travelers have returned home to find burglars have had a field day at their house. The best bet is to have the person who is looking after your house check the machine regularly for messages, or, you can call in, say every week to check for yourself. If your machine has a toll-saver feature, set it before you leave; it'll save you some money on long-distance charges.

• Leave a copy of your itinerary with a relative or friend should it be necessary to contact you in case of an emergency. Some people contact their consulate when traveling in a foreign country. This can be particularly helpful when traveling in dangerous or unstable regions, but is otherwise unnecessary.

• If you are like most of us, you'll have bills due while you're traveling, especially if you will be away for a month or more. Consider doubling up on payments, if you can afford it. American Express card members can pay their monthly tabs without much trouble since their offices are just about everywhere on the planet. Bank cards like Visa or MasterCard are another story. The bank card folks usually aren't keen on accepting credit card payments overseas. Some banks even try to charge ridiculous fees to send a payment to the States. Once, your editor was off on a three-month trip and left three separate envelopes with the pet sitter. Each envelope contained a check with an estimated payment to a single credit card company. Each envelope had a note on it with the date it should be mailed. Well, the pet sitter mailed all of them about a week into the editor's trip! The credit card company applied all the payments to that one month. That went over like the proverbial lead balloon. The bottom line? If you want it done right, do it yourself. Take pre-addressed envelopes with you and drop them in the mail a week or so before your payment is due. It'll mean standing in line at the post office to get the correct postage, but for a little peace of mind, it's worth it. And while we're on the subject of mail, some people might consider this tacky, but making up mailing labels to take along is a great time-saver when writing to friends and relatives.

• Think about purchasing travelers checks or cash of the country in which you'll be arriving. Having $50 or $100 in local currency for hopping a cab or grabbing a bite, sure beats standing in line at the money exchange after a long flight and leaves you with one-less-task to worry about.

• Consider putting together a "snack pack" for those picnics in the park or rolling feasts on the train. Take along some travel silverware, a collapsible cup and of course, the ubiquitous Swiss Army Knife (make sure you get the one with the corkscrew so you can sample the wines of the world). You can buy these items in Europe, but except for the Swiss Army Knife, it's probably cheaper to get them before you leave the States.

• Find out if your insurance policies cover you for theft, loss, accident, and illness while you are in another country. If yes, write down the procedures to follow in case an incident occurs.

• If you're thinking about traveling to a country where there's been some unrest, you might want to check with the State Department's hot line first, (202) 647-5225 from a touch-tone phone, or on their Web site, http://travel.state.gov.

• The Centers for Disease Control and Prevention has a hot line offers health information about destinations worldwide. Call (404) 332-4559, or visit their Web site, http://www.cdc.gov. Once in the site, select Travelers' Health menu, then the Blue Sheet option.

On the Road: A few Precautions

Traveling in Europe's major cities is probably just as safe — or more so — than visiting large cities in the U.S., but it's always a good idea to review a few tips and sharpen your awareness skills before heading out the door.

• Pickpockets thrive in crowded train and metro stations, so always keep close tabs on your passport, important documents, money and tickets. Never store these valuables in a railway station locker. Keep them with you always. And on night trains, especially in couchettes, keep them on your person, if possible. If you have a compartment, always lock the door. Reports have surfaced that luggage theft is on the rise in Europe, so always keep your bags locked and consider buying a bicycle lock to attach them to the overhead rack in your compartment or the luggage rack at the end of the car. These precautions are especially important to follow when traveling around Mexico, Latin America, Africa and Asia, but really, theft can happen anywhere. Travel-accessory stores sell all kinds of money belts, pouches and hidden wallets that will keep your valuables out of reach from most would-be thieves. If you don't have such a store in your area, call Magellan's for a catalogue, (800) 962-4943. This mail-order house has anything and everything for the traveler, from "hidden wallets" to Swiss Army Knives and compact shortwave radios.

• Watch your bags at train stations, or when getting out of cabs. You may be approached by strangers who offer to help take your bags inside or to the train. Don't succumb, unless they are uniformed railway employees, which is pretty unlikely these days because station porters have gone the way of the dodo bird. Instead of toting your bag to the train, the "good Samaritans" might just dash off into the crowd with it and ruin your trip. This isn't just a European phenomenon. It can happen in just about any major city around the world, from Los Angeles to Moscow. In recent years European railway stations and the surrounding neighborhoods have become hangouts for the homeless and for drug sellers. Most of them are looking for a handout and are harmless, but as the sun goes down crime around the stations goes up. Be aware. Don't stray into deserted areas.

• Grab-and-run thieves scope-out people who let cameras and shoulder bags dangle invitingly; reduce the odds of theft by carrying a small backpack. Sometimes thieves will roll by on a bicycle or in a car, then grab your bag or camera and scoot off. Keep your eyes open.

• Tales abound about people getting stripped to their skivvies by gypsies in Paris. It can happen anywhere, though, from Rome and Budapest to Florence. Look out for groups of young people who seem to appear from out of nowhere, waving papers or other things in your face to distract you. One such group allegedly tossed a baby at an unsuspecting tourist. Instinctively, when he reached out to catch the child, the bandits attacked like a swarm of bees, robbing him before he knew what happened.

• Don't tempt hotel staffers by leaving valuables lying around. If it's really valuable, leave it in the hotel safe, if there is one. Otherwise, keep things like cameras and video recorders with you. Leave your expensive jewelry at home.

• Don't leave luggage sitting in the car overnight, where it's visible, if you're taking the rail/drive route. You're just asking for trouble.

• Always file a police report, if you do get robbed. Otherwise you won't get reimbursed by your travel insurance company, if you purchased a policy.

• If someone comes up to you and whispers in your ear about a real deal on rail or air tickets or offers an incredible exchange rate for your dollars, just say no. The tickets are probably phony and the money is possibly counterfeit. Black market currency exchangers have been known, too, to work with a partner to relieve you of your hard-earned travel money. Think twice. Is the "deal" really worth it?

• When taking a cab, ask the driver to estimate the fare to your destination, before leaving the stand. Some cabbies thrive on taking advantage of tourists.

Travelers with Disabilities

If you're a physically disabled traveler, you may think tht rail travel outside North America is out of the question. Not so. While many countries still have a long way to go to provide access to everyone, Europe has made great strides in this area.

As new generations of rail cars are introduced, it's getting easier for travelers in wheelchairs to enjoy European train travel. Many stations have access ramps and more are being built. Some trains have wheelchair lifts, special seating areas and specially-equipped toilets.

On international routes all Eurostar and some InterCity (IC) and EuroCity (EC) trains are wheelchair-friendly. CityNightLine trains have a special compartment. Here's a rundown of the countries with the best access:

       Denmark: IC and Lyn trains

       France: TGVs and many other long-distance services

Germany: ICE trains, all EC, IC and IR trains
Italy: Pendolino, many EC and IC trains
Republic of Ireland: Dublin's suburban rail system (not all stations); most
mainline trains
Netherlands: Most trains
Sweden's X2000s, most IC and IR trains and some sleeping cars
Switzerland: All IC trains, most EC trains and some regional trains

The following countries offer accessibililty on only a few routes: Austria, Poland, Great Britain and the Republic of Ireland (although most trains are accessible, improvement is needed because generally wheelchair passengers must sit in the vestibule, away from other pasengers). Bulgaria, Czech Republic and Slovakia, Greece, Hungary, Spain and Turkey provide little if no accommodations for travelers in wheelchairs.

If you're thinking about taking an overnight train, there are some viable options for travelers in wheelchairs, from expensive compartments to reasonably-priced couchettes, where up to six people share the compartment. Keep in mind, though, railway coaches that haven't been modernized may lack accessible restrooms.

To avoid surprises, it's best to consult with your travel agent or rail-pass supplier for the latest information about whether the trains you plan to ride can accommodate wheelchairs. Also, ask them about accessible hotels. Many of Europe's smaller properties don't even have elevators, much less elevators large enough for a wheelchair. And, remember, too, that the first floor isn't usually on the ground floor, but up a flight of stairs.

The key to an enjoyable trip is to plan as far in advance as possible. Here are some useful tips and sources for more information. Cyber surfers can check out this Web site geared to travelers with disabilities: http://www.disabled-travel.com.

• If you are a wheelchair user, try to take the narrowest wheelchair you can find. If you can live without a motorized chair, you'll reduce your luggage load. Otherwise, consider a motor add-on device that fits your lightweight chair. And if you are taking a motorized chair, make sure you buy new batteries before hitting the road. Label the batteries and your chair with your name and address.

• If you're taking a wheelchair, consider new tires. In Europe, traditional air-filled inner tubes provide more shock resistance on cobblestones.

• Take along a tube repair kit, just in case you get a flat tire. The kit should include: bicycle wrenches, puncture repair kit, a tire changing kit and cheap garden gloves. Forget taking a pump. Bicycles shops are common in Europe.

• If you need a car with hand-controls for rail/drive, check and double-check with the rental company that this type of vehicle is actually available; they are few and far between overseas. London and Paris are good bets for finding a car equipped with hand controls.

• Don't plug your electric wheelchair into the hotel's razor plugs. Since they only handle 15-watt appliances, you'll blow a fuse and ruin your equipment.

• Take a narrowing device so you can get through doors skinnier than your wheelchair. Use a 12-inch long quarter-inch chain with a snap hook at each end that attaches through holes in each wheel axle brace. Shortening the chain as needed by moving the hook to a different link, and re-attaching it will pull the wheels together and narrow the chair

• Bring along a wheelchair backpack for carrying cameras, maps, snacks, etc. A small lock on the pack will keep it free from pickpockets..

Check out these sources to learn more about accessible travel.

• Global Access - A Network for Disabled Travellers - R Stricher and M Gacioch, this is an interactive community-based internet site, which enables travellers with disabilities to gain information from other travellers: http://www.geocities.com/paris/1502

• Mobility International, P.O. Box 10767, Eugene, OR 97440, Phone: (541) 343-1284. Offers a quarterly newsletter, Over the Rainbow,($15 per year). It details worldwide travel resources and opportunities for disabled people.

• SATH (Society for the Advancement of Travel for the Handicapped), 347 Fifth Ave., Ste. 610, New York, NY 10016. Phone: (212) 447-7284. Their quarterly newsletter, Access to Travel ($13 per year) focuses on disabled travel.

• Travelin' Talk, P.O. Box 3534, Clarksville, TN 37047. Phone: (615) 552-6670. For disabled travelers who want to network and share their travel experiences.

• The Very Special Traveler, P.O. Box 756, New Windsor, MD 21776. Phone: (410) 635-2881. Editor, Beverly Nelson's quarterly newsletter shares personal insights from her many trips while listing the latest in resources.

• For videos geared to disabled travelers, contact these companies: Rand McNally, 2515 E. 43rd St., Chattanooga, TN 37407, Phone: (800) 234-0679. House of Tyrol Inc., P.O. Box 909, Cleveland, GA 30528, Phone: (800) 241-5404. International Video Network , 2246 Camino Ramon, San Ramon, CA 94583, Phone: (800) 669-4486.

What Weather to Expect

These general descriptions of seasonal weather patterns may be at least moderately helpful in your planning of where to go and when.

• North America and Europe
Spring: April-June, Summer: July-September, Fall: October-December. Winter: January-March. Weather patterns vary greatly between the north and south and east and west.

• Mexico and Central America
These regions range from tropical to desert. While there isn't much rain in the deserts, it can be very rainy in the tropical zones from May through October.

• South America, Australia and New Zealand
Spring: October-December, Summer: January-March, Fall: April-June, Winter: July- September. The climate in these regions can range from temperate to tropical to sub-Antarctic. Expect high humidity and often heavy rain, in tropical zones between December and February.

• Asia
Year-round tropical heat in Hong Kong, India, Indonesia, Malaysia, the Philippines, Singapore, Thailand, and the South Pacific islands. Typhoon season is June-September in Japan, August to mid-October in Taiwan. The monsoon months in India are June-August. The rainy season in most of Asia is May-September but is June-November in the Philippines.
• North Africa Extremely hot, except December-February in Egypt.

• Middle East
Israel has mild Mediterranean temperatures year round. Iran, Iraq, Jordan, Lebanon, and Syria have four seasons similar to those in North America and Europe.

Customs Procedures and Duty-Free Shopping

It is good to know a few things about customs regulations before you begin your journey. Foreign-made articles taken abroad from the U.S. are subject to duty each time they are brought back into the U.S., unless you have acceptable proof of prior possession such as a bill of sale, insurance policy, jeweler's appraisal, or receipt of purchase. Watches, cameras, tape recorders, or articles identified by serial number or permanently affixed markings may be taken to the U.S. Customs office nearest you and registered before departure. The certificate of registration is valid for all future trips. This may be a slight hassle obtaining, but it is an effective way of being reassured if you travel with highly valuable or duty-susceptible items.

As for duty-free shopping, items in "duty-free" shops in major airports are not always the bargains they are played up to be. Only by comparison shopping can you be sure whether it is worthwhile buying that Hermés scarf, Mont Blanc pen, or Sony Walkman at the duty-free shop. Cigarettes and alcohol do tend to be well-priced. Remember that duty within EU countries has been erased. There is complete free trade. Furthermore, upon returning to your home country (non-EU) you may sometimes find that you must pay duty on your "duty-free" purchases. Duty-free means only that the airport store from which you made a purchase did not have to pay a duty when it bought the article.

To know what you can and cannot bring back to the country of your residence and what the duty tax (if any) will be when returning with articles purchased abroad, request a copy of the helpful booklet "Know Before You Go" published by the U.S. Customs Service, Custom Information Section, 6 World Trade Center, New York, N.Y. 10048.

Only a fool tries to smuggle through customs an article on which there is an embargo or outright ban or attempts to avoid paying duty for something that is subject to import tax. If caught, the penalty when entering the United States can be a combination of having the article seized, paying a fine on the amount of the U.S. value, and being subject to criminal prosecution. For example, if you buy a $1,000 piece of jade in Hong Kong and don't declare it, you'd be in violation of the 1993 law that stipulates that there is an exemption only on the first $400 of goods entering the U.S. which were purchased anywhere outside the U.S. other than the U.S. Virgin Islands, American Samoa, and Guam. After that first $400, the flat duty for the next $1,000 is 10 percent. Technically you would owe a duty of $60. In trying to avoid this $60 tax, you could lose the jade, be forced to pay a fine of $1,000, and face a jail sentence.

Another point: Do not try to bring home fruits, vegetables, plants, animal or fish products, or any perishable foods that cannot be cleared by your country's agriculture department. Without such clearance, it is a certainty such items will be confiscated and you may be subject to a fine. One traveler from Portland recently returned from Paris to the U.S. carrying the uneaten apple from his airline meal. He did not declare this food item and was fined $50 in Newark Airport. At Boston's Logan Airport, Agriculture Department officials use beagle dogs to sniff out smuggled foods and plants.

Overcoming Jet Lag

When your trip involves between a five- and nine-hour time change, those first few days of your overseas trip can be sluggish. There are ways, though, that you can greatly reduce the fatigue of jet lag and be more energetic sooner on your journey.

First, when traveling in a closed compartment such as airplanes or train compartments, drink as much water as you can to overcome dehydration resulting from lack of fresh air or from airconditioning. Remember that the more alcoholic beverages you absorb, the faster your body dehydrates. It's wiser to eat lightly or at least refrain from overeating if you want to feel better upon arriving. Dress comfortably by wearing loose clothing. Exercise as much as possible in flight or when in a closed compartment for a long time.

At one time SAS and Lufthansa published concise booklets describing exercises that can be performed by passengers while seated. Northwest Airlines shows an in-flight aerobics video on its overseas flights. If you don't mind seeming ridiculous, mimic the motions involved in rowing a boat and picking apples from an overhead branch. Rise up and sit down repeatedly. Alternately, raise your knees to your elbows. Nod your head and turn it vigorously from side to side. Turn your hands at the wrist while spreading and closing your fingers. Lift your heels up and then place them down firmly, while placing pressure on your toes. With toes up, rotate your feet in large circles. European travelers of course will think you've lost your marbles, but as the French are so fond of saying while shrugging shoulders and pursing lips, "Tant-pis" (What the heck!). You'll feel fine tomorrow.

Traveling by Night

There are some advantages to traveling by night train. You can hop from one place to another without sacrificing daytime activities in either the departure city or the arrival city. Also, by traveling at night in a regular sitting compartment, not in an extra-fare couchette or sleeping compartment, the holder of a Eurailpass can make a substantial contribution to a budget by dispensing with room rent. Attention: Even on comfortable trains, a night in a seat is not going to leave you in the best of moods in the morning. And, although you can wash in train bathrooms, the water is cold and not drinkable, the hygienic state of things is not always up to snuff, especially at the end of a long journey, and the movement of the speeding train makes it a bit tough to shave or put on or take off makeup.

On some trains the seats in the regular sitting compartments can be adjusted so that your seat and the one facing you either come together or nearly meet, and many who are fortunate enough to be in a compartment that is not full are able to stretch out. This is one technique for eliminating hotel bills, which many students and other economy-prone tourists have used successfully. However, if the seat opposite you is occupied, both you and the other passenger are going to spend the night sitting up. On a packed night train from Cairo to Luxor, a student from Philadelphia bragged of actually sleeping in the luggage rack above the seats. In the summer, be prepared to see everything.

The offsetting drawbacks of night trains are considerable. The pleasant act of meeting and conversing with Europeans and tourists from other parts of the world is reduced when you travel at night. And, of course, the scenery is severely dulled. If you are a light sleeper by nature, it's probable that you won't sleep well on trains, and certainly not while curled up in a seat.

Train sleeping accommodations vary from one European country to another, but generally they consist of communal *couchette* compartments (seats converted into berths at night) or private sleeping car compartments (beds). A blanket and a pillow are provided for each berth in a couchette compartment. There is no way to tuck the blanket in. It just slides around during the night. The sheet is often a fitted pouch which functions as top sheet and bottom sheet–you slip in between the halves. Some people undress fully or partially for bed, but a lot of this depends on your own sense of comfort in that each couchette in second class consists of six bunks, three on each side with a bottom, middle, and upper berth each. Privacy is thus minimal, yet dignity is never sacrificed.

The first-class couchette is a berth with four instead of six bunks (consisting of two rows of two bunks each). First-class couchettes are rare birds, though. France seems to have the most, but only for domestic travel. You might run into a few in Italy, but like France, they aren't used on international routes. Travelers also report seeing women-only couchettes in Germany. With either a first- or second-class ticket or with a train pass, the 1997 price per berth was around $25 for a first- or second-class couchette.

New vriations of the couchette are appearing on European trains. For instance, German Railways introduced a small fleet of Talgo couchette cars on its InterCity Night services. The design is based on the traditional Pullman sleeping car, once the staple of American railroading. The cars consist of a series of alcoves with pairs of seats staggered on each side of a central aisle. At night, the seats are converted into a single berth. Another berth folds down from the wall above. For privacy, the berths are screened off by curtains.

Private sleeping compartments come in several varieties, from first-class doubles with an upper and lower berth, to two types of single compartments; one is roomier than the other. Second-class sleepers have several configurations, from an upper and lower berth set-up to two upper berths to a compartment with three berths. These are usually called T2s or T3s. On most night trains, toilet facilities are located at one or both ends of the car.

Standard, or traditional, services, while following the compartment configurations above are generally operated using older cars, equipped with your basic power plug and a wash basin. You'll find them with names like *Wagons-Lits* or *Voiture-Lits* in French or in German, *Schlafwagen.* The newer and faster trains are sometimes roomier and have both 220- and 110- volt current, whereas the older trains only have the local 220.

EuroNight trains are a cut above traditional trains and that's reflected in a ticket price that's about 10 percent higher. For the higher price, first-class travelers are treated to such nicities as complimentary welcome drinks, snacks, bottled water, special soaps and continental breakfast. And you'll probably sleep better on one of these trains because they only make one or two station stops throughout the night—some don't stop at all after a certain time. Specials are regularly offered in conjunction with these trains, like day rooms at 50 percent off the regular night rate, or a 30 percent discount on a Europcar-InterRent car rental.

European rail authorities have stated repeatedly that specific prices for these sleeping car compartments (which vary in different areas of Europe) will not be available until the moment the reservation is confirmed. It is fair to estimate using the 1997 prices. Sleeping compartments: Paris-Zurich, per-person first-class fare $141, second class, $96; single first-class compartment $148, double compartment $64 per person. Paris-Amsterdam, single first-class compartment $127, or $73 per person in a double compartment. Florence-Paris $89 per person, double, single $188. Rail fare ranges from $72-$235 first class and from $56-$156 second class.

If you're thinking of reserving a sleeping compartment, keep a couple of things in mind. If you buy from a supplier like Rail Europe before you leave the States, they often will quote the same price for a compartment in either class, so obviously, if you've got a Eurailpass, you'll want the first-class compartment. Sometimes, though, the fare is less when you book in Europe. If you need to follow a tight schedule, it's probably best to book sleepers in advance and avoid the hassles of standing in line just to save a little money.

Something solo travelers should keep in mind when booking a compartment is that unless you specifically ask for a single compartment, you could be assigned to a double, which means that you might end up sharing it with another traveler. European railways usually match up travelers of the same sex. In Russia, however, this is not the case. Berths are assigned in the order the reservation was made, so men and women often end up sharing a compartment.

Bargain hunters will like the *Cabine 8* semi-couchette, not necessarily for comfort, but because there's no extra charge to stretch out (sort of) and sleep (or try to) on an overnight trip. Cabine 8s are treated like seats so there's no supplement due. But there's not a seat in sight in a Cabine 8 compartment. In fact, you can't even sit up in in the curvy recliner-like stationary bunks, because the railroad has crammed eight of these contraptions resembling accommodations that would look more at home on a spaceship than a train, into each second-class compartment. After awhile, being in a constant "recliner" mode wears a little thin. Still, you can't beat the price, and you can probably get a few more winks than sitting up in a seat all night. You'll find these quirky cars in France operating on the following schedules: Paris-Basel train #468/9 (*Cook's Timetable* 380); Paris-Brest train #3626/7/8 (*Cook's Timetable* 281); Paris-Quimper train #3627, 3727 (*Cook's Timetable* 285).

In recent years, hotel-trains have popped up on the night-train scene, serving business centers in Austria, Germany, Switzerland and Spain. The idea is to leave in the evening so you'll arrive at the beginning of the business day to get a jump on appointments or sightseeing.

Accommodations range from reclining seats to deluxe compartments with private baths and separate sitting areas, and a complimentary "welcome aboard" drink. And these modern trains aren't short on gadgets, from hair dryers to phones and fax machines. There's even a reception desk for guests—just like at a hotel.

Passengers in reclining seats are served continental breakfast at their seat, while other passengers receive a full breakfast in their compartment or the dining car.

Here's a look at some hotel trains.

• **InterCityNight (ICN)** These are Talgo Pendular trains and in late 1997, they were operating on three routes within Germany: Berlin-Bonn, Berlin-Munich, Munich-Hamburg. In *Komfort* class, passengers check in at the reception desk, then head to their double or single compartment. Each compartment has a shower, wash basin and toilet. For daytime use, the lower bed converts to two seats. *Tourist* class offers comfortable reclining seats. The trains have a restaurant and bistro. In 1997, a one-way ICN ticket (Berlin-Bonn or Berlin-Munich) without a rail pass cost about $144 per person in a double compartment. The fare for railpass holders in Komfort class was only $59. Tourist class passengers paid about $101 without a pass, but only $10 with a pass. On the Hamburg-Munich route, fares were slightly lower.

• **CityNightLine (CNL)** These trains connect Dortmund and Vienna, Hamburg and Zurich, Zurich and Berlin/Dresden. The CNL trains offer several sleeper options. *Grande class* compartments are very large and have two fixed beds, two chairs, a shower, washbasin and toilet. *Comfort* class has two berths that turn into seats, and a washbasin. The train also has some four-berth family compartments. Sleeperette seats are available for those not booking a compartment. CityNightLine trains have a restaurant and a lounge. The 1997 one-way per-person fares for most destinations were Grande class, $240 without a rail pass, $127 with a pass; Comfort class $203 without a pass, $108 with a pass; bunk space cost $158 with a pass, $84 without one. Sleeperette seats were $101 without a pass, but just $10 with one. This fare is 50 percent less than was charged in 1996.

• **Spanish Tren Hotel** Talgo Pendular trains are used on Tren Hotel routes connecting Paris to Madrid and Lisbon, as well as Barcelona to Paris, Zurich and Milan. Besides the international routes, they also serve the Madrid-Barcelona and Barcelona-Seville market. *Gran Clase* compartments have showers and toilet facilities. *Turista Clase* offers four-berth compartments. Without a rail pass, the per-person one-way cost for a Gran Clase compartment between Madrid and Paris was $232, in 1997; Turista Clase was $208 per person. Passholders paid $125 for

Gran Clase, while Turista class cost $111.

A new night service, NightStar, was scheduled to begin operating in early 1998, but it appears, at press time, that it will either be delayed or scrubbed completely. The plan was to link Britain and the Continent with overnight service. Trains from cities to the north and west of London were supposed to link up with Eurostar trains in London, which would continue on to destinations like Paris, Brussels, Amsterdam and Cologne, arriving in these cities at the start of the business day. Regional Eurostar day services to Paris were also facing delays at press time. Check with your travel agent or Rail Europe for the latest information.

Note that neither *couchettes* nor compartments are included in the Eurailpass or any national train passes.

Don't worry about oversleeping or missing your early morning destination. You can always rely on being awakened, and not so gently, by the voice of a stationmaster bellowing over the public address system at stops along the way. Twenty minutes or so before you arrive at your destination, the train conductor will rap his knuckles on the door of your compartment and yell something like, "Leipzig, twenty minutes." When the train crosses international borders during the night, it is completely normal for the train conductor to collect passports before everyone goes to sleep. He will present the documents to the border police and return them to you in the morning. This avoids unnecessary disturbances. With the easing of internal European borders with the EU (European Union), border crossings have become extremely lax, although some routes in the summer are watched more closely for potential drug and terrorist movements.

Baggage

Karl Baedeker wrote in 1891, in the fourteenth edition of his *Switzerland Handbook For Travelers*: "The traveler will save both time and money by planning his tour carefully before leaving home. A super abundance of luggage infallibly increases the delays, annoyances, and expenses of travel. To be provided with enough luggage, and no more, may be considered the second golden rule for the traveler."

Criticism you will hear most about rail travel in Europe concerns the problems of storing and handling luggage. Don't count on being able to get a porter; many small cities don't have them. Nearly all the large cities with porters have too few. Some stations provide self-service carts, but the stations which do so often don't have enough of them at peak times. Some stations provide self-service carts, but the stations that do so often don't have enough of them at peak times. Also, many stations charge a dollar or two to use the carts. Make sure you have enough change on hand.

An effective procedure if you travel in pairs is for one of you to guard your luggage while the other hurries toward the station to find a cart and returns to the track with it.

When boarding a train, you want to avoid the difficulty of hauling your luggage down the narrow corridors of several cars. Before your train arrives, examine the train diagram on the platform. The sequence of cars and the platform location for each car are indicated for all long-distance trains. Try to place yourself and your luggage at the correct site for boarding your car. This little procedure will simplify your life.

On many trains there is a storage area for luggage at one or at both ends of the car. On most trains you have to store your baggage on a rack above your seat, which tends to be very high. Lifting a 30-pound (or heavier) weight above one's head can be a physical strain for the elderly or those who have a physical disability.

On the whole, it is much better to travel with two small, relatively lightweight suitcases or duffel bags per person than with one monstrous case. The small ones are easier to lift, and there's a better chance of being able to store them under the seat or in station lockers.

Some trains have a baggage car, although the newer and faster trains have baggage services in which the luggage, bikes, etc., don't necessarily travel on the same train with you. Using the traditional baggage car is almost always inconvenient, and although the charge is reasonable—about $6 per piece, with a limit of 66 pounds each—it is more expensive than having your cases with you in your own car or in your compartment. Also, unless you verify that your luggage is to travel on the same train as you, it may go on another train, possibly arriving a day after your arrival. If you want luggage to arrive at your destination prior to your arrival, you can arrange to send it in advance and it will be held in the "checked luggage" room at your destination. Usually, no charge is made for the first two or three days of storage, however, after that, a small daily fee must be paid when claiming the bags.

Additionally when your bags are in the baggage car, you don't have access to them, and you may have to wait up to 30 minutes for your cases to be unloaded. In some countries, a well placed tip can help convince the porter to unload your gear surprisingly fast. Waiting for cases to be unloaded, in turn, delays you in getting to the room reservation desk at the tourist accommodation office inside the station, a delay that can cost you getting a decent room that night. Every minute counts in obtaining an available room during peak travel days in the high season. Waiting at the baggage car also delays you in getting into what can often be a very long line for taxis.

When you arrive in a city with more luggage than you need for that destination, savvy travelers opt to store excess stuff in a station locker. Others wisely return to the station the night before their departure so as to store luggage in a locker and facilitate the haul to the station the following morning.

Although there are baggage checkrooms at nearly all major rail stations, using a checkroom instead of a rental locker eats up precious time you could have used more pleasantly and productively. There are frequently long lines both when you leave your luggage and again when you are claiming it. If you use checkrooms instead of rental lockers, be sure to leave yourself adequate time prior to your train's departure to retrieve your suitcases. And, although these check-rooms are secure, it isn't all that reassuring leaving any valuables in unlocked luggage.

The most convenient and safest method of storing luggage is to place it in a 24-hour rental locker. Unfortunately the lockers present their own set of problems. Several European stations have too few lockers, have strict time limitations, and are too small for large bags. Again, small suitcases make better sense.

Another wise maneuver is to have small change on hand for each country you visit. It goes without saying, the lockers in each country work only with the local coins. You cannot use a *kroner* in France, or a *franc* in Denmark!

Eating on Trains

Food in the dining cars tends to be expensive, and the choice can be limited, although in the last few years the quality of food services has radically improved. In restaurant cars of *de luxe* trains, the lunch is a fixed menu, very tasty, and highly caloric. On ordinary trains, the restaurant car food is adequate…but still a bit pricey. On the French TGV, the bar cars are very comfortable and the choice and quality of the sandwiches is surprisingly good. Not only can you buy sandwiches and drinks, you can purchase newspapers and magazines, telephone cards for the phones onboard, cognac, and some gift items.

Dining in the restaurant car of a train speeding across Europe has to be one of the most graceful and elegant experiences in life. If you can manage to relax about the prices and not see the linen table cloth and heavy silverware as pretensions but as remnants of an old European style, you should have a jolly good time.

Here are a few examples of meals (with prices) on major European train routes. Amsterdam-Paris *Etoile du Nord* serves crayfish, duck or lamb chops, potatoes *Lyonnaise*, steamed vegetables, cheeses and rolls, and pastry for a cool $55. Dinner on the Oslo-Bergen trip may include salad, poached salmon with boiled potatoes, and beer for $42. Dinner on the Paris-Lisbon run of the *Sud Express* can be $36 for vegetable soup, wild turkey with rice, fava beans, flan and fruit, and coffee. Tuck in your napkin and enjoy. You can't do this between Albany and Buffalo! Note that on many trains, you must reserve a seat in the restaurant car for the entire trip if you want lunch or dinner.

Both budget travelers and many of those who can't afford the meals served on trains buy their food at a market or delicatessen or one of those great French charcuteries before they board a train. A hunk of cheese and some bread, salads, meats, patés, fruits, and wine can make for a copious and sensuous, yet informal eating experience.

Before making the 12-hour ride from Copenhagen to Amsterdam, try buying a dozen, delicious smorre-brod sandwiches in a shop just a block from the Copenhagen station. The variety includes shrimp, salmon, ham, chicken, and beef, all garnished with tasty cucumbers, asparagus, and tomatoes. Two people can can buy enough provisions for four meals for about $36. If you find the idea of "picnicking" attractive, you can ask your hotel or *pensione* to pack a lunch for you, or you can purchase food either at a store near the station, in a restaurant at the station, from a food market inside the station, or, along the way, from vendors that push carts up and down the platforms at many station stops.

You will find restaurants and food stores located in many principal rail stations. Food stores in the Copenhagen, Stuttgart, Vienna, and Zurich rail stations offer meat, cheeses, salads, breads, pastries, etc., that are excellent. In Germany, most shops close at 18:00, so the main train station is the best bet for buying food after hours.

Remember in any case that it's always a good idea to bring along some food and a bottle of water on a long journey.

Car-Sleeper Express Service

Europe's "Car-Sleeper Express Service" is one of the fastest growing train services in Europe today. Essentially you can sleep in a *couchette* or sleeping compartment on the same train that carries your auto. You can also ship your car ahead on an "Auto Express" while you ride on another train, and find your car waiting for you at your destination. Started by French Rail in 1957, this service is now offered in Austria, Belgium, Britain, Holland, Italy, Spain, and Germany, and links cities in those countries as well as in Portugal and Switzerland. The system annually moves more than 500,000 people and more than 160,000 cars. Inquire with the national rail offices or agents in your country. If you are buying a car in Europe with the idea of using it overseas and then shipping it home, this service might be very useful. The *Thomas Cook European Timetable* lists these trains in Table 1 (international services) and Table 2 (countrywide services).

Airport-City Rail Connections

Here is a handy list of fast train travel times in minutes between major cities and their airports.

Amsterdam (17-21 minutes)
Barcelona (16-22)
Brussels (23)
Frankfurt (17)
London (50 minutes from Heathrow, 42 minutes from Gatwick)
Malaga (12)
Paris (33-39 minutes from De Gaulle, 23-28 minutes from Orly)

Rome (30)
Vienna (31-40)
Zurich (10)
(For a complete listing see Table 5 in the *Thomas Cook European Timetable*.)

Lost Money and Passports

Losing or having your money or passport stolen is a certain way to spoil at least a part of your trip. The best precaution is to carry a minimal amount of cash at one time. Traveler's checks and major credit cards are safer. With the advent of ATM machines, it's even esier to obtain cash overseas, and often, as with credit card purchases, the ATM's give a better exchange rate then a bank. Remember to record the numbers in a safe place. Also guard your return airplane ticket as closely as your cash, traveler's checks, and passport. Each year, approximately 3,000 U.S. passports are stolen and another 11,000 are lost. There is an increasingly aggressive market for American and European passports in Latin America and Asia, so take precautions.

If, despite all your safeguards, you discover that your passport has been taken or is simply missing, don't panic. Here's what you do. First, notify the local police and obtain a signed copy of the police report. Take this document to the local office of your country's consulate. It is not necessary to go to your embassy: It is your consulate, not your embassy, that will assist you by issuing a replacement passport. Obtaining a replacement is expedited if you can provide the passport number. Otherwise, you might have a few days to wait. If, in addition to the passport number, you have a certified copy of your birth certificate or certificate of citizenship, the consulate usually can issue a new passport the same day without telexing or wiring the State Department back home. In order to issue a new passport, two ID photos are required. Note that U.S. passport requirements include very specific dimensions for photos, which are obtainable at only certain photographers or photo stores. Consulates always have a list of places that can make these photos in each foreign city.

Obviously, it's best not to lose your papers. The delay of missed connections, additional hotel bills, and taxis (to police, consulate, photographer, airline office, etc.) can amount to a terrible expense.

Day Rooms

Many non-Europeans are unfamiliar with an extremely convenient service called "day rooms" available at some rail stations. With this accommodation, the tenant has privacy, a place to change clothes, and sometimes even bathing facilities. Some day rooms have beds. The advantages of a rail station day room over a conventional hotel room are that it is usually cheaper and it is located at the station.

Last-Minute Checklist

Here are several important tips that can greatly increase the pleasure (or reduce the struggle) of your international travel.

• Carry as little luggage as possible. You will arrive at many rail stations where it is a long walk from the train to the taxis (often requiring walking up and down stairs) and will find that there are neither porters nor carts. If the luggage you take is a burden, bring along a lightweight folding luggage rack.

• Bring a bottle of mineral water on any long trip. Most trains only provide drinking water in the bar car.

• Pack soft-ply toilet paper, wash-and-dry packets, and plastic bags. The bags are useful for storing leftover food items, wet soap and damp or dirty laundry.

CHAPTER 6

EURAILPASS EUROPE

AUSTRIA

Getting on Track in Austria

• Tourist information: Austrian National Tourist Office, New York office, P.O. Box 1142, New York, NY 10108-1142. Telephone (212) 944-6880, fax (212) 730-4568. Los Angeles office, 11601 Wilshire Blvd., Suite 2840, Los Angeles, CA 90025. Telephone (310) 477-2038, fax (310) 477-5141. Montreal, Canada office, 1010 Sherbrooke Street West, Suite 1410, Montreal, Quebec H3A 2R7, Canada, telephone (514) 849-3708, fax (514) 849-9577. Toronto office, 2 Bloor Street East, Suite 3330, Toronto, ON M4W 1A8, Canada, telephone (416) 967-3381, fax (416) 967-4101. Vienna office, Osterreich Werbung, A-1040 Vienna, Margaretenstrasse 1, Austria. E-mail: anto@aol.com. On the Web: http://www.anto.com.

• Public holidays: January 1, New Year's Day, January 6, Epiphany, Easter, Easter Monday, May 1, Labor Day, Ascension Day, Whit Monday, Corpus Christi Day, August 15, Assumption Day, October 26, National holiday, November 1, All Saints Day, December 8, Immaculate Conception, December 25, Christmas Day, December 26, St. Stephen's Day.

• Summer time: Austria changes to Summer Time on the last Sunday of March and converts back to Standard Time on the last Sunday of September.

• Currency: Austrian Shilling (AS). At press time, $1 was worth approximately AS 12.78.

Overview of Austria's Trains

Train travel in Austria promises to be not only an aesthetically exciting experience but an informative one as Austria has recently become a jumping off point for travel and trade with the rapidly evolving central and eastern European countries. When heading north, east, and south from Vienna, western travelers are destined to meet up with Hungarians, Czechs, Slovaks, Bulgarians, Romanians, and Russians, Europe's new travelers.

The Austrian Federal Railway, called ÖBB (Österreichische Bundesbahnen) is well known for being on time and for providing clean and efficient service, although in the summer months the most popular routes can be overflowing with travelers attracted by the captivating Alps and enchanting music festivals. While travel between the major cities is swift and regular, the local mountain trains can be painfully slow although blissfully scenic. Train travel in Austria on the whole is a pleasant experience although in the words of one Viennese publisher, Austria can be tiring in that the Austrians tend to look inward as if the whole world were Austrian.

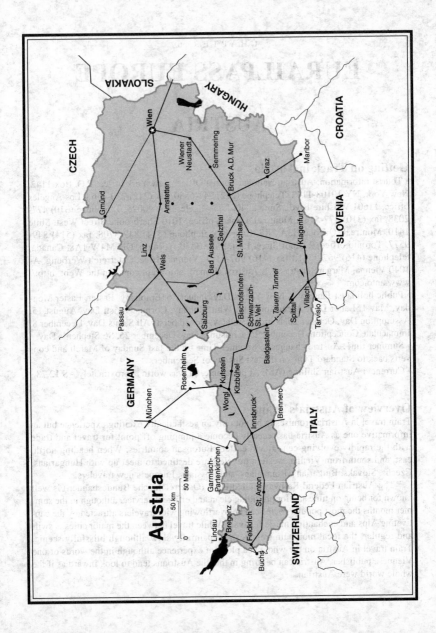

General Rail Information

• Children under six travel free. Half-fare for children between the ages six and 14. Travelers over 15 must pay full fare.

• Special "through tickets" are required for "privileged trains," which cross German or Italian borders from one part of Austria to another without border formalities (customs, passport and currency control). These trains do not allow passengers to board or leave the train in Germany or Italy.

• The second-class couchette cars on most Austrian internal routes and on some international services have four berths per compartment instead of six. A supplement of 33 percent over the price of a couchette in a six-berth compartment is charged for them. Inquire about this when reserving a couchette.

• You'll find these trains in Austria: EuroCity, international express trains and superior-service within the country; EuroNight, high-quality overnight trains; InterCity, express trains that run within the country;

The signs you will see at rail stations in Austria are:

ABFAHRT	DEPARTURE
ANKUNFT	ARRIVAL
AUSGANG	EXIT
AUSKUNFT	INFORMATION
BAHNHOF	STATION
BAHNSTEIG	PLATFORM
DAMEN	WOMEN
EINGANG	ENTRANCE
FAHRKARTEN-SCHALTER	TICKET OFFICE
FAHRPLAN	TIMETABLE
GEPACKAUFBEWAHRUNG	BAGGAGE CHECKROOM
GLEIS	TRACK
HERREN	MEN
PLATZ RESERVIERUNG	SEAT RESERVATION
RAUCHER	SMOKING COMPARTMENT
SCHLAFWAGEN	SLEEPING CAR
SPEISEWAGEN	RESTAURANT CAR

AUSTRIA'S TRAIN PASSES

European East Pass See Eastern Europe

Austrian Railpass Sold worldwide by travel agencies, by Rail Europe, and by DER Tours/GermanRail.

Also sold in Austria at travel agencies and rail stations. Vouchers for this pass are sold at many major rail stations near the Austrian border (such as Munich and Zurich), to be exchanged for Rabbit Card after entering Austria.

This pass is valid for unlimited travel on all Austrian Federal Railway lines and on state and private rail lines in Austria any three days within 15 days.

	Adult		Child**	
	1st Cl.	2nd Cl.	1st Cl.	2nd Cl.
3 days in 15	$145	$98	$72.50	$49
Add's Rail Day (5 max.)	$ 21	$15	$10.50	$7.50

**Child prices for children 4-12 years of age. Children under four free.

Bonuses: 50 percent discount on steamers of Donauschiffahrt Wurm & Köck operating between Passau and Linz. 40 percent discount on bicycle rental in over 130 railway stations in Austria. 20 percent discount on steamers of DDSG operating between Melk, Krems and Vienna. 10 percent discount on Schneeberg rack railway,15 percent on Schafberg rack railway, 20 percent on steamers on the lake Wofgansee and steamers operating on Lake Constance. Also receive a 50 percent discount on bicycle rental from selected rail stations..

Senior Citizen Half-Fare In 1998, women 60 and over and men who are 65 and older can buy train and bus tickets at half-price after purchasing a Senior Citizen's Identification for 350 Austrian schillings, available at all rail stations and major post offices in Austria, and also at the Hauptbahnhof stations in Frankfurt, Munich and Zurich.

The ID (valid for one calendar year) can also be obtained by mail by sending a travelers check in the amount of $37 or equivalent, a photostat of the passport page which has a picture and states the holder's age, plus one passport-size photo to: OBB Verkehrseinnahmen-und Reklamationsstelle, Mariannengasse 20, A-1090 Wien, Austria.

The Austrian tourist office says they will accept a personal or bank check sent to the address in Vienna that's currently in the Eurail Guide. The card is valid for a calendar year (Jan. 1-Dec. 31)

This discount is *not* valid on municipal transit lines (subway, trolley, bus).

Bundesnetzkarte (National Network Pass) Sold only in Austria. Unlimited train travel in all of Austria. The 1997 *first*-class prices were: $590 for one month. *Second*-class: $430.

Kilometer Bank Sold only in Austria. Valid for *both* first and second-class seats. May be used by 1–6 persons traveling together on trips of over 70 km one way. Can be used in first or second-class. The conductor deducts trip distance for each passenger age 16 or older. Only half the distance is charged for each child age 6–15. No charge for children under age six.

The 1997 prices were: 2,000 km (1,243 miles) A S2,400 (approx. $240), 3,000 km (1,865 miles) AS 3,540 (approx. $354). Call the tourist office for 1998 prices.

The maximum kilometers charged against this pass for any one trip are 600. Any number of kilometers above that are free.

For *first-class* use, one kilometer is counted as 1.5 kilometers.

EURAILPASS BONUSES IN AUSTRIA

Free transportation on two rack railways, Puchberg am Schneeberg–Hochschneeberg and St. Wolfgang–Schafbergspitze, also the steamers on Lake Wolfgang.. Reduction of 50 percent on Lake Constance steamers, and 50 percent off Linz–Passau (and v.v.) daytrips on "Wurm and Kock" ships.

ONE-DAY EXCURSIONS AND CITY-SIGHTSEEING

Here are 23 one-day rail trips that can be made comfortably from Innsbruck, Linz, Salzburg and Vienna, returning to them in most cases before dinnertime. Notes are provided on what to see and do at each destination. The number after the name of each route is the *Cook's Timetable* reference. Additionally, we have listed 17 scenic rail trips.

Innsbruck

Innsbruck, in the province of Tyrol, is a marvelous winter resort. Two Winter Olympics were staged here, in 1964 and 1976. The city is an excellent gateway to many cable railway trips (Hungerburg, Hafelekar, Igls, Patscherkofel). In town, see the 28 bronze statues around the enormous and magnificent tomb of Maximilian I in the 16th-century Court Church (Hofkirche) and the effigy of King Arthur there. Also view the silver altar at the Silver Chapel.

Take a look at the roof on Goldenes Dachl. Dating from the 16th century, it has some 2,657 gold plated tiles. Next, head for the Museum of Tyrolean Folk Art, considered the most important collection of costumes and rustic furniture in Austria. The Folk Art museum is open 09:00-17:30 and during July and August 19:00-21:00 evenings, and on Sunday, 09:00-12:00. Admission is $1.79-$5. Other places worthy of a visit include the 18th-century Roman-style Triumphal Arch, Reisenrundgemalde, a huge circular fresco depicting the Battle of Bergisel, and the 18th-century Imperial Palace. Stop by the Tyrolean Regional Museum in the Arsenal of Emperor Maxmillian I, or Bergisel Kaiserjager, home to the museum of the Tyrolean Imperial Light Infantry. Enjoy splendid views, too, of the city and surrounding mountains. There's an excellent art collection of Archduke Ferdinand II at Schloss (castle) Ambras, which is open daily except Tuesday, April 1 through October 31, 10:00-17:00, admission $0.93-5.58. Take the shuttle bus from Maria-Theresien-Strausse (Attes-Landhaus) to the castle. It leaves every hour from 10:00. Walk on the wild side at the Alpenzoo, where you can see an assortment of alpine animals, about 2,000 in all. Alpenzoo is open 09:00-18:00 during the summer; admission $2.80 and $6.50.

Linz

Linz is on the Danube, halfway between Vienna and Salsburg, and was an important trading center. Its historic center has been superbly restored with a large pedestrian zone and elegant patrician houses.

Visit the schloss where Emperor Fredrich III lived, with its Upper Austrian Regional Museum collections of prehistoric and Roman antiquities, medieval armor and weapons, musical instruments and regional arts and crafts, open Tuesday-Saturday 10:00–18:00, Sunday 10:00–16:00. Or, drop by Martinskirche, one of Austria's oldest churches.

The medieval, Renaissance and Baroque exhibits in the City Museum at 7 Bethlehemstrasse, are available for viewing Monday-Friday 09:00–18:00, Saturday and Sunday 15:00–17:00.

Take the 16-minute two-mile tram ride from Urfahr Station to the 1,722 feet high summit of Postlingberg on the south side of the Danube, to visit the Town Hall and see the view from there. The Pöstlingbergbahn, as the train is called, heads up the hill from 05:20 to 20:00 and down the hill from 05:40 to 20:20 Monday-Saturday and on Sunday the schedule, going up, starts at 06:40 with the last tram at 20:00. Return trips start at 07:00 and run until 20:20. Trams run every 20 minutes and an adult round trip costs around $5. The tram has been running since 1898, and made the Guiness Book of Records as Europe's steepest tram. In 1742, the first stone was laid for the twin-spired church at the summit.

Kremsmunster, an enchanting small town established in 777, is a 30-minute drive south of Linz. Visit it in order to see the treasures in the monastery. It houses a fabulous library as well as an exceptional museum of natural history and early scientific instruments, a picture gallery, an art gallery, a fine collection of stained glass, and an armory.

Among its more than 100,000 rare books, 886 incunabula (books produced before movable type was invented in the 16th century), and 910 old manuscripts are two famous "jewels" of the 230-foot-long library, dating from the 8th and 9th century, the splendidly illuminated parchments called Codex Millenarius Major and Codex Minor. All four large rooms of the library are furnished with beautiful baroque bookcases.

Take the kids for a ride on the "Grottenbahn," Europe's longest grotto railway. The setting is a fairy tale, a legend about the orphan Cindi. The Grotto Railway is housed in a tower which was once part of the fortifications on Pöstlingberg. The Dragon Angelus brings its passengers through a brightly illuminated fairy tale world. On the lower level is a scale model of Linz Main Square. The side streets of the model contain scenes from well known fairy tales. The Grotto Railway is open from the Saturday before Holy Week until November 2nd (All Souls Day). During the summer it runs daily from 09.00 to 18.00. Adults pay AS 45, children pay AS 20.

Salzburg

"The artistic capital of not only Europe but the whole world." That's what Austrian writer Stefan Zweig had to day about Salzburg. With the cornucopia of art and music available year-round, capped off by the grand Salzburg Festival which lasts nearly a month and a half in the summer, the hills really are alive with music in and around Salzburg.

Get in tune with a visit to the most amusing place in Europe, the 17th-century Hellbrunn Palace. The 12th-century fortress, 500 feet above the town (Festung Hohensalzburg), has a 16th-century 200-pipe barrel organ (played three times every day). Forty-minute guided tours start every 15 minutes 09:00–17:30 daily in July and August.

Guided tours of the incredibly opulent rooms in The Residenz, the 17th-century city palace of Salzburg's archbishops, start at 10:00 and leave every half-hour, except between 12:00 to 13:00, until 15:00, Monday-Friday. The gallery of paintings in The Residenz (including Titian and Rembrandt) is open daily 10:00–17:00.

See the painted ceilings in the 17th-century Festspeilhaus or the collection of Mozart musical instruments and family memorabilia in the Mozart Museum, his birthplace (9 Getreidegasse), open daily 09:00–19:00. The vast musical library at Bibliotheca Mozartiana. St. Sebastian's Cemetery (Linzergasse 41) is a haven for music lovers. Other interesting Salzburg sights include the well-preserved cathedral on Domplatz, the Gothic cloister in the 9th-century Benedictine Abbey of St. Peter and the baroque Universitatskirche, or. Collegiate Church, on Universitatsplatz.

Twice daily, the melodies of Mozart ring out from the carillon chimes at Residenz, where, from the 7th century, archbishops lived. Then there's the ancient marketplace, Alter Markt, the marble Angel Staircase and the Salzburger Barock-Museum in the 17th-century Schloss Mirabell, and the marvelous gardens there. Look for a superb collection of prehistoric objects, fossils and meteorites at the Natural History Museum. It's open daily from 09:00 to 17:00.

Take the cable car to the top (5,800 feet) of Untersberg for a breathtaking view of Salzburg and the Alps. There are other good views of the city and river from Hettwer Bastion and also from the top of Monchsberg, Kapuzinerberg and Gaisberg.

Vienna (Wien)

When you think of Vienna, two things come to mind, the Vienna Boy's Choir, founded by the Emperor Maxmilian I and the famous high-stepping Lipizzaner stallions of the Spanish Riding School at Hofburg. That's just for starters, though. Vienna has so much to offer, it could take weeks to scratch the surface. A good place to start is Vienna's main tourist office (38 Kartnerstrasse), to find out what's going on around town. It's open daily 09:00–19:00.

For those arriving by air, there is frequent rail service between the city's Schwechut Airport (Flughafen) and Vienna's Nord station. Trains start running at 05:03. The last train from Vienna to the airport is 21:33 and the last train from the airport is 22:23. Generally trains run every 30 minutes, with more frequent departures at peak times. The ride takes 31-40 minutes.

Scope out a great view of the city by marching up the 365 steps of the 13th-century Saint Stephen's Cathedral, to the top of the south steeple. The steeple is open daily 09:00–16:30. Another great view is from the top of the Donauturm (Danube Tower), or from the hills in the Vienna Woods. Vienna's most elegant shopping streets are two pedestrian malls that run south and east from St. Stephen's: Karntnerstrasse and Graben. Three-hour boat trips on the Danube Canal operate daily except Monday at 10:00, 13:00 and 16:30 from Schwedenbrucke, a bridge that is a 15-minute walk from St. Stephen's.

See the Opera House. The Art Gallery. The Burgtheater. The Rathaus (City Hall). The Giant Ferris Wheel and the miniature railway in the Prater amusement park.

Guided tours of some of the 1,400 rooms in Schonbrunn Castle, Vienna's Versailles, are offered daily 09:00–12:00 and 13:00–16:00. It is a 20-minute ride from Burgring on streetcar # 58. Most of the castle is accessible for wheelchair users.

Visit Tierpark, the zoo, in the Schonbrunner Schlosspark. From March, it's open daily, 09:00-17:30. Check out the museums of modern art in Palais Liechtensten and in Schweizer Garten. For a peek at the crown jewels of the Holy Roman Empire (crafted around 962), the crown of the Austrian Empire (1602, before 1804 merely the family crown of the Habsburgs), the Burgundian treasure (15th century) and the treasure of the Order of the Golden Fleece, take train D, J, 1, 2 or bus 57A to Burgring and Schatzkammer. Schatzkammer is open daily except Tuesday 10:00-18:00. Admission is about $4.90.

At the Imperial Palace are the offices of the Austrian president, an international convention center, the chapel where the Vienna Boy's Choir sings mass on Sundays and religious holidays, the hall in which the Lipizzan stallions of the Spanish Riding School perform, various official and private apartments and several museums and state rooms which are open to the public.

The Museum of Fine Arts (or Kunsthistorisches Museum) at 1, Maria-Theresien-Platz, has an excellent Picture Gallery that's open daily except Monday 10:00-18:00, Thursday, 10:00-21:00. The museum's Egyptian and Near Eastern Collection, Collection of Greek and Roman Antiquities, Collection of Sculpture and Decorative Arts (partly not opened to the public) and Coin Cabinet are available for viewing daily except Monday, 10:00-18:00. General admission is $4; expect to pay about $8 for special exhibits. Much of this museum is accessible to visitors using wheelchairs. Ride any of these transit lines to the museum: U2: Babenbergerstrasse, U3: Volkstheater, tram D, J, 1, 2, bus 57A: Burgring.

The many art museums in Belvedere Palace (medieval, baroque and modern art), open Tuesday-Sunday from 10:00 to varying afternoon hours, Buy a pass for all the museums for about $5.35. The Historical Museum of the City of Vienna, 4, Karlsplatz, offers 20 centuries of memorabilia. Open daily except Monday 09:00-16:30; free admission on Fridays (except holidays) until 12 noon. U, tram, bus: Karlsplatz/Oper.

The Sigmund Freud Museum, where the founder of psychoanalysis lived and practiced for many years, is at 9, Berggasse 19. Open July to September 09:00-18:00, October to June 09:00-16:00 Admission, $5.35. Tram D: Schlickgasse, tram 37, 38, 40, 41, 42: Schwarzspanierstrasse, bus 40A: Berggasse.

The great paintings (Hieronymus, Bosch, Rubens, Titian, Van Dyck) at the Academy of Fine Arts (Akademie der bildenden Künste) , 1, Schillerplatz 3, open Tuesday, Thursday and Friday 10:00–14:00, Wednesday 10:00–13:00 and 15:00-18:00, Saturday, Sunday and holidays 09:00–13:00. Admission: $2.50. U, tram, bus: Karlsplatz/Oper, tram D, J, 1, 2, bus 57A: Burgring.

Check out the exhibits at the Austrian National Library, Grand Hall (Österreichische Nationalbibliothek, Prunksaal). At 1, Josefsplatz 1, its operating hours from mid-May to late October are Monday-Saturday 10:00-16:00. Sundays and holidays 10:00-13:00. General admission $3.35, special exhibitions $5. U, tram, bus: Karlsplatz/Oper, U1, U3: Stephansplatz, U3: Herrengasse

If streetcars are your interest, stop by the Vienna Streetcar Museum (Strassenbahnmuseum) 3, Erdbergstrasse 109. Until early October, open Sat, Sun, public holidays, 09:00-16:00. (Subject to closure additional days, phone first, 7909-44 903.) U3, tram 18, 72: Schlachthausgasse. Sightseeing is also available with Oldtime Tram tours until October 5. Tickets: Information Office of the Wiener Linien (underground station Karlsplatz), phone 7909-44 026. Approximate cost per person, $16.70.

Vienna's largest outdoor food market (Naschmarkt) runs between Rechte Wienzeile and Linke Wienzeile.

Sightseeing flights over Vienna operate from the Schwechat Airport.

Take trolley car # 38 from Schottentor (in central Vienna) to **Grinzing**, the wine-tasting village. Continue from there on bus # 38A to the small Church of St. Joseph on the top of the 1,585-feet high

Kahlenberg, from where Hungary and Czechoslovakia can be seen on clear days.

Save some money on Vienna sightseeing with the Vienna Card. For only AS 180 (about $15), you'll get unlimited travel on the underground, buses (except night buses) and trams for 72 hours, plus a discount on Vienna Airport Lines' shuttle bus from the airport in the city center or reverse for AS 60 each way instead of the usual AS 70. The card also offers discounts 100 museums, sights, theaters, concerts, shops, restaurants, cafés and Heurigen (wine taverns), restaurants, cafés and Heurigen (wine taverns). You can by it at your Vienna hotel, at Tourist Information Offices (i.e., 1st District, Kärntner Strasse 38, daily 09:00-19:00), at Vienna Transport (Wiener Linien) sales counters and information offices (e.g. Stephansplatz, Karlsplatz, Westbahnhof, Landstraße/Wien Mitte) or from outside Vienna with your credit card by phone 011 43-1-798 44 00-28.

In the following timetables, where a city has more than one rail station we have designated the particular station after the name of the city (in parentheses). **Where no station is designated for cities in Austria, Switzerland and West Germany, the station is "Hauptbahnhof."**

Innsbruck - Bregenz - Innsbruck   950

| Dep. Innsbruck | 06:31 (1) | 08:39 (1) | Dep. Bregenz | 12:43 (1) | 15:24 (2) |
| Arr. Bregenz | 09:10 | 11:13 | Arr. Innsbruck | 15:41 | 18:24 |

(1) Restaurant car. (2) Plus other departures from Bregenz at 16:43 (1), 18:43 (1), 20:43 (1) and 21:42, arriving Innsbruck 19:21, 21:21, 23:21 and 00:35.

Sights in **Bregenz**: Divided into two sections, features of the lower town include the lakeshore, the shopping district and the Voralberg Museum. The upper town has churches. Situated on the shore of the Bodensee (Lake Constance), easy day trips can be made from here to Innsbruck, Munich, Salzburg and Zurich.

The annual Music Festival (light opera and ballet on an unusual water stage in the lake) runs mid-July to mid-August. Take the funicular to the top (3,200 feet) of Pfander Mountain for a spectacular view of Bodensee, the Rhine River and the town of Lindau (see notes about Lindau under "Munich-Lindau"). The funicular runs 08:30–20:00 (until 22:00 in mid-summer). Steamboats are operated on the lake from early April to early October.

Innsbruck - Igls - Innsbruck   Suburban Train

Four miles from Innsbruck by suburban railway is the great ski resort of Igls.

Innsbruck - Kitzbuhel - Innsbruck   960

Dep. Innsbruck   09:25 (1)   11:25 (2)   13:25 (1)
Arr. Kitzbuhel   60-65 minutes later

Sights in **Kitzbuhel**: This is one of the major winter resorts in the Alps. Cable cars take you from Kitzbuhel to many mountaintops. The city has one museum, some old churches.

Dep. Kitzbuhel   11:29(1)   13:29 (2)   15:29 (1+3)
Arr. Innsbruck   60-65 minutes later

(1) Light refreshments. (2) Restaurant car. (3) Plus other departures from Kitzbuhel at 17:30 (2), 19:29 (1), and 21:29 (1).

Innsbruck - Mayrhofen - Innsbruck   890, 950, 955

All of the Jenbach–Mayrhofen and v.v trains are second class only.

890

Dep. Innsbruck   09:30   13:30   15:30
Arr. Jenbach   09:50   13:50   15:50
Change from a standard-gauge train to a narrow-gauge train; Table 955
Dep. Jenbach   10:22   14:22   16:22 (1)
Arr. Mayrhofen   10:11   15:18   17:18

Sights in **Mayrhofen**: This is a popular winter resort, with horse sleighs.

955

Dep. Mayrhofen   13:40   15:40   17:40   19:10 (2)
Arr. Jenbach   14:35   16:35   18:35   20:10
Change from a narrow-gauge train to a standard-gauge train; Table 890
Dep. Jenbach   15:00   17:00   19:00   21:00
Arr. Innsbruck   20 minutes later

(1) Steam trains operate on this route from June 1 to the end of Sept. Depart Jenbach 10:47 or 14:52 and arrive Maryhofen 12:10 and 16:10. Leave Mayrhofen 12:47 or 16:47, arrive in Jenbach 14:02 and 18:02 (2) This segment is operated by bus.

Innsbruck - Munich - Innsbruck   890

Dep. Innsbruck	06:18	08:37 (1)	10:34
Arr. Munich	08:25	10:30	12:30

• • •

Dep. Munich	13:29 (1)	15:29 (1)	19:29 (1)
Arr. Innsbruck	15:22	17:22	21:22

(1) Reservations required. Restaurant car.

Innsbruck - St. Anton - Innsbruck   950

Dep. Innsbruck	06:31 (1)	07:35 (1)	08:39 (1)	10:39 (1)	12:41 (1)
Arr. St. Anton	07:53	09:01	09:57	12:56	13:56

Sights in **St. Anton:** A popular ski center since 1907, located at the eastern end of the 6-mile-long Arlberg Tunnel. The enormous number of ski lifts here offer a great variety of slopes.

Dep. St. Anton	12:06 (1)	14:06 (1)	16:06 (1)	16:58 (1+2)
Arr. Innsbruck	13:21	15:21	17:19	18:24

(1) Restaurant car. (2) Plus other departures from St. Anton at 18:06 (1), 20:06 (1), 22:06, and 23:14.

Innsbruck - Salzburg - Innsbruck (via Zell-am-See)   950, 960

The route via Zell-am-See is one of the most scenic rides in Austria, as well as a trip to an interesting destination. Exceptionally beautiful views of gorges, lakes, mountains and rivers.

All of these trains have a restaurant car.

	960	960	950	960
Dep. Innsbruck	07:38 (1+2)	09:25 (1)	09:30 (3)	13:25 (1+4)
Dep. Zell-am-See	09:19	11:19	-0-	15:19
Arr. Salzburg	10:55	12:55	11:29	16:55

Sights in **Zell-am-See:** Minutes by bus from year-around glacier skiing.

	950	960	950	960	950
Dep. Salzburg	12:31 (3)	13:05 (1)	14:31 (3)	17:05 (1)	16:31 (3+5)
Dep. Zell-am-See	-0-	14:42	-0-	18:42	-0-
Arr. Innsbruck	14:30	16:35	16:30	20:35	18:30

(1) Of the two routes between Innsbruck and Salzburg, this train takes the more interesting one (via Zell-am-See), one of the most scenic rail trips in Austria. (2) Change trains in Bischofshofen. Restaurant car. (3) Via Kufstein. Restaurant car. (4) Plus other departures (schedule 950) from Innsbruck at 11:30 (3) and 13:30 (3), arriving Salzburg 13:29 and 15:29. (5) Plus other Salzburg departures at (schedule 950) 18:31 (3) and 21:22 (3), arriving Innsbruck 20:30 and 23:23.

Linz - Munich - Linz   67

All of these trains charge a supplement for first-class which includes seat reservation fee and have a restaurant car.

Dep. Linz	07:40	10:40	Dep. Munich	16:25	18:25
Arr. Munich	10:35	13:36	Arr. Linz	19:20	21:20

Linz - Salzburg - Linz   950

Not all of these trains have a restaurant car.

Dep. Linz   Frequent times from 05:10 to 23:15
Arr. Salzburg   1 to 2 hours later

• • •

Dep. Salzburg   Frequent times from 03:20 to 21:32
Arr. Linz   1 to 2 hours later

Linz - Vienna - Linz   950

Most of these trains have a restaurant car.

Dep. Linz   Frequent times from 04:34 to 22:55
Arr. Vienna (Westbf.) 1½ to 2 hours later

• • •

Dep. Vienna (Westbf.) Frequent times from 05:10 to 23:30
Arr. Linz   1½ to 2 hours later

Salzburg - Zell-am-See - Innsbruck - Salzburg   950, 960

The route via Zell-am-See is one of the most scenic rides in Austria, as well as a trip to an interesting destination. Exceptionally beautiful views of gorges, lakes, mountains and rivers.

These trains have a restaurant car, unless designated otherwise.

	950	960	950	960	950
Dep. Salzburg	06:23 (1)	07:05 (2+3)	08:31 (1)	09:05 (2+3)	10:31 (1)
Dep. Zell-am-See	-0-	08:42	-0-	10:42	-0-
Arr. Innsbruck	08:30	10:35	10:30	12:35	12:30

Sights in **Zell-am-See**: Minutes by bus from year-around glacier skiing.

	950	960	950
Dep. Innsbruck	13:30 (1)	13:25 (2)	15:30 (1+3)
Dep. Zell-am-See	-0-	15:19	-0-
Arr. Salzburg	15:29	16:55	17:29

(1) Via Kufstein. (2) Of the two routes between Salzburg and Innsbruck, this train takes the most interesting one (via Zell-am-See), one of the most scenic rail trips in Austria. (3) Plus other departures from Innsbruck at frequent times from 17:19 to 23:34.

Salzburg - Kitzbuhel - Salzburg   860

All of these trains have a restaurant car.

	07:05	09:05	09:40	11:40
Dep. Salzburg	07:05	09:05	09:40	11:40
Arr. Kitzbuhel	09:29	11:29	12:51	14:51

Sights in **Kitzbuhel**: See notes about Kitzbuhel under "Innsbruck–Kitzbuhe."

	13:09	14:31	17:09	18:31	20:31	00:47
Dep. Kitzbuhel	13:09	14:31	17:09	18:31	20:31	00:47
Arr. Salzburg	16:21	16:55	20:21	20:55	22:55	03:05

Salzburg - Linz - Salzburg   950

Most of these trains have a restaurant car.

Dep. Salzburg	Frequent times from 05:02 to 21:32
Arr. Linz	80 minutes later

• • •

Dep. Linz	Frequent times from 05:10 to 23:15
Arr. Salzburg	80 minutes later

Salzburg - Munich - Salzburg 890

All of these trains charge a supplement for first-class which includes a reservation fee and have a restaurant car, unless designated otherwise.

Dep. Salzburg	04:12 (1)	04:35 (1)	10:38	12:06 (4)
Arr. Munich	06:03	06:13	12:20	13:36

• • •

Dep. Munich	11:38 (3)	13:25 (4)	15:25 (4)	16:25 (4)	17:38 (2+5)
Arr. Salzburg	13:22	14:55	16:55	17:55	19:22

(1) No supplement charged. No restaurant car. (2) No supplement charged. Light refreshments. (3) Light refreshments. (4) Restaurant car. (5) Plus other Munich departures at 18:25, 19:38 (2), 20:34 (1), 21:38 (2) and 23:14 (1), arriving Salzburg 19:55, 21:21, 22:28, 23:22 and 00:57.

Salzburg - Schafbergspitze - Salzburg   962, 963

A very scenic one-day trip that includes views of the eight-mile-long **Wolfgangsee (Lake Wolfgang)**, the warmest lake in Austria (79 degrees in summer). The narrow-gauge steam rack railway climbs 5,682 feet to the top of the **Schafberg**, from where there are glorious views of 13 lakes and many mountains. The ride from Schafbergspitze back to St. Wolfgang must be booked immediately on arrival at the summit. This railway operates May to October.

Bus. 962

Dep. Salzburg	06:45 (1)	08:15	09:15	11:25	12:15	13:15
Arr. Strobl	07:54	09:19	10:29	12:39	13:29	14:29

Change buses 963

Dep. Strobl	08:15 (1)	09:40 (1)	10:40 (1)	12:40	13:55	14:40
Arr. St. Wolfgang	08:30	09:55	10:55	12:55	14:10	14:55

Change to steam rack railway; Table 963

Dep. St. Wolfgang	Train operates when it has at least 20 passengers.
Arr. Schafbergspitze	40 minutes after departing St. Wolfgang

• • •

Dep. Schafbergspitze	At random times
Arr. St. Wolfgang	39 minutes after departing Shafbergspitze

Change to bus 963

Dep. St. Wolfgang	10:10	12:10	13:14	15:15	16:15 (4+5)
Arr. Strobl	10:25	12:25	13:29	15:30	16:30

Change buses 962

| Dep. Strobl | 10:41 (2) | 12:41 | 13:41 (3) | 15:41 | 16:45 |
| Arr. Salzburg | 11:55 | 14:00 | 14:55 | 16:55 | 17:55 |

(1) Runs daily, except Sundays and holidays. (2) Runs Monday-Friday, except holidays. (3) Operates mid-July to mid-September. (4) Mid-July to late September: runs daily. Late September to mid-July: runs daily, except Sundays and holidays. (5) Plus other St. Wolfgang departures at 17:15 (4), 18:20 and 20:00 (3), arriving Salzburg 18:55, 19:55 and 21:35.

Salzburg - Vienna - Salzburg   950

Marvelous views of the Alps and pretty farmland on this ride.

All of these trains have a restaurant car.

| Dep. Salzburg | 06:00 | 07:00 (1) | 08:10 | 09:10 (1) | 10:10 | 11:05 (1) |
| Arr. Vienna (Westbf.) | 09:35 | 09:55 | 11:42 | 12:35 | 13:35 | 14:18 |

* * *

| Dep. Vienna (Westbf.) | 13:28 (1) | 14:28 (1) | 15:28 (1) | 16:28 (1) | 17:20 (1+2) |
| Arr. Salzburg | 16:50 | 17:50 | 18:50 | 19:03 | 20:28 |

(1) Supplement charged for first-class includes reservation fee. (2) Plus other Vienna departures at 18:28, 19:28, 20:28 and 21:25, arriving Salzburg 21:50, 23:19, 23:50 and 00:33.

Vienna - Baden - Vienna   Tram

A local tram runs at frequent times from the center of Vienna to Baden and v.v.

Sights in **Baden**: Only 16 miles from Vienna, Baden is an alternative to staying in Vienna.

Famous since the 1st century for the curative powers of its hot sulphur springs. Many of the rooms in hotels here have a faucet in the bathroom that carries mineral water. See the Baroque Trinity Column. Try your luck in the Casino in Kurpark.

Visit the house where Beethoven lived, at 10 Rathausgasse, open daily except Thursdays, May–September, 09:00–11:00 and 15:00–17:00.

Vienna - Budapest - Vienna   1200

| Dep. Vienna (Sud.) | 07:00 (1) | Dep Budapest (Kel.) | 16:58 | 18:57 (2+5) |
| Arr Budapest (Kel.) | 9:25 | Arr. Vienna (Sud.) | 20:00 (3) | 21:22 |

(1) Restaurant car. (2) Reservation required. Restaurant car. (3) Arrives Vienna's Westbahnhof rail station. (4) Plus other Budapest departures at 18:57 (1+2) and 21:45, arriving Vienna 21:22 (Sud.) and 00:44 (Westbf).

Vienna - Graz - Vienna   980

All of these trains have light refreshments.

Dep. Vienna (Sudbf.)	05:55	07:55	09:55	11:55
Dep. Bruck a.d. Mur	08:01	10:06	12:01	14:01
Arr. Graz	08:35	10:40	12:35	14:35

• • •

Dep. Graz	13:25	15:25	17:25 (1)
Dep. Bruck a.d. Mur	14:03	16:03	18:03
Arr. Vienna (Sudbf.)	16:05	18:05	20:05

(1) Plus other departures from Graz at 19:25 and 21:25, arriving Vienna 22:05, and 00:05 .

Sights in **Graz**: A 2½-hour motorcoach sightseeing tour of Graz starts from in front of the Opera House weekdays at 10:00, June through September.

From the main square (Hauptplatz) with its many vegetable, fruit and flower markets, go to the arcades with shops in the 17th-century Luegghaus. Then to the City Hall (Rathaus) to see the city's symbol, a carved white panther.

Follow Neutorgasse to the Joanneum (state Museum of Styria), one of the world's oldest museums, to see its archaeological collection, library, paintings and exhibits of Styrian crafts (09:00–12:00 daily, 14:30–17:00 Monday, Wednesday and Friday).

Continue on Landhausgasse and Herrengasse to the splendid Renaissance Landhaus. Next door, in the four-story, 17th-century Styrian Armory (Zeughaus) is an exhibit of 17th-century armor (for both men and horses) said to be the best and largest collection in Europe (same hours as the Joanneum). Its 32,000 weapons include complete suits of armor, guns, helmets, swords, lances, shields and breastplates.

Walk on Opernring to the outstanding Opera House and then through marvelous Stadtpark with its fantastic double-spiral Gothic staircase and cross the Glacis to visit the city's oldest church (13th century), Leekirche, the Church of the Teutonic Order.

Pass the castle and see the Diocesan Museum and Treasury in the 15th-century cathedral. Across a narrow street is the 17th-century Mausoleum of Emperor Ferdinand II and his mother (Maria of Bavaria), open 11:00–12:00 and 14:00–15:00 from May to September, only 11:00–12:00 the rest of the year.

Don't miss the folk dance by carved wood figures performing at 11:00 and 18:00 on the 400-year-old clock in Glockenspielplatz. Nearby is the 116-foot-high belfry which has a four-ton bell that the people here call "Liesl." See the exhibits of regional costumes, tools, folk art, etc., in the Volkskundemuseum (Folk Art Museum of Styria) open Monday, Wednesday and Friday 14:30–17:00.

Cable cars leave every 15 minutes from 38 Kaiser Franz Josef Kai for the 350 foot ascent to the top of Schlossberg (Castle Hill), from where there is a great view of Graz, its suburbs, the Mur Valley and the Alps.

Drink Schilcher (the local rose wine) and Steiermark beer. Local food specialties to sample are: Steierische Wurzelfleisch (pork shoulder), Sulmtaler Krainer (smoked pork

sausage) and Steierische Brettljause (a dish of bacon, sausage, cheese, peppers and tomatoes served on a wooden platter).

Take the tram #1 to **Eggenberg** to see the hunting museum in the 17th-century castle
there. Go to the top of Castle Hill (Schlossberg) by foot or funicular for a great view of
Graz and tour the Bell Tower and Clock Tower, where the big hands show the hour and the
small hands the minutes.

Take a local bus to nearby **Stubing**, which has the largest open-air museum in Austria
(ancient wood churches, peasants' homes). Another tour goes to **Koflach**, where a stud farm
that is an auxiliary of Vienna's Spanish Riding School has been breeding thoroughbred horses
since 1798.

Vienna - Linz - Vienna   950

Most of these trains have a restaurant car.

Dep. Vienna (Westbf.)	Frequent times from 05:10 to 23:30
Arr. Linz	2 hours later

• • •

Dep. Linz	Frequent times from 04:43 to 22:55
Arr. Vienna (Westbf.)	2 hours later

Vienna - Melk - Vienna   Train Ride + Danube Boat Trip 950 + 955

The Melk-Vienna boat is covered by Eurailpass.

Train 950			Danube Steamship 955	
Dep. Vienna (Westbf.)	08:33 (1)	12:45	Dep. Melk	15:15 (2)
Arr. Melk	09:40	13:55	Arr. Vienna	20:45 (3)

(1) Light refreshments. Second class only. (2) Operates from late April to late October (3) Arrives at
Vienna's Reichsbrucke.

Sights in **Melk**: Walk from the rail station up the hill to the Abbey, built in 1133 but
completely reconstructed 1702 to 1736. English-language guided tours are offered
sometimes. There is a splendid view of the Danube from the terrace.

At the top of the stone Emperor's Stairway is the 644-foot-long Emperor's Corridor, off which are several rooms whose doors are made of highly decorated rare wood
and in which many treasures are displayed. Also on this floor are the magnificently

decorated Marble Hall (actually faux marble stucco), the gilded bookcases of inlaid wood in the Library (over 85,000 books and 1,200 manuscripts from the 9th to the 15th centuries), and the Abbey church with a pulpit made entirely of gold.

A restaurant at the Abbey serves a hearty lunch. For the return trip to Vienna by boat, go to the main river dock, not to the dock below the abbey.

Vienna - Salzburg - Vienna   950

All of these trains have a restaurant car.

Dep. Vienna (Westbf.)	05:50 (1)	06:28	07:20 (1)	07:28	08:50	09:20 (1+2)
Arr. Salzburg	08:55	09:50	10:28	10:55	11:55	12:28

•   •   •

Dep. Salzburg	14:05	15:10	15:32 (1)	16:10	17:10	17:32 (1+3)
Arr. Vienna (Westbf.)	17:35	18:34	18:45	19:35	20:35	20:45

(1) Supplement charged for first-class includes reservation fee. (2) Plus other departures from Vienna at 09:28 (1), 10:28 and 11:20, arriving Salzburg 12:50, 13:50 and 14:28. (3) Plus other Salzburg departures at 18:05, 18:10, 19:32 (1), 20:05, 20:25 and 21:32 (1), arriving Vienna 21:18, 21:35, 22:45, 23:15, 24:00 and 00:50.

Vienna - Sopron - Vienna   1200

A day-trip into Hungary.

Dep. Vienna (Sud)	07:00	10:07 (2)		Dep. Sopron	14:20	15:50 (3)
Arr. Gyor	08:07 (1)	11:36		Arr. Gyor	15:23	17:15 (1)
Dep. Gyor	08:58	12:20		Dep. Gyor	16:50	18:21
Arr. Sopron	09:55	13:25		Arr. Vienna (Sud)	18:30	20:00 (2)

(1) Change trains in Gyor. (2) Vienna Westbahnhof. (3) Plus another Sopron departure at 18:15, arriving Vienna (Sud) 21:22.

Sights in **Sopron**: A 900-year-old architectural treasure, with 240 perfectly preserved historic buildings. The Castle has a Roman foundation and a Norman basement. Visit the 13th-century Goat Church and Church of St. Michael. The 15th-century synagogue. St. George Church. Holy Ghost Church. The 16th-century Lyceum. The 18th-century Trinity Statue. The rococo Erdody Palace. Many museums: Liszt, Stonework, Pharmacy, Guild History, and Fabricius House.

SCENIC RAIL TRIPS

Innsbruck - Brennero 595

The beautiful mountain scenery here can be seen either on an easy one-day round trip from Innsbruck or as a portion of the Innsbruck–Verona–Milan route.

Dep. Innsbruck	06:36 (1)	9:28 (2)	13:28 (4)	14:06 (3)	15:28 (4)
Arr. Brennero	07:18	10:04	14:04	14:48	16:04

• • •

Dep. Brennero	07:30	11:59 (4)	15:59	17:30 (3)
Arr. Innsbruck	08:12	12:32	16:32	18:12

(1) Second-class only. (2) Restaurant car. (3) Runs Monday-Friday, except holidays. Second class. (4) Supplement charged for first class includes reservation fee. Restaurant car.

Innsbruck - Buchs 950

The excellent mountain scenery here can be seen either on an easy one-day round trip from Innsbruck or as a portion of the Innsbruck–Zurich route.

All of these trains have a restaurant car, unless designated otherwise.

Dep. Innsbruck	06:31 (1)	08:39 (1)	12:41 (2)	14:41(2)
Arr. Buchs	09:08(2)	11:08	15:08	17:08

• • •

Dep. Buchs	10:52 (2)	12:31 (1+2)	14:52 (2)	16:04 (1+3)
Arr. Innsbruck	13:19	15:21	17:19	19:21

(1) Change trains in Feldkirch. (2) Supplement charged for first-class includes reservation fee. (3) Plus other Buchs departures at 18:52 (1), and 22:53, arriving Innsbruck 21:21, and 01:35.

Innsbruck - Bruck an der Mur - Vienna 975, 980

This indirect route from Innsbruck to Vienna, traveling south of the main line (via Linz), offers excellent mountain scenery. As the schedules below indicate, a stopover of up to seven hours in Bruck an der Mur is possible.

All of the trains have a restaurant car or light refreshments unless designated otherwise.

975

Dep. Innsbruck	07:38	11:25	15:25
Arr. Bruck an der Mur	12:54	16:54	20:54
Change trains 980			
Lv. Bruck an der Mur	13:03	17:03	21:03
Arr. Vienna (Sudbf.)	15:05	19:05	23:05

Sights in **Bruck an der Mur**: Located in the Styrian Alps, at the meeting of the Mur and Murz rivers, on the main route between Vienna and Graz. See the 17th-century Wrought Iron Well, the outstanding example of Styrian ironwork, the parish church and examples of houses from the 15th and 16th century.

Innsbruck - Feldkirch - Innsbruck   950

Very good mountain scenery. As the schedules below indicate, a two- to eight-hour stop-over in Feldkirch is possible.

All of these trains charge a supplement, have a restaurant car, unless designated otherwise.

Dep. Innsbruck	06:31	07:35 (1)	10:39	12:41	14:41	16:39
Arr. Feldkirch	08:45	10:05	12:48	14:51	16:51	18:48

Sights in **Feldkirch**: A medieval town, next to the Swiss border. See the Old Town and Marketplace. The 12-foot-thick walls at the 16th-century Schattenburg Castle. The local museum, open daily except Wednesday afternoon.

Dep. Feldkirch	11:13	13:13	15:13	15:54	17:13	19:13
Arr. Innsbruck	13:21	15:21	17:19	18:24	19:21	21:21

(1) No supplement charged.

Innsbruck - Garmisch - Zugspitze   895, 898

The outstanding mountain scenery here can be seen either on an easy one-day round trip from Innsbruck or as a portion of the Innsbruck–Munich route.

For the first way:

895

Dep. Innsbruck	07:07	07:59	09:03	10:58	11:47
Arr. Garmisch	08:25	09:27	10:26	12:25 (1)	13:24

The following schedule allows one to ride one cable route to the summit of Zugspitze and ride a different cable route back to Garmisch.

Change trains 898

Dep. Garmisch	08:35	09:35	10:35	11:35	12:35	14:35
Arr. Eibsee	09:15	10:15	11:15	12:15	13:15	15:15

Change to cable railway

Dep. Eibsee	Every 30 minutes from 08:00 to17:30
Arr. Zugspitze	10 minutes later

(1) As the Garmisch departures show, there is time to lunch in Garmisch and take a later train to Eibsee and Zugspitze. See departures above.

Return to Garmisch on a different cable railway.

In 1997, all of the times Zugspitze-Zugspitzplatz-Garmisch were estimated.

898

Trains operate between Zugspitze and Zugspitzplatz every 30 minutes from 10:00 to 16:00; trains stop in Eibsee, where you can change to a Garmish train.

•   •   •

Change trains 895

Dep. Garmisch	11:29	12:26 (1)	14:25	16:01 (2)	16:25
Arr. Innsbruck	12:50	13:57	15:57	17:40	17:58

(1) As the Garmisch departures show, there is time to lunch in Garmisch and take a later train to Innsbruck or Munich. (2) Supplement charged. Restaurant car. Note: Other cable cars serve this area, too, operating between Eibse and Zugspitzgipfel (Eibse-Seilbahn), Zugspitzplatt and Zugspitzgipfel summit (Gletscherbahn) and Ehrwald-Obermoos (bus connection to/from Ehrwald station) to Zugspitzgipfel. Always check locally with the cable railway company before venturing out, as these schedules are subject to the whimseys of the weather.

Here is the schedule for continuing on from Garmisch to Munich.

895

Dep. Garmisch	11:34	12:25	13:25	14:27	15:34	16:27 (1)
Arr. Munich	12:52	13:52	14:52	15:53	16:53	17:54

(1) Plus other departures from Garmisch at 17:33, 18:33, 19:34, 20:29 and 21:34.

Innsbruck - Salzburg - Innsbruck   950, 960

The good canyon, lake, river and mountain scenery on this route can be seen either on an easy one-day round trip from Innsbruck (see details under "Innsbruck–Zell am See–Salzburg –Innsbruck"), or as a portion of the Innsbruck–Vienna route (see below).

Innsbruck - Vienna   950

These schedules will take you across Austria.

All of these trains have a restaurant car, unless designated otherwise.

Dep. Innsbruck	05:00	07:42	09:30	11:30	13:30	15:30 (1)	17:30
Arr. Vienna (Westbf.)	09:55	12:55	14:45	16:45	18:45	20:45	22:45

(1) Plus another departure from Innsbruck at 19:30, arriving Vienna 00:50.

Linz - Selzthal - Amstetten - Linz   950, 975, 976

The Selzthal–Amstetten portion of this easy one-day circle trip affords fine river, canyon and mountain scenery. There are good views of the colorful **Enns Valley**.

All of the Linz–Selzthal and v.v. trains have light refreshments. All of the Selzthal–Amstetten and v.v. trains are second-class only. All of the Amstetten–Linz and v.v. trains have a restaurant car.

975
Dep. Linz	07:57	11:57	15:57	
Arr. Selzthal	09:37	13:35	17:35	
Change trains 976				
Dep. Selzthal	10:29	12:27	14:28	16:37
Arr. Amstetten	12:51	15:04	17:08	18:39
Change trains 950				
Dep. Amstetten	12:47	14:22	16:19	18:47
Arr. Linz	13:29	15:02	17:02	19:29

The same trip can be made in reverse, using this schedule:

950
Dep. Linz	08:34	10:34	12:34	14:34
Arr. Amstetten	09:16	11:16	13:16	15:16

Change trains 976

| Dep. Amstetten | 09:21 | 10:52 | 16:50 |
| Arr. Selzthal | 11:26 | 13:20 | 19:34 |

Change trains 975

| Dep. Selzthal | 12:24 | 14:24 | 16:24 | 18:24 |
| Arr. Linz | 15:03 | 17:03 | 18:03 | 21:03 |

Salzburg - Zell-am-See - Innsbruck   950, 960

There are exceptionally beautiful views of canyon, lakes, mountains and rivers on one of the most scenic rides in Austria. Schedules for this trip appear earlier in this section under both "Innsbruck–Salzburg" and "Salzburg–Innsbruck."

Salzburg - Gmunden - Stainach - Salzburg   950, 960, 965

There is fine mountain and lake scenery on the Gmunden–Stainach portion of this circle trip.

950

| Dep. Salzburg | 06:00 (1) | 12:10 (1) |
| Arr. Attnang | 06:53 | 12:58 |

Change trains 965

Dep. Attnang	07:16 (2)	13:11 (2)
Dep. Gmunden	07:35	13:30
Dep. Bad Ischl	08:19	14:13
Dep. Hallstatt	08:43	14:38
Dep. Bad Aussee	09:01	15:09
Arr. Stainach	09:35	15:46

Change trains 960

| Dep. Stainach | 09:39 (3) | 20:31 (4) |
| Arr. Salzburg | 11:43 | 22:39 |

(1) Restaurant car. (2) Second-class only. (3) Supplement charged for first-class includes seat reservation fee. Light refreshments. (4) Light refreshments.

Sights in **Gmunden**: A colorful little town. Artistic pottery has been made here since the 15th century. See the porcelain-tiled clock tower of the Renaissance Town Hall in the main square (Rathausplatz). Stroll from there along the beautiful flowerbeds and chestnut trees of the Esplanade to the yacht harbor and lakeshore beach. Walk on the breakwater to the Ort Chateau, built on a small island.

Sights in **Bad Ischl**: A popular mineral water spa since 1822; center of the Salzkammergut resort region. Visit the home of composer Franz Lehar, now a museum, then stop by the Imperial Villa.

Sights in **Hallstaat**: One of Europe's oldest permanent settlements, it dates back to the 5th-century B.C. The local museum traces the prehistoric stages of this region's culture.

See the colorful houses (blue, red, yellow or beige), every balcony and window festooned with flowers. It is a short walk to several waterfalls. Close to one that rushes through the town is a 16th-century church that has a splendidly carved late-Gothic altar. Drop by the Bone House in the village, near the parish church, for a look at a unique collection of neatly piled, gaily decorated skulls. The skulls belong to generations of villagers; there has never been enough land here for a cemetery.

Sights in **Bad Aussee**: This was the center of the salt region in the 15th century and is still popular for health-inducing brine baths. Bad Aussee is both a summer resort and winter sports area. There are many picturesque lakes here.

Salzburg - Vienna   950

Marvelous views of the Alps and pretty farmland. See schedules for Vienna–Salzburg.

Salzburg - Villach - Salzburg   970

The excellent canyon and mountain scenery on this ride can be seen either on an easy one-day round trip from Salzburg or as a portion of the Salzburg–Venice route.

For the first way:

Dep. Salzburg	07:14 (1)	09:14 (1)	11:14 (1)	13:14 (1)	15:14 (2)
Arr. Villach	10:00	12:00	14:00	16:00	18:00
		•	•	•	
Dep. Villach	10:02 (2)	12:00 (2)	14:00 (1)	16:00 (1)	18:00 (1)
Arr. Salzburg	12:46	14:46	16:46	18:46	20:46

(1) Light refreshments. (2) Supplement charged for first-class includes reservation fee. Restaurant car

Here is the schedule for going from Salzburg to Italy:

88

Dep. Salzburg	09:14 (1)
Arr. Venice (Mestre)	15:39
Arr. Venice (S.L.)	15:50

(1) Supplement charged. Restaurant car.

The very scenic Klagenfurt–Udine–Trieste portion of the Vienna–Trieste route is described under "Vienna–Trieste." A departure from Salzburg can connect with that trip at Villach.

Vienna-Puchberg am Schneeberg-Hochschneeberg-Vienna 980, 981

Book the ride from Hoshschneeberg back to Puchberg immediately on arrival at the summit.

These schedules operate Monday-Friday.

(Unsere Bahn) 980

Dep. Vienna (Sud)	06:55	07:55	09:55	10:55	11:55	13:55
Arr. Wiener Neustadt	07:32	08:32	10:32	11:32	12:32	14:32

Change trains 981

Dep. Wiener Neustadt	07:36	08:36	10:36	11:36	12:36	14:38
Arr. Puchberg	08:24	09:24	11:24	12:24	13:24	15:23

Change to steam rack railway

Dep. Puchberg (Puchberg-Hochschneeberg services run May-October subject to demand)

Arr. Hochschneeberg (time varies depending on seasonal schedule)

Sights in **Puchberg**: Located at the foot of the mountain called Schneeberg, the eastern edge of the Alps. A summer and winter resort. Popular for water cures and weight-loss treatment.

Sights in **Hochschneeberg**: At 5,900 feet, there are good views and a restaurant at the peak.

Dep. Hochschneeberg (time varies depending on seasonal schedule)
Arr. Puchberg (Hochschneeberg-Puchberg services run May-October subject to demand.)

Change trains 981

Dep. Puchberg	15:38	16:38	17:38	18:38	-0-	19:38
Arr. Wiener Neustadt	16:23	17:23	18:23	19:23	-0-	20:23

Change trains 980

Dep. Wiener Neustadt	16:34	17:34	18:34	19:30	-0-	20:30
Arr. Vienna (Sud)	17:20	18:20	19:20	20:05	-0-	21:05

Vienna - Bruck an der Mur - Innsbruck 960, 970, 980

This indirect route from Vienna to Innsbruck, traveling south of the main line (via Linz), offers excellent mountain scenery. The schedules allow a stopover in Bruck an der Mur.

980

Dep. Vienna (Sud)	08:55 (1)	10:55 (1)
Dep. Bruck an der Mur	11:01	13:01
Arr. Villach	13:50	15:50
Change trains 970+960		
Dep. Villach	14:00	16:00
Dep. Bischofshofen	15:56 (2)	17:56 (2)
Arr. Innsbruck	18:35	20:35

(1) Light refreshments. (2) Restaurant car.

Sights in **Bruck an der Mur**: See "Innsbruck–Bruck an der Mur."

Vienna - Klagenfurt - Udine - Trieste   88

The marvelous farm and lake scenery on this route includes **Worthersee**, a lake fed by warm springs that is very popular for swimming and boating, and the beautiful coastline from Udine to Trieste.

The great Worthersee resort area is open June through mid-September. The region around **Klagenfurt** has attractive lakes, rolling hills and wildlife parks.

Even if you don't stay there, at least watch for that area a few minutes before the stop at Klagenfurt. An early departure from Vienna is recommended in order to be able to see the Adriatic shore approaching Trieste in the afternoon sunlight.

The comfortable local train from Udine hurtles downhill too fast to permit picture-taking, but you will have a memory of that truly beautiful scene forever. Have a seat on the right-hand side of the train for the best possible view.

Not only is Trieste a worthwhile one-day stopover, it is also ideal as a base for several short rail trips into Yugoslavia such as Villa Opicina, Sezana, Pivka, Postojna and Ljubljana. While staying in Trieste, it is also easy to make a one-day rail excursion to see the sights in Udine.

88

Dep. Vienna (Sud.)	07:30 (1)	12:55
Dep. Klagenfurt	11:40	17:22
Arr. Udine	14:17	20:10
Change trains		
Dep. Udine	15:37	20:30
Arr. Trieste	16:41	21:43

(1) Supplement charged for first-class includes reservation fee. Restaurant car.

Sights in **Trieste:** City buses go to Miramare Castle, Maximilian and Charlotte's lovely seaside palace. Constructed in 1856, it has been restored. The fine library and much of the original furniture are exhibited. Charlotte returned here after their tragic brief time as rulers of Mexico, made insane by Maximillan's death. The Piazza deli'Unita is reminiscent of Piazza San Marco in Venice. Also visit the 15th-century Castello di San Giusto. 14th-century Cathedral of San Giusto, ruins of a Roman amphitheater and the Civic Museum of History and Art. Take a taxi or bus from the rail station up to the 15th-century Castello di San Giusto for views of the city and to see the collection of weapons and armor there. It is a scenic 30-minute bus trip (#45, from Piazza G. Oberdan) to visit Grotta Gigante, a cave large enough to contain St. Peter's Cathedral.

If you are starting from Salzburg, refer to this schedule:

88

Dep. Salzburg	09:14 (1)
Arr. Udine	14:17
Change trains	
Dep. Udine	15:37
Arr. Trieste	16:41

(1) Supplement charged.

Now for the one-day excursion to Udine:

Trieste - Udine - Trieste 606

Dep. Trieste	07:17	08:12 (1)	08:17 (2)	09:17	10:10 (1)	12:17
Arr. Udine	08:22	09:38	9:35	10:22	11:36	13:31

Sights in **Udine**: The collection of paintings in the Civic Museum and Gallery, a 20-minute walk from the rail station.

Tiepolo's paintings are featured in both the Bishop's Palace and the cathedral. Visit Piazza della Liberta.

Dep. Udine	12:27 (1)	13:37	14:16	15:37 (1)	16:27 (2+3)
Arr. Trieste	13:43	14:44	15:42	16:41	17:41

(1) Runs Sundays and holidays only. (2) Runs daily, except Sundays and holidays. (3) Plus other departures from Udine at 17:37, 18:56, 19:37 and 20:30, arriving Trieste 18:41, 20:22, 20:41 and 21:43.

Danube Cruise 995

Dep. Vienna (Reich.)	08:30 (1)		Dep. Linz	09:00 (2)
Arr. Durnstein	14:00		Arr. Durnstein	16:20 (3)
Arr. Linz	-0-		Arr. Vienna (Schif.)	20:45

(1) Runs Sunday only, early May-late September. Sailing depends on minimum number of passengers. Vienna Reichsbrucke is near Vorgartemstrabe U-Bahn station (line U1). Cruises from Vienna operate from early

May to late October. (2) Operates Tuesday, Thursday and Sunday from late April to late October. (3) Change vessels in Dunstein. This schedule operates on Sunday only, from early May to late September. Sailing depends on minimum number of passengers. Note: Since the departure from Vienna doesn't have a connection to Linz, consider this alternative. Take a train from Vienna's Franz Joseph station at 05:05 to Krems an der Donau, arriving there at 06:43. At 09:00, a DDSG ship leaves the docks for Linz, arriving there at 19:15.

Sights in **Durnstein**: This small, fortified town is at the foot of a ridge surrounded by vineyards. Richard the Lion Hearted was held for an enormous ransom in the town's castle, from which there is a wonderful view of Durnstein and the valley below it. Stroll down the interesting main street; the town's main highlight is the parish church.

INTERNATIONAL ROUTES
FROM AUSTRIA

Innsbruck, Salzburg and Vienna are the Austrian gateways for travel to Germany (and on to Copenhagen). Vienna is also the access point for many Eastern European destinations such as Poland, Czechoslovakia (with connections to Russia), Hungary, Romania and Yugoslavia. From Yugoslavia there are connections to Bulgaria, Greece and Turkey. Due to the continued unrest in the region, we don't recommend taking this route to Bulgaria, Greece or Turkey, at this time. Innsbruck, Salzburg and Vienna are also starting points for trips to Italy. Additionally, Innsbruck is the gateway to Switzerland, where connections can be made to Belgium, France, Holland and Luxembourg.

Innsbruck - Munich   895

Dep. Innsbruck	07:59	09:03	10:58	11:47	13:51	14:58 (1)
Arr. Mittenwald	09:03	10:02	11:55	12:51	14:50	15:53
Dep. Mittenwald	09:05	10:04	12:03	13:03	15:03	16:01
Arr. Garmisch	09:27	10:26	12:25	13:25	15:25	16:23
Dep. Garmisch	09:34	10:28	12:27	13:34	15:34	16:27
Arr. Munich	10:52	11:52	13:52	14:52	16:53	17:54

(1) Plus other departures from Innsbruck at 15:51, 16:58, 19:01 and 21:05, arriving Munich 18:54, 19:55, 21:53 and 23:52.

Vienna - Salzburg - Munich   67

There are departures from Salzburg in addition to those shown here, at frequent times from 04:08 to 23:38 (Table 890).

Dep. Vienna (West)	05:50 (1)	08:50 (1)	09:28 (2)	11:28 (2+3)
Arr. Salzburg	09:00	12:01	12:45	14:45

Dep. Salzburg	09:05	12:06	13:05	15:05
Arr. Munich (Hbf.)	10:35	13:36	14:36	16:36

(1) Supplement charged for first-class includes reservation fee. Restaurant car. (2) Change trains in Salzburg. Restaurant car on both trains. Salzburg-Munich: supplement charged. (3) Plus other departures from Vienna at 15:50 (1), 18:28 (1+4) and 23:30 (5) and departing Salzburg at 19:05, 22:36, and 04:12 (4), arriving Munich 20:36, 00:20 and 06:03. (4) Change trains in Salzburg. (5) Has first- and second-class coaches and second-class couchettes.

Vienna - Prague - Berlin   60

Dep. Vienna (Sud.)	07:10 (1)	11:10 (1)
Arr. Prague (Hole)	12:18	16:29
Arr. Berlin (Licht.)	-0-	21:10

(1) Supplement charged for first-class includes reservation fee. Restaurant car.

Vienna - Warsaw (or Kiev) - Minsk - Moscow   94a

Both of these trains carry only sleeping cars.

94 a

Dep. Vienna (Sudbahnhof)	21:25
Dep. Warsaw (Centralna)	07:48
Dep. Warsaw (Wschodnia)	10:20
Arr. Kiev	- 0 - (1)
Arr. Minsk	21:58
Arr. Moscow (Smolenskaya)	09:27

(1) Day 3.

Vienna - Budapest - Bucharest   61, 890

Dep. Vienna (Westbf.)	09:07 (1)	10:07 (1+2)	14:35 (1+2)	20:07 (1+2)
Arr. Budapest (Keleti)	11:58	12:58	17:14	22:58
Change trains				
Lv. Budapest (Keleti)			18:15 (3)	(4)
Arr. Bucharest (Nord)	-0-	-0-	07:51	13:36

((1) Restaurant car. (2) Restaurant car. Supplement charged. (3) Carries sleeping cars. (4) No train change Budapest. Carries restaurant Vienna-Budapest and Curtici-Burharest. Carries sleepers and couchettes, second-class coach. Arrives Bucharest (Nord) 13:36 on day two.

Vienna - Belgrade and Athens   61, 97

61

Dep. Vienna (Westbf.)	10:07 (1)	23:25 (1+3)
Arr. Belgrade	20:34	09:45 (2)
Change trains 945		
Dep. Belgrade	-0-	19:15 (1+5)
Arr. Thessaloniki	-0-	09:56
Dep. Thessaloniki	-0-	11:06 (1)
Arr. Athens	-0-	16:51 (4)

(1) Supplement payable. Restaurant car. (2) Day 3 from Vienna. (3) Carries a sleeping car. Also has couchettes. Coaches are second-class only. (4) Day 4 from Vienna. (5) Departs from Belgrade's Centar rail station. Carries a sleeping car. Also has couchettes. **Note:** Due to the ongoing situation in Serbia, travel through the region is not advisable at this time. Passengers making international trips on this route must have proper visas or will not be allowed to travel. Expect delays.

Vienna - Belgrade - Istanbul   61

This train carries a sleeping car and has couchettes to Belgrade. The Vienna-Istanbul portion has couchettes and second-class coaches.

Dep. Vienna (West.)	23:25 (3)
During summertime,	
set your watch back one hour.	
Arr. Belgrade	09:33 (1)
All year,	
set your watch forward two hours.	
Dep. Belgrade	10:00 (1)
Arr. Istanbul	08:30 (2)

(1) Day 2 from Vienna. (2) Day 2 from Belgrade. (3) Supplement payable. **Note:** Due to the ongoing situation in Serbia, travel through the region is not advisable at this time. Passengers making international trips on this route must have proper visas or will not be allowed to travel. Expect delays.

Innsbruck - Verona and Milan or Venice 70

Dep. Innsbruck	01:42 (1)	09:28 (2)	11:28 (3+4)	
Arr. Verona (P.N.)	05:34	13:05	15:05	
Change trains				
Dep. Verona (P.N.)	06:58	-0-	15:33 (4)	15:26 (4)
Arr. Milan (Cen.)	-0-	14:50	-0-	16:55
Arrive Venice (S.L.)	08:45	-0-	16:55	-0-

(1) Direct train to Venice. No train change in Verona. Has couchettes. Coach is second-class. (2) Direct train to Milan. No train change in Verona. Supplement charged for first-class includes reservation fee. Restaurant car. (3) Restaurant car. (4) Supplement charged for first-class includes reservation fee.

Innsbruck - Verona - Bologna - Florence - Rome 70

Dep. Innsbruck	23:45(1,4)	11:28 (2,3)	22:40 (1)
Arr. Verona (P.N.)	03:38	15:05 (6)	02:35
Arr. Bologna	05:28 (5)	16:34	04:20
Arr. Florence (SMN)	09:10	17:49	-0-
Arr. Rome (Ter.)	-0-	19:50	08:15

(1) Carries a sleeping car. Also has couchettes. (2) Light refreshments. (3) Supplement charged for first-class includes reservation fee. Restaurant car. (4) Has couchettes. Coaches are second-class. (5) Change trains in Bologna. (6) No train change in Bologna.

Vienna - Nurnberg - Frankfurt - Cologne 66

All of these trains charge a supplement and have a restaurant car, unless designated otherwise.

Dep. Vienna (Westbf.)	08:20	10:20	12:20	14:20
Arr. Nurnberg	13:28	15:28	17:28	19:28
Arr. Frankfurt	15:39	17:39	19:39	21:39
Arr. Cologne	18:05	20:05	22:05	00:05

Vienna - Salzburg - Munich - Paris   32

Dep. Vienna (West.)	08:50 (1)	15:50 (2)	20:28 (3)	23:30 (4)
Dep. Salzburg	12:06	19:05	23:55	04:12
Arr. Munich (Hbf.)	13:35	20:46	-0-	05:56
Change trains				
Dep. Munich	13:46	21:00 (3)	-0-	07:46 (2)
Arr. Paris (Est.)	22:22	07:07	10:24	16:23

(1) Direct train to Paris. No train change in Munich. Restaurant car. (2) Supplement charged for first-class includes reservation fee. Restaurant car. (3) Direct train to Paris. Carries a sleeping car. Also has couchettes. Coach is second-class. Restaurant car. (4) Has couchettes.

Vienna - Venice   88

Dep. Vienna (Sud.)	12:55	19:30 (2)	20:10 (2+3)	22:45 (4)
Arr. Venice (S.L.)	21:52	04:00 (5)	04:36	08:42

(1) Restaurant car. (2) Supplement payable. Carries a sleeping car. Also has couchettes. (3) Late May to early-June runs daily. Early-June to late September runs Thursday, Friday and Saturday. (4) Supplement payable. Carries a sleeping car. Also has couchettes. Coach is second-class. (5) Runs Monday, Tuesday, Wednesday, Sunday from early June to late September.

Innsbruck - Zurich   86

There is marvelous Alpine scenery on this route. About 2½ hours before reaching Zurich, the train passes through one of Europe's longest rail tunnels, the 6.3-mile-long Arlberg.

Dep. Innsbruck	04:24 (1)	08:39 (2)	12:41 (3)	14:41 (4+5)
Arr. Zurich	08:25	12:25	16:25	18:26

(1) Carries a sleeping car. Also has couchettes. (2) Restaurant car Innsbruck to Feldkirch. Change trains in Feldkirch at 10:52. (3) Supplement charged for first-class includes reservation fee. Restaurant car. (4) Supplement charged for first-class includes reservation fee. Has a first-class Observation Car. Restaurant car. (5) Plus other departures from Innsbruck at 18:39 (3+2), arriving Zurich 22:50; change trains in Feldkirch and Sargans.

BENELUX
BELGIUM, NETHERLANDS and LUXEMBOURG

Getting on Track in Belgium, Netherlands and Luxembourg

• Tourist information: **Belgium:** Belgium Tourist Office, 780 Third Avenue, Suite 1501, New York, NY 10017. Telephone (212) 758-8130, fax (212) 355-7675. E-mail inquiries: belinfo@nyxfer.blythe.org. On the Web: http://www.visitbelgium.com/ or http://www.nmbs.be. **Netherlands:** Netherlands Board of Tourism, 225 North Michigan Avenue, Suite 1854, Chicago, IL 60601, telephone (toll-free) 888 2 HOLLAND (24 hours), (312) 819-1500, fax (312) 819-1740. E-mail inquiries: GO2Holland@aol.com. On the Web: http://www.nbt.nl/holland/. By press time, another easier-to-remember Web site should be on line: http://www.goholland.com
Luxembourg: Luxembourg National Tourist Office, 17 Beekman Place, New York, NY 10022. Telephone (212) 935-8888, fax (212) 935-5896. E-mail inquiries: luxnto@aol.com. On the Web: http://www.luxuk.demon.co.uk/ (this site is geared to travelers from the UK, but also has lots of good general information); http://www.luxembourg-city.lu/ (this site zooms in on Luxembourg City's offerings).

• Public holidays: **Belgium:** New Year's Day, January 1, Easter, Easter Monday, April 13 Labor (or May) Day, May 1, Ascension Day, May 21, Whit Monday, June 1, National Day, June 23, Independence Day, July 21, Assumption Day, August 15, All Saints Day November 1st (Sunday; observed Monday), Armistice Day (World War !), November 11, Christmas Day, December 25. (NOTE: When any holiday falls on Sunday, the following day is also a holiday.). **Netherlands:** New Year's Day, January 1, Good Friday, Easter, Easter Monday, Queen's Birthday, April 30, Liberation Day (in May), Ascension Day (in May), Whit Sunday and Monday, Christmas Day, December 25, Boxing Day, December 26. **Luxembourg:** New Year's Day, January 1, Carnival, February 23, Easter, Easter Monday, April 13 Labor (or May) Day, May 1, Ascension Day, May 21, Whit Monday, June 1, National Day, June 23, Assumption Day, August 15, Luxembourg City Kermesse (observed only in Luxembourg City), August 31, All Saints Day November 1st (Sunday; observed Monday) Christmas Day, December 25, St. Stephen's Day, December 26.

• Summer time: Belgium, Holland and Luxembourg change to Summer Time on the last Sunday of March and convert back to Standard Time on the last Sunday of September.

• Currency: **Belgium**: Belgian franc, written BEF or "f" or "Bf." At press time, $1 equaled f37.5020. **Netherlands**: Guilder, abbreviated as "f" or "Dfl." At press time, $1 equaled f2.0494. **Luxembourg:** Luxembourg franc. It is written as "f" or "flux" and has the same rate as the Belgian franc. Both are commonly and widely used in the country. At press time, $1 equaled f38.0300.

Belgium, Netherlands & Luxembourg

NETHERLANDS

BELGIUM

GERMANY

LUXEMBOURG

FRANCE

North Sea

Waddenzee

IJsselmeer

40 km

0   40 Miles

Leeuwarden

Groningen

Alkmaar

Zwolle

Bentheim

Oldenzaal

Haarlem

Amsterdam

Den Haag

Amersfoort

Utrecht

Arnheim

Hoek Van Holland

Emmerich

Rotterdam

Nijmegen

Kleve

Roosendaal

Eindhoven

Kalden-
Kirchen

Oostende

Venlo

Brugge

Antwerp

Gent

Köln

Bruxelles

Maastricht

Lille

Liège

Aachen

Tournai

Namur

Quévy

Jeumont

Gouvy

Aulnoye

Gouvy

Arlon

Luxembourg

Longuyon

Thionville

Overview of Benelux Trains

Although the term Benelux is still widely used to signify Belgium, the Netherlands, and Luxembourg, these three little nations cannot really be spoken about as one entity. It is true that in Flemish Belgium and the Netherlands the people speak more or less the same language and that the currency in Belgium and Luxembourg is interchangeable, but, nonetheless, train travel in these three countries and tourism in general are distinct. The Dutch Railways (Nederlandse Spoorwegen, NS) are highly dependable and although not as fancy or high-tech as the French or German trains, wholly efficient and pleasant. The Belgian National Railways, which like everything else in Belgium has a Flemish (Nationale Maatschappij der Belgishche Spoorwegen, NMBS) and French name (Société Nationale des Chemins de fer Belges, SNCB), runs mostly without incident, although has been known to halt services at times of national labor strikes. The train and bus network of the Luxembourg National Railways (Society Nationale des Chemins de fer Luxembourgeois) covers more than 870 miles. A sprawling network of railway buses covers areas not served by trains.

General Rail Information
Belgium
• Children under six travel free on Belgian trains, children ages six to 11 pay half-fare, children 12 and over must pay full fare.
• There is frequent train service from Brussels' (Central) (05:41 to 23:14) and Brussels (Nord) (05:45 to 23:18) from Brussels (Nord) to the National Airport [Table 401] and from the Airport to Brussels: 05:24 to 23:43. The trip from Brussels Central takes 19 minutes, from Nord, 15 minutes.

Holland
• Children under four travel free on Dutch trains, children ages four to nine pay half-fare, children 10 and over must pay full fare.
• A 17 to 21-minute train ride between Amsterdam's Central rail station and Schiphol Airport [Table 451] runs frequently between 00:07 and 23:49.
• Seat reservations are available only on international trains to, from, or via France, Germany and Luxembourg.

Luxembourg
• Children under four travel free on Luxembourgois trains, children ages four to 11 pay half-fare, children 12 and over must pay full fare.
• Buses run every 15-30 minutes between Luxembourg's Gare Centrale and Findel Airport [Table 5].

The signs you will see at rail stations in Belgium, Holland and Luxembourg are:

	BELGIUM and LUXEMBOURG	HOLLAND
Arrival	Arrivee	Aankomst
Departure	Depart	Vertrek
Exit	Sortie	Uitgang
Information	Renseignements	Inlichtingen
Luggage Check-Room	Consigne	Hetbagagedepot
Men	Messieurs	Heren
Restaurant Car	Wagon-Restauran	Restauratie-Wagen
Sleeping Car	Wagon-Lit	Slaapcoupe
Smoking Compartment	Fumeurs	Rokers
Station	Gare	Station
Timetable	Horaire	Spoorboekje
Track	Quai	Spoor
Women	Dames	Dames

EURAILPASS BONUSES

A 35 percent reduction on the Ostend-Ramsgate ferry operated by Régie Belge des Transports Maritimes. A 30 percent reduction on the full fares of the Stena Line for the ferry crossing between Hoek van Holland and Harwich.

BENELUX TOURRAIL PASS

This pass is for any five days of unlimited travel out of a one month period on all the rail lines of Belgium, Holland and Luxembourg, plus railway buses in Luxembourg. Sold at the rail stations of all three countries and also by the U.S. and Canadian offices of the Netherlands Board of Tourism ((800) 598-8501) (Holland shop, open 09:00-17:00 Monday-Friday, Central Time), Rail Europe and DER Travel.

	2 Adults**		1 Adult	
	1st Cl.	2nd Cl.	1st Cl.	2nd Cl.
5 days in 1 month	$163	$116.50	$217	$155

*Valid for five days of unlimited travel within a 30-day period on the rail lines of Belgium, Holland and Luxembourg   **Price per person based on two people traveling together; fare includes 50 percent companion discount. Children under four: Free.

Junior Benelux Tourrail Pass*
                      2nd Cl. only
5 days in 1 month $104
*Junior Pass available to passengers who are under 26 on their first day of travel.

BELGIUM'S TRAIN PASSES

The following passes and cards are sold at Belgian railway stations.

Tourrail Pass Good for unlimited rail travel in Belgium any five days during one month. The card is available year-round and the validity period may start on any day of the month. Children under six travel free. These prices are valid until January 31, 1998.

First Class	BFr 3,170
Second Class	BFr 2,060

Fixed Price Reduction Card For first- or second-class travel at half-price within a one-month period. Begin using the card any day of the month. First class or second class BFr 590.

The Go Pass Sold at Belgian railway stations. Provides 10 second-class trips for passengers aged six to twenty-five. The pass is valid for six months and can't be used before 07:45, except weekends, public holidays and in July and August. BFr 1,390.

Multi Pass This pass is geared to groups of two to five people traveling together. At least one member of the group should be 26 years old or under. The pass provides two single journeys or one round trip in second class, and is valid for two months. Travel must begin after 07:45.

Maximum 3 people	BFr 1,230
Maximum 4 people	BFr 1,390
Maximum 5 people	BFr 1,540

Golden Railpass Provides six single trips in first or second class for travelers 60 and over. Passengers 55 and up and under 12 who are traveling with the pass-holder can use the pass, too. It's valid for one year and you can start using it on the day of your choice.

First Class	BFr 1,890
Second Class	BFr 1,230

Belgium has other interesting programs for the rail traveler, including the Train + Bike package, which includes rail fare and a bike rental, or, B-Daytrips that combine rail, tram, metro or bus tickets with entry to tourist attractions like museums or amusement parks.

HOLLAND'S TRAIN PASSES

The Holland Rail Pass and Public Transport Link passes are sold by U.S.A. and Canadian travel agencies and the office of Netherlands Board of Tourism (see phone and address information at beginning of chapter).

Holland Railpass*

	Adult		Youth**
	1st Cl.	2nd Cl.	2nd Cl.
3-Day	$ 88	$ 68	$ 56
5-Day	$140	$104	$ 73

*Good for unlimited rail travel in Holland within 30 days. **Must be age 25 or under.

Public Transport Link Available only in combination with the Holland Rail Pass, above. Provides unlimited use of city buses and streetcars throughout Holland. Sold in conjunction with 3- and 5-day passes; $13 and $21 respectively.

PASSES SOLD ONLY IN HOLLAND

These passes are sold at rail stations and accredited travel agencies. A "Public Transport Link" that provides unlimited use of all city transit services throughout Holland (buses and streetcars) is available only in combination with all of the following passes, except "Multi Rover." Prices are the same for both adults and children.

Rail Idee Ticket Netherlands Railways offers during the spring and summer months 72 one-day excursions from Amsterdam to interesting destinations. Eurailpass holders pay only for the non-rail portions of these trips and for admission fees. Available year-round; prices vary depending on destination.

An example is the day that starts with a train ride from Amsterdam to Koog-Zaandijk to first see wood houses from the 17th and 18th century, brought there from many parts of Holland and then a variety of windmills, some of which still operate. After you visit the Zaandam Clockwork Museum, where Dutch clocks from 1500 to 1850 are displayed, you take a 45-minute boat ride along other old houses and windmills. Coffee or a soft drink and a pancake at a restaurant are included in the price.

One Month Rail Pass Unlimited train travel for one month (example: June 3–July 2). The prices below are from 1997; 1998 prices were unavailable at press time.

Adult		Youth*	
1st Cl.	2nd Cl.	1st Cl.	2nd Cl.
911 guilders	608 guilders		486 guilders

*Through age 18.

Rail Rover   One day of unlimited train travel. During June, July and August, it is valid all day, any day. From September through May: valid only after 09:00 on Monday–Friday, all day on Saturday and Sunday. Priced for two–six persons.

The 1997 (1998 prices unavailable at press time) first-class prices: 132 Dutch florins for two persons, Dfl-159 for three, Dfl-180 for four, Dfl-205 for five, and Dfl-228 for six. Second-class: Dfl-88, Dfl-105, Dfl-120,   Dfl-135, and Dfl-150. Day train ticket for children aged 4-11; $2 first/second class.

Schiphol Airport Roundtrip   (1998 prices unavailable at ptess time.) In 1997, round-trip ticket between Central Station, Amsterdam and Schiphol Airport was $12 first class, $8 second class. Children, four and up paid same price.

LUXEMBOURG'S SPECIAL TICKETS

Valid on both trains and all public buses, including Luxembourg-City buses. Not valid for journeys departing from or arriving at border stations. Children under age six travel free.

Benelux Tourrailpass*

	2 Adults**		1 Adult	
	1st Cl.	2nd Cl.	1st Cl.	2nd Cl.
5 days in 1 month	$163	$116.50	$217	$155

*Valid for five days of unlimited travel within a 30-day period on the rail lines of Belgium, Holland and Luxembourg. **Price per person based on two people traveling together; fare includes 50 percent companion discount. Children under four free.

Junior Benelux Tourrail Pass*

	2nd Cl. only
5 days in 1 month	$104

*Junior Pass available to passengers who are under 26 on their first day of travel.

The following rates are valid until at least June 1998.

Short-Distance Ticket   Valid for a trip of up to one hour; 40 Luxembourg francs. A one-month ticket: is 700 Luxembourg francs.

Book of 10 Short-Distance Tickets   320 Luxembourg francs.

One-Day Long-Distance Ticket   Valid for unlimited travel throughout the country from the time first used on one day until 08:00 the next morning; 160 Luxembourg francs.

Book of 10 Long-Distance Tickets   640 Luxembourg francs. A one-month ticket is 1,050 Luxembourg francs.

Group Pass For groups of 10 or more persons. If a round trip is in one day, the price is 80 Luxembourg francs. It is 160 Luxembourg francs per person if return takes place on the following day.

Senior Citizen Half-Fare Half-fare is available only to Luxembourg residents 60 years and up.

ONE-DAY EXCURSIONS AND CITY-SIGHTSEEING

Here are 52 one-day rail trips that can be made comfortably from three major Benelux cities (Amsterdam, Brussels and Luxembourg City), returning to them in most cases before dinner time. (Five of these trips offer, in addition to interesting destinations, scenic fields of flowers in bloom mid-March through May.) Notes are provided on what to see and do at each destination. The number after the name of each route is the *Thomas Cook Timetable*. Three other one-day trips are recommended for exceptional scenery.

Schedules for international connections conclude this section.

Amsterdam

Trains depart Amsterdam's Central rail station around the clock for Schiphol (the airport) and from Schiphol to Amsterdam. Departures are frequent; the journey takes 17-21 minutes.

The tourist office in the Central rail station is open daily 08:45–23:00, Easter to September 30.

Your city sightseeing in Amsterdam should include the following museums, which are open Tuesday-Saturday 10:00–17:00, Sundays and holidays 13:00–17:00. Rijkmuseum (State Museum) collection of Rembrandt, Rubens, Goya and El Greco paintings (42 Stadhouderskade). Also exhibited there are Dresden china, delftware, tapestries, prints, furniture, doll houses and sculpture.

See the works of Chagall, Cezanne, Picasso, Calder, Pollack, Rodin, Braque and Warhol at the Stedelijkmuseum (Municipal Museum), 13 Paulus Potterstraat. A complete spectrum of Van Gogh paintings plus several by Gauguin and Toulouse-Lautrec at the Museum Vincent van Gogh (7–11 Paulus Potterstraat). The display of Indonesian and Far Eastern art and anthropology at the Tropical Museum.

The National Shipping Museum (1–7 Kattenburgplein) displays some 300 ship models, many atlases and charts, and 5,000 books. You'll find Rembrandt's house at 4–6 Jodenbreestraat; check out the nearby flea market. Exhibits depicting the city's history since its founding in 1270 are at the Amsterdam Historical Museum (92 Kalversraat).

Learn about the history of Jews in Holland since 1590, at the Jewish Historical Museum (4 Nieumarkt). See the altar and organ at the attic church of the 17th-century Amstelkring Museum (40 Oudezijds Voorburgwal), the last of the "hidden" Catholic churches in Holland, with interesting 17th- and 18th-century furniture.

Visit the Anne Frank House (263 Prinsengracht), open Monday-Saturday 9:00–17:00 and on Sundays and holidays 10:00–17:00. Take a 75-minute ride in a glass-roofed canal boat, starting at the piers in front of Central rail station or at Stadhouderskade, near the Rijksmuseum.

Other sightseeing possibilities include the Royal Palace, Tower of Tears, Nieuwe Kerk on the Dam, open Monday-Saturday 10:00–17:00, Sunday 12:00–15:00 and the Mint Tower. Free samples await at tour's end at the Heineken Brewery, open Monday–Friday from 09:30. The flower market (Bloemenmarkt), is open Monday–Friday. Visit a diamond-cutting factory.

The Theater Museum (168 Herengracht) is open Tuesday–Friday 11:00–17:00, Saturdays, Sundays and holidays 11:00–17:00. See Willet Holthuyen Museum (5 Herengracht), a classical 17th-century canal house, elegantly furnished in the style of Holland's Golden Age. Open Monday-Saturday 09:30–17:00, Sundays and holidays 13:00–17:00.

Take an inexpensive half-day bus tour to the heart of the tulip district. It is near Aalsmeer, less than 45 minutes from Amsterdam. Visit the daily Aalsmeer Flower Auction, close to Amsterdam's Schiphol Airport. The peak time at the auction is 08:00–10:00.

Brussels

Sightseeing starts in Grand Place, the ornate town square with many gilded buildings. Inside Hotel de Ville (Town Hall), there is a tapestry museum open daily in Summer, Monday–Friday in Winter. Next to it is a reproduction of a 17th-century brewery. See the 15th-century Notre Dame des Victoires church and the 17th-century Flemish houses in nearby Place du Grand Sablon.

The marvelous Place Parc de Bruxeles gardens and lakes is worth a stop. The Royal Palace, at one end of this park, is open daily except Monday 09:30–16:00 for about six weeks during summer. The Belgian Parliament is at the other end of the park.

One of the world's best collections of 15th- and 16th-century Flemish and Dutch paintings (Rubens, Brueghel, Bosch) is exhibited at the Museum of Ancient Art & Modern Art on Rue de la Regence, open daily except Monday 10:00–17:00.

Nearby, is a collection of rare musical instruments in the Royal Conservatory of Music at the Petit Sablon (also on Rue de la Regence), open Tuesday, Thursday and Saturday 14:30–16:30, Sunday 10:30-22:00, Wednesday 20:00–22:00.

View the collection of paintings by both medieval masters (one section devoted entirely to Bruegel) and also those of later centuries through the 19th, in the Beaux Arts Museum at 3 Rue de la Regence. Then go through a short passageway to the new (1984) Modern Art Museum (Henry Moore, Dali, Magritte, Delvaux). Both museums are open daily except Monday 10:00–17:00.

See the impressive array of African art in The Royal Museum of Central Africa, 12 km east, in Tervuren Park & Arboretum, or the view from the Palais de Justice. Also visit the Law Courts. Tapestries are on display in the 13th-century Cathedral of St. Michael.

Brussels has plenty of museums to keep you busy, from the Brussels City Museum, Museum of Arms and Armor and the museum of sculptures by Constantin Meunier, whose work depicts the dignity of laborers. Or there's the Postal Museum, the Royal Greenhouses and the Brueghel Museum, in the house where the painter lived the last six years of his life.

The Railway Museum is on the mezzanine of Brussels' Nord rail station. For art nouveau head to the Horta Museum at 25 Rue Americaine, open daily except Mondays and holidays 14:00–17:30.

The most famous gourmet food emporium here is the Rob store at Boulevard de la

Woluwe 28. (Take the subway from the center of town to the Tomberg stop and then bus #42, which stops in front of Rob.) Fruits from all over the world, an assortment of 25 ordinary and exotic pates (baby boar!), eel cooked in green sauce, snails marinated in wine sauce, numerous fish (live trout, Scotch salmon, Norwegian lobsters), 600 different wines, 35 types of mustard, chocolates galore.

Take a bus to **Waterloo,** the site of Napoleon's defeat at the Battle of Waterloo; it's about a 10-mile ride.

Luxembourg City

Visit the Citadel, with its 53 forts connected by 16 miles of tunnels. The fish market is the site of the city's oldest buildings. Visit the Museum of History and Art or the State Museum; it's open daily except Monday 10:00–12:00 and 14:00–18:00. Other interesting places include the Palais Grand-Ducal. the splendid view from the bridge that crosses the River Alzette and the Palais Municipal, on the Place d'Armes. The Municipal Art Gallery is open daily except Monday during summer, only on Saturday and Sunday the rest of the year. Visit City Hall then wander through the old quarter, Pfaffenthal, with its medieval buildings. The Fort of Three Acorns, Malakoff Tower, the Church of St. Michael and Notre Dame Cathedral are also interesting spots to visit. Look at the Three Towers and you'll see where the outer limits of the town were in 1050. The 4th-century Chapel of St. Quirinus is one of the oldest shrines in Christendom. General Patton's grave is in the U.S. Military Cemetery, three miles away, at **Hamm.**

Visit the Tramway and Bus Museum at 63, Rue de Bouillon It's open every Thursday, Saturday, Sunday and public holiday from 1.30 to 5.30 p.m. Closed between Christmas and New Year's Day. Other visits on request. From the States, phone 011 32 2 4796 - 2385, fax 011 32 2 45 47 01.

If you're planning to visit lots of museums and other attractions, consider purchasing a one-, two- or three-day Luxembourg Card. With the card, you can take in some 34 varied activities and attractions such as Luxembourg City's guided City Promenade and the National Museum of Natural History. In the Moselle region, the card opens the door to the Wine Museum in Ehnen and the tourist train in Remich. The price of the card also includes transport on all trains and buses throughout the country. Discounts to other attractions are another card benefit. For instance, card-holders can take 30 percent off the fare for these trips: *Petrusse Express* tourist train in Luxembourg City, *M.S. Marie-Astrid* Moselle Pleasure Boat (Grevenmacher - Schengen) and *Musel* Moselle Pleasure Boats in Remich A one-day card costs about f300 for one adult, a two-day card f500 and three days f700 (about $7.89, $13.15 and $18.40).

In the following timetables, where a city has more than one rail station we have designated the particular station after the name of the city (in parentheses).

On day trips from Amsterdam that we have designated "H-L," you will see in the area between Haarlem and Leiden, from mid-March through May, fields of tulips, narcissus, crocus and other bulb flowers in bloom. The region is known as the "Champs de Fleurs" (Fields of Flowers).

Amsterdam - Alkmaar - Amsterdam   470

Dep. Amsterdam	every 30 minutes from 05:37 to 23:22
Arr. Alkmaar	30 minutes later

Sights in **Alkmaar**: The Friday Cheese Market, from the end of April until the end of September, 10:00–12:00. The organ at St. Lawrence Church.

Dep. Alkmaar	every 30 minutes from 05:11 to 23:36
Arr. Amsterdam	30 minutes later

Amsterdam - Alkmaar - Haarlem - Amsterdam   465, 470, 480

It is easy to visit both Alkmaar and Haarlem in a single day-trip.

470
Dep Amsterdam	twice each hour
Arr. Alkmaar	30 minutes later
Change trains 465	
Dep. Alkmaar	twice each hour
Arr. Haarlem	28 minutes later

480
Dep. Haarlem	twice each hour
Arrive Amsterdam	19 minutes later

Amsterdam - Amersfoort - Amsterdam   490

Dep. Amsterdam	Frequent times from 06:06 to 23:36
Arr. Amersfoort	34 minutes later

Sights in **Amersfoort**: A beautiful citadel town with many canals and ancient streets. Popular among antique collectors and for taking side trips to **Spakenburg** (a quaint fishing village on the old Zuider Zee), **Laren** (to visit the Singer Museum), **Zeist** (to see the beautifully-furnished castle there), **Baarn** (to visit Palace Soestdijk, the residence of the former Queen Juliana, **Muiden** (to see the 15th-century moated castle, Muiderslot).

Dep. Amersfoort	Frequent times from 06:14 to 23:57
Arr. Amsterdam	34 minutes later

Amsterdam - Antwerp - Amsterdam   18

Dep. Amsterdam	Frequent times from 06:30 to 21:30
Arr. Antwerp (Cen.)	2 hours and 20 minutes later

Sights in **Antwerp:** To the right of the rail station is one of the best zoos in the world, set in a beautiful garden. It is open daily 08:30–17:00. Walk through the maze of streets called Grote Markt (art galleries, bakeries, fruit stalls, antique shops).

You can watch diamonds being cut and polished at Diamond Land, 33 Appelmanstraat, open daily except Sunday 09:00–18:00. There is a good exhibit of the history of diamonds at the Provincial Museum of Safety, 28–30 Jezusstraat, open Wednesday-Saturday 10:00–17:00, with demonstrations on Saturday 14:00–17:00.

Visit the large Gothic cathedral, Onze Lieve Vrouwe. Open April through mid-October: Monday-Friday 12:00–17:00, Saturday 12:00–15:00, Sunday 13:00–17:00. The rest of the year: Monday 14:00–17:00, Saturday 12:00–15:00, Sunday 13:00–17:00.

Flemish, Italian, French, Dutch and German masterpieces in the Gallery of Fine Arts, open daily except Monday 10:00–17:00. Rubens House, with many of his paintings, at 9–11 Wapper, open daily 10:00–17:00. The 16th-century printing shop in the Plantin-Moretus Museum. The Marine Museum.

Other places of interest: Mayer van den Bergh Museum, Folklore Museum, Town Hall,. Guild Houses, Vieille Bourse (the Old Stock Exchange), Rockox Mansion, the view of Antwerp from the 24th floor of Torengebouw.

Now a classy suburb of Antwerp, **Middelheim** was first settled in the 14th-century. Houses more than 300 statues (by Henry Moore, Vic Gentil, Charles Leplae and many other great sculptors) in the 30-acre Middelheim Open-Air Museum of Sculpture, founded in 1950. It is 30 minutes by bus #17, #27 or #32, from Antwerp's Central rail station. Ask the bus driver to tell you where to get off. The walk to the sculpture park is 15 minutes from there, passing many splendid mansions.

One can begin circling the park-museum by starting either toward the left of the entrance (in the direction of the statue of Balzac) or to the right, along a tree-shaded stream and through a lawn that has many statues.

The park (admission free) is open daily 10:00 to sunset about 17:00 in winter, 21:00 in summer.

Dep. Antwerp (Cen.)	Frequent times from 06:49 to 21:46
Arr. Amsterdam	2 hours and 20 minutes later

Amsterdam - Apeldoorn   490, 492

Dep. Amsterdam (Cen.)	6 minutes after every hour/half-hour from 07:06 to 22:06
Change trains in Amersfoort	
Arr. Apeldoorn	1 hour and 10 minutes later

Sights in **Apeldoorn:** From the rail station, take bus #102, #104 or #106 to the Het Loo Palace. Set in the 27,000-acre Royal Forest, the palace was a private residence for the Dutch royal family until it became a state museum in 1971.

Both the lavish, enormous palace and the geometric patterns of its extraordinary gardens are well worth visiting. Seventeenth-century tapestries, magnificent furniture, exceptional Delft pottery and fine paintings (Rembrandt, Vermeer, van Ruisdael) are exhibited in the palace.

Dep. Apeldoorn	26 minutes and 58 minutes after every hour from 05:58/06:26 to 23:26

Change trains in Amersfoort

Arr. Amsterdam (Cen.)	1 hour and 10 minutes later

Amsterdam - Arnhem - Amsterdam   470

Dep. Amsterdam (Cent.)	Frequent times from 06:48 to 23:49
Arr. Arnhem	60–70 minutes later

Sights in **Arnhem:** See the collection of several farm villages, depicting rural lifestyles from the 18th to early 20th centuries, at the Netherlands Open-Air Museum; almost three square miles to explore. Colored arrows direct visitors to one-, two- and four-hour tours. Open April–October, Monday-Friday 09:00–17:00, Sunday 10:00–17:00. At the craft exhibits, wood shoes are chiseled, bread is baked, baskets and paper are made. See a blacksmith at his forge. Don't fail to try the little pancake balls called "poffertjes," and then eat some pannekoeken (traditional Dutch pancakes) and wafelen (waffles).

Also visit the 16th-century Grootekerk (Ptotestant Church) and the extensively-restored Eusebiuskerk, a Gothic church. See the Duivelshuis (devil's house). The best collection of Van Gogh is at the Kroller-Muller Museum in the nearby National Park. Special buses go the several miles from the rail station to the museum and surrounding 13,300-acre national park during June, July and August. The museum is open Tuesday–Saturday 10:00–17:00, Sunday 11:00–17:00.

Dep. Arnhem	Frequent times from 06:39 to 23:09
Arr. Amsterdam (Cent.)	60–70 minutes later

Amsterdam - Bonn   28, 912, 913

All of the Amsterdam–Cologne and v.v. trains charge a supplement.

28

Dep. Amsterdam (Cen.)	07:00 (1)	08:00 (1)	09:00 (1+3)	10:00	11:00 (3)
Arr. Cologne (Koln)	09:41	10:55 (4)	11:41	12:55 (4)	13:41

Change trains 912 or 913

Dep. Cologne	09:58	11:13	11:58	13:13	13:58
Arr. Bonn	10:36	11:40	12:36	13:40	14:36

Sights in **Bonn**: See notes about Bonn under "Cologne–Bonn"

912 or 913

Dep. Bonn	11:27	15:27	17:15	18:15	20:27
Arr. Cologne	11:59	15:59	17:45	18:45	20:59
Change trains 28					
Dep. Cologne	12:16 (1)	16:16 (1)	18:02 (1)	19:02 (1)	21:16 (1)
Arr. Amsterdam	14:52	18:52	20:52	21:52	23:52

(1) Restaurant car. (2) Light refreshments. (3) Change trains Cologne; restaurant car. (4) direct train.

Amsterdam - Brussels - Amsterdam 18

Dep. Amsterdam	06:30	07:30	08:30	09:30	10:30	11:30
Arr. Brussels (Nord)	09:21	10:21	11:21	12:21	13:21	14:21
Arr. Brussels (Cen.)	09:26	10:26	11:26	12:26	13:26	14:26
Arr. Brussels (Midi)	09:30	10:30	11:30	12:30	13:30	14:30

•   •   •

Dep. Brussels (Midi)	13:10	14:10	15:10	16:10	17:10	18:10 (1)
Dep. Brussels (Cen.)	13:14	14:14	15:14	16:14	17:14	18:14
Dep. Brussels (Nord)	13:19	14:19	15:19	16:19	17:19	18:19
Arr. Amsterdam	16:04	17:04	18:04	19:04	20:04	21:08

(1) Plus other departures from Brussels (Midi) at 19:10, 20:10 and 21:10, arriving Amsterdam 22:04, 23:04 and 00:04.

Amsterdam - Cologne 28

All of these trains charge a supplement.

Amsterdam	07:00 (1)	08:00 (1)	09:00 (1)	10:00 (1)	11:00 (1)
Arr. Cologne	09:41	10:55	11:41	12:55	13:42

•   •   •

Dep. Cologne	12:16 (1)	14:16 (1)	16:16 (1)	18:02 (1)	19:02 (1)
Arr. Amsterdam	15:51	16:52	18:52	20:52	21:52

(1) Restaurant car.

Amsterdam - Delft - Amsterdam (H-L)   450

Dep. Amsterdam (Cen.)   Frequent times from 00:22 to 22:41
Arr. Delft   55 minutes later

Sights in **Delft**: The tourist information office (on the main square) provides a brochure outlining a walking tour all of the city's principal sights.

See the 14th-century New Church, where members of the Dutch royal family are buried. The Mausoleum of William the Silent at the 15th-century New Church. The 17th-century Prinsenhof (Princes Court), housing the Municipal Museum. Tetar van Elven Museum, containing the works of Vermeer and Pieter de Hoogh. Old Church. The Grain Market. Town Hall. The Old Delft Canal.

The Delft Pottery Factory ("De Porceleyne Fles") at 196 Rotterdamsweg is open May–September 09:00–17:00 Monday-Saturday and 13:00–18:00 on Sunday. It is open 09:00–17:00 Monday–Saturday from October through April. Its tour includes visiting a showroom, a shop and exhibits of antique tiles and mural ceramics.

Dep. Delft   Frequent times from 00:25 to 23:56
Arr. Amsterdam (Cen.)   55 minutes later

Amsterdam - Den Haag - Amsterdam (H-L)   450

Dep. Amsterdam   2–3 times each hour from 05:23 to 23:41
Arr. Den Haag (H.S.)   45–50 minutes later

Sights in **Den Haag**: Binnenhof, a complex of palaces and courtyards, including the 13th-century Hall of Knights (an 118-by-56-foot banquet hall where Holland's Parliament meets every September), and Gevangenpoort, Holland's 14th-century prison.

Mauritshui is an art gallery filled with the works of Rembrandt, Vermeer and Rubens. The finest collection in the world of 19th-century Dutch art is at the Gemeente Museum. There's an excellent collection of Rembrandts at the Bredius Museum. Other places worthy of a visit include the Peace Palace, the Hidden Church, at 38 Molenstraat, the Mesdag Museum, Costume Museum, Municipal Museum and the miniature city of Madurodam, with everything on a scale of 1/25th life size.

View the marvelous paintings in the Johan de Witt Huis at Kneuterdijk 6, open Monday-Saturday 10:00–17:00, and on Sundays and holidays 11:00–17:00, or the more than 1,000 puppets and marionettes at the Puppet Museum. Den Haag is also graced with some five miles of wide, beautiful beaches.

Dep. Den Haag (H.S.)   2–3 times each hour from 05:02 to 00:36
Arr. Amsterdam   45–50 minutes later

Amsterdam - Den Haag + Utrecht - Amsterdam (H-L) 450, 491, 480

It is possible to visit both Den Haag (see sightseeing notes above) and Utrecht in one day.

450

| Dep. Amsterdam | Frequent departures from 05:23 to 23:41 |
| Arr. Den Haag (**H.S.**) | 45–50 minutes later |

Change trains and rail stations 491

| Dep. Den Haag (**Cen.**) | Frequent times from 00:11 to 23:42 |
| Arr. Utrecht | 40 minutes later |

Change trains 480

| Dep. Utrecht | Frequent times from 00:02 to 23:32 |
| Arr. Amsterdam | 30 minutes later |

For those who prefer the direct trip to Utrecht and to have more time there, refer to notes under "Amsterdam–Utrecht"

Sights in **Utrecht**: The 13th-century Dom Cathedral, and the view from the top of its 465 steps (300 feet high). In fall, winter and spring the tower is open only on weekends. Nearby is the Music Box and Street Organ Museum on Achter de Dom, open Tuesday-Saturday 11:00-16:00. Next door is the Museum of Contemporary Art at 14 Achter de Dom.

Take in the museum of mechanical instruments, at 38 Lange Nieuwstraat or the Netherlands Railway Museum, at 6 Van Oldenberneveltlaan, open Tuesday–Saturday 10:00–17:00, Sundays 13:00–17:00. Stop by the 11th-century St. Peter's Church or view the paintings and Viking ship in the Centraal Museum at 1 Agnietenstraat, open Tuesday-Saturday 10:00–17:00, Sundays and holidays 14:00–17:00.

The ancient fish market, Vis Markt, an institution at the same location since the 12th century. The largest medieval art collection in Holland is at the Museum of Religious Art in Het Catherijneconvent (St. Catherine's Church and Convent).

A collection of 180 musical instruments ("from music box to barrel organ") is displayed at the van Speeldos tot Pierement Museum. Other museums include the Gold, Silver and Clock Museum, Museum of Contemporary Art and Museum of the Insurance Business.

Nearby interesting villages: **Breukelen**, for which New York's Brooklyn was named; the village has beautiful castles, 17th-century mansions, **Oudewater**, famous for its stork colony and three-aisle church, and **Loenen**, known for its 18th-century houses and their lovely gardens.

Amsterdam - Dusseldorf - Amsterdam 28

All of these trains charge a supplement.

Dep. Amsterdam (Cen.)	07:00 (1)	08:00 (1)	09:00 (1)	10:00 (1)	11:00 (1)
Arr. Dusseldorf	09:18	10:30	11:18	12:30	13:18

Sights in **Dusseldorf**: See notes about Dusseldorf under "Cologne–Dusseldorf"

Dep. Dusseldorf	12:37 (1)	14:37 (1)	16:37 (1)	18:26 (2)	19:26 (1+3)
Arr. Amsterdam (Cen.)	14:52	17:51	18:52	20:52	21:52

(1) Restaurant car.   (2) Light refreshments.   (3) Plus another Dusseldorf departure at 21:37 (1).

Amsterdam - Enkhuizen - Amsterdam   461

Local trains run every 30 minutes 07:19–23:49 for the 62-minute trip north from Amsterdam's Central rail station. Trains depart Enkhuizen every 30 minutes 08:09–23:08 for the 64-minute trip back to Amsterdam.

It is a four-minute walk from the Enkhuizen rail station to its ferry dock. Boats depart every 15 minutes to the 700-acre Zuider Zee Open Air Museum, open summer months 10:00–17:00.

This museum consists of 130 houses, portraying life and work from 1880 to 1932. Allow at least two hours to tour it. Then take a 10-minute walk to the Binnenmuseum, an indoor complex of 15 exhibition halls displaying fine examples of furniture, fishing boats, toys and other items. It is open mid-February to December 31: Monday–Saturday 10:00-17:00, Sunday 12:00–17:00.

Amsterdam - Gouda - Amsterdam   467

Dep. Amsterdam	First train at 6:22, then 22 minutes after each hour, from 07:22 to 22:22
Arr. Gouda	50 minutes later

Sights in **Gouda**: Stained-glass in Sint Janskerk. The 15th-century Town Hall. The famous Thursday cheese market.

Dep. Gouda	17 minutes after each hour, from 06:17 to 23:17
Arr. Amsterdam	50 minutes later

Amsterdam - Haarlem - Amsterdam   450

Dep. Amsterdam (Cen.)	Twice each hour, from 06:41 to 00:22
Arr. Haarlem	14 minutes later

Sights in **Haarlem**: It is only a few minutes' walk from the rail station to town center and Grote Markt, where jousting tournaments took place in the Middle Ages. Nearby is the

14th-century Town Hall and many cafes.

Works by Franz Hals and many other great painters plus Delft tiles, Flemish wallpaper made of gilded and painted panels of leather, silver tankards and candlestands, pikes and swords, and stained and painted glass windows are found at the Frans Hals Museum at 62 Groot Heiligland (Note the address. That is the only mark outside the building!). This museum is only a 20-minute walk from the rail station, or take buses 1, 2, 3, 5, 6, 70 or 71.

In St. Bavo's, Holland's most beautiful church, hear the massive 5,000-pipe Baroque organ (ivory and tortoise shell keyboard) built in 1738 by Christiaan Muller. Mozart played it when he was 10 years old. It can be heard Sundays at 10:00 and 19:00, also at free concerts Tuesday at 20:15.

Take a look a the World Clock at 88 Wagenweg. Teyler's Museum at 16 Spaarme (open Tuesday- Saturday 10:00–17:00), exhibits Dutch, Italian and French paintings from the 16th to 20th centuries, as well as antique musical instruments, telescopes and globes.

Dep. Haarlem	Twice each hour, from 07:05 to 01:15
Arr. Amsterdam (Cen.)	14 minutes later

Amsterdam - Hoorn - Amsterdam   461

Dep. Amsterdam	Freq. times 06:19-00:26	Dep. Hoorn	Freq. times 05:34-00:33
Arr. Hoorn	40 minutes later	Arr. Amsterdam	40 minutes later

Sights in **Hoorn**: The full-scale enactment of 17th-century trades and crafts in Hoorn's "Old Dutch Market" takes place in the Rodesteen Square on Wednesdays mid-June to mid-August: folk dances and stalls with basket weaving, net mending and the making of wood shoes. Daily from mid-June to mid-August (plus Saturdays and Sundays from mid-August through mid-September), a steam train with antique coaches operates between Hoorn and **Medemblik**.

See Hoorn's 17th-century mansions and warehouses, the collection of paintings and antiques in the West Friesian Museum, the 17th-century Weighhouse or the 16th-century Hospital of St. John. Visit the two medieval churches: Noorderkerk and Oosterkerk. Also of interest: the 16th-century St. Mary Tower and East Gate, remains of the original fortification and the 17th-century almshouse, St. Pietershof.

Amsterdam - Leiden - Amsterdam (H-L)   450

Dep. Amsterdam	Frequent times during all 24 hours
Arr. Leiden	33 minutes later

Sights in **Leiden**: Pieterskerk, the church where the Pilgrim fathers worshipped for 10 years before setting sail for America in 1620. The University. The Royal Arms Museum. The National Museum of Antiquities. The Municipal Museum. The National Ethnological Museum. The nearby flower center, called **Keukenhof**.

Dep. Leiden   Frequent times during all 24 hours
Arr. Amsterdam   33 minutes later

Amsterdam - Maastricht - Amsterdam 480

All of these trains have light refreshments.

Dep. Amsterdam   06:33 (1) Plus frequent times daily 07:33-22:03
Arr. Maastricht   2½ hours after departing Amsterdam

Sights in **Maastricht**: The 6th-century St. Servatius Church, oldest church in Holland, where Charlemagne occasionally attended mass. There is a large statue of him in the rear of the church. Shoppers from not only nearby Dutch cities but even from Belgium, France and Germany come to the Market Day (produce and pastries) at Town Hall Square, Fridays 08:00–13:00.

See the carved wood columns of the choir in the 10th-century Basilica of Our Gracious Lady. The many 17th- and 18th-century houses on the Stokstraat Quarter, each having a plaque that shows the construction date, the owner's name and his trade. Some of the old houses are now antique shops, art galleries and boutiques. Try the local Limburger cheese and gingerbread in one of the sidewalk cafes on famous Vrijthof Square.

Take a bus from the rail station for the short trip to the Mount St. Peter caves, consisting of 200 miles of labyrinths where people hid during a Spanish invasion in 1570. It was originally a sandstone quarry, worked from Roman times until the end of the 19th century. Since 1584, famous visitors (Napoleon, Archduke Ferdinand of Spain, Voltaire, Sir Walter Scott) have scratched their signatures on the walls of the very cold and very damp caves.

Dep. Maastricht   Frequent times from 05:27 to 20:31
Arr. Amsterdam   2½ hours later

(1) Runs Monday–Friday, except holidays.

Amsterdam - Paris - Amsterdam   18

Both of these trains charge a supplement.

| Dep. Amsterdam (Cen.) | 07:19 (1) | Dep. Paris (Nord) | 17:37 (2) |
| Arr. Paris (Nord) | 12:05 | Arr. Amsterdam (Cen.) | 22:28 |

(1) Runs daily. Light refreshments. (2) Reservation required. Runs daily, except Saturday. Light refreshments..

Amsterdam - Rotterdam - Amsterdam (H-L)   450, 467, 452

Dep. Amsterdam	Frequent times during all 24 hours
Arr. Rotterdam (Cent.)	60–70 minutes later

Sights in **Rotterdam**: The Netherlands Tourist Information Bureau has offices all over Holland. Look for its "VVV" sign.

Don't miss the view of the city and port from the top of the 340-foot high Euromast, open daily 09:00–22:00 March 15–October 14, and 09:00–18:00 October 15–March 14. Nearby, Heineken's Brewery (Crookswijksesingel 50).

There's a fantastic collection of 15th-to-19th-century Flemish and Dutch paintings and a wing of modern sculpture and art (Van Gogh and Kandinsky to the present day) as well as objects of glass, pewter, silver, lace, furniture and tiles in the Boymans-van Beuningen Museum (Mathenesserlaan 18–20).

Devices used by smugglers to defraud customs, are on display at the Profesor van der Poel Tax Museum (Parklaan 14). The collection of globes, ships and atlases in the Maritime Museum (Leuvehaven 1). Many old vessels are open to visitors.

The 75-minute harbor boat trip circles one of the world's largest ports. Boats depart every 45 minutes from Willemsplein Landing.

Stroll through the noteworthy Lijnbaan shopping center. Hear a free lunchtime concert every day at De Doelen, an enormous complex of music and congress halls, just across from the Central rail station.

Unwind in the 10,000-acre Zuiderpark, Plaswijck Park, Zuiderparkgordel, Het Park, and the Kralingse Bos (woods). See the wide variety of trees in Arboretum Trompenburg.

Visit the collection of elephants, orangutans, tigers (Sumatran, Siberian and Bengal), great apes, reptiles and seals in the Blijdorp Zoo (open 09:00–17:00).

Enjoy the many statues located throughout the city, particularly Mastroianni's "Kiss," at the Central Railroad Station. Visit "De Ster," a working windmill (spice and snuff grinding) near Kralingse Lake.

A collection of folk art of primitive cultures from the non-Western world is housed at the Museum of Ethnology (Willemskade 25). The Rotterdam Historical Museum in the Schielands Huis (Korte Hoogstraat 31) has an extensive display of interiors from the 17th, 18th and 19 century. Rotterdam has many art galleries, including Lijnbaan Centrum (Linjbaan 165) and Kunstzaal (Zuidplein 120) and the Henrik Chabot Museum. The city also has a 14th-century church, St. Laurenskerk.

Nearby **Delfshaven** is the port from which the Puritans started their voyage to the New World, sailing from there on July 22, 1620, before boarding the Mayflower off the English coast. The group spent its last night praying in Delfshaven's Reformed Church, now called Pelgrimvaderskerk (Pilgrim Fathers' Church). A stained-glass window and a plaque there commemorate the Pilgrims' sailing. Visit the "De Dubbelde Palmboom" Museum (with everyday objects used centuries ago in Rotterdam) and a pewter workshop in the Sack Carriers guildhouse. The enormous hydraulic project of the Haringvliet sluices can be seen in nearby **Stellendam**.

Dep. Rotterdam (Cent.)	Frequent times during all 24 hours
Arr. Amsterdam	60–70 minutes later

Amsterdam - Rotterdam + Den Haag - Amsterdam (H-L) 450, 452, 467

This circle trip allows seeing only a few of the sights in Rotterdam (see notes in preceding listing) and in Den Haag (see notes earlier in this section), but one can see something of both Rotterdam and Den Haag in this one-day trip.

Dep. Amsterdam (Cen.)	Frequent times during all 24 hours
Arr. Rotterdam (Cen.)	65 minutes later
Dep. Rotterdam (Cen.)	Frequent times during all 24 hours
Arr. Den Haag (Hbf.)	16–24 minutes later
Dep. Den Haag	Frequent times during all 24 hours
Arr. Amsterdam (Cen.)	45–60 minutes later

Amsterdam - Utrecht - Amsterdam (H-L) 470

Dep. Amsterdam	Frequent times from 05:47 to 23:49
Arr. Utrecht	36–44 minutes later

Sights in **Utrecht**: see notes about sightseeing in Utrecht under "Amsterdam–Den Haag + Utrecht–Amsterdam"

Dep. Utrecht	Frequent times each hour from 06:16 until 00:16
Arr. Amsterdam	36–44 minutes later

Amsterdam - Zwolle - Amsterdam 490

All of these trains have light refreshments.

Dep. Amsterdam	Hourly, from 06:36 to 23:36
Arr. Zwolle	70 minutes later

Sights in **Zwolle**: Hear the famous Schnitger Organ in the magnificent St. Michael's Church. There are many beautiful buildings in this more than 700-year old town on the

Ijssel River. This is a popular base for taking side trips to **Hattem** (great for local arts and crafts) and **Giethoorn** (the Venice of Holland, where everything moves on water).

Dep. Zwolle	Hourly, from 07:48 to 22:48
Arr. Amsterdam	70 minutes later

Brussels - Aachen - Brussels 400

All of these trains have light refreshments.

Dep. Brussels (Midi)	06:47	07:47	09:48	10:48	12:07 (1)
Dep. Brussels (Cen.)	06:52	07:52	09:52	10:47	-0-
Dep. Brussels (Nord)	06:57	07:57	09:57	10:52	12:16
Arr. Aachen	08:43	09:43	11:53	12:43	13:55

Sights in **Aachen**: Charlemagne's 8th-century treasury at the cathedral contains an extraordinary collection of German medieval ecclesiastical gold and silver, including the Shrine of the Virgin Mary, completed in 1236. The Grand Coronation Chamber in Town Hall.

Dep. Aachen	13:03	14:10	15:03	16:07 (1)	17:03	19:03 (2)
Arr. Brussels (Nord)	14:47	15:49	16:47	17:49	18:47	20:47
Arr. Brussels (Cen.)	14:52	15:53	16:52	-0-	18:51	20:51
Arr. Brussels (Midi)	14:55	15:57	16:55	18:03	18:54	20:54

(1) Restaurant car. (2) Plus another Aachen departure at 21:03, arriving Brussels (Nord) 22:47.

Brussels - Amsterdam - Brussels 18

Dep. Brussels (Midi)	Frequent times from 06:10 to 21:10
Dep. Brussels (Cen.)	4 minutes after departing Midi station
Dep. Brussels (Nord)	4 minutes after departing Central station
Arr. Amsterdam	3 hours after departing Brussels (Midi)

Sights in **Amsterdam**: See notes about sightseeing in Amsterdam.

Dep. Amsterdam	Frequent times from 06:30 to 22:15
Arr. Brussels (Nord)	3 hours later
Arr. Brussels (Cen.)	4 minutes after arriving Nord station
Arr. Brussels (Midi)	4 minutes after arriving Central station

Brussels - Antwerp - Brussels 410

Dep. Brussels (Midi)	Frequent times from 05:42 to 23:10
Dep. Brussels (Cen.)	4 minutes later
Dep. Brussels (Nord)	4 minutes after departing Central station
Arr. Antwerp (Cen.)	45 minutes after departing Brussels (Midi)

Sights in **Antwerp**: See notes about sightseeing in Antwerp under "Amsterdam–Antwerp–Amsterdam"

Dep. Antwerp (Cen.)	Frequent times from 05:30 to 23:19
Arr. Brussels (Nord)	40 minutes later
Arr. Brussels (Cen.)	4 minutes after arriving Nord station
Arr. Brussels (Midi)	4 minutes after departing Central station

Brussels - Brugge - Brussels 400

Dep. Brussels (Nord)	Frequent times from 05:47 to 23:19
Dep. Brussels (Cen.)	4 minutes after departing Nord station
Dep. Brussels (Midi)	7 minutes after departing Central station
Arr. Brugge	60 minutes after departing Brussels (Midi)

Sights in **Brugge**: The splendid view from the top of the 255-foot-high 13th-century Belfry (365 steps), with its famous 47-bell carillon, in the city's main square, Markt. The Belfry's tower is closed 12:00–14:00. The interesting 15th-century Town Hall and 15th-century Recorders' House are on this square. The tourist office is in the nearby Government Palace. (Many cafes are located in this area.)

At the 12th-century Basilica of the Holy Blood, a phial said to contain a few drops of Christ's blood is displayed on Fridays. It was brought to Brugge in 1150 from the Second Crusade. Also there: a fine display of gold, silver and copper artwork. Open daily, except between 12:00–14:30.

See the lace, pottery, gold pieces, musical instruments and weapons in the 15th-century mansion that houses the Gruuthuse Museum. Also of note are the small museum in the 13th-century Saint Saviour's Cathedral and the black slate and gilded brass 16th-century effigies and Michelangelo's white carrara marble Madonna with Child statue in the Church of Our Lady. Behind the Church, see Dutch masterpieces at the Groeninge Museum (open daily 09:30–12:00 and 14:00–17:00).

A collection of Old Flemish School paintings is at the Hans Memling Museum, in a section of the 13th-century Hospital of St. John (open 09:00–12:30 and 14:00–18:00 in summer, 09:00–12:00 and 14:00–16:00 the rest of the year). Look for paintings and silverwork at the Archer's Guild of St. Sebastian. Ter Buerze, the world's first stock exchange, is now a bank, on the corner of Acadamiesstraat and Vlamingstraat.

St. John's, the most beautiful of Belgium's 140 functioning windmills, was built in

1770. Nearby is the beach resort **Knokke-Heist** (many hotels, shops and nightclubs).

Canal boats leave from several docks for half-hour cruises with English-language guides.

Dep. Brugge	Frequent times from 05:17 to 22:50
Arr. Brussles (Midi)	One hour later
Arr. Brussels (Cen.)	10 minutes after arriving Midi station
Arr. Brussels (Nord)	3 minutes after arriving Central station

---

Brussels - Cologne (Koln) - Brussels   20

Dep. Brussels (Midi)	06:43	07:43	09:48	10:48	12:07 (1)
Dep. Brussels (Cen.)	4 minutes after departing Midi station				
Dep. Brussels (Nord)	5 minutes after departing Central station				
Arr. Cologne	09:42	10:42	12:42	13:42	14:42

• • •

Dep. Cologne	13:14 (1)	14:14	15:14 (1)	16:14	18:14 (2)
Arr. Brussels (Nord)	15:49	16:44	17:49	18:44	20:44
Arr. Brussels (Cen.)	15:57	16:55	-0-	18:54	20:54
Arr. Brussels (Midi)	15:57	16:59	18:03	18:59	20:59

(1) Supplement charged. Restaurant car. (2) Plus another Cologne departure at 20:14, arriving Brussels (Nord) 22:44.

Brussels - Gent (Ghent) - Brussels   400

Dep. Brussels (Nord)	Frequent times from 05:47 to 23:19
Dep. Brussels (Cen.)	4 minutes after departing Nord station
Dep. Brussels (Midi)	5 minutes after departing Central station
Arr. Gent (St. Pieters)	40–50 minutes after departing Nord station

Sights in **Gent**: Located at the confluence of the Lys and Scheldt rivers. Flanked by many canals lined with 15th-century gabled buildings.

The Gent Tourist Office, in the 14th-century Town Hall, is near the 14th-century belfry and the 15th-century Cloth Hall, where a 20-minute sound and light program commemorates ancient Gent. Two-hour walking tours start at the tourist office. A 30-minute boat tour on the canals gives a fine perspective of Gent's past.

See the superior collection of paintings at the Fine Arts Museum, the collection of furniture at the Museum of Decorative Arts and reproductions of medieval Gent homes, ironwork, costumes and weapons at the Byloke Museum.

The fantastic altarpiece in St. Bavo's Cathedral is worth a stop. West from it is Graseli, the city's oldest port, lined by famous guild houses. Gent's other medieval harbor, Koornlei, is on the opposite bank from Graseli. Many of the old houses there were restored and reconstructed at the beginning of the 20th century.

See the foreboding dungeons and torture chambers in the 12th-century Gravensteen (Castle of the Counts), modeled eight centuries ago on forts visited by Philip of Alsace when he led Crusaders in Syria. Sint Jorishof, built in 1228 and operated as a hotel since the 15th century, is believed to be the oldest hotel in Europe, with 70 rooms in the original building.

The largest indoor plant and flower show (nearly seven acres) is held in Gent in April, every five years. The 32nd show takes place from April 22 to May 1, 2000.

Dep. Gent (St. Pieters)	Frequent times from 04:47 to 23:50
Arr. Brussels (Midi)	28–35 minutes later
Arr. Brussels (Cen.)	6 minutes after arriving Midi station
Arr. Brussels (Nord)	3 minutes after arriving Central station

Brussels - Liege - Brussels 400

Dep. Brussels (Midi)	Frequent times from 05:48 to 23:47
Dep. Brussels (Central)	4 minutes later
Dep. Brussels (Nord)	6 minutes after departing Brussels (Central)
Arr. Liege (Guillemins)	69-82 minutes after departing Brussels (Midi)

Sights in **Liege**: There are many museums on and near Rue Feronstree. The wonderful collection of illuminated manuscripts, ancient Roman pottery, tapestries, medieval sculpture and ancient coins in the Musee Curtius (do not miss seeing the enormous twin fireplaces in the large hall on the second floor). In a building at the rear of the Curtius is the Musee du Verre, which has an incredible collection of ancient Egyptian and Roman glassware.

See the exhibit of very beautiful guns in the Musee d'Armes, on nearby Quai de Maestricht. Clocks, tapestries, wood paneling, chandeliers, leather-covered walls, porcelain, kitchen utensils and furniture are featured in the Musee d'Ansembourg. Impressionist and expressionist paintings (Courbet, Corot, Chagall, Gauguin and Picasso) are on exhibit at the Musee des Beaux-Arts. The Aquarium.

If time permits, visit the town's aquarium or the columned courtyard at the Palais des Princes-Eveques. Stroll La Roture, the city's old quarter and visit the colorful Sunday market at La Batte. Shop the boutiques on Rue Pont de I'lle and Rue Vinave de I'lle.

Dep. Liege (Guillemins)	Frequent times from 04:24 to 23:12
Arr. Brussels (Nord)	60–70 minutes later
Arr. Brussels (Central)	6 minutes after arriving Nord station
Arr. Brussels (Midi)	3 minutes after arriving Central station

Brussels - Luxembourg - Brussels 430

Dep. Brussels (Midi/Zuid)	21 minutes after each hour, from 05:21 to 20:21
Dep. Brussels (Cen.)	6 minutes after departing Brussels Midi-Zuid
Dep. Brussels (Nord)	3 minutes after departing Brussels Central
Arr. Luxembourg	2½ hours after departing Brussels Midi/Zuid

Dep. Luxembourg	27 minutes after each hour, from 05:27 (2) to 20:27
Arr. Brussels (Nord)	2¼ hours later
Arr. Brussels (Cen.)	5 minutes after arriving Brussels Nord
Arr. Brussels (Midi/Zuid)	4 minutes after arriving Brussels Central

(1) Additional departures from Midi/Zuid station at 07:15 and 12:16 (both charge a supplement and have a restaurant car) do not stop at Central station. (2) There are additional departures from Luxembourg at 12:10, 17:01, 20:06, 04:09, 06:13, 06:56 which (except for the 20:06) do not stop at Brussels Central. All have a restaurant car (except the 08:14). The 17:01 and 20:06 departures charge a supplement.

Brussels - Namur - Brussels 430

Dep. Brussels (Midi)	Frequent times from 05:21 to 22:47
Dep. Brussels (Central)	4 minutes later (1)
Dep. Brussels (Nord)	6 minutes after departing Brussels Central
Arr. Namur	One hour after departing Brussels Midi

Sights in **Namur**: The silver art in Sisters of Our Lady Convent. The fortress. The baroque 18th-century cathedral. The Diocesan Museum. The extremely elegant Casino, featuring gastronomic feasts.

Dep. Namur	Frequent times from 04:49 to 22:22
Arr. Brussels (Nord)	49 minutes later
Arr. Brussels (Central)	6 minutes after arriving Nord station (1)
Arr. Brussels (Midi)	4 minutes after arriving Central station

(1) A few trains do not stop at Brussels' Central rail station.

Brussels - Paris - Brussels 18

All of these trains charge a supplement and all trains have light refreshments

| Dep. Brussels (Midi) | 07:07 | 08:05 | 10:07 | 12:07 |
| Arr. Paris (Nord) | 09:05 | 10:05 | 12:05 | 14:05 |

| Dep. Paris (Nord) | 14:40 | 16:37 | 17:37 | 18:40 (1) |
| Arr. Brussels (Midi) | 16:38 | 18:37 | 19:38 | 20:38 |

(1 Plus other Paris departures at 19:40 and 23:16 (2), arriving Brussels 21:41 and 04:35. (2) Has couchettes.

Brussels - Tournai - Brussels   425

Dep. Brussels (Nord)	06:57	08:01	09:03	10:03	10:57	12:01
Dep. Brussels (Cen.)	4 minutes after departing Nord station					
Dep. Brussels (Midi)	6 minutes after departing Central station					
Arr. Tournai	08:03	09:08	10:08	11:08	12:02	13:10

Sights in **Tournai**: One of Belgium's leading art towns. Pick up a free map and brochure at the city tourism center, at Vieux-Marche-aux-Poteries 14, open Monday–Friday 09:00–19:00, Saturday and Sunday 10:00–13:00 and 15:00–18:00. English-speaking guides are available for a fee.

Tournai is best seen on foot, and the place to start is at the Grand Place, a square that is lined with reconstructed medieval guild houses, of which the Cloth Hall is dominant. Nearby is the 236-foot-high 12th-century Belfry. Its 16th-century 43-bell carillon is played daily at 11:30.

Visit the 12th-century 435-foot-long Romanesque cathedral, particularly to see its 13th-century Ile-de-France Gothic choir and many fine paintings in several of its chapels. The remains of two 12th-century murals there are extraordinary.

Also see the 13th-century gilded copper Shrine of Our Lady, decorated with silver figures that depict scenes from the life of the Virgin...and a 7th-century Byzantine cross studded with rubies, emeralds and pearls with what is said to be a fragment of the cross on which Jesus died imbedded in its back.

From Easter until the end of September, the cathedral is open 08:30–18:00. The rest of the year: 08:30–16:30. Its treasury is open from Easter until the end of September 10:00–12:00. Rest of the year: 10:00–12:00 and 14:30–16:30. Walk across the Scheldt River and see the earliest examples in Western Europe of bourgeois houses of the Romanesque period as well as Gothic houses dating from the 14th and 15th century. From the Pont des Trous (one of the oldest bridges in Europe), view the five mammoth cathedral towers at dusk, silhouetted against the sky.

Dep. Tournai	Once per hour 04:27 to 22:32
Arr. Brussels (Midi)	58 minutes later
Arr. Brussels (Cen.)	5 minutes after arriving Midi station
Arr. Brussels (Nord)	3 minutes after arriving Central station

Luxembourg - Basel - Luxembourg   385

Before 1991, departure at 05:28 from Luxembourg made this excursion more practical than it is today.

Both of these trains charge a supplement and have a restaurant car.

Dep. Luxembourg	10:01	Dep. Basel (SNCF)	16:23
Arr. Basel (SNCF)	13:39	Arr. Luxembourg	19:56

Sights in **Basel**: Superb Holbein, Delacroix, Gaugin, Matisse, Ingres, Courbet and Van Gogh paintings in the Kunstmuseum on St. Alban Graben. The collection of 18th-century clothing, ceramics and watches in the Kirschgarten. The Historical Museum in the Franciscan church in Barfusserplatz. Shop on Freiestrasse.

See the 16th-century town hall, the fishmarket and the 15th-century New University. Take a boat excursion from the pier in the back of Hotel Three Kings. See the view of the city from the Wettstein Bridge. Visit Munsterplatz.

Luxembourg - Bonn - Luxembourg   910, 912, 915

915			*910*		
Dep. Luxembourg	09:40	10:33	Dep. Bonn (Hbf.)	15:47	16:30
Arr. Koblenz	11:48	12:37	Arr. Koblenz	16:23	17:10
Change trains 912			*Change trains 915*		
Dep. Koblenz	11:56	12:56	Dep. Koblenz	16:55	17:19
Arr. Bonn (Hbf.)	12:56	13:56	Arr. Luxembourg	19:04	19:23

Luxembourg - Brussels - Luxembourg   430

Dep. Luxembourg	06:27	07:07 (1)	07:27	08:27	09:27	
Arr. Brussels (Nord)	09:12	09:32	10:12	11:12	12:12	
Arr. Brussels (Cen.)	5 minutes after arriving Brussels Nord					
Arr. Brussels (Midi)	4 minutes after arriving Brussels Central					
Dep. Brussels (Midi)	13:21	14:21	15:21	16:21	17:21	18:21 (2)
Dep. Brussels (Cen.)	4 minutes after departing Brussels Midi					
Dep. Brussels (Nord)	5 minutes after departing Brussels Central					
Arr. Luxembourg	16:15	17:15	18:15	19:15	20:15	21:15

(1) Runs Monday-Friday, except holidays. (2) Plus other Brussels (Midi) departures at 19:11 and 19:21, arriving Luxemburg 21:49 and 22:15.

Luxembourg - Clervaux - Luxembourg   439

The best view (from the viaduct) as you depart Luxembourg City is from the left-hand side of the train.

Dep. Luxembourg	08:10	10:10	12:10
Arr. Clervaux	08:55	10:55	12:57

Sights in **Clervaux**: This is the Ardennes area, where the Battle of the Bulge was fought in December, 1944. It is a 15-minute walk from the rail station, along the river, to the center of town. You cross a bridge over the river to get to the office of the miniature golf course. This is also the tourist information office, open from late March to late September 10:00–12:00 and 14:00–18:00.

Pick up a copy of the brochure about the "Family of Man" exhibition of Edward Steichen photos. This world-famous American photographer was born in Luxembourg. Then, go to see that collection at DeLannoi Castle, which also has the Battle of the Bulge Museum and its monument—one of General Patton's U.S. Army tanks. It also has an exhibit of castle models.

The Castle is open 10:00–17:00 June through September (13:00–17:00 on Sundays and bank holidays the rest of the year). Have a pleasant lunch at the Castle's restaurant.

See the view from the Benedictine Abbey of St. Maurice.

Dep Clervaux	12:51	14:51	17:51	19:36	20:51
Arr. Luxembourg	13:39	15:39	18:39	20:24	21:39

Luxembourg - Cologne (Koln) - Luxembourg   915

All of these trains have light refreshments

Dep. Luxembourg	09:40	10:33	14:33
Arr. Cologne	11:45	13:48	17:46

• • •

Depart Cologne	06:10	10:10	16:10
Arr. Luxembourg	09:23	13:23	19:23

Luxembourg - Dusseldorf - Luxembourg   910, 915

915			*910*	
Dep. Luxemb'g	09:40	10:33 (2)	Dep. Dusseldorf	15:44 (2)
Arr. Koblenz	11:48	12:37	Arr. Koblenz	17:05
Change trains 910			*Change trains 915*	
Dep. Koblenz	12:06 (1)	13:12 (1)	Dep. Koblenz	17:19 (2)
Arr. Dusseldorf	13:30	14:20	Arr. Luxemb'g	19:23

(1) Restaurant car. (2) Light refreshments.

Luxembourg - Frankfurt - Luxembourg　910, 915

915			*910*		
Dep. Luxemb'g	10:33 (1)	14:33 (1)	Dep. Frankfurt	13:50 (2)	14:50 (2+3)
Arr. Koblenz	12:37	16:37	Arr. Koblenz	15:12	16:12
Change trains 910			*Change trains 915*		
Dep. Koblenz	12:49 (2)	16:49 (2)	Dep. Koblenz	15:19 (3)	17:19 (1)
Arr. Frankfurt	14:08	18:08	Arr. Luxemb'g	19:04	19:23

(1) Light refreshments. (2) Supplement charged includes reservation fee. Restaurant car. (3) Change trains in Trier (arr. 16:40-dep. 18:11).

Luxembourg - Koblenz - Luxembourg　915

Dep. Luxembourg	09:40	10:33	14:33	20:33
Arr. Koblenz	11:48	12:37	16:37	22:38

Sights in **Koblenz**: A pedestrian tunnel goes from the front of the rail station to the city tourist information office, open mid-June to mid-October Monday–Saturday 08:30–20:00, Sunday 13:30–19:00. For a small fee you can obtain hotel reservations, a city map and a "Tour of the City" brochure. See where the Moselle and Rhine rivers meet. Visit the Old Town, St. Castor's Church and the Middle Rhine Museum.

Dep. Koblenz	06:10 (1)	11:19 (1)	16:55	17:19 (1)
Arr. Luxembourg	09:23	13:23	19:04	19:23

(1) Light refreshments.

Luxembourg - Liege - Luxembourg　439

Dep. Luxembourg	08:10	10:10	12:10	
Arr. Liege (Guillemins)	10:36	12:34	14:34	
		• • •		
Dep Liege (Guillemins)	13:08	16:08	17:48	19:08
Arr. Luxembourg	15:39	18:39	20:24	21:39

Luxembourg - Mainz - Luxembourg　910, 915

915				
Dep. Luxembourg	09:40	10:33 (1)	14:33 (1)	20:33 (1)
Arr. Koblenz	11:48	12:37	16:37	22:38

Change trains 910

| Dep. Koblenz | 11:56 (4) | 12:49 (4) | 16:49 (4) | 22:49 (4) |
| Arr. Mainz | 12:46 | 13:39 | 17:39 | 23:43 |

Sights in **Mainz**: The art collection in the cathedral. The Museum of the Central Rhineland. The rare books in the World Museum of Printing in the Romischer Kaiser. The restored Baroque mansions on the Schillerplatz and Schillerstrasse, in the Kirschgarten. Old Town. The sculptures in the Diocesan Museum.

Dep. Mainz	05:52 (4)	14:16 (4)	16:16 (4)
Arr. Koblenz	06:47	15:06	17:06
Change trains 915			
Dep. Koblenz	07:19 (1)	15:19 (1+3)	17:19 (2)
Arr. Luxembourg	09:23	19:04	19:23

(1) Light refreshments. (2) Restaurant car. (3) Change trains in Trier. (4) Supplement charged includes reservation fee. Restaurant car.

Luxembourg - Metz - Luxembourg 390

| Dep. Luxembourg | 05:25 (2) | 07:23 (1) | 08:02 (2) | 10:01 (3) |
| Arr. Metz | 45 minutes later | | | |

Sights in **Metz:** The fantastic rail station here looks like a castle because it was built for Kaiser Wilhelm II when he was Germanifying this region. The imperial apartments in the station were arranged for the Kaiser to enjoy his obsession with train-spotting.

See the oldest church in France, the 4th-century Pierre-aux-Nonains.

The largest stained-glass windows in the world are found in the 16th-century Cathedral of Saint Etienne. The cathedral was formed by joining two 12th-century churches into a single building. Its contemporary Marc Chagall and Jacques Villon stained-glass are exceptional.

See the Gallo-Roman antiquities in the city's Art and History Museum (Musee d'Art et d'Histoire) . Walk across the 13th-century Porte des Allemands (Gate of the Germans).

| Dep. Metz | 11:45 (1) | 16:06 (5) | 19:11 (3) | 20:04 (4) | 21:12 (6) | 23:00 (7) |
| Arr. Luxembourg | 45 minutes later | | | | | |

(1) Runs Sunday only. (2) Runs daily, except Sundays and holidays. Light refreshments. (3) Supplement charged. Restaurant car. (4) Supplement charged. (5) Restaurant car. (6) Runs daily, except Saturday. Supplement charged. (7) Light refreshments.

Luxembourg - Mulhouse - Luxembourg   385

Both of these trains charge a supplement and have a restaurant car.

Dep. Luxembourg	10:01	Dep. Mulhouse	16:49
Arr. Mulhouse	13:14	Arr. Luxembourg	19:56

Sights in **Mulhouse:** France's largest collection of antique cars, and one of the best collections in the world of old autos is found at the Musee Nationale de l'Automobile. About 500 cars are on exhibit, ranging from an 1878 steam-powered Jacquot to a magnificent 12-liter Bugati Royale. It is open daily except Tuesday 10:00–18:00.

The Museum of Fabric Printing (Musee de l'Impression sur Etoffes) displays textile arts at 3 Rue des Bonnes-Gens. There are 8,000,000 fabric samples as well as drawings of printed and woven fabrics in its 1,700-volume library. April–December the museum is open daily 10:00–12:00 and 14:00–18:00. January–March, same hours, but closed Tuesdays.

Visit France's largest and best railroad museum (Musee Francais du Chemin de Fer), open daily at Rue Alfred de Glehn. Its exhibits include passenger cars, freight cars, and steam, diesel and electric locomotives.

Luxembourg - Paris - Luxembourg   390

Dep. Luxembourg	05:25 (1)	07:23 (2)	08:02 (3)
Arr. Paris (Est)	09:14	11:03	11:41
		• • •	
Dep. Paris (Est)	17:16 (4)	18:20 (5)	19:49
Arr. Luxembourg	20:52	22:06	23:48

(1) Supplement charged. Runs daily, except Sundays and holidays. Light refreshments. (2) Runs Sunday only. (3) Runs daily, except Sundays and holidays. Light refreshments. (4) Supplement charged. (5) Supplement charged. Runs daily, except Saturday.

Luxembourg - Saarbrucken - Luxembourg   — *via Trier*   915

These schedules allow stopping-over in Trier for sightseeing on the ride to/from Saarbrucken.

Dep. Luxembourg	09:40	10:33 (1)	14:33 (1)
Arr. Trier	10:26	11:15	15:15
Change trains			
Dep. Trier	10:40 (1)	11:36 (1)	15:36 (1)
Arr. Saarbrucken	11:41	10:43	16:42

These schedules allow stopping-over in Trier for dinner en route back to Luxembourg:

Dep. Saarbrucken	11:15 (1)	12:15 (1)	17:15 (1)
Arr. Trier	12:18	13:15	18:19
Change trains			
Dep. Trier	12:40 (1)	18:40 (1)	
Arr. Luxembourg	13:23	19:23	

(1) Light refreshments.

Luxembourg - Saarbrucken — *via Metz* 385, 386, 390

These schedules allow stopping-over for sightseeing in Metz en route to/from Saarbrucken.
386

Dep. Luxembourg	06:19 (1)	07:15 (2)	07:50 (1)	10:01 (3)
Arr. Metz	07:12	08:06	08:46	10:43
Change trains 390				
Dep. Metz	07:51 (4)	08:44 (5)	10:00 (6)	11:54 (7)
Arr. Saarbrucken	08:53	09:53	10:56	12:46

These schedules allow stopping-over in Metz for lunch or dinner en route back to Luxembourg:

390

Dep. Saarbrucken	13:13 (7)	17:13 (7)	18:25 (8)
Arr. Metz	14:02	18:07	19:21
Change trains 386			
Dep. Metz	17:02 (2)	19:02 (2)	20:16 (1)
Arr. Luxembourg	17:53	19:48	21:02

(1) Second class only; runs Monday-Saturday, except holidays. (2) Second class only, runs Monday-Friday, except holidays. (3) Schedule 385, supplement payable. (4) Runs Monday-Saturday through late June and from Sept. 1. (5) Daily from late June to Sept. 1. (6) Runs daily, except Sundays. (7) Supplement payable. Restaurant car. (8) Runs Monday-Saturday, except holidays.

Luxembourg - Strasbourg - Luxembourg 385

Both of these trains charge a supplement and have a restaurant car.

Dep. Luxembourg	11:29 (1)		Dep. Strasbourg	17:46
Arr. Strasbourg	13:11		Arr. Luxembourg	19:56

(1) Monday-Friday, except holidays.

Luxembourg - Trier - Luxembourg   915

Dep. Luxembourg	09:40	10:33	14:33
Arr. Trier	10:26	11:15	15:15

Sights in **Trier**: There are more Roman monuments here than in any other German city: the 4th-century Porta Nigra (Black Gate), baths dating from the 2nd and 4th century, an amphitheater with roots in the 1st century, and the 4th-century Roman palace, Palastula (with its throne room of Roman emperors), now a Lutheran church. See the "Holy Coat of Trier," said to be Christ's robe, in the Romanesque cathedral, started in the 6th century.

See Roman and medieval relics in the Municipal Museum. Stroll around Peter's Fountain in the market square. Nearby, visit the 17th-century Electoral Palace and 18th-century Kasselstatt Palace.

Dep. Trier	12:40	15:09	18:38
Arr. Luxembourg	13:23	19:04	19:23

Luxembourg - Ettelbruck - Vianden - Luxembourg   439 +
Government timetable

The Ettelbruck–Viandin bus leaves from the front of the Ettelbruck rail station. Re-check the bus schedules!!

Dep. Luxembourg	08:10	12:10	14:10
Arr. Ettelbruck	08:28	12:28	14:28
Change to bus			
Dep. Ettelbruck	08:35	13:14	14:52
Arr. Vianden	09:03	13:38	15:15

Sights in **Vianden**: Leave the bus at the first stop, the Hotel Oranienburg. At the end of the day, board the bus at Gare Routiere (the bus station) for the ride back to Ettelbruck. Most of the attractions in Vianden are closed 12:00–14:00.

Walk uphill from the Hotel Oranienburg to the large and very interesting castle, open daily March-December; open weekends only in January and February.

Leave the castle at 12:00 and have lunch before visiting the home of Victor Hugo. Take the chairlift across the river to the top of a hill from which there are good views of the castle, dam and valley. After descending, walk across the top of the dam.

See the rococo altar in the 13th-century Church of the Trinitarians. Visit the exhibits of folklore and ancient household items in the Museum of Rustic Arts.

Bus

Dep. Vianden	14:34	16:26	18:10	20:31
Arr. Ettelbruck	15:05	16:55	18:38	21:01

Change to train

Dep. Ettelbruck	15:16	18:16	20:01	21:16
Arr. Luxembourg	15:39	18:39	20:24	21:39

SCENIC RAIL TRIPS

Most of the scenic rail trips of the Benelux countries are in Holland, and all of those are included in the list of one-day round trips from Amsterdam preceding this section. They are the train rides between Amsterdam and Delft, Den Haag, Leiden, Rotterdam and Utrecht.

The scenery on these trips is best from mid-March through May: fields of tulips, narcissus, crocus and other bulb flowers in bloom. The region is known as "Champs de Fleurs" (Fields of Flowers).

Three other scenic trips in the Benelux countries are listed in this section. All are noteworthy for beautiful river scenery.

Brussels - Liege - Jemelle - Luxembourg 400, 420, 430

See fine farm and river scenery by taking an indirect route from Brussels to Luxembourg.

400

Dep. Brussels (Midi)	10:18	11:18	12:18	13:18
Dep. Brussels (Cen.)	4 minutes after departing Midi station			
Dep. Brussels (Nord)	6 minutes after departing Central station			
Arr. Liege (Guill.)	11:40	12:40	13:40	14:40
Change trains 420				
Dep. Liege (Guill.)	07:23	09:59	18:47	01:53 (1)
Arr. Namur	08:04	10:39	19:25	02:31
Change trains 430				
Dep. Namur	13:12 (1)	14:24	15:24	16:24
Dep. Jemelle	-0-	15:04	16:04	17:04
Arr. Luxembourg	14:49	16:15	17:15	18:15

(1) Supplement charged. Restaurant car.

Luxembourg - Liege 439

There is excellent farm and river scenery on this easy one-day roundtrip. See Luxembourg timetables above.

Brussels - Namur - Dinant - Namur - Luxembourg   210, 430

This is a spur off the Brussels-Luxembourg route. Break up the ride from Brussels to Luxembourg (or vice versa) to see some great farm and river scenery. This is also an easy one-day round trip from Brussels.

For the first way (showing both directions):

Dep. Brussels (Midi)	08:42 (1)	09:42 (1)	Dep. Luxembourg	08:27	09:27
Dep. Brussels (Cen.)	08:46	09:46	Arr. Namur	10:17	11:17
Dep. Brussels (Nord)	08:53	09:53	*Change trains*		
Arr. Namur	09:42	10:42	Dep. Namur	10:47 (1)	11:47 (1)
Arr. Dinant	10:15	11:15	Arr. Dinant	11:15	12:15
Change trains			*Change trains*		
Dep. Dinant	10:27 (1)	11:27 (1)	Dep. Dinant	11:27 (1)	12:27 (1)
Arr. Namur	10:55	11:55	Dep. Namur	12:00	13:00
Change trains			Arr. Brussels (Nord)	12:49	13:49
Dep. Namur	11:24	12:24	Arr. Brussels (Cen.)	12:56	13:56
Arr. Luxembourg	13:15	14:15	Arr. Brussels (Midi)	13:00	14:00

(1) Daily from June 1 through August 31.

Here is the Brussels one-day round trip   210

All of these trains run Monday–Friday except holidays.

Dep. Brussels (Midi)	08:42	09:42	Dep. Dinant	14:27	16:27
Dep. Brussels (Cen.)	08:46	09:46	Arr. Namur	15:00	17:00
Dep. Brussels (Nord)	08:53	09:53	Arr. Brussels (Nord)	15:49	17:49
Arr. Namur	09:42	10:42	Arr. Brussels (Cen.)	15:56	17:56
Arr. Dinant	10:15	11:15	Arr. Brussels (Midi)	16:00	18:00

INTERNATIONAL ROUTES
FROM BELGIUM

Brussels is the Belgian gateway for rail travel to London, Amsterdam, Basel (with connections to Zurich and Milan), Cologne (with connections to Hamburg and Copenhagen) and Paris (with connections to Madrid).

Brussels - Amsterdam 18

Many of these trains have light refreshments.

Dep. Brussels (Midi)	10 minutes after each hour, from 06:10 to 23:10
Dep. Brussels (Cen.	4 minutes after departing Midi station
Dep. Brussels (Nord)	4 minutes after departing Central station
Arr. Amsterdam	3 hours later

Brussels - Basel - Milan 43

Dep. Brussels (Midi)	07:15 (1)	19:11 (2)
Dep. Brussels (Nord)	8 minutes after departing Midi station	
Arr. Basel (SNCF.)	14:02	02:00
Arr. Milan (Cen.)	19:25	07:10

(1) Supplement charged. Restaurant car. (2) Coaches are second-class. Runs Friday and Saturday only.

Brussels - Cologne (Koln) 20

Dep. Brussels (Midi)	06:47	07:47	09:48	10:48	12:07 (1)	13:48
Dep. Brussels (Cen.)	06:52	07:52	09:52	10:52	-0-	13:52
Dep. Brussels (Nord)	06:57	07:57	09:57	10:57	12:16	13:57
Arr. Cologne	09:42	10:42	12:42	13:42	14:42	16:42

Dep. Brussels (Midi)	16:54 (1)	18:08 (1)	18:47	20:03 (1)
Dep. Brussels (Cen.)	16:58	18:12	18:52	-0-
Dep. Brussels (Nord)	17:03	18:18	18:57	20:12
Arr. Cologne	19:42	20:42	21:55	22:42

(1) Supplement charged. Restaurant car.

Brussels - London via Oostende   (Jetfoil)   12

The schedules shown below are for late May to late September, unless designated otherwise. All of these ships require reservation, charge a supplement and have light refreshments.

Dep. Brussels (Nord)	09:47	11:35	14:47	17:47 (1)
Dep. Brussels (Midi)	09:59	11:45	14:59	17:59
Arr. Oostende	11:09	12:48	16:09	19:09
Change to boat				
Dep. Oostende	11:50	14:15	17:20	19:50

Set your watch back one hour, except from late September to late October.

Arr. Ramsgate	12:45	16:25	18:15	20:45 (1)
Arr. London (Vic.)	15:17	18:17	20:20	23:15

(1) Runs Sunday only.

Brussels - London   (Eurostar)   12

All Eurostar trains require a reservation; check in a minimum of 20 minutes before departure. All trains have meal and buffet service. When traveling Brussels-London, set your watch ahead one hour, London-Brussels, back one hour; Schedules reflect the time change.

Dep. Brussels Midi/Zuid	07:31 (1)	08:27	10:31	12:31	1528
Arr. Lille Europe	08:42	09:37	11:42	13:41	16:39
Arr. Ashford	-0-	09:41	-0-	-0-	16:41
Arr. London Waterloo	09:39	10:43	12:43	14:43	17:43

Dep. Brussels Midi/Zuid	17:22	18:27 (2)	19:27 (3)	19:52 (4)
Arr. Lille Europe	18:33	19:37	20:37	-0-
Arr. Ashford	18:37	19:42	20:41	21:07
Arr. London Waterloo	19:39	20:03	21:43	22:09

(1) Runs Monday-Saturday. (2) Runs daily except Saturdays. (3) Runs Monday-Friday. (4) Runs Saturday and Sunday.

Brussels - Luxembourg 430

See "Brussels-Luxembourg" under Luxembourg.

Brussels - Paris 18

Dep. Brussels (Nord)	01:25 (1)	-0-	-0-	09:22 (3)
Dep. Brussels (Midi)	01:40	07:07 (2)	08:05	10:07
Arr. Paris (Nord)	06:56	09:05	10:05	12:05

Dep Brussels (Nord)	11:22 (3)	13:22 (3)	15:22 (3)	16:22 (3)
Dep. Brussels (Midi)	12:07	14:07	16:02	17:07
Arr. Paris (Nord)	14:05	16:05	18:05	19:05

Dep. Brussels (Nord)	17:22 (3)	18:22	19:22 (3)	20:22 (3)
Dep. Brussels (Midi)	18:02	19:00	20:02	21:07
Arr. Paris (Nord)	20:05	21:05	22:05	23:05

(1) Has couchettes. (2) Runs Monday–Friday. Light refreshments. (3) Change trains, Brussels Midi. Note: Except first departure, 01:25; light refreshments. Trains between Brussels Midi and Paris charge a supplement.

INTERNATIONAL ROUTES
FROM HOLLAND

Amsterdam is the Dutch gateway for rail travel to London, Basel (with connections to Zurich and Milan), Cologne, Hamburg (with connections to Copenhagen) and Paris (and a connection to Madrid). Notes on the route to London appear under "London–Amsterdam" in Great Britain chapter.

Amsterdam - Brussels 18

Dep. Amsterdam	Frequent times from 06:30 to 22:15
Arr. Brussels (Nord)	3 hours later
Arr. Brussels (Cent.)	4 minutes after departing Nord station
Arr. Brussels (Midi)	4 minutes after departing Central station

Amsterdam - Cologne (Koln) - Mainz - Basel 73

Look for lots of castles in the Koblenz–Mainz area as the train travels alongside the Rhine River. En route to Basel, sit on the left-hand side for the best views of marvelous Rhine River scenery.

All of these trains charge a supplement.

Dep. Amsterdam	07:00 (1+2)	08:00 (3)	09:00 (2+3)	11:00 (3+4)
Arr. Cologne	09:41	10:57	11:38	13:42 (2)
Dep. Cologne	10:00	11:00	12:00	14:00 (3)
Arr. Koblenz	10:53	11:53	12:53	14:51
Arr. Mainz	11:42	12:42	13:46	15:42
Arr. Basel (SBB)	14:48	15:55	16:37	18:43

(1) Light refreshments. (2) Change trains in Cologne. (3) Restaurant car. (4) Plus other Amsterdam departures at 13:00 (1+2), 15:00 (1+2) and 20:05 (5). (5) Carries sleepers and couchettes.

Amsterdam - Osnabruck - Bremen - Hamburg - Copenhagen 22

Both of these trains have couchettes.

Dep. Amsterdam (Cen.)	20:14 (1)	19:00 (2)
Arr. Bremen	00:47	01:27
Arr. Hamburg (Hbf.)	01:50	02:35
Arr. Copenhagen	07:30	08:30

(1) Operates late June to late August. (2) Change trains in Duisburg.

Amsterdam - Luxembourg 400, 439, 480

480	
Dep. Amsterdam	07:33
Arr. Maastricht	10:04
Change trains 400	
Dep. Maastricht	10:24
Arr. Liege	10:55
Change trains 439	
Dep. Liege	11:08
Arr. Luxembourg	13:39

Amsterdam - London via Hoek van Holland (regular ferry)   15

Dep. Amsterdam	05:23 (1+3)	13:52 (1)
Arr. Hoek van Holland	06:35	15:00
Change to ferry		
Dep. Hoek van Holland	06:49	16:10 (2)
Set your watch back one hour		
Arr. Harwich	09:55 (2)	18:50
Change to train		
Dep. Harwich	10:35	19:35
Arr. London (Liverpool)	11:48	20:46

(1) Light refreshments. (2) Reservation required. (3) Operates Monday-Saturday.

Amsterdam - Brussels - Paris   18

Dep. Amsterdam (Cen.)	06:30	08:30	10:30	11:30	12:30
Dep. Antwerp (Berch.)	08:53	10:49	12:49	13:49	14:49
Arr.. Brussels (Nord)	09:22	11:22	13:22	14:22	15:22
Arr. Brussels (Midi)	09:31 (1)	11:31 (1)	13:31 (1)	14:31 (1)	15:31 (1)
Dep. Brussels (Midi)	10:07	11:57	14:07	15:07	16:02
Arr. Paris (Nord)	12:05	14:05	16:05	17:05	18:05

Dep. Amsterdam (Cen.)	13:30	14:30	15:30	16:30	22:15 (2)
Dep. Antwerp (Berch.)	15:53	16:53	17:53	18:53	00:54
Arr. Brussels (Nord)	16:22	17:22	18:22	19:22	01:25
Arr. Brussels (Midi)	16:31 (1)	17:31 (1)	18:31 (1)	19:31 (1)	01:34
Dep. Brussels (Midi)	17:07	18:07	19:05	20:07	01:52
Arr. Paris (Nord)	19:05	20:05	21:05	22:05	06:56

(1) Change trains Brussels Midi. Supplement charged. Light refreshments. (2) Has couchettes. Note: All trains between Brussels Midi and Paris Nord, except the 22:15 departure, requires payment of a supplement. These trains have light refreshments available, as do most Amsterdam-Brussels trains.

INTERNATIONAL ROUTES
FROM LUXEMBOURG

Luxembourg City is a gateway for rail travel to London, Amsterdam, Basel (with connections to Zurich and Milan), Brussels, Cologne, Koblenz (with connections to Frankfurt), and Paris. (Notes on the routes from Amsterdam, Brussels and Paris to London appear in Chapter 7.)

Luxembourg - Amsterdam   400, 439, 480

439

Dep. Luxembourg	16:10 (1)
Arr. Liege	18:36

Change trains 400
Dep. Liege   18:48
Arr. Maastricht   19:21
Change trains 480
Dep. Maastricht   19:31
Arr. Amsterdam   22:00

Luxembourg - Basel   40

Dep. Luxembourg	01:18 (1)	10:01 (2)	14:59 (2)	19:01 (3)
Arr. Basel (SBB)	05:20	13:39	18:25	22:39

(1) Carries a sleeping car. Also has couchettes. (2) Supplement charged. Restaurant car. (3) Restaurant car.

Luxembourg - Brussels   430

Dep. Luxembourg	04:09	05:27 (1)	06:27	07:07 (1)	08:27 (2)
Arr. Brussels (Nord)	6:40	08:12	09:12	09:32	11:12
Arr. Brussels (Cen.)	-0-	08:17	09:17	09:38	11:17
Arr. Brussels (Midi)	06:49	08:21	09:21	09:42	11:21

(1) Runs Monday–Friday, except holidays. (2) Plus other frequent departures from Luxembourg at 27 minutes after each hour from 09:27 to 20:27.

Luxembourg - Cologne   915

Dep. Luxembourg	09:40	10:33 (1)	14:33 (1)
Arr. Cologne	13:03	13:46	17:46

(1) Light refreshments.

Luxembourg - Paris   390 *via Metz*

Dep. Luxembourg	08:02 (1+2)	10:01 (4)	13:08 (5+6)
Arr. Metz	08:46	10:43 (3)	13:55
Dep. Metz	08:50	10:54	14:20
Arr. Paris (Est)	11:41	13:42	17:11

(1) Runs Monday-Friday, except holidays. Light refreshments. (2) Direct train. No change in Metz. (3) Change trains in Metz. Supplement payable. (4) Reservation required. Restaurant car. (5) Direct train. No change in Metz. Supplement payable. (6) Plus other departures from Luxembourg at 16:34 (5+7), 17:24 (5), arriving Paris 20:23, 21:05. (7) Runs daily except Saturdays.

FRANCE

Getting on Track in France

• Tourist information: French Government Tourist Office, 444 Madison Avenue, 16th Floor, New York, NY 10022. Telephone (212) 838-7800, fax (212) 838-7855. E-mail inquiries: pubinfo@fgtousa.org. Chicago office, 676 North Michigan Avenue, Suite 3360, Chicago, IL 60611. Telephone (312) 751-7800 (recorded message only). North Americans also can phone (900) 990-0040 for 50 cents/minute charge, or, fax (312) 337-6339. Beverly Hills office, 9454 Wilshire Boulevard, Suite 715, Beverly Hills, CA 90212. Telephone (310) 271-6665 (10:00-16:00 Pacific time), fax (310) 276-2835. Quebec office, 1981 Avenue McGill College, Suite 490, Montreal, Quebec QC H3A 2W9, Canada. Telephone (514) 288-4264, fax (514) 845-4868. E-mail inquiries: mfrance@passeport.com Toronto office, 30 Saint Patrick Street, Suite 700, Toronto, Ontario M5T 3A3 Canada. Telephone (416) 593-4623, fax (416) 979-7587. On the Web: http://www.francetourism.com/, also http://www.maison-de-la-france.com:8000/index.html.

• Public holidays: In that train schedules differ between working days and holidays, and many trains do not run at all on holidays, a list of such days in France can be especially useful. Also, those trains which operate on holidays are often filled, and it is necessary to make reservations for them long in advance. When at all possible, avoid train travel in France on holidays, long weekends, and the first and last day of the Paris-region's school vacations!

January 1	Jour de l'An (New Year's Day)
Late March/April	Pâques (Easter)
Monday after Easter	Lundi de Pâques (Easter Monday)
May 8	Fête de la Victoire 1945 (V.E. Day)
Sixth Thursday after Easter	Ascension (Ascension) Day)
Second Monday after Ascension	Pentecôte (Pentecost)
July 14	Fête nationale/14 juillet (Bastille Day)
August 15	Fête de l'Assomption (Feast of the Assumption)
November 1	Toussaint (All Saints' Day), Halloween
November 11	Fête de l'Armistice (Veteran's Day)
December 25	Noël (Christmas)

• Currency: Franc (FF). At press time, $1 was worth FF6.14.

Overview of French Trains

Travelers who return home from Europe without having ridden a French train, are poorer for the experience. For over a decade the French National Railway, (Société Nationale de Chemins de Fer Français, SNCF) has been a leading force in international train travel, revolutionizing European rail with its streamline TGV (Train à Grande Vitesse).

The TGV almost didn't make it off the drawing board, though, when SNCF proposed the idea in the late 1960s. It didn't get any government funding then because the concept

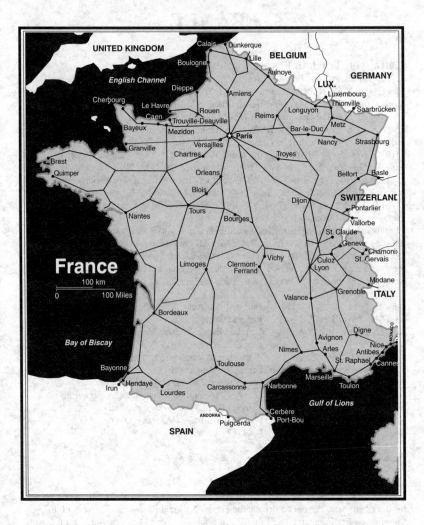

wasn't considered innovative enough. Maglev was the technology du jour then and the government felt that steel wheel/steel rail technology had gone as far as it could. But the folks at SNCF didn't give up on their idea of creating a high-speed rail system that was compatible with the existing railroad infrastructure. The plan was to build a dedicated right-of-way for high-speed sprints to the outskirts of a city, then use existing trackage for the last few miles and pull in to an existing station. As we all know now, the plan was a winner, and because building new stations and track was limited, it also saved SNCF millions of francs. Popular with passengers from the get-go, it didn't take long for the orange and white speedsters to give the airlines a run for their money on the first route, Paris to Lyon. While the rest of SNCF's routes barely broke even, the TGV turned a profit and paid for itself in just a few years. Finally, the French government recognized that SNCF's idea wasn't so bad after all, and provided funding for future TGV routes.

The French high speed train has not only shrunk the country's borders, its cars are being exported and integrated into foreign rail systems as far and wide as China and Korea. The TGV has cut the traveling time in half between Paris and, for example, Marseilles, 900 kilometers away, to a little over four hours instead of eight. The TGV Southeast line currently serves the Paris-Lyon-Marseilles line to the south with branches reaching Nice to the southeast and Perpignan to the southwest, Geneva and Lausanne in the east, Lille and Calais to the north, and the newer ultra high-speed Bordeaux Atlantic line to the southwest. High speed train travel is expanding rapidly in Europe. Eurostar TGVs already serve Disneyland Paris via the Channel Tunnel (as do conventional TGVs) and for the first time last year, a Eurostar "ski train" made a weekly London-Bourge St. Maurice trip to the French Alps. Another TGV, Thalys, has shaved time off the Paris-Brussels-Amsterdam route; a German extension will follow soon, as will other high-speed routes throughout the European network.

The TGV requires reservations, which can be made in most travel agencies, all train stations, and at home with the Minitel, the home-style on-line computer that most French households and offices have perched in their hallways and desktops. Seat reservations for regular trains are also recommended during busy periods. Practically all French towns and cities and a large majority of even the rural villages are served by the SNCF. Although there has been a move away from Paris as the central transportation hub of France, the City of Lights still functions as the pivot point for much of French travel, especially internationally bound. New, smaller hubs are gaining importance, such as Lyon and Lille, which is particularly well situated for train traffic to the U.K., Belgium, Holland, and northern Germany. The Paris suburb to the south, Massy, now functions as a changing station for north-south passengers to avoid Paris. Marne la Vallée Chessy, TGV Hte. Picardie, and Charles de Gaulle TGV, have all been designed to move passengers across the country without having to transit in congested Paris.

France isn't all express trains and TGVs, though. Set aside some time to ride the little country puddle-jumpers such as the Nice-Digne line or the open-air train to La Rhune, in France's Basque country. You'll probably be the only American on board!

In a nutshell, the train as a vehicle of transportation in France is both an excellent means of seeing some of the finest scenery in Europe and a model of contemporary European efficiency.

General Rail Information

• Paris has nine main rail stations, six principal stations and three specialized stations designed for cars, etc., all of them connected to subway and commuter train (Métro and RER) lines. All offer a wide range of services: bars and restaurants, refreshment stands, lockers, business services, telephone and postal facilities, newsstands and information booths (sporadically staffed).

• SNCF Train Information (by phone)

General information: 01 45.82.50.50; information for inter-city trains, from 07:00 to 22:00, 08 36 35 35 35. Information in English 08 36 35 35 39.

Reservations: Grandes Lignes (national & international lines), 01 45.82.50.50, Ile de France (regional lines), 01 45.65.60.00 or 01 40 52 75 75, Minitel 36 15 SNCF. Open daily from 08:00-20:00.

• French rail tickets purchased in France are valid for travel any day within two months from the date of purchase. Train tickets obtained before arrival in France are valid for six months.

• Passengers using a French train ticket purchased in Europe must validate it (composter) in one of the many orange-colored machines located at the entrance to the platforms before boarding a train. Failure to do so may result in a stiff fine—train travel within France is essentially based on the honor system. In most cases a conductor will check your tickets anyway. You can purchase tickets on board, but you pay a supplement. A person holding a non-validated European ticket is subject to a fine. All tickets purchased outside Europe are exempt from having to be validated.

• Since September 1996, SNCF has had a program to compensate travelers if a train arrives at its destination at least 30 minutes late. This program applies to mainline trains, and you must have traveled at least 100 km. If a train is 30-60-minutes late, passengers are instructed about how to obtain vouchers for future travel. If the delay is between 30 and 60 minutes, passengers will receive a voucher worth 25 percent of the original fare. If the delay is over 60 minutes, a voucher is issued for 50 percent of the fare. The compensation applies only when the liability of the delay lies with SNCF. Certain routes are not covered such as Eurostar, Thalys, Talgo; they have their own programs.

• As for time changes, travelers should note that France turns its clocks ahead on the last Sunday of March and converts back to Standard Time on the last Sunday of September.

• French train travel is graced by scores of internal regulations and new specialized services stipulating tariffs and days and times for reduced-fare travel. Children under four travel free. Half-fare for children from 4 to 11. Children 12 and over must pay full fare. (See J8 and J30 details listed under Discount Train Travel in France.) Fare reductions are available on trains with a special family card (See Carte Kiwi details under Discount Train Travel in France).

• Semi-Couchettes. Some compartments on French trains have eight semi-inclined bunks (instead of seats) on these routes: Paris-Brest, Paris-Quimper and Paris-Basel. For reservation purposes, these "Cabine 8" bunks are treated as seats and no supplement is charged. In 1997 the supplement for a regular couchette was 90FF, for a reclining seat, 20FF.

• Family compartments. In many trains, if you are a group of at least four paying passengers including a child of under 16 years old, travelling in second-class accommodation (seats, couchettes or sleeping berths), you can reserve a compartment designed for families.

These compartments can be reserved on payment of the following fees: day trains 160 francs, night trains 540 francs (prices as of late 1997). Since the number of these compartments is limited, you should make your reservation in advance. A list of trains offering this facility can be found in the *Guide Famille*. Many French trains also have a nursery area, with changing tables and bottle-warmers, and a play area for older children.

• There is no charge for taking a bicycle on a train. You can rent a bicycle at many French train stations. For more information get the *Guide du Train et du Vélo*. The SNCF publication is available at train stations.

• Passengers traveling first class on the TGV have these meal options available at their seats: Breakfast; served between 07:00 and 08:30, lunch, served between 11:30 and 13:30, and dinner, served between 19:00 and 20:30. Reserve your meal when you make a reservation.

• Look for SNCF personnel wearing red jackets. They'll provide you with information and also serve as porters. You shouldn't have to pay more than FF30 for up to three bags.

• Costs for storing luggage for a 24-hour period in a French railway station: left-luggage office, FF30-35 per piece; key-operated locker, FF5-20; electronically-operated locker 15-30 FF. Sometimes the electronic-type lockers are unavailable for security reasons..

• Track down a copy of *Le guide du TGV*. It tells you all there is to know about travelling on the world's fastest trains; find it at railway stations.

• Tips for disabled travelers. Before you leave home ask the tourist office to obtain a copy of the guide for disabled travelers, *Voyageur à Mobilité Réduite*. If you're already in France, the guide is available at all the major stations. It provides excellent descriptions of SNCF's equipment and services that the railway can offer, as well as information about special fares available to disabled passengers and their companions. Since not all trains are equipped to carry wheelchairs, call SNCF or a French travel agency to ensure that the train you want to ride is accessible. In the U.S., Rail Europe or your travel agent can help with this. A wheelchair space is provided on the TGV and Corail trains to allow you to travel in your wheelchair. This space is located in first class, but second-class ticket holders can also use it. If you wish to catch a TGV train you must reserve the wheelchair space. Your reservation will guarantee you assistance at the station. You can reserve several hours before departure in stations, SNCF travel shops and travel agencies. You also can buy your ticket and reserve your wheelchair space by telephone, and have your ticket mailed directly to your hotel, with no extra charge. It's also a good idea to make reservations for conventional trains. Follow the same procedure as you would to reserve TGV space. In certain locations, specially adapted vehicles are available to transport wheelchair passengers within the city limits. For information, contact Groupement pour l'Insertion des personnes Handicapées Physiques (G.I.H.P.), Bureaux Parisiens, 98 rue de la porte jaune, 92210 Saint-Cloud. Phone 01 41 83 15 15 or contact the town hall of the location concerned. To help you prepare your journey, a toll-free number for "SNCF Accessibilité Service" will provide information about accessible facilities at around 300 stations within the mainline "Grandes Lignes" network and greater Paris. Call 0800 15 47 53 (France only).

• Animals pay half fare of a second-class ticket or FF28 if the animal is under six kilos and is carried in a bag measuring not more than 45 x 30 x 25 cm.

• If you want to travel with your car or motorcycle on the train, the SNCF has a complete list of destinations applicable to this service. Auto Train is a European network of special trains, generally overnight, carrying passengers with vehicles on journeys up to 900 miles. In Paris, reservations can be made by calling 08 36 35 35 35 Otherwise, inquire at:

Gare Austerlitz (Tolbiac): 01 45 82 73 62.

Gare de Lyon (Bercy): 01 53 33 60 11

Gare Montparnasse (Vaugirard): 01 40 48 14 72.

(For the phone numbers above, the 01 is to be used when dialing in France; drop the "0" when dialing from the States, i.e., 011 33 1 + 8-digit number)

Signs you are likely to see at rail stations in France:

ARRIVÉE	ARRIVAL
CONSIGNE	BAGGAGE CHECKROOM
DAMES	WOMEN
DÉPART	DEPARTURE
ENTRÉE	ENTRANCE
FUMEURS	SMOKING COMPARTMENT
GARE	STATION
HORAIRE	TIMETABLE
LOCATION DE PLACE ASSISE	SEAT RESERVATION OFFICE
MESSIEURS	MEN
QUAI	PLATFORM
RENSEIGNMENT	INFORMATION
SORTIE	EXIT
VOIE	TRACK
VOITURE-LIT	SLEEPER CAR
VOITURE-RETSA	RESTAURANT CAR

Connections with Great Britain

With the opening of the EuroTunnel underneath the English Channel, which accommodates train cars as well as private vehicles, the war for passengers is heated. Ferryboat companies and hydrofoil services continue the battle to maintain market share by reducing prices, offering attractive specials, and increasing services. Airlines are scrambling, too. The EuroTunnel option is undoubtedly the fastest and easiest way to go between England and France. If you're railing and driving you and your car can travel through the tunnel aboard Le Shuttle, EuroTunnel's vehicle-carrying trains. From door-to-door, it takes about thirty minutes. Passenger train service through the tunnel on "Eurostar" began in late 1994 and there are now trains leaving almost every hour. When Eurostar first started running, the price of a Eurostar ticket could break a budget traveler's bank. These days, though, Eurostar has specials for everyone from students to seniors to Eurailpass holders. And if you're footloose-and-fancy-free, without set travel plans, sometimes you can pick up really good deals on Eurostar tickets in Europe. Recent prices for a one-way London-Paris ticket ranged from $69 to $79. For more information on UK-France connections, see the chapter for Great Britain. For information about Le Shuttle trains through the tunnel, write to BP 69, 62231 COQUELLES or telephone 011 (33) 21 00 60 00 in France, or in Britain, 011 44 1303 273 300. An information and reservation number in Paris is: 44 94 80 80. U.S. toll-free rail information: 1-800-EUROSTAR. See Chapter 2 "Le Shuttle Through Channel Tunnel" for additional phone numbers and Web sites.

DISCOUNT TRAIN TRAVEL IN FRANCE

The SNCF publishes a color-coded calendar of travel days and times and prices that shows when to travel for the best discounts and when discounts are just so-so. Here, in order of largest discount to smallest, are the days: Jour bleue: Saturday noon through Sunday 15:00. Jour blanche: Friday noon through Saturday noon, and Sunday 15:00 through Monday noon. Plus holidays. Jour rouge: Principal days of departure If you have access to the Web, SNCF's excellent official site has a wealth of information about riding their trains. There's a copy of the "jour bleue" calender, schedules (even to obscure towns), and details about the latest special deals. Log on at: http://www.sncf.fr/.

The SNCF also publishes a free *Guide des prix Réduits* (*Guide to Reduced Priced Train Travel*). Here are the principal reduced ticket possibilities for those traveling without a Eurailpass: Discounts depend on destinations, dates, and times.

• **Train Verts** Some 200 TGV trains and other mainline trains offer a 15 percent discount off the basic fare. Also these Train Verts, including TGVs, do not require a reservation. If you do choose to make a reservation, the reservation fee is included for TGVs. For other trains, the reservation fee in 1997 was FF20. Guides, available at most SNCF stations or French travel agencies, list all the timetables and prices for the Train Verts; guides specific to the TGV indicate which TGVs apply to this program. SNCF suggests getting a copy of *Mode d'emploi Trains Verts,* a booklet that lists routes that aren't in the other publications. This guide is available at rail stations, SNCF shops and appointed travel agencies. If you ride a TGV Vert without a reservation, SNCF suggests that you select first the two rows of seats located near to each end of the car because they are very often not reserved. If you don't find any seats available, don't hesitate to ask the conductor to help you find a seat, if any are available.

• **12-25 Card**: Replaces Carrissimo Card. Youth fares, 12-25 years old, 25-50 percent. In 1997, the card was priced at FF270, was valid for one year, and entitled the user to get discounts on unlimited travel in first and second class. A small photo is required for the card. Good for 25-50 percent off of basic TGV fares; seats are limited. Discounts on other trains are based on SNCF's color-coded calender and generally range from 25 to 50 percent. The card also offers a 20 percent discount on Avis car rentals for those who are of driving age.

• **Decouverte 12-25**: For travelers aged 12 to 25, who don't plan to do a lot of traveling, this fare offers a 25 percent discount off the basic fares of mainline and TGV trains. Some restrictions may apply, depending on travel date.

• **Carte Kiwi**: When traveling with children (even one child) discounts can go to 50 percent. Some Carte Kiwi advantages: A child under four years of age (the holder of the "Kiwi" card) can be seated free of charge on a separate seat; a dog or cat can be taken free of charge by the holder of the Carte Kiwi; discounts on selected Avis car rentals. Without a Carte Kiwi, children under four travel free, but cannot occupy a seat without paying extra. Another option to the Carte Kiwi is "Bambin." In 1997, this fare allowed a child of under four years old to have his/her own seat for 50 francs; included the price of the reservation. This fare is available on all trains and in both first and second class.

• **Carte Vermeil Quatre Temps and Plein Temps**: Senior citizen discounts for the over-60 bracket. The cards are each valid for one year, and entitle the user to discounts of 20-50 percent off the basic first- or second-class fare on regular mainline trains and TGVs. Discounts on regular trains are based on SNCF's color-coded calender; TGV seats are limited. The Quatre Temps card offers four journeys within France at reduced fares. In 1997, the card cost FF143. The Plein Temps card cost FF279 in 1997 and entitled the user to unlimited trips within France at reduced rates. It also entitled users to 30 percent off fares in 23 European countries that participated in the Rail Europ Senior program.

• **Decouverte J8 and J30; Decouverte Deux:** These fares replace the Joker tickets and offer up to a 40 percent discount when reservations are made between two months and 30 days with the J30 fare and two months and eight days before departure for the J8 fare. This fare does not apply to trains that charge a supplement; other restrictions may apply. A brochure, *Guide Decouverte J30 et J8*, available at train stations, lists complete route and fare information. The Decouverte Deux fare offers up to a 25 percent discount off the basic fare when two people travel together.

• **Sejour Fare:** This fare offers a 25 percent discount for first- or second-class travel aboard mainline and TGV trains. The ticket is issued for a return or a circular trip including at least 1000 km. Travel must include a Sunday or a part of Sunday (or a holiday) away, and within two months after the departure date of the outward journey. Space on TGV trains is limited; reductions on other trains are based on SNCF's color-coded calendar.

• SNCF has many other discount options, including the seasonal pass, Modulopass, available in three-, six- or 12-month increments, for first- or second-class travel. The pass offers discounts of up to 50 percent. Businesspass is a pass in the name of your company or organization enabling businesses to profit from up to a 50 percent discount when 25 or more round-trip tickets are purchased. The Temporis, which offers discounts to travelers making at least 16 trips within a 19 to 31 day period, and ABO 8, a special offer of up to 75 percent off for travelers making at least one round-trip journey per week on the same route.

THE FRENCH TGV:
FASTEST TRAINS ON EARTH

Since 1981, France has operated the world's fastest trains, the *Train à Grande Vitesse*, which can run up to 320.2 mph and are operated commercially at between 186-220 mph. Try this on for size. On the 126-mile Paris-Le Mans line, the TGV takes only 55 minutes while regular trains need one hour and fifty minutes! In the nineties, one speaks more of the opening of new services and lines than the high speed, which is a given, a banal detail in daily European travel. Seat reservations are required for practically all TGV trains—and are particularly essential on peak days and at peak hours. Standing is not allowed on TGVs. Hundreds of destinations are served by TGVs, with more on the way. And in the last few years a handful of ultramodern stations have opened, serving Paris' Charles de Gaulle Airport, Lyon's Satolas Airport, and Lille's "Europe" station, through which Paris-London Eurostars pass. Essentially, this network is progressing faster than any annual guidebook can accurately report on!

Although certain supplements for certain trains may be in effect, pass holders should only count on the modest reservation fee of about 30 FF.

The usual composition for a TGV is 386 seats: 111 in first-class, 275 in second-class. Each TGV has a bar car with snack and drink services as well as providing international press and telephone cards. Meals are brought to seats in some of the first-class cars, however, in most cases, those interested in dining should indicate such and proceed to the dining car at the set dinner hour.

The initial 1981 TGV service (Paris-Lyon, Paris-Dijon and Paris-Geneva) was expanded in 1983 to include Paris-Marseilles, Paris-Montpelier and Paris-Annecy-Grenoble. A TGV service Paris-Lausanne (with cross-platform transfer in Lausanne for trains to Milan) began in 1984. Service Paris-Grenoble started in 1985, Paris-Le Mans and Paris-Tours in 1989. The nineties has brought an excellent TGV Atlantic line serving Poitier, La Rochelle, Bordeaux, Nantes and Quimper. The northern route, one of the most promising extensions to the system in that it connects Paris with the cities of northern Europe, boasts of an exceptionally rapid and regular Paris-Lille service in one hour.

FRENCH TRAIN PASSES

The French national passes are sold everywhere in the world, except in France—at travel agencies and offices of Rail Europe (U.S.A. and Canadian addresses listed in introduction). Here are the most widely used and advantageous passes available for France:

France Railpass Unlimited train travel for any three days within one month. The 1998 prices are: $195 for first-class and $165 for second-class; when two people travel together, it's $156 per person first class, $132 per person second class. Up to six additional days may be added at $30 per day for first or second class. Half-fare for children age 4-11.

France Railpass Youth Unlimited second-class travel for passengers under the age of 26 on their first date of travel. Any four days of travel within two months costs $150. Up to six additional rail days may be added at $25 per day.

Bonus information was unavailable for 1998 at press time. In 1997, both passes included the following bonuses:
• 50 percent discount off travel on the Nice-Digne scenic private rail line.
• Special fares for travel aboard Eurostar, Thalys and Artesia trains.
• 50 percent off 2+1 Paris Visite tours when purchased in conjunction with a France Railpass.

France Rail 'n Drive This program offers three days of rail travel with a two-day Avis car rental, within one month. Purchase up to six more rail days plus additional car days (no limit on car days). Third and fourth passengers pay only for the three-day rail pass.

Car Categories	2 Adults*		1 Adult		Add'l Day
	1st Cl.	2nd Cl.	1st Cl.	2nd Cl.	Car
A Economy	$189	$174	$259	$234	$45
B Compact	$209	$194	$309	$274	$65
C Intermediate	$229	$214	$349	$314	$85
D Compact/Auto.	$239	$224	$359	$324	$95
Add'l rail day (6 max.)	$30	$30	$30	$30	

*Price based on two people traveling together.

France Rail 'n Fly Prices for 1998 were unavailable at press time. In 1997, the pass offered three days of unlimited train travel plus one day of air travel anywhere in France (any four days) within one month. Up to six extra rail days could be added for $30 per day ($15 per day, children 2-11). When two adults traveled together, the fare was $230 first class, $210 second class. For one adult, first class was $275, $255 second. Children ages 2-11 paid $195 for first-class, $175 for second-class. Adults and children could purchase one additional day of air travel for $95, either first or second class.

France Fly Rail 'n Drive Prices for 1998 were unavailable at press time. In 1997, the program offered three rail days, one air day and two car-rental days, within one month. Per person rates for two adults traveling together started from $279 first class, $259 second class. One adult, $359 first class, $339 second class. Additional rail days (up to six) were $30 per person. Extra car days, per person, were priced from $45, air vouchers $95 (no limit on additional air/car days). Third and fourth passengers paid for the rail and air portion of the package. Children aged 2-11 paid a child fare for the rail and air portion of the package. Children under two were free.

ONE-DAY EXCURSIONS AND CITY-SIGHTSEEING

Here are 63 one-day round-trip rail excursions that can be made comfortably from French cities, with return travel in most cases before dinner time. The comments provided on the major sites and events at each destination are designed to give travelers only a basic idea and a few suggestions of what to see. More specific guides are recommended for more in-depth and specialized discussion of these cities. Note that the number after the name of each route corresponds to the *Thomas Cook Timetable* of the same number.

Avignon

This walled city, the tourist capital of Provence, can be entered through 14 different gates. You can obtain a city map or a personal guide at the Syndicat d'Initiative (41 Cours Jean-Jaurès). During the 14th century, Avignon was briefly the papal headquarters of the Roman Catholic Church when it was unsafe for a series of French popes to be in Rome. Take the one-hour tour of the Palace of the Popes, open daily January-March 09:00-12:45 and 14:00-18:00 April-late August 09:00-19:00 late August-September 09:00-20:00 October 09:00-19:00 November-December 09:00-12:45 and 14:00-18:00. Next to the palace is the 12th-century Cathedral of Notre-Dame-de-Doms. Outside the palace you can board "Circuit #2," a 54-seater trackless train pulled by a gasoline-powered locomotive that operates March through October; it departs daily, every 15 minutes. This route climbs to the top of a hill overlooking the palace (a great view of the city and the Rhone Valley) and through the colorful Rocher Dom Gardens, where passengers can get off and return to the palace on a later train. "Circuit #1" operates March through September and runs daily 10:00-19:00 for a 30-minute ride through the city's shopping streets and renovated old quarters. Initial boarding for this train (every 35 minutes) is at Palace Square. See the 13th to 16th-century Italian-school religious paintings in the 14th-century Petit Palais museum, open daily except Tuesday 9:30-11:30 and 14:00-18:00. Other medieval buildings worth seeing are the 12th-century St. Ruff Church and the 14th-century Gothic St. Didier Church. See the Roman sculptures and mosaics (some dating back 3,000 years) in the Lapidary Museum (housed in the 17th-century Jesuit Church), open daily except Tuesday 10:00-11:55 and 14:00-18:00. Cross the Rhone River by walking or driving over the bridge to Villeneuve-les-Avignon and admire the view of Avignon from the other side of the river. An accredited guide-interpreters service from the Avignon Tourist Office give theme guided tours of the town, from October to March, and tours of Avignon and its surroundings, on request.

All-day bus tours from Avignon to many interesting places in this area can be taken from in front of the rail station. One tour includes Roman ruins at St. Remy, the village of Les Baux (sculptured during the Middle Ages from the top a stone hill), and the Roman theater in Arles. In nearby Orange, there is a Roman Triumphal Arch and an amphitheater built during the reign of Augustus. Don't forget that each summer in July and August Avignon hosts the most important theater festival in France. The population of the town multiples ten fold and it's nearly impossible to find a room if you haven't booked in advance. But, the drama is excellent.

For more information about Avignon, contact the Office du Tourisme, 41 Crs Jean Jaurès-84000 Avignon, France, telephone 011 33 4 90 82 65 11, fax 011 33 4 90 82 95 03. On the Web: http://vaucluse.com/avignon.

Bordeaux

Bordeaux turns its shoulders away from Paris and believes in its own supreme importance. A lively and wealthy port city, Bordeaux, of course, is one of the capitals of the French wine industry. Information about tours of the port and an excellent city map for making a walking tour of Bordeaux are available at the tourist office, 12 Cours du 30 Juillet. The opera, parks, hotels, Roman ruins and 18th-century mansions are in the northern sector of the city. Museums, churches and fine shops are in the southern part of Bordeaux. See the Maritime Museum, on the Quai de la Douane, the wonderful Louis XV houses on rue Fernand Philippart, and the modern stained-glass in the 14th-century St. Michel Church on Place Dubourg. The view of Bordeaux from the top of that church's tower shouldn't be missed. The large 15th-century bell tower, Grosse Cloche, the 13th-century Gothic St. Andres Cathedral, and the Musée des Beaux Arts, open daily except Tuesday 10:00-12:00 and 14:00-18:00, are key sites. Many tourists admire the fans with mother of pearl, ivory and silver handles (plus Medieval furniture, costumes and ceramics) in the Musée des Arts Decoratifs (39 rue Bouffard), open daily except Tuesday 14:00-18:00.

Do not miss seeing the array of fruits, cheeses, wild game and many exotic foods at the market on Place des Grands Hommes. The fantastic carved plants and the swan boat in the Jardin Public provide an easygoing afternoon activity. The Maison des Vins at 1 Cours du 30 Juillet, where you can obtain information on visiting nearby famous wineries, is a useful stop. See the lovely 18th-century Opera House, the Grand Theatre by architect Victor Louis, the Museum of Painting and Sculpture, the Numismatic Museum, the Museum of Old Bordeaux, and the Bonie Museum of Far Eastern Art.

For more information about Bordeaux, contact their Office du Tourism, 12 Cours du 30 Juillet, 33080 BORDEAUX CEDEX, telephone 011 331 5 56 00 66 10/00 66 12, fax 011 33 5 56 00 66 11. Open all year Monday-Friday 09:00-12:00 and 14:00-18:00. On the Web: http://www.mairie-bordeaux.fr. This Web site is in French.

Lyon

France's culinary capital, Lyon, is second to Paris in size and importance in the country. Occasionally, two trains depart from the same track at Lyon's Perrache rail station standing in opposite directions. Be sure to stand at the correct end (North or South) of the track in order to board the train you want to ride. Check the departure signs at the underground passageway. Do not rely merely on a track number when departing from Perrache rail station!

Next to the North passageway of Track A is a take-out restaurant, handy for provisioning your trip. A metro connects Perrache and Lyon's other rail station, Part-Dieu; change trains at Charpennes.

If you try to keep from eating at the spectacular Nouvelle Les Halles food market—65 tantalizing stalls of meat, poultry, fish, produce, cheese, bread, pastry, coffee, tea, spices, wine and candy—you are certain to fail. Too tempting. Open 07:00-19:00 Monday-Saturday and 07:00-12:00 on Sunday. Here, you can buy pheasants in plumage, partridges, wild ducks, quail, snipe, frog legs, four varieties of oysters, shrimp, eel, cod and sole. There are goose, duck and game patés. Do not fail to sample the three Lyon specialties: Morteau de Jesu (pork meat in a pig's foot casing), the peppery pink and white salami, and the garlicky Lyon sausage. The wine here is magnificent. It has been said that Lyon has three rivers: the Rhone, the Saone, and the Beaujolais. You are in Burgundy country.

Stroll for a few hours through the winding streets of the three-block wide half-mile long ancient section (Vieux Lyon) and see the magnificent 15th-century Renaissance mansions. Much information is available in the booklet *Guide du Vieux Lyon* sold everywhere in the city. Take the funicular to the 19th-century Basilica of Notre Dame de la Fourviere to see the extraordinary mosaics on its floors, walls and nave. The view from either the terrace behind it or from the observatory above it is marvelous. Then walk downhill to the Gallo Roman Museum (open daily except Monday and Tuesday 09:30-12:00 and 14:00-18:00), built into the side of a hill next to several Roman ruins. Its exhibits include objects from prehistory to the end of the Roman Empire, as well as elaborate floor mosaics and scale models of ancient Lyon. Walking further downhill brings you to the Cathedral of St. Jean, which has 13th-century stained glass and a 500-year-old astrological clock that performs a tableau at 12:00, 13:00, 14:00 and 15:00. The exhibits in the History Museum at the nearby Palais Gadagne cover the period from where the Gallo Roman Museum leaves off, including carved Renaissance furniture, prints, Nevers glazed pottery, and documents from the French Revolution. The adjoining Puppet Museum at 10-14 rue de Gadagne, honors Laurent Mourguet, a destitute weaver who, in seeking to attract customers with a puppet show, invented the character Guignol, whose name has come to symbolize children's afternoon puppet theater everywhere in France. Both museums are open daily except Tuesday 10:45-18:00.

In the more modern area of the city, grab bus #13 from the rail station, through the main shopping streets, to the Place de la Croix Rousse and then proceed by foot to Place des Terreaux to see the 17th-century City Hall, the 19th-century Opera House and the Fine Arts Museum. This museum, featuring works of Rodin, Renoir, Gauguin, Monet, Delacroix, Courbet and Corot, is open daily except Monday and Tuesday 10:30-18:00. Do not miss the Italian fountain with its four bronze horses, sculptured by the same Bartholdi who created the Statue of Liberty. The Musée des Tissus (34 rue de la Charite), open daily except Monday 10:00-17:30, houses a nearly 2,000-year-old collection of Oriental and European silks and velvets. It displays Persian carpets hung in a room that is 28 feet high. Next door, there is a fine collection of silver objects, kitchen utensils, Louis XIV furniture, tapestries and enamels in the Museum of Decorative Arts, open daily except Monday 10:00-12:00 and 14:00-17:30. Visit the Museum of Printing and Banking (13 rue de la Poullaillerie), open daily except Monday and Tuesday 09:30-12:00 and 14:00-18:00, and the Museum of Medicine in Hotel-Dieu on rue de l'Hopital, closed Monday. And, certainly treat yourself to a full and leisurely Lyonnais lunch and dinner.

For a pleasant getaway from Lyon take a local Lyon (Part-Dieu)-Valence train to Tain-Hermitage-Tournon, between Valence and Vienne, then pick up the Vivarais Railway to Lamastre. This privately-run railway operates both steam and diesel trains though delightful mountain scenery near Lyon. Eurailpasses are not accepted, though. Trains leave Tournon at 10:00 (steam), 10:50 and 14:30 (weekends, holidays) and 18:10. From Lamastre trains leave at 08:00, 15:30 (steam) and 17:00 (weekends, holidays) Diesel trips take between 60 to 75 minutes, steam about two hours. Service is stepped up in July and August Lyon-Valence trains operate frequently. For more information and current ticket prices, write CFTM, 2 Quai Jean Moulin, 69001 Lyon, France. Or call 011 33 04 78 28 83 34, fax 011 33 04 72 00 97 67. The *Cook Timetable* reference for these trains is 350 and 394.

Lyon's main tourist office, Pavillon du Tourisme, is at Place Bellecour B.P. 2254, telephone 04 72 77 69 69.

Marseilles

If scenes from The French Connection flutter to mind, you'd not be wholly wrong. Marseilles, France's oldest city, is a Mediterranean sea port with a strong flavor of North Africa, Italy, and the middle East. Yet it can only be French. Enjoy the sun, the pastis, the mixture of southern laziness and Latin fervor. There are plenty of fancy shops on Canebiere, the main street. Visit the dungeon from which Monte Cristo escaped, at Chateau d'If, reached by launch from the Quai des Belges. Most of the museums in Marseilles are closed Tuesday. Among the interesting museums are the Maritime Museum, on the ground floor of the Palais de la Bourse (Stock Exchange), the Fine Arts Museum and Natural History Museum in the Palais de Longchamps, the Roman Docks Museum, the Museum of Old Marseilles, the Museum of Mediterranean Archaeology, and the Lapidary Museum, both in the Park of Borely. There are fine views of the harbor from Fort St. Jean and Fort St. Nicolas. Don't neglect just sitting out on a terrace and ordering a Ricard with ice and watching the people as you eat olives. This is the south of France.

Contact the Marseille Office du Tourisme for more information, 4 La Canebière-13001 Marseille, telephone 011 33 4 91 13 89 00, fax 011 33 4 91 13 89 20. On the Web: http://www.mairie.marseille.fr

Nice

Aside from being France's retirement enclave, Nice has lots to offer travelers. See the priceless antiques, lavish carpets and exceptional paintings and sculptures in the Hotel Negresco at 37 Promenade des Anglais, the long and delightful avenue that follows the sea. Hotels and outdoor restaurants dot the wide boulevards. The Jules Cheret Museum of Fine Arts, 33 Avenue des Baumettes (behind the Promenade des Anglais), has many of Cheret's paintings. The Matisse Museum, 164 Avenue des Arenes, has guided tours in English. Note that most of the museums in Nice are closed either Monday or Tuesday.

You also might want to take in the War Memorial. The view of the Bay of Angels from the Naval Museum, and the Bellanda Tower are memorable things to see. The Marc Chagall National Museum, off Avenue Docteur Menard, the Roman Baths, the Terra Amata Prehistory Museum, and the 15,000 species of seashells at the Musée Internationale de Malacologie are definitely worth your time. Take the lift to the Colline du Chateau fortress ruins. One drawback about the Nice area and the famed Cote d'Azur is the nerve-wracking traffic in the summer months. And in recent years, the area around the main train station, Nice Ville, has been overrun with homeless types; the cafeterias next to and across the street from the station have had to hire security guards so diners can eat in peace. Be extra vigilant with your belongings around the station.

Try the Nicoise cuisine: pissaladiere (the local pizza), socca (a pancake), ratatouile (sauteed eggplant, onions, tomatoes and squash), le poulet farci aux figues (roast chicken stuffed with fresh figs), and of course salade nicoise. Nice is full of inexpensive restaurants with great fixed-price meals.

Save money on museum visits with the French Riviera Museum Pass (La Carte Musée). It includes unlimited admission to 58 museums and other sights along the Côte d'Azur such as the Musée Picasso in Antibes or the famous monastery at Saorge. The pass is valid for three or seven consecutive days. The three-day pass cost 70 FF in 1997, the seven-day pass, 140FF. You can visit as many museums/attractions as you wish during the three or seven days. Buy the pass at participating museums and monuments, at tourist offices and at FNAC stores. There's a tourist office at Nice Ville station. During the summer, it's open from 08:00 to 20:30 Monday-Saturday, Sunday until 19:00

Here's a trip suggestion from Nice: If the call of different kind of adventure is ringing in your ears, consider hopping a ferry from Nice (or Marseille or Toulon) to the island of Corsica. Don't expect to find any TGVs or fast expresses here, or even a first-class coach. Corsica is the place to go if you're looking for local color and slow-and-easy little narrow-gauge country trains that stop for cows and sheep. Scenery runs the gamut, from the seashore to the mountains. The only downside is that Corsican Railways (Chemins de Fer de la Course) doesn't honor Eurailpasses. Travelers with InterRail passes are entitled to discounts, though.

Lines run from Bastia to Ajaccio and Bastia to Calvi. In some cases you have to change trains at Ponte Leccia to get to Calvi; this could involve a two- to three-hour wait between trains. The peak-season schedule runs from late June to late September, with four daily departures/returns between Bastia and Ajaccio and two Bastia-Calvi departures/returns. *Cook* Table 393 shows these schedules: Bastia to Ajaccio: 07:20, 09:05, 14:30 and 15:50. Ajaccio to Bastia: 07:00, 09:00, 14:30, 16:05; trip time approximately four hours. Bastia to Calvi: 08:45, 16:35. Bastia to Calvi: 06:20, 14:30; trip time approximately three hours. Tickets sell from about $10 to $25, depending on the distance traveled.

Ferries sail from Nice, Marseilles and Toulon to the Corsican ports of Ajaccio, Bastia, Calvi, Ile Rousse and Propriano. The major ferry company is SNCM. (Ferries also leave from the Italian ports of Genoa, La Spezia and Livorno.) Ferry passage from French ports costs between 211FF and 286FF one way, depending on the travel date. Discounts are available for children and seniors. (Fares from Italian ports run from 130FF to 210FF.) Expect an average daytime crossing from Nice to Bastia to take 6-7 hours; overnight crossings take around 12 hours. Italian crossings are shorter, for example, from Livorno, it's about 5-6 hours.

So, what's there to do on Corsica besides taking train rides? Enjoy the fantastic beaches, hike the island's many trails, do some mountain biking, visit museums, take in a festival, shop for local folk art, savor the local wines and cuisine .

Ajaccio is Corsica's largest city as well as cultural center. It's also the birthplace of Napoléon. Look for the famous equestrian statue of Napoléon surrounded by his four brothers on the Place de Gaulle. Bastia, the second largest city has lots of attractions such as the old port that overlooks the old town, the 17th-century church of St. Jean Baptiste and the Chapel of the Conception which were magnificently decorated in the 18th century and the Museum of Corsican Ethnography in the Genovese Governor's Palace. Don't miss the Citadel in Calvi, with 13th-16th-century ramparts which stand on a rocky promontory that juts out to the sea. The Gulf of Porto surrounded by red granite cliffs, is also beautiful, especially at sunset.

Corsican wines are as colorful as the island itself. Try the local sausages, smoked hams and salamis with an Italian influence. Wild boar, goat and lamb are popular, as is tripe. Fish and shellfish are found in abundance. Cheese and dishes prepared with sweet chestnuts are another specialty. Try the sweet after-dinner drink, cedratine.

A bit of advice about traveling to Corsica. Don't go in July or August unless you've reserved a room. June is your best bet. A possible itinerary would be to visit Nice, then ferry over to Corsica, then return to the Continent via Italy.

Paris

For travelers arriving in Paris for the first time, a more in-depth guide book is advised. Paris is one of the few destinations on earth that continues to mesmerize visitors. The myths that Paris generate are all true. Paris enchants and it annoys, it fulfills all expectations, and it demands that you return. It is welcoming and it is cold. It is a city to fall in love in and a city that nurtures melancholia.

Arriving in Paris by Air

Odds are, if you're flying in from the States, you'll land at Aeroport Roissy-Charles De Gaulle, which is about 16 miles north of Paris. Don't even think about taking a cab into Paris unless you've got deep pockets. Figure on spending about $50 (add another 30 percent if you're traveling after 19:00!), plus extra francs for luggage weighing over 10 pounds. Besides, you're here to ride trains, right? Well, you might as well start at the airport. If you're going into downtown Paris, the suburban rail system, RER (Reseau Express Regional) (Line B), will take you there in about 35-40 minutes. Catch the free shuttle bus (navette) from the airport to the SNCF station, just minutes from the airport. A one-way ticket costs FF46 (children 4-10 years old FF32). Trains run every 7-15 minutes from 04:55 to 23:52. Main stops in Paris include Gare du Nord, Chatelet les Halles and St. Michel Notre Dame. Line B connects with other RER lines, the metro and train stations.

Now that the TGV stops at Roissy-Charles de Gaulle Airport, travelers can bypass Paris when heading to destinations like Lyon, Montpellier, Nice and Lille Europe, where it's an easy transfer to a London-bound Eurostar or trains to Brussels and beyond.

Paris' other airport, Orly, is about 7.5 miles south of town. There are a couple of options for getting away from the airport. OrlyVal is a state-of-the-art automatic metro that takes about 30 minutes to downtown and involves a connection with RER Line B at Antony Station. Once in Paris, the RER connects with the metro and the train stations. OrlyVal operates from 06:30-21:15, Monday-Saturday and 07:00-22:55 on Sunday, with departures every 4-7 minutes. One way Orly to Paris costs FF54 (children 4-10 years old FF27).

The other option is OrlyRail, RER line C. This involves taking a shuttle from the airport terminal to Pont de Rungis Aeroport d'Orly, then picking up the train. Trains run every 15 minutes from 05:04 to 23:34 and stop in Paris at Austerlitz, St. Michel Notre Dame, Musée D'Orsay and Champ de Mars Tour Eiffel; Line C also makes connections with the metro and train stations. The trip takes about 40 minutes. One-way fare, FF28.50 (children 4-10 years old: FF19.50).

Both of these airports also have a variety of bus and shuttle services, including the Air France shuttle, OrlyBus, RoissyBus, hotel and other shuttles and the municipal bus system, RATP.

Getting Around Paris

As for getting around, the city is particularly fortunate in that its famous Métro is ubiquitous. There is virtually nowhere you can't get to by metro, RER or tram, and the prices are reasonable. Here's a look at some of the tickets and passes available for getting around Paris.

• Individual tickets: They cost FF8 per trip and can add up fast if you'll be doing lots of riding. They're good on buses, the metro and RER within the city limits. Outside the city limits there's a series of zones that determine how much fare you'll pay.

• Carnet: This is a packet of 10 tickets that sells for FF48. You don't have to be a math whiz to figure out that this is definitely a better deal over individual tickets.

• Formule 1: This card is valid for one day with an unlimited number of trips by metro, RER, bus, SNCF suburban trains, the Montmartre Funicular and the late-night buses. Buy the card at the Paris Convention and Visitors Bureau (main office) and in all metro stations. Prices weren't available for 1998 yet, but last year the pass cost FF40.

• Paris Visite: This card is valid for one-to-five consecutive days over one-to-eight zones. It takes in the entire RATP, RER, Paris and Ile de France SNCF networks as well as for the Noctambus, Orlybus, Orlyrail and Roissyrail. When you purchase the pass in Paris you get all sorts of deals in addition to unlimited transportation on the above services. How about a two-for-one coupon on a Canauxrama canal boat tour? Or two-for-one to the top of Montparnasse tower, or to the wine museum? Or hop a train to Disneyland Paris or Versailles. The possibilities are limitless. Buy Paris Visite passes at the Paris Convention and Visitors Bureau (main office), in Metro stations, RER/SNCF stations and air terminals. Fares are based on zones. Prices for 1-8 zones range from FF50-FF150 for one-day pass, FF85-FF220 for two days, FF120-FF270 three days and FF170-FF350 for a five-day pass. Rail Europe also sells a version of Paris Visite. They offer four choices. In 1997, a card valid for two consecutive days cost $40, for two consecutive days plus one flexible day, the cost was $53. Two consecutive days and two flexible days cost $66 and two consecutive days plus three flexible days came to $79. The passes were good for unlimited travel in the greater Paris region, including Disneyland Paris, Versailles and the airports. If you buy from Rail Europe (800 4-EURAIL), it must be in conjunction with another Rail Europe purchase. There's another company in the States, Marketing Challenges International, that sells Paris Visite tickets for one to five days. Call them at (212) 529-9069.

• Carte Orange: If you'll be in Paris for a week or more, the best deal is the Carte Orange. It comes in validity periods of one week (hebdomadaire) from Monday to Sunday or one month (mensuelle) from the first day of each calendar month. You'll need a passport-size photo in order to get this pass (photo machines are found in most metro stations). Recent prices for at 1-2 zone one-week pass good for travel on buses, metro and RER: FF75 second class, FF113 first class; a pass for 1-8 zones cost FF225 second class, FF413 first class. One month: FF255 1-2 zones second class, FF383 1-8 zones first class; 1-8 zones cost FF770 second class, FF1403 first class. Usually one or two zones is sufficient for most travelers.

The metro has 15 lines; each is numbered. Metro trains generally operate from 05:30 (departure point) to 00:30 (departure point). Paris also has two tram lines, T1 between Bobigny-Pablo Picasso to Saint Denis and T2 between La Defense and Issy-val-de-Seine Unlike most metro lines, trams travel on surface streets, so you'll get a different perspective of the city. The RER operates between 05:30 and midnight. On the bus side, the first departure from the terminal is 06:30, the last bus from the terminal, 20:39. Some lines operate at night up to: 00:30. The Noctambus operates from 01:00 to about 05:00 departing from Châtelet.

For information about the RATP network (Paris Urban Transport System), call 01 43 46 14 14 (06:00-21:00). For information in English call 08 36 68 41 14 (this call will cost 2,23 F/minute). Also look for RATP information kiosks at major railway stations.

For a more detailed discussion of Paris and its transportation, consult *Paris Inside Out* (Houghton-Mifflin, 1995).

Paris Train Stations and the Directions They Serve

Always double-check the station for any departure from Paris!

Gare du Nord: Home base for Channel Tunnel Eurostars to/from London; serves the north, including the Channel ports, where trains connect with ferries and hover crafts from Britain; also services Belgium, Holland and the Scandinavian countries.

Gare de l'Est: Serves the east, Nancy and Strasbourg, and Germany and eastern Europe, including ex-Yugoslavia and Moscow. (The former Paris-Frankfurt train now continues to Leipzig.)

Gare d'Austerlitz: Serves the southwest; Bordeaux, Toulouse, and Spain and Portugal via Orleans, Tours, Poitiers and Angouleme.

Gare St. Lazare: Serves Normandy and boat trains to/from Dieppe.

Gare Montparnasse: Serves western France, especially Brittany.

Gare de Lyon: Serves southwestern France, Switzerland, Italy and Greece.

Bus service connects these Paris rail stations:

Between Gare Austerlitz and Gare de l'Est, Gare du Nord and Gare Saint Lazare, Gare de Lyon and Gare de l'Est, Gare du Nord and Gare Saint Lazare, Gare du Nord and Gare de Lyon and Gare Austerlitz, Gare de l'Est and Austerlitz, Gare du Nord and Gare Saint Lazare.

Sightseeing, Attractions and Shopping

Here are a few basic ideas of things to see in Paris. Use this list simply as a jumping off point.

• Musée d'Orsay, the converted train station on the Left Bank which served the Paris-Orleans line in the 19th century and became a museum in 1987, now houses much of the impressionists and early 20th century French collection, and should excite train travelers and art lovers alike. Its main attractions: works by Monet, Van Gogh, Renoir, Pissarro. A great place to start your Parisian visit. RER: Line C Musée d'Orsay. Metro: Solferino. Summer: 09:00-18:00. Winter: 10:00-18:00. Open to 21:45 on Thursdays. Closed on Mondays, January 1, May 1, and December 25.

• Louvre (open Monday and Wednesday 09:00-21:45, Thursday-Sunday 09:00-18:00, closed Tuesdays and some public holidays). The Pyramid, designed by I.M. Pei has modernized the feel of this classic world-important museum; it was unveiled in 1989. Louvre redevelopment continues. The new Richelieu Wing opened in November 1993, a new exhibition area followed, and the Grand Louvre was finished in 1997. Metro: Palais Royal-Musée du Louvre.

• Montmartre area and the stunning Sacre Coeur church. Do this at sunset (the Eiffel Tower glimmers) or night. Metro: Lamarck Caulaincourt.

• Eiffel Tower, which needs no introduction. Open 09:30-11:30. July/August: 09:00-midnight. RER: Line C Champ-de-Mars-Tour Eiffel. Metro: Bir Hakeim, Trocadéro.

• The obelisk at Place de la Concorde where Marie Antoinette was guillotined. Metro: Concorde.

• Arc de Triomphe. Experience an excellent rooftop view of Paris. At the top of the Champs-Elysée. Open summer: 10:00-17:30. Winter: 10:00-17:00. Closed on public holidays. RER: Line A Charles-de-Gaulle/Etoile-Metro: Charles-de-Gaulle/Etoile.

• La Grande Arche-Paris la Defénse. Panorama with a view of the historic route: Arc de Triomphe-Cour Carrée du Louvre. The arch is open in summer 09:00-19:00 Monday-Friday. Saturdays, Sundays and public holidays 09:00-20:00. Winter: 09:00-18:00. Besides Le Grande Arche, there's a sports center and a gigantic shopping center (hundreds of stores and restaurants!). RER Line A La Défense exit "La Grande Arche." Metro: Grande Arche de la Défense.

• Stained-glass windows at St. Chapelle. Open summer 09:30-18:00. Winter 10:00-16:30. Closed on public holidays. RER: Lines B-C Saint-Michel, Notre Dame. Metro: Cité.

• Deportation Monument behind Notre Dame Cathedral. RER: Lines B-C Saint-Michel, Notre-Dame. Metro: Cité.

• Luxembourg Gardens. Go for a stroll or a jog or a pony ride. Paris at its most Parisian. RER: Line B Luxembourg.

• Pompidou Center. France's most significant cultural center, library, and public meeting place. Open 10:00-22:00. Closed on Tuesdays. 12:00-22:00 Saturdays, Sundays, and public holidays. RER: Lines A-B-D Châtelet-Les-Halles. Metro: Hôtel de Ville, Rambuteau.

• Orangerie Museum, with its 150 works of impressionist painters including Renoir, Matisse, Cezanne, Picasso and Utrillo. Open 09:45-17:15. Closed on Tuesdays and public holidays. RER: Line C Invalides, Musée d'Orsay. Metro: Concorde.

• Les Invalides and its Army Museum, where the preserved body of Napoleon is on exhibit. Enormous collection of uniforms, weapons, war trophies, flags, books, manuscripts and paintings. And, the Eglise du Dome (containing Napoleon's Tomb). Open daily 10:00-18:00 April-September and 10:00-17:00 October-March. A fine sound-and-light show is presented nightly, April-September. RER: Line C Invalides. Metro: Varenne, Invalides.

• Rodin Museum, at Hotel Biron. The gardens are delightful. Don't miss "The Thinker." The Rodin Museum, 77 rue de Varenne, is open daily except Monday 09:30-17:45. Also closed January 1, May 1 and December 25. RER: Line C Invalides. Metro: Varenne.

• Tour Montparnasse offers an excellent view of Paris from its 650-foot-high observation deck. Open summer 09:00-23:30. Winter 10:00-22:00. Metro: Montparnasse-Bienvenue.

• Flower markets on the Ile de la Cité, the rue de Buci, rue Mouffetard in the Latin Quarter and Place Louis-Lépine-adjoining quays. Flowers sold Monday-Saturday from 07:30. Metro: Cité.

• Flea Markets (marché aux puces). Porte de Clignancourt, Saturday, Sunday and Monday, 07:00-19:30. Metro: Porte de Clignancourt. Porte de Vanves, Saturday-Sunday 14:00-19:30 (new goods), 07:00-19:30 (used goods) Metro: Porte de Vanves. Porte de Montreuil, Saturday, Sunday and Monday, 07:00-19:00. Metro: Porte de Montreuil.

• Cité des Sciences et de l'Industrie. A tribute to science, industry and technology. Includes an aquarium and planetarium. Open daily 10:00-18:00, except Monday. Metro: Porte de la Vilette.

• Eugene Delacroix Museum, 6 rue de Furstenberg, is the artist's last home and studio. Open 09:45-17:00, closed Tuesdays. Metro: Saint-Germain-des-Pres.
• Musée National d'Art Moderne (Modern Art Museum), Centre d'Art et de Culture Georges Pompidou. Displays national collections from 19045 to present day. Open 12:00-22:00, 10:00-22:00 Saturday, Sunday. Closed Tuesday and May 1. RER: Lines A-B-D-Châtelet-Les-Halles. Metro: Rambuteau.
• Musée de la Musique la Villette. A rich collection of musical instruments from the 16th century to modern times. Open 12:00-18:00, 10:00-18:00, Sunday, Thursdays until 21:30. Closed Monday.
• Musée des Arts Decoratifs (Decorative Arts Museum) Next to the Louvre, the museum houses displays of interiors from the Middle Ages to the present day. Open 12:30-18:00 Wednesday-Saturday, Sundays 12:00-18:00. Closed on Mondays, Tuesdays and public holidays. Metro: Palais-Royal-Musée du Louvre, Tuileries.
• Honoré de Balzac Museum, 47 rue Raynouard, is open daily except Mondays and holidays and public holidays, 10:00-17:40. Metro: Passy, La Muette.
• Paris Opera House. It's one of the most beautiful monuments of the Second Empire. Open 10:00-17:00. Metro: Opera. Two of Paris' major department stores, Printemps and Galleries Lafayette, are within walking distance of the opera house. Open 09:30-19:00; open Thursday until 21:00. RER: Line A Auber. Metro: Chaussée d'Antin. Printemps stays open until 22:00 on Thursday.
• Samaritaine is another legendary Paris department store, 19, rue de la Monnaie. Open 09:30-19:00 Monday-Saturday; stays open until 22:00 Thursdays. Kick back with a cappuccino or a snack at the rooftop eatery and enjoy an awesome view of the Seine and Eiffel Tower. Metro: Pont Neuf. For a spirited shopping experience, go to Tati, the French low-budget clothing store. The largest store (Metro: Barbes Rochechouart) is a real free-for-all as hordes of shoppers fight for a place at the overflowing bins of clothing. There are separate buildings for women's, men's and children's clothing, plus another building for housewares. The clothes are hardly haute couture, but the price is right; a great place to pick up inexpensive togs for traveling
• Theater tickets. These two kiosks sell same day theater tickets at half price: 15, place de la Madeleine, 12:30-20:00 Tuesday-Saturday, Sunday 12:30-16:00; Metro: Madeleine, and at the RER station at Châtelet-Les Halles, 12:30-19:30. Closed on Sundays, Mondays and public holidays.
• Other noteworthy museums include the Musée de la Mode et du Costume, 10 Ave. Pierre Premier de Serbie, the Archaeological Museum, electronic exhibits at the Musée Branly, Chinese and Japanese artifacts at the Musée Dennery, the Museum of French Bread, the Museum of Police History, the Musical Instruments Museum, the large poster collection in the Musée de l'Affiche et la Publicité (at the Decorative Arts Museum, 107 rue de Rivoli). 17th and 18th-century furniture in the Musée Carnavalet, 23 rue de Sevigne, open daily except Monday 10:00-17:40. Consider buying the Museum & Monument Pass, which gives a free and direct access to the permanent collections housed in 70 museums and monuments in Paris and the Ile de France region. Passes are sold at participating museums and monuments, major metro stations, the Tourist Information Bureau (Carrousel du Louvre), the Paris Tourist Bureau, 127 avenue des Champs-Elysées, Paris 8e (open daily from

09:00 to 20:00), and at railway station tourist bureaus. The museum pass does not include entry to exhibitions or guided visits. Prices in 1997 were: one-day pass FF70, three-day pass, FF140, five-day pass FF200. The passes are for consecutive days.

Other Attractions

• The Marais district, the oldest section of Paris, a maze of narrow 16th-century streets, should not be overlooked. It can be examined by starting at the Pompidou Center and walking along rue Rambuteau to rue des Francs-Bourgeois, a street named in the 15th century, describing its poor residents who were exempt from paying taxes. Interesting documents (the order sending Marie Antoinette to the guillotine, the 1944 law giving French women the right to vote, etc.) can be seen in the History of France Museum at 60 rue des Francs-Bourgeois, open daily except Tuesdays and holidays 14:00-17:00. Metro: Rambuteau.

Among the many elegant town mansions (called hotels in the 15th century) worth seeing in the Marais are Hotel d'Albret, Hotel de Fourcy, and Hotel de Lamignon (all on rue des Francs-Bourgeois). Then take note of the Hotel Merle and Hotel de Chatillon (along rue Payenne), and follow the signs leading to the Hotel Sale on rue de Thorigny, which house in great elegance and perfect sophistication the Picasso Museum, open Wednesday 10:00-22:00, Thursday-Monday 10:00-17:15. There is an extraordinary collection of stuffed animals, furniture carved with animal figures, and silver encrusted riffles at the Hunting and Nature Museum, in the Hotel Gueneguad at 60 rue des Archives, open daily except Mondays and holidays 10:00-17:30. By walking down rue du Parc Royal, you pass the pink and white Hotel Duret de Chevry. Turn right to go down rue de Sevigne so as to pass by Hotel Le Peletier St. Fargeau and Hotel Carnavalet, now the Museum of French Interior design, open daily except Monday 10:00-17:40. Then visit the Maison de Victor Hugo (6 Place des Vosges), situated in the corner of one of Paris's most charming and elegant old world squares, open daily except Mondays and holidays 10:00-17:40. Next, walk down rue de Birague and onto rue St. Antoine in order to see Hotel Sully (at Number 62). By walking rue Mahler until it reaches rue des Rosiers, you arrive at the center of the Jewish district and the most famous delicatessen in Paris, Jo Goldbergs, at Number 7. Don't miss Chez Marianne, slightly further down the rue des Rossiers, for it is here that you'll experience the soul (and Tunisian deli delights) of the neighborhood, under the welcoming acceuil of owners Marianne and her philosopher/poet/grocer husband André. Nearby is the unusual Art Deco synagogue on the rue Pavee. The rue Simon-le-Franc will lead you back to the Pompidou Center.

• At the 14-acre Père Lachaise Cemetery (Metro: Père-Lachaise) are the graves of Edith Piaf, Gertrude Stein, Alice B. Toklas, Colette, Sarah Bernhardt, Isadora Duncan, Simone Signoret, Frederick Chopin, Oscar Wilde, Honore de Balzac, Ferdinand de Lesseps (promoter of the Suez Canal), and Jean Francois Champollion (interpreter of the Rosetta stone). Upstaging them all though is the cult hangout and graffiti-sprawled grave of myth-making rock star Jim Morrison, who came to Paris to attempt to become an obscure philosophical poet and died there in 1971. Opened in 1804, it is the oldest of the four main cemeteries in Paris. It is open mid-March to mid-November Monday-Saturday 07:30-18:00, the rest of the year 08:30-17:30. On Sundays and holidays: mid-November to mid-January 09:00-18:00, the rest of the year 08:30-17:30. Other cemeteries of note include Montparnasse cemetery (Metro: Raspail) in which such notables as Jean-Paul Sartre, Simone de Beauvoir, and Samuel Beckett rest in peace and Montmartre cemetery, the last resting place of Vigny, Stendhal, Poulbot, Berlioz and Jouvet. Metro: Place de Clichy.

• Take a cruise along Paris' Canal Saint-Martin. In a couple of hours, you'll see a whole different side of the city, as you float beneath bowers of trees and through locks to Parc de la Vilette, where you can get off and visit the Cité des Sciences et de l'Industrie (Museum of Science and Industry). Canauxrama operates trips several times per day along Canal Saint-Martin, as well longer trips. Boats leave from 13, Quai de la Loire (Metro: Jaurès) Reservations are recommended; the trip takes about two hours costs about $25 one way. Telephone 01 42 39 15 00, fax: 01 42 39 11 24.

• For the recreation-minded traveler, Paris offers some prime swimming pools. Swimmers can chose from a wide variety of pools in this city. The 50-meter Piscine Georges-Vallerey, located next to the Porte des Lilas metro station was built for the 1924 Olympic Games and has a transparent roof that is opened in sunny weather. The underground Piscine Suzanne Berlioux at Les Halles, near the Pompidou Center, is another modern 50-meter facility. Aquaboulevard de Paris is an indoor-outdoor amusement park (sand beaches, wave machines, slides, toboggans, mock tropical islands and lagoons) is near the metro Balard. The former Piscine Pontoise re-opened after renovations in 1990 with the new name Piscine du Quartier Latin. The famous Piscine Deligny located on a moored barge on the Left Bank of the Seine, burned down in 1993 and has yet to be restored. Joggers can practice their habit in the Jardin du Luxembourg, Parc Monceau, or—although on the edges of town—the expansive and verdant Bois de Vincennes or Bois de Boulogne, which doubles up after dark as a commercial meeting grounds for amorous encounters of every sort.

• If you've got kids (or you still feel like one), don't pass up Disneyland Paris. Take RER Line A to Chessy-Marne-La-Vallée.

• As for cuisine, not only is Paris a feast of fine dining, its gourmet shops have the power of overwhelming visitors with the elegance and beauty of its window presentations. The prices will send you spinning, but there's no charge to look. The most famous of these fine shops is Fauchon on the Place de la Madeleine and its neighbor Hediard. Across the Place is La Maison de Truffe (19 Place de la Madeleine), where truffles, foie gras and caviar are the rule, and next door you'll be amazed by the Creplet-Brussol fromagerie featuring a cool 250 varieties of cheeses. Caviar Kaspia hosts fine caviar from Iran and Russia, with the Marquise de Sevigne specializing in sinfully rich and stunning fine chocolates for nearly 100 years. All this on Place de la Madeleine, which houses as well a kiosque for same-day half price theater tickets (see details on earlier page about buying half-price tickets).

For additional information on Paris and its surroundings contact:
Office du Tourisme et des Congrès de Paris
127, av des Champs-Elysées
75008 PARIS
Tel: 49.52.53.54, fax: 49.52.53.00
Metro stop for tourist office: Etoile/Georges V.
Also check this Web site: http://www.paris.org.

Strasbourg

Strasbourg, Alsace's capital, had a history of being an historical pawn, Strasbourg was French until 1872, German 1871-1918, French 1918-1940, German again 1940-1944, and has been French since 1944. Currently the seat of the European parliament, Strasbourg has gained continental importance over the last ten years. On rue de la Rape, visitors will find the city's majestic 13th-century Cathedral of Notre-Dame. All of its stained-glass windows date either from the 12th, 13th or 14th century. Its famous 60-foot-high astronomical clock, which calculates eclipses, sunrises and sunsets into eternity, comes alive on the hour and quarter-hour, when figures appear from and return into its interior. The clock's major performance is at 12:30. It is then that the Four Ages of Man pass before Death, and the 12 Apostles move past the figure of Jesus. As he blesses them, a mechanical rooster flaps its wings and crows three times.

There is an extraordinary view of the city from a platform 217 feet above street level, at the top of the cathedral's 328-step spiral staircase. From April-September, a fabulous sound-and-light show is presented inside the cathedral: illuminated stained-glass windows, bells tolling, organ music, the whole works for an enchanting Alsatian evening.

There are three fine museums in the 18th-century Chateau des Rohans (next to the cathedral): a collection of Monet, Renoir, El Greco, Goya and Tintoretto in the art gallery; the relics in the Archaeological Museum; and a display of clocks, ironwork, earthenware and porcelain in the Museum of Decorative Arts. More recently, Strasbourg opened up a new museum of contemporary works.

Next to the Rohans is a 14th-century building that houses wonderful 11th to 17th-century Alsatian art in the Musée de l'Oeuvre Notre-Dame. Next to it is the Modern Art Museum. All of these museums are open daily except Tuesday 10:00-12:00 and 14:00-18:00.

You might want to take the one-hour sightseeing mini-train ride that starts at the south side of the cathedral. It runs every half-hour, late March to the end of October. There are also cruises on the Rhine (90 minutes, three hours, and 11 hours) starting in front of the Palais des Rohans, and nearby Musée Alsacien, 23 Quai St. Nicholas, which houses impressive rooms dating from the early 17th century (furnished with marvelous utensils, stoves, wooden molds and pottery from the same era).

In all cases, treat yourself to a choucroute garni, an elaborate and copious Alsatian dish of sauerkraut, sausage, potatoes, and pork. Order an Alsatian white wine and you'll never regret stopping in Strasbourg.

Tours

Although much of the old city was destroyed in the 1944 bombings, Tours is worth a stop. One option is to take a 90-minute walk from the Tours rail station along Boulevard Heurteloup to rue Nationale. Turn right and go up one side of rue Nationale to the bridge that stretches over the Loire. Return along the opposite side of rue Nationale. Cross Boulevard Heurteloup and go one block further. Turn left onto rue de Bordeaux, and follow it directly back to the rail station. This will give you a fine overview of the city.
Stop in and see the fine collection of paintings in the Musée des Beaux-Arts.

A pamphlet called *The Loire Valley by Train* may be obtained from the information desk at many French rail stations. It shows schedules of trains from Tours (not provided in *Cook*) that stop at stations near 12 different castles. The train to Azay-le-Rideau continues to Chinon. Another train goes to Amboise, Chaumont (Onzain), Blois and Beaugency. A third train goes to Villandry (Savonnieres), Langeais, Samur and Angers. A fourth train goes to Loches and a fifth goes to Chenonceaux. These train rides range from 10 to 70 minutes in each direction. Most are less than 30 minutes. There are also bus tours from Tours to the castles.

EXCURSIONS AND CITY-SIGHTSEEING

In the following tables, when cities host more than one rail station, the name of the particular station has been designated in parentheses after the name of the city. Don't assume that the station from where you depart is the same as the station where you arrived. Doing so may cause you to miss your train.

Note: Renovation of Paris's Gare du Nord was completed in late 1993. Now it serves two functions: one part of the station handles all long-distance trains (including TGVs) servicing Lille and the northern regions of France. The other, exclusively designed for traffic to the Channel Tunnel, includes a duty-free area and a customs baggage check for passengers traveling to Great Britain.

Avignon - Antibes - Avignon   79

| Dep. Avignon | 04:56 (1) | 05:17 (2) | Dep. Antibes | 20:07 (3) | 20:23 (4) |
| Arr. Antibes | 08:52 | 09:19 | Arr. Avignon | 00:05 | 00:10 |

(1) Runs daily, except Friday and Saturday. (2) Runs Friday and Saturday. (3) Runs Monday-Friday. (4) Runs Saturday and Sunday.

Sights in **Antibes**: The exhibit of 231 Picasso paintings at the special Picasso Museum in Grimaldi Castle, on Place Mariejol. Open daily except Tuesday 10:00–12:00 and 15:00–18:00.

Avignon - Arles - Avignon   350

| Dep. Avignon | 06:41 | 06:47 (1) | 06:58 (2) | 10:51 (3) | 15:06 | 16:18 | 17:15 (2) |
| Arr. Arles | 20 minutes later | | | | | | |

Sights in **Arles**: The ancient Roman cemetery, Alyscamps, that contains 400,000 sarcophagi, hand-carved granite caskets. The 21,000-seat Roman arena (open 08:30-19:00 in summer, 09:00-12:00 and 14:00-18:00 the rest of the year). The museum of Pagan Art, in St. Anne Church on Place de la Republique (open 09:00-12:30 and 14:00-19:00 in summer, 10:00-12:30 and 14:00-17:30 the rest of the year). The Roman Theater, open 08:30-12:00 and 14:00-18:00. The Forum, built during Augustus' rule. The Thermae, from Constantine's era. The 12th-century Cloister in the marvelous Romanesque Church of Saint-Trophime.

Dep. Arles   11:51   15:06   16:17 (4)   17:46   20:10 (5)   22:14
Arr. Avignon   20 minutes later

(1) Friday only early June-late September. (2) Runs Monday-Friday, except holidays. (3) Runs daily through mid-September. (4) Friday only. (5) Sunday only.

Avignon - Lyon - Avignon   350

Dep. Avignon	06:35 (1)	07:31 (2)	07:56	10:14
Arr. Lyon (Part Dieu)	08:46	09:08	10:08	12:15

Dep. Lyon (Part Dieu)	14:03 (3+4)	17:13 (3+4)	18:51 (5)	19:19 (2+6)
Arr. Avignon	15:58	19:12	20:44	20:55

(1) Runs Monday-Saturday, except holidays. (2) TGV. Reservation required. Supplement charged . Restaurant car. (3) Runs to late June and from early September. (4) Light refreshments. (5) Friday only. (6) Plus other departures from Lyon at 20:20 (5), 21:04 (7) and 23:57, arriving Avignon 22:18, 23:22 and 01:55. (7) Runs Friday and Sunday.

Avignon - Marseille - Avignon   350

Dep. Avignon	08:25 (1)	10:51 (2)	11:37 (3)	11:58
Arr. Marseille (St. Ch.)	50–60 minutes later			

Dep. Marseille (St. Ch.)	14:04 (1)	14:20	16:59	17:29 (1)
Arr. Avignon	50–60 minutes later			

Dep. Marseille (St. Ch.)	18:01 (1)	19:00	22:04	22:47	23:23
Arr. Avignon	50–60 minutes later				

(1) TGV. Reservation required, supplement charged. (2) Daily through mid-September. Monday-Friday, except holidays from mid-September. (3) TGV. Reservation required, supplement charged. Runs Monday-Thursday.

Avignon - Monaco (Monte Carlo) - Avignon   350, 360

350			*360*	
Dep. Avignon	08:25 (1)	10:28 (1)	Dep. Monaco	19:09
Arr. Marseille	09:20	11:24	Arr. Nice	19:26
Change trains 360			*No train change*	
Dep. Marseille	09:35	12:11	Dep Nice	19:56
Arr. Nice	12:08	14:34	Arr. Marseille	22:28
Change trains			*Change trains 350*	
Dep. Nice	12:18	14:55	Dep. Marseille	22:38
Arr. Monaco	12:40	15:19	Arr. Avignon	23:51

(1) TGV. Reservation required. Supplement charged. Light refreshment car.

Avignon - Nimes - Avignon   355

Dep. Avignon	07:31	10:58	11:22	12:14 (2)	14:10 (1)
Arr. Nimes	25 minutes later				

Sights in **Nimes:** Many Roman ruins in excellent condition, such as the 1st-century amphitheater (seating 24,000 people) in the center of the city, used in recent years for bullfights to entertain Spanish migrant workers. The construction of the arena was done by fitting large stones together without the use of mortar. The arena is open 08:00-19:00 in summer, 09:00-12:00 and 14:00-17:00 the rest of the year. Also see the beautiful 1st-century rectangular temple, Maison Carree, and its collection of Roman sculptures, open 09:00-20:00 in summer, 09:00-12:00 and 14:00-18:00 the rest of the year. The view of Nimes from the oldest Roman building, Tour Magne, on a hill outside the city. A few miles away is the enormous Pont du Gard Roman aqueduct. Visit the collection of Iron Age and Roman objects in the Archaeological Museum. Stroll through the 18th-century Garden of the Fountain.

Dep. Nimes	11:56	13:35 (3)	13:57 (1)	14:28 (1)	14:49	15:51
Arr. Avignon	25 minutes later					

· · ·

Dep. Nimes	16:31	17:36 (3)	18:59	20:07 (4)	23:43
Arr. Avignon	25 minutes later				

(1) TGV. Reservation required. Supplement charged. Light refreshments. (2) Runs daily, except Sundays and holidays. Light refreshments. (3) Runs Monday-Friday except holidays. (4) Runs Friday and Sunday.

Avignon - Orange - Avignon   350

Dep. Avignon	07:56	09:48 (1)	12:23	13:55 (1)	15:28 (2)
Arr. Orange	15 minutes later				

Sights in **Orange**: See the 10,000-seat Roman Theater (open 09:00-18:30 in summer, 09:00-12:00 and 13:00-17:00 the rest of the year) and the ancient walls of the old city. The Roman Triumphal Arch.

Dep. Orange	11:10 (1) 14:43 (3) 16:00	17:21 (4)	20:13 (1)	21:21 (5)
Arr. Avignon	15 minutes later			

(1) Runs Monday-Saturday, except holidays. (2) Light refreshments. (3) TGV. Supplement payable. (4) Runs Monday–Friday, except holidays. (5) Runs daily, except Saturday.

Bordeaux - Bayonne and Biarritz - Bordeaux 302

Dep. Bordeaux (St. Jean)	07:03	10:34 (1)	13:07 (1)
Arr. Bayonne	09:06	12:14	14:43
Arr. Biarritz	10 minutes after arriving Bayonne		

Sights in and around **Bayonne**: This is the Cote Basque's leading port and private yacht harbor. Visit the cathedral, Basque Museum, Chateau-Viex, Museum Bonnat. Exhibits tracing Basque history and customs (farm tools, household objects, costumes) are in the Musée Basque, at 1 Rue Marengo. Whatever you do, don't leave Bayonne without stopping by Chocolat Cazenave for a cup of world-class hot chocolate and other sweets. It's in the shadow of the cathedral at 19, rue Port Neuf (closed Mondays).

Bayonne is also a good base for taking train trips around Basque country. St. Jean Pied de Port is only five miles from the Spanish border and was the last stop in France for pilgrims heading south to visit the tomb of Saint James in Santiago de Compostela. This is a puddle-jumper train, where you'll rub elbows with the locals. Emerald farmlands and forests dot the landscape, and the town, with its cobblestone streets is filled with artist studios and souvenir shops. Another worthwhile train adventure is to La Rhune, a supposed mystical mountain on the French-Spanish border. The wooden two-car trains wind their way into the clouds, passing little streams, crater-like rocks and tiny wild Basque horses called *pottoks*. At the top, in Spain, you can see all the way to the ocean, when it's clear. Have a snack at the small bar. Hike the hillsides. Trains leave from Col de Saint Ignace daily July-September and on weekends and holidays May, June and October to mid-November. Trains run every 30 minutes from 10:00 to 17:30 and the trip takes about 35 minutes; round trip $10. In Col de Saint Ignace, across from the station, is Le Pullman Bar/Restaurant. As the name implies, there's a railway atmosphere here. The food's good, too. In summer, buses run from Saint Jean de Luz (take the train there from Bayonne). The rest of the year, though, you're on your own. A cab will set you back about $35 round trip. Tours, operated by Le Basque Pullman, leave from Saint Jean de Luz; phone 05 59 26 03 37. Renting a car is always another option. This area is filled with fascinating places to visit, from the "village of the witches," to nearby caves and cozy country inns. Hotel Arraya in Sare (near Col de Saint Ignace) is an excellent choice for a couple of quiet nights in the country; enjoy a gourmet meal in the hotel restaurant. From the U.S., dial 011 33 59 54 20 46, fax 011 33 59 54 27 04. From $88, double with bath.

Sights in **Biarritz:** France's snootiest beach resort since 1854. Golf, tennis and every type of water sport are popular here. There are many spas offering thalassotherapy. See the food market. A small grocery store called Maison Arosteguy stocks 120 types of Scotch whiskey and what has been described as "a dizzying array" of Armagnacs. A marvelous way to toast a special occasion is with a stay at the spectacular Hotel du Palais, once the summer palace of Napoleon III and his wife Empress Eugenie. It's a bit pricey, but worth every cent, especially when you're lulled to sleep by the crashing waves outside your window. Very romantic. For information about the Palais call (800) 223-6800.

Dep. Biarritz	14:52 (1)	17:51 (1)	18:02 (2)	18:56 (3+4)
Dep. Bayonne	10 minutes after departing Biarritz.			
Arr. Bordeaux (St. Jean)	16:37	19:38	20:28	20:40

(1) TGV. Reservation required. Supplement charged. Light refreshments. (2) Runs Sundays and holidays only. (3) TGV. Reservation required. Supplement charged. Runs Sundays only. (4) Plus another departure from Biarritz at 23:34, arriving Bordeaux 01:58.

Bordeaux - Carcassonne - Bordeaux   321

Light refreshments are offered on all trains.

Bordeaux (St. Jean)	06:38	11:49	14:44
Arr. Carcassonne	09:50	15:01	18:03

Sights in **Carcassonne:** The most interesting walled city (actually double-walled) in France and Europe's best preserved relic of the Middle Ages. The inner wall, built by the Romans in the 2nd century, bears 29 towers. The 13th-century French outer wall has 17 towers and barbicans (fortified castles). It is a 30-minute walk from the rail station to the walled city. There is both bus and taxi service.

To the south are the ruins of five other walls erected by France in medieval days as additional protection from attack by the Spaniards. As you stand on the walkways at the top of the French wall, it is easy to imagine yourself shooting arrows through the narrow slits or dropping hot oil on the marauders below.

See the Narbonnaise Gate and drawbridge. Nearby is a bust of Dame Carcas, for whom the city is named. Carcassonne had been under siege by Charlemagne. She gathered the little grain the starving people had and scattered it to livestock in view of the soldiers who were by then weary of the months they had been waiting for the people inside the impregnable walls to capitulate.

Her bold act convinced the soldiers that the people could last much longer, and Charlemagne abandoned his attempt to starve-out the town.

Inside the Basilica of St. Nazare are many stone carvings depicting scenes from the fort's history, magnificent stained-glass windows regarded by many as the finest in southern France, and the rectangular tombstone of Bishop Radulph. Also see the 12th-century Countal Castle.

| Dep. Carcassonne | 15:57 | 18:17 | 20:17 |
| Arr. Bordeaux (St. Jean) | 19:01 | 21:45 | 23:35 |

Bordeaux - Limoges - Bordeaux   305

| Dep. Bordeaux (St. Jean) | 10:54 | 13:57 | 15:43 | 18:10 (1) |
| Arr. Limoges | 13:11 | 16:47 | 18:01 | 20:45 |

Sights in **Limoges**: Tours of the famous porcelain and enamel factories are free, by applying to the Syndicat de la Porcelain, 7 Rue du General Cerez. Visit the Adrien Dubouche Museum, with its great collection of ceramics. See the Municipal Museum's display of china made in Limoges from the 12th century to the present. Visit the Cathedral of Saint Etienne.

| Dep. Limoges | 14:43(2) | 18:19 | 21:05 |
| Arr. Bordeaux (St. Jean) | 17:22 | 20:36 | 23:35 |

(1) Operates daily except Saturdays.   (2) Change trains in Perigueux Monday-Friday early July to late August.

Bordeaux - Lourdes - Bordeaux   302

| Dep. Bordeaux (St. Jean) | 07:03 (1) | 11:06 (2) | 13:11 (3) | 17:00 (2) | 19:06 (4+8) |
| Arr. Lourdes | 10:06 | 13:30 | 15:56 | 19:28 | 21:37 |

Sights in **Lourdes**: A 14-year-old girl, Bernadette Soubirous, had numerous visions here in 1858, in the Massabielle grotto. The underground spring in the grotto is believed by many to have miraculous qualities. About 3,000,000 people come here every year, many of them disabled or diseased and hoping to be cured.

The immense underground church seating 20,000 was inaugurated in 1958.

On the other side of the torrent called Gave de Pau there is an interesting 14th-century castle which was used as a prison from 1643 until the early 19th century.

| Dep. Lourdes | 15:01 (2) | 16:19 | 17:43 (5) | 18:54 (6) | 19:36 (7+9) |
| Arr. Bordeaux (St. Jean) | 17:25 | 19:19 | 20:07 | 22:08 | 22:51 |

(1) Operates early July–late August. (2) TGV. Reservation required. Supplement charged. Light refreshments. (3) Light refreshments. (4) TGV. Runs Friday only. Reservation required. Supplement charged. Light refreshments. (5) Runs Sundays only. TGV. Reservation required. Supplement charged. Light refreshments. (6) Runs late June to late August. (7) Runs Sunday only. (8) Plus another Bordeaux departure at 20:54, arriving Lourdes 23:22. (9) Plus another Lourdes departure at 22:49, arriving Bordeaux 01:58. For those overnighting in Lourdes, there are other departures from Lourdes at 07:48 (2), 10:17 and 11:19 (2).

Bordeaux - Nantes - Bordeaux   291

Dep. Bordeaux (St. J.)	06:39	10:32 (1)	
Arr. Nantes	11:05	14:25	

•   •   •

Dep. Nantes	13:53 (1)	18:12	19:39 (2)
Arr. Bordeaux (St. J.)	18:08	22:17	23:25

(1) Light refreshments. (2) Early July to early September: runs daily, except Friday. Early September to early July: runs Friday and Sunday.

Sights in **Nantes**: This was a commercial center under the Romans. The Normans pillaged the town in 834. After having been partly destroyed in World War II, its railway was placed underground.

This is an important seaport and shipbuilding center. See the extraordinary white marble Renaissance tomb of Francois II, duke of Brittany, in the cathedral that was bombed during World War II. The church was restored, only to have its roof almost entirely destroyed by fire in 1972. The tomb was not harmed.

Tour the medieval castle that was rebuilt in 1466, Chateau des Ducs de Bretagne and its museums (entrance on the Rue des Etats). Guided tours are offered every half-hour, daily during July and August from 10:00–12:00 and 14:00–18:00. The rest of the year there are only three tours a day, and the castle is closed on Tuesday. The castle is surrounded by a moat and has a drawbridge at its entrance.

Visit the Jules Verne Museum (the author was born in Nantes in 1828), open daily except Tuesday 10:00–12:00 and 14:00–17:00. See the exceptional paintings in the Fine Arts Museum (10 Rue Georges Clemenceau), open daily except Tuesday and national holidays 10:00–12:00 and 13:00–17:45.

Stroll through the Passage Pommeraye, a decorative three-level shopping arcade. Visit the Jardin des Plantes, a botanical garden and formal French park, with grottos, waterfalls, statues, ponds, 400 varieties of camellias, and 19th-century greenhouses, containing many orchids.

There are three-hour boat cruises on the **Erbe River**, leaving from 24 Quai de Versailles at 12:30 (lunch), 14:30 and 20:00 (dinner).

Bordeaux - Narbonne - Bordeaux   320

All of these trains have light refreshments.

Dep. Bordeaux (St. Jean)	06:38	11:49	Dep. Narbonne	19:46
Arr. Narbonne	10:18	15:30	Arr. Bordeaux (St. Jean)	23:35

Sights in **Narbonne:** The cloister adjacent to the Palace of the Archbishops. The choir of the incomplete Cathedral of Saint-Just.

Bordeaux - Toulouse - Bordeaux   320

Dep. Bordeaux (St. Jean)	05:58 (1)	06:38	08:25	11:15 (2)
Arr. Toulouse (Matabiau)	08:49	08:56	11:12	13:12

Sights in **Toulouse: The** Basilica of Saint Sernin, displaying the remains of 128 saints, including six of the apostles and a thorn from the Crown of Thorns. It also has seven extraordinary 11th-century marble bas reliefs and the Meigeville Door, a 12th-century sculpture of apostles watching Christ ascend to heaven surrounded by angels.

Other places worth a visit include the exceptional collection of busts of Roman emperors at Musée Saint Raymond on Place St. Sernin, the Roman and medieval sculptures in the Musée des Augustins, 21 Rue de Metz, the beautiful 14th-century Church of the Jacobins and the popular art of the region and the history of Toulouse, at the Musée du Vieux-Toulouse, 7 Rue du May.

See Chinese, Japanese and Indian art at the Musée Georges Labit, 43 Rue des Martyrs de la Liberation. St. Etienne Cathedral. Visit two 16th-century homes, Hotel de Bernuy and Hotel d'Assezat, and take in the view of the city from the tower of the latter.

Check with the Office de Tourisme (Donjon du Capitole, Square Charles de Gaule, 31000 Toulouse) about walking and bus tours of the city.

Obtain the tourist office's brochure describing 16 different one-day bus sightseeing excursions to nearby interesting places. All of these trips start at 08:00 and arrive back in Toulouse between 19:00–20:30.

Consider a tour to these places of interest: the 16th-century Chateau de Saint-Genies-Bellevue; to Cordes, a 13th-century walled town, to see marvelous Gothic houses and the quality arts and crafts sold at 14th Marketplace; Albi, where Toulouse-Lautrec was born in 1864, to see more than 600 of his works; then to Chateau de Latours for tasting Gaillac wine.

Every year, from the end of June to late September, both an international Piano Festival featuring noted soloists and a series of orchestral concerts (jazz to Beethoven) are presented in Toulouse.

Barges can be rented to tour the 17th-century Canal du Midi all the way to the Mediterranean. Visitors can also rent motorboats and rowboats.

Dep. Toulouse (Matabiau)	13:54 (3)	16:24 (2)	16:48 (2)	17:24 (4)	19:10 (2+5)
Arr. Bordeaux (St. Jean)	16:01	18:24	19:01	19:30	21:45

(1) Runs daily, except Sundays and holidays. (2) Light refreshments. (3) TGV. Reservation required. Supplement charged. (4) TGV. Reservation requires. Supplement charged. Runs daily except Saturday. (5) Plus another departure from Toulouse at 21:15 (2), arriving Bordeaux 23:35.

Bordeaux - Tours - Bordeaux   300

All of the Bordeaux–St. Pierre-des-Corps and v.v. trains are TGV, require a reservation, charge a supplement and have light refreshments, unless designated otherwise.

Dep. Bordeaux (St. Jean)	07:08	12:08	
Arr. Tours	09:46	14:58	

• • •

Dep. Tours	13:49 (1)	15:15	19:37 (2)
Arr. Bordeaux (St. Jean)	16:48	17:53	22:21

(1) Fridays only. (2) Daily except Friday.

Dijon - Beaune - Dijon 339

Dep. Dijon	07:34	09:14	11:29	12:30	14:39 (1)	16:07
Arr. Beaune	20 minutes later					

Sights in **Beaune**: The wine capital of Burgundy. Popular for its old houses along narrow, cobbled streets. Famous for Burgundian food: coq au vin, game birds, terrines of veal and pork, snails, salamis, sausages, terrines of salmon and sole. Hotels and restaurants here are booked months in advance.

Visit the many great wineries in this locale, such as Chateau de Meursault, Marche aux Vins and Maison Patriarche. Persuade your hotel to sell you $100 tickets to one of the 17 "grand dinners" at the Clos de Vougeot, sponsored by the Confrerie des Chevaliers de Tastevin. See the priceless art collection in the 15th-century Hotel-Dieu. The other attractions there are the 28 red-canopied and red-curtained beds that were used five centuries ago, the original 15th-century furnishings in the 160-foot-long Paupers' Room, the ancient pharmacy and kitchen, fantastic tapestries and rare pewter.

See the 15th-century tapestries in the Notre Dame Church.

Many hot-air balloon trips are available in this area.

Dep. Beaune	13:25 (1)	15:36	17:14	17:43 (2)	19:22	21:09
Arr. Dijon	20 minutes later					

(1) Runs daily, except Sun. and holidays. (2) Runs Friday and Saturday only. (3) Runs Mon.-Fri., except holidays. (4) Runs Sat., Sun. and holidays.

Dijon - St. Claude - Dijon 375

Dep. Dijon	06:30 (1)	16:49	Dep. St. Claude	16:34 (2)	18:22 (3)
Arr. St. Claude	09:31	20:06	Arr. Dijon	19:45	22:35

(1) Runs Mondays-Saturdays, except holidays. (2) Runs Monday-Thursday. (2) Runs Sundays and holidays only. Change trains in Mouchard.

Sights in **St. Claude**: The 15 manufacturers of smoking pipes who are located here have made this "the pipe capital of France." They produce 1,600,000 briar pipes annually. A walk down Rue du Pre and its extension, Rue du Marche, takes you past many pipe shops to the Pipe Museum, at 1 Rue Gambetta. It's visited by 35,000 people June–September (the only months the museum is open); open 09:30–11:30 and 14:00–19:00.

Across from the Pipe Museum is St. Claude's Cathedral.

The Genod factory, at 13 Fauborg Marcel, allows visitors daily except Saturdays, Sundays and holidays 09:30–11:30 and 14:00–18:00. One of the pipe shops, La Tabatiere at 8 Rue du Pre, has pipes ranging in price from $5 to $1,400.

Limoges - Les Eyzies de Tayac 306

Dep. Limoges	12:54		Dep. Les Eyzies	22:54
Arr. Les Eyzies	14:35		Arr. Limoges	00:58

Sights in **Les Eyzies de Tayac:** This is the prehistoric capital of Europe. The tourist information office and the famous cave paintings are a short walk from the rail station.

Lyon - Annecy - Lyon 367

En route, the train splits. Some cars go to Annecy, others to Grenoble. Be sure to sit in a car marked "Annecy" (pronounced Ahn-see).

Dep. Lyon (Part-Dieu)	06:37	08:11
Arr. Annecy	09:04	10:38

Sights in **Annecy**: This is a beautiful lake resort. See the 12th-century Island palace. The shops in the old quarter.

Dep. Annecy	12:30 (1)	15:54	17:13
Arr. Lyon (Part-Dieu)	14:25	18:12	19:23

(1) Light refreshments.

Lyon - Dijon - Lyon 373

Dep. Lyon (Perrache)	06:41	09:16	-0-
Dep. Lyon (Part-Dieu)	06:51	09:26	12:24 (1)
Arr. Dijon	08:33	11:04	14:05

Sights in **Dijon**: Town Hall, formerly the palace of those swashbuckling dukes of Burgundy and now one of the richest museums in France. The Church of Notre Dame. The

13th-century Cathedral of St. Benigne archaeological museum. The Palace of Justice. The Magnin Museum. The 14th-century Chartreuse de Champmol, with its famous chapel portrait and Moses Fountain. Rude Museum.

Don't fail to have lunch in Dijon, France's food and wine capital.

Dep. Dijon	12:17	15:35 (1)	17:05 (2)	19:17	20:47
Arr. Lyon (Part-Dieu)	13:58	17:07	18:45	20:57	22:28
Arr. Lyon (Perrache)	-0-	-0-	18:56	21::08	22:39

(1) Light refreshments. (2) Runs daily, except Fridays.

Lyon - Geneva   372

There are many scenic canyons on this ride.

Dep. Lyon (Perrache)	07:30 (1)	09:24 (1)	12:16 (1)
Dep. Lyon (Part-Dieu)	07:39	09:33	12:26
Arr. Geneva (Cornavin)	09:40	11:26	14:14

* * *

Dep. Geneva (Cornavin)	16:24	19:28 (1)	21:54 (1)
Arr. Lyon (Part-Dieu)	17:47	20:55	23:46
Arr. Lyon (Perrache)	18:12	21:20	-0-

(1) Light refreshments.

Lyon - Grenoble - Lyon   341

Dep. Lyon (Part-Dieu)	07:10 (1)	08:17 (2)	10:15 (2)	12:27	14:15
Arr. Grenoble	08:31	09:41	11:38	13:50	15:44

Sights in **Grenoble**: The information office outside the rail station offers maps, guides and city bus tickets. See the monumental Calder sculpture at the rail station. The very rich (Utrillo, Picasso, Rubens) art museum in the 16th-century Palace of Justice. The contemporary art museum's collection of Delaunay, Picasso, Matisse and many surrealists.

Fine paintings in the Musée des Beaux Arts at Place de Verdun (Corot, Renoir, Monet, Roualt, Picasso, Utrillo). The Stendhal Museum, devoted to Grenoble's native son and greatest writer, whose real name was Henri Beyle. The Museum of the Resistance, in the house where Stendhal was born on Rue Jean-Jacques Rousseau. At the Municipal Library, see the "Catholicon" (printed by Gutenberg in 1460), Stendhal's manuscripts, and more historic papers.

The geometrical gardens and three fountains in Place Victor Hugo, Grenoble's prettiest square, locale of expensive shops and sidewalk cafes. The Natural History Museum, in the

Jardine des Plantes. The 17th-century Church of St. Laurent. The City Gardens.

Take the cable car ride up to Guy Pape Park for a marvelous view of the city below and the fields surrounding Grenoble. While at the top, visit the military museum in the 19th-century fort, the Bastille, and the Auto Museum.

Walk back to Grenoble, downhill, through the Jardine des Dauphines.

Another walk on the way down leads to a collection of Alpine artifacts (antique cradles, beds, chests, backpacks, school rooms) at the Musée Dauphinois, in a 17th-century cloister.

If you plan to spend a day or two in Grenoble, there's a scenic trip on a private railway that's easy to make from here. La Mure's electric trains, operated by Chemin de fer de la Mure, run daily from mid-May to mid-September and on weekends from mid-April to mid-May and mid-September to mid-October. Leave Grenoble at 08:42 for St. Georges de Commiers. You'll arrive there at 09:02. At 09:45 pick up the train to La Mure. The last train leave La Mure at 17:00, arriving in St. Georges at 18:30. The next train leaving for Grenoble is 20:38, leaving enough time to explore St. Georges or have an early dinner. Arrival in Grenoble is 21:01. The *Cook* schedules for this trip are 364 and 394. The La Mure-St. Georges portion of the trip is not covered by the Eurailpass. For the latest fares contact Chemin de fer de la Mure, 38450 St. Georges de Commiers, France. From the States, dial 011 33 04 76 72 57 11, fax 011 33 04 76 72 47 43. Within France, drop the 011 33 0.

Dep. Grenoble	13:05	16:00	16:58	17:25	18:14 (4)
Arr. Lyon (Part-Dieu)	14:28	17:26	18:19	19:03 (3)	19:32

• • •

Dep. Grenoble	19:15	21:06	21:55 (5)
Arr. Lyon (Part-Dieu)	20:45	22:59 (3)	23:23

(1) Runs Monday–Friday, except holidays. (2) Runs daily, except Sundays and holidays. (3) Arrives at Lyon's Perrache rail station. (4) Runs daily, except Saturday. (5) Runs Sunday only.

Lyon - Marseille - Lyon   350

Dep. Lyon (Perrache)	08:35	-0- (1)		
Dep. Lyon (Part Dieu)	-0-	09:57		
Arr. Marseille (St. Ch.)	11:59	12:23		

• • •

Dep. Marseille (St. Ch.)	15:54 (2)	16:59 (3)	18:01 (2)	19:00 (4+5)
Arr. Lyon (Part Dieu)	18:34	20:08	20:38	-0-
Arr. Lyon (Perrache)	-0-	-0-	-0-	22:22

(1) TGV. Reservation required. Supplement charged. Runs Monday-Thursday, except holidays. Restaurant car. (2) TGV. Reservation required. Supplement charged. Light refreshment. (3) Light refreshments. (4) Arrives at Lyon's Perrache rail station. (5) Plus another Marseille departure at 21:36 (4), arriving Lyon 01:24.

Lyon - Paris - Lyon 340

All of these trains are TGV, require reservation, charge a supplement and have a restaurant car or light refreshments.

Dep. Lyon (Per.)	05:48 (1)	06:18 (1)	06:48 (1)	07:49	08:44 (2)
Dep. Lyon (P-D)	06:00	06:30	07:00	08:00	09:00
Arr. Paris (Lyon)	08:16	08:34	09:04	10:10	11:04

• • •

Dep. Paris (Lyon)	14:00	15:00	16:48 (3)	17:00	17:30 (4+5)
Arr. Lyon (P-D)	16:04	17:04	18:52	19:04	19:34
Arr. Lyon (Per.)	16:14	17:15	19:03	19:15	19:48

(1) Runs Monday–Friday, except holidays. (2) Runs daily, except Sundays and holidays. (3) Runs Friday only to mid-July and from mid-August. (4) Runs Monday-Friday, except holidays to mid-July and from mid-August. (5) Plus other departures from Paris at 19:30 (1), 20:00 and 20:48, arriving Lyon (P-D) 21:40, 22:04 and 22:52.

Lyon - Tours - Lyon 290

Dep. Lyon (Perrache)	06:35 (1)	-0-
Dep. Lyon (Part-Dieu)	06:45	09:11 (2)
Arr. Tours	11:42	14:13

• • •

Dep. Tours	15:47 (2)	18:21 (3)
Arr. Lyon (Part-Dieu)	20:48	23:16
Arr. Lyon (Perrache)	20:58	23:26

(1) Runs Monday and Saturday only. (2) Light refreshments. (3) Runs Friday and Sunday. Light refreshments.

Lyon - Vienne - Lyon 350

Dep. Lyon (Perrache)	07:57 (1)	12:04 (1)	12:24 *(plus frequent times through the day)*
Arr. Vienne	18-22 minutes later		

Sights in **Vienne**: Many good Roman ruins. The Temple of Augustus and Livia, a large amphitheater, and the pyramid which once marked the center of a Roman coliseum. Ancient jewels and bronze and ceramic relics on exhibit at the Museum of Fine Arts. Try to dine at one of the world's most famous restaurants, Pyramide, open daily except Tuesday and closed November through mid-December.

Dep. Vienne	13:59	16:58	17:48 (1)	18:29 (2)	21:45 (3)	22:00
Arr. Lyon (Perrache)	18-22 minutes later					

(1) Runs Monday–Friday, except holidays. (2) Runs daily except Saturdays. (3) Runs Sundays and holidays only.

Marseille - Aix-en-Provence   362

Dep. Marseille (St. Ch.)	07:49	13:16	17:08
Arr. Aix-en-Provence	35-40 minutes later		

Sights in **Aix-en-Provence**: The remarkable Vasarely Museum; the 18th-century quarter of the city.

Dep. Aix-en-Provence	11:31	16:23	20:44
Arr. Marseille (St. Ch.)	35-40 minutes later		

Marseille - Antibes - Marseille   360

Dep. Marseille (St. Ch.)	09:35	12:11	13:16
Arr. Antibes	11:49	14:19	15:30

Sights in **Antibes**: See notes under "Avignon–Antibes"

Dep. Antibes	14:10	14:35	16:25 (1)	18:31	20:41
Arr. Marseille (St. Ch)	16:18	16:45	18:38	21:35	23:01

(1) Light refreshments.

Marseille - Cassis - Marseille   SNCF timetable

Dep. Marseille (St. Ch.)	08:45	09:50	11:41	12:15	14:57
Arr. Cassis	30 minutes later				

Sights in **Cassis:** A fishing village and beach resort. There are many small restaurants here offering "the catch of the day" prepared so as to please any gourmand. The activities in Cassis are topless sunbathing, sailing, swimming, snorkeling, diving and fishing.

The municipal Casino is open daily 15:00-20:00. The "calanques" (coves) of **Port Miou**, **Port Pin** and **En-Vau** can be visited by foot or by boat.

Dep. Cassis	12:05	13:05	13:43	14:20	16:18 (1)
Arr. Marseille (St. Ch.)	30 minutes later				

(1) Plus other departures from Cassis at 17:12, 18:03, 19:17, 20:47 and 21:59.

Nice - Antibes - Nice   360

Dep. Nice	Frequent times from 05:18 to 00:20
Arr. Antibes	16–30 minutes later

• • •

Dep. Antibes	Frequent times from 05:41 to 00:42
Arr. Nice	16–30 minutes later

Nice - Cannes (and Grasse) - Nice   360

Dep. Nice	Frequent times from 05:18 to 00:20
Arr. Cannes	40 minutes later

Sights in **Cannes:** Stroll along Promenade de la Croisette to see the beautiful beach and splendid yachts, all the way to the Palm Beach Casino. Take boat rides on the Bay of Cannes or to the **St. Honorat** and **St. Marguerite** islands. On the latter, you can visit the prison that held the Man in the Iron Mask.

There is also a short boat trip to **Lerins**, where the 5th-century Monastery of the Cistercians is located. It is said that St. Patrick began his evangelical tour of Europe from there. Visit the 10th-century castle, Castrum Canois, on a mountain that overlooks Cannes. It houses the Museum of Mediterranean Civilization.

La Napoule is a few miles west of Cannes. The attraction there is the Chateau de la Napoule Art Foundation, one of the finest art galleries on the Riviera, open daily except Tuesday, with guided tours in the afternoon.

Sights in **Grasse:** Take the 50-minute bus ride from Cannes' rail station to nearby Grasse, the perfume capital of France. Many of the 35 perfume factories there are open to visitors. One of them, Parfumerie Fragonard, is only a five-minute walk from the Grasse bus terminal. Near it is a Perfume Museum. The nearby hillsides are covered with wildflowers and jasmine every Spring.

Dep. Cannes	Frequent times from 05:27 to 00:29
Arr. Nice	40 minutes later

Nice - Marseille - Nice   360

These trains have light refreshments, unless designated otherwise.

Dep. Nice	05:55	06:16 (1)	08:15	09:01	10:26 (2)
Arr. Marseille (St. Ch.)	08:21	08:48	10:47	11:29	12:45

• • •

Dep. Marseille (St. Ch.)	13:16	15:27	15:55	16:50	17:37 (3)
Arr. Nice	15:43	17:54	18:16	19:07	20:04

(1) No light refreshments. (2) Plus other Nice departures at 11:41, arriving Marseille 14:08 and 13:05, arriving 15:38. (3) Plus other Marseille departures at 18:40, 20:11 and 22:55, arriving Nice 21:32, 22:37 and 00:46.

Nice - Monaco (Monte Carlo) - Nice   360

Dep. Nice	Frequent times from 06:07 to 00:10
Arr. Monaco	20–25 minutes later

• • •

Dep. Monaco	Frequent times from 05:20 to 23:55
Arr. Nice	20–25 minutes later

Nice - Saint Raphael - Nice   360

Dep. Nice	Frequent times from 05:50 to 22:32
Arr. St. Raphael	60 minutes later

Sights in **Saint Raphael**: An excellent Riviera beach resort. Good golfing, hiking and sailing here. There is a gambling casino.

Dep. St. Raphael	Frequent times from 05:57 to 23:55
Arr. Nice	60 minutes later

Paris - Angers - Paris   280

All of these trains are TGV, require a reservation, charge a supplement and have light refreshments, unless designated otherwise.

Dep. Paris (Mont.)	07:50 (1)	08:55	09:50	11:25
Arr. Angers (St. L.)	09:18	10:25	11:25	13:01

Sights in **Angers**: Located on Promenade du Bout du Monde (Walkway of the World's End), is the massive 13th-century castle (Chateau d'Angers), with its 17 towers. It houses the world's finest collection of medieval and Renaissance tapestries. Don't fail to see the supreme tapestry, "The Apocalypse." It was 430 feet long and about 20 feet high when it was woven in the 14th century. Unbelievably produced in less than seven years. What we can view today is 350 feet long and 15 feet high 8,600 square feet. What remains are 67 of the original 84 panels and four of the original six scenes showing a bearded figure sitting on a stone dais.

The Angers tapestry illustrates the text of the Book of Revelation, complete with the four horsemen (the last of which is death), followed by hell.

It is in the second half of the tapestry that we are shown the ultimate destruction (Judgment Day): shipwrecks, rains of fire, many-headed beasts (including a dragon that has seven heads and 10 horns), the fall of Babylon, the extinction of both the sun and the moon, and the descent of Jerusalem from heaven to earth, where it becomes the eternal dwelling of those who are blessed. The miracle of the tapestry is its survival.

Dep. Angers (St. L.)	12:01	14:11	15:16	17:07	18:08 (2)
Arr. Paris (Mont.)	13:35	15:50	16:50	18:45	19:50

(1) Operates late August to mid-July. Runs daily, except Sundays and holidays. (2) Plus other Angers departures at 19:27 (3), 19:48, 20:54 (4) and 21:12. (3) Runs Sundays only. (4) Runs Monday-Friday, except holidays.

Paris - Basel - Paris   380

Dep. Paris (Est)	07:30 (1)	08:41 (2)	11:40 (3)	13:35 (4)	16:59 (2+5)
Arr. Basel (SNCF)	12:11	14:05	16:33	18:36	21:40

•   •   •

Dep. Basel (SNCF)	00:28 (6)	08:23 (7)	12:53 (3)	16:48 (8)	18:30 (2)
Arr. Paris (Est)	06:46	13:13	18:14	21:36	23:49

(1) Supplement charged. Runs daily, except Sunday. Light refreshments. (2) Supplement charged. Light refreshments. (3) Light refreshments. (4) Runs Monday-Friday, except holidays. Light refreshments. (5) Plus another Paris departure at 22:38 (6) arriving Basel 04:56. (6) Carries first- and second-class sleepers, second-class couchettes and second-class coaches. (7) Supplement payable. Restaurant car. (8) Runs daily except Saturday. Supplement payable. Light refreshments.

Paris - Bayeux - Paris   270

All of these trains have light refreshments, unless designated otherwise.

Dep. Paris (St. Laz.)	09:08 (1)	12:25 (2)
Arr. Bayeux	11:16	14:27

Sights in **Bayeux**: The world-famous 230-foot-long, 20-inch-wide embroidered tapestry, sewn by Queen Mathilda (wife of William the Conqueror) and her friends for 10 years after the 1066 Battle of Hastings, both to commemorate the Norman conquest of England and her husband becoming king of England. On public view in Bayeux since 1077, it consists of 58 scenes that include 626 people, 37 ships, 33 buildings and 730 animals while also depicting 11th-century life.

The battle waged by Duke William of Normandy involved transporting 10,000 Normans across the English Channel in 400 ships.

One of the world's greatest works of art, "Queen Mathilda's Tapestry" has been exhibited daily 09:00–19:00 (except Christmas and New Year's Day) in a museum which opened in 1983 after two years of construction. As many as 2,300 people enter the museum on some days, including hordes of schoolchildren that begin arriving at 10:00.

The tapestry is mounted on a horseshoe-shaped frame, sealed inside unbreakable glass. Its humidity and temperature are regulated. Except for the light directed at the tapestry, the rest of the hall is entirely dark. A 15-minute description can be heard over earphones in many languages.

Other local attractions are the World War II Battle of Normandy Museum (next to the British Military Cemetery) and the three-spired Notre Dame Cathedral. There are views of a magnificent seascape from its high center tower.

Dep. Bayeux	15:00 (2)	18:19 (2)	19:37 (2)	20:56 (3)
Arr. Paris (St. Laz.)	17:02	20:51	21:45	23:27

(1) Runs Saturdays, Sundays and holidays. Light refreshments. (2) Runs Monday-Friday, except holidays. (3) runs Sundays and holidays only. Light refreshments.

Paris - Bayeux - Caen - Paris 270

As shown below, it is possible to combine a visit from Paris to both Bayeux and Caen in one day.

Dep. Paris (St. Lazare)	06:54 (1)	09:08 (2)	Dep. Bayeux	17:20 (3)
Arr. Bayeux	09:25	11:16	Arr. Caen	17:40

Sights in **Bayeux**: See notes above.

Sights in **Caen**: Although much was destroyed here during the 1944 Normandy invasion battle, numerous historical buildings have been preserved. Hotel d'Escoville, the "Chateau." The 11th-century Abbaye aux Hommes and Abbaye aux Dames. The Museum. The church of Saint Sauveur. The Palace of Justice. Try these regional specialties: tripe, berlingots, cider, Calvados.

Take bus #12 from the rail station three miles to the "Normandy Memorial and Museum for Peace." It documents both the 1944 Battle of Normandy and the resulting Allied march from here to Berlin with original war films, photos, huge animated maps and vivid re-creations of battle scenes. Open daily except the first two weeks of January. The hours during June, July and August are 09:00-22:00. During the rest of the year: 09:00-19:00. The last entry allowed is 75 minutes before closing time.

Dep. Caen	18:49 (4)	19:40 (5)	20:27 (5)	21:31 (5)
Arr. Paris (St. Laz.)	20:49	21:36	22:34	23:27

Here are schedules leaving more time in Caen.

Dep. Paris (St. Laz.)	07:12 (6)	08:40 (1)	09:08 (2)	10:43 (8)
Arr. Caen	08:56	10:45	10:57	12:27

• • •

Dep. Caen	14:24 (6)	17:50 (3)	18:39 (1)	19:55 (1+7)
Arr. Paris (St. Laz.)	16:33	19:35	20:51	21:45

(1) Runs Monday-Friday, except holidays. (2) Operates Saturdays, Sundays and holidays. (3) Runs Monday-Thursday. (4) Sundays only. (5) Runs Sundays and holidays. (6) Operates Monday through Friday. (7) Plus other Caen departures at 20:27 (5) and 21:31 (5), arriving Paris (St. Laz.) 22:34 and 23:27.

Paris - Blois - Paris 296

Dep. Paris (Aust.)	07:32 (1)	09:49 (2)	11:58
Arr. Blois	09:01	10:39	12:45

Sights in **Blois**: St. Louis Cathedral. Church of Saint Nicolas. Church of Saint Vincent. Church of Saint Saturin, and its curious cemetery. The Alluye Manor.

Visit the Castle of Blois, the palace of Catherine de Medici during the 16th century. From late March to late September, a sound-and-light show is presented there every evening. The other two fine Chateaux here are Chambord and Bracieux (Herbault-en-Sologne). For lunch in Blois, try the regional specialties: Rillettes, Loire fish, great local wines and cheeses.

Dep. Blois	13:40 (3)	15:43	18:53 (2)	19:37 (4)	20:20 (5)	21:07 (6)
Arr. Paris (Aust.)	15:18	17:29	20:27	21:39	22:03	22:40

(1) Light refreshments. (2) Runs late June to late August. (3) Rims Saturdays only. (4) Runs Sundays and holidays only. (5) Runs Saturday only. Operates to late June and from late August. (6) Runs Sunday only.

Paris - Tours - Paris 295

Here are schedules for having more time in Tours than when combining a trip from Paris to both Blois and Tours.

All of these trains are TGV, require a reservation, charge a supplement and have light refreshments, unless designated otherwise. The trains travel at 186 mph on some portions of this route.

Dep. Paris (Mont.)	07:00	07:40 (1)	09:00	10:45	12:15
Arr. Tours	08:11	08:49	10:05	11:51	13:25

• • •

Dep. Tours	13:02	14:37	16:06	17:14 (2)	17:45
Arr. Paris (Mont.)	14:10	15:45	17:15	18:25	18:55

Dep. Tours	19:47 (3)	20:22 (1)	20:59 (3)	21:57 (1)	22:07 (3)
Arr. Paris (Mont.)	20:55	21:35	22:10	23:05	23:20

(1) Runs daily, except Sundays and holidays. (2) Runs daily, except Saturday. (3) Runs Sunday only.

Paris - Bordeaux - Bayonne - Biarritz - Paris   302

All of these trains are TGV, require reservation, charge a supplement and have light refreshments, unless designated otherwise.

Dep. Paris (Mont.)	07:00	08:05 (1)	10:00		
Arr. Bordeaux (St. Jean)	10:31	11:03	13:02		
Arr. Bayonne	12:14	-0-	14:43		
Arr. Biarritz	12 minutes after arriving Bayonne				

• • •

Dep. Biarritz	14:52	-0-	16:34 (2)	17:51 (2)	18:56 (2)
Dep. Bayonne	15:02	-0-	16:51	18:01	19:06
Dep. Bordeaux (St. Jean)	16:37	17:25	18:18	19:38	20:40
Arr. Paris (Mont.)	19:55	20:30	21:30	23:05	23:45

(1) Runs daily, except Sundays and holidays. (2) Runs Sunday only.

Paris - Bourges - Paris   315

Dep. Paris (Austerlitz)	07:21 (1+2)	09:06 (2)
Arr. Vierzon	08:41	10:44
Arr. Bourges	09:12	11:19

Sights in **Bourges**: A key gateway to the chateau area of the Loire Valley, Bourges is a living history museum.

The beautifully preserved stained glass windows in the Cathedral of St.-Etienne are a dazzling play of red against magenta and deep blue, located in a narrow hall that is 387 feet long, 136 feet wide, and an amazing 130 feet high. "Spellbinding" is the only way to describe these windows that depict the Bible's great morality stories. The cathedral's restored 17th-century organ is the best one of France. The l'Archeveche Garden is near the cathedral. See the medieval houses below the cathedral on a stroll along the town's winding, cobbled streets.

Visit the 15th-century Palace of Jacques Couer, open daily 9:00–12:00 and 14:00–18:00 (closes at 17:00 November–March). See the collection of Roman artifacts and antique ceramics at the Musée de Berry in the 15th-century Hotel Cujas (4 Rue des Arenes), open daily except Tuesday 10:00–12:00 and 14:00–18:00 (Sunday: only 14:00–18:00).

The Museum of Decorative Arts in the 16th-century Hotel Lallemant (6 Rue Bourbonnoux) is open daily except Tuesday 10:00–11:30 and 14:00–16:30. The Municipal Garden and the garden at the City Hall, formerly the residence of a 17th-century archbishop.

Dep. Bourges	17:46 (2)	18:35 (3)	19:52 (4)
Arr. Vierzon	18:09	19:06	20:22

Change trains

Dep. Vierzon	18:28	19:25 (3)	20:26 (5)
Arr. Paris (Austerlitz)	20:20	21:33	22:22

(1) Runs daily, except Sun. and holidays. (2) Direct train. No change in Vierzon. (3) Runs Monday-Friday, except holidays. (4) Runs Friday and Sunday. (5) Runs Sunday only.

Paris - Brussels - Paris   18

Dep. Paris (Nord)	07:40 (1)	10:40 (1)	14:40 (1)
Arr. Brussels (Midi)	09:38	12:38	16:38

• • •

Dep. Brussels (Midi)	14:07 (1)	15:07 (1)	16:02 (1)	17:07 (1)	18:07 (2)	19:05 (1+3)
Arr. Paris (Nord)	16:05	17:05	18:05	19:05	20:05	21:05

(1) Thalys high-speed train. Reservation required. Supplement charged. Light refreshments. (2) Daily except Saturdays. Operates daily late June to early September. (3) Plus additional departures from Brussels at 20:07 and 21:07, arriving in Paris 22:05 and 23:05.

Paris - Chantilly - Paris   SNCF Timetable

Dep. Paris (Nord)	Frequent times from 06:31 to 23:01
Arr. Chantilly	30–40 minutes later

Sights in **Chantilly:** (Pronounced "Shawnteeyee") The 16th-century castle, actually two chateaux, has been called "the most beautiful house in France." It stands in a lake and is surrounded by magnificent gardens and a large forest.

Of the two routes from the rail station to the castle, the shortest distance (and most pleasant stroll) is to walk 30 minutes via a trail through tall trees and then across the large lawn infield of the racecourse, locale during the first two weeks of June every year for a very elegant horse-racing meet.

The two attractions are the chateau's Conde Museum and its Living Museum of the Horse. Among the fine objects exhibited in the Conde are priceless collections of art spanning 1,000 years; 13,000 books beginning with 10th-century manuscripts, paintings (Delacroix, Fouquet, Ingres, Rembrandt, Clouet, Raphael, Rosselli, Greuze) and furniture, all on an estate of 17,000 acres that contain forests, farms, a racetrack with stadium, and a golf course.

Between April 1 and September 30, the chateau is open daily except Tuesday 10:30–18:00 (until 17:00 the rest of the year).

Between April 1 and October 31, the Grand Stables are open daily except Tuesday 10:30–17:00 (13:00–17:00 the rest of the year). Riders wearing 18th-century costumes perform at 12:00, 15:00 and 17:00 April 1 to October 31 (at 14:30 and 16:00 the rest of the year).

See the spectacle of the Tuesday and Saturday fox hunts.

| Dep. Chantilly | Frequent times from 05:52 to 23:16 |
| Arr. Paris (Nord) | 30–40 minutes later |

Paris - Chartres - Paris 276

| Dep. Paris (Montpar.) | 07:01 (1) 08:56 (2) 09:24 (3) 09:57 (4) 11:14 12:59 (3) |
| Arr. Chartres | 50–60 minutes later |

Sights in **Chartres:** The main attraction is the magnificent 13th-century cathedral, third largest in the world, exceeded in size only by St. Peter's and Canterbury. Its stained-glass is unrivaled. Open daily 07:30–19:30, it is a short stroll from the rail station.

Also see the ancient process that was used to make the cathedral's stained glass, at the Stained Glass Center, next to the cathedral, open daily except Monday 10:00–18:00.

A city map and details on a self-guided walking tour of Chartres is available at the Tourist Office, across from the cathedral. The tourist office is open Monday–Saturday 09:30–12:30 and 14:00–18:30, and on Sunday 10:00–12:00 and 15:00–19:00 (closed Sundays, November–April).

Malcom Miller has conducted his world-renowned English-language tour of the cathedral since 1958 (at 12:00 and 14:45). He usually offers two different tours.

Other sights: the Former Collegiate Church, the Church of St. Aignan, the Church of St. Aignan, the Church of St. Martin-au-Val and the Church of St. Foy.

Picassiete's Garden was built by a street sweeper out of pieces of garbage (broken bottles, enameled tiles, stones)…similar to Watts Tower in Los Angeles. A bus goes within a few blocks of it, two miles north from the center of Chartres.

| Dep. Chartres | 11:04 14:03 15:13 (2) 16:43 18:45 |
| Arr. Paris (Montpar.) | 50–60 minutes later |

(1) Runs daily, except Saturday and holidays. (2) Operates early July to early September. (3) Runs Saturdays only, early July to late August. (4) Runs daily, late June to late August.

Paris - Cologne (Koln) - Paris 25

Both of these trains charge a supplement and have a restaurant car.

| Dep. Paris (Nord) | 07:25 | Dep. Cologne | 17:08 |
| Arr. Cologne | 12:51 | Arr. Paris (Nord) | 22:35 |

Paris - Compiegne - Paris   255

| Dep. Paris (Nord) | 07:07 (1) | 07:25 (2) | 12:16 (1) |
| Arr. Compiegne | 50–60 minutes later | | |

Sights in **Compiegne**: Town Hall. Vivenel Museum. Hotel Dieu. The 7th-century Beauregard Tower. The "Clairere de l'Armistice" in Compeigne Forest, where Marshal Foch signed the 1918 armistice for France…and Adolph Hitler received the June 21, 1940 surrender of France.

Beautiful furnishings and decorations can be seen in the first drawing room, family drawing room, Emperor's library, music room, Empress's bedroom, a series of dining rooms, the hunting gallery, and the ornate ballroom at the Chateau built by Louis XV in the late 18th century.

| Dep. Compeigne | 10:35 | 13:13 | 19:18 | 20:12 (3) | 21:13 (4) |
| Arr. Paris (Nord) | 50–60 minutes later | | | | |

(1) Runs daily, except Sundays and holidays. (2) Restaurant car. (3) Runs Sunday only. (4) Runs Sundays and holidays only.

Paris - Dijon - Paris   370

All of these trains are TGV, require reservation, charge a supplement and have a restaurant car or light refreshments, unless designated otherwise.

Dep. Paris (Lyon)	07:18	10:24 (1)	12:18	
Arr. Dijon	08:58	12:08	13:59	
		• • •		
Dep. Dijon	14:49	18:11	20:02	22:38 (2)
Arr. Paris (Lyon)	16:30	19:57	21:42	00:18

(1) Runs Monday–Friday, except holidays. (2) Runs Friday and Sunday.

Paris - Evreux - Paris   270

| Dep. Paris (St. Laz.) | 08:07 | 09:18 (1) | 10:10 (2) | 11:00 (3) | 12:32 (4) |
| Arr. Evreux | 09:13 | 10:26 | 11:06 | 12:09 | 13:36 |

Sights in **Evreux**: The Cathedral of Notre Dame, a jumble of architectural styles due to having been built over a period of six centuries: from the 11th to the 17th. Goldsmith work in the Church of Stain Taurin. The ancient Eveche. The tower of The Clock. For lunch, try the Norman cuisine.

Dep. Evreux	12:16 (5)	14:32 (1+6)	15:36 (5)	17:56 (4)	18:04 (2+6)
Arr. Paris (St. Laz.)	13:12	15:29	16:33	18:53	19:01

(1) Runs Saturday only. (2) Runs Saturdays, Sundays and holidays. (3) Runs daily except Saturday. (4) Runs Monday-Friday, except holidays. (5) Runs Monday-Friday, except holidays. Light refreshments. (6) Light refreshments.

Paris - Fontainebleau - Paris   370

Dep. Paris (Lyon)	Frequent times from 06:02 to 22:45
Arr. Fontainebleau-Avon	40 minutes later

Take the 10-minute bus ride from the rail station to the palace, open 08:00 to sunset, daily except Tuesdays.

Sights in **Fontainebleau:** It is advisable to plan on an entire day here for seeing the magnificent 16th-century palace that many kings of France occupied, and the parks and gardens surrounding it. There are guided tours of the palace 10:00–12:30 and 14:00–18:00. Many visitors bring a picnic lunch.

Dep. Fontainebleau-Avon	Frequent times from 05:24 to 22:37
Arr. Paris (Lyon)	30–40 minutes later

Paris - Granville - Paris   275

Dep. Paris (Montpar.)	07:06 (1)	08:18 (2)
Arr. Granville	10:39	12:07

Sights in **Granville:** This is a lively seaside town near Le-Mont-Saint-Michel, with remarkably high tides and sandy beaches. The marina here can accommodate 1,000 yachts. The Regional Nautical Center offers instructions in sailing and wind surfing.

The aquarium (with exhibits of sea life, shells and mineral stones) is along the walk to the lighthouse. The **Chausey Islands** can be seen from the shore, and there is daily boat service to them.

Visit the Church of Notre Dame. Try your luck in the Casino.

Dep. Granville	14:09 (1)	14:40 (3)	18:14 (4)	19:01 (4)
Arr. Paris (Montpar.)	17:40	18:20 + 18:31	21:56	22:50

(1) Runs Monday–Friday, except holidays. (2) Runs Saturdays, Sundays and holidays. Light refreshments. (3) Runs Saturday and Sunday/holidays. (4) Runs Sundays only. Light refreshments.

Paris - Limoges - Paris   310

Dep. Paris (Aust.)	07:02 (1)	07:21 (2)	09:06 (3)	10:18 (3)	10:21(4)
Arr. Limoges	10:40	10:15	12:36	13:11	13:11

• • •

Dep. Limoges	14:41 (5)	17:01 (6)	18:30 (7)	19:49 (8)	20:57 (9)
Arr. Paris (Aust.)	18:12	20:11	21:20	23:04	23:49

(1) Runs Sunday only to late June and from early Sept. (2) Runs Monday-Saturday. (3) Runs late June to late August. (4) Runs late to June and from early Sept. (5) Runs daily to late June and from early Sept. Light refreshments. (6) Runs daily except Saturdays. Light refreshments. (7) Runs daily except Saturdays. Supplement payable. Light refreshments. (8) Runs Sunday only. Light refreshments. (9) Runs Friday and Sunday. Light refreshment.

Paris - Lyon - Paris   340

All of these trains are TGV, require reservation, charge a supplement and have a restaurant car or light refreshments.

Dep. Paris (Lyon)	06:10 (1)	06:30 (1)	07:00 (2)	07:30	08:00 (1)
Arr. Lyon (P.D.)	08:20	08:34	09:04	09:41	10:04

Dep. Lyon (P.D.)	14:00 (3)	15:00	16:00	17:00	17:30 (1)
Arr. Paris (Lyon)	16:04	17:04	18:04	19:10	19:37

Dep. Lyon (P.D.)	18:00	18:48	20:00	20:30 (4)	21:45 (4)
Arr. Paris (Lyon)	20:04	20:58	22:04	22:34	23:55

(1) Runs Monday–Friday, except holidays. (2) Runs Monday-Saturday. (3) Operates Saturdays, Sundays and holidays. (4) Runs Sunday only.

Paris - Nancy - Paris   390

Dep. Paris (Est)	06:50 (1)	07:50 (2)	08:18 (3)	10:50 (4)
Arr. Nancy	09:34	10:27	11:23	13:31

Sights in **Nancy:** The Ducal Palace, with its museum of this city's 2,000-year history at 64 Grande Rue is open daily except Tuesdays and holidays 10:00–12:00 and 14:00–18:00. Its exhibits include a room on the history of Jews in this region.

See the Church of the Cordeliers, the 14th-century Porte de la Craffe, oldest monument in Nancy, the wrought-iron grillwork and fountains in Place Stanislas or the Lovely 18th-century houses on Place de la Carriere.

Visit the model rooms of early 20th-century interior decor at the Musée de l'Ecole, 36–38 Rue Sergent Blandan, open daily, except Tuesdays and holidays. April–September: 10:00–12:00 and 14:00–18:00. October–March: 10:00–12:00 and 14:00–17:00. Much work by Emile Galle, Jacques Gruber, Eugene Vallin and other Art Nouveau artisans is exhibited there: glass bowls, tables, fireplaces, tooled leather wall coverings, inlaid bed headboards and footboards, inlaid chests, Galle's fantastic glass mushroom lamp, and the extraordinary Louis Majorelle grand piano, inlaid with irises and waterlillies.

Majorelle's house, a few blocks away at 1 Rue Majorelle (open Monday-Friday except holidays 8:30–12:00 and 13:00–18:00), is well worth visiting to see the exterior and interior ceramic work and the Gruber stained glass windows there.

Visitors can also see examples of Galle and Daum vases, lamps and other glass objects at the Musée Beaux-Arts, Place Stanislas, open daily except Tuesdays and holidays 10:00–12:00 and 14:00–18:00.

Pepiniere is a 57-acre park with gardens, a small zoo, and a restaurant.

Dep. Nancy	13:37 (2)	14:40 (3)	15:52 (5)	17:22 (6)	18:29 (7+8)
Arr. Paris (Est)	16:23	17:55	18:33	20:06	21:09

(1) Supplement charged. Operates early September to early July. Runs Mon-Fir, except holidays. Light refreshments. (2) Supplement charged. Restaurant car. (3) Light refreshments. (4) Runs daily, except Sundays and holidays. Light refreshments. (5) Runs Monday–Friday, except holidays. Light refreshments. (6) Runs daily, except Saturday. (7) Supplement payable. Light refreshments. Runs daily except Saturday, to early July and from early Sept. (8) Plus another Nancy departure at 19:36 (2), arriving Paris 22:22.

Paris - Nantes - Paris 284

All of these trains are TGV, require reservation, charge a supplement and have light refreshments.

Dep. Paris (Mont.)	06:45 (1)	07:15 (2)	08:55	10:55 (3)
Arr. Nantes	08:47	09:33	11:05	12:59

Sight in **Nantes**: See notes under "Bordeaux–Nantes"

Dep. Nantes	12:16 (3)	14:44 (3)	16:25 (4)	17:25 (3)	19:06 (4+5)
Arr. Paris (Mont.)	14:25	17:00	18:45	19:30	21:25

(1) Operates late August to early July. Runs Monday–Friday, except holidays. (2) Early July to late August: runs daily, except Sundays and holidays. Late August to early July: runs Monday–Friday, except holidays. (3) Operates late June to late August. (4) Runs Monday-Saturday. (5) Plus other departures from Nantes at 19:53 (6), 20:02 (6) and 21:41 (6). (6) Runs Sunday only.

Paris - Neuilly - Paris (Paris Metro/RATP)

Take the Metro from Paris' Champs-Elysees station. **Neuilly** is the fourth stop.

The attraction here is The Museum of Women at 12 Rue de Centre, open daily except Sunday 14:30–18:00. The one guided tour starts at 15:00. Among the exhibits is the lavishly decorated bed used by France's most famous prostitute during the reign of Napoleon III, the Marchioness de La Paiva. While the bed cost her 10,000 gold francs, she recovered this expense quickly. She charged her clients 10,000 gold francs a night.

There is also the corset that Marie Antoinette wore in prison while waiting to be guillotined, a bronze cast of ballet dancer-choreographer Katherine Dunham's feet, a silk jacket that belonged to the last empress of China, a letter written by Nobel prize-winner Marie Curie, and many other curiosities.

Paris - Reims - Paris 392

Dep. Paris (Est)	07:16 (1)	08:04 (2)	10:58 (3)	12:18
Arr. Reims	08:55	09:36	12:31	13:52

Sights in **Reims**: See the 13th-century Cathedral of Notre Dame (open daily 07:30–19:30), longer and higher than Notre Dame in Paris. Most of this city was destroyed in World War I, and restoration of the cathedral was not completed until 1938.

See church treasures in the Palais du Tau (2 Place du Cardinal-Lucon), open 10:00–12:00 and 14:00–18:00. The Porte Mars 13th-century Arch. Saint Remi Basilica (open daily 08:00–18:30). Nearby, the great collection of 16th–19th-century weapons in the St. Remi Museum (53 Rue Simon), open daily 14:00–18:30.

The Church of St. Jacquet. The museum at the Church of St. Denis.

See champagne processed. The public is invited to visit the Taitinger and Pommery caves.

Dep. Reims	12:33	16:28 (1)	17:24 (4)	19:00 (4)	20:28
Arr. Paris (Est)	14:09	18:08	19:06	20:36	22:04

(1) Runs Monday-Friday, except holidays. (2) Runs Saturday only. (3) Runs Monday-Saturday, except holidays. (4) Runs daily except Saturday.

Paris - Rouen - Paris 269

Dep. Paris (St. Laz.)	06:40 (1)	07:29 (1)	08:16 (1)	09:15 (2)
Arr. Vernon	07:20	08:09	09:04	-0-
Arr. Rouen (Rive Dr.)	07:51	08:40	09:46	10:23

Sights in **Rouen**: Walk out of the rail station and then down Rue de Jeanne D'Arc about 1½ miles. Turn right onto Rue de la Grosse Horloge and continue a short distance to the remodeled ancient, large central market, Vieux Marche, the place where Joan of Arc was tied to a stake and burned. This is now the Church of St. Joan, built in 1977. It is in the shape of an upside-down boat and has magnificent stained-glass windows that were saved from the Church of Saint-Vincent, bombed during World War II. Try the regional specialty (terrine of duck) in one of the nearby restaurants.

Then, go back along Rue de la Gross Horloge (crossing Rue de Jeanne D'Arc). Straight ahead is the gigantic, ornate clock for which the street was named. The clock presents a spectacle of moving figures when each hour strikes.

Past the famous clock is the cathedral, with its renowned Carillon of 56 bells. Nearby, see the sculptures on the doors of the Church of Saint-Maclou.

See the stained-glass windows in the Church of St. Godard and the Church of St. Patrice.

Visit the remains of a building located below the Palace of Justice. It was either an 11th- century Jewish school or a synagogue. See the Hebrew graffiti written on the walls there more than 900 years ago, the elaborate carved columns and the two inverted Lions of Judah. It is open only on Saturdays.

The rose window of the Gothic Church of St. Ouen. The collection of fine faience ware for which Rouen was once famous, in the Museum of Fine Arts. The Gallo-Roman artifacts in the Museum of Antiquities. The late Gothic and Renaissance Bourgtheroulde mansion. The collection of old street signs and other ironwork pieces in the Musée Le Secq.

From Rouen, it is an easy bus trip to the colorful harbor at **Honfleur**.

Take a bus or taxi from Vernon about four miles to Giverny, to visit the home and spectacular garden of painter Claude Monet, both of them open daily except Monday, 10:00-18:00 April 1 through October 31.

Dep. Rouen (Rive Dr.)	12:06 (3)	12:51 (4)	14:08 (3)	14:53 (3+4)
Dep. Vernon	12:53	-0-	14:52	-0-
Arr. Paris (St. Laz.)	13:41	14:01	15:42	16:04

Dep. Rouen (Rive Dr.)	16:42 (5)	17:16 (1)	18:19 (6)	19:17 (6+7)
Dep. Vernon	17:32	18:04	19:01	-0-
Arr. Paris (St. Laz.)	18:25	18:48	19:50	20:26

(1) Runs Monday–Friday, except holidays. (2)) Plus other departures from Paris at 10:48 (3) and 12:40 (3), arriving Rouen 12:04 and 13:47. (3) Runs Monday-Saturday, except holidays. (4) Light refreshments. (5) Runs Sundays and holidays only. (6) Runs Sunday only. (7) Plus other departures from Rouen at 20:20 (8), 20:47 (1) and 21:25 (6), arriving Paris 21:58, 21:48 and 22:55. (8) Runs Saturday only.

Paris - Strasbourg - Paris   390

This ride is along the Marne, with clear views of the area near famous World War I battlefields.

Dep. Paris (Est)	06:50 (1)	07:50 (2)	08:18
Arr. Strasbourg	10:48	11:41	12:50

Dep. Strasbourg	15:55 (3)	17:10 (4)	18:20 (2)	19:16
Arr. Paris (Est)	20:06	21:09	22:22	23:31

(1) Supplement charged. Runs Monday-Friday, except holidays. Runs to early July from early Sept. Light refreshments. (2) Supplement charged. Restaurant car. (3) Runs daily except Saturday. Light refreshments. (4) Supplement charged. Light refreshments. Runs daily except Saturday. Operates to early July from early Sept.

Paris - Tours - Paris   295, 296

This one-day excursion appears immediately following "Paris–Blois–Tours–Paris"

Paris - Trouville and Deauville - Paris   270

Dep. Paris (St. Laz.)	08:07 (1)	08:49 (2)	10:04 (3)	12:00 (4)
Arr. Trou Deau	10:13	10:51	11:48	13:59

Sights in **Trouville**: There is no chance of obtaining hotel rooms here in summer without advance reservation. One of France's most beautiful swimming beaches. A gambling casino. Marvelous seafood.

Sights in **Deauville**: One of France's most beautiful swimming beaches. Two racetracks. Lovely gardens. To explore the Norman countryside, you can rent a car at the Deauville rail station.

Take a bus six miles to **Honfleur**, the beautiful fishing village that inspired many Impressionist paintings. Very crowded in July and August. Stroll along the bank of its old harbor on the English Channel. Visit the Eugene Bodin Museum (paintings of the Saint Simeon school) and the Marine Museum in the 14th-century Church of St. Etienne.

Dep. Trou Deau	14:16 (5)	17:39 (6)	19:31 (7+8)
Arr. Paris (St. Laz.)	16:07	19:26	21:21

(1) Operates late June to early September. Runs Monday-Friday, except holidays. (2) Runs Saturdays, Sundays and holidays. (3) Operates early July to late August. (4) Runs Monday-Friday, except holidays. (5) Runs Saturdays, Sundays and holidays, late June to late August. (6) Runs Sundays only, late June to late August. (7) Runs Sunday only. (8) Plus other departures from Trou Deau at 20:21 (3) and 21:05 (9), arriving Paris 22:31 and 22:49. (9) Runs Saturdays, Sundays and holidays.

Paris - Troyes - Paris   380

Dep. Paris (Est)	07:03 (1)	08:00 (2)	08:41 (3)	12:38	13:28 (4)
Arr. Troyes	08:35	09:37	10:14	14:13	14:54

Sights in **Troyes**: This is the Champagne area. The most interesting places here are located along the 30-minute walk from the rail station to St. Pierre Cathedral, which has marvelous 13th, 14th and 16th-century stained glass.

See the museum of tools used in French crafts at the 16th-century Hotel de Mauroy, on Rue de la Trinite. The 16th-century religious art and the hosiery museum, both at the Musée de l'Hotel de Vauluisant. The mansions of Autry, des Ursins and Marisy. The Museum of Fine Arts, with its solid collection of 17th–18th-century paintings and 13th–14th-century sculptures.

The 12th-century manuscripts in the Library. The Pharmacy Museum. The Archaeology Museum. The Natural History Museum

Dep. Troyes	12:08 (5)	12:42 (6)	16:42 (7)	17:56 (5)	19:27 (5+8)
Arr. Paris (Est)	13:43	14:13	18:14	19:43	21:10

(1) Runs daily, except Sundays and holidays. Supplement payable. (2) Runs Sundays and holidays only. (3) Supplement payable. Light refreshments. (4) Runs Saturday, Sunday and holidays. (5) Runs Monday–Friday, except holidays. Light refreshments. (6) Runs Saturday only. (7) Light refreshments. (8) Plus other departures from Troyes at 20:36 (4), 20:55 (9) and 22:00 (3), arr. Paris 22:19, 22:24 and 23:49. (9) Runs Sunday only. Light refreshments.

Paris - Versailles - Paris 274

To reduce the often long wait for a guided tour, phone 01 30 84 74 00 to get the schedule and arrive 90 minutes before the desired tour. Some of the tours (taking either one or two hours) are given in English.

Dep. Paris (Austerlitz/RER C))	Frequent times from 05:30 to 00:30.
Arr. Versailles (Rive Gauche)	37 minutes later

Other RER Line C trains from Austerlitz stop at Versailles Chantiers; if you want to go to the chateau, take a train that stops at Rive Gauche. These RER trains also stop at St. Michel Notre Dame.

Versailles is also reached by suburban trains from Paris St. Lazare, which stop in Versailles at the Rive Droite station, or from Paris Montparnasse to Versailles Chantiers. This trip generally take about 14 minutes. Additionally, you can take the Metro to Pont de Sevres, then catch bus 171 to Versailles.

Sights in **Versailles**: The fabulous palace where Louis XV lived like a king, and the elegant 250 acres of gardens here. Open daily except Mondays 09:00-18:30 (summer), 09:00-17:30 (winter). Bring a picnic lunch and eat in the gardens, by the mile-long Grand Canal.

During the time of Louis XV, about 5,000 members of the nobility lived in the palace's private apartments. Versailles became a museum in 1837.

Among its highlights are: the 237-foot-long by 33-foot-wide Hall of Mirrors (in which

17 mirror-lined arcades reflect 17 corresponding arched windows), throne room, Queen's chambers, chapel, theater, the apartments of Madame de Pompadour and Madame du Barry, and the rooms named for Venus, Mercury, Diana and Mars.

The private apartment of the king can be seen only as a part of the guided tours of the palace, which start at various times from 09:45 to 15:30. However, most of the great rooms, such as the Hall of Mirrors and the King's bedroom, can be visited without a guide from 09:45 until the palace closes. Books are sold that make it possible to see and appreciate the palace without a guide.

| Dep. Versaille | Frequent times from 06:30 to 01:30 |
| Arr. Paris (Austerlitz) | 39 minutes later |

If you visit Versaille in the morning, it is possible to also see Chartres in early afternoon. There are frequent trains for the 30-minute ride from Versaille to Chartres.

TRIPS TO THE RIVIERA

Unless designated otherwise, all of these trains are TGV, require reservation, charge a supplement and have light refreshments or restaurant car.

Paris - Marseille - Paris 350

Dep. Paris (Lyon)	06:54 (1)	08:24	10:54	12:06	13:18 (2)
Arr. Marseille (St. Ch.)	11:24	12:42	15:14	16:30	17:43
		•	•	•	
Dep. Marseille (St. Ch.)	06:15	07:38	09:02	12:40	14:54 (3)
Arr. Paris (Lyon)	10:40	11:57	13:27	16:58	19:15

(1) Runs Monday–Friday, except holidays. (2) Plus other departures from Paris at 15:18, 16:42, 17:42, 20:27 and 22:33, arriving Marseille 19:42, 21:06, 21:59, 04:55, and 07:08. (3) Plus other departures from Marseille at 17:29, 18:49, 21:36 and 22:38, arriving Paris 21:52, 23:22, 06:24 and 07:12.

Paris - Nice - Paris 360

All of these trains are TGV, require reservation, charge a supplement and have light refreshments, unless designated otherwise.

| Dep. Paris (Lyon) | 07:54 | 11:06 | 20:27 (1) |
| Arr. Nice | 14:24 | 17:36 | 08:12 |

• • •

| Dep. Nice | 09:52 | 15:40 | 18:42 (2) | 19:42 (3) |
| Arr. Paris (Lyon) | 16:24 | 22:16 | 06:24 | 07:12 |

(1) A non-TGV train that has second-class couchettes and second-class coach cars. Operates Sunday only. (2) A non-TGV train that carries first- and second-class couchettes and second-class coach cars. Runs Sunday only. (3) A non-TGV train that carries sleeping cars and first- and second-class couchettes. No coaches.

SCENIC RAIL TRIPS

Chamonix - Vallorcine - Chamonix 572

Good mountain scenery on this short ride. It is easy to combine this with the one-day round-trip from Geneva to Chamonix.

| Dep. Chamonix | 07:55(1) | 09:22 (2) | 09:51 | 11:58 | 13:04 | 15:10 (3) | 17:01 (4) |
| Arr. Vallorcine | 08:26 | 09:55 | 10:23 | 12:30 | 13:37 | 15:41 | 17:32 |

• • •

| Dep. Vallorcine | 09:36(4) | 10:38 (2) | 11:42 (4) | 12:47 | 14:38 (5) | 15:58 (4) | 17:01 (5) |
| Arr. Chamonix | 10:06 | 11:09 | 12:13 | 13:19 | 15:09 | 16:29 | 17:34 |

(1) Runs from early June to late June and from early Sept. to late Sept. (2) Operates late June to late August. (3) *Mont Blanc Express*. Has observation cars. Runs late June to late Sept. (4) *Mont Blanc Express*. Has observation cars. (5) Operates late June to late September.

Limoges - Toulouse - Limoges 310

Recommended for mountain scenery. This can be seen either as an easy one-day round-trip between Limoges and Toulouse or as a portion of the route from Paris to Toulouse (and v.v.) via Limoges.

| Dep. Limoges | 09:38 (1) | 13:15 (2) | 16:53 (3) | | |
| Arr. Toulouse (Mat.) | 13:00 | 16:45 | 20:25 | | |

• • •

| Dep. Toulouse (Mat.) | 13:41 (4) | 14:05 (5) | 17:34 (6) | 18:03 (7) | 19:29 (8) |
| Arr. Limoges | 16:48 | 17:35 | 20:55 | 21:30 | 22:58 |

(1) Runs Sunday only. (2) Light refreshments. (3) Supplement charged. Light refreshments. (4) Light refreshments. (5) Runs Friday & Sunday. (6) Runs Monday–Thursday. (7) Runs Friday only. (8) Runs Saturday, Sunday and holidays.

Here is the schedule for the Paris-Toulouse route:

All of the TGV trains in this table depart/arrive at Paris Montparnasse rail station. All of the TGVs require a reservation and charge a supplement.

310

Dep. Paris (Aust.)	07:21 (1)	10:21 (3)	13:54 (4)	17:00 (5)	17:44 (6)
Dep. Limoges	10:17 (2)	13:15	16:53	20:07	20:47
Arr. Toulouse (Mat.)	13:49	16:45	20:25	23:26	23:59

Dep. Paris (Aust.)	21:09 (7)	22:18 (8)	22:56 (9)
Dep. Limoges	00:55	02:12	02:59
Arr. Toulouse (Mat.)	04:21	07:03	07:00

* * *

Dep. Toulouse (Mat.)	00:35 (10)	01:40 (11)	06:26 (12)	07:42 (1)	10:33
Dep. Limoges	04:00	04:57	09:54	10:59	14:19
Arr. Paris (Aust.)	07:44	08:35	13:09	13:55	17:14

Dep. Toulouse (Mat.)	13:41	14:05 (13)	17:34 (14)	23:15 (15)
Dep. Limoges	17:01	17:37	20:57	-0-
Arr. Paris (Aust.)	20:14	21:17	00:04	07:05

(1) Runs Monday-Saturday. Light refreshments. (2) Change trains in Brive (arr. 11:17, dep. 11:3). (3) Runs to late June and from early Sept. Light refreshments. (4) Supplement charged. Light refreshments. (5) Supplement charged. Runs daily, except Saturday. (6) Supplement charged. Runs Friday. Light refreshments. (7) Has couchettes. (8) Runs Fridays. Runs Monday-Thursday late June to late August. Has couchettes and sleepers. (9) Runs Friday and Sunday. Has second-class couchettes and first- and second-class coaches from late June to late August. (10) Has first- and second-class couchettes and second-class coaches. (11) Runs late June to late August. Carries first- and second-class couchettes and second-class coaches. (12) Runs on Monday only, to late June and from early Sept. Light refreshments. (13) Runs Friday and Sunday. (14) Runs Monday-Thursday. (15) Carries sleepers and couchettes only, no coaches.

Lyon - Geneva 372

This trip is noted for scenic canyons. See details under "Lyon."

Marseille - Nice - Monaco (Monte Carlo) 360

Great views of the Mediterranean seashore.

Dep. Marseille	06:15 (1)	09:35	12:11	13:16	15:27 (2)
Arr. Nice	09:02	12:08	14:34	15:43	17:54

Change trains

Dep. Nice	09:10	12:18	14:55	16:09	18:07
Arr. Monaco	09:39	12:43	15:19	16:50	18:30

• • •

Dep. Monaco	11:12 (1)	12:45	16:45	18:06 (1)	21:46 (1)
Arr. Nice	11:33	13:08	17:07	18:24	22:00

Change trains

Dep. Nice	11:41	13:55	17:58	18:35	22:23
Arr. Marseille	14:08	16:18	20:28	21:13	00:56

(1) Direct train. No train change in Nice. (2) Light refreshments.

Narbonne - Carcassonne   320, 321

Outstanding farm and vineyard scenery. Easy to make as a one-day round-trip or can be covered in the route from Narbonne to Toulouse and Bordeaux.

Dep. Narbonne	06:49 (1)	08:24	09:44 (2)	12:06 (2)	15:25 (2)
Arr. Carcassonne	40–45 minutes later				

Sights in **Narbonne**: The Cloister adjacent to the Palace of the Archbishops. The choir of the incomplete Cathedral of Saint-Just.

Sights in **Carcassonne**: See notes under "Bordeaux–Carcassonne."

Dep. Carcassonne	09:50 (2)	12:19 (2)	12:46 (2)	15:01 (2)	18:03 (3)
Arr. Narbonne	40–45 minutes later				

(1) Runs Monday-Friday, except holidays. (2) Light refreshments. (3) Plus other departures from Carcassonne at 19:43 (2) and 21:54 (2).

Here is the daytime viewing schedule for the Narbonne-Bordeaux route:

321

Dep. Narbonne	08:24	09:44	11:56	15:25 (1)
Arr. Toulouse (Matabiau)	09:41	11:07	13:15	16:41

Change trains 320

Dep.. Toulouse	09:47	11:13	13:23	16:48
Arr. Bordeaux (St. Jean)	11:58	13:34	15:49	19:01

• • •

320

Dep. Bordeaux (St. Jean)	06:38	08:25	11:49 (1)	14:44
Arr. Toulouse (Matabiau)	08:56	11:12	14:05	17:06

Change trains 321

Dep.. Toulouse	09:01	11:29	14:10	17:11
Arr. Narbonne	10:18	12:45	15:30	18:31

(1) Light refreshments.

Nice - Cuneo   581

There is spectacular scenery on the 74-mile-long Nice–Cuneo rail route through the Alps and the **Roya Valley**, a service that first became operational in 1928. Severe damage during World War II caused it to be closed in 1940, and it was not re-opened until the winter of 1979. An outstanding feat of engineering, this line is a succession of very high viaducts, bridges and 60 tunnels that span 27 miles of this route, interspersed with sections that look down into deep valleys. This route has attracted many tourists.

Dep. Nice	07:25	12:28		Dep. Cuneo	10:00 (1)	16:10 (1)
Arr. Breil	08:28	13:37		Arr. Breil	11:20	17:57
Change trains				*Change trains*		
Dep Breil	08:36	13:47		Dep. Breil	11:25	18:05
Arr. Cuneo	10:20	15:28		Arr. Nice	12:23	19:05

(1) Direct train. No train change in Breil.

Nice - Digne - Nice   361

This is a very scenic ride up the beautiful **Var Valley** on a self-propelled single car narrow-gauge train operated by Chemins de Fer de la Provence. Eurailpasses are accepted on this route. There is a great drop in temperature between sea-level Nice and 1,955-foot-high Digne. The scenery includes canyons, chateaus and forests. The train follows the route Napoleon took when he returned from exile in Elba in 1815. Plaques and monuments along the way mark that event.

Dep. Nice (Sud)	06:42	09:00	12:43
Arr. Digne	09:53	12:12	16:02

Sights in **Digne**: A popular mineral bath resort. See the 15th-century Cathedral of Saint Jerome. Many fruit orchards. Digne is famed for the lavender cultivated here.

Dep. Digne	10:33	13:58	17:25
Arr. Nice (Sud)	13:49	17:15	20:35

Lyon - Torino (and Rome)   365, 44

The Culoz-Modane portion of this trip offers outstanding lake and mountain scenery. The train goes through the 8.5-mile-long Mont Cenis Tunnel, constructed in 1871.

Both of these trains have light refreshments.

Dep. Lyon (P-D)	07:20		Dep. Torino (P.N.)	13:00
Dep. Culoz	N/A		Dep. Modane	14:20
Arr. Modane	09:41		Dep. Culoz	N/A
Arr. Torino (P.N.)	11:00		Arr. Lyon (P-D)	16:40

Toulouse - La Tour-de-Carol - Toulouse   312

Excellent mountain and canyon scenery.

Dep. Toulouse (Mat.)	07:52	10:15	Dep. La Tour	10:40	13:35
Arr. La Tour	10:26	12:49	Arr. Toulouse (Mat.)	13:07	16:13

Toulouse - Limoges - Toulouse   310

Recommended for mountain scenery. This route can be seen either as an easy one-day round-trip between Toulouse and Limoges or as a portion of the ride Toulouse–Paris and v.v. trip.

Dep. Toulouse (Mat.)	07:42 (1)	10:33 (2)	11:01 (3)	13:41 (4)	14:05 (5)
Arr. Limoges	10:56	14:15	14:22	16:58	17:35
		•	•	•	
Dep. Limoges	13:15	16:53 (6)	20:47 (7)		
Arr. Toulouse (Mat.)	16:45	20:25	23:59		

(1) Runs Monday-Saturday. Light refreshments. (2) Runs daily. Light refreshments. (3) Operates late June to late August. Runs daily. (4) Runs daily except Saturday. (5) Operates Fridays and Sundays. (6) Supplement charged. Light refreshments. (7) Runs Saturday only. Light refreshments.

INTERNATIONAL ROUTES
FROM FRANCE

Paris is the French gateway for rail travel to Amsterdam, Bern (and on to Zurich and Vienna), Brussels, Cologne, Geneva, London and Madrid. Notes on the routes to London (other than Eurostar) appear in Chapter 7.

From Marseille, there is rail service to Barcelona and Genoa (and on to Milan and Rome). From Paris, there are trains London to Amsterdam, Barcelona, Bern, Brussels, Cologne, Geneva, Genoa, Lisbon, Madrid, Milan and Rome.

Nice - Marseille - Narbonne - Barcelona   81, 355, 656

Dep. Nice	05:50 (1, 7)	10:26 (4, 6)	-0-	12:04 (5)
Dep. Marseille	08:31	12:57 (1)	-0-	14:36
Arr. Montpellier	-0-	14:26	-0-	-0-
Dep. Montpellier	-0-	15:09 (6)	-0-	-0-
Arr. Narbonne	11:52 (7)	-0-	-0-	17:36
Dep. Narbonne	12:15	16:00	-0-	18:11
Arr. Port Bou	13:40	18:05	-0-	19:56
Dep. Port Bou	14:30 (2, 9)	18:28	19:15 (1, 9)	20:16
Arr. Barcelona (P. de G.)	17:07 (8)	19:16 (3)	21:43 (3)	22:20 (3)

(1) Light refreshments. (2) Second-class only. (3) Arrives at Barcelona's Sants rail station. (4) Timetable 81. Change trains at Montpellier. (5) Timetable 81. Change trains at Narbonne Light refreshments. (6) Restaurant car. Supplement payable (7) Timetable 355. Change trains in Narbonne. (8) Arrives Barcelona Sants 17:13. (9) Timetable 656.

Marseille - Nice - Genoa - Milan - Rome   90

There is marvelous Mediterranean coastal scenery on this route.

Dep. Marseille (St. Ch.)	-0-	05:12	06:15
Arr.. Nice	07:11 (1)	08:19	09:02
Dep.. Nice		08:21	10:04 (3)
Arr. Ventimiglia	-0-	08:59	-0-
Dep.. Ventimiglia	-0-	09:30 (2)	-0-
Arr. Genoa (P.P.)	11:40	11:47	13:10
Arr. Milan (Cen.)	13:45	-0-	14:50
Arr. Rome	-0-	16:56	-0-

Dep. Marseille (St. Ch.)	15:55	17:37 (3)	-0-
Arr. Nice	18:16	20:00	-0-
Dep. Nice	18:26 (3)	20:35 (3, 4)	-0-
Arr. Genoa (P.P.)	21:19	00:28	-0-
Arr. Milan (Cen.)	23:00	-0-	-0-
Arr. Rome	-0-	06:48	-0-

(1) Operates early-June to late September. (2) Change trains in Ventimiglia. Supplement payable. Light refreshments. (3) Change trains in Nice. Supplement payable. (4) Carries a sleeping car. Also has couchettes. (5) Light refreshments.

Paris - London (Eurostar)   10

All Eurostar trains require a reservation. Meal service is available. Minimum check-in time is 20-minutes. When traveling Paris-London, set your watch back one hour; London-Paris, ahead one hour. Schedules reflect the time change.

Dep. Paris (Nord)	06:37 (1)	07:16 (1)	08:13 (1)	08:07 (2)	09:10 (1)
Dep. Calais	08:04	-0-	-0-	09:34	-0-
Arr. Ashford	-0-	-0-	09:11	09:11	-0-
Arr. London (Waterloo)	08:46	09:09	10:13	10:30	11:09

Dep. Paris (Nord)	09:10 (2)	09:43	10:19 (1)	10:19 (2)	11:43
Dep. Calais	-0-	-0-	-0-	-0-	-0-
Arr. Ashford	-0-	10:41	-0-	-0-	-0-
Arr. London (Waterloo)	11:26	11:43	12:13	12:30	13:43

Dep. Paris (Nord)	12:19 (1)	12:19	13:04	14:16(3)	14:49 (4)
Dep. Calais	-0-	-0-	14:31	-0-	-0-
Arr. Ashford	-0-	-0-	14:08	-0-	-0-
Arr. London (Waterloo)	14:13	14:30	15:09	16:09	16:43

Dep. Paris (Nord)	15:19	16:07	17:10	18:19	19:19
Dep. Calais	-0-	17:34	-0-	-0-	-0-
Arr. Ashford	-0-	17:11	18:11	-0-	20:14
Arr. London (Waterloo)	17:13	18:13	19:13	20:13	21:13

Dep. Paris (Nord)	20:07	20:49 (3)	21:13
Dep. Calais	-0-	-0-	-0-
Arr. Ashford	21:11	-0-	22:11
Arr. London (Waterloo)	22:13	22:43	23:16

(1) Runs Monday-Saturday. (2) Runs Sunday only. (3) Runs Fridays and Sundays. (4) Runs daily except Saturdays. (5)

Paris - Amsterdam   18

See "Amsterdam–Paris."

Paris - Basel   380

See "Basel-Paris."

Paris - Bordeaux - Lisbon   46, 300

This train has couchettes Paris-Lisbon, plus a sleeping car, coaches and a restaurant car Irun-Lisbon.

Dep. Paris (Austerlitz)	13:39
Dep. Bordeaux (St. J.)	18:13
Set watch back one hour	
Arr. Irun	20:52
Change trains	
Dep. Irun	22:00
Arr. Lisbon (S. Apol.)	11:25 Day 2

Paris - Bordeaux - Madrid   46, 300

Dep. Paris (Mont.)	10:00 (1)	20:00 (2)
Dep. Bordeaux (St. J.)	13:07	-0-
Set your watch back one hour		
Arr. Irun	15.27	
Dep. Irun	15:45	-0-
Arr. Madrid (Cham.)	22:05	08:48

(1) TGV Paris-Irun. Talgo Irun-Madrid; operates daily except Saturday. Connection in Irun is not guaranteed. Supplements payable on both legs of journey. Light refreshments. (2) Departs from Paris Austerlitz. Hotel Train, special supplements payable. Restaurant car.

Paris - Brussels - Amsterdam   18

Unless noted otherwise, these are Thalys high-speed trains that require a reservation and payment of a supplement. Light refreshments are available on most trains.

Dep. Paris (Nord)	07:04 (1)	07:40 (2)	10:40 (2)	11:40	12:40
Arr. Brussels (Midi)	09:04	09:38	12:38	13:38	14:41
Change trains					
Dep. Brussels (Midi)	09:10	09:45	12:45	14:10	15:07
Arr. Amsterdam	12:04	12:28	15:28	17:08	18:04

Dep. Paris (Nord)	14:40 (2)	16:37	17:37 (2)	18:40 (3)	23:16 (2+4)
Arr. Brussels (Midi)	16:38	18:37	19:38	20:38	04:35
Change trains					
Dep. Brussels (Midi)	16:45	19:07	19:45	21:07	04:47
Arr. Amsterdam	19:28	22:04	22:28	00:04	08:02

(1) Runs Monday–Friday. (2) Direct train. No train change in Brussels. (3) Runs daily except Saturday. (4) Carries second-class couchettes and first- and second-class coaches.

Paris - Cologne - Hamburg - Copenhagen   25

Dep. Paris (Nord)	07:25 (1)	16:34 (2)	21:31 (3)
Arr. Cologne	12:51	21:49	-0-
Change trains			
Dep. Cologne	13:10 (1)	21:59	-0-
Arr. Hamburg (Hbf.)	17:07	02:35	07:08 (4)
Change trains			
Dep.. Hamburg	18:27	02:45	07:30
Arr. Copenhagen	22:59	08:30	11:59

(1) Supplements charged all trains. Restaurant car. Light refreshments Hamburg-Copenhagen train. (2) Direct train to Copenhagen. No train change in Cologne. Operates late May to late September. Carries a sleeping car. Also has couchettes. Coach is second-class. Restaurant car. (3) Direct train to Hamburg. Does not call on Cologne. (4) Change trains in Hamburg. Supplement payable Hamburg-Copenhagen.

Paris - Geneva 372

All of these trains are TGV, require reservation and charge a supplement.

Dep. Paris (Lyon)	07:12 (1)	10:18 (1)	14:40 (2)	17:18 (1)	19:12 (1)
Arr. Geneva (Corn.)	10:55	13:57	18:19	20:57	22:52

(1) Restaurant car. (2) Light refreshments.

Paris - Dijon - Lausanne - Milan - Genoa - Rome or Venice 44, 82

44

Dep. Paris (Lyon)	07:18 (1)	12:18 (1)	17:54 (1)
Arr. Lausanne	11:18	16:10	21:47
Change trains 82			
Dep. Lausanne	12:42 (2)	16:42 (1)	22:29 (5)
Arr. Milan (Cen.)	14:56 (3)	19:45 (4)	-0-
Arr. Genoa (P.P.)	-0-	-0-	-0-
Arr. Rome (Ter.)	-0-	-0-	09:40
Arr. Venice (S.L.)	18:55	22:55	-0-

(1) TGV. Reservation required. Supplement charged. Restaurant car. (2) Pendolino train. Supplement payable. (3) Train to Venice departs 16:05. Supplement payable. (4) Train to Venice Departs 20:05. Supplement payable. (5) Supplement payable. Carries sleeping cars, couchettes, second-class coach.

THE FERRY-CROSSING TO IRELAND

Paris - Le Havre - Rosslare and Paris - Cherbourg - Rosslare
269, 270 (Train), 2010, 2060 (Ferry)

Operated by Irish Ferries Company. Passage *only* (without a seat or a berth) is free all year with a Eurailpass; passengers are responsible for port taxes, which are payable in the local currency. Reservations are required for cabin space, and in July and August for all types of accommodation.

Fares for 1998 were unavailable at press time. In 1997, peak season ran from June 21-August 31. The standard single one-way fare for ferry passage only, Rosslare-Le Havre or Rosslare-Cherbourg was $160. With a first-class rail ticket, the Paris-Cherbourg portion of the trip cost an additional $69, or an additional $50 for a second-class rail ticket. A first-class Paris-Le Havre ticket cost an additional $49, second class $36. Another $7 was added for a seat on the ferry. Six-berth cabins were $10 per person, four-berth cabins $12-26 per person, three-berth cabins, $28 per person, two-berth cabins $32-44 per person, deluxe suites $75 per person.

In 1997, off-season was May 1-June 20 and September 1-September 30. Passage only, Le Havre-Rosslare or Cherbourg-Rosslare was $110. With first-class rail between Paris and Cherbourg, it was $179, $160 second-class rail; the Paris-Le Havre-Rosslare trip wat $159 with first-class rail, $146 second-class rail. Student and senior fares are also available.

There is no winter ferry service from early November to early March. There are sailings to and from Cork, Ireland during June, July and August. Days of operation and departure times vary during five different periods of the year.

For 1998 schedules, prices and reservations, contact the North American agent: Scots-American Travel Advisors, (201) 768-1187, fax (201) 768-3825, 26 Rugen Drive, Harrington Park, NJ 07640.

GERMANY

Getting on Track in Germany

• Tourist information: German National Tourist Office, New York office, 122 East 42nd Street, 52nd Floor, New York, NY 10168-0072. Telephone: (212) 661-7200, fax: (212) 661-7174. E-mail inquiries: gntony@aol.com. Chicago office, 104 S. Michigan Avenue, Chicago, IL 60603-5978. Telephone (312) 644-0723. Los Angeles office, 11766 Wilshire Boulevard, Los Angeles, CA 90025. Telephone (310) 575-9799, fax (310) 575-1565. E-mail inquiries: gntolax@aol.com. Toronto office, 175 Bloor Street East, North Tower, Suite 604, Toronto, Ontario M4W 3R8, Canada. Telephone (416) 968-1570, fax (416) 968-1986. E-mail inquiries: germanto@idirect.com. On the Web: http://www.germany-tourism.de.

• Public holidays: New Year's Day, Epiphany (January), Good Friday through Easter Monday (four days in March or April; dates vary), Ascension Day (April or May; date varies), Whit Monday (May or June; date varies), Corpus Christi Day (June; date varies), and Christmas Day and Boxing Day (25–26 December). Additionally, there are many religious and other holidays celebrated in certain German states. Check with the tourist office to see what holidays may occur during your visit.

• Currency: Deutschmark (DM). At press time, $1 equalled DM1.75.

Overview of German Trains

Most of Germany's trains are operated by Deutsche Bahn Aktiengesellschaft, or DB. Train travel in Germany has changed radically since the Berlin wall came down and the Bundesrepublik reunified with the former East Germany. Although tremendous building projects have begun to help the eastern part of the country catch up materially with the west, there is still a vast gully between the two. Trains equipped to go twice as fast must slow down in parts of the east due to old and ill-maintained tracks. Cities like Berlin, Leipzig, Weimar, and Dresden are now easily connected to the major western German cities of Munich, Frankfurt, Hannover, Hamburg, etc. The DB is highly efficient and well equipped. The railway's InterCity Express (ICE) trains are similar to the French TGVs, but because the coaches are wider, there's even more room to stretch out. Most passenger seats are equipped with audio systems, and some have video monitors as well. And like their French counterparts, Germany's all-white speedsters (a splashy pink racing stripe adds a nice touch), run regularly between the major cities in record time and are teched-out with business conference rooms and on-board telephones.

Night services have been retooled in Germany, with the introduction of InterCityNight (ICN) trains. These trains, which operate within Germany, are rolling hotels, with compartments equipped with showers and private toilets. Trains have full-service dining cars and more personalized service than on conventional night trains. EuroNight trains also serve the overnight market, but with fewer amenities than ICNs.

Along with its fast trains, Germany has an array of railways, including funiculars, that course through glorious mountain segments. These gems should not be overlooked.

Generally, fares in Germany are reasonable by U.S. standards, but a Eurailpass is probably your best bet here for keeping costs down. Second class is an alternative, but it can be crowded.

In Germany the train station functions as the hub of most downtown areas and after 18:30 when stores close in German cities, the train station (hauptbahnhof) is pretty much the only place to buy groceries, wine, etc.

General Rail Information

• Children under four travel free. Half-fare for children 4-11. Children 12 and over pay full fare.

• Germany has an alphabet soup of trains for the taking. Here's a look at what all the letters mean: ICE: InterCity Express; high-speed trains (165 mph) at premium fares; EC: EuroCity, international express train, supplement charged; IC: InterCity, long-distance express train, supplement charged; IR: InterRegio, regional express trains, refurbished equipment; S-Bahn: urban trains; ICN: InterCityNight: Hotel-class overnight trains within Germany; premium fares charged; carries coaches with reclining seats, sleeping compartments (all with private showers/toilets) and a restaurant car; EN: EuroNight, a cut above regular sleeping cars; within this category, CityNightLine is similar to ICN, but only deluxe compartments have showers and toilets.

• A premium is charged for travel on ICE and ICN trains. Fast InterCity and EuroCity trains, connecting 50 important cities along five major rail routes, have easy cross-platform connections in such cities as Cologne, Wurzburg, Mannheim and Dortmund. The DM6 supplement charged for IC and EC trains includes the cost of a seat reservation. Where timetable footnotes indicate that a supplement is charged by a particular train, a passenger using a Eurailpass or German Flexipass does not have to pay the extra charge. (All of those passes are also valid on all commuter rail services in major German cities.) The IC supplement must be paid when using the Inter-Rail Card, available only to residents of Europe. Some of the InterCity trains have top speeds of 125 mph while ICE trains travel at speeds of up to 165 mph. A conference compartment in them can be rented for the cost of four first-class tickets. Worldwide telephone calls can be made from all IC and ICE trains.

• Cyclists can rent bikes (April 1–October 31) at very low daily rates; turn them in at any of 400-odd stations, and hire another two-wheeler elsewhere on the railroad's system. Railway stations and tourist offices carry brochures that explain the bicycle program.

• Porter service may be reserved in advance at many rail stations, including those at the Dusseldorf and Frankfurt airports. A program began in 1987 to install conveyor belts at stairways in 130 rail stations as well as escalators which can accommodate baggage carts in all major stations.

• Disabled travelers will find that Germany has better-than-average facilities in most public places. For a listing of specific hotels and resorts that offer special services, write to the Touristik Union International, Postfach 610280, 3000 Hannover 61.

• The signs you will see at rail stations in Germany are the same as those listed earlier in this chapter under Austria.

GERMANY'S TRAIN PASSES

EuroCity and InterCity supplements are included in the prices listed below for all German train passes. Travelers arriving in Germany by airplane can validate all of them and also Eurailpass at the airport rail ticket office after exiting the customs area and use them for the rail trip from the airport to the city.

All of the following passes are sold worldwide outside Germany by travel agencies and by German Rail. Similar programs are offered by Rail Europe and DER Travel. All of them are 'flexible,' valid for one month (example: July 3 to August 2). Prices for 1998 were unavailable at press time. The 1997 prices are shown below.

German Railpass	First Class	Second Class
5 days in 1 month	$276	$188
10 days in 1 month	$434	$304
15 days in 1 month	$562	$410

A second-class Youthpass (under age 26 on first day of travel) cost $146, $200 and $252.

German Rail Twinpass	First Class	Second Class
5 days in 1 month	$414	$282
10 days in 1 month	$650	$456
15 days in 1 month	$842	$615

(prices for two people traveling together)

German Rail Youthpass	(second-class travel only, under 26 years of age)
5 days in 1 month	$146
10 days in 1 month	$200
15 days in 1 month	$252

German Railpass bonuses: In 1997, included free travel on KD River Steamers on selected routes and free travel on certain bus lines operated by Deutsche Touring and Europabus.

German Rail 'n Drive Pass 1998 information was unavailable at press time. In 1997, the pass provided seven or eight days of travel within Germany in one month. Included four or five days of first- or second-class rail travel plus three days of Hertz rental car with unlimited mileage. Extra car days could be added.

When two people traveled together, the cost of the seven-day pass started at $208 per person. This included second-class rail travel and an economy car with a manual transmission. For one person traveling alone, a seven-day pass with first-class rail travel and a compact automatic or intermediate-sized car with manual transmission, started at $418. Prices for the eight-day pass ranged from $238 to $458. Additional car days cost $49-$69 per person, depending on the type of car rented. Third or fourth passengers needed only to purchase a five-day German Pass, which cost $188 second class, $272 first class. Children under four were free. Children 4-11 paid half the adult rail pass price.

Wunder Card Available from DB in Germany. Offers nine days of unlimited coach-class travel for around DM222, 16 days for close to DM300 (first class is slightly more); the card gives holders free bike rentals, discounts on river steamer voyages, and reduced fares on round-trips to Berlin.

The Senior Pass (Senioren) Available from DB in Germany. Entitles travelers over 60 years of age to 50 percent reductions for a year. Pass-A costs DM75 and is valid Monday–

Saturday (Fridays excepted); Pass-B, good throughout the week, costs DM110; the RES-Stamp costs DM20 more, but it entitles holders of both passes to reductions of 30–50 percent in 18 European countries. Bring your passport for proof of age.

BAHNCARDS

They allow 50 percent discount. Prices for 1998 were unavailable at press time. The 1997 prices below are for *first* class. *Second*-class is 50 percent less. The cards are good for one year.

BahnCard DM480.

BahnCard fur Ehepartner (for married couples) DM240 for first person, DM120 for the partner.

BahnCard fur Familien (for families — parents and all children) DM240.

BahnCard fur Kinder (for children age 4–11) DM120.

BahnCard fur Jugendliche/Teens (for youths age 12–17) DM120.

BahnCard fur Junioren (for youths age 18-22) DM240.

BahnCard fur Senioren (for persons age 60 and older) DM240.

ONE-DAY EXCURSIONS AND CITY-SIGHTSEEING

Here are 90 one-day rail trips that can be made comfortably from cities in Germany, returning to them in most cases before dinnertime. Brief notes highlight sightseeing options at each destination. The number after the name of each route corresponds to the *Thomas Cook Timetable*. Details on 19 other rail and bus trips recommended for exceptional scenery. Schedules for international connections conclude this section. Sightseeing tours to Chemnitz (formerly Karl Marx Stadt), Dresden and Potsdam start in Berlin at Parkplatz Rankestrasse, near the Kurfurstendamm. For reservations, contact Deutsches Reiseburo, Kurfurstendamm 17, Berlin W. 30, Germany.

The eight base cities for one-day excursions include Berlin, Cologne, Dresden, Frankfurt/Main, Hamburg, Hannover, Leipzig and Munich.

Berlin

Two-hour and four-hour tours of West Berlin begin at 10:00 and occur at frequent intervals during the day, from 220 Kurfurstendamm, 216 Kurfurstendamm, and opposite from the bombed-out Gedachtniskirche (Memorial Church). Or, see Berlin a different way: by boat. Tourists haven't discovered Berlin's rivers or canals yet. During the Cold War, many of the canals and rivers were blocked to prevent people escaping to the West. Today the waters of the Havel River, Tegeler See and Wannsee bustle with tour boats.

Stern-und Kreisschiffahrt (Sachtlebenstr. 60, Tel. 30/536-3600) is one of the best-known river excursion companies in Berlin. Their three-hour Historische Stadfahrt trip along the Spree offers views of the Pergamon Museum, the Reichstag, and the Royal Library, then traverses what used to be the Soviet zone. Or, take the five-hour Seerunderfahrt tour. It leaves every day at 11:30 and circles southeastern Berlin on the Spree and Dahme rivers, the Langersee, the Seddinsee, the Muggelsee, and the Grosser Muggelsee.

The stroll down tree-lined Kurfurstendamm is almost mandatory, to observe the city's fine stores, theaters, cafes, movie houses and bars. See the zoo (started in 1843) and aquarium, one of Europe's oldest and best animal exhibits, open daily until dusk. The New National Gallery at Potsdamerstrasse 50, open daily except Monday 09:00–17:00.

The bust of Nefertiti and other important items in the Egyptian Museum at 70 Schloss Strasse, closed Friday. The rooms and gardens of Charlottenburg Castle, closed Monday, opposite the Egyptian Museum. The 1936 Olympic Stadium. The German History Museum, in the reconstructed Reichstag Building, on Paul-Lobe Strasse, open daily except Monday 10:00–17:00. The tent-shaped Philharmonic Hall.

See modern paintings at Brucke Museum, Bussardsteig 9, open Monday–Friday 11:00–17:00. Masterpieces by Durer, Cranach the Elder and Holbein the Younger, at the Dahlem Museum, Arnimallee 23–27, open Tuesday-Sunday 09:00–17:00. Models of everything that floats, flies or rolls, at the Transport Museum, Trebbinerstrasse 9, open Tuesday–Friday 09:00–18:00 and on Saturday and Sunday 10:00–18:00.

Exhibits about many modern architects in the Bauhaus Museum, Klingelhoferstrasse 13, open daily except Tuesday 11:00–17:00. The best collection of Durer drawings in Germany is at the Kupferstichkabinett.

Visit the sixth floor (called Feinschmecker Etage —"the gourmet's floor") of Kaufhaus des Westens (called KaDeWe "Kah-day-vay" by local people), a large department store on Tauentzienstrasse. It is the largest food store in Europe: 500 sales clerks dispensing 30,000 different products. Fruits and vegetables sold there include limes from Brazil, rare wild mushrooms from France and Poland, avocados from Israel, tiny beans from Kenya, tomatoes from Spain, apples from Hungary.

They sell 1,500 kinds of meats (250 varieties of salami). Then there are also eels, crawfish, catfish and carp. Live lobsters are delivered to the store in tank trucks. You will also find 400 types of bread. Three separate counters for 1,800 varieties of cheese from France, Italy and other countries. Eighteen kinds of herring salad. It also has 28 restaurants, counter services and stand-up bars.

Store hours are: 9:00–18:30 on Monday, Tuesday, Wednesday and Friday; 9:00–20:30 on Thursday; 9:00–14:00 on most Saturdays. KaDeWe has 30,000 customers on an ordinary day. Before holidays, there are 100,000 customers in a single day.

The Weissbierstube Restaurant in the Berlin Museum is acclaimed for its bounteous buffet tables. Both the Restaurant and the Museum are open daily except Mondays 11:00–18:00.

To see East Berlin, take the elevated railway from West Berlin's Zoo rail station to its Friedrichstrasse station. On leaving Friedrichstrasse station, turn right and walk three blocks to reach Berlin's famous boulevard, Unter den Linden, and the enormous Soviet embassy. A few blocks further, at the end of the boulevard, is the classical Brandenburg Gate and the ruins of the Berlin Wall. Last year, the famous Hotel Adlon reopened with much fanfare. Next to the Brandenburg gate, the Adlon was hopping in the 1920s with such guests as Henry Ford, John D. Rockerfeller, Charley Chaplin and Mary Pickford. The 1932 movie "Grand Hotel," with Greta Garbo and John Barrymore, was patterned after the hotel. After the Communists took over in 1945, though, the hotel ended up on the wrong side of the Berlin Wall. A few days after the takeover, a fire broke out, destroying most of the building. It was rebuilt, but never returned to its original luster. At its lowpoint in the 1970s, the once-fabulous hostelry became a dormitory. By 1984, most of the building had been torn down. Today, from about $233 per night, you can stay at the resurrected Adlon in a room where the ceilings are gold-leaf and the furnishings are cherry and other rich woods.

Also see the reconstructed St. Hedwig's Cathedral. The National Gallery. The 18th-century State Opera. The tremendous collection of Oriental, Greek and Roman antiquities, the Market Gate of Milet and the impressive Pergamon Altar, all at the Pergamon Museum on Bodestrasse, open Wednesday and Thursday 09:00–18:00 and Friday 10:00–18:00.

The Palace of the Republic. Bode Museum. The Altes Museum. The tiny 14th-century church, Marienkirche. The Museum of German History.

Getting around Berlin is easy on the U-Bahn (underground) and the S-Bahn (surface). The Touristen Karte, valid for 24 hours of travel on mist buses, S-bahn, and subway lines within the city, is a good buy. Check out other transit ticket options by picking up a brochure called the *Schnellbahnnetz*. Purchase tickets at Berlin Public Transport (BVG, U-Bahn Kleistpark 8), at the Bahnhof Zoologischer Garten on the Hardenbergplatz, or at the Tourist Information Office at Tegel Airport.

Cologne (Koln)

All museums are closed on Monday.

It is a 10-minute bus ride from the Cologne/Bonn Airport to the center of Cologne.

Your city-sightseeing in Cologne should include, above all, the cathedral, very near the rail station. Started in 1248 and not completed until 1880, it houses the world's largest reliquary, containing relics of the three kings, the Magi, as well as a splendid collection of illuminated books, vestments, ivories and liturgical articles. These can be seen Monday–Saturday 09:00–17:00, Sundays and holidays 12:30–17:00.

The best time to be inside the cathedral is at the Sunday 10:00 mass, when the ceremony starts with a procession of church elders dressed in robes of burgundy, crimson and rose, and wearing white, embroidered, starched linen. If you climb the 502 steps to the top of the spire, past the nine giant bells, you will see a magnificent view of Cologne, The Rhine River and the Rhine Valley.

Near the cathedral, explore ancient Cologne. The Praetorium, a palace for Roman governors several centuries before Christ, located in the basement of the town hall, open daily 10:00–17:00. Its entrance, difficult to find, is across from the Restaurant-Bar-Cafe Oldtimer at 110 Kleine Budengasse. See the 3rd-century Dionysus mosaic (once the dining hall floor of a Roman house) in the Roman Museum, open Tuesday–Sunday 10:00–20:00.

Also on view there is an outstanding collection of Roman glass, cooking utensils and 4th-century jewelry. Visit the 3rd-century Roman tower.

See the collection of paintings by Cologne masters of the 13th–17th and 19th centuries in the Wallraf Richartz Museum (1 Bischofsgartenstrasse, between the cathedral and the Hauptbahnhoff), open Tuesday, Wednesday and Thursday 10:00–20:00. On Friday, Saturday and Sunday 10:00–18:00. Modern art is exhibited in the Ludwig Museum (same address and hours). Visit the zoo. The 15th-century Gurzenich. The Metropolitan Historical Museum. The town hall. St. Pantaleon Church. St. Andreas Church. Relics and treasures in the Golden Room at the Church of St. Ursula. The luxury shops on Hohestrasse and Schildergasse.

Cologne's transit network is made up of buses, trams and local trains. A 24-hour or multi-day transit pass is your best bet here; the fare structure can be complicated. Pass prices are based on the number of zones in which you want to travel.

Dresden

View works of Raphael, Rembrandt, Rubens, Tintoretto, Van Eyck, Vermeer and other great 16th and 17th-century painters at the Picture Gallery in the Semper Building of Zwinger Palace. Another excellent collection of paintings in the National Gallery.

Hear the Silberman organ (242 years old in 1997) at the cathedral, Hofkirche. Visit the baroque opera house. The zoo in Stadtpark (also called Volkspark). The Block House. Dresden Palace. The Japanese Castle. The treasures at the Albertinium Museum. The Palace of Culture. Take the cable car to Weisser Hirsch for the view of Dresden from the top of that hill.

It is a 17-mile ride by suburban railway from Dresden to **Meissen**. See the 15th-century castle (Albrechtsburg) and the cathedral there. Shop in Meissen for Dresden china and Albrecht porcelain.

Dresden has two railway stations, Dresden Hauptbahnhof is on the southern side of town; Dresden-Neustadt to the north. The first station is most convenient for seeing the sights. Dresden also has a good-sized bus and tram system.

Frankfurt

There is frequent rail service from Frankfurt's Hauptbahnhof rail station to the city's airport and vice versa (12-minute travel time) operates from 04:41 to 23:58. Frequent trains per hour continue beyond the airport station to Mainz and Wiesbaden. Trains also depart the airport at frequent times for Bonn, Cologne, Dortmund, Dusseldorf, Koblenz, Ludwigshafen, Luxembourg, Mannheim, Nurnberg, Trier and Wurzburg. The fare to/from the airport is DM3.60 (slightly higher during rush hour) versus about $20 by taxi.

Bus tours that cover the city's most interesting places depart daily from the south side of the main rail station at 10:00 and 14:00. The tours run about two and a half hours. Most museums in Frankfurt are closed on Monday.

See the house where Goethe was born in 1749 (23 Grosser Hirschgraben), open daily: April–September, 09:00–18:00, October–March, 09:00–16:00. Next to it, the Goethe Museum (books, pictures, furniture and manuscripts associated with the writer) in the Grosser Hirschgraben, open Monday–Saturday 09:00–18:00, Sunday 10:00–15:00. The new (1991) Jewish Museum at 14–15 Untermainkal, in the former Rothschild Palace, is open daily except Monday.

The zoo, one of the world's greatest, at Am Tiergarten, open 08:00–19:00 in Sum- mer, 08:00–18:00 in October, 08:00–17:00 in Winter. Its Exoticarium (aquarium and reptile house) is open until 22:00. Buses #10, #13 and #15 go to the zoo.

The emperor's coronation hall in the Romer complex at medieval Romerberg Square. The wonderful doors in the 13th-century Leonhardskirche. The 13th-century chapel of Saalhof in the remains of the palace of Frederick Barbarossa. Cloth Hall. The Botanical Garden. The pews and murals in the Cathedral of St. Bartholomew. The Church of St. Nicholas. The Church of St. Paul. Senckenberg Museum, the largest natural history museum in West Germany, open 09:00–16:00. The collection of Dutch primitives and 16th-century German masters at the Stadel Art Institute and Municipal Gallery, open daily except Monday 10:00–17:00. The Liebighaus Exhibition of Sculpture.

The Museum of Plastic Art. The changing exhibits of European silver, porcelain, furniture and glass from the Middle Ages to the present time and also an Asian collection (3rd to 19th century) at the Museum of Arts and Crafts. The Henninger Tower in Sachsenhausen, the old quarter of the city (across the Main River, near the commercial district). The Postal Museum. The major shopping streets: Zeil and Kaiserstrasse.

The palm trees, other tropical plants, and Alpine gardens in the city's central park, Palmengarten. Nine miles away in **Offenbach,** center of West Germany's leather industry, is the German Leather Museum, open daily 10:00–17:00.

Sightseeing is easy by subway, streetcar and bus. Two major transit centers are Hauptwache and Bahnhof. The fare is DM1.30. During rush hour it rises to DM2.70. A 24-hour ticket will save you some money. They cost DM8 (half-price for children) and offer unlimited travel; including to the airport.

Hamburg

Most museums in Hamburg are closed Monday. See the port, one of the busiest in the world. There are splendid views of the enormous port from Stintfang Hill. Visit Hagenbeck Zoo, the first cageless zoo in the world, at Stellingen Gardens. St. James Church, with its famous organ, built in 1693. Rathausmarkt Square. The models of Old Hamburg, the port and the city's railway system, in the Museum of the History of Hamburg.

The Counting Houses in the business quarter, around Burchardplatz. The notorious Reperbahn, or "red-light district. The view of the city from the Michel Tower of St. Michaelis Church. The Museum of Decorative Arts. The Botanical Garden. The "Sight and Sound" performances during summer in the Planten un Blomen park. Take a flight over the city from Fuhlsbuttel Airport.

Use Hamburg's S-Bahn, U-Bahn or buses to get around town. A variety of transit passes and tickets are available to visitors.

Hannover

The bus ride between Langenhagen Airport and Hannover's rail station takes 30 minutes. The bus terminal is located next to Track #14.

See the collection of art (from the Middle Ages to the beginning of the 20th century) in the Niedersachsische Landesgalerie. Modern painting and sculpture in the Sprengel Museum (Max Beckmann, Paul Klee, Pablo Picasso).

For an interesting two-hour walking tour of Hannover, obtain the detailed brochure available at both of the rail station's two tourist information offices. Walk out of the station to the statue in front of it and start to follow the painted red line which leads to Passerelle (a pedestrian mall), the 19th-century opera house, the old city wall, Town Hall, and Hannover's oldest (16th century) half-timbered structure.

See the bronze doors by Marcks at Market Church. The outstanding collection of Egyptian antiquities in the Kestner Museum. The prehistoric objects in the Museum of Lower Saxony.

Take a short walk from the central rail station to the station under Kropke Cafe and, from there, tram #1 or #2 to the absolutely fantastic baroque Royal Gardens of Herrenhausen. Its ornamental fountains perform in summer Monday–Friday, 11:00–12:00 and 15:30–16:30. See them 10:00–12:00 and 15:30–17:30 on Saturdays and Sundays.

Next to Herrenhausen is the natural park, Georgengarten. Nearby, see the exotic plants in the greenhouses at Berggarten.

Take streetcar #6 from the central rail station to Hannover's outstanding zoo.

Leipzig

The circa-1915 Leipzig railway station is one of Europe's largest terminal stations. From the station, set off for the area around Markt Place, about a 10-minute walk. Visit the Museum of the History of Leipzig in the Renaissance Old Town Hall. The 17th-century stock exchange (Alte Bourse), rebuilt in 1963. The weighinghouse (Alte Waage), where taxes were levied on imported goods. Auerbachs Keller, the old tavern on which Goethe based the locale of his Faust drama. Bach's tomb, at St. Thomas Church. The Museum of Fine Arts.

West of Markt Place is the church where Johann Sebastian Bach is buried. Bach composed in that church the last 27 years of his life. Also see Gohliser Schlosschen, a rococo palace. Gohlis, the home of the poet Schiller. The opera house in Karl Marx Platz. It is impossible to find a room in Leipzig during the semiannual (March and September) trade fairs that attract visitors from all over the world.

Leipzig has a good network of trams, and most of them converge at Willy-Bradt-Platz, next to the main train station. An S-Bahn circles the city. A variety of transit passes and tickets are available here.

Munich (Munchen)

A metropolitan train connects Munich's Hauptbahnhof and Ostbahnof rail stations. It is a 10-minute bus ride between Munich's Riem Airport and the Hauptbahnhof rail station, where the city's monthly program of events (theaters, museums, exhibits, concerts, plays, etc.) can be obtained. The program is also sold at newsstands.

Most museums in Munich are closed on Monday. There are more than 50 — on coins, ethnology, theater, applied arts, hunting and fishing, folk music, graphic arts, mineralogy, Egyptian art, toys, fire fighting, beer making, prehistory, porcelains, paleontology, puppets, photography, even chamber pots.

See the works of Durer, El Greco, Raphael, Holbein, Rembrandt and many other great 14th-to-18th-century painters at Alte (Old) Pinakothek, at 27 Barer Strasse, open Tuesday-Sunday 09:00–16:30, and on Tuesday and Thursday 07:00–21:00. The Neue (New) Pinakothek at 29 Barer Strasse (same days and hours as the "Old" museum) has a collection of 19th and 20th-century artists. The paintings of Kandinsky, Marcs and Klees in the Lenbachhaus, at 33 Luisen Strasse, open daily except Monday 10:00–18:00.

The 15th-century Frauenkirche Cathedral, and the view of Munich from its north tower. Then later the view of Frauenkirche from the top of Neue Rathaus (New City Hall), where at 11:00 every day the mechanical figures in its bell tower perform a tournament of knights, a medieval royal wedding, and a dance. There are other fine views of Munich from Olympia Tower.

The paintings of Cezanne, Gauguin, Renoir and other impressionists at the Haus der Kunst at 1 Princregenten Strasse, open daily except Monday 09:00–16:30. On Thursday, it is also open 19:00–21:00. For the Haus der Kunst and gallery area, use bus #55 and get off at Königinstr. See Wittelsbach Fountain.

The fine exhibits and planetarium at Deutsches Museum, considered the best scientific museum in the world, open daily 09:00–17:00. It is across the Ludwigsbrucke, on an island in the Isar River Displays of 16,000 items. For the Deutsches Museum and Ludwig's Bridge, use tram #18.

The view of the Alps from the top of Peterskirche. The best collection of tapestries and wood carvings in Germany, at the Bavarian National Museum. Munich's most famous beer palace, Hofbrauhaus.

The Schatzkammer in the Residenz palace (which houses the enormous Festaal and many museums that are open Tuesday–Saturday 10:00–16:30, Sunday 10:00–13:00), and the flower gardens in the park north of it. Words cannot describe the fabulous beauty of the Festaal.

At Schloss (Castle) Nymphenburg: the porcelain in the showrooms of Nymphenburger Porzellan Manufaktur, open daily except Monday 10:00–12:00 and 13:30–16:00. Also visit the park outside the castle. Located on the outskirts of Munich, Nymphenburg can be reached by taking the U-1 subway to the end of that line (Rotkreutzplatz) and transferring to the #12 streetcar. Alternate lines from the center of Munich are streetcars #17 or #21, or buses #41 or #42.

See the history of Munich in the Isartorplatz Museum. The impressive Renaissance Michalskirche on the Neuhauserstrasse pedestrian mall. Ancient Greek and Roman sculpture in the Glyptothek (Konigsplatz 3), open Tuesday, Wednesday, Friday and Sunday

10:00–16:30, on Thursday 12:00–20:30. Nearby, the Staatliche Antikensammlungen (State Collection of Antiquities) at Konigsplatz 1, open Tuesday and Thursday–Sunday 10:00–16:30, on Wednesday 12:00–20:30.

The collection of Medieval art and sculpture, arts and crafts, applied arts, folk art and folklore at the Bayerisches Nationalmuseum (Bavarian National Museum), at Prinzregenstrasse 3, open daily except Monday 09:30–17:00. Nearby, an exhibit of late 19th-century Herman painters in Schackgalerie at Prinzregenstrasse 9, open daily except Tuesday 09:00–16:30.

Visit Schwabing, the Latin quarter (take U-3, U-6 or U-2 and disembark at the fork formed by Ungererstr and Leopoldstr). See the palaces on Ludwigstrasse and the history of Bavarian Motor Works (aircraft, motorcycles, automobiles) in the BMW Museum, open daily 09:00–16:00.

Infamous Dachau is a 40-minute ride by commuter train S-2 or bus #11. Although there are no guides at Dachau, an exhibit there details the operation of the concentration camp, and an English-language film is shown at 11:30 and 15:30.

Since 1870, an Alois Dallmayr food store has offered gourmet delicacies in Munich. It added a restaurant in 1978. As Fauchon's in Paris does, Dallmayr (15 Dienerstrasse) has a vast section of imported foods. Its most notable feature, however, is the enormous array it offers of West Germany's finest lunch meats, 22 varieties of smoked fish, and 27 types of bread.

Nearly everything edible can be found at Dallmayr's: local and imported fruits, cooked meats and poultry, live fish swimming in marble tanks, wines, more than 50 different salads, 200 different chocolates, 120 different sausages, 18 types of ham, and they also sell special cigars.

If you eat none of the splendid food there, at least see the statues, marble pillars and mounted deer heads that decorate the interior of the store. Another famous food emporium is Kafer's, at 73 Prinzregenten, Germany's largest delicatessen and caterer. Both stores have an excellent restaurant.

The Viktualienmarkt, behind St. Peter's Church, is one of Europe's largest outdoor food markets. Two blocks long, it has operated since 1807: fruits, vegetables, poultry, cheeses, herbs, breads, pastries, wines, plants and flowers. It is open Monday–Friday 07:00–18:30, Saturday 07:00–17:00. Friday and Saturday are its busiest days. It is closed on Sundays.

The Most practical way to visit Neuschwanstein and Linderhof Castles is by taking the train-and-bus excursion operated by EurAide on Wednesday and Saturday during June, July and early August. Passengers depart Munich at 07:35, returning there 17:30. For information and advisable advance reservations, write to EurAide, Bahnhofplatz 2, Am Gleissll, 80335 Munchen 2, Germany. Telephone: (089) 59-38-89

Munich's 24-hour transit pass sells for DM10. For twice the price, you can extend your travels to take in all the transit network's zones. Pick up a copy of *Rendezvous with Munich* for all the latest transit information.

In the following timetables, where a city has more than one rail station, we have designated the particular station after the name of the city (in parentheses). Where no station is designated for cities in Austria, Switzerland and Germany, the station is "Hauptbahnhoff."

Reservations are advisable on most German trains!

Berlin - Chemnitz (formerly Karl Marx Stadt) - Berlin   835

All of these trains have light refreshments. Reservation is advisable for them.

Dep. Berlin (Lichtenberg)	07:32	11:32
Dep. Berlin (Schonefeld)	07:49	11:49
Arr. Chemnitz	10:08	14:08

Sights in **Chemnitz:** This was an East German post-World War II showplace new city before the 1990 unification of West and East Germany.

Dep. Chemnitz	13:57	15:57	17:57
Arr. Berlin (Schonefeld)	16:14	18:14	20:14
Arr. Berlin (Lichtenberg)	23 minutes later		

Berlin - Dresden - Berlin   840

All of these trains charge a supplement that includes reservation fee and have a restaurant car, unless designated otherwise.

Dep. Berlin (Licht.)	06:46	08:46	10:46	12:46	
Arr. Dresden (Hbf.)	08:48	10:37	12:37	14:37	

• • •

Dep. Dresden (Hbf.)	13:17	15:17	17:17	19:17	21:26
Arr. Berlin (Licht.)	15:10	17:10	19:10	21:10	23:14

Berlin - Erfurt - Berlin   850

Reservation is advisable for all of these trains. All of them have light refreshments, unless designated otherwise.

Dep. Berlin (Lichtenberg)	07:27	09:27	11:27
Dep. Berlin (Schonefeld)	20 minutes after departing Lichtenberg rail station		
Arr. Erfurt	10:57	12:57	14:57

Sights in **Erfurt:** The exquisite Gothic and German Renaissance houses. The cathedral, where Martin Luther was ordained in 1507. The bridge, on which 33 houses stand. St. Severin Church.

Dep. Erfurt	12:58	14:58	16:58	18:58
Arr. Berlin (Schonefeld)	16:05	18:05	20:05	22:05
Arr. Berlin (Lichtenberg)	20 minutes later			

Berlin - Frankfurt   900

All of these trains charge a supplement that includes reservation fee and have a restaurant car.

Dep. Berlin (Zoo)	05:58	08:00	10:00	12:00	14:00	16:00 (1)
Arr. Frankfurt (Hbf.)	10:43	12:43	14:43	16:43	18:43	20:43
			•	•	•	
Dep. Frankfurt (Hbf.)	07:15	09:15	11:15	13:15	15:15	17:15 (2)
Arr. Berlin (Zoo)	12:01	14:01	16:01	18:01	20:01	22:01

(1) Plus another Berlin departure at 18:00, arriving Frankfurt 22:53. (2) Plus another Frankfurt departure at 19:15, arriving Berlin 00:03.

Berlin - Hamburg   840

All of these trains charge a supplement that includes reservation fee and have a restaurant car.

Dep. Berlin (Zoo)	06:27	07:27	09:27	12:27	14:27	16:27 (1)
Arr. Hamburg (Hbf.)	08:51	09:52	11:52	14:47	16:47	18:47
		•	•	•		

Dep. Hamburg (Hbf.)	06:58	09:03	11:03	13:03	15:03	17:03 (2)
Arr. Berlin (Zoo)	09:32	11:32	13:32	15:32	17:32	19:32

(1) Plus other Berlin (Hbf.) departures at 18:27 and 20:27, arriving Hamburg 20:52 and 21:52. (2) Plus other Hamburg departures at 1903 and 20:40, arriving Berlin (Hbf.) 21:32 and 23:12.

Berlin - Hannover   810

All of these trains charge a supplement that includes reservation fee and have a restaurant car, unless designated otherwise.

Dep. Berlin (Zoo)	07:13	09:13	11:13	
Arr. Hannover	09:54	11:54	13:54	
	•	•	•	
Dep. Hannover	16:04	18:04	18:22	20:07
Arr. Berlin (Zoo)	18:51	20:51	21:20	22:55

Berlin - Leipzig - Berlin   850

Dep. Berlin (Zoo)	05:38 (1)	07:40 (1)	09:40 (1)
Arr. Leipzig	07:30	09:34	11:32
	•	•	•
Dep. Leipzig	14:22 (2)	16:22 (2)	18:22
Arr. Berlin (Licht.)	16:19	18:19	20:19

(1) Reservation advisable. Restaurant car. (2) Supplement charged includes reservation fee. Restaurant car.

Berlin - Munich and Munich - Berlin   875

All of the day trains charge a supplement that includes reservation fee and have a restaurant car.

Dep. Berlin (Hbf.)	07:40	09:40	11:40	13:40	15:40
Arr. Munich	15:06	17:06	19:06	21:16	23:06
		•	•	•	
Dep. Munich	06:52	08:49	10:52	12:52	14:52
Arr. Berlin (Hbf.)	14:19	16:19	18:19	20:19	22:19

Berlin - Potsdam - Berlin 810

There are frequent trains from Berlin's Zoo station 05:10 to 23:55 for this 20-minute ride. From Potsdam: 06:35 to 23:53. Reservations are advisable.

Sights in **Potsdam:** The Concert Room and the great paintings in the picture gallery at the 18th-century Sans Souci Palace. The 17th-century palace, Cecillienhof, where Truman, Attlee and Stalin signed the Potsdam Agreement in 1945.

Berlin - Rostock - Berlin 835

Reservation is advisable for all of these trains.

Dep. Berlin (Lichtenberg)	06:47 (1)	08:47 (1)	10:47 (1)	12:47 (1)
Arr. Rostock	09:22	11:22	13:22	15:22

Sights in **Rostock:** East Germany's largest seaport. See St. Mary's Church. The ancient town hall.

Dep. Rostock	12:31 (1)	14:31 (1)	16:31 (1)	18:31 (1)	20:31
Arr. Berlin (Lichtenberg)	15:08	17:08	19:08	21:08	23:08

(1) Light refreshments.

Berlin - Stralsund - Berlin 835

Dep. Berlin (Licht.)	07:41	09:41	11:41
Arr. Stralsund (Hbf.)	10:51	12:49	14:51

Sights in **Stralsund:** Many old red-brick buildings and churches along the city's quaint Hanseatic streets.

Dep. Stralsund (Hbf.)	13:07	15:00	17:08	19:08
Arr. Berlin (Licht.)	15:44	18:16	20:16	22:16

Berlin - Rostock - Warnemunde - Berlin   835, DB Timetable

Dep. Berlin (Licht.)	06:47 (1)	08:47 (1)	16:47 (1)	18:47 (1)
Arr. Rostock	09:22	11:22	19:22	21:22
Arr. Warnemunde	Transfer to local train; frequent around-the-clock departures; arrive approximately 20 minutes later.			

Sights in **Warnemunde:** A famous beach resort. A ferry connection to Denmark.

Dep. Warnemunde	Board local train; frequent around-the-clock departures; arrive Rostock approximately 20 minutes after departure.			
Dep. Rostock	04:31 (1)	10:31 (1)	14:31 (1)	18:31 (1)
Arr. Berlin (Licht.)	07:08	13:08	17:08	21:08

(1) Light refreshments.

Cologne - Aachen - Cologne   800

Dep. Cologne	07:14 (1)	08:14 (2)	09:14 (1)	10:50	11:14 (1)
Arr. Aachen	08:00	08:55	09:56	11:46	12:00

· · ·

Dep. Aachen	12:53 (1)	13:58 (2)	14:12	15:53 (1)	17:12	18:12 (1+3)
Arr. Cologne	13:42	14:42	15:11	16:42	18:11	19:11

(1) Light refreshments. (2) Supplement charged includes reservation fee. Restaurant car. (3) Plus other Aachen departures at 18:12, 18:56 (2), 19:12, 19:58 (2), 21:12 (2), 21:35 (1), 21:55 (2) and 22:02.

Cologne - Amsterdam - Cologne   28

All of these trains charge a supplement that includes reservation fee and have light refreshments.

Dep. Cologne	07:09	08:16	10:16	12:16
Arr. Amsterdam	09:54	10:52	12:52	14:52

· · ·

Dep. Amsterdam	15:00	17:00	19:00	20:05
Arr. Cologne	17:41	19:41	21:41	23:48

Cologne - Bonn - Cologne   910

Dep. Cologne	Frequent times from 01:39 to 23:58
Arr. Bonn	22 minutes later

Sights in **Bonn:** Beethoven-Halle and the museum at Bonngasse 20, where Beethoven was born in 1770. Drachenfels Mountain and the castle ruins that Byron immortalized. The 13th-century Remigius Church. Jesu Church. The view of the Rhine and Siebengebirge from Alte Zoll. The university in the Electors' Castle. Poppelsdorf Castle. The Rhineland Museum. The Collegiate Church and Cloister. Take a cruise boat on the Rhine River to see the Siebengebirge Mountains.

Dep. Bonn	Frequent times from 01:49 to 23:45
Arr. Cologne	22 minutes later

Cologne - Brussels - Cologne   20

Dep. Cologne	06:30 (1)	07:14	09:14 (1)		
Arr. Brussels (Nord)	08:50	09:44	11:32		
Arr. Brussels (Cen.)	-0-	-0-	-0-		
Arr. Brussels (Midi)	09:01	09:54	11:42		
	•	•	•		
Dep. Brussels (Midi)	12:07 (1)	13:48	15:55	16:54	18:08 (1+2)
Dep. Brussels (Cen.)	-0-	-0-	-0-	-0-	-0-
Dep. Brussels (Nord)	12:16	13:57	16:03	17:03	18:17
Arr. Cologne	14:42	16:42	19:25	19:42	20:42

(1) Supplement charged includes reservation fee. Restaurant car or light refreshments. (2) Plus other departures from Brussels Midi/Zuid at 18:47, 20:03 (1), arriving Cologne 21:59 and 22:42.

Cologne - Dortmund - Cologne   800

Dep. Cologne	Frequent times from 03:16 to 23:16
Arr. Dortmund	70 minutes later

Sights in **Dortmund:** The view of the city from the top of the Television Tower. Westphalia Park. The Ostwall Museum.

Dep. Dortmund	Frequent times from 03:44 to 22:38
Arr. Cologne	70 minutes later

Cologne - Dusseldorf - Cologne   800

There is frequent rail service between Dusseldorf's rail station and its airport. Travel time is 12 minutes (Table 699).

| Dep. Cologne | Frequent times from 03:16 to 23:11 |
| Arr. Dusseldorf | 24–28 minutes later |

Sights in **Dusseldorf:** Many sensational modern buildings, replacing the 85 of the city that was destroyed in World War II. See the Paul Klee collection at Kunsttammlung Nordhein-Westfallen. The Aquarium at the Museumbunker am Zoo.

The collection of 18th-century Meissenware and 20th-century art (Kadinsky, Chagall, Braque, etc., with 90 works by Paul Klee) at the 18th-century Jagerhof Castle in the 30-acre Hofgarten (park), open daily except Monday 10:00–17:00 (until 20:00 on Wednesday).

The large collection of Goethe memorabilia (30,000 items: first editions, paintings, manuscripts) at the Goethe Museum, also in Hofgarten, open daily except Monday 10:00–17:00. An enormous collection of paintings in the Kunstmuseum.

The more than 4,000 manuscripts in the Heinrich Heine Institute, Bilkerstrasse 14, open daily except Monday 10:00–17:00. Near Altstadt ("Old Town"), stroll the half-mile long shopping street, Konigsallee (called "the Ko").

Take the 75-minute boat trip on the Rhine to Zons. Boats leave every 60 minutes 13:30–17:30 from the Rathausufer, at the edge of Old Town.

Take the 30-minute tram ride (#1 and #18, from Jan-Welem-Platz) to the 18th-century Benrath Castle, surrounded by spectacular English-style and French- style gardens.

Sample the eight local beers in Old Town and try the local food specialties: reibekuchen, a potato pancake; halve hahn, a caraway cheese eaten with mustard on roggelchen, small loaves of rye bread; spanferkel brotchen, slices of roast suckling pig served on a roll; bratwurst with hot mustard; and blutwurst, a black pudding served with raw onions.

| Dep. Dusseldorf | Frequent times from 05:09 to 23:29 |
| Arr. Cologne | 24–28 minutes later |

Cologne - Frankfurt - Cologne   910

All of these trains have a restaurant car or light refreshments.

| Dep. Cologne | Frequent times from 05:54 to 23:10 |
| Arr. Frankfurt | 2–2½ hours later |

• • •

| Dep. Frankfurt | Frequent times from 05:44 to 22:15 |
| Arr. Cologne | 2–2½ hours later |

Cologne - Hamburg - Cologne 800

All of these trains charge a supplement that includes reservation fee and have a restaurant car, unless designated otherwise.

Dep. Cologne	06:18	07:03	08:09	09:10	10:09	11:10
Arr. Hamburg (Hbf.)	09:45	11:07	12:07	13:07	14:07	15:07

Dep. Cologne	12:09	13:10	14:09	15:10	16:09	17:10 (1)
Arr. Hamburg (Hbf.)	16:07	17:07	18:07	19:07	20:07	21:07

Dep. Hamburg (Hbf.)	03:12	04:53	05:53	06:53	07:53	08:53
Arr. Cologne	07:57	08:49	09:50	10:50	11:49	12:55

Dep. Hamburg (Hbf.)	09:53	10:53	11:53	12:53	13:53	14:53 (2)
Arr. Cologne	13:49	14:49	15:49	16:50	17:49	18:49

(1) Plus other Cologne departures at 18:07, 19:10, 20:10 and 21:59. (2) Plus other Hamburg departures at 15:53, 16:53, 17:53 (3), 18:53 and 19:53.

Cologne - Heidelberg - Cologne 910

Reservation is advisable for all of these trains, and they have light refreshments.

Dep. Cologne	07:10	09:10
Arr. Heidelberg	10:02	12:02

Sights in **Heidelberg:** Take a short cable-car ride from the town center to see the gardens, library, Great Terrace, Fat Tower, Elizabeth Gate, Freidrich's Wing, the Otto-Heinrich Wing, the Mirror Room Wing, the 10-room German Pharmaceutical Museum and the Great Vat (said to be the world's largest wine barrel, holding 55,000 gallons), all at Heidelberg Castle.

Visit Germany's oldest (13th century) university, immortalized in "The Student Prince" opera. The astounding 16th-century carved wood Altar of the Twelve Apostles in the Kurpfalzisches Museum. The Jesuit Church. The Church of the Holy Ghost, where visitors often hear impromptu organ concerts. The 16th-century wood-carved Windsheim Altar (Christ and the Twelve Apostles) plus many rooms furnished with period pieces and paintings in the Palatine Museum at the Palais Morass. Knight's Mansion. Student's Jail.

From Easter into October, there are boat trips on the **Neckar River** that begin each morning and afternoon, with views of many medieval villages and fortresses. It is only a 20-minute bus ride to **Neckargemund**, where you can wander ancient cobbled streets and see the view of the river and the countryside from Zum Ritter, a restaurant operating since 1579.

| Dep. Heidelberg | 13:55 | 17:51 |
| Arr. Cologne | 16:46 | 20:30 |

Cologne - Koblenz - Cologne   910

Most of these trains charge a supplement that includes reservation fee and have a restaurant car.

| Dep. Cologne | Frequent times from 01:39 to 23:58 |
| Arr. Koblenz | 60 minutes later |

Sights in **Koblenz:** Where the Rhine and Moselle rivers meet. See Old Town, St. Castor's Church, the Middle Rhine Museum, Stolzenfels Castle, the 18th-century Prince Electors' Palace, the regional and Rhenish museums in the 19th-century Ehrenbreitstein Fortress, the wine village.

Visit the 13th-century castle, the 18th-century Mint Master's House, the 18th-century Baroque Franconian Royal Palace, the 13th-century Romanesque Church of Our Lady, the 15th-century Altes Kaufhaus. The 16th-century Schoffenhaus.

The very scenic 4½-hour Koblenz–Cochem boat trip on the Mosel River is covered by Eurailpass. Views include hillside vineyards and quaint "wine villages." There is a magnificent castle in Cochem.

A popular detour is to get off the boat before it arrives in Cochem—at Moselkern—and walk 45 minutes through the forest to Burg Eltz, one of Europe's loveliest castles. Then take a train from Moselkern to Cochem, and return to Koblenz from Cochem either by boat or by a 45 minute train ride.

| Dep. Koblenz | Frequent times from 01:18 to 23:12 |
| Arr. Cologne | 60 minutes later |

Cologne - Luxembourg - Cologne   915

Reservation is advisable for these trains, unless designated otherwise.

| Dep. Cologne | 06:10 | 08:10 (1) | 10:10 |
| Arr. Luxembourg | 09:23 | 13:23 | 13:23 |

• • •

| Dep. Luxembourg | 09:40 | 10:33 | 14:33 |
| Arr. Cologne | 13:03 | 13:46 | 17:46 |

(1) Change trains in Trier. Two-hour layover to explore Trier.

Cologne - Mainz - Cologne   Boat   910, 914

Here is a way to combine a cruise on the Rhine with a scenic rail trip.

Have lunch and Rhine wine on board the 09:00 boat just before arriving Mainz. Early in the trip, you can see Drachenfels Castle, near Bonn. During the Koblenz–Bingen portion of this cruise, you will see the best scenery on the Rhine, many hilltop castles, and the Lorelei.

914

Dep. Cologne (Rheingarten)	09:00 (1)
Dep. Bonn	09:40
Dep. Koblenz	11:05
Dep. Bingen	12:30
Arr. Mainz	13:15

(1) Hydrofoil boat express service. *Not* covered by Eurailpass. Supplement charged. Operates late-March to late October.

Sights in **Mainz:** The art collection in the 1,000-year-old cathedral. Adjacent to it is the Gutenberg Museum, with the first printed bible and where a movie on the inventor's life can be viewed. Also visit the Museum of the Central Rhineland. See rare books in the World Museum of Printing in the Romischer Kaiser. Restored Baroque mansions are on the Schillerplatz and Schillerstrasse, in the Kirschgarten. Old Town and sculptures in the Diocesan Museum are worth a look.

Then for the train ride back to Cologne:

All of these trains charge a supplement that includes reservation fee and have a restaurant car.

910

Dep. Mainz	14:16	19:47	21:22	22:23
Arr. Koblenz	15:06	20:37	22:12	23:12
Arr. Bonn	15:39	21:10	22:45	23:45
Arr. Cologne	15:59	21:30	23:05	00:05

Here is the schedule for visiting Mainz by taking the train both ways:

910

Dep. Cologne	Frequent times from 01:39 to 23:58
Arr. Mainz	2 hours later

• • •

Dep. Mainz	Frequent times from 00:28 to 22:23
Arr. Cologne	2 hours later

Cologne - Mannheim - Cologne   910

All of these trains charge a supplement that includes reservation fee and have a restaurant car, unless designated otherwise.

Dep. Cologne	06:27	07:00	07:27	08:00	08:27 (1)
Arr. Mannheim	08:52	09:25	09:52	10:25	10:52

(1) Plus other frequent departures from Cologne at 09:00 to 21:25.

Sights in **Mannheim:** The Squared Town. The first thing that strikes you about Mannheim is its "Squareness." Built to be a fortified town, it was designed as a chessboard of 144 residential blocks, each known by a letter and number that identifies its position on the grid.

See the Fine Arts Museum, Reiss Municipal Museum, the cathedral, Europe's largest Romanesque church. Visit the water tower, the old town hall and parish church in the Marketplatz, also the castle.

Dep. Mannheim	Frequent departures from 03:36 to 20:34
Arr. Cologne	2½ hours later

Cologne - Siegen - Cologne   808

Dep. Cologne	Every other hour 08:19-22:19
Arr. Siegen	1½ hours later

Sights in **Siegen:** The Upper Castle, with its Rubens paintings (he was born here) in the Siegerland Museum, which also offers the history of this region and a tour of the old iron mine under the castle's cellar. See the crypts of the Princes of Nassau-Orange in the castle.

Dep. Siegen	Every hour 08:09-22:09
Arr. Cologne	1½ hours later

Cologne - Trier - Cologne   915

Dep. Cologne	06:10	08:10	10:10	Dep. Trier	15:17	17:17
Arr. Trier	08:37	10:38	12:38	Arr. Cologne	17:46	19:46

Dresden - Berlin - Dresden 840

All of these trains charge a supplement that includes reservation fee and have a restaurant car, unless designated otherwise.

Dep. Dresden (Hbf.)	07:15 (1)	08:30 (2)	11:17 (3)
Arr. Berlin (Licht.)	09:20	10:31	13:10

* * *

Dep. Berlin (Licht.)	12:46 (3)	14:47 (3)	16:46 (3)	18:46	21:32
Arr. Dresden (Hbf.)	14:37	16:37	18:37	20:37	23:30

(1) Supplement payable. Restaurant car. (2) Arrives Berlin Zoo Station. (3) Reservation advisable. Restaurant car.

Dresden - Chemnitz (formerly Karl Marx Stadt) - Dresden 880

Reservation is advisable for all of these trains, unless designated otherwise.

Dep. Dresden (Hbf.)	07:34 (1)	09:34 (1)	10:34 (2)	11:34 (1)	12:34 (3)
Arr. Chemnitz	08:47	10:47	11:48	12:47	13:48

Sights in **Chemnitz**: An East German post-World War II showplace *new* city.

Dep. Chemnitz	11:56 (2)	12:57 (1)	13:56 (2)	14:57 (1)	15:56 (2+4)
Arr. Dresden (Hbf.)	13:14	14:14	15:14	16:14	17:14

(1) Light refreshments. (2) Reservation not available. (3) Runs daily except Sundays & holidays. (4) Plus other Chemnitz departures at 16:57 (1), 18:57 (1), 19:56 (2), 20:57 (1) and 22:02 (2), arriving Dresden 18:14, 20:14, 21:13, 22:14 and 23:16.

Dresden - Leipzig - Dresden 840

Dep. Dresden (Hbf.)	07:25 (1)	10:00
Dep. Dresden (Neu.)	8 minutes after departing Hauptbahnhof.	
Arr. Leipzig	08:45	11:35

* * *

Dep. Leipzig	13:24 (1)	14:28	17:24 (1)	18:04 (1)	21:1 (1)
Arr. Dresden (Neu.)	14:34	15:55	18:42	19:37	22:45
Arr. Dresden (Hbf.)	8 minutes later				

(1) Reservation advisable. Restaurant car.

Frankfurt - Basel - Frankfurt 910

All of these trains charge a supplement that includes a reservation fee and have a restaurant car, unless designated otherwise.

Dep. Frankfurt (Hbf.)	07:47	08:47	09:47	10:05 (1)
Arr. Mannheim	08:26	09:26	10:26	10:42
Change trains				
Dep. Manheim	08:33	09:33	10:33 (1)	10:44
Arr. Basel (Badisch.)	10:45	11:45	12:45	12:55
Arr. Basel (SBB)	7 minutes later			

* * *

Dep. Basel (SBB)	14:14	15:14	16:14	17:14	18:14 (2)
Dep. Basel (Badisch.)	7 minutes later				
Arr. Mannheim	16:25	17:26	18:25	19:26	20:26
Change trains					
Dep. Mannheim	16:32	17:32	18:32	19:32	20:32
Arr. Frankfurt	17:11	18:11	19:11	20:11	21:11

(1) Direct train. No train change in Mannheim. (2) Plus another departure from Basel at 19:14, arriving Frankfurt 22:15.

Frankfurt - Bremen - Frankfurt 900, 816

All of these trains charge a supplement that includes a reservation fee, unless designated otherwise. Unless designated otherwise, the Frankfurt–Hannover (and v.v.) trains have a restaurant car—and the Hannover–Bremen and (v.v.) trains have light refreshments.

750
Dep. Frankfurt	06:03	08:19	08:57	10:19
Arr. Hannover	08:28	10:40	11:08	12:40
Change trains 816				
Dep. Hannover	09:44	11:44 (1)	12:19 (1)	13:44
Arr. Bremen	10:48	12:48	13:41	14:48

Sights in **Bremen:** It is an easy walk, down Bahnhofstrasse, from the rail station to the fine buildings in Market Square (Am Markt). Starting there at the 18-foot-high statue of Roland (Sculpted in 1404), following the white dots on the sidewalk will lead you to most of the city's important places. The statue faces the 11th-century St. Peter's Cathedral, open daily to tourists, except Saturday afternoon and Sunday morning.

Close by the cathedral, the 17th-century city hall offers free guided morning tours daily, except Sunday. The interesting features in its upstairs hall are the oak-beamed ceiling, portraits of Holy Roman emperors from Charlemagne to Sigismund, and ship models. Also see the exceptional woodcarving in its Golden Chamber.

The largest rathskeller in Europe, serving only German wine (500,000 bottles a year), located under the city hall, has been a tavern, restaurant and wine cellar for over 500 years. More than 800 people can be seated there. Very crowded at noon, it offers a choice of more than 500 wine varieties and vintages from Germany's 11 main wine areas. Its bottles and casks include vintages from as far back as 1653.

Behind the city hall is the 13th-century Liebfrauenkirche (Church of Our Lady), whose seven new stained glass windows were installed in 1966. It is open daily, but closed 12:30–14:00.

Walk from Market Square down Bottcherstrasse to see the Porcelain Carillon and Atlantic House, decorated with Zodiac signs.

The Ubersee (Overseas) Museum, across from the rail station at 13 Bahnofplatz, has exhibits of ethnology, world trade and natural history, gathered in the Middle Ages by Bremen ships. It is open daily, except Monday 10:00–18:00.

Visit the Focke Museum of Folklore and the Municipal Weights and Measures Office. See the old workshops, inns and houses in the Schnoor residential area.

Near Martini Church, 90-minute boat tours of Europe's third largest port depart five times a day in summer, at the river end of Bottcherstrasse.

In Bremerhaven, 36 miles away where the Weser River meets the North Sea, there is a maritime museum called Schiffahrts on Van Ronzelenstrasse. It is open daily, except Monday.

816

Dep. Bremen	13:10 (1)	14:16 (1)	15:10	16:15	17:18 (2)
Arr. Hannover	14:14	15:15	16:14	17:15	18:41
Change trains 900					
Dep. Hannover	14:50	15:50	16:50	17:50	19:18
Arr. Frankfurt	17:01	18:01	19:01	20:01	21:42

(1) No supplement. (2) Plus another Bremen departure at 19:01, arriving Frankfurt 23:04.

Frankfurt - Brussels - Frankfurt 21

Dep. Frankfurt	06:50 (1)	08:50 (2)	Dep. Brussels (Midi)	14:48 (2)	16:54 (2+3)
Arr. Cologne	09:05	11:05	Arr. Cologne	17:42	19:42
Change trains			*Change trains*		
Dep. Cologne	09:14 (1)	11:14 (2)	Dep. Cologne	17:54 (1)	19:54 (1)
Arr. Brussels (Midi)	11:42	13:54	Arr. Frankfurt	20:08	22:08

(1) Supplement includes a reservation fee. Restaurant car. (2) Light refreshments. (3) Plus another Brussels departure at 18:08 (1), arriving Frankfurt 23:21.

Frankfurt - Cologne - Frankfurt 910

From Mainz to Bonn, the cliffs on both sides of the Rhine are topped by ruins of ancient castles. This portion of the river is crowded with barges, sailboats, recreational motorboats, ferries and cruise ships.

All of these trains charge a supplement that includes a reservation fee and have a restaurant car, unless designated otherwise.

Dep. Frankfurt	06:58	07:50	08:50	09:39	10:39		
Dep. Mainz	07:28	08:22	09:22	10:22	11:22		
Dep. Bonn	08:59	09:45	10:45	11:45	12:45		
Arr. Cologne	09:24	10:05	11:05	12:05	13:05		

• • •

Dep. Cologne	12:54	13:54	14:54	15:54	16:54	17:54	18:54 (1)
Dep. Bonn	13:14	14:14	15:14	16:14	17:14	18:14	19:14
Dep. Mainz	14:39	15:39	16:39	17:39	18:39	19:39	20:39
Arr. Frankfurt	15:08	16:08	17:08	18:08	19:08	20:08	21:08

(1) Plus other departures from Cologne at 19:54, 20:26, 21:00 and 21:26, arriving Frankfurt 22:08 23:00, 23:21 and 23:50.

Frankfurt - Dusseldorf - Frankfurt 800

All of these trains charge a supplement that includes a reservation fee and have a restaurant car, unless designated otherwise.

Dep. Frankfurt	06:51	09:51			
Arr. Dusseldorf	09:39	12:32			

• • •

Dep. Dusseldorf	13:27	15:27	18:27	19:27	20:03 (1+2)
Arr. Frankfurt	16:08	18:08	21:08	22:08	23:00

(1) No supplement charged. Runs Monday-Saturday. (2) Plus another Dusseldorf departure at 20:50, arriving Frankfurt 23:50.

Frankfurt - Essen - Frankfurt 800

All of these trains charge a supplement that includes a reservation fee and have a restaurant car, unless designated otherwise.

Dep. Frankfurt	06:16	07:50	09:50
Arr. Essen	09:48	10:59	12:59

Sights in **Essen**: One of the leading German collections of 18th, 19th and 20th-century art (Menzel, Delacroix, Renoir, Gaugin, Vlaminck, Kandinsky, Klee, Rothko, Rodin) at the Folkwang Museum. The 10th-century cathedral and its collection of priceless 10th and 11th-century processional crosses, the 9th-century Golden Madonna (oldest Western statue of the Virgin Mary), and the sword of Cosmas and Damian, the martyr saints.

The chronicle of the Krupp family and business in the Annex at Villa Hugel, former residence of the Krupp family. The 12th-century castle, Burg Altendorf. The Four Horsemen bronze door on the 11th-century Marktkirche, Protestant since 1563.

Dep. Essen	15:01	15:55 (1)	16:32 (1)	18:01	19:30 (2)
Arr. Frankfurt	18:08	19:08	20:08	21:08	23:00

(1) Change trains in Cologne. (2) No supplement. Light refreshments.

Frankfurt - Hamburg - Frankfurt 903

All of these trains charge a supplement that includes a reservation fee and have a restaurant car, unless designated otherwise.

Dep. Frankfurt (Hbf.)	06:03	07:57	08:57	09:57	
Arr. Hamburg (Hbf.)	09:52	11:22	12:22	13:22	
		• • •			
Dep. Hamburg (Hbf.)	14:36	15:36	16:36	18:36	19:36
Arr. Frankfurt (Hbf.)	18:01	19:01	20:01	22:01	23:04

Frankfurt - Hannover - Frankfurt 900

All of these trains charge a supplement that includes a reservation fee and have a restaurant car, unless designated otherwise.

Dep. Frankfurt	06:03	07:57	08:19	08:57	09:57	10:19
Dep. Hannover	08:28	10:08	10:38	11:08	12:08	12:39

. . .

Dep. Hannover	14:50	15:18	15:50	16:50	17:18	17:5 (1)
Arr. Frankfurt	17:01	17:38	18:01	19:01	19:38	20:01

(1) Plus other Hannover departures at 18:50, 19:18 and 21:28 (2), arriving Frankfurt 21:01, 21:42 and 23:46. (2) Runs daily except Saturday.

Frankfurt - Heidelberg - Frankfurt   910

Reservation is advisable for all of these trains, and they have light refreshments.

Dep. Frankfurt	Every 2 hours from 07:51 to 21:51
Arr. Heidelberg	One hour later

. . .

Dep. Heidelberg	Every 2 hours from 07:17 to 21:17 + 23:10
Arr. Frankfurt	One hour later

Frankfurt - Kassel - Frankfurt   900

All of these trains charge a supplement that includes a reservation fee and have a restaurant car.

Dep. Frankfurt (Hbf.)	Every hour from 07:15 to 21:15
Arr. Kassel (Wil.)	1½ hours later

Sights in **Kassel**: Take bus #13 to see the enormous 233-foot-high copper statue of Hercules, the 19th-century Wilhelmshohe Castle, and the art museums (Rembrandt, Durer, Rubens) inside the Castle. Open daily except Monday, March–October, 10:00–17:00. Also see the collection of Brothers Grimm memorabilia in the City Museum. They wrote their fairy tales here. Other interesting sights are the 18th-century Orangery Palace in Karlsaue Park, the paintings in the Landesmuseum, the Tapestry Museum, the Fredericianum Museum and the world's only wallpaper museum.

Dep. Kassel (Wil.)	Every hour from 06:15 to 21:15 (1)
Arr. Frankfurt (Hbf.)	1½ hours later

(1) Plus another departure from Kassel at 22:34, arriving Frankfurt 00:05.

Frankfurt - Luxembourg - Frankfurt   910, 915

All of the Frankfurt–Koblenz (and v.v.) trains charge a supplement that includes reservation fee. Reservation is advisable for the Koblenz-Luxemburg (and v.v.) trains, unless designated otherwise.

910			*915*		
Dep. Frankfurt	05:45	09:50 (1)	Dep. Luxembourg	10:33 (2)	14:33 (2)
Arr. Koblenz	07:07	11:12	Arr. Koblenz	12:37	16:37
Change trains 915			*Change trains 910*		
Dep. Koblenz	07:19 (2)	11:19 (2)	Dep. Koblenz	13:49 (1)	17:49 (1)
Arr. Luxembourg	09:23	13:23	Arr. Frankfurt	15:08	19:08

(1) Restaurant car. (2) Light refreshments.

Frankfurt - Mainz - Frankfurt   910

All of these trains charge a supplement that includes a reservation fee and have a restaurant car or light refreshments.

Dep. Frankfurt	50 minutes past each hour from 06:50 to 21:0
Arr. Mainz	32 minutes later
Dep. Mainz	39 minutes past each hour from 07:39 to 21:39
Arr. Frankfurt	31 minutes later

Frankfurt - Mannheim - Frankfurt   910

All of these trains charge a supplement that includes reservation fee and have a restaurant car or light refreshments.

Dep. Frankfurt	Frequent times from 05:30 to 23:08.
Arr. Mannheim	40 minutes later

• • •

Dep. Mannheim	Frequent times from 06:15 to 22:34.
Arr. Frankfurt	41 minutes later

Frankfurt - Munich - Frankfurt   930

All of these trains charge a supplement that includes reservation fee and have a restaurant car.

Dep. Frankfurt	06:25	07:47 (1)	08:47	09:47			
Arr. Munich	09:46	11:18	12:18	13:18			

Dep. Munich	12:41	13:41	14:41	15:41	16:41	17:38 (2)	19:41 (3)
Arr. Frankfurt	16:11	17:11	18:11	19:11	20:11	21:11	23:16

(1) Runs Monday–Saturday. (2) Runs daily, except Saturday. (3) Plus another Munich departure at 20:46, arriving Frankfurt 00:44.

Frankfurt - Nurnberg (and Bayreuth) - Frankfurt   920

All of these trains charge a supplement that includes reservation fee and have a restaurant car or light refreshments.

Dep. Frankfurt	Every hour from 07:19 to 22:23
Arr. Nurnberg	2 hours and 10 minutes later

Sights in **Nurnberg**: The bronze and silver Sebaldusgrab, excellent stained glass and the carved tomb of Saint Sebaldus, for whom the 13th-century church is named. Take a guided tour of the Kaiserburg (Imperial Castle), Burggrafenburg and Imperial Stables in the fort. See the Albrecht Durer Haus, with copies of his paintings. The kitchen is as it was, when the artist lived there from 1509 to 1528. Open daily except Monday 10:00–13:00 and 14:00–17:00. Also see the Rosette window, wood carvings and statues in St. Lorenz Kirche.

Visit the 14th-century Frauenkirche in the marketplace, where the moving figures in the clock perform every day at 12:00. Then lunch at a bratwurst restaurant. One is located next to St. Sebaldus Church; another is behind the rebuilt 17th-century Rathaus (City Hall). There are guided tours of 14th-century catacombs (torture chamber and dungeons) in the Rathaus.

Also visit the Alstadt Museum, the collection of toys, doll houses and other works in the German National Museum and the 40 gold figures of artists, emperors, philosophers, prophets and popes around the 14th-century Schoner Brunnen (Beautiful Fountain) at Hauptmarkt, where farmers sell their produce from stalls.

On the little island in the Pegnitz River is the Holy Ghost Hospital, locale of the legendary Till Eulenspiegel. Disguised as a doctor, this is where the 14th-century peasant clown told the man in charge of the hospital that he could cure all the patients in one day. The hospital authorities believed Till was a miracle worker when the patients rose from their beds and left the hospital after he whispered in each one's ear. He told the patients: "Those of you who are the most sick are going to be burned into a powder the hospital will use to heal the others."

Visit the collection of porcelains and the model of Old Nurnberg at Fembo House (The

City Historical Museum), 15 Burgstrasse, open daily except Monday 10:00–17:00. The best collection of old trains in West Germany (including Germany's first locomotive) is in Nurnberg's Transport Museum, open Monday-Saturday 10:00–17:00 (closes at 16:00 in Winter) and Sunday 10:00–13:00. Toys from all over the world are exhibited at Spielzeug Museum, open daily except Monday 10:00–17:00.

From Nurnberg, it's a short trip to Bayreuth, site of a five-week annual (over 100 years) Wagner opera festival at Festspielhaus, every year from late July to late August at 16:00.

Marvelous sights in nearby **Bayreuth**: Haus Wahnfried, Wagner's home. The breathtaking opera house. The Orangerie castle, open daily 10:00–11:30 and 13:30–15:00. Eremitage Park.

Dep. Nurnberg	Every hour from 08:31 to 20:31
Arr. Frankfurt	2 hours and 10 minutes later

Here are the connections between Nurnberg and Bayreuth:
There is great river and canyon scenery on the Nurnberg-Pegnitz portion of this trip.

886

Dep. Nurnberg	49 minutes after each hour from 05:49 to 23:49		Dep. Bayreuth	10 minutes after each hour from 05:10 to 22:10
Dep. Pegnitz	40 minutes later		Arr. Pegnitz	18 minutes later
Arr. Bayreuth	16 minutes after Pegnitz		Arr. Nurnberg	40 minutes after Bayreuth

---

Frankfurt - Siegen - Frankfurt   807

Dep. Frankfurt	08:03 (1)	10:03 (1+2)	Dep. Siegen	13:53	15:53 (3)
Arr. Giessen	08:43	10:43	Arr. Giessen	14:44	16:44
Change trains			*Change trains*		
Dep. Giessen	09:15	11:15	Dep. Giessen	15:16 (1)	17:11 (1)
Arr. Siegen	10:06	12:06	Arr. Frankfurt	15:57	17:57

(1) Light refreshments. (2) Plus another departures from Frankfurt at 12:03 (1), arriving Siegen 13:47. (3) Plus other departures from Siegen at 17:53 and 19:53, departing Giessen 19:16 (1) and 21:16 (1), arriving Frankfurt 19:57 and 21:57.

Frankfurt - Strasbourg - Frankfurt   904, 945

904			727		
Dep. Frankfurt	07:40 (1)	11:38 (1)	Dep. Strasbourg	09:44	18:02
Arr. Offenburg	09:56	13:56	Arr. Offenburg	10:13	18:28
Change trains 945			*Change trains 904*		
Dep. Offenburg	11:28 (2)	17:28 (2)	Dep. Offenburg	14:04 (1)	20:04 (1)
Arr. Strasbourg	12:07	18:07	Arr. Frankfurt	16:20	23:23

(1) Reservation advisable. Light refreshment. (2) Change trains in Kehl.

Frankfurt - Stuttgart - Frankfurt 930

All of these trains charge a supplement that includes reservation fee and have a restaurant car.

Dep. Frankfurt   Every hour from 07:27 to 21:47
Arr. Stuttgart   One hour and 20 minutes later

Sights in **Stuttgart:** Outstanding contemporary architecture, built since World War II. The Schillerplatz flower and vegetable market (Tuesday, Thursday and Saturday). Also on Schillerplatz, Swabian art and culture from the Middle Ages to Art Nouveau, at the Wuerttemberg Provincial Museum in the Altes Schloss. Europe's most modern planetarium, opened in 1977.

The largest Picasso collection in Germany (among the 4,000 paintings from the 14th-to-20th-century), at the State Gallery, Konrad Adenaur Strasse 32. The Daimler-Benz Automobile Museum, admission only by advance appointment. The Museum of Natural History, in Rosenstein Palace.

Dep. Stuttgart   Every hour from 05:51 to 21:51
Arr. Frankfurt   One hour and 20 minutes later

Frankfurt - Wiesbaden 919

Dep. Frankfurt   Frequent times from 05:00 to 23:30
Arr. Wiesbaden   33-40 minutes later

Sights in **Wiesbaden:** One of Europe's top mineral bath resorts. See Brunnenkolonnade, the longest colonnade in Europe.

Dep. Wiesbaden   Frequent times from 06:33 to 20:33
Arr. Frankfurt   33-40 minutes later

Hamburg - Berlin - Hamburg 840

See "Berlin-Hamburg."

Hamburg - Bremen - Hamburg 800

All of these trains charge a supplement that includes reservation fee and have a restaurant car or light refreshments.

Dep. Hamburg (Alt.)	Every hour from 05:38 to 19:38
Dep. Hamburg (Hbf.)	15 minutes later
Arr. Bremen	70 minutes after departing Altona rail station.

* * *

Dep. Bremen	Every hour from 07:15 to 23:15
Arr. Hamburg (Hbf.)	52 minutes later
Arr. Hamburg (Alt.)	14 minutes after arriving Hauptbahnhof rail station.

Hamburg - Munich and Munich - Hamburg 900

Germany introduced its 165-mph InterCity Express (ICE) trains on this route in 1991. The air-conditioned luxury train's coaches have phone service, restaurant/bistro cars and seats fitted with earphones that carry a choice of music. The supplement charged to ride ICE trains includes the reservation.

Dep. Hamburg (Hbf.)	07:08	10:08	11:08	12:08	13:08 (1)
Dep. Hannover	08:28	11:30	12:28	13:30	14:28
Dep. Kassel	09:22	12:25	13:22	14:25	15:22
Dep. Augsburg	12:10	15:32	16:10	17:32	18:10
Arr. Munich	12:41	16:07	16:41	18:06	18:41

* * *

Dep. Munich	07:14	09:14	09:52	11:17 (2)
Dep. Augsburg	07:46	09:46	10:24	11:46
Dep. Kassel	10:38	12:38	13:35	14:38
Dep. Hannover	11:33	13:33	14:33	15:33
Arr. Hamburg (Hbf.)	12:52	14:52	15:42	16:52

(1) Plus other Hamburg departures at 14:08, 15:08 and 17:08. (2) Plus other Munich departures at 13:17, 13:52, 15:17, 17:16 and 19:17.

Hamburg - Lubeck - Hamburg 825

Dep. Hamburg (Hbf.)	Frequent times from 06:02 to 23:15
Arr. Lubeck	40 minutes later

Sights in **Lubeck**: All museums here are closed Monday. April–September, they are open other days 10:00–17:00, October–March 10:00–16:00. It is an easy walk from the rail station down Konrad Adenauer Strasse, over the Puppenbrucke bridge, and straight ahead to the museum of the city's history in Holstentor, the immense 15th-century fort. Particularly interesting there is the model of the town as it was in 1650.

Nearby, just off Holstenstrasse, is the 15th-century St. Peter's Church. There is a marvelous view of the city and its harbors from the top of the church's 165-foot-high tower. Also see the elegant chapel in the 14th-century St. Mary's Church. Across the square from it is Buddenbrookshaus, at 4 Mengstrasse, where Thomas Mann was born. Although it is now a bank, some of the upstairs rooms can be visited during the hours the bank is open.

There are dozens of interesting alleys and little passageways here with lovely cottages, shops and restaurants. See the mansions on Grosse Petersgrube, Engelsgrube, Fischergrube and Mengstrasse. See the 19th and 20th-century paintings, handicrafts and sculptures in the Bennhaus, a magnificent 18th-century merchant's house. The city's main museum is in St. Anne's Convent.

Cruise boats that go around the city and harbor leave from the front of Hotel Jensen (Trave Landing) daily in spring, summer and fall every half hour from 10:00 to 18:00.

Dep. Lubeck	Frequent times from 06:03 to 00:03
Arr. Hamburg (Hbf.)	40 minutes later

Hannover - Berlin - Hannover   810

All of these trains charge a supplement that includes reservation fee and have a restaurant car, unless designated otherwise.

Dep. Hannover	06:07	08:07	10:07		
Arr. Berlin (Zoo)	08:49	10:51	12:51		

•   •   •

Dep. Berlin (Zoo)	13:13	15:13	17:13	18:40	20:11
Arr. Hannover	15:54	17:54	19:54	21:37	22:45

Hannover - Bremen - Hannover   816

Dep. Hannover	07:44 (1)	08:19	09:44	10:19	11:44	12:19
Arr. Bremen	08:49	09:41	10:48	11:41	12:48	13:41

• • •

Dep. Bremen	13:10	14:16	15:10	16:16	17:18	18:16 (2)
Arr. Hannover	14:14	15:15	16:14	17:15	18:41	19:15

(1) Runs Monday-Saturday. Light refreshments. (2) Plus other departures from Bremen at 19:10, 20:18, 21:10, 22:18 and 23:18.

Hannover - Celle - Hannover   904

Reservation is advisable for most of these trains.

Dep. Hannover	Frequent times from 05:18 to 20:49
Arr. Celle	21 minutes later

Sights in **Celle:** The beautifully decorated chapel and wonderful French Garden at the 13th-century Duke's Palace. The 14th-century Marienkirche. The exhibit of the local life and farm culture in the Bomann Museum. The heavy wood-beamed ceilings and quality wood panelling in the 14th-century Rathaus (Town Hall), oldest tavern in Northern Germany. The Lower Saxony stud farm, home of the famous Hannoverian horses.

The 480 half-timbered houses, some dating back to the 15th century, many with carved beams. The Apiary Museum at the Institute for Bee Research. The nearby Wienhausen Monastery. Regional food specialties are *heidschnuckenbraten* (roasted lamb), *meissendorfer spiegelkarpfen* (carp) and *burgdorfer spargel* (asparagus). There are steamer cruises on the **Aller River.**

Dep. Celle	Frequent times from 06:49 to 22:53
Arr. Hannover	21 minutes later

Hannover - Dortmund - Hannover   800

All of these trains charge a supplement that includes reservation fee and have a restaurant car.

Dep. Hannover	06:58	07:58	08:58	09:58	10:58	11:58	
Arr. Dortmund	08:35	09:31	10:34	11:31	12:34	13:31	

• • •

Dep. Dortmund	13:23	14:23	15:23	16:23	17:23	18:23	19:23
Arr. Hannover	15:01	16:01	17:01	18:01	19:01	20:01	21:05

Hannover - Dusseldorf - Hannover 800

Dep. Hannover	09:58 (1)	11:58 (1)	13:58 (1)	
Arr. Dusseldorf	12:22	14:22	16:22	

• • •

Dep. Dusseldorf	15:39 (1)	17:39 (1)	19:32 (2)	20:32
Arr. Hannover	18:04	20:04	22:04	23:07

(1) Supplement payable. Restaurant car. (2) Operates Monday-Friday.

Hannover - Frankfurt - Hannover 904

All of these trains have light refreshments.

Dep. Hannover	06:12	08:12	10:12	12:12	14:12	16:11
Arr. Frankfurt	09:38	11:38	13:38	15:38	17:38	19:38

• • •

Dep. Frankfurt	12:23	14:23	16:23	18:23	00:20 (1)
Arr. Hannover	15:47	17:47	19:47	21:47	04:23

(1) Has first-class and tourist-class sleepers, plus second-class couchettes and first- and second-class coaches. No food service.

Hannover - Goslar - Hannover 860

Dep. Hannover	06:34	07:34	08:34	09:34	11:14 (1)	13:14 (1)
Arr. Goslar	07:55	08:55	09:55	10:55	12:41	14:41

Sights in **Goslar**: The many 13th–16th-century half-timbered buildings and 19th-century houses. The Eagle Fountain. The five 13th-century churches. The chandeliers of reindeer horns in the 15th-century town hall. The 16th-century towers and old city walls. The 11th-century Imperial Palace. The museums of natural science and antiquities.

Goslar is a popular base for touring the Harz Mountains.

Dep. Goslar	12:11(1)	13:31(1)	15:02(2)	16:02	17:02 (3)	18:02	19:02 (4)
Arr. Hannover	13:19	14:46	16:22	17:22	18:22	19:22	20:22

(1) Light refreshments. (2) Runs daily, except Sunday and holidays. (3) Runs daily except Saturdays. (4) Plus another Goslar departure at 21:02.

Hannover - Hamburg - Hannover   904

All trains offer light refreshments, unless noted otherwise.

Dep. Hannover	06:49	07:49	08:02	08:49	09:49	10:49
Arr. Hamburg (Hbf.)	08:22	09:22	10:02	10:22	11:20	12:22

• • •

Dep. Hamburg (Hbf.)	14:40	15:40	16:40	17:40	18:40 (1)	19:40(1)
Arr. Hannover	16:10	17:11	18:10	19:11	20:10	21:11

(1) Plus other departures from Hamburg at 19:27, and 21:38, arriving Hannover 21:40 and 23:18.

Hannover - Hameln - Hannover   809

Dep. Hannover	Every hour from 06:50 to 22:50
Arr. Hameln	47 minutes later

Sights in **Hameln:** Every Sunday at noon (mid-May through mid-September), see the reenactment of the Pied Piper leading children through the town square. Approximately 80 actors in historical costumes participate in the 30-minute performance.

Take a 90-minute guided walking tour from the tourist information office. A stroll through the surrounding woods is pleasant. Or, try a steamboat trip on the **Weser River**.

Dep. Hameln	Every hour from 07:21 to 22:22
Arr. Hannover	47 minutes later

Hannover - Hildesheim - Hannover   860

Dep. Hannover	Every hour from 05:34 to 21:34
Arr. Hildesheim	30-35 minutes later

Sights in **Hildesheim**: See the supposedly 1,100-year-old rose tree (more likely 300–500 years old) which survived World War II bombings that literally destroyed the city, on the grounds of the 11th-century cathedral.

The cathedral houses marvelous 11th-century art, particularly the two wings of the bronze door cast in 1015, showing eight scenes from the Old and New Testaments.

Also see the Egyptian and Greco-Roman objects, as well as the collection of episcopal silverware and Chinese porcelain, in the Roemer und Pelizaeus Museum. The 12th-century painted ceiling in the 11th-century St. Michael's Church. The 15th-century Tempelhaus.

The Gothic town hall. The collection of 15th-century books and official records dating back to the 12th century at the Stadtarchiv.

Take a local train for the short ride to **Nordstemmen** and then it is a 20-minute walk from that rail station to see the medieval castle, Schloss Marianburg.

Dep. Hildesheim Every hour from 06:50 to 21:50
Arr. Hannover   30-35 minutes later

Hannover - Kassel - Hannover   900

There is beautiful **Fulda River Valley** scenery 20 minutes before arriving in Kassel.

All of these trains charge a supplement that includes reservation fee. Most of them have a restaurant car.

Dep. Hannover   Frequent times from 05:21 to 21:25
Arr. Kassel (Wil.) 55-60 minutes later

Dep. Kassel (Wil.) Frequent times from 06:38 to 22:45
Arr. Hannover   55-60 minutes later

Hannover - Luneburg - Hannover   904

Dep. Hannover	07:49 (1)	08:02	08:49 (1)	09:49 (1)	10:49 (1)	11:49 (1)
Arr. Luneburg	08:51	09:24	09:48	10:51	12:22	13:22

Sights in **Luneburg**: The 18th-century crane at the waterfront. Guided tours of town hall, constructed over five centuries (1300-1800). The 17th-century Ducal Palace. The view of the town from Kalkberg (Chalk Mountain).

The 15th–16th-century wood carvings and paintings and the 16th–18th-century organs in the three churches that have survived out of the city's 14 original churches: St. Johannis, St. Michaelis and St. Nicolai. There are magnificent tombs of the town's most important citizens inside St. Johannia, the oldest church here. The sound of its organ is unique.

Don't miss seeing the 12th-century monastery, slightly more than one mile northeast of the town.

Dep. Luneburg	14:12 (1)	15:08 (1)	16:08 (1)	17:08 (1)	18:09	19:08 (1+2)
Arr. Hannover	15:11	16:10	17:11	18:10	19:10	20:10

(1) Light refreshments. (2) Plus another departure from Luneburg at 20:08 (1), arriving Hannover 21:11.

Leipzig - Berlin - Leipzig 850

Dep. Leipzig	08:22 (1)	10:22 (1)	12:22 (1)	14:22 (1)	
Arr. Berlin (Hbf.)	12:47	14:47	16:47	18:47	

• • •

Dep. Berlin (Hbf.)	11:03 (1)	13:03 (1)	15:03	19:27 (2)	21:23 (3)
Arr. Leipzig	15:34	17:34	19:34	23:29	23:28

(1) Supplement payable. Restaurant car. (2) Leaves from Berlin Lichtenberg. Light refreshments. (3) Departs from Berlin Lichtenberg. No food service.

Leipzig - Chemnitz (formerly Karl Marx Stadt) - Leipzig 878

Dep. Leipzig	08:24	10:28	12:24		Dep. Chemnitz	11:59	13:59	16:59 (1)
Arr. Chemnitz	80-87 minutes later				Arr. Leipzig	80-87 minutes later		

(1) Plus other departures from Chemnitz at 17:59, 19:59 and 21:03, arriving Leipzig 80-87 minutes later.

Sights in **Chemnitz**: An East German post-World War II showplace new city.

Leipzig - Dresden - Leipzig 840

Dep. Leipzig	06:47	08:28	09:24 (1)	10:28	11:24 (1)	12:28
Arr. Dresden (Neu.)	08:09	09:55	10:34	11:55	12:42	13:56
Arr. Dresden (Hbf.)	8 minutes later					

• • •

Dep. Dresden (Hbf.)	12:20 (1)	14:20 (1)	15:25 (1)	16:20 (1)	18:20 (1+2)
Dep. Dresden (Neu.)	8 minutes later				
Arr. Leipzig	13:45	15:45	16:45	17:45	19:45

(1) Supplement payable. Restaurant car. (2) Plus another departure from Dresden (Hbf.) at 21:22 arriving 22:47.

Leipzig - Erfurt - Leipzig 850

Dep. Leipzig	08:54 (1)	10:54 (1)	12:54 (1)	
Arr. Erfurt	10:12	12:12	14:12	

• • •

Dep. Erfurt	13:44 (1)	15:44 (1)	17:44 (1)	19:44 (1+2)
Arr. Leipzig	15:12	17:12	19:12	21:12

(1) Supplement charged includes reservation fee. Restaurant car. (2) Plus another departure from Erfurt at 21:44 (1), arriving Leipzig 23:12.

Leipzig - Naumburg - Leipzig 850

All of these trains charge a supplement that includes reservation fee and have a restaurant car, unless designated otherwise.

Dep. Leipzig	07:38	09:38	11:38	13:38
Arr. Naumburg	40 minutes later			

Sights in **Naumburg**: A gem of a medieval village.

Dep. Naumburg	11:36	13:36	15:36	17:36	19:36	21:36	22:28
Arr. Leipzig	40 minutes later						

Leipzig - Rostock - Leipzig Local Schedule

Reservation is advisable for all of these trains. All of them have light refreshments.

Dep. Leipzig	08:00	12:00 (1)	Dep. Rostock	14:45 (2)	18:45
Arr. Rostock	13:36	17:16	Arr. Leipzig	19:57 (1)	00:05

(1) Change trains in Magdeburg (arr. 09:39–dep. 09:50). (2) Change trains in Ludwigslust (arr. 17:48–dep. 17:54).

Sights in **Rostock**: Eastern Germany's largest seaport. St. Mary's Church. The ancient town hall.

Leipzig - Schwerin - Leipzig 840

Reservation is advisable for all of these trains, and all of them have light refreshments, unless designated otherwise.

Dep. Leipzig	08:50	10:50	Dep. Schwerin	15:29	19:27
Arr. Schwerin	12:26	14:26	Arr. Leipzig	19:19	23:19

Sights in **Schwerin**: The opera house. The fine castle.

Munich - Augsburg - Munich   905, 930

Most of these trains charge a supplement that includes reservation fee and have a restaurant car or light refreshments.

Dep. Munich (Hbf.)	Frequent times from 05:38 to 23:55
Arr. Augsburg	30–40 minutes later

Sights in **Augsburg**: An ancient castled city, complete with splendid Gothic gate, moat, tower and ramparts. The Tourist Information Office, 7 Bahnhofstrasse, is open Monday-Friday 09:00–18:00, Saturday 09:00–13:00.

See the palatial, eight-story, 17th-century city hall. Next to it is the 11th-century Perlachturm, a belltower. The oldest (12th century) Romanesque stained-glass in the world, great 11th-century bronze doors, four altarpieces by Holbein and a huge 11th-century bronze portal with scenes from the Old Testament in the 10th-century cathedral.

Just north of the cathedral, on Frauentorstrasse, is the Mozart Museum (closed on Tuesday) in the house where the composer's father lived.

Schaezlerpalais, at 46 Maximilianstrasse, is an 18th-century 60-room mansion that houses the Municipal Art Collections (Rubens, Rembrandt, Veronese, Tiepolo) and has a richly ornamented rococo ballroom on the second floor. The ballroom leads to an adjacent building that has a dazzling collection: Lucas Cranach, Holbein the Elder, Albrecht Durer. Both museums are open daily except Monday 10:00–16:00.

Also see the 15th-century Basilica of St. Ulrich and St. Afra, the largest and most impressive church in Augsburg. The collection of manuscripts and drawings in the Municipal Library. See the city's three 16th-century fountains. Maximilianstrasse is considered by many to be the best Renaissance street in Germany.

Dep. Augsburg	Frequent times from 05:39 to 23:65
Arr. Munich (Hbf.)	30–40 minutes later

Munich - Bamberg - Munich   875

All of these trains charge a supplement that includes reservation fee and have a restaurant car.

Dep. Munich (H.)	06:52	08:49	10:52	Dep. Bamberg	16:43	18:43	20:43
Arr. Bamberg	09:13	11:13	13:13	Arr. Munich (H.)	19:06	21:15	23:06

Sights in **Bamberg**: A major port on the Rhine-Main-Danube Canal that connects the North Sea with the Black Sea. One of the few towns not damaged in World War II.

Visit the town hall, located in the center of the bridge that crosses the Regnitz River. The 16th-century Geyerworth Castle. A history museum is located in the 16th-century Ratsstube. Nearby is the Old Imperial Court and the 17th-century Concordia House.

Walk 10 minutes up the hill to Domplatz (Cathedral Square), location of the 13th-century Imperial Cathedral, to see many masterpieces of German medieval and early Renaissance sculpture (especially the 13th-century life-sized Knight of Bamberg astride his horse). Also see the 16th-century tomb of Henry II with sculpted bas-relief panels showing scenes from his and his wife's life, the dazzling carved-wood Marienaltar, the tile floors, frescoes and 18th-century French tapestries in the Neue Residenz, the 15th and 16th-century German paintings in the museum there, and its 18th-century rose garden.

The cathedral is open dawn to sunset, daily except holidays. The Neue Residenz is open 09:00–12:00 and 13:30–17:00 (16:00 October through March). See the paintings of more than 600 different medicinal herbs in the ceiling of St. Michael, an 11th-century church.

Munich - Bayreuth - Munich   886, 905

All of the Munich–Nurnberg (and v.v.) trains charge a supplement that includes reservation fee and have a restaurant car.

905			886		
Dep. Munich (Hbf.)	06:52	08:49 (1)	Dep. Bayreuth	14:10	16:10 (2)
Arr. Nurnberg	08:32	10:32	Arr. Nurnberg	15:08	17:08
Change trains 886			Change trains 905		
Dep. Nurnberg	08:49	10:49	Dep. Nurnberg	15:26	17:26
Arr. Bayreuth	09:45	11:45	Arr. Munich (Hbf.)	17:06	19:06

(1) Plus another departure from Munich at 10:52, arriving Nurnberg 12:32, arriving Bayreuth 13:45. (2) Plus other departures from Bayreuth at 18:10 and 20:10, arriving Nurnberg 19:08 and 21:08, arriving Munich 21:15 and 23:06.

Sights in **Bayreuth**: Sight of a five-week annual (over 100 years) Wagner opera festival at Festspielhaus, every year from late July to late August, at 16:00. See Haus Wahnfried, Wagner's home. The breathtaking opera house. Eremitage Park. The Orangerie castle, open daily 10:00–11:30 and 13:30–15:00.

Munich - Frankfurt - Munich   930

All of these trains charge a supplement that includes reservation fee and have a restaurant car.

Dep. Munich (Hbf.)	06:41	07:38	08:38	09:38	
Arr. Frankfurt	09:53	11:11	12:11	13:11	
		•	•	•	
Dep. Frankfurt	15:47	16:47	17:47	18:47	19:47
Arr. Munich (Hbf.)	19:11	20:11	21:11	22:11	23:11

Munich - Heidelberg - Munich 930

All of these trains charge a supplement that includes reservation fee and have a restaurant car.

Dep. Munich (Hbf.)	06:46	08:46	10:46
Arr. Heidelberg	09:52	11:51	13:51

Sights in **Heidelberg**: See notes under "Cologne–Heidelberg"

Dep. Heidelberg	15:07	16:07	17:07	18:07
Arr. Munich (Hbf.)	18:01	19:01	20:01	21:01

Munich - Innsbruck - Munich 890

Dep. Munich (Hbf.)	07:29 (1)	09:29 (1)	11:29 (1)		
Arr. Innsbruck	09:222	11:22	13:22		
		•	•	•	
Dep. Innsbruck	12:37 (1)	14:37 (1)	16:37 (1)	18:37 (1)	20:37 (1)
Arr. Munich (Hbf.)	14:30	16:30	18:30	20:30	22:30

(1) Supplement charged that includes reservation fee. Restaurant car.

Munich - Lindau - Munich 935

There are good views of the Allgau region and fine mountain scenery on this easy one-day round-trip.

Dep. Munich (Hbf.)	06:19	06:50	08:15 (1)	08:19
Arr. Lindau	09:14	09:50	10:22	11:14

Sights in **Lindau**: An island resort town in the Bodensee (Lake Constance), third largest lake in central Europe and actually a part of the Rhine River. Departure times for the sightseeing boat can be obtained at the tourist information office across from the rail station.

See the 13th-century lighthouse, Mangturm. The beautiful 15th-century Old Town Hall on the Reichplatz. The Fountain of Linavia. The casino. The collection of furniture, arms, paintings and folk art in the 18th-century mansion that now houses an art museum called Stadtische Kunstsammlungen, open Tuesday–Saturday 09:00–12:00 and 14:00–17:00, also Sunday 10:00–12:00.

The 15th-century homes on Hauptstrasse, a pedestrian-only road. Enjoy a mid-day repast at one of the many sidewalk cafes along that street. The only existing wall mural by Hans Holbein The Elder, done between 1485 and 1490, depicting the Passion of Jesus, can be seen in the 11th-century St. Peter's Church. Visit the wine tavern in the 16th-century Pulverturm (Gun Powder Tower). Walk on the breakwater to the New Lighthouse and climb its 108-foot-high tower for a breathtaking view of the Alps.

Dep. Lindau	12:45	15:37 (1)	18:45 (2)
Arr. Munich (Hbf.)	15:28	17:48	21:28

(1) Supplement charged includes reservation fee. Restaurant car. (2) Plus other departures from Lindau at 19:37 (1) and 20:43, arriving Munich 21:54 and 23:29 (3). (3) Second class only.

Munich - Mainz - Munich   910

All of these trains charge a supplement that includes reservation fee and have a restaurant car.

Dep. Munich (Hbf.)	06:46	08:46	10:46		
Arr. Mainz	10:47	12:47	14:47		
		•	•	•	
Dep. Mainz	14:14	15:14	16:14	17:14	19:14
Arr. Munich (Hbf.)	18:11	19:11	20:11	21:11	23:11

Munich - Mannheim - Munich   930

All of these trains charge a supplement that includes reservation and have a restaurant car.

Dep. Munich (Hbf.)	Frequent times from 05:38 to 23:17
Arr. Mannheim	3 hours later
	• • •
Dep. Mannheim	Frequent times from 07:54 to 20:27
Arr. Munich (Hbf.)	3 hours later

Munich - Nurnberg - Munich   905

All of these trains charge a supplement that includes reservation and have a restaurant car, unless designated otherwise.

Dep. Munich (Hbf.)	07:52	08:34	09:52	10:52	11:52
Arr. Nurnberg	09:32	11:10	11:32	12:32	13:32
		•	•	•	

Dep. Nurnberg	13:26	14:26	15:26	16:26	17:26	18:26	19:26 (1)
Arr. Munich (Hbf.)	15:06	16:06	17:06	18:06	19:06	20:06	21:15

(1) Plus other departures from Nurnberg at 20:26, 21:26 and 22:26, arriving Munich 22:06, 23:06 and 00:06.

Munich - Oberammergau - Munich   895, 897

There is very good mountain and lake scenery on the Murnau–Oberammergau portion of this trip.

895

Dep. Munich (Hbf.)	08:00	09:00	10:00	11:00	12:00
Arr. Murnau	08:53	09:59	10:53	11:57	12:53

Change trains 897

Dep. Murnau	08:56	10:00	11:05	12:05	13:07
Arr. Oberammergau	43 minutes later				

Sights in **Oberammergau**: Every year ending in zero (2000, 2010, etc.), the famous Passion Play is staged. Three hundred years ago the villagers here promised to produce this play every 10 years if the Black Plague ended. In the interval between decades, you can still see the unique theater and enjoy this interesting woodcarving capital of Bavaria. There is time to take a bus trip and see the lapis lazuli, gilt and crystal in King Ludwig II's glorious palace, Schloss Linderhof.

897

Dep. Oberammergau	11:07	12:07	13:07	14:07	15:07	16:07	17:07 (1)
Arr. Murnau	40 minutes later						

Change trains 895

Dep. Murnau	11:57	12:53	13:57	14:53	15:58	16:53	18:00
Arr. Munich (Hbf.)	12:52	13:52	14:52	15:53	16:53	17:54	18:54

(1) Trains run hourly until 23:07 and all but the last departure connect with trains departing Murnau.

Munich - Regensburg - Munich   880

Dep. Munich (Hbf.)	07:48	09:48	11:48
Arr. Regensburg	09:14	11:14	13:14

• • •

Dep. Regensburg	13:34	14:44	16:44	19:34	21:38
Arr. Munich (Hbf.)	15:01	16:16	18:16	21:01	23:06

Sights in **Regensburg:** Founded by the Celts in about 500 B.C., Regensburg was made into an impregnable fort by the Romans in 179 A.D. How amazing that it still exists, intact! Its location on the Danube River made this city Germany's gateway to the Balkans and the Orient for several centuries.

Undamaged during World War II, this is the largest and most perfectly preserved medieval city in Germany.

Because most of the streets here are too narrow for modern vehicles and also because its size is only one mile by a half-mile, Regensburg is ideal for strolling. A half-day guided walking tour is offered by the municipal tourist office, located in the 14th-century Rathaus (City Hall). Many guided tours of the city hall's ornate rooms are offered daily.

The ancient Roman 23-foot-high wall surrounding the city is built of enormous limestone blocks without mortar, and it runs more than a mile long. Christian tombstones here date back to the 4th century. The city's forum, temples, mint, and pottery and tile factories served a population of 12,000 in Roman times. This was also one of the most important cities in the German Holy Roman Empire from the 10th through the 18th centuries.

You will not even scratch the surface in a one-day visit. In order to see all of the 26 Romanesque and Gothic churches and the wonderful artwork displayed in them would require several weeks, and, there is much more than those churches to see here.

Walk over the 12th-century Steiner Brucke (Stone Bridge), one of the greatest engineering marvels of the Middle Ages. Riverboat rides on the Danube start near the Stone Bridge.

Visit St. Peter's Cathedral to see its lace-work spires and its collection of sacral art dating back to the Middle Ages and the Renaissance, especially the 13th-century gem-and-pearl-encrusted crucifix.

Hear the boys' choir (called "cathedral sparrows," they sing both secular and liturgical songs) in the adjacent Niedermunster. Famous since the year 975, the choir can be heard Sundays and holidays at the 09:00 mass.

See the 20 medieval tower houses (some are 12 stories high), especially the 13th-century Goldener Turm on Wahlenstrasse and the Bamberger Turm on Watmarkt, near the City Hall. The Golden Cross, a magnificent hotel since the 16th century.

The Municipal Museum at Dachauplatz has several paintings by Albrecht Altdorfer, considered to be the world's first landscape painter and founder of the Danubian School in the 16th century. The collection there also includes Celtic, Roman, early German and medieval artifacts.

The 9th and 10th-century sculptures and tombs in the 5th century St. Emmeramskirche are notable. There are many illuminated manuscripts and more than 200,000 ancient books in the adjacent abbey.

The enormous monastery at St. Emmerams's (named for a martyred 7th century missionary monk) is presently the palace of the princes of Thurn-und-Taxis. After Napoleon secularized the abbey in 1808, that family bought it and converted it into their palace. It is worth visiting to see the priceless art in its many lavishly decorated rooms.

The Thurn-und-Taxis family invented postal service in the 15th century and used a network of stage coaches. There is a very interesting stable museum across from St. Emmeram's, with exhibits of silver and gold harnesses, equestrian paintings and 19th-century coaches.

Also near this church is the Diozesan Museum, which houses 1,000 years of ecclesiastical art.

The Shipping Museum is located on the other side of the Danube River. Weinstube zur

Stritzelback at No. 6 Watmarkt has been an inn since the 13th century. (Stritzel is a salty roll.)

There is an exhibit of 17th-century mathematical instruments, astronomical tools and manuscripts that were used by the mathematician and astronomer Johann Kepler at No. 5 Keplerstrasse, the house in which he died in 1630.

Sample the chocolate pralines called "Barbara's kisses" at Cafe Prinzess (No. 2 Rathausplatz), Germany's oldest pastry shop and coffeehouse. It opened in 1686.

Try the fist-sized, white radishes that the locals eat as beer snacks.

Munich - Salzburg - Munich 890

These trains charge a supplement that includes reservation fee and have a restaurant car, unless designated otherwise.

Dep. Munich (Hbf.)	07:49	08:33 (2)	09:38 (1)	10:33 (2)	11:25	13:38 (1)
Arr. Salzburg	09:29	10:28	11:22	12:28	12:55	15:52

· · ·

Dep. Salzburg	13:05	13:33 (2)	14:38 (1)	15:05	16:38 (1)	17:33 (2+3)
Arr. Munich (Hbf.)	14:36	15:28	16:21	16:36	18:21	19:28

(1) No supplement charged. Reservation advisable. Light refreshments. (2) Reservation not available. No supplement. No restaurant car. (3) Plus other departures from Salzburg at 18:38, 19:05, 19:33 (2), 20:38 (1) and 21:33, arriving Munich 20:20, 20:36, 21:28, 22:20 and 23:28.

Munich - Stuttgart - Munich 930

Many of these trains charge a supplement that includes reservation fee and have a restaurant car.

Dep. Munich (Hbf.)	Frequent times from 05:38 to 20:45
Arr. Stuttgart	2–3 hours later

· · ·

Dep. Stuttgart	Frequent times from 06:00 to 22:14
Arr. Munich (Hbf.)	2–3 hours later

Munich - Tegernsee and Schliersee - Munich   893

Take a local train from Starnberger Bahnhof (the northern annex of Munich's Hauptbahnhof station) for this 37-mile ride that takes 72 minutes.

At the northern end of Tegernsee (an exceptionally beautiful lake) is **Gmund**, not to be confused with the two Austrian villages also named Gmund. A mile away from this Gmund is a smaller lake, **Schliersee**. It is only a four-mile walk around Schliersee.

There is a lovely view of the lake from the ruins of Hohenwaldeck Castle and also from one of the many benches along the lake's shore. Sports (tennis, sailing, swimming) are very popular in this area.

The Taubenstein mountain railway goes to an area that provides extensive mountain hiking. Wandering through the Weissachau wildlife preserve, with its rare flowers, is worthwhile. Local food specialties in this region are white sausage, liver loaf, big white radishes and spicy Miesbacher cheese.

Sights in **Tegernsee**: The concerts (May–September) in the enormous Baroque dining hall of the Castle. The large collection of rustic furniture, weapons, craft utensils, traditional costumes and ancient books in the Tegernsee Museum. Try the beer in the Hofbrauhaus, located in the Museum building. Ludwig Schieffer of Cologne tells us the beer there is better than which is sold at Munich's famous Hofbrauhaus.

See the drawings, illustrations, sketches and caricatures by Olaf Gulbransson at the Kurpark Museum. Visit the lakeside gambling casino at **Wiessee,** across the lake.

Take the 10-minute boat trip (every half hour) across the lake to Wiessee. Both Tegernsee and Wiessee have been popular for centuries for their curative mineral waters, laden with iodine and sulphur. Swimming in the pristine lake is marvelous.

Take the cable car from nearby **Rottach-Egern** to the top of **Wallberg** for a view of the Tegernsee Valley and Austria's highest peak, the **Grossglockner**.

Munich - Ulm - Munich   930

All of these trains charge a supplement that includes reservation fee and have a restaurant car or light refreshments.

Dep. Munich   Frequent times from 05:38 to 21:46
Arr. Ulm   70–80 minutes later

Sights in **Ulm**: The Bakery Museum (tools, library, artwork pertaining to bread) on Fuersteneckerstrasse. The display there includes breads made in ancient Egypt and in the Middle Ages. Open Monday-Friday 10:00–12:00 and 15:00–17:30.

The 14th-century Gothic cathedral has one of the highest towers in the world (528 feet) and a ceiling that is 100 feet above the central nave. When you hear an organ recital here (8,000 pipes!), you will experience an incredible affect from the exceptional acoustics. Don't miss seeing the magnificent 15th-century carving on the choir stalls.

The views of the Alps while climbing the 528-feet-high tower are breathtaking. (You don't have to make the entire ascent.)

The 17th-century Schworhaus, where town council members once took their oaths to perform their duties (where they were "sworn in").

Arts and crafts from this region are displayed in the Ulmer Museum, open Tuesday–Saturday 10:00–12:00 and 14:00–17:00, Sunday 10:00–13:00 and 14:00–17:00. See the 15th-century fountain, Fischkasten, at the Marktplatz. Also on that square is the 14th-century Town Hall with an exceptional astronomical clock on its east wall.

Visit Metzgerturm, Ulm's 14th-century leaning tower. Cross the bridge to New Ulm and walk along the Jahnufer promenade to see good views of the old city.

| Dep. Ulm | Frequent times from 06:12 to 23:12 |
| Arr. Munich | 70–80 minutes later |

Munich - Wurzburg - Munich 905

All of these trains charge a supplement that includes reservation fee and have a restaurant car.

| Dep. Munich (Hbf.) | 07:14 | 07:52 | 09:52 | 11:17 |
| Arr. Wurzburg | 09:34 | 10:31 | 12:31 | 13:34 |

Sights in **Wurzburg**: Vineyards and wineries galore. The tourist information center is located in Falcon House, on the square where bratwurst, vegetables, fruits and flowers are sold. See the Main-Franconia Museum (sculptures, wine presses, etc.) in the 13th-century Miarienberg Fortress.

The view of the city from the restaurant at the Fortress. The rococo garden in the nearby Schloss Veitshochheim. The 12 statues of saints on the Old Main Bridge. Pilgrimage Church. The Tiepolo ceiling and the Emperor's Hall, in the Residenz. Neumunster Church. The cathedral. The fine sculptures in the Mainfrankisches Museum at the Festung. Take a boat trip on the River Main to see **Randersacker** and **Sommerhausen**, both of them located in one of Germany's most important wine regions. Pfuelben, Sonnenstuhl and Tuefelskeller are among the leading wineries here.

Sights in **Randersacker**: There are many scenic walking tours near the **Main River** and through vineyards. Stroll the narrow Medieval streets lined with baroque houses. Many sculptures here (madonnas and pietas). See the Balthasar garden-pavilion. Try the delicious franconian meat and sausages. Fishing and many other watersports here.

Sights in **Sommerhausen:** Famous since the Middle Ages for wine-making. Its coat- of-arms features a radiant sun above a cluster of grapes. Its old town walls, gates and towers make it one of the most beautiful towns in the region. Sailing and motor boating are popular here. Visit the Rechteren-Limpurgsche Castle and the ancient City Hall.

Dep. Wurzburg	12:25	13:27	14:24	15:27	16:24	17:27 (1)
Arr. Munich (Hbf.)	14:43	16:06	16:41	18:06	18:41	20:07

(1) Plus other Wurzburg departures at 18:24, 19:27, 20:24, and 21:27, arriving Munich 20:44, 22:06, 22:44 and 00:06.

Munich - Zurich - Munich   75

Both of these trains charge a supplement that includes reservation fee and have a restaurant car.

Dep. Munich (H.)	08:15	Dep. Zurich	17:45
Arr. Zurich	12:26	Arr. Munich (H.)	21:54

SCENIC RAIL TRIPS

Cologne - Koblenz - Bullay - Cologne   915

There is beautiful farm, mountain and vineyard scenery on this easy one-day trip through the Moselle Valley. Very good river scenery on the Koblenz–Bullay portion.

Reservation is advisable for all of these trains; light refreshments are available.

Dep. Cologne	08:10	10:10	12:10	14:10
Dep. Koblenz	09:19	11:19	13:19	15:19
Arr. Bullay	50 minutes later			

•   •   •

Dep. Bullay	09:54	11:54	13:54	15:54
Arr. Koblenz	10:37	12:37	14:37	16:37
Arr. Cologne	57 minutes later			

Cologne - Mainz   910

See the fine mountain, vineyard and Rhine River scenery. Complete schedules appear under the "Cologne–Mainz–Cologne" one-day excursion.

Cologne - Giessen - Frankfurt - Koblenz - Cologne   807, 910

View excellent mountain scenery on this circular circuit.

807

Dep. Cologne	08:19	10:19	12:19			
Arr. Giessen	10:44	12:44	14:44			
Change trains						
Dep. Giessen	11:16 (1)	13:16 (1)	15:16 (1)			
Arr. Frankfurt	11:57	13:57	15:57			
Change trains 650						
Dep. Frankfurt	12:50 (2)	14:50 (2)	16:50 (2)	17:50 (2)	18:50 (2)	19:50 (2+3)
Dep. Koblenz	14:12	16:12	18:12	19:12	20:12	21:12
Arr. Cologne	15:05	17:05	19:05	20:05	21:05	22:05

(1) Light refreshments. (2) Supplement charged includes reservation fee. Restaurant car. (3) Plus another departure from Frankfurt 21:50 (2), arriving Cologne and 00:05.

Dresden - Bad Schandau - Dresden   1110

For best views of the **Elbe River** en route to **Bad Schandau**, sit on the left side of the 50-minute suburban train as it goes down the **Elbe Canyon**. Then, take a local tramway from the center of Bad Schandau into the mountains of the Sachsischer Schweiz to the **Lichtenhainer Waterfall**.

Frankfurt - Koblenz - Cologne - Giessen - Frankfurt   807, 910

Here is the Frankfurt version of the circle trip shown on the previous trip:

910

Dep. Frankfurt	07:50 (1)	09:50 (1)	11:50 (1)	13:50 (1)
Dep. Koblenz	09:12	11:12	13:12	15:12
Arr. Cologne	10:05	12:05	14:05	16:05
Change trains 807				
Dep. Cologne	10:19	12:19	14:19	16:19
Arr. Giessen	12:44	14:44	16:44	18:44
Change trains				
Dep. Giessen	13:16 (2)	15:16 (2)	17:16 (2)	19:16 (2)
Arr. Frankfurt	13:57	15:57	17:57	19:57

(1) Supplement charged includes reservation fee. Restaurant car. (2) Supplement charged includes reservation fee. Light refreshments.

Frankfurt - Freiburg - Donaueschingen - Basel   910, 938, 945

The train runs through the heart of the Black Forest. Very good mountain scenery on this spur of the Frankfurt–Basel route.

910		*938*	
Dep. Frankfurt	09:51	Dep. Donau.	15:17
Arr. Karlsruhe	11:14	Arr. Freiburg	16:18
Change trains 945		*Change trains 945*	
Dep. Karlsruhe	11:59	Dep. Freiburg	17:02(1)
Arr. Freiburg	13:04	Arr. Basel (SBB)	17:45
Change trains 938			
Dep. Freiburg	13:40		
Arr. Neu. Schwarz.	14:25		
Change trains 938			
Dep. Neu. Schwarz.	14:32		
Arr. Donau.	15:21		

(1) Supplement charged includes reservation fee. Restaurant car.

Koblenz - Giessen   807, 906

There is fine river scenery on this easy one-day round-trip. This area can also be seen by taking an *indirect route* from Koblenz to Frankfurt. For the first way:

906					
Dep. Koblenz	08:14 (1)	09:14	10:54 (2)	12:54	14:54
Arr. Giessen	10:38	11:38	12:48	14:48	16:48
			• • •		
Dep. Giessen	11:12	12:22 (3)	13:12	15:12	17:12
Arr. Koblenz	13:06	14:46	15:08	17:06	19:06

Here is the long route to Frankfurt which offers the same scenery:

906					
Dep. Koblenz	08:54 (2)	10:54 (2)	12:54	14:54	16:54
Arr. Giessen	10:48	12:48	14:48	16:48	18:48
Change trains 807					
Dep. Giessen	11:16 (4)	13:16 (4)	15:16(4)	17:16 (4)	19:16 (4)
Arr. Frankfurt	11:57	13:57	15:57	17:57	19:57

(1) Runs Monday-Friday, except holidays. (2) Runs daily except Sundays and holidays. (3) Runs Saturdays, Sundays and holidays. (4) Reservation advisable. Light refreshments.

Here is the schedule for the reverse of the Koblenz–Frankfurt trip on previous page:

807

Dep. Frankfurt	08:03 (1)	10:03 (1)	12:03 (1)	14:03 (1)	16:03 (3)
Arr. Giessen	08:43	10:43	12:43	14:43	16:43
Change trains 906					
Dep. Giessen	09:12 (2)	11:12	13:12	15:12	17:12
Arr. Koblenz	11:06	13:06	15:08	17:06	19:06

(1) Light refreshments. (2) Runs daily, except Sundays and holidays. (3) Plus another Frankfurt departure at 18:03, arriving Koblenz 21:06.

Munich - Garmisch - Innsbruck - Munich   890, 895

There is fine mountain scenery on this easy one-day circle trip.

895

Dep. Munich (Hbf.)	08:00	10:00	12:00	14:00
Arr. Garmisch	09:16	11:16	13:16	15:16
Arr. Mittenwald	09:59	11:50	13:50	15:48
Arr. Innsbruck	10:59	12:50	14:51	16:50
Change trains 890				
Dep. Innsbruck				
(via Kufstein)	12:37 (1)	14:37 (1)	16:37 (1+2)	
Arr. Munich (Hbf.)	14:30	16:30	18:30	

(1) Supplement charged includes reservation fee. Restaurant car. (2) Plus other departures from Innsbruck at 17:10 (1), 18:37 (1), 20:37 (1) and arriving Munich 19:15, 20:30, 22:30.

Garmisch - Zugspitzplatt - Zugspitzgipfel (summit) - Garmisch

The following schedule allows one to take one route to the summit of Zugspitze and a different route back to Garmisch.

This is a local schedule that does not appear in the *Thomas Cook European Timetable.*

Cog train

Dep. Garmisch	07:39	08:39	09:39	10:39	11:39	12:39	13:39	14:39	15:39
Arr. Eibsee	08:15	09:15	10:15	11:15	12:15	13:15	14:15	15:15	16:15
Arr. Zugspitzplatt	08:55	09:55	10:55	11:55	12:55	13:55	14:55	15:55	16:55

Change to cable car

Dep. Zugspitzplatt   Hourly departures are timed to meet incoming trains
Arr. Zugspitzgipfel   Approximately 20 minutes later

• • •

Dep. Zugspitzgipfel   Hourly departures are timed to meet departing trains
Arr. Zugspitzplatt   Approximately 20 minutes later

Change cable cars

Dep. Zugspitzplatt   Hourly departures are timed to meet arriving cable cars
Arr. Schneefernerhaus   Approximately 4 minutes later

Change to cog train

Dep. Schneefernerhaus	10:00	11:00	12:00	13:00	14:00	15:00	16:00	17:00	18:00
Arr. Garmisch	11:20	12:20	13:20	14:20	15:20	16:20	17:20	18:20	19:20

Munich - Nurnberg - Heilbronn - Heidelberg   905, 924, 925, 926

This schedule follows the route of the "Castle Road" and "Romantic Road" bus trips.

The 09:52 and 11:52 Munich departures must be made only Monday–Friday except holidays because of connection in Crailsheim.

905

Dep. Munich	07:52 (1)	09:52 (1)	11:52 (1)
Arr. Nurnberg	09:32	11:32	13:32
Change trains 925			
Dep. Nurnberg	09:43 (2)	11:43 (2)	13:43 (2)
Arr. Crailsheim	10:35	12:35	14:35
Change trains 926			
Dep. Crailsheim	10:41 (3)	12:41	14:41
Arr. Heilbronn	12:04	14:04	16:10

Sights in **Heilbronn**: More than 80 percent of the pre-World War II buildings in this city of 110,000 in the heart of Germany's wine country was obliterated by Allied bombing planes in 1944. The wine festival (one week in September) attracts 300,000 people every year.

924

Dep. Heilbronn	12:14 (4)	14:14 (5)	16:14 (5)
Arr. Heidelberg	13:41	15:41	17:41

(1) Supplement charged includes reservation fee. Restaurant car. (2) Reservation advisable. Light refreshments. (3) Runs Monday–Friday, except holidays. (4) Second class only. Runs Monday-Friday, except holidays. (5) Second class only.

Munich - Salzburg 890

This route offers good mountain scenery and is an easy one-day round-trip. See schedules earlier in this section, under "One-Day Excursions."

Offenburg - Konstanz - Offenburg 904

This trip is recommended for exceptional mountain scenery.

Dep. Offenburg	09:56 (1)	11:56 (2)	13:56 (2)	17:56 (2)	
Arr. Konstanz	12:13	14:13	16:13	20:13	
	•	•	•		
Dep. Konstanz	07:47 (2)	11:49 (2)	13:49 (2)	15:49 (2)	17:49 (2)
Arr. Offenburg	10:04	14:04	16:04	18:04	20:04

(1) Operates Monday-Saturday. Reservation advisable. Light refreshments. (2) Light refreshments.

Offenburg - Singen - Schaffhausen - Offenburg   904, 939, 945, 946

Excellent Black Forest scenery on this route. This trip can also be made as a detour en route from Frankfurt to Basel.

Reservation is advisable for all of the Offenburg-Singen (and v.v.) trains, and all of them have light refreshments.

946

Dep. Offenburg	07:58	09:58	11:58	13:58	15:58
Arr. Singen	09:50	11:50	13:50	15:50	17:50
Change trains 939					
Dep. Singen	12:09	14:09	16:09	18:09	
Arr. Schaffhausen	12:28	14:28	16:28	18:28	

•   •   •

Dep. Schaffhausen	11:33	13:33	15:33	17:33	19:33
Arr. Singen	11:51	13:41	15:51	17:51	19:51
Change trains 946					
Dep. Singen	12:12	14:12	16:12	18:12	20:49
Arr. Offenburg	14:02	16:02	18:02	20:02	22:37

Here is the detour from the Frankfurt-Basel ride:

904

Dep. Frankfurt	07:50 (1)	09:50 (1)		*Change trains 939*		
Arr. Offenburg	09:56	11:56		Dep. Singen	12:09	14:09
Change trains 946				Dep. Schaffhausen	12:28	14:28
Dap. Offenburg	09:58	11:58		Arr. Basel (Bad.)	13:45	15:46
Arr. Singen	11:59	13:50				

(1) Reservation advisable. Light refreshments.

Wurzburg - Zurich   84, 921

There is exceptional Black Forest scenery on this ride.

921

Dep. Wurzburg	06:53	08:29	10:39	12:39		
Arr. Stuttgart	09:17	10:46	13:00	15:00		
Change trains 84						
Dep. Stuttgart	09:45 (1)	11:46 (1)	13:46 (1)	15:46	16:46	18:46
Arr. Zurich	12:47	14:47	16:47	18:47	19:47	21:47

(1) Reservation required. Light refreshments.

RHINE RIVER CRUISES

A variety of cruising on the Rhine is offered. The complete five-day *down*stream route (from Basel to Amsterdam or Rotterdam) and the complete six-day *up*stream route (Amsterdam or Rotterdam to Basel) are offered April to October.

A shorter portion (Rotterdam-Strasbourg and vice versa) is also available April to October. It is four days downstream and five upstream.

Still another service (three days downstream and four upstream), between Amsterdam or Rotterdam and Mainz, is offered April to September.

On any of these, passengers may stop-over at points en route and resume the journey later (Cologne, Koblenz, etc.).

The most popular stretch of the Rhine (Koblenz to Mainz and Frankfurt) is covered by the Eurailpass. This is the portion famed for scenic vineyards and hilltop castles. The *entire* Rhine trip is *not* covered by Eurailpass. However, with a Eurailpass there is *no* charge for either the boat trip or train ride Mainz–Cologne or Cologne–Mainz.

The scenery between Mainz and Koblenz can be seen as well from a train as from a boat because the track on this run goes along the river bank.

Here are the schedules for taking the boat *Mainz–Cologne* and returning to Mainz by train the same day:

914 *(Boat)*		910 *(Train)*	
Dep. Mainz	09:00 (1)	Dep. Cologne (Hbf.)	19:54 (2)
Arr. Koblenz	14:20	Dep. Koblenz	20:49
Arr. Cologne (Rheing'n)	19:30	Arr. Mainz	21:39

(1) Operates early May to early October. (2) Supplement charged includes reservation fee. Restaurant car.

Here are the schedules for taking the hydrofoil *Cologne-Mainz* and returning to Cologne by train the same day:

914 *(Hydrofoil/extra charge)*		910 *(Train)*	
Dep. Cologne (Rheing'n)	09:00 (1)	Dep. Mainz	14:22 (2)
Arr. Koblenz	11:05	Dep. Koblenz	15:12
Arr. Mainz	13:15	Arr. Cologne (Hbf.)	16:05

(1) Operates late March to early October. Runs daily, except Monday. Supplement charged. (2) Supplement charged includes reservation fee. Restaurant car. Plus other departures from Mainz at frequent times from 14:24 to 22:24.

THE ONE-DAY RHINE HYDROFOIL
CRUISE ROUND TRIP

Cologne - Mainz - Cologne   914

Operates late March to late October. Runs daily. Hydrofoil supplement charged.

Dep. Cologne (Rheing'n)	09:00	Dep. Mainz	14:25
Arr.. Koblenz	11:05	Dep. Koblenz	16:20
Arr. Mainz	13:15	Arr. Cologne (Rheing'n)	18:05

SCENIC BUS TRIPS
COVERED BY EURAILPASS

Both of these extremely popular bus trips are covered by Eurailpass: "Romantische Strasse" **Romantic Road)** and "Burgenstrasse" **(Castle Road)**. Advance seat reservations should be made at least three days before travel date. They can be obtained at no cost by writing to: Deutsche Touring GmbH, Am Roemerhof 17, 60486 Frankfurt/M. 90, Germany, or by phoning: 011 49 69 7 90 32 81; fax 011 49 69 7 90 32 19 (When dialing from within Germany, drop the 011 49 and add a 0 before the 69). Be sure to indicate the dates you want to journey, which of the two different lines you want to travel, where you will start and end your trip, and the number of seats you want.

Passengers are allowed to break the journey at as many stops as they desire on both bus lines, and we recommend some specific places to do so in the text that follows. If that is your plan, be sure to provide all the specific dates this will involve when requesting a reservation. For additional information about hotels and activities in the area, contact Touristik Arbeitgemeinschaft, Romantische Straße, Marktplatz, 91550 Dinkelsbühl, Germany. Phone 011 49 98 51 9 02 71 or fax 011 48 98 51 9 02 79.

The two lines connect in **Rothenburg**, making it easy to ride on all or part of both trips. Lodging in Rothenburg is good quality, but the supply is small and the demand very great. The Encyclopedia Britannica calls Rothenburg "probably the finest surviving example of a medieval town." It has been there for 1,000 years. Its 30 watchtowers and many dungeons, churches, patrician homes, ornamental fountains and market squares are perfectly preserved.

The town's most important buildings are on the old Market Square: the Town Hall, Virgin's Pharmacy (Marienapotheque), the lovely stone fountain (Herterichbrunnen), the ancient city council drinking hall, and the mechanical clock that performs at 11:00, 13:00 and 14:00.

According to the Meistertrunk Legend, when the town was under siege in the 17th century, the commander of the victorious Imperial Army was given his first taste of wine by the inhabitants. He offered to spare the lives of the city officials if any of them could empty in one drink the content of a tankard holding almost one gallon. One burgermeister rose to the challenge, accomplished the feat, and even quaffed more. The 3.24 liter Meistertrunk tankard is on display in the town's Reichstadt Museum. The legend is recreated every year in a pageant held on Whit Sunday, seven weeks after Easter.

Statues of the seven deadly sins and seven virtues adorn the Baumeisterhaus, on Schmiedgasse, near Market Square. This chiseled house is well worth seeing. The torture museum at the Dominican Nunnery is another attraction in the town.

Rothenburg has 15 hotels with 11 to 145 rooms each. It is an ideal stopover either for breaking the Romantische Strasse ride into two days or for transferring from or to the Burgenstrasse ride.

Also a recommended stopover on the Romantische Strasse ride is **Dinkelsbuhl,** another finely preserved medieval town with a surfeit of gates, bastions, towers, a moat equipped with floating swans and a sharp sense of ancient history. Its major pageant is every July, complete with sword dances and historic tableaux.

Augsburg is an ancient castled city. See notes under "Munich–Augsburg."

Castle Road   927

This bus trip operates from mid-May to late September.

Dep. Heidelberg	08:00		Dep. Rothenburg	16:50
Arr. Rothenburg	13:10		Arr. Heidelberg	20:40

Romantic Road   927

The portion of this bus trip which has the principal sights is Wurzburg–Augsburg (and v.v.). A stewardess-guide is provided for that part of the two schedules shown below.

These buses operate daily from early April to late October.

Dep. Frankfurt	08:00	-0-	Dep. Munich	09:00	-0-
Dep. Wurzburg	10:00	-0-	Dep. Fussen	-0-	08:00
Arr. Rothenburg	12:45 (1)	-0-	Dep. Augsburg	10:30	11:00
Dep. Rothenburg	14:30	-0-	Arr. Dinkelsbühl	12:45 (1)	12:45 (1)
Arr. Dinkelsbühl	15:25 (1)	-0-	Dep. Dinkelsbühl	14:00	14:00 (2)
Dep. Dinkelsbühl	16:15	16:15	Arr. Rothenburg	14:40 (1)	14:40 (1)
Arr. Augsburg	18:20	18:00	Dep. Rothenburg	16:15	16:15
Arr. Munich	19:50	-0-	Arr. Wurzburg	18:30	18:35
Arr. Fussen	-0-	20:40	Arr. Frankfurt	20:30	20:30

(1) Meal stop. Time to stroll. (2) Change buses.

SPECIAL RAIL TRIP FROM FUSSEN

For a marvelous extension from Fussen, here is a train trip that offers superb scenery: alpine meadows, deep river gorges, mountains. One of the most spectacular one-day rail routes in Europe.

Bus. German table.

Dep. Fussen	09:30	12:50
Arr. Reutte	10:03	13:43
Change to train 898		
Dep. Reutte	12:23	14:27
Arr. Garmisch	13:24	15:22
Change trains 895		
Dep. Garmisch	13:29	15:26
Arr. Innsbruck	14:51	16:50
Change trains 950		
Dep. Innsbruck	15:30 (1)	17:30 (1)
Arr. Salzburg	17:29	19:29

(1) Supplement charged includes reservation fee. Restaurant car.

INTERNATIONAL ROUTES FROM GERMANY

The German gateway for travel to Amsterdam and Brussels (and on to London) is Cologne. Frankfurt and Cologne are the access points to Paris (and on to Barcelona and Madrid). Frankfurt is also the starting point for travel to Basel and Zurich, Milan and Genoa, as well as to Warsaw.

Munich and Nurnberg are gateways for trips to Vienna (where you can make connections to Belgrade and Budapest), and Bologna (with connections to Rome or Venice). Nurnberg and Berlin are departure points for getting to Prague. Berlin and Hamburg are the gateways to Copenhagen (and on to Oslo and Stockholm).

Berlin - Copenhagen   50

Dep. Berlin (Zoo)	06:27 (1)	10:27 (2)	23:14 (3)
Arr. Copenhagen	14:20	17:59	09:45

(1) Supplement payable. Light refreshments. (2) Change trains in Hamburg. Supplement payable both trains. Restaurant car Berlin-Hamburg, light refreshments Hamburg Copenhagen. (3) Leaves from Berlin Lichtenberg. Change trains in Malmo. First- and second-class sleepers, second-class couchettes and second-class coaches available Berlin-Malmo. Malmo-Copenhagen train operates Monday-Saturday.

Berlin - Prague   60

Reservations are advisable for all of these trains; they have a restaurant car, unless designated otherwise.

Dep. Berlin (Licht.)	06:46	08:46	10:46	12:46
Arr. Prague (Hole.)	11:39	13:39	15:39	17:20
Arr. Prague (Hlavni)	-0-	-0-	-0-	17:41

Dep. Berlin (Licht.)	16:46	19:45 (1)
Arr. Prague (Hole.)	21:30	01:09
Arr. Prague (Hlavni)	21:41	-0-

(1) No restaurant car

Berlin - Warsaw   56

Dep. Berlin (Licht.)	08:04 (1)	16:36 (1)	22:41 (2)
Arr. Warsaw (Centralna)	14:32	22:55	06:29
Arr. Warsaw (Wschodnia)	14:44	22:10	-0-

(1) Reservation required. Supplement charged includes reservation fee. Restaurant car. (2) Carries first and second-class sleepers, plus a restaurant car.

Cologne - Amsterdam   28

Sit on the right-hand side for best views of the marvelous Rhine River scenery.

All of these trains charge a supplement that includes reservation fee and have a restaurant car, unless designated otherwise.

Dep. Cologne	07:08	08:16	10:16	12:16	14:16	16:16	18:02 (1)
Arr. Amsterdam	09:54	10:52	12:52	14:52	16:52	18:52	20:52

(1) Plus other departures from Cologne at 19:02 and 21:16, arriving Amsterdam 21:52 and 23:52.

Cologne - Basel - Zurich   73

Dep. Cologne	07:00 (1)	08:00 (1)	09:00 (1)	11:00 (1)	12:00 (1+3)
Arr. Basel (SBB)	11:45 (2)	12:45 (2)	13:45	15:45 (2)	16:45
Arr. Zurich	13:00	14:03	15:00	17:00	18:03

(1) Supplement charged includes reservation fee. Restaurant car. (2) Change trains in Basel. (3) Plus other Cologne departures at frequent times from 13:00 to 17:00 plus.

Cologne - Brussels   20

Dep. Cologne	06:30 (1)	07:14	11:14	12:14 (2)
Arr. Brussels (Nord)	08:50	09:44	13:44	14:44
Arr. Brussels (Midi)	09:01	09:54	13:54	14:55

(1) Supplement charged includes reservation fee. Restaurant car. (2) Plus other departures from Cologne at 13:14 (1), 14:14, 15:14 (1), 16:14, 18:14 and 20:14, arriving Brussels Nord 15:49, 16:44, 17:49, 18:44, 20:44 and 22:44.

Cologne - Paris   25

Dep. Cologne	08:14 (1)	13:14 (2)	17:08 (3)
Arr. Paris (Nord)	13:29	18:05	22:35

(1) Supplement charged. Restaurant car. (2) Change trains in Brussels. Cologne-Brussels has light refreshments, Brussels-Paris has a restaurant car. Supplement charged Brussels-Paris; reservation required. (3) Supplement charged. No train change in Brussels. Restaurant car.

Munich - Bologna - Florence - Rome   70

Dep. Munich (Hbf.)	09:29 (1)	20:30 (2)	21:25 (3)	23:40 (2)
Arr. Bologna	16:34	04:20	05:28	07:50
Arr. Florence (SMN.)	17:49	05:35	-0-	09:10
Arr. Rome (Ter.)	19:50	08:15	-0-	-0-

(1) Supplement charged includes reservation fee. Restaurant car. (2) Carries a sleeping car. Also has couchettes. Coach is second-class. (3) Has couchettes. Coach is second class.

Munich - Salzburg - Vienna 67

Dep. Munich (Hbf.)	06:00 (1)	07:25 (2)	09:25 (3)	11:25 (2+4)
Arr. Salzburg	07:45	08:55	10:55	12:55
Arr. Vienna (Westbf.)	-0-	12:35	14:18	16:35

(1) Change trains in Salzburg. Light refreshments. (2) Supplement charged. Restaurant car Munich-Salzburg. Change trains Salzburg. Salzburg-Vienna, light refreshments. (3) Supplement charged. No train change in Salzburg. Restaurant car. (4) Plus other Munich departures at 13:25 (2), 15:25 (2), 16:25 (3), 18:25 (3) and 23:19 (5). (5) Has second-class couchettes and first- and second-class coaches.

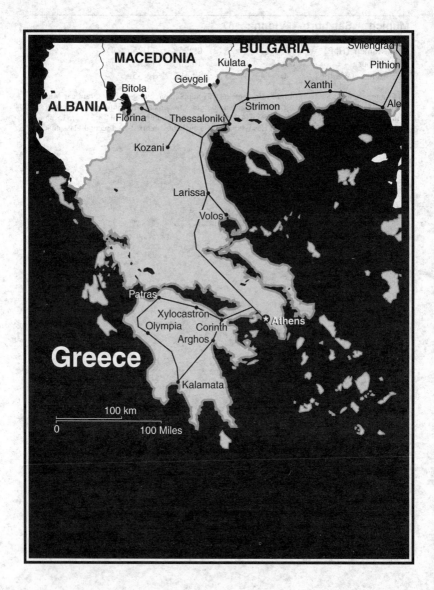

GREECE

Getting on Track in Greece

• Tourist information: Greek National Tourist Organization, Los Angeles office, 611 West Sixth Street, Suite 2198, Los Angeles, CA 90017. Telephone (213) 626-6696-9, fax (213) 489-9744. Chicago office, 168 North Michigan Avenue, Suite 600, Chicago, IL 60601. Telephone (312) 782-1084, fax (312) 782-1091. New York office, 645 Fifth Avenue, Olympic Tower, New York NY 10022. Telephone (212) 421-5777, fax (212) 826-6940. E-mail inquiries: gnto@greektourism.com. On the Web: http://www.greektourism.com. Note: This site was under construction at press time. Keep checking. It should be ready soon! Meanwhile, the Greek railway, OSE, has an official Web site at: http://www.ose.gr/.

• Public holidays: New Year's Day, January 1, January 6 (Epiphany), March 25 (Independence Day), Greek Good Friday, Greek Good Saturday, Greek Easter, Greek Easter Monday, May 1 (Labor Day), August 15 (Virgin Mary's Day), Ash Monday, October 28 (National Day), Christmas, December 25, December 26 (Boxing Day).

• Summer time: Greece changes to summer time on the last Sunday of March and converts back to standard time on the last Sunday of September.

• Recommended reading: For an in-depth look at riding the rails in Greece, pick up a copy of *Greece by Rail* by Zane Katsikis. Throughout the book's 266 pages, the author examines rail services in each region of the country. Along with the rail information is a lively history of the railway, interesting moments in Greek history, a list of major ferry routes and recommendations for accommodations in most cities and towns. *Greece by Rail* is published by Globe Pequot U.S./Bradt Publications U.K., and retails in the U.S. for 17.95.

• Currency: Drachma (drs). At press time, $1 equaled 285 drs.

Overview of Greek Trains

In the days before the conflicts in Yugoslavia, many Eurailpass travelers took the train to Athens via Belgrade and Thessaloniki. While the situation is somewhat better these days, trains still are experiencing frequent delays and with countries constantly shuffling entry requirements, you might get stuck in transit if you don't have the proper visas. The best route to Greece is to ride the train to the Italian port of Brindisi, Ancona or Bari and ferry across to Corfu and then continue by rail to the Greek capital via Patras. Ferries also leave from Venice and Trieste. Only ferries from Brindisi, though, are covered by the Eurailpass. These voyages are long but not unpleasant.

Considered the birthplace of Western civilization, Greece is one of those magical places that sets the mind to wandering. It doesn't take much, a stroll through ancient ruins where gentle breezes seem to whisper secrets of the past, a day in a small village that percolates along at the pace of a century ago, a fiery-red Greek isle sunset. Fortunately, trains can take you just about everywhere—except, of course, to the islands—in this fascinating land of mythology, philosophy and a history that won't quit.

Often, travelers think of Greek trains as third-rate and snaillike. Sometimes they were (and still are) right, but in recent years major improvements have been made, with new, air-conditioned rolling stock and fast InterCity trains linking major cities.

Like just about everywhere else on the planet, prices have gone up in Greece. Deals still exist, though, especially if you travel in the off season or stick to smaller towns.

Often, travelers think of Greek trains as third-rate and snaillike. Sometimes they were (and still are) right. In recent years, though, the Hellenic Railways Organisation (OSE), the state-owned railway has made major improvements, adding new, air-conditioned rolling stock and fast InterCity trains linking major cities. InterCity (IC) trains offer either non-stop or limited-stop service The OSE maintains travel offices in most major cities. In Athens, dial Larissa Central Station for information, 01 82 37 000, in Thessaloniki, 031 51 75 17.

Some tips to make your Greek holiday a pleasant one: Brush up on the history and mythology of Greece before you go...Take a stab at learning the Greek alphabet; it'll help you find your way around...Antiques can't be exported, so don't spend your money on that must-have bauble, only to have it confiscated when you leave the country; reproductions are okay...For those of you who might get caught up in the passion of smashing plates or glasses in restaurants, à la Zorba the Greek, better think twice. Depending on how much damage you do, it'll cost from $100 to $2,000!...Try to attend a Greek folk dance or local festival. They're usually held year-round; ask for a schedule from the tourist bureau...Entrance is free on Sundays to all public museums, archeological sites and other places of national heritage. Museums and archaeological sites usually close earlier in the day during the winter months...Don't get upset if a taxi driver won't take you where you want to go. Your editor was trying to get to a train station one day, but all the drivers emphatically said no! Finally, one cabby solved the mystery: "You're on the wrong corner!" Often they won't take you if the destination is not far enough or if it's not on their way...Did you know that Greece is a country full of caves? Reportedly, Greece has the largest number and variety of caves in the world. The action of time and water has carved out passages in the country's rocks, creating over 7,500 dry caves, potholes, subterranean rivers and caves containing lakes and waterfalls, stalagmites, stalactites and columns created over thousands of years from the calcium deposits of droplets of water...And finally, though they're devoid of trains, it's still worth a trip to a Greek Island, even if its only one a thirty-minute ferry ride from Pireaus. Unless you like crowds, avoid islands like Crete or Santorini in the summer.

General Rail Information

• Most Greek trains have first- and second-class coaches. Reservations are recommended on most express trains. Supplements for InterCity trains (IC) are based on the distance traveled and can cost up to 3,700 drs.

• Children under four travel free if they do not occupy a separate seat.

GREECE'S TRAIN PASSES

Sold worldwide outside Greece by travel agencies and Rail Europe.

Greek Flexipasses Unlimited *first-class* train travel. The 1998 adult prices are: $86 for any three days in one month, $120 for any five days in one month. Children: $58 and $85. The child's fare is for children aged 6 to 12. Children under the age of six travel free. DER Travel (800) 782-2424 offers a 10 percent discount off the above fares for travel January 1-March 31 and October 1-December 31.

Greek Flexipass Rail'n Fly In 1998, travelers receive unlimited rail travel in first or second class and a one way or round trip flight between Athens and any of the Greek islands served by Olympic Airways. Airport taxes aren't included and must be paid locally.

	Adults		Child Fare	
	1st Cl.	2nd Cl.	1st Cl.	2nd Cl.
3 days/1 month	$163 (1)	$143 (1)	$97 (1)	$87 (1)
3 days/1 month	$202 (2)	$192 (2)	$108 (2)	$104 (2)

Additional flight coupons: Adult $56, Child (2-12) $26, Child (under 2) $5.60.

(1) Includes a one-way air ticket. (2) Includes a round-trip air ticket.

Greek Flexipass Fly Rail 'n Drive This Rail Europe program offers three first-class rail days, two air days and two car days within one month. It includes a round-trip flight coupon for a trip to/from Athens and any of the Greek Islands served by Olympic Airways. Airport taxes are not included.

Car Categories	2 Adults* 1st Class	1 Adult 1st Class	Add'l Days Car
A Economy	$278	$338	$55
B Compact	$298	$368	$75
C Intermediate	$308	$388	$85

Vergina Flexipass This pass offers unlimited first- or second-class rail travel on the Greek Railways, plus a number of bonuses: a one-night-stay in an Athens hotel (category A or B depending on the class of rail pass) with breakfast included; lunch on an InterCity train (except Peloponnese); overnight accommodations in a sleeper compartment on the night train between Athens and Thessaloniki or vice versa, with breakfast included. There's also a choice of one of these excursions: a one-day cruise to the islands of Aegina, Poros, Hydra (buffet lunch included), or an excursion to Argolis or Delphi, or a city tour of Athens including the Museum of the Acropolis. Travelers also may add flight coupons for a one-way flight to all Greek islands serviced by Olympic Airways. Refer to the Rail'n Fly plan for flight coupon prices. DER Travel offers the same 10 percent off-season discount for this pass as for the Greek Flexipass. The age ranges for children's fares shown above also apply to this pass. See the previous page for details.

	Adults		Child Fare	
	1st Cl.	2nd Cl.	1st Cl.	2nd Cl.
3 days/1 month	$276	-	$251	-
5 days/1 month	$328	$263	$276	$242
10 days/2 months	$550	$416	$452	$377

The passes described below can be purchased only in Greece, at travel agencies and main rail stations.

Greek Senior Card Valid for one year from date issued (except 10 days before and after Easter, 10 days before and after Christmas, and July 1 to September 30. For persons age 60 or older on the day that identity card or passport is presented. Allows five free journeys plus 50 percent discount for unlimited number of journeys after the first five. Prices for 1998 were unavailable at press time. In 1997 a first-class card cost 6,000 drachmas, 4,000 drachmas for second-class.

Group Discount A 30% discount is granted to groups of 10 or more persons.

EURAILPASS BONUSES IN GREECE

• The ferry crossing from Patras to Brindisi (see note under "Italy") aboard Adriatica di Navigazione or Hellenic Mediterranean Lines.

ONE-DAY EXCURSIONS AND CITY-SIGHTSEEING

Here are nine one-day rail trips that can be made comfortably from Athens and Thessaloniki, returning to them in most cases before dinnertime. Notes are provided on what to see and do at each destination. The number after the name of each route is the Cook's timetable.

Details on two longer rail trips in Greece follow the one-day excursions. Schedules for international connections conclude this section.

Athens (Athínai)

From 07:30 to sunset, and from 21:00 to 24:00 on nights of a full moon, visit the Parthenon, the elegant temple of the Wingless Victory and the Erechtheion at the ancient Acropolis. The monuments there can be seen 07:30–16:45 daily. The adjacent museum is closed Tuesday. Then walk northwest to the partly restored ancient Agora to see the best preserved Doric temple in Athens, the Hephaistos, also known as the Thesseion.

Also near the Acropolis are: The old theater of Dionyssos. The gravestones and sculptures in Kerameikos, the city's ancient cemetery. The Corinthia-style columns of the Temple of Olympian Zeus. Hadrian's Arch. The all-marble Athenian Stadium, where the Olympic Games were revived in 1896. The Clock of Kyrrestos, showing the prevailing wind on each of its eight sides, standing in Aerides Square, named for the function of the clock. The Roman Forum.

Walk downhill to the Monastiraki area, where the daily "flea market" is held. See the view of Athens from the white chapel of Agios Georgios on the Hill of Lycabettus, climbed either by foot or by cable car.

Athens' best-known museums are the National Archaeological Museum at 1 Tositza

Street; the collection of ancient coins at the Numismatic Museum, next to the Archaeological Museum; the Acropolis Museum (noted above), the Byzantine Museum at 22 Vassilis Sophias Avenue (closed Monday), for its collection of icons; the Museum of Greek Popular Art (closed Monday); the Museum of the Ancient Agora excavations in the Stoa, an ancient commercial community at Attalus (closed Tuesday). The work of contemporary Greek painters and sculptors in the National Gallery at 60 Vas Constantinou (closed Monday). The more than 2,000 items relating to the social and religious customs of Romanlot and Sephardic Jews in the Jewish Museum (third floor at 36 Amalias Avenue), open daily except Saturday 09:00–13:00. Displays include the reconstructed interior of a provincial synagogue, religious articles, costumes and objects of everyday life.

The 28 exhibit rooms at the fantastic Benaki Museum in central Athens (Vasilisis Sophias Avenue at Koumbari Street), arranged chronologically, cover the entire spectrum of Greek culture from the early Bronze Age to the start of the 20th century: gold, ornaments, jewelry, portraits, statues, embroidery, icons, rare 17th and 18th-century bibles, and 8 centuries (10th to 18th) of Islamic art that includes ceramics, textiles and wood carvings. The Benaki is open daily except Tuesday 08:00 to 14:00.

Figurines of white marble from the Cycladic islands (in the Aegean Sea), created 5,000 years ago, in the Goulandris Museum of Cycladic Art (4 Neophytou Douka Street), open Monday–Friday 10:00-16:00, Saturday 10:00–15:00.

A collection of weapons since the Neolithic Age in the War Museum (Vasilisis Sophia Avenue at Rizari Street), open Tuesday-Saturday 09:00–14:00, Sunday 9:30–14:00. Nineteenth-century arts and crafts (woodcarving, needlework, naive painting) at the Museum of Greek Folk Art (17 Kydathineon Street), open daily except Monday 10:00–14:00.

The collection (from the Archaic period through the Middle Ages) of stone sculptures, ceramics, bronzes and exceptionally beautiful icons in the Canellopoulos Museum (below the Acropolis, at Theorias and Panos streets), closed Tuesday, open other weekdays 08:45–15:00, Sundays 09:30–14:30.

There are sound-and-light performances in English at Pnyx Hill every night at 21:00. When it ends, cross the road and see native dances of Greece, performed nightly at 22:15 on the Hill of Philopappus.

For Greek arts and handicrafts (ceramics, hand-woven fabrics, alabaster articles, embroideries, hand-carved wood furniture), shop on the streets around Syntagma Square, the center of the city.

Athens has a 14-mile rail line, the Athens-Pireaus Electric Railway (ISAP) that connects the suburb of Kifissia with central Athens and the port of Pireaus. Ride the entire line for a feel of the area; one way takes about an hour. Or use ISAP to sight-see. For the Acropolis, exit Thission, then walk about 10 minutes to the entrance. Explore Athens' markets near Monastiraki station or the National Archeological Museum, about 10 minutes from Victoria station. The ride's a bargain at 100 drachmas, about 41 cents. The ISAP (soon to be known as Metro Line 1) operates every five to ten minutes between 05:00 and midnight daily. With only one in five residents owning cars, it's no wonder two more rail lines are under construction; they should be complete sometime in 1998.

Athens - Arghos - Athens 1450

Dep. Athens	06:29 (1)	07:24	10:35 (1)	15:26 (1)	16:02
Arr. Arghos	09:20	10:17	13:26	18:20	18:51

Sights in **Arghos:** The museum, with its archaeological exhibits. From there, it is a 15-minute walk to the ancient theater, carved into the hillside, and to some Roman ruins. A five-mile taxi ride to the 800 B.C. ruins of Tiryns is well worth the small fare. At the birthplace of Hercules you will see the ruins of Greece's oldest recognizable temple: underground galleries polished for many centuries by the woolly backs of innumerable sheep who sought shelter there during storms. Massive Cyclopean walls.

Dep. Arghos	11:03 (1)	15:11 (1)	18:52	20:03 (1)
Arr. Athens	13:55	17:58	21:42	22:48

(1) Light refreshments.

Athens - Corinth (Korinthos) - Athens 1450

Watch 80 minutes after departing Athens for the same view described above, under "Athens–Arghos." The arrival in Corinth is in the "modern" Corinth, built after the 1858 earthquake.

Dep. Athens	06:29 (1)	07:24	08:49 (1)	09:37 (1)	10:35 (2)
Arr. Corinth	08:20	09:19	10:22	11:35	12:26

Sights in **Corinth:** The 2500-year old Temple of Apollo. The Kato Pirini Fountain. The rostrum from which St. Paul preached Christianity to the Corinthians.

Dep. Corinth	07:28	09:00(1)	12:05 (1)	12:52(1)	14:17 (1)	18:29 (1)	19:54 (3)
Arr. Athens	09:17	10:32	13:55	14:46	15:49	20:01	21:42

(1) Light refreshments. (2) Plus other departures from Athens at 12:07 (1) and 14:06. (3) Plus other departures from Corinth at 20:33, 21:03, and 22:24.

Athens - Kalamata - Athens 1450

Dep. Athens	06:29 (1)	09:37 (1)	10:35 (1)	15:26 (1)
Arr. Kalamata	13:02	19:40	17:08	22:00

Sights in **Kalamata:** The exhibits at the museum in the Kyriakos mansion, ranging from Stone Age weapons to Venetian mirrors and coins as well as relics from the 1821 War of Independence. The Byzantine-style Church of Aghii Apostoli. The splendid view from the

Frankish castle and, descending from there, see the handmade silk articles at the convent. Aghios Haralambos, one of the finest Byzantine churches in the area, is a short distance east of the convent. Stroll along the seafront.

Dep. Kalamata	07:20 (1)	11:27	16:19
Arr. Athens	14:18	18:27	22:48

(1) Light refreshments.

Athens - Pirghos - Olympia - Athens 1450, 1455

Most of this trip is alongside the sea, through green fields of citrus and olive trees. Between Athens and Corinth, the train goes across a bridge that spans the Korinthos Canal, which separates northern Greece from Peloponesia.

1450

Dep. Athens	08:49 (1)	09:37 (2)
Arr. Pirghos	13:53	16:31
Change trains 1455		
Dep. Pirghos	14:10 (3)	19:20 (3)
Arr. Olympia	14:46	19:56

Sights in **Olympia:** The first Olympic Games (776 B.C.) were held here and continued here every four years for the next 12 centuries. See the stadium. The fine Olympic Museum, with its marvelous Hermes of Praxiteles sculpture. The temples of Hera and Zeus.

1455

Dep. Olympia	07:21 (3)	09:46 (3)	16:11 (3)
Arr. Pirghos	07:57	10:22	16:50
Change trains 1450			
Dep. Pirghos	08:22 (2)	10:46 (1)	17:00 (1)
Arr. Athens	14:46	15:49	22:04

(1) Light refreshments. Supplement charged. (2) Light refreshments. (3) Narrow-gauge railway; second class only.

Athens - Diakopto - Kalavrita - Athens 1450

Dep. Athens	06:29 (1)	08:49 (3)	09:37 (1)	12:07 (3)	14:06 (3)
Arr. Diakopto	09:43	11:29`	13:10	14:47	16:46
Change trains					
Dep. Diakopto	09:50 (2)	11:52 (2)	13:26 (2)	15:25 (2)	17:30 (2)
Arr. Kalavrita	10:59	13:01	14:35	16:34	18:39

The 750 mm narrow-gauge rack railway between Diakopto and Kalavrita, built between 1889 and 1896 is a fascinating 22 km climb through the Vouraikos gorge. Diakopto, is seaside resort on the coast of Northern Peloponnese (about 169 km from Athens). The little train starts its climb shortly after leaving Diakopto. Following the gorge, the train clings to rocky precipices, trundles over viaducts, cruises through short tunnels and even over a large waterfall. Travelers rave about the 8 km section of the route leading to Mega Spileon station, saying the scenery is among the most spectacular in Europe.

Extra trains run during the summer, weekends and holidays. Talks are underway about extending the line to Helmos, a ski area 14 km from Kalavrita.

Sights in **Kalavrita**: Take a cab to the monastery of Agia Lavra. See the mural on the wall of the primary school; it's dedicated to the martyred towns of the world. Kalavrita was the site of a horrible massacre during World War II. In December 1943, Austrian Nazi soldiers murdered the entire male population of the town, because they were incensed at losses to Greek resistance groups. In the main square, the church's clock is frozen at the time of the massacre, 14:34. Greece by Rail author, Zane Katsikis, recommends Villa Kalavrita for an overnight stay. It has suites and rooms in a new building across from the rail station. In Greece, dial 0692 22 712 or 22 845.

Dep. Kalavrita	10:13 (2)	11:47 (2)	13:21 (2)	15:20 (2)	17:25 (2)	19:30 (2)
Arr. Diakopto	11:22	12:56	14:30	16:29	18:34	20:37
Change trains						
Dep. Diakopto	11:30 (1)	13:09 (3)	15:17 (1)	17:22 (3)	19:25 (2)	21:02 (1)
Arr. Athens	14:46	15:49	18:58	20:01	22:04	00:06

(1) Light refreshments. (2) Narrow-gauge rack railway. Second class only. (3) Supplement payable. Light refreshments.

Athens - Patras - Athens   1450

Dep. Athens	06:29 (1)	08:49 (2)	09:37 (1)	14:06 (2)	15:26 (1+3)	
Arr. Patras	10:44	12:15	14:18	17:34	19:57	

• • •

Dep. Patras	07:06 (2)	10:25 (1)	12:22 (2)	13:54 (1)	16:35 (1)	18:38 (1+4)
Arr. Athens	10:32	14:46	15:49	18:58	20:01	22:04

(1) Light refreshments. (2) Supplement payable. Light refreshments. (3) Plus other departures from Athens at 18:20 (1), 22:19 (1), arriving Patras 21:47 and 02:12. (4) Plus other departures from Patras at 19:58, arriving Athens 00:16.

Sights in **Patras:** Cross the street in front of the rail station to the park. Then walk from the Trion Fountain along Ayiou Nijulauo to the steps that ascend to the Patras Acropolis for a fine view of Patras, the surrounding mountains and the port, third largest of Greece.

After descending the steps, go to the left along Georgiou Street to the old Roman Theater, the Odeon. Another walk from the Trion Fountain is to the Archaeological Museum to see its collection of exhibits from the Mycenean, Geometric, Archaic and Roman periods. Also worth seeing are the Venetian castle and Greece's largest church, St. Andrews's. See the Clock of Patras, made entirely of flowers. Visit the century-old Achaia Clauss Winery, the leading producer of Greek wines.

Athens - Piraeus - Athens   Transit Timetable

Subway trains depart every few minutes from the southbound section of a combined north-and-south platform at Athens' Omonia Square rail station for the 20-minute ride to Piraeus. Be certain, at the same platform, you are not boarding the northbound train for Kifissia. There is also ordinary train service from Athens to Piraeus.

Sights in **Piraeus:** One of the largest ports on the Mediterranean. Ships sail daily from here to almost all the Aegean islands and to many other Greek ports. The two small adjoining ports of Zea and Mikrolimano are for pleasure craft. Bus #20 goes to those ports. The bus terminal is to the left of the rail station. See the neoclassical style Municipal Theater and the exhibits in the Archaeological Museum. The Maritime Museum, closed Monday, exhibits 13,000 items reflecting 5,000 years of Greek seafaring. Plays are performed at the open-air Theater of Kastella in the summer.

Thessaloniki - Kavala - Thessaloniki   1420

All of the Thessaloniki-Drama (and v.v.) trains have light refreshments.

1420

Dep. Thessaloniki	07:25 (1)	08:25 (2)	13:45 (1)
Arr. Drama	10:10	12:08	16:25
Change to bus (local sched.)			
Dep. Drama	10:00	16:00	18:00
Arr. Kavala	10:30	16:30	18:30

Sights in **Kavala:** The view from the Byzantine Fort. The colossal 16th-century aqueduct, Kamares. Imaret, the group of Moslem buildings constructed a short time prior to the 1821 War of Independence. The ancient relics in the Archaeological Museum. Beautiful beaches.

Dep. Kavala	08:00	12:00	16:00	18:00
Arr. Drama	08:30	12:30	16:30	18:30
Change to train 1420				
Dep. Drama	10:14 (1)	14:15 1)	17:45 (2)	20:12 (2)
Arr. Thessaloniki	12:55	18:07	21:14	22:54

(1) Supplement payable. Light refreshments. (2) Light refreshments.

SCENIC RAIL TRIPS

Athens-Thessaloniki and Thessaloniki-Athens   1400, Greek Timetable

From **Tithorea** to **Domokos,** the train winds along **Mt. Iti** and **Mt. Orthrys,** providing a panoramic view of many valleys and high mountains and, at one point, of the sea in the distance. Then the train goes along **Pinios River** and passes through **Tembi Valley.** About one hour before arriving **Katerini** (Athens–Thessaloniki), you can see on the left side of the train 9,000-foot-high **Mt. Olympus.**

Dep. Athens (Larissa)	07:02 (1)	08:24 (2)	10:10 (6)	13:05 (1)	14:24 (3)	17:05(1+4)
Dep. Tithorea	-0-	10:25	-0-	-0-	16:26	
Dep. Katerini	12:06	14:30	-0-	18:01	20:33	22:10
Arr. Thessaloniki	13:10	15:41	16:00	19:15	21:45	23:15

Sights in **Thessaloniki:** Second largest city in Greece. See the ruins of the Roman Baths, north of the Church of Agios Demetrios. The Roman market and theater. Nymphaion, the ancient circular building. The Arch of Galerius. The unique mosaics in the 4th-century Rotunda, at the intersection of Agiou Georgiou and Filippou streets.

The two surviving early Christian churches: the 4th-century Ahiropiitos and the 5th-century Osios David. The 15th-century White Tower. The collection of prehistoric to Byzantine items in the Archaeological Museum on YMCA Square. Articles from the past three centuries at the Folklore and Ethnological Museum, 68 Vasilisais Olgas.

Dep. Thessaloniki	08:02 (2)	11:06 (6)	13:26 (1)	17:04 (1)
Dep. Katerini	09:12	-0-	14:31	18:08
Dep. Tithorea	13:35	-0-	-0-	N/A
Arr. Athens (Larissa)	15:34	16:51	19:36	23:14

Dep. Thessaloniki	18:27 (2)	22:25 (3)	23:35 (5)
Dep. Katerini	19:38	23:38	00:51
Dep. Tithorea	23:47	03:54	04:54
Arr. Athens (Larissa)	01:46	05:57	06:51

(1) Reservation required. Supplement charged. Light refreshments. (2) Restaurant car. (3) Light refreshments. (4) Plus other departures from Athens at 23:17 (5) arriving Thessaloniki 06:25. (5) Carries first- and second-class sleepers and second-class couchettes. (6) This is the fast *Hermes Express* InterCity train. Lunch at your seat is available for purchase. In late 1997, a one-way first-class ticket cost 10,060 dra., round trip, 17,890 dra.; a one-way second-class ticket was 8,020 dra., round trip 14,920 dra.

INTERNATIONAL ROUTES FROM GREECE

Thessaloniki is Greece's gateway to Central Europe (and on to Western Europe), as well as to Turkey (and on to the Middle East).

NOTE: These trains travel through Serbia. Due to the ongoing political situation there, trains are subject to long delays or cancellation. There's also some risk in traveling through this area. Additionally, passengers without proper visas may not be allowed to continue their journey by train. Consider taking the alternate ferry route via Italy; details follow this entry.

Athens - Belgrade - Budapest   61, 70, 97, 1400

...Plus Salzburg, Vienna, Munich or Venice

	1400	1400 +97	97
Dep. Athens	10:10 (1)	23:17 (2)	13:05
Arr. Thessaloniki	15:55	06:25 (3)	19:15
Dep. Thessaloniki	-0-	19:30	19:30

Set your watch back one hour from late September to early April, two hours from early April to late September.

Arr. Belgrade	-0- (3)	08:18	08:18
Change trains			
Dep. Belgrade	-0-	09:05 (4)	09:05 (4)
Arr. Budapest (Keleti)	-0-	16:18 (5)	16:18 (6)
Change trains		*61*	*61*
Dep. Budapset (Keleti)	-0-	16:58	16:58
Arr. Vienna (Westbf.)	-0-	20:00	20:00
Arr. Salzburg	-0-	23:50	23:50
Change trains			
Dep. Salzburg	-0-	03:52 (6)	03:52 (6)
Arr. Munich	-0-	06:03 (7)	06:08 (7)
Change trains 70			
Dep. Munich	-0-	07:29 (8)	07:29
Arr. Venice (SL)	-0-	14:55	14:55

(1) Supplement payable. Light refreshments. At-seat meals available. (2) Carries sleeping cars, couchettes and coaches. (3) Day 2. (4) No train change in Belgrade. (5) Day 3. (6) Has sleeping cars, couchettes, second-class coaches. Reservation required. (7) Day 4. (8) Change trains in Verona. Both trains require payment of a supplement and carry dining cars.

Athens - Patras - Brindisi   87, 1450

The Patras-Brindisi boat trip is covered by Eurailpass and Eurail Youthpass but only if you go on the ships of Adriatica di Navagazione or Hellenic Mediterranen. Information for 1998 wasn't available at press time, but in 1997, there was a $15 high-season charge for travel from early June to late September. A reservation fee of $3 was in effect throughout the year.

WARNING: The employees of other lines intimate that their ships honor the two passes and then charge fees after the boat leaves the pier.

With or without a Eurailpass or Eurail Youthpass, a reservation theoretically can be made on day of departure or day before departure but it is very unlikely that space will be available (particularly during July and August) unless a reservation is made many weeks in advance of departure date.

Those gambling on making a reservation after arriving in Patras can make application January 1 to June 9 and October 1 to December 31 only at the Adriatica di Navagazione or Hellenic Mediterranean embarkation offices in Patras. From June 10 to September 30, those without advance reservations can apply also to any Patras travel agency that displays in its window the green badge "Eurail Information—Eurailpass." Before boarding, all passengers must check with the shipping line office at the pier to have their tickets checked, settle port taxes due and obtain the required Embarkation Ticket.

Another fee is charged for aircraft type seats, Pullman berths and cabins. Port taxes are not covered by the Eurailpass and must be paid in drachmas. Passengers without advance reservations must obtain the Embarkation Ticket at least two hours prior to the ship's departure time. The ferry companies reserve the right to cancel a reservation when that is not done and to give the space to a standby passenger.

Readers reported to us in 1997 that Adriatica and Hellenic ships are often older, slower and more crowded then the ferries of other lines. They also report that these ships are often not as clean as those of other lines. *Greece by Rail's* author, Zane Katsikis, highly recommends the ferry companies that sail to/from Ancona because they offer the newest ships and more convenient and frequent schedules than the Brindisi route. The extra money is worth it, he says.

For a view first of the Corinthian Canal and then the Corinthian Gulf, sit on the right side of the train between Athens and Patras.

1450

Dep. Athens	06:29 (1)	08:49 (2)	09:37 (1)	14:06 (2)	15:11 (3+4)
Arr. Patras	10:44	12:15	14:18	17:34 (3)	19:32

It is a 20-minute walk from the rail station to the harbor.

Change to boat. Check Cook's Table 2270 for sailing dates.

Dep. Patras Harbor	19:00	22:00	
Arr. Brindisi	10:00	15:30	Both arrivals are on day 2

(1) Light refreshments. (2) Supplement charged. Light refreshments. (3) Plus other departures from Athens at 15:26 (1) and 18:20 (2), arriving Patras 19:57 and 21:47.

Athens - Thessaloniki - Istanbul 1400, 1420

Both of these trains have light refreshments.

1400
Dep. Athens   23:17 (1)
Arr. Thessaloniki   06:25
Change trains 1420
Dep. Thessaloniki   07:25 (2)
Arr. Istanbul   21:43 Day 2 (Reservation recommended)

(1) Carries first- and second-class sleepers and second-class couchettes. (2) Supplement charged. Light refreshments.

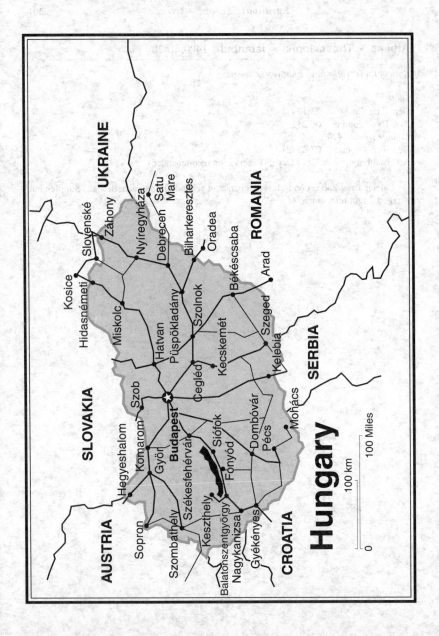

HUNGARY

Getting on Track in Hungary

• Tourist Information: Hungarian Tourist Board, c/o Embassy of the Republic of Hungary, Office of the Commercial Counsellor, 150 East 58th Street, 33rd floor, New York, NY 10155. Telephone (212) 355-0240, fax (212) 207-4103. E-mail inquiries: huntour@gramercy.ios.com or tourinform@hungary.com. On the Web: http://www.hungary.com/tourinform/.

• Public holidays: New Year's Day, January 1, March 15 (Day of the 1848 Revolution), Easter and Easter Monday, April 4 (Liberation Day), May 1 (Labor Day), Whit Monday (June), August 20 (St. Stephen's/Constitution Day), October 23 (Republic Day), November 7 (Revolution Remembrance Day) and Christmas, December 25-26.

• Currency: Forint (Ft.). At press time, $1 equalled Ft.196.3. NOTE: Convert money only at official exchange offices. Hang on to exchange receipts; no more than half the amount exchanged (up to $50) can be reconverted. Stay away from illegal black market money converters, you'll get ripped-off. Guaranteed!

Overview of Hungary's Trains

Most of Hungary's trains are operated by Magyar Államvasutak (MAV; Hungarian State Railways). The state's ownership dates from 1868. The Gyor-Sopron line is operated by Gyor-Sopron-Ebenfurthi Vasut. A few narrow-gauge lines remain and they are run by a group called Allami Erdei Vasutak.

Hungary has always held a special place for travels in the East. Even in the days of the communist bloc, Budapest remained the most popular holiday destination for eastern visitors. Thus, it wasn't surprising that Hungary became the first of the former communist countries to join the Eurail pass system countries, becoming the seventeenth. Just behind Prague in its massive tourist attraction to western travelers, Budapest offers cultural splendor and aesthetic pleasure, full-bodied red wine, peppery food, lively folk music, and an atmosphere of openness. Budapest represents all the positive aspects of Prague without the excess of grotesque commercialism. Prices have increased, but are still manageable. Just a jump away from Vienna, Hungary was always the first step into the East. Aside from the train, many travelers opt for the pleasant Danube river trip between the two cities via Bratislava by hydrofoil, which can be convenient (but sometimes less so). One British historian recently reported that the five-hour river trip is almost always delayed due to insufficient water level on the Danube. The boat slows to a standstill waiting for the water level to rise. You might just prefer the train.

Ethnically unique, Hungarians are of Finno-Ugrian descent and speak Magyar, linguistically related only to Finnish and Estonia. There are slightly more than 10 million people in Hungary, of which two-thirds are Catholic. The once vibrant Jewish population of nearly 800,000 today stands at just 10 percent of that, representing nonetheless the largest Jewish community today in Eastern Europe. Hungary has one of the highest rates of suicide in the world, and also performs the highest per capita amount of abortions.

Literary and cultural life is intense with more writers in Hungary per capita than in any other European country. The president of Hungary himself is a leading contemporary writer.

If you need to unwind from the stresses of work or travel, you've come to the right place. Hungary is teeming with spas and thermal baths. Budapest alone has nearly 200 thermal springs. Try to get a one-hour massage in the States for a mere $15, and that's considered expensive in Hungary. Among the cities with spas are Hévíz, Budapest, Sarvar, Györ, Debrecen and Eger.

As more travelers venture into Eastern Europe, Hungary's infrastructure is taking a beating. Hotel construction is having a hard time keeping up with the influx of tourists. Budapest has the most first-class and deluxe hotels of any Eastern European capital, but room shortages still occur. Book as far in advance as possible. A popular alternative is to take a room in a private residence. Find private rooms through travel agencies or representatives at the train station. Be careful of accepting offers of rooms from people you meet on the street; sometimes they work out, sometimes they don't. Often, the rooms aren't in the city, and require a metro or bus ride to the suburbs.

Train travel aboard MAV trains, aside from the Eurail passes, has gone up substantially in price over the last five years. In general, international connections and access in Hungary are excellent. There are direct rail links between Budapest and 25 capital cities of Europe, and 54 scheduled international trains arrive every day in Budapest. All international trains have dining, sleeping and couchette cars. Most international express trains arrive and depart from the Keleti Railway Station (east). Destinations include Vienna Westbahnhof, Bucharest (via Arad), Belgrade, Poland, Prague, Bratislava and northern Hungary. Trains using Buda's Déli Railway Station (south) serve Vienna Südbahnhof, Zagreb, Balatan Lake, Pécs and western Transdanubia. Trains from Nyugati Railway Station (west) provide service to Bucharest (through Oradea), the Danube Bend, the Great Plain, Bratislava and Prague.

Vienna makes an excellent gateway to Hungary, with eight trains per day to Budapest; some schedules make the trip in about three hours. These trains include the *Liszt Ferenc* from Dortmund and Nuremberg, the *Orient Express* from Paris and Munich, and the *Wiener Waltzer* from Basel and Innsbruck. Special EuroCity return-trip fares between Vienna and Budapest exist, as well. There are also many local trains that run between smaller cities in Austria and Hungary; reservations are not needed. The Prague-Budapest voyage is made in nine hours, a popular route among Eurailers. One traveler sharing his Prague-Budapest overnight train experience reported that he woke in the night "to find the porter had chained the car doors shut. We were on a siding somewhere around Brataslavia. He was able to make me understand he had wanted to sleep and to insure the safety of his charges had chained and padlocked the doors."

Some travelers recommend first class for its comfort; others prefer second class where it's easier to encounter local people. The *Balt-Orient* and *Meridian* express trains serve Budapest from Berlin, Prague and Bratislava, and then continue east to Romania and Bulgaria. There are daily Budapest-Warsaw connections on the *Bathory* and *Polonia* express trains depending which route you choose. The *Bem* express train from Szczecin, Poznan and Wroclaw serves Budapest via Trencin. The *Varsovia* arrives from Gdansk. For Czech and Slovak connections, see those chapters in this guide. Train connections with points further east include the *Ovidius Express*, which runs from the Black Sea at Constanta, and the *Claudiopolis* train via Cluj to Budapest. The *Corona* from Brasov arrives in Budapest 14 hours later. For points south, Budapest is a hub. The Budapest-Belgrade express train currently is a strange shuttle for all sorts of traffic. To Croatia there is the Budapest-Zagreb express train (*Adriatica, Agram, Drava,* and *Ma*estral). If you plan on departing from Budapest for a journey by train through Russia and China, see David Stanley's comments on and recommendation of Star Tours in Budapest, which is published in his excellent Lonely Planet edition on Eastern Europe. Says Stanley, "Once you have your train ticket and reservations you can apply for a Chinese tourist visa (allow three days for processing), then a Russian transit visa ($60 U.S.), which you may be able to get in one day. If time is short, ask for the Russian train via Manchuria, which eliminates the need for a Mongolian transit visa (another three days' processing). Three-day Ukrainian transit visas are usually available at the border for $50." In any case, train travelers experience a rush of excitement just thinking about such journeys.

There is also a car–train service operating on the Vienna-Budapest Eastern Station-Thessaloniki route during the main tourist season, July 1 to September 25. Car loading time at Budapest Keleti Station: 10:00 to 10:30 for an 11:00 departure. Arrives Thessaloniki 09:45 the next morning. At Thessaloniki, car loading takes place from 17:45 to 18:45 for a 19:30 departure. Arrival in Budapest is 16:28 the next day.

The Keleti and Déli railway stations are both on the M2 metro line (seven stops).

Other Intercity and express trains from Budapest to the major tourist regions in Hungary include Northern Transdanubia, Lake Balaton (north shore), Southern Transdanubia, Northern Hungary, and Great Plain.

A Budapest company called Nostalgia Trains Ltd. organizes specialized train trips in the summer months. Contact: Nostalgia Ltd., H-1055 Budapest, Teréz krt. 55. Telephone/fax: (36) 1/269-5242.

Of special interest are fifteen narrow-gauge specialized railways operating in Hungary, generally from May to September. For information phone TOURINFORM at 117-9800

Obtain specialized information on Hungary through the *Hungary Report.* Find it on the Web at: http://www.yak.net/hungary-report/ or http://www.isys.hu/hrep/9708/index.htm. You can reach *Budapest Week* at 100324.141@compuserve.com and/or Central Europe Today (free online) by E-mail at cet-info@eunet.cz, or on the Web at http://www.enet.hu/bpweek/. The following site will connect you with other Hungarian-based news and travel publications: http://www.hungary.com/English/hudir/News/Econ_News/. For other up-to-date sources of information on Hungary consult the *Budapest Business Journal* at 100263.213@compuserve.com If Compuserve is your Internet provider, you can reach the *Budapest Sun* at 100275.456@compuserve.com or http://www.ceo.cz/bpsun.html). Please note that some of these sites might not be accessible at times, or even for a day or two. Additionally, we have found that not all Internet providers are created equal. If you can't access any of these addresses, contact your Internet provider.

The Hungary Report writes about a local train service that operates from Budapest to Csepel Island to the south of the city and to the nearby towns of Szentendre and Ráckeve. Here you can experience the majestic Danube River Bend.

Transportation buffs will be pleased to note that the first underground railway or public subway on the continent, Millenary Underground Railway (the second in the world after London's) was built in Budapest in the late 1800s and was restored to its original state for its 100th anniversary.

Additionally, the Funicular from the Buda side of the Chain Bridge to the Buda Castle Palace has been operating since the turn of the century. Fantastic views from topside.

General Rail Information

• Most trains offer first- or second-class seating. Certain international trains may not be used to make trips within Hungary.

• Railpass holders don't have to pay the supplement for InterCity or EuroCity trains, just the reservation fee. The supplement charge for those without a pass was Ft.250.

• Budapest's three major train stations are Déli Railway Station (south) in Buda, telephone 175-6293, Keleti (east), in Pest, telephone 113-6835, and Nyugati (west), also in Pest, dial 149-0115. All have metro stops.

• Always reconfirm your departure station or you might miss the train. Check, too, that the entire train is going to depart. It might look like one long train, then the first half takes off, leaving you in a coach going nowhere anytime soon, despite the sign on the side of the train showing your destination!

• For information on international fares, call: 122-8035.

HUNGARY'S TRAIN PASSES

Hungarian Flexipass First class only, unlimited train travel. The 1998 adult prices are: $64 for any five in 15 days, and $80 for any 10 days in a month (example June 3–July 2). Half-fare for children age 5–14. Children under five travel free. Sold worldwide by travel agencies and Rail Europe, 800-4-EURAIL.

ONE-DAY EXCURSIONS AND CITY-SIGHTSEEING

Budapest

The city is divided into two cities, Buda and Pest, by the Danube, and locals and tourists alike will playfully disagree about which they like better and for what reasons. The great width of the river in Budapest contributes to the split personality of the city. Buda in general is the historically endowed side while Pest is the commercially vibrant side. The city's public transportation system is highly expansive and efficient, reaching far on both sides of the river with key lines converging at Deák tér.

The theater district is focused on Andrassy út, and the offering of theatrical performances on any given night is impressive. Go see a play in Hungarian! You'll never have been more concentrated on the acting and set design than during those two hours of pure Magyar bliss.

In Buda, a visit up Castle Hill is a must. Here, the vestiges of medieval Budapest lurk. There are several possibilities for exploring the Buda Hills around the city: the Cogwheel Railway from Városmajor (two stops from Moszkva tér on the No. 56 tram) to Széchenyi Hill and the chair lift (libegé) from Zugliget (at the terminus of No. 28 bus from Moszkva tér) to the lookout on János Hill (Budapest's highest point: 526 meters) are two good approaches. Plan to visit both the National Gallery and the Historical Museum, both of which are located in the Palace of Buda Castle. From the castle you can catch the funicular down to the tunnel under Castle Hill at the foot of the famous Chain Bridge.

On Gellert Hill, above the Hotel Géllert, which, besides being known for its unusual swimming pool that made artificial waves, was a hotbed for high-end espionage in the 1960s and 70s, you'll find the Citadella, a fort built by the Austrians, now a hotel and commemoration to the Soviet soldiers who gave their lives to liberate Hungary in 1945. In 1956, a bronze statue of a soldier on this spot was knocked down, but was later restored. From here you are afforded the finest view Budapest has to offer. On the Pest side of the world you'll want to visit the City Park, the Grand Circus, the Budapest Zoo, the Museum of Fine Arts, and St. Stephen's Basilica. For a picturesque visit of the city, try riding the newly restored Number 2 Tram on the Pest side of the river.

A fun activity for the family is a ride on the Children's Railway. This narrow-gauge railway runs a distance of 12 kilometers through the Buda forests. Don't overlook the very lovely Margaret Island and its spacious 112-acre park. Special pedal-operated vehicles for two to six persons can be hired for a ride in the park.

Budapest's excellent bus, metro, suburban railway and tram system is easy to use. The metro has three lines; all meet at Deák tér. The suburban train, HÉV, runs north from Batthyány tér metro station. One- to three-day passes, good from midnight to midnight and on all transit systems, including HÉV (only to city limits, though), are sold at selected metro stations and cost between $4 and $6. Validate single-fare tickets, or risk a fine. Pleading the ignorant tourist doesn't always work with fare inspectors.

Györ

Well connected by express train, halfway between Budapest and Vienna, Györ is Hungary's third-largest city. With an interesting old town, historic churches and the striking new Kisfaludy Theater, Györ is worth a stop. Called the Town of Four Rivers, it's situated where the Raba, Rabca, Marcal and Mosoni-Duna rivers join. Highlights in this 2,000-year-old city include a 12th-century cathedral and the remains of a castle with cannons intact. Györ is also known for its thermal baths.

Fertod

The Esterházy Palace with its more than 100 rooms and grand Versailles-style baroque details merits a visit to Fertod.

Szeged

This gateway town to and from Romania and the former Yugoslavia is best known for its paprika salami and the Votive Church, which was built in the 1920s in remembrance of the devastating flood of 1879 that changed the face and history of Szeged.

Lake Balaton

This long and lively lake, the largest freshwater lake in Europe, is a popular summer swimming resort and family vacation spot. The south shore is sandier and more developed while the north shore is more scenic and historically rich. For ecological reasons motorboats are prohibited, making the lake ideal for sailing. There is constant train traffic between Balaton and Budapest, a train route around the lake and numerous passenger and car ferries. Keszthely, at the western end of the lake, is a large town with lots of lakefront and boating services. Siófok and Balatonszentgyörgy are also accessible by train and offer lakeside pleasures. Lake Balaton is an easy day trip from Budapest, but consider staying a night or two. Lodgings around the lake run the gamut from private rooms to hostels and hotels.

Hévíz

Hévíz is famous for its thermal lake, Gyógy. Water temperatures average 30 degrees Celsius at the surface. In winter, the haze off the water renders the experience particularly strange and appealing. In addition, there are lake baths and thermal baths in Hévíz; most are open year-round.

Kecskemét

A perfect day trip from Budapest, this central Hungarian town is best known for its fruit production, especially its production of apricot brandy. Art Nouveau buildings dot the main square; the Cifrapalato, a ceramic covered palace, is the most elaborate. Stop by the Museum of Naive Artists to view original paintings by self-taught Hungarian artists; paintings are reasonably priced. Kecskemét is a good base for a visit to nearby Bugac and Kiskunság National Park.

Pécs

In the Southern Transdanubian part of Hungary near Croatia, Pécs is Mediterranean in feel. Pécs is on the direct line to Zagreb and thus has become a departure point for Croatian travel. The first King of Hungary, Stephane I, proclaimed Pécs a bishopric in the year 1009. Reminders of the 1543-1686 Turkish occupation include two former mosques and lots of Ottoman architecture. The cultural scene comes alive in the summer with dance recitals, plays among the ruins of Tettye and classical-music concerts in the basilica.

Budapest - Kecskemét - Szeged - Budapest   1260

As these schedules show, it is possible to visit both Kecskemét and Szeged in the same day.

Dep. Budapest (Nyugati)	07:20 (1)	10:30 (3)	11:20 (1)	14:30 (4)
Arr. Kecskemét	08:32 (2)	11:55	12:32 (2)	15:55
Arr. Szeged	09:27	12:55	13:27	17:00

• • •

Dep. Szeged	05:30	06:35 (1)	09:30 (3)	13:30 (5)
Dep. Kecskemét	06:32	07:32 (2)	10:32	14:32
Arr. Budapest (Nyugati)	07:54	08:45	11:54	15:54

(1) Supplement payable. (2) Light refreshments. (3) Runs daily except Sundays and holidays. (4) Plus other Budapest departures at 16:30, 18:25 and 19:20 (1+2), arriving Szeged 19:00, 20:55 and 21:27. (5) Plus other Szeged departures at 15:30, 18:35 (1+2), 19:40 (6) and 20:26 (7), arriving Budapest 17:58, 20:45, 22:57 and 23:24. (6) Runs Monday-Friday except holidays. Second class. (7) Runs Saturdays, Sundays and holidays.

Budapest - Lake Balaton (Siófok and Balantonszentgyörgy)
and v.v. 1230

It is a short train and bus ride to reach Hungary's most popular resort area, the 46-mile-long **Lake Balaton** is circled with spas, motels and campgrounds along its 118 miles of shoreline. Great sailboating and fishing here. Frequent ferries link the many towns on both sides of the lake.

Dep. Budapest (Déli)	07:10	08:10	13:10	15:10	17:10 (1)
Dep. Siófok	08:49	09:54	15:00	16:48	18:54
Arr. Balatonszentgyörgy	09:56	11:23	16:24	17:56	20:04

* * *

Dep. Balatonszentgyörgy	06:29	08:08	11:24	12:25	15:20 (2)
Dep. Siófok	07:33	09:31	12:37	13:51	16:48
Arr. Budapest (Déli)	09:08	11:13	14:13	15:28	18:33

(1) Plus another Budapest departure at 19:10, arriving Balatonszentgyörgy 22:01. (2) Plus other Balatonszentgyörgy departures at 16:25, 17:37 and 20:17 arriving Budapest 19:33 (3), 20:33 and 22:48 (3). (3) Arrives Budapest Keleti rail station.

INTERNATIONAL CONNECTIONS
FROM HUNGARY

Budapest is Hungary's gateway for many rail destinations, including Belgrade, where continuing service to Athens and Istanbul is available, Moscow, Prague (pick up connecting trains here to Berlin and Scandinavia), Vienna (connections to the rest of Western Europe), and Zagreb, gateway to Italy.

Budapest - Belgrade 1360

Dep. Budapest (Keleti)	05:50 (1)	11:00 (2)	13:30 (3)	15:55 (1)	23:55 (4)
Arr. Belgrade	12:52	18:35	20:34	22:47 (3)	08:21

(1) Supplement payable. (2) Reservation required. (3) Restaurant car. (4) Carries sleeping cars and couchettes. Reservation required.

Budapest - Moscow　94c

This train carries only sleeping cars.

Dep. Budapest (Keleti)　　　16:20
Arr. Moscow (Kievski)　　　10:09　Day 3

Budapest - Vienna　1200

Dep. Budapest (Keleti)	06:00 (1)	09:12 (2)	10:50 (1)	12:42 (2)
Arr. Vienna (Westbf.)	09:00	12:07 (1)	14:00	15:30 (1)

Dep. Budapest (Keleti)	15:25 (1)	16:68 (1)	18:57 (1+2)
Arr. Vienna (Westbf.)	18:30	20:00	21:22 (3)

(1) Restaurant car. (2) Reservation required. Supplement charged. (3) Arrives Vienna's Sudbahnhof station.

Budapest - Prague　1160

Dep. Budapest (K.)	06:25 (1)	10:25 (1)	14:45 (1)	18:55 (2)	21:30 (2)
Arr. Prague (Hlav.)	-0-	-0-	-0-	-0-	06:42 (3)
Arr. Prague (Hole.)	14:20	18:18	22:45	03:41	-0-

(1) Supplement payable. Restaurant car. (2) Supplement payable in Slovakia. (3) Carries sleeping cars, couchettes and coaches.

IBERIAN PENINSULA
(SPAIN AND PORTUGAL)

Getting on Track in Spain and Portugal

• Tourist information: **Spain:** Tourist Office of Spain, New York office, 666 Fifth Avenue, 35th floor, New York NY 10103. Telephone (212) 265-8822, fax (212) 265-8864. E-mail: fdbksp@eclipse.here-i.com. California office, 8383 Wilshire Blvd., Suite 960, Beverly Hills, CA 90211. Telephone (213) 658-7188 or 658-7192, fax (213) 658-1061. On the Web: http://www.okspain.org/. **Portugal:** Portuguese National Tourist Office, New York office, 590 Fifth Avenue, 4th Floor, New York, NY 10036-4704. Telephone (212) 354-4403, toll-free in USA, 800-PORTUGAL, fax (212) 764-6137. Washington office, 1900 L Street, Suite 310, Washington, DC 20036. Telephone (202) 331-8222, fax (202) 331-8236. On the Web: http://www.ua.pt/turismo/.

• Public holidays: A list of holidays is helpful because some trains will be noted later in this section as *not* running on holidays. Also, these trains which operate on holidays are filled, and it is necessary to make reservations for them long in advance.

Spanish Holidays

January 1	New Year's Day		Ascension Day
January 6	Epiphany		Corpus Christi Day
March 19	Saint Joseph's Day	June 29	St. Peter and St. Paul
	Maundy Thursday	July 18	National Holiday
	Good Friday	July 25	Saint James' Day
	Easter	August 15	Assumption Day
	Easter Monday (Barcelona)	October 12	Columbus Day
April 1	Victory Day	November 1	All Saints Day
May 1	St. Joseph Artisan Day	December 8	Immaculate Conception
		December 25	Christmas Day

Portuguese Holidays

January 1	New Year's Day	August 15	Assumption of Our Lady
	Shrove Tuesday	October 5	Anniversary of the
	Good Friday		Proclamation of the
	Easter		Portuguese Republic
May 1	Labor Day	November 1	All Saints Day
	Corpus Christi Day	December 1	Restoration of Independence
June 10	Day of The Race	December 8	Immaculate Conception
	(Portuguese National Day)	December 25	Christmas
	St. Anthony's Day (Lisbon)		

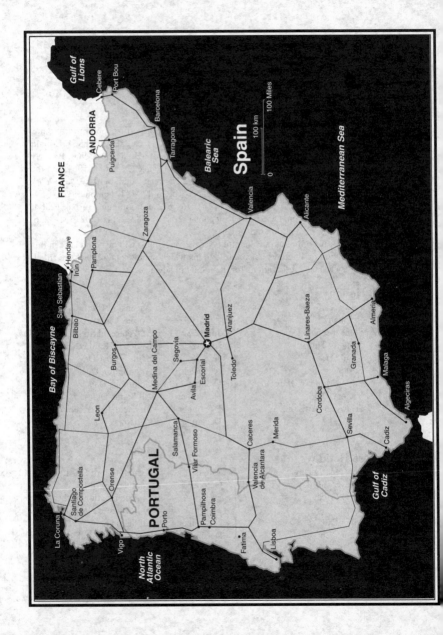

• Summer time: Portugal is one hour earlier than Spain all year. Portugal is on the same time as England nearly all year, except for a few weeks in the Spring and Fall. Both Portugal and Spain change to Summer Time on the last Sunday of March and convert back to Standard 12:00 in Portugal and 13:00 in Spain. Time on the last Sunday of September. During Summer Time, when it is 12:00 in England, it is 12:00 in Portugal and 13:00 in Spain.
• Currency: **Spain:** Peseta (pta(s). At press time, $1 equalled 153.5 ptas. **Portugal**: Escudo. At press time, $1 equalled 184.14 escudos.

Overview of Spanish and Portuguese Trains

It has become increasingly difficult to speak of Spain and Portugal as a single entity, as each country's tourist industry and infrastructure has progressed independently. Spain, of course, had a big year in 1992 when it hosted the Olympics in Barcelona, the World Expo in Seville, and the seat of the European Cultural Capital in Madrid, that resulted in some modernization projects for the festivities. Lisbon was the Cultural Capital of Europe in 1994 and some development and expansion has occurred there as well

Train travel in Spain is highly varied in that you can zoom across central and south Spain from Madrid to Seville in rocket time or take what seems like days to creek 50 kilometers across the Basque country or Galicia. Spain and Portugal have the broadest gauge railroad tracks in Western Europe. It is therefore necessary in most crossings from Spain into France (at Irun/Hendaye, Port Bou/Cerbere, or La Tour-de-Carol) to change trains. A few trains running between Spain and France are adaptable to either gauge.

Spain's trains are operated by Red Nacional de los Ferrocarriles Españoles, better known as RENFE. Portugal's trains are operated by Caminhos de Ferro Portugueses, or CP. Below is information that will come in handy for riding the rails of both Spain and Portugal.

General Rail Information

• Children under four travel free in Portugal and Spain if they do not occupy a separate seat. Half-fare for children 4-11 includes use of a separate seat. Children 12 and over must pay full fare.
• Do not discard a ticket during the journey. Frequently, the ticket is collected at the termination of a ride. If it is not presented at the destination rail station, the passenger must purchase a second ticket.

Spain:
• Spain offers a complicated mix of services and fares. Most trains have first- and second-class seating. First-class sleeping cars in Spain have single-berth and two-berth compartments. Second-class sleeping cars have three-berth tourist compartments, except the Paris-Madrid and Barcelona Talgos, which have tourist compartments with four berths. There is a supplemental charge for air-conditioned sleeping cars. Neither berths nor this supplement are covered by Eurailpass. Hotel trains (Euronight or EN) are becoming popular for international travel to/from Spain. They have special pricing structures and often include en suite accommodations such as a shower and toilet in the compartment. Among the trains under the EN banner: *Francisco de Goya,* Madrid-Paris v.v., *Joan Miro,* Barcelona-Paris v.v., *Pablo Casals/Salvadore Dali,* Barcelona-Zurich-Milan v.v. Some Spanish trains have second-class couchette cars, with six-berth compartments, as are also available in other Western European countries. In 1997, the charge for a couchette, above the ticket price, was 1,300 ptas.

• Many categories of trains are operated in Spain: InterCity daytime expresses (though supplements are usually charged for these trains, Eurailpass/Spanish Railpass holders normally just pay the required reservation fee); Tilting Talgo equipment operates on quality express trains (supplements are charged); Alta Velocidad Española (AVE), high-speed trains (to 300/kph) that operate over standard-gauge tracks between Madrid and Seville; Euromed trains, similar to AVE, operate on broad-gauge lines along the east coast at speeds of up to 200/kph; and Talgo 200 (T200), used on both high-speed and broad-gauge lines (a special fare structure applies to AVE, Euromed and T200 trains; some discounts are available to Eurailpass/Spanish Railpass holders). Spain also has a network of local trains sold under the name Regional Exprés. Reservations are often available for these trains up to 15 days before a travel date.

• Many Spanish train tickets include the price of a lunch or dinner, a fact that is wise to determine this in advance of a trip.

• For most Spanish trains, it is necessary to reserve a seat and have one's ticket stamped with the train number and departure date. Even when traveling with a Eurailpass or a Spanish pass, an endorsed ticket should be obtained for trains requiring them.

• Every year, some tourists using Eurailpass or a Spanish pass report being ejected from a Spanish train either just before its departure or at a station en route to their destination for failing to obtain the required endorsed tickets. A person using a pass has been indoctrinated with the idea that he or she need not have either a ticket or (when riding an ordinary train) a seat reservation. This is confirmed everywhere in Europe outside Spain. Unaware of the Spanish Railway regulation, the passenger blithely steps aboard a train in Spain without having the ticket or reservation required there. A ticket can be obtained without charge by presenting a Eurailpass or a Spanish pass. If the train is not exceptionally crowded that day and the conductor appears before the train departs, the passenger is told to get off the train, go back into the rail station, and obtain the required endorsed ticket. Frequently, the notice to do this is given so close to the departure time that the train leaves before the passenger is able to return to it. If the train departs before the conductor has discovered the omission of an endorsed ticket, often the passenger is forced to leave the train at the next stop to obtain a ticket. If that stop is typically brief, the train leaves that station before the passenger is able to return to the train.

• The justification for the Spanish ticket-and-reservation requirement is that Spain's first-class fares are substantially lower (about 60 percent) than what French National Railways charges for the seven-hour trip from Paris to Avignon or what Norwegian State Railways charges for the eight-hour Bergen-Oslo trip. The demand for Spain's limited number of express train seats far exceeds the supply. Only by issuing endorsed tickets can they control the situation. Reservations can be made at RENFE offices both in the major rail stations and at numerous locations outside the station, as well as at various travel agencies in Spanish cities. Making train reservations in Spain is very easy. More than 90 percent of the stations in Spain are hooked-up with a computer in Madrid, making it usually possible to arrange at one time all of your reservations for train trips in Spain. Reservations can be made as much as two months in advance. Timetable information can be obtained at offices of RENFE and at Spanish travel agencies. Tell the clerk at the train information window your departure date, train number (which you can find in the rail station on the list of departures) and/or departure time, destination and number of seats required. You will be handed a form which you then take to a ticket window, where you will be handed a seat reservation computer card. It will show either an exact seat number or the symbol SR (Seat Reserved) under the column Asiento. If it is marked SR, the conductor will tell you which seat to occupy after you board the car designated on the reservation computer card.

Do not board a Spanish non-local train without a seat reservation!

• In Spain, Rail Club Lounges are special rail station waiting rooms that have television sets, a bar, telephones, magazines and daily newspapers. These lounges are located at Madrid's Chamartin and Atocha stations, Barcelona's Sants, Valencia's Termino, and at the rail station in Bilbao, Cordova, Malaga, Vigo and Zaragoza. These lounges are available to passengers who are ticketed for international trains: Madrid-Paris, Barcelona-Geneva, Barcelona-Paris, Barcelona-Bern…and also for domestic travelers holding first-class tickets for sleeping compartments as well as for coach seats on any Talgo or InterCity train.

• Check out RENFE's official site on the Web: http://www.renfe.es/renfe1/homglish.htm.

Portugal:

• Most Portuguese trains have first- and second-class seating. First-class sleeping cars in Portugal have single and double-berth compartments. Second-class Portuguese sleeping cars have three-berth compartments. Seat reservations cost 300.00 escudos, first or second class.

• Among the types of trains operating in Portugal are Alfa and Intercidades (comparable to InterCity trains in other countries; higher fares are applied to these trains) and Inter-Regional. Reservations are recommended for Inter-Regional trains. Reservations are required for travel on international trains.

• Check out Portugal's official railway site: http://www.cp.pt/.

In order to avoid waiting in the wrong line for Spanish tickets and seat reservations, take note of these signs you will find in large Spanish rail stations:

TRENES DE SALIDA INMEDIATE	TRAINS READY TO DEPART
VENTA PARA HOY	TRAINS LEAVING LATER IN THE DAY
VENTA ANTICIPADA	TRAINS LEAVING ON A FUTURE DAY

Other **Spanish** rail station signs:

ANDEN	PLATFORM
ASIENTO	SEAT
BILLETTE	TICKET
CABALLEROS	MEN
COCHE-CAMA	SLEEPING CAR
COCHE-LITERA	COUCHETTES
COCHE-COMEDOR	RESTAURANT CAR
ENTRADA	ENTRANCE
ESTACION	STATION
HOMBRES	MEN
HORARIOS DE TRENES	TIMETABLES
LARGO RECORRIDO	LONG DISTANCE

LLEGADA	ARRIVAL
OFICINA DE INFORMACION	INFORMATION OFFICE
RESERVA	SEAT RESERVATION
SALA DE CONSIGNA	BAGGAGE CHECKROOM
SALIDA	DEPARTURE (EXIT)
SENORAS	WOMEN
TREN CON SUPLEMENTO	TRAIN WITH SURCHARGE
VIA	TRACK

Signs you will find in **Portuguese** rail stations:

CARRUAGEM-CAMA	SLEEPING CAR
CARRUAGEM-RESTAURANTE	RESTAURANT CAR
CHEGADA	ARRIVAL
ESTACAO	STATION
HOMENS	MEN
HORARIO DOS CAMINHOS	TIMETABLES
PARTIDA	DEPARTURE
PLATAFORMA	PLATFORM (TRACK)
SAIDA	EXIT
SENHORAS	WOMEN

SPAIN'S TRAIN PASSES

Spain Flexipass and Spainrail'n Drive are sold both in Spain (at travel agencies and the offices of RENFE—the Spanish Railway) and also outside Spain worldwide by travel agencies and Rail Europe. Purchasers must prove by passport that they are *not* residents of Spain.

Spain Flexipass Unlimited train travel.

	Adult	
	1st Cl.	2nd Cl.
3 days in 2 months	$190	$150
Add'l rail day (7 max.)	$ 40	$ 32

Children 4-11, half adult fare. Under four, free.

Spain Rail'n Drive Offers three rail days and a two-day Avis car rental within two months. The third and fourth person sharing the car need only pay for rail passes.

Car Categories	2 Adults* 1st Cl.	1 Adult 1st Cl.	Add'l Day Car
A Economy	$239	$289	$55
B Compact	$249	$329	$75
C Intermediate	$259	$339	$85
E Small Automatic	$289	$389	$105
Extra rail days (2 max.)	$40	$40	

* Price per person for two people traveling together.

All of the following are sold only in Spain, at main rail stations and travel agencies. Contact the tourist office for 1998 prices.

Family Card   For at least three persons from the same family or living at the same address, a discount is given on train tickets for "Blue " periods of the day or all-day to certain destinations on certain trains. Not valid for high speed or inter-regional trains. The passholder pays full fare. All adults except the passholder receive 50 percent discount on tickets. For children 4–11 the discount is 75 percent. Valid for one year from date of purchase. Proof by marriage certificate or any other certifying documents is required.

Golden Card   (Senior Citizen and Disabled Person Discount) For persons 60 and older and disabled persons of any age —*and who are residents of Spain*. One must first purchase a "Tarjeta Dorada" (Gold Card) at any rail station or Renfe ticket office. Proof of age (passport, etc.) required. Valid for one year. With the Gold Card, there is a 40 percent discount in "Blue " periods of the day or 25 percent discount all-day. Discounts for AVE and other premium services may vary.

Under 26   For travelers under age 26. Valid for two months. Cannot be used for high speed trains. Allows discounts up to 15 percent.

Round-trip Discount   A 30 percent discount on both first-class and second-class round trips on high speed trains if both trips are on the same day, 20 percent discount if both trips are on different days within two months. There is a 10 percent discount for inter-regional trains. Discounts for other trains depend on destination and time of day.

PORTUGAL'S TRAIN PASSES

Portuguese Railpass   Unlimited *first*-class train travel. The 1998 prices are: $99 for any four days within 15 days, $155 for any seven days within 21 days. Children under 15 pay half the adult fare. Under four, free (up to two children per adult transportation if seat reservations or supplement for sleeper not required.

All of the following are sold only in Portugal, at main rail stations and travel agencies:

Tourist Ticket   Unlimited train travel for any class. The 1998 prices are: Adult fares: seven days 18,000 escudos, 14 days 29,200 escudos, 21 days 41,200 escudos. Children (aged 4 through 11) and seniors 65 and over: seven days 9,000 escudos, 14 days 14,600 escudos, 21 days 20,600 escudos.

Senior Citizen Discount   Persons 65 or older receive a 30 percent discount.

Family Ticket   For three or more family members traveling together. Valid for trips covering a minimum of 150 km (93 miles). Passports and documents proving family relationship must be presented. One person must pay full fare. Half-fare for others who are age 13 or older. One-quarter fare for children 4–12. Children under four travel free.

Group Tickets Available throughout the year to 10 or more people in a group who travel a minimum of 80 km (50 miles) one way, and 160 km (100 miles) round trip. Group members didn't have to travel in the same class. Two children count as one adult passenger. A group of 15 to 50 people get one free ticket. Groups of 10 to 24 adult passengers receive a 20 percent discount, 25 to 49 passengers, 25 percent discount and 50 or more 30 percent.

Children's fares Children under four ride free, as long as they sit on a parent's or guardian's lap. If they occupy a seat they pay half-fare. Children four through eleven are half-fare.

For rail schedule and fare information while in Portugal, call the Portuguese Railroad Company (CP), 888-4025, between 08:00 and 23:00.

EURAILPASS BONUSES

Information was not available for 1998 at press time. In 1997, there were no Eurailpass bonuses in Portugal or Spain. There was a 20 percent reduction on ferry crossings operated by Trasmediterranea between Barcelona and Palma de Mallorca and Valencia and Palma de Mallorca.

ONE-DAY EXCURSIONS AND CITY-SIGHTSEEING

Here are 43 one-day rail trips that can be made comfortably from 13 major Spanish and Portuguese cities, returning to them in most cases before dinner-time. Notes are provided on what to see and do at each destination. The number after the name of each route is the *Cook's* timetable.

The 13 base cities are: Barcelona, Cordoba, Granada, Leon, Lisbon, Madrid, Porto, Regua, San Sebastian, Seville, Tarragona, Valencia and Vigo.

This section concludes with details on 15 rail trips recommended for exceptional scenery plus seven trips to/from Madrid, information about two interesting and luxurious tourist trains, *Al Andalus* and *Transcantabrico*, and the international rail connections from Portugal and Spain.

Barcelona

There is rail service (Table 654) between the center of Barcelona (Sants rail station) and the city's airport every 30 minutes from 05:43 to 22:13. The rail service from the airport to the city is every 30 minutes from 06:10 to 22:40.

Local trains, not requiring seat reservations, depart from Barcelona's underground Pas de Gracia and Sants rail stations. Faster express trains, requiring seat reservations, also depart from Pas de Gracia and from Sants, as well as from Barcelona's Termino station.

A guided walking-tour audiocassette (and Walkman adaptable to one or two headphones) can be rented from Libreria de la Virreina, at Rambla 99. It is closed Sunday of one week and Saturday of the alternate week. Open 10:00-14:00 and 16:30-20:30.

Your sightseeing here can be divided into covering four separate areas of Barcelona. In the Gothic Quarter: The cloisters in the 14th-century cathedral (La Seu), the Episcopal Palace, Palacio de la Generalidad, many elegant 14th and 15th-century palaces, the Federico Mares Museum. The Picasso Museum.

The Montjuic Hill area, where thousands of visitors gathered at Olympic Stadium for the 1992 games, is booming with museums and galleries. Visit the National Art Museum of Catalunya. It has one of the best collections of Romanesque art in the world, including the works of El Greco, Velasquez and Rembrandt. See the latest finds at the Archaeological Museum in Palacio Real or handicrafts and architecture representing every region of Spain in the Spanish Village. Also in this area is the Miro Foundation, featuring sculptures and paintings of Joan Miro (a Barcelona-Paris hotel train bears her name!).

In the Tibidado area: Pedralbes Palace, Pedralbes Monastery, and the view all the way to Montserrat and the Pyrenees. Take a funicular ride up the hill.

In the modern city center: Stroll the mile-long Ramblas, from Plaza de Cataluna to Plaza Puerta de la Paz at the waterfront, with its Columbus monument. You will enjoy seeing the numerous stalls selling hundreds of varieties of birds, the many stands with flowers and plants, the very large central food market, cafes offering tapas (the local and varied between-meal snacks), and at least half the population of Barcelona. Visit the Picasso Museum, for exhibits of his early Impressionist works.

Another rewarding walk, in the opposite direction, is along beautiful Paseo de Gracia, from Plaza de Cataluna to Avenida del Generalismo Franco (also called "Diagonal," its original name), to see luxury shops, decorative sidewalks designed by Dali, and several buildings created by Barcelona's most radical and inventive architect, Antoni Gaudi.

In Plaza Gaudi, you must see the uncompleted and absolutely unique church, La Sagrada Familia, the architect's most important work. It was started in 1884. Because of lack of funds, Barcelonians believe construction will not be finished until 100 years from now.

What has been constructed in the last 100 years is well worth seeing: the four lofty towers (nearly 300 feet tall), the Nativity and Passion facades with the Tree of Life supported by the central arch, and the wrought-iron plants in the side chapels of the completed crypt.

Although public transportation is not available to the Gaudi-designed park, Parque Guell, we suggest you take a taxi there to see it and to see the view of Barcelona from its elevated plaza. The paths in this park are decorated with concrete pillars that imitate trees and vines. Also see the colorful undulating bench surfaced with broken ceramic pieces, on the plaza. And the gigantic tiled frog fountain on the steps leading down from the park's plaza.

Regular city tours include only the church and one apartment building designed by Gaudi. A guided tour of most of his projects is offered by the Municipal Tourist Office (Avenida Paralelo 202) for both individuals and groups.

Lisbon

Santa Apolonia is Lisbon's rail station for departure to Madrid and beyond (to France and the rest of Europe). It has currency exchange and hotel reservation services.

See the beautiful Avenida de Liberdade. The Tower of Belem (monument to Portugal's sailors). The view from the bi-cultural St. George's Castle, built by the Visigoths in the 5th century and by the Moors in the 9th century. Largo das Portas do Sol (Sun Gateway), one of the seven gates into the ancient Arab City. Santa Cruz quarter. Alfama Quarter. Salazar Bridge.

The lovely Praco de Rossio. The marvelous collection of priceless Middle Eastern and European tapestries, jewelry, ceramics, and Dutch, Spanish, Italian and 15th to 18th-century Portuguese paintings in the Ancient Art Museum (9 Rua das Janelas Verdes). The more than 3,000 art treasures (Rembrandt, Fragonard, Corot, many Impressionists, Egyptian sculpture, Persian art) in the Gulbenkian Museum (45 Avenida de Berna). Across the park from it is the Gulbenkian Center of Modern Art (Rua Dr. Nicolau Bettencourt).

Edward VII Park. The zoological garden. The botanical garden. The Museum of Modern Art. The Municipal Museum. The greatest collection in the world of royal coaches in the Belem Palace at Praca Afonso de Albuquerque. The flea market. The Military Museum. The collection of 17th and 18th-century Portuguese and Indo-Portuguese furnishings in the Museum of Decorative Arts (2 Largo das Portas do Sol).

The Maritime Museum, in the west wing of Jeronimos Monastery. Jeronimo's Church. The cathedral. House of Facets, its front entirely faced with dark stones that have been cut into diamond-like facets.

A trip to Lisbon wouldn't be complete without a ride or two on one of the city's electric trams. Lisbon is one of the few cities in the world to maintain such an extensive network of them. Some of the little yellow trams date back to the early part of the century. The older equipment is joined by modern light rail vehicles, quite a contrast. Seven tram routes scale Lisbon's seven hills overlooking the Tagus River. Most of Lisbon's important sights and museums are just a tram ride away. Buy a *Passe Turistico* (Tourist Pass) from transit information booths at railway stations or kiosks around town. Passes range from a one-day variety ($3-$3.25), to three, four or seven days ($8.75-$14). The passes are good for unlimited travel aboard trams, metros and buses. You'll need to show your passport in order to buy the pass. Besides the trams, there are three funicular routes–Gloria, Bica and Lavra–plus the Santa Justa Elevator. All lines connect the downtown area with the upper parts of the city.

Lisbon-based American writer, Joseph Abdo, has written an excellent guide to the trams, *Tram Tours of Lisbon*. The slim 134-page book's second edition was published in 1996, and was sponsored by the transit agency, Carris, so it is very accurate. It's a must-have for the serious tram rider. Each line is described, station-by-station. There are tips for buying passes and tickets and schedule information, also lots of good color photos. You can order the book directly from the author for $15 (includes postage). He will accept personal checks, but will wait for them to clear before sending the book. Contact Joseph Abdo at Rua São João da Mata 5-3°, 1200 Lisboa, Portugal. Telephone/fax 351-1 60 61 49. His E-mail address is jcabdo@ip.pt.

Madrid

There is train service connecting Madrid's Chamartin and Atocha stations. A Eurailpass *can* be used on it. At Chamartin station, look for the track marked "Linea de Atocha y Guadalajara." At Atocha, go to the separate small station, a short walk from the main station. "Atocha-Apeadero" is a lower level at Atocha rail station.

Take in Madrid's "Golden Triangle" of museums. Start with the world-famous Prado Museum, with its breathtaking collection of some 3,000 great paintings and 400 sculptures. Next stop, the 19th-century Villahermosa Palace. It houses about 750 pieces of Old Masters, Impressionists and post-Impressionists. Most of the collection was purchased by Spain from the large collection of Baron Thyssen-Bornemisza. The museum now bears the baron's name. The third part of the triangle is the Reina Sofia Art Center. It's about a half-mile from the Prado and features works of modern artists such as Dali, Gris, Miro and Picasso.

There is more art to be seen in the mid-18th-century Royal Palace on Plaza de Oriente. Gaze at Tiepolo frescos, Ribera portraits, the many tapestries and carpets and the more than 400 antique clocks (keeping perfect time). Visit the Royal Pharmacy and Royal Armory, complete with suits of decorated armor. The Music Museum has five instruments made by Stradivari. Other fascinating rooms in the palace are the State Apartments and Chapel, Apartments of Queen Maria Cristina of Hapsburg, the private apartments, library and numismatic museum. The Royal Carriage Museum is near the west gate. The palace is often closed to the public for official functions, so check in advance before venturing there.

Additional interesting sights in Madrid are the botanical garden. The Bullfighting Museum. Descalzas Reales Convent where you can see the oldest creche in Spain. The Archaeological Museum. The Folk Museum. The Americas Museum. Retiro Park. University City. Plaza de Espana, with its stone monument to Cervantes. The Royal Tapestry Factory (closed Sunday during August). If you're in Madrid between May and October, hop aboard the Strawberry Train for a 75-minute jaunt to Aranjuez and the Bourbon Royal Palace.

Check out the restaurants around the oval-shaped Puerta del Sol, Madrid's commercial center. Head to a taverna, or *tasca*, for *tapas*, appetizers of cheese, olives or seafood. If you're used to eating dinner at an early hour, better fill up on tapas. Dinner in Madrid doesn't really get rolling until at least 21:00!

San Sebastian

An excellent seaside resort that became fashionable in the 19th century. The Goya and El Greco collection at San Sebastian Picture Gallery. Santa Maria Church. San Telmo Museum. The aquarium and Oceanographic Museum in Sea Palace, open daily 10:00–3:30 and 15:00–20:00. The picturesque fishing village nearby. Climb up Mount Urgull for a view of the bay from the Castle of Santa Cruz de la Mota.

Seville

The city of Don Juan and Carmen. You must not miss seeing Corpus Christi Cathedral, largest Gothic cathedral in the world and the site of Columbus' tomb.

The 14th-century Alcazar Palace with its magnificent chambers, particularly the room where foreign ambassadors were received. Its colorful mosaics and tiles, delicate wrought-iron and carved wood ceilings are spellbinding. You can see nearby Segovia from the tower of Isabella's castle. Allow time to stroll through the elaborate gardens there: bronze and marble statues, lovely fountains and the extraordinary Pavilion of Carlos V.

On one side of the Alcazar is a university, formerly Antigua Fabrica de Tobacos, the tobacco factory Bizet immortalized in his opera, Carmen. On the other side of the Alcazar is Barrio de Santa Cruz, with its ancient buildings and narrow streets. Once a refuge for Jews fleeing the Inquisition, now it is a fashionable residential section of Seville.

You can enjoy spending many hours in Maria Luisa Park, seeing the beautiful buildings, gardens, pools and fountains there. Particularly noteworthy is the magnificent Plaza de Espana.

Other notable sights in Seville: The 12th-century La Giralda Tower, a minaret when the Moors ruled here (open only on Sundays and holidays 11:00–14:00). The 12-sided Tower of Gold. Meander along the city's cobbled streets to see many picturesque homes.

RESERVATIONS ARE STRONGLY ADVISED
ON ALL SPANISH TRAINS!!

In the following timetables, where a city has more than one rail station we have designated the particular station (in parentheses).

Barcelona - Blanes - Barcelona   657 Costa Brava Resorts

Go to the "Estacion de Cercanias" (suburban section of Barcelona's Termino rail station) to board the train for Blanes. Seat reservations are *not* required for this ride. Board well before departure time to avoid standing for 90 minutes.

All of these trains are second class only.

Take a bus or taxi from Blanes' rail station to the center of the village. It is a half-mile walk there from the station.

Dep. Barcelona (Sants)	Every 30 minutes from 06:10 to 22:18
Arr. Blanes	90 minutes later

Sights in **Blanes**: Stroll the waterfront. See the aquarium and botanical garden, near the location of the daily fish auction, at 17:00. The Gothic fountain. The Church of Santa Maria. The view of the Bay of Blanes from the ruins of the castle on San Juan Mountain. it is a short drive to many popular beaches: Santa Catalina, Fanals, Lloret and Tossa.

Sights in **Lloret de Mar**: See the remains of the Tower of the Moors. The colored tiles that decorate the Church of San Roman. The 11th-century castle at the beach. There is an active nightlife here (discotheques, nightclubs and casinos).

Sights in **Tossa de Mar**: Exhibits of Roman archaeology, modern paintings and sculptures (Catalan and foreign), and a 1933 painting of the town by Marc Chagall in the Town Museum, open 10:00–13:00 and 17:00–20:00. See the view from the lighthouse.

Dep. Blanes	Every 30 minutes from 06:11 to 21:39
Arr. Barcelona (Sants)	90 minutes later

Barcelona - Girona - Barcelona   656

All of these trains are second class, unless designated otherwise.

Dep. Barcelona (Sants)	07:10 (1)	08:05 (2)	09:10	10:20	11:15 (2)
Dep. Barcelona (P. de G.)	-0-	08:10	09:15	10:25	11:20
Arr. Girona	08:34	09:36	10:26	11:35	12:25

Sights in **Girona**: The collection of paintings, sculptures, ceramics, glass objects, coins and silverware at the art museum in the former Episcopal Palace, open 10:00–13:00 and 16:30–19:00. Exhibits of local history and art in the Museum of the History of the City, open Monday–Saturday 10:00–14:00 and 17:00–19:00, Sundays and holidays 9:30–14:30.

The museum in the magnificent 14th-century cathedral has such outstanding exhibits as the 11th-century Tapestry of Creation, the 10th-century Book of the Apocalypse, and the 10th-century Arab chest of Hisham II, the oldest Hispanic-Arab work of silver. It is open daily 10:00–13:00 and 15:30–18:00.

The Provincial Archaeological Museum is open daily 10:30–13:00 and 16:30–19:00.

Visit the 12th-century Arab Baths. See Sobreportes, the ancient gate. Stroll on the narrow 17th-century streets.

Dep. Girona	11:50 (2)	12:31	13:27	14:26	15:38 (3)
Arr. Barcelona (P. de G.)	13:11	13:39	14:49	15:38	17:07
Arr. Barcelona (Sants)	13:17	13:45	14:55	15:44	17:13

(1) Reservation advisable. Light refreshments. (2) Second class only. (3) Plus other departures from Girona at 16:28, 17:26 (2), 18:25, 19:01 (4), 20:21 (1), 20:40 (2), 21:12 (5), 21:29 (2) arriving Barcelona (Sants) 17:45, 18:55, 19:45, 20:15, 21:43, 22:12, 22:20 and 22:49 (2). (4) Runs Fridays only. (5) Talgo service. Restaurant car.

Barcelona - Lerida (Lleida) - Barcelona   650

It is advisable to make a reservation for this ride well in advance of departure date. Although departures are from other stations, go to Barcelona's Triunfo rail station to make this reservation. On boarding, find a seat on the left side so as to have a good view of the restored 13th-century hilltop Seo Antiqua Cathedral before the arrival in Lerida.

Reservation advisable for all of these trains, unless designated otherwise.

Dep. Barcelona (Paseo de Gracia)	-0-	-0-
Dep. Barcelona (Sants)	07:30 (1)	08:30 (2)
Arr. Lerida	09:24	10:16

Sights in **Lerida**: The archaeological museum, in the Antiguo Hospital de Santa Maria, where the tourist office is located. A walking tour is easy with the city map available there. See the old Byzantine-Gothic-Moorish 13th-century cathedral. The Palacio de la Paheria. Stroll the maze of narrow streets in the interesting old section on the right bank of the Segre River, and visit the 12th-century Alcazaba (castle).

Dep. Lerida	15:45 (3)	18:37 (2)	20:35 (2)	21:18 (1)
Arr. Barcelona (Sants)	18:00	20:30	22:35	23:05
Arr. Barcelona (Paseo de Gracia)	18:08	-0-	-0-	-0-

(1) Restaurant car. (2) Reservation advisable. Supplement charged. Restaurant car. (3) Light refreshments.

Barcelona - Montserrat - Barcelona   Local Table

This trip is not covered by Eurailpass.

Dep. Barcelona (P. Espanya)	Every 2 hours from 09:11 to 15:11
	(Summer: until 17:11)
Arr. Martorell-Enllac	50–60 minutes later
Change to cable car	
Dep. Martorell-Enllac	Every 15 minutes from 10:00 to 17:45
Arr. Monistrol (Monastery)	5 minutes after departing Martorell-Enllac

Sights in **Montserrat**: The 9th-century mountaintop monastery, still occupied by hundreds of Benedictine monks, is 3,700 feet above a valley. It ranks with Zaragoza and Santiago de Compostela as one of the most important pilgrimage sites in Spain. See the Grotto of the Virgin, the Mirador, the Chapel of San Miguel and the Chapel of Santa Cecilia. Then take a funicular to the Grotto of San Juan Garin and an aerial tram to the 4,000-foot-high Hermitage of San Jeronimo, from where you will have a view of the Eastern Pyrenees.

Dep. Monistrol (Monastery)	Every 15 minutes from 10:00 to 17:45
Arr. Martorell-Enllac	5 minutes after departing Monistrol
Change to train	
Dep. Martorell-Enllac	Every 2 hours from 11:26 to 19:26
	(Summer: from 09:26)
Arr. Barcelona (P. Espanya)	50–60 minutes later

Barcelona - Sitges - Barcelona   654a

Frequent local trains run from Barcelona's Paseo de Gracia and Sants stations to Sitges, a 30-minute trip.

Sights in **Sitges:** The 18th-century furnishings at Casa Llopis. Antique dolls collected from every part of Europe, in the Lola Anglada Museum. El Greco paintings at the Cap Ferrat Museum.

Barcelona - Tarragona - Barcelona   650

Frequent local trains run from Barcelona's Paseo de Gracia and Sants stations to Tarragona, a 90-minute trip.

Sights in **Tarragona:** Relics of pre-Roman, Roman, Visigothic and Moorish cultures.

It is a short, but severely uphill, walk from the rail station to the long promenade, Balcon del Mediterraneo, from which there is a marvelous view of the sea. Two strolling streets start at each end of the "balcony." The first is Rambla del Generalismo. The other is Rambla de San Carlos.

We suggest you rest a while at one of the many sidewalk cafes on either Rambla. Then, start your walking tour of Tarragona by going two blocks from the "balcony," down Rambla de San Carlos to where it intersects with San Augustin. Turn right (the street name changes to "Mayor") and walk one-quarter mile to the 12th-century cathedral, worth seeing for its large and architecturally unique Cloisters, influenced by Roman, Gothic and Moorish styles.

Next, return to Rambla de San Carlos and turn right. Walk down it two blocks until it intersects with Abalto. Turn right and walk uphill, alongside the Roman wall. You will then be on the semicircular Paseo Arqueologico walk, from which there are excellent views of the countryside surrounding Tarragona.

At the end of this walk, bear to the right and come downhill on Avenida de la Victoria for five minutes until you reach Plaza del Rey. There, you can visit the museum in the 1st-century B.C. Pretoria and also see the marvelous mosaics and ancient coins in the archaeological museum.

Across from Plaza del Rey is the Roman Amphitheater. Having completed a circle, you will again be at Balcon del Mediterraneo, and it is all downhill to return to the rail station.

Granada - Malaga - Granada   666, 666a

Between Bobadilla and Malaga, the train travels through the spectacular **El Chorro Gorge**.

Dep. Granada	08:05 (1)		Dep. Malaga	13:35 (2)	18:15 (2)
Arr. Bobadilla	08:51		Arr. Bobadilla	14:33	19:11
Change trains 666a			*Change trains 666*		
Dep. Bobadilla	10:17 (2)		Dep. Bobadilla	14:37 (2)	20:05 (1)
Arr. Malaga	12:13		Arr. Granada	15:35	21:15

(1) Restaurant car. (2) Reservation advisable.

Sights in **Malaga**: Winter sun. The 9th-century Alcazaba Moslem palace and the ruins of Gibralfaro Castle, two fortresses that made Malaga a major stronghold in the Middle Ages. The Fine Arts Museum. Sagrario, an unusual rectangular church that was originally a mosque. The cathedral.

Lisbon - Algarve Resorts

The 100-mile Algarve (Lisbon-Vila Real de Santo Antonio) coastline, famous for its many popular resorts, consists of several centuries-old fishing villages and offers championship golf courses, tennis, horseback riding and all the watersports (windsurfing, fishing, water skiing, yachting).

Lisbon - Vila Real or Lagos   699

There is boat service from **Vila Real** to **Ayamonte** (Spain) approximately three times per hour during the summer; less frequent in winter. The trip takes about 10 minutes. Boat schedules are listed in *Cook's* Table 669.

Boat			Train		
Dep. Lisbon			Dep. Vila Real	-0-	06:00 (5)
(Ferry Ter.)	07:25 (1)	07:55 (2)	Dep. Faro	-0-	07:20 (6)
Arr. Barreiro	07:55 (9)	08:25	Dep. Albufeira	-0-	07:49
Change to train			Dep. Lagos	06:55 (4)	-0-
Dep. Barreiro	08:05	08:35	Arr. Tunes	07:44 (3)	07:55
Arr. Tunes	11:00	12:17	Dep. Tunes	-0-	08:00
Dep. Tunes	11:04	12:29	Arr. Barreiro	-0-	10:59
Arr. Lagos	12:10	13:23	*Change to boat*		
Arr. Albufeira	-0-	12:28	Dep. Barreiro	-0-	11:10
Dep. Faro	-0-	13:02	Arr. Lisbon		
Arr. Vila Real	-0-	14:07	(Ferry Ter.)	-0-	11:40

(1) Plus other Lisbon departures for Tunes, Albufeira, Faro and Vila Real at 13:20 (6), 17:30 (6), 18:50 (7) and 23:05. (2) Plus other departures for Tunes and Lagos at 17:30 (3), 18:50 and 23:05 (3) (3) Change trains in Tunes. (4) Plus other Lagos departures at 13:30 (8), 17:00 (8) and 22:30. (5) Plus other Via Real departures at 06:35 (8) and 21:40 (6+8). (6) Reservation required. (7) Reservation advisable. (8) Light refreshments. (9) Runs daily July 1-August 31.

Sights in **Lagos**: This historic town was the center for the Portugal–Africa trade. See the marvelous tiles in the baroque Chapel of San Antonio.

Sights in **Albufeira**: The Moorish ambiance here is striking. This is a very "arty" place. Has a colorful market.

Sights in **Faro**: The ancient church. The old quarter.

Lisbon - Setubal and Lisbon - Evora   698, 699

Boat	698	699	698	698	698
Dep. Lisbon (Ferry Ter.)	05:45	07:55 (1)	15:15	19:20	23:05
Arr. Barreiro	06:15	08:25	15:45	19:50	23:35
Change to train					
Dep. Barreiro	06:20	08:35 (1)	16:00	20:05 (2)	23:50
Arr. Setubal	-0-	09:03	-0-	-0-	-0-
Arr. Evora	07:45	-0-	18:10	21:58	01:58

Sights in **Setubal**: The paintings in the town's museum. Next to it, the lovely Church of Jesus. The view from the 16th-century Saint Philip's Castle, while having lunch there. Many sardine canneries, some of them open to the public. The maritime museum. Take an inexpensive taxi ride to the nearby (5½ miles) Palmela Castle.

Sights in **Evora**: Portugal's "Museum City." The Tourist Information Office faces the main square, Praca Do Giraldo. See the beautiful Temple of Diana, oldest Roman remains on the Iberian Peninsula. Visit the excellent regional museum in what was once the Bishop's palace. The 17th-century monastery, now an inn called Pousada dos Loios. The Church of St. Francis, where the walls are decorated with the skulls and bones of nearly 5,000 monks.

	698	699	699	698
Dep. Evora	09:02 (2)	-0-	-0-	14:28 (1+3)
Dep. Setubal	-0-	08:10	11:49 (1)	-0-
Arr. Barreiro	09:40	08:57	12:17	15:10
Change to boat				
Dep. Barreiro	10:00	09:05	12:35	15:25
Arr. Lisbon (Ferry Ter.)	30 minutes later			

(1) Light refreshments. (2) Reservation required. Light refreshments. (3) Plus another departure from Evora at 21:58 (1), arriving Lisbon 22:45.

Lisbon - Coimbra - Lisbon   694, 695

The trains below (Table 695) all require a reservation and have light refreshments, unless noted otherwise. Table 695 trains all stop at Coimbra B. Shuttle trains between Coimbra B and Coimbra meet most trains. Running time between the two towns is about 10 minutes. Cook's Table 694 has local trains departing hourly from 05:14 to 23:14 (return from 06:41 to 20:21). Travel time for these trains is longer, at just over four hours.

Dep. Lisbon						
(S. Apol.)	07:03	08:00	08:06 (1)	09:05 (1)	11:00	12:05 (1)
Arr. Coimbra	09:24	10:07	10:27	11:41	13:07	14:41

Sights in **Coimbra**: Walk uphill to the 13th-century cathedral, one of the finest Romanesque buildings in Portugal. Continue to the treasures at the Machado do Castro Museum. At the top of the hill is the 13th-century university, where you must see the gilded carved stone and wood and the baroque library. Also see the silver shrine in the magnificent interior of the New Convent of St. Clara. The Almedina Gate. Nearby, the Roman ruins at Conimbriga. Try the local food specialty, roasted suckling pig (leitao).

Dep. Coimbra	12:23	15:26	17:06	17:54 (1)	18:26 (2)	19:54 (1)
Arr. Lisbon						(3)
(S. Apol.)	14:30	17:30	19:25	20:25	20:30	22:25

(1) Reservation not required. (2) Supplement charged. (3) Plus other departures from Coimbra at 20:26 (2), 21:25 and 21:56, arriving Lisbon 22:30, 23:30 00:30.

Lisbon - Estoril and Cascais - Lisbon　691

A scenic seashore ride that costs about one U.S. dollar.

All of these trains run daily, except Sundays and holidays.

Dep. Lisbon (Cais do Sodre)	Frequent times from 05:30 to 02:30
Arr. Estoril	35 minutes later
Arr. Cascais	5 minutes after departing Estoril

Sights in **Estoril:** Portugal's major beach resort. Try your luck in the gambling casino. Enjoy a wonderful seafood dinner.

Sights in **Cascais:** Bloodless bullfights on summer Sundays. Surf fishing. Wednesday is market day, on the street that veers right from the rail station. There are taxis that will take you to Sintra (see "Lisbon–Sintra").

Dep. Cascais	Frequent times from 05:30 to 02:30.
Dep. Estoril	5 minutes later
Arr. Lisbon (Cais do Sodre)	35 minutes after departing Estoril

Lisbon - Fatima - Lisbon　Railway Timetable

Dep. Lisbon (S. Apol.)	08:06	17:03 (1)	Dep. Fatima	10:35 (1)	20:45 (1)
Arr. Entroncamento	09:15	-0-	Arr. Entroncamento	-0-	-0-
Change trains			*Change trains*		
Dep. Entroncamento	10:10	-0-	Dep. Entroncamento	-0-	-0-
Arr. Fatima	10:38	18:20	Arr. Lisbon (S. Apol.) 13:08	22:25	

(1) Direct train. No train change in Entroncamento.

Sights in **Fatima:** Millions of pilgrims have come here from all over the world to worship at one of the world's most famous Marian Shrines.

Lisbon - Porto (Oporto) - Lisbon   695

Reservation is required for all these trains and they have light refreshments, unless designated otherwise.

Dep. Lisbon (S. Apol.)	07:00 (1)	08:00	09:05	11:00 (2)
Arr. Porto (Campanha)	10:00	11:25	13:20	14:25

Sights in **Porto**: The more than 80 wine stores occupying all of the Vila Nova de Gaia quarter. The 12th-century cathedral. The three great bridges: Dom Louis, Dona Maria and Ponte da Arrabida. Portugal's oldest chapel, Sao Martinho de Cedofeita. The gilded wood-carvings in the Church of San Francisco.

The Church of the Clerigos, with its 10-story tower. The city's many beautiful gardens. The 15th-century Church of Santa Clara. The Moorish Hall of the Stock Exchange. The 14th-century convent-fortress, Leca do Bailio Abbey. The fine paintings, sculpture, porcelain and jewelry at the Soares dos Reis Museum. The folklore objects of this region in the Ethnological Museum.

Dep. Porto (Campanha)	14:10 (3)	16:10	17:10 (3)	19:10 (4)	20:05
Arr. Lisbon (S. Apol.)	17:30	20:25	20:30	22:30	23:30

(1) Runs Monday-Friday except holidays. Supplement charged. Light refreshments. (2) Restaurant car. (3) Supplement payable. (4) Runs daily except Saturdays.

Porto - Braga - Porto   696

Dep. Porto (Cam.)	06:22 (1)	09:35	11:15	12:06
Arr. Braga	08:11	11:14	12:08	13:25

Sights in **Braga**: The most interesting buildings are on the narrow street that runs from Arco da Porta Nova to the Praca da Republica. (It changes its name along the way.)

See the beautiful Santa Barbara Gardens. The treasury at the cathedral (gold and ivory crosiers, also damask and velvet vestments embroidered with heavy gold thread). The museum in the Casa dos Biscainhos. The terraced gardens that ascend uphill to the church of Bom Jesus.

Dep. Braga	12:39	14:17 (2)	17:26	21:11 (2)
Arr. Porto (Cam.)	13:30	15:40	18:28	22:52

(1) Runs daily except Sundays and holidays. (2) Runs daily except Saturday.

Lisbon - Sintra - Queluz - Lisbon   691

All of these trains run daily, except Sundays and holidays.

Dep. Lisbon (Rossio)	Frequent times from 06:07 to 02:07
Arr. Sintra	45 minutes later

Sights in **Sintra**: An outstanding old town, nestled on a mountaintop. There are many antique and craft shops on this village's winding, narrow streets. Take the "Sintra–Vila" bus from the rail station to the city's tourist office, where guide books and maps are available.

Use inexpensive taxis to see the view from the 19th-century Palacio de Pena, the Moorish castle, the Palacio Real, and the marvelous gardens at the Palacio de Monserrate. The palaces are closed on Tuesday.

Dep. Sintra	Frequent times from 05:08 to 22:23
Arr. Queluz	12 minutes later

Sights in **Queluz**: The beautiful gardens, the monument to Maria I and the exquisite restaurant at the 18th-century Palacio de Queluz, a miniature Versailles.

Dep. Queluz	Frequent times from 05:39 to 01:38
Arr. Lisbon (Rossio)	37 minutes later

Madrid - Aranjuez - Madrid   659, 660

	659	659	660	660	659
Dep. Madrid (Cham.)	-0-	-0-	09:05 (2)	10:30 (3)	-0-
Dep. Madrid (Atocha-Cer.)	-0-	-0-	09:20	10:45	-0-
Dep. Madrid (P. de Atocha)	06:30 (1)	08:53	-0-	-0-	12:20
Arr. Aranjuez	07:07	09:27	09:48	11:13	12:55

Sights in **Aranjuez**: The Museum of Royal Robes, the luxurious interiors of the Porcelain Room (walls and ceilings covered with red and green figures depicting Chinese and Japanese themes), the intricately chiseled Moorish interior of the Arab Chamber, the more than 200 drawings from the Ching Dynasty in the Chinese Print Room, and the Throne Room all in the Royal Palace, which has guided tours that are usually in Spanish. See the bed of Queen Isabella II, inlaid with carvings, floral decorations and bronze ornaments.

There are guided tours of the magnificent furnishings in the 18 rooms at the 18th-century Casa del Labrador, where a 19th-century clock in the form of Hadrian's Column is exhibited in the sculpture gallery. (A ruby and pearl-studded star strikes the hour by spiraling up and down the column.) Platinum, gold and bronze decorations are displayed in the Platinum Chamber. There are many silk wall tapestries in this palace.

The Pastere and Island gardens. The collection of royal ships in the Casa de Marinos.

The 300-acre forest, called Jardin del Principe (Prince's Garden). The Fountain of Hercules and the Fountain of Bacchus in the park called Jardin de la Isla.

	659	*660*	*659*	*660*	*660*
Dep. Aranjuez	13:29	15:24 (4)	16:30 (5)	17:19 (4)	19:17 (6)
Arr. Madrid (P. de Atocha)	14:05	-0-	17:05	-0-	19:51
Arr. Madrid (Atocha-Cer.)	-0-	15:57	-0-	17:49	-0-
Arr. Madrid (Ch.)	-0-	16:11	-0-	18:03	20:04

(1) Runs Monday-Saturday. (2) Talgo service. Supplement charged. Runs Saturday only. (3) Talgo service. Supplement charged. Runs daily except Saturday. (4) Talgo service. Supplement charged. (5) Additional departures 20:23 and 22:07 (7). (6) Second class only. Reservations available 15 days in advance. (7) Runs Saturday and Sunday.

Madrid - Avila - Madrid   675, 680

	675	*675*	*680*	*675*	*680*
Dep. Madrid (Cham.)	08:00 (1)	09:00 (2)	10:00 (3)	11:30 (4)	13:30 (5)
Arr. Avila	09:25	10:20	11:21	12:58	14:53

Sights in **Avila**: There are bus and inexpensive taxi services from Avila's rail station to the city center, about one mile from the station. Take a stroll on the 1½-mile-long 11th-century walls that circle Avila to best see the 88 semicircular towers and more than 2,300 battlements (11:00–13:00 and 16:15–18:00, closed weekday afternoons from October through April).

Also see the El Greco painting and the enormous (nearly 200 pounds) silver monstrance in the fortress cathedral. The baroque 17th-century Convent of St. Teresa. The Basilica of St. Vincent.

	680	*675*	*680*	*680*	*675*
Dep. Avila	13:26 (6)	16:15 (2)	17:30 (5)	18:40 (7)	19:50 (2+9)
Arr. Madrid (Cham.)	14:55	17:40	19:10	20:30 (8)	21:20

(1) Supplement charged. Light refreshments. (2) Talgo service. Supplement charged. Light refreshments. (3) Second class. Light refreshments. (4) Regional Express. Reservations available. (5) Second class only. (6) Second class only. Runs daily except Saturday. (7) Second class only. Operates Monday-Friday, except holidays. (8) Plus other Avila departures at 21:10 (10) and 21:50 (3), arriving Madrid 22:40, 23:20 (9) Plus other Avila departures at 20:45 (1) and 22:15 (11), arriving Madrid 22:20 and 23:50. (10) Operates Friday only. (11) Operates Sunday only.

Light refreshments. (3) Second class. (4) Supplement charged. (5) Plus other Avila departures at 20:57 (2) and 21:49, arriving Madrid 22:29 and 23:26.

Madrid - Burgos - Madrid   680

Dep. Madrid (Ch.)	09:20 (1)	10:00	Dep. Burgos	17:18 (1)	19:03 (2)	19:20
Arr. Burgos	12:30	13:26	Arr. Madrid (Ch.)	20:50	22:10	23:30

(1) Second class. Light refreshments. (2) Supplement charged. Light refreshments.

Sights in **Burgos**: The many interesting chapels in the magnificent 13th-century Cathedral of Santa Maria. The remains of Spain's greatest hero, El Cid, and those of his wife, are buried here. See the archaeological museum. Stroll 15 minutes on Paseo del Espolon, from the 14th-century Arch of Santa Maria to the statue of El Cid.

To see the Royal Monastery of Las Huelgas, only a few minutes outside Burgos, take a bus from Plaza de Jose Antonio.

Madrid - Cuenca - Madrid 659

| Dep. Madrid (Ato.) | 08:53 | 12:20 | Dep. Cuenca | 14:39 | 18:34 (1) |
| Arr. Cuenca | 11:20 | 14:43 | Arr. Madrid (Ato.) | 17:05 | 20:58 |

(1) Plus another Cuenca departure at 20:05 (2), arriving Madrid 22:49. (2) Runs Saturdays and Sundays.

Sights in **Cuenca**: The tourist office (Calderon de la Barca 28) is only a five-minute walk from the rail station.

Strolling down the winding lanes and narrow footpaths is marvelous. See the old houses hanging from sheer cliffs in this 15th-century setting. The best modern art museum in Spain, Museo de Arte Abstrato. Wonderful El Greco paintings and 15th and 16th-century altarpieces in the cathedral. A few steps away from the cathedral, the collection of coins, statues and Roman mosaics at the Archaeological Museum in a restored 14th-century granary.

Paleolithic red paintings of bison, wild boars, horses and archers at La Pena del Escrito National Monument.

Madrid - San Lorenzo del Escorial - Madrid 675

Although the stop for San Lorenzo del Escorial doesn't appear in Cook's, you can take a local train from Madrid that's bound for Ávila. The stop for El Escorial is less than an hour from Madrid. From El Escorial, take a bus to the monastery; it's about a 2 km ride.

Dep. Madrid (Ato.)	11:15	14:15	Dep. Escorial	16:55	19:25
Dep. Madrid (Ch.)	11:30	14:30	Arr. Madrid (Ch.)	17: 40	20:10
Arr. Escorial	12:15	15:15	Arr. Madrid (Ato.)	17:55	20:25

Sights in **San Lorenzo del Escorial**: Burial place of Spanish kings and queens. The Royal Monastery of San Lorenzo del Escorial, an enormous granite fortress (300 rooms), has more than 1,600 paintings (many of the finest Velasquez and El Greco) and murals, and it houses the Charter Hall Royal Library, containing 60,000 volumes.

See the Philip II apartments, the Throne Room, apartments of the Bourbon kings, Whispering Hall, Casita del Principe, and the Basilica.

The basilica was intended to copy St. Peter's in Rome, filled with gilt and marble carvings. Its four enormous pillars are 100 feet in circumference and support a cupola more than 300 feet high. Life-size bronze figures (royal families) surround the 100-foot-high altar.

The 18th-century Prince's Cottage has nine elaborately furnished rooms. Don't miss seeing the famous cross by Benvenuto Cellini and paintings by El Greco, Ribera and Velasquez in the church.

The circular, domed Royal Pantheon, crypt for most of the Spanish kings since the 17th century. Thirty feet underground, it contains 26 charcoal-gray marble coffins, in five tiers, and is illuminated by Italian baroque candelabra. Lesser royalty rest in white marble coffins in other rooms.

In planning a visit here, keep in mind that this enormous 16th-century building covers eight acres. It is open 10:00–13:00 and 15:30–18:30 (18:00 in winter).

Also visit the nearby monumental Valley of the Fallen, memorializing those who died in Spain's civil war. A 492-foot-high cross of concrete faced with stone marks this crypt containing more than 100,000 bodies. Its 900-foot-long basilica is a tunnel into the mountain. You can ride to the top of the cross in an elevator.

Madrid - Salamanca - Madrid   671

All of these trains are second class only.

Dep. Madrid (Ch.)	09:30	16:35	Dep. Salamanca	17:35	20:20 (1)
Arr. Salamanca	01:00	20:05	Arr. Madrid (Ch.)	20:55	23:40

(1) Runs Sunday only.

Sights in **Salamanca:** The Convent of San Sebastian. The church and cloister at St. Stephens Monastery. The 15th and 16th-century houses around the beautiful Plaza Mayor.

The oldest part of the city is the area between Plaza Mayor and the Tormes River. En route to the river, the 12th-century Church of St. Martin is on Plaza del Corrillo. Opposite it is the 15th-century Casa de las Conchas, named so because its facade is covered with 400 stone conch shells.

A few minutes walk from it is the third oldest university in Europe (after Oxford and Bologna), founded in 1218. A stone staircase leads to the university's magnificent library which has 60,000 books from the 16th to 18th centuries and ancient manuscripts going as far back as 1059.

The city's old and new cathedrals stand side by side behind the university. A magnificent altar and an elaborate ceiling are the highlights of the new cathedral, begun in 1513. Its 16th-century organ still works.

Madrid - Segovia - Madrid   671

All of these trains are second class only.

Dep. Madrid (Chamartin)	08:03	10:03	12:03	14:03	15:03 (1)
Arr. Segovia	116-132 minutes later				(2)

• • •

Dep. Segovia   12:55   14:55   16:55   18:55   20:55
Arr. Madrid (Chamartin)   116-132 minutes later

(1) Runs daily, except Sundays and holidays. (2) Plus other Madrid departures at 16:03, 18:03 and 20:03.

Madrid - Toledo - Madrid   671

Seat reservations are not required or obtainable for this ride. Board early to avoid standing for entire ride. The walk from Toledo's rail station to downtown is long. It's best to take a bus or taxi.

All trains are second class.

Dep. Madrid (Atocha-Cercarias)   07:05 (1) 08:25 (1) 09:39 (2) 10:25   12:25 (3)
Arr. Toledo   72-82 minutes later

Sights in **Toledo**: The most spectacular cathedral in Spain (750 stained-glass windows, priceless church clothing, jeweled ornaments, hundreds of tapestries, and paintings by Goya, El Greco, Velasquez, Tintoretto, Murillo and Titian). The house of El Greco, with a superb collection of his paintings. The 15th-century palace of the Duchess of Lerma. The Church of Santo Tome, containing El Greco's "Burial of the Count of Orgaz."

The Sefardi Museum in the 14th-century El Transito Synagogue. The Provincial Museum of Archaeology and Fine Arts in the 16th-century Hospital de Santa Cruz. The Army Museum in the Alcazar (fortress).

The Museum of Santa Cruz. Cristo de la Luz, the church first built in the 11th century as a Mosque (on the site of the ruins of a Visigothic church). It was then converted into a Catholic church in the 12th century. The works of Spain's leading modern sculptor, in the Vitorio Macho Museum. Most of Toledo's museums and other attractions are open from 10:00 to 18:00 (19:00 in summer); they usually close for lunch from 13:30 to 16:00.

Dep. Toledo   12:30   14:30   16:30   18:30   21:00(1)
Arr. Madrid (Atocha-Cercarias)   72-82 minutes later

(1) Runs Monday-Friday except holidays. (2) Runs daily except Saturdays. (3) Plus other Madrid departures at 14:25 (4), 14:35 (1), 16:25, 18:09 (4) and 18:25 (1). (4) Runs Saturdays, Sundays and holidays.

Madrid - Valladolid - Madrid   675

Dep. Madrid (Cham.)   08:00 (1)   11:30   14:30
Arr. Valladolid   10:27   14:01   17:01

Sights in **Valladolid**: The National Museum of (Wood) Sculpture in San Gregorio College, founded in the 15th century by the confessor to Isabella, one of the finest museums in Spain; open Tuesday–Saturday 10:00–14:00 and 16:00–19:00. Its life-size 15th–16th-century carvings are famous for their emotive and natural expressions, swirling draperies, and their realistic, vivid colors.

These sculptures were carved for religious processions and also to fill many of the magnificent and very complex altars that still remain in churches and museums throughout Spain. Visit the adjacent Church of San Pablo.

Sculptures, carvings and massive gold and silver objects are exhibited at the cathedral in a museum that is open Tuesday–Friday 10:00–13:30 and 16:30–19:00; on Saturdays, Sundays and holidays 10:00–14:00.

See Vivero Palace, where Ferdinand and Isabella were married in 1474. The magnificent ceilings and wood sculptures at the National Museum of Sculpture, in the 15th-century Colegio de San Gregorio. The wood sculptures in the 15th-century Convent of Santa Clara. The 15th-century Palace of Santa Cruz.

Cervantes' House, where he spent the last years of his life. Simancas Castle, seven miles from Valladolid. Charles V converted the castle into a storehouse for state records. It holds 8,000,000 documents that provide a history of Spanish administration from the 16th through the 20th century.

Dep. Valladolid	15:11 (1)	18:26 (1)	18:45 (1)	19:43 (1)
Arr. Madrid (Cham.)	17:40	11:10	21:20	22:20

(1) Supplement charged. Light refreshments.

Madrid - Zaragoza - Madrid   650

All of these trains charge a supplement and have light refreshments unless otherwise noted.

Dep. Madrid (Chamartin)	07:00	09:00	11:00
Arr. Zaragoza (Portillo)	09:55	11:55	14:00

Sights in **Zaragoza**: The Tapestry Museum in the cathedral. The Exchange. Aljaferia, an 11th-century Moorish palace. The Basilica de Pilar. The Goya and El Greco paintings at the Museo de Pintura.

Dep. Zaragoza (Portillo)	14:20	16:00	17:30 (1)	19:00	20:00
Arr. Madrid (Chamartin)	17:35	19:05	20:50	22:00	23:05

(1) Runs daily except Saturdays.

San Sebastian - Biarritz - Bayonne - San Sebastian   46, 302

46

Dep. San Sebastian (Donastia)	08:22
Arr. Hendaye	08:52
Change trains 302	
Dep. Hendaye	09:40 (1)
Arr. Biarritz	10:07
Arr. Bayonne	10:18

•   •   •

302

Dep. Bayonne	14:01 (2)	14:43 (1)	15:10	20:09
Dep. Biarritz	14:10	14:55	15:19	20:21
Arr. Hendaye	14:34	15:18	15:43	20:43
Change trains 46				
Dep. Hendaye	-0-	-0-	20:47	-0-
Arr. Irun	14:40	15:27	20:52	20:56
Change trains				
Dep. Irun	15:45 (3)	15:45 (3)	22:00	22:00
Arr. San Sebastian (Donastia)	16:00	16:00	22:17	22:17

(1) TGV. Reservation required. Supplement charged. Light refreshments. (2) Daily except Sundays and holidays. (3) Supplement payable. Reservation required. Light refreshments.

San Sebastian - Bilbao - San Sebastian   678

*This the second-class FEVE narrow-gauge rail trip is **not** covered by Eurailpass. Other trains, which depart/arrive Bilbao's Concordia rail station, run on this route at frequent times not listed in Cook. All schedules listed here require a train change in Ermua. Additional departures are available before and after times listed.*

Dep. San Sebastian (Amara)	08:12	Dep. Bilbao (Axturi)	12:15	18:15
Arr. Bilbao (Axturi)	12:05	Arr. San Sebastian (Amara)	15:40	21:40

Sights in **Bilbao**: The Fine Arts Museum. The Biscay Historical Museum. The Begona Sanctuary.

San Sebastian - Burgos - San Sebastian   680

All of these trains have light refreshments.

Dep. San Sebastian	08:32	08:45
Arr. Burgos	11:19	12:13

• • • •

Dep. Burgos	16:52	18:44 (1)
Arr. San Sebastian	20:07	21:37

(1) Supplement charged.

San Sebastian - Pamplona - San Sebastian 652

Both of these trains have a restaurant car.

Dep. San Sebastian (Dona.)	10:35	Dep. Pamplona	19:51
Arr. Pamplona	12:23	Arr. San Sebastian (Dona.)	21:10

Sights in **Pamplona**: The 14th-century Gothic cathedral, with its cloisters and Diocesan Museum. The Navarre Museum. The running of the bulls through the city's streets, every year from early July to mid-July.

Seville - Cadiz - Seville 665

All of these trains are second class, unless designated otherwise.

Dep. Seville (S. Justa)	06:35 (1)	07:55 (1)	09:99	10:00 (1)
Arr. Cadiz	08:28	09:43	10:44	11:43

Sights in **Cadiz**: The African environment. The Fine Arts Museum. The Museum of Archaeology and Art. The cathedral, with its monumental Silver Tabernacle, decorated with almost 1,000,000 jewels. The Historical Museum.

Dep. Cadiz	14:00 (2)	15:13 (3)	16:25	18:45 (4)
Arr. Seville (S. Justa)	15:45	17:02	17:57	20:55

(1) Runs Monday-Friday except holidays. (2) Runs daily except Sundays and holidays. (3) Runs daily except Saturday. (4) Plus other departures from Cadiz at 19:05, 19:30 and 20:00 (3) arriving Seville 20:50, 21:17 and 21:45.

Seville - Cordoba - Seville 665

Dep. Seville (S. Justa)	07:00 (1)	08:15 (2)	08:50 (3)	09:40 (3)	11:00 (1+4)
Arr. Cordoba	07:41	09:38	10:15	10:48	11:41

Sights in **Cordoba**: One thousand years ago, this was the most important city west of Constantinople (today's Istanbul). Its 200,000 houses *then* were double those of today. See the array of marble, jasper, onyx and granite on the 80 marble columns in the 8th-century Mosque, built on top of what was first a Roman temple and later a Catholic church, before the Moors seized Cordoba.

Following the recapture of the city by the Spaniards and in the conversion of the building to a church again, most of the original 1,000 marble columns were removed to provide space for a nave and a high altar. Called "Mezquita," its interior is illuminated by 4,000 bronze and copper lamps. Its ceiling is carved cedar. Its mosaics are made from 35 tons of glass bits. The mosque is closed 12:00–16:00, and the Alcazar palace fortress is closed 12:00–17:00.

Also see the 14th-century synagogue. The Fine Arts Museum. The Museum of Julio Romero de Torres. The Museum of Cordoban art, with its Bullfight Museum. The Provincial Archaeological Museum, one of the most important archaeological collections in Spain. The Roman Bridge, built in the time of Emperor Augustus. The home of the Marques de Viana, with its 14 flower-filled patios.

Dep. Cordoba	12:41 (1)	13:30 (5)	15:41 (1)	17:00 (6)
Arr. Seville (S. Justa)	13:25	15:16	16:25	18:24

(1) High-speed AVE service. Supplement charged. Restaurant car. (2) Restaurant car. (3) InterCity or Talgo service. Supplement charged. Restaurant car. (4) Plus other Seville departures at 12:54 and 14:00 (1) (5), arriving Cordoba 14:30 and 14:41. (5) Second class only. (6) Plus other departures from Cordoba at 17:48 (1), 18:11 (3), 18:50 (3), 19:41 (1) and 20:13, arriving Seville 18:30, 19:21, 20:15, 20:25 and 21:34.

Seville - Granada - Seville   666a

Both of these schedules are for regional trains.

Dep. Seville (S. Justa)	08:15	Dep. Granada	17:20
Arr. Granada	12:13	Arr. Seville (S. Justa)	21:12

Sights in **Granada**: The indescribable Alhambra complex, consisting of the Royal Palace, adjacent Partal Gardens, the 9th-century Alcazaba watchtower fortress and, a quarter of a mile away, the Generalife (summer palace of Moorish caliphs), one of Europe's greatest gardens.

At the Royal Palace, be sure to see the Court of the Mexuar, the Hall of the Ambassadors, the Court of the Myrtle Trees, the Hall of the Two Sisters, the Court of the Lions, the Royal Baths and the Daraxa courtyard. The Mocarabes Gallery and Abencerrrajes Gallery are near the Court of the Lions.

The Partal Gardens are a series of terraces featuring roses, poinsettias, orange and lime trees, lilies, bougainvillea and carnations.

Also see the crypts of Ferdinand and Isabella in the cathedral's Royal Chapel. The Fine Arts Museum and Hispano-Moorish Museum in Charles V's palace. The Royal Hospital. Casa Castril.

Seville - Jerez - Seville 665

Dep. Seville (S. Justa)	0635 (1)	07:55 (2)	09:00	10:00 (2)
Arr. Jerez	07:47	08:59	10:07	11:03

Sights in **Jerez**: A 3,000-year-old city, famous for its horses, beautiful women and sherry wine. Its renowned Andalusian horses, bred from Spanish mares and stallions, which the Moorish invaders brought here more than 1,500 year ago, do not date as far back as the wine does. Phoenicians started the vineyards here in 1100 B.C. Later, Romans began the vinting of sherry. Many of the best wineries offer tours that conclude with tasting.

See the annual September Wine Festival. Its opening ceremony takes place on the steps that lead into the 17th-century Collegiate Church of Santa Maria. Next to it is the 11th-century Moorish fort, the Alcazar.

Also visit the 15th-century San Dionisio Church. See the exhibit of Punic, Roman and Arabic pottery, tombstones, household implements and statues in the Archaeological Museum that occupies two small rooms inside Chapter House on tiny Plaza de la Asuncion, across from San Dionisio Church.

Look for the 7th-century B.C. Corinthian helmet, believed to be the oldest Greek artifact ever found in Spain.

Dep. Jerez	14:43 (3)	15:58 (4)	16:59	18:39 (5)
Arr. Seville (S. Justa)	15:45	17:02	17:55	19:42

(1) Second class only. Runs Monday-Friday, except holidays. (2) Runs Monday-Friday, except holidays. (3) Runs daily except Sundays and holidays. (4) Runs daily except Saturdays. (5) Plus other Jerez departures at 19:26, and 20:05 (2), arriving Seville 20:30, and 21:17.

Seville - Malaga (via Bobadilla) - Seville 666a

Both of these schedules are for regional.

Dep. Seville (S. Justa)	08:15	Dep. Malaga	18:15
Arr. Malaga	11:05	Arr. Seville (S. Justa)	21:12

Sights in **Bobadilla:** An elegant modern resort, designed to resemble an Andalusian village. Recitals on a pipe organ that has 1,595 pipes are presented in a copy of a 16th-century church.

Seville - Torremolinos - Seville   666a, 667

666a		*667*	
Dep. Seville (S.B.)	08:05	Dep. Torrenmolinos	17:04
Arr. Malaga	11:05	Arr. Malaga	17:27
Change trains 667		*Change trains 666a*	
Dep. Malaga	11:30	Dep. Malaga	18:15
Arr. Torremolinos	11:53	Arr. Seville (S.B.)	21:12

Sights in **Torremolinos**: Characters from all over the world, on and around this resort's five-mile beach.

Tarragona - Tortosa - Tarragona   655

Dep. Tarragona	07:23 (1)	09:03	10:34 (2)	12:03	14:30 (3)
Arr. Tortosa	08:32	10:05	11:40	13:04	15:34

Sights in **Tortosa**: St. Louis College, founded in 1554 by Charles V for Moors converting to Christianity. The cathedral. The bishop's palace.

Dep. Tortosa	13:24	15:50	17:20 (4)	17:11	18:48 (5)
Arr. Tarragona	14:28	16:59	18:27	18:02	19:55

(1) Second class. Runs daily except Sundays and holidays. (2) Second class only. (3) Second class only. Runs Monday-Friday. (4) Runs daily except Saturday. (5) Plus another Tortosa departure at 19:31 (2), arriving Tarragona 20:54.

Valencia - Alicante - Valencia   655

Dep. Valencia (Nord)	08:00	10:10	Dep. Alicante (Ter.)	17:40 (1)	18:40 (2)
Arr. Alicante (Ter.)	09:54	11:45	Arr. Valencia (Nord)	19:30	21:00

(1) Supplement charged. (2) Plus other Alicante departures at 19:20 and 23:37, arriving Valencia 21:40 and 02:00.

Sights in **Alicante**: The avenue lined with date palms, part of the complete African atmosphere. The huge Moorish castle. Take the 26-mile bus trip to Elche to see the only palm forest in Europe.

Alicante - Benidorm - Denia - Alicante   658

There is marvelous scenery on a one-class narrow-gauge train that runs from Alicante (via **Benidorm**), to **Denia** and there is time to take it (13:15–17:57) before returning to

Valencia. *Not covered by Eurailpass.*

A special tourist train called "Limon Express" (*not covered by Eurailpass* and for which *Cook's* does not carry a timetable) runs between Benidorm and **Gata de Gorgos** on Wednesday and Friday. Taking "Limon Express" requires arriving Alicante the prior day and overnighting in Alicante.

Departing 08:00 from Alicante's FGV rail station, arriving Benidorm 09:08. Change to "Limon Express." Depart Benidorm 09:50 for this round-trip, arriving back in Benidorm 13:50. Depart Benidorm 14:51, arriving Alicante (FGV) 15:57.

Tickets for "Limon Express" (sold by Alicante travel agencies) include visiting a guitar factory, and visiting Gata de Gogos, and a half-bottle of sparkling wine.

Valencia - Cuenca - Valencia   659

Dep. Valencia (Nord)	08:12	11:12	Dep. Cuenca	14:43	18:27
Arr. Cuenca	11:33	14:39	Arr. Valencia (Nord)	17:54	21:54

Sights in **Cuenca**: See notes under "Madrid–Cuenca"

Valencia - Murcia - Valencia   655

All of these trains are second class.

Dep. Valencia (Nord)	07:35	Dep. Murcia	17:16	22:10 (1)
Arr. Murcia	11:33	Arr. Valencia (Nord)	21:00	02:00

(1) Light refreshments.

Sights in **Murcia**: The Moorish granary. The 14th-century Gothic-Romanesque cathedral. Glass, pottery and leather factories.

Valencia - Tarragona - Valencia   655

Dep. Valencia (Nord)	06:12 (1)	07:05 (1)	08:40 (2)
Arr. Tarragona	08:57	09:00	10:30
		• • •	
Dep. Tarragona	15:21 (2)	18:49 (2)	19:56 (1)
Arr. Valencia (Nord)	18:30	20:57	23:30

(1) Light refreshments. (2) Supplement charged. Light refreshments.

SCENIC RAIL TRIPS

Here are 15 exceptionally scenic rail trips in Spain and Portugal.

Barcelona - La Tour-de-Carol - Villefranche - Perpignan - Barcelona 314, 355, 653, 656

Passengers on the famous La Tour-de-Carol-to-Villefranche narrow-gauge service (called "The Yellow Train") may ride either in modern cars, an antique car or a completely open car, which John Zucker of New York City recommends for best glimpses of beautiful Pyrenees mountain scenery.

This very scenic route can be traveled either as a one-day circle trip from Barcelona (see following schedules) or when going from Spain to France. (A Perpignan–Marseille train with a connection in Montpellier [Table 355] departs Perpignan 16:47, arriving in Marseille 21:19.)

You pass the popular **Mont-Louis** and **Font-Romeu** ski resorts and then ride alternately along very narrow ledges and also on very high bridges as the line crisscrosses canyons before arriving in the ancient walled-city of **Villefranche-de-Conflans**, a few miles from the **Vernet les Bains** sulfur-bath spa. The train-change in Villefranche is an easy cross-platform transfer.

The One-Day Circle Trip

All of these trains are second class.

653			*Change trains 355*	
Dep. Barcelona (Sants)	06:15	09:18	Dep. Perpignan	18:31
Arr. La Tour de Carol	09:49	12:42	Arr. Port Bou	19:24
Change to narrow-gauge			*Change trains 656*	
"Yellow Train" 314			Dep. Port Bou	20:20 (2)
Dep. La Tour de Carol	10:46	13:20	Arr. Barcelona (P. de G.)	22;14
Dep. Font-Romeu	12:13	14:27	Arr. Barcelona (Sants)	22:20
Arr. Villefranche	13:30	15:42		
Change trains 314				
Dep. Villefranche	17:11	17:11(1)		
Arr. Perpignan	18:00	18:00		

(1) Plus another Villefranche departure at 18:15, arriving Perpignan) 19:03. (2) Talgo service. Supplement charged. Restaurant car.

Barcelona - Massanes - Blanes - Barcelona   657

Fine coastline and mountain scenery on this easy one-day circle excursion. There are no tourist restaurants in Massanes or Blanes. All trains are second class.

Dep. Barcelona (Sants)	06:10	07:12 (1)	and hourly until 19:12 (1+2)		
Arr. Massanes	about 103 minutes later				

•   •   •

Dep. Massanes	06:26	06:55	07:25	07:55	08:22 (1)
	and hourly until 20"23 (1+3)				
Arr. Barcelona (Sants)	about 103 minutes later				

(1) Change trains at Blanes. (2) Plus other Barcelona departures at 19:42, 20:12 and 20:42. (3) Plus another departure from Massanes at 21:25.

Barcelona - Zaragoza - Madrid   650

There are many ancient towns, castles, mountains and gorges to see on this route.

Dep. Barcelona (Sants)	08:30 (1)	10:30 (2)	12:00 (1)	15:33 (1)	23:00 (3)
Arr. Zaragoza	11:55	14:15	15:55	18:55	03:33
Arr. Madrid (Cham.)	14:50	17:49	19:05	22:00	08:00

(1) Supplement charged. Light refreshments. (2) Light refreshments. (3) Runs daily except Saturday. Carries a sleeping cars, second-class coach. Light refreshments.

Barcelona - Puigcerda   312, 653

There is beautiful Pyrenees mountain scenery on this portion of the Barcelona–Toulouse route. As shown below, this trip also can be made as a one-day excursion from Barcelona.

All of these trains are second class, unless designated otherwise.

653

Dep. Barcelona (Sants)	06:15	09:18	15:16
Arr. Puigcerda	09:43	12:36	18:17
Arr. La Tour-de-Carol	09:49	12:42	18:24
Change trains 312			
Dep. La Tour-de-Carol	10:40	13:35	19:36
Arr. Toulouse (Mat.)	13:07	16:13	22:25

Here is the easy one-day excursion Table 653

All of these trains are second class only.

Dep. Barcelona (Sants)	06:15	09:18	15:16
Arr. Puigcerda	09:43	12:36	18:17
Arr. La Tour-de-Carol	09:49	12:42	18:24

• • •

Dep. La Tour-de-Carol	11:07	13:21	18:59
Dep. Puigcerda	11:14	13:28	19:06
Arr. Barcelona (Sants)	14:27	16:36	22:09

Barcelona - Tarragona

This trip is noted for excellent scenery along the Mediterranean coastline. See "Barcelona" schedules for times.

Barcelona - Valencia

There are good views of the Mediterranean shoreline on this ride. See "Barcelona" schedules for times.

Cordoba - Malaga - Cordoba   666

View scenic canyons on this trip, an easy one-day excursion from Cordoba.

All of these trains are second class, unless designated otherwise.

Dep. Cordoba	06:45	12:16 (1)
Arr. Malaga	09:24	14:30

Sights in **Malaga**: See notes under "Granada–Malaga"

Dep. Malaga	12:55 (1)	15:40 (1)	19:32 (2)	20:25 (3)	22:50 (4)
Arr. Cordoba	15:07	17:02	21:20	23:02	01:35

(1) Light refreshments. Has both first and second-class coaches. (2) Daily except Sundays and holidays.
(3) Restaurant car. (4) Light refreshments.

Leon - Oviedo - Leon   677

Very good mountain scenery on this one-day round trip.
Sights in **Leon**: The stained-glass windows in the cathedral and the 11th-century Church of
San Isidoro.

Dep. Leon	08:00 (1)	11:55 (2)	Dep. Oviedo	11:43 (2)	13:07
Arr. Oviedo	10:15	13:55	Arr. Leon	13:35	15:40

(1) Light refreshments. (2) Supplement charged. Light refreshments.

Leon - Monforte   675

The Leon–Monforte route is recommended for mountain scenery.

Both of these trains are second class only.

Dep. Leon	04:32	Dep. Monforte	17:30
Arr. Monforte	08:30	Arr. Leon	21:27

Lisbon - Porto - Redonela - Vigo - Lisbon   695, 696

695		*696*	
Dep. Lisbon (S. Apol.)	11:00 (1)	Dep. Vigo	13:50 (2)
Arr. Porto (Campanha)	14:25	*Set watch back one hour*	
Change trains 696		Arr. Porto (Campanha)	16:00
Dep. Porto (Campanha)	15:14 (2)	*Change trains 695*	
Set watch forward one hour		Dep. Porto (Campanha)	17:10 (3)
Arr. Vigo	19:24	Arr. Lisbon (S. Apol.)	20:30

(1) Reservation required. Restaurant car. (2) Light refreshments. (3) Supplement payable. Light refreshments.

Porto - Viana do Castelo - Vigo   696

Schedules allow stopping over in Viana on the Porto–Vigo route.

Reservation is advisable for all of these trains. All of these trains have light refreshments.

Dep. Porto (Camphanha)	07:40	15:14	18:57
Arr. Viana do Castelo	09:18	16:41	20:19
Arr. Vigo	12:02	19:24	23:16

Sights in **Viana do Castelo**: A pretty, little fishing resort. Walk along the twisting road lined with pine and eucalyptus trees, up to the Basilica of Santa Luzia for marvelous views (or take the funicular).

See a collection of ceramics for which Portugal is famous, at the Municipal Museum. The Renaissance buildings in the Praca da Republica. The church of Sao Domingos.

Dep. Vigo	08:20	13:50
Arr. Viana do Castelo	09:11	14:41
Arr. Porto (Camphanha)	10:39	16:00

Porto - Regua - Porto   697

There is good river scenery on this easy one-day round trip.

Dep. Porto (S. Bento)	08:45	10:48 (1)	12:16 (2)	13:32	14:35 (1+3)
Dep. Porto (Campanha)	08:52	10:56	12:22	13:39	14:43
Arr. Regua	11:21	12:50	14:28	16:13	16:49

•   •   •

Dep. Regua	11:21 (1)	13:14	15:00 (1)	16:25 (1)	17:55 (4)
Arr. Porto (Campanha)	13:32	15:19	16:41	18:46	20:01
Arr. Porto (S. Bento)	13:39	15:25	16:48	18:53	20:08

(1) Reservation advisable. Light refreshments. (2) Runs daily, except Sundays and holidays. (3) Plus another daytime Porto (S. Bento) departure at 16:20, arriving Regua 18:41. (4) Plus other Regua departures at 19:07 and 21:15 (1), arriving Porto (S. Bento) 21:40 and 23:42.

Barcelona - Valencia - Barcelona   655

Dep. Barcelona (Franca)	-0-	-0-	-0-
Dep. Barcelona (P. de G.)	-0-	-0-	-0-
Dep. Barcelona (Sants)	07:00	08:00 (1)	09:00 (2)
Arr. Valencia (Nord)	09:57	11:26	11:57

Dep. Barcelona (Franca)	14:04 (3)	16:40 (3+5)
Dep. Barcelona (P. de G.)	14:13	16:50
Dep. Barcelona (Sants)	14:30	17:00
Arr. Valencia (Nord)	18:08	20:38

Dep. Valencia (Nord)	02:00 (4)	06:12	08:40 (1)
Arr. Barcelona (Sants)	07:30	10:10	11:33
Arr. Barcelona (P. de G.)	-0-	-0-	13:35
Arr. Barcelona (Franca)	-0-	-0-	-0-

Dep. Valencia (Nord)	13:10 (3)	15:05 (3)	16:05 (2+6)
Arr. Barcelona (Sants)	16:30	18:33	19:03
Arr. Barcelona (P. de G.)	16:42	18:42	-0-
Arr. Barcelona (Franca)	-0-	-0-	-0-

(1) Reservation *required*. Supplement charged. Restaurant car. (2) Light refreshments. (3) Supplement charged. Light refreshments. (4) Carries sleeping cars, couchettes and second-class coaches. Light refreshments. (5) Plus other departures from Barcelona 18:33 (2+7), 19:00 (8), arrives Valencia 23:07 and 22:30. (6) Plus other departures from Valencia at 16:44 (9), 17:15 (3), 19:30 (10), arrives Barcelona 19:03, 20:52 and 23:25. (7) Departs Barcelona Sants, arrives Valencia Cabanyal. (8) Departs Barcelona Sants. (9) Restaurant car. (10) Arrival time Barcelona Franca; also stops at Sants and Gracia..

Madrid - Barcelona - Barcelona - Madrid   650

Many ancient towns, castles, mountains and canyons to see on this route.

Dep. Madrid (Cham.)	07:00 (1)	11:00 (1)	12:00 (1)	14:00 (4)	16:00 (4+5)
Arr. Barcelona (Franca)	14:31	18:00 (2)	19:48 (3)	20:30	22:55

• • •

Dep. Barcelona (Franca)	10:06 (1)	14:04 (8)	23:00 (7)
Arr. Madrid (Cham.)	17:35	22:18	08:00

(1) Light refreshments. (2) Arrives Barcelona Sants; also stops Barcelona P. de Gracia. (2) Arrives Barcelona Sants. (4) Talgo service. Supplement charged. Light refreshments. Arrives Barcelona Sants. (5) Plus other Madrid departures at 22:00 (6) and 23:00 (7), arriving Barcelona 07:00 and 08:00. (6) Carries sleeping cars and couchettes, second-class coaches, has light refreshments. (7) Operates daily except Saturday. Carries sleepers, Gran Clase, couchettes and second-class coaches. Light refreshments. (8) Talgo service. Supplement charged. Light refreshments. Arrives at Madrid's P. de Atocha.

THE MAJORCA ONE-DAY RAIL TRIP

If you are planning on visiting the island of Majorca, you will enjoy this rail trip.

This narrow-gauge, easy one-day trip goes through olive groves before tunneling through a mountain and emerging high above **Soller**. At the tunnel exit, the train stops for 10 minutes to allow passengers to enjoy the view before it spirals downhill to Soller. A quaint tram makes the short ride from Soller to the seaside and **Puerto de Soller**.

Don't forget, if you're traveling with a Eurailpass, you are entitled to a 20 percent discount on ferry crossings operated by Transmediterranea between Barcelona and Palma de Majorca and Valencia and Palma de Majorca.

Palma - Soller   662

*This ride is **not** covered by Eurailpass.*

| Dep. Palma | 08:00 | 10:40 | 13:00 | 15:15 | 19:45 (1) |
| Arr. Soller | 55 minutes later | | | | |

• • •

| Dep. Soller | 06:45 | 09:15 | 11:50 | 14:10 | 18:30 (1) |
| Arr. Palma | 55 minutes later | | | | |

(1) January 1-April 30 and November 1-December 31.

THE TRIP TO ANDORRA

Barcelona - La Tour-de-Carol - Andorra la Vella   653, 313

All of these trains are second class only.

653

| Dep. Barcelona (Sants) | 06:15 | 09:18 | 15:16 |
| Arr. La Tour-de-Carol | 09:49 | 12:42 | 18:24 |

Change to a bus (weather permitting) 313

| Dep. La Tour-de-Carol | -0- | 13:00 | 18:50 (1) |
| Arr. Andorra la Vella | -0- | 14:05 | 21:00 |

Sight in **Andorra la Vella**: Capital of the quaint, tiny (50,000 population) co-principality, governed jointly by the French government and the Spanish Bishop of Urgel. Both the Spanish peseta and the French franc are legal currency here.

The country's main export is postage stamps, created for philatelists. Small ski resorts and duty-free shops are the main attraction for the 6,000,000 tourists who come here every year. Located in the eastern Pyrenees, the country's mountain peaks reach heights of 9,800 feet.

Lying in one of Andorra's six valleys, this is the country's market town (179 square miles). Catalan (the language of the Barcelona area), Spanish and French are spoken here.

313 (Bus)

Dep. Andorra la Vella	07:45	14:00
Arr. La Tour-de-Carol	09:50	17:00
Change to train 653		
Dep. La Tour-de-Carol	11:07	18:59
Arr. Barcelona (Sants)	14:27	22:09

((1) Operates July 1 to September 28. Subject to confirmation.

THE MADRID ROUTES

Madrid is the hub of the Iberian Peninsula, with spokes going from it to the major cities of Spain and Portugal: Barcelona, Bilbao, Cordoba, Lisbon, San Sebastian, Santiago de Compostela, Seville and Valencia. Here are the schedules for reaching those cities from Madrid:

Madrid - Barcelona - Barcelona - Madrid

Covered under the description of scenic trips.

Madrid - Bilbao   680

Dep. Madrid (Chamartin)	15:45 (1)	22:45 (2)
Arr. Bilbao (Abando)	21:25	07:30

Sights in **Bilbao**: This is the largest Basque city. A major port and industrial city.

Dep. Bilbao (Abando)	16:25 (3)	23:30 (2)
Arr. Madrid (Chamartin)	22:05	07:50

(1) Supplement charged. Light refreshments. (2) Carries a sleeping car. Also has couchettes. Coaches are second class. (3) Runs daily except Saturdays.

Madrid - Lisbon　670

Both of these trains charge a supplement and have light refreshments.

Dep. Madrid (Chamartin)	22:35 (1)
Dep. Madrid (Atocha)	-0-
Set your watch back one hour.	
Arr. Lisbon (S. Apolonia)	08:40

• • •

Dep. Lisbon (S. Apolonia)	22:00 (1)
Set your watch forward one hour.	
Arr. Madrid (Atocha)	-0-
Arr. Madrid (Chamartin)	08:35

(1) Hotel train. Carries sleeping cars, couchettes, first- and second-class coaches. Restaurant car.

Madrid - San Sebastian　680

Dep. Madrid (Cham.)	10:00 (1)	15:45 (2)	23:00 (3)
Arr. San Sebastian	16:23	21:37	07:30

• • •

Dep. San Sebastian	08:32 (4)	13:32 (1)	16:01 (5)	23:07 (3)
Arr. Madrid (Cham.)	14:55	20:50	22:05	07:50

(1) Light refreshments. (2) Runs Monday-Saturday. Light refreshments. (3) Carries sleeping cars, couchettes, second-class coaches; light refreshments. (4) Runs daily except Saturdays. Light refreshments. (5) Runs daily except Saturdays. Supplement charged. Light refreshments.

Madrid - Santiago de Compostela　672

Dep. Madrid (Cham.)	14:00 (1)	21:45 (2)
Arr. Santiago	21:19	07:12

• • •

Dep. Santiago	09:52 (3)	13:47 (4)	22:25 (2)
Arr. Madrid (Cham.)	17:35	21:30	08:35

(1) Supplement charged. Light refreshments. (2) Carries a sleeping car. Also has couchettes. Coaches are second class. Restaurant car. (3) Runs Saturday only. Supplement charged. Light refreshments. (4) Runs daily, except Saturday. Supplement charged. Light refreshments.

Sights in **Santiago de Compostela**: One of the three most sacred places in Christendom, ranking equally with Jerusalem and Rome since 812. It is believed that this is the repository of St. James (Santiago), a cousin of Jesus, son of Mary's sister, and the first follower of Jesus to attain martyrdom.

After witnessing the crucifixion, James came to Spain in A.D. 44, converted nine Iberians to Christianity, was visited at Zaragoza by the Virgin Mary, returned to the Holy Land, and was beheaded there by King Herod Agrippa.

The legend which has generated the pilgrimage to Santiago de Compostela for the past 1,100 years is that, after the decapitation in Jerusalem, his body was disinterred and found to have the head intact. The body was brought to Spain's west coast in A.D. 44.

Eight centuries later, a hermit saw a bright star (stela) over a vacant field (compo). Excavations were conducted, and the remains of James were found. Since that event, pilgrims have come to this shrine by horse and in vehicles, as well as on foot (from as far as Scandinavia) to pray and meditate here.

See the majestic cathedral built in the 12th century. It has a beautiful baroque sculptured Obradoire facade. See the carved Romanesque 12th-century Door of Glory and touch the grooves left in the central pillar by the fingers of millions of pilgrims over the centuries. Visit the Archaeological Museum in the basement, the art pieces in the Treasury, the collection of tapestries with designs by Goya and Rubens in the many halls of the cathedral's Tapestry Museum. Also see the gigantic 6-foot-tall, 118-pound brass censer in the cathedral's library.

In the early pilgrimage years, it was difficult for priests to tolerate the odor of worshippers from afar who had gone unbathed for weeks and months. The censer here, called Botafumeiro (smoke-thrower), masked the noxious odors.

A custom that originated in the early days of pilgrimages here is perpetuated today. On feast days, this censer is brought into the cathedral, filled with incense, hung by ropes from the dome 104 feet above the floor, and swung in an arc, barely passing over the heads of people standing in the cathedral. It is easy to explore Santiago de Compostela on foot. See the marvelous view of the town from Alameda Park. Santa Maria del Sar, one of the more than 40 churches here, is a splendid example of 12th-century Romanesque architecture.

Madrid - Seville   665

The introduction of high-speed trains (in excess of 156 mph) on this route in 1992 reduced this trip from six hours to two and a half hours. Called AVE (Tren de Alta Velocidad Espanola), they go between Madrid's Atocha rail station and Seville's Santa Justa station, on the grounds of the 1992 World Expo.

The three classes on an air-conditioned AVE train are: "Club" (the most luxurious, with boutiques and fax, video and secretarial services), "First" (equivalent to first class on a French TGV), and "Tourist" (similar to TGV second class, but with larger and lower windows. Each AVE has a cafeteria and a bar. The trains have telephones and are accessible to disabled travelers. Club and First class passengers receive complimentary papers and entry to AVE Club Rooms at stations.

Here is an example of the range of one-way Madrid-Seville fares for off-peak, normal and peak travel times during 1997:

Tourist Class	8,000/9,000/9,600 ptas.
First Class	11,600/13,300/13,900 ptas.
Club Class	14,000/16,100/16,800 ptas.

These discounts were offered in 1997: 20 percent off the purchase of a round-trip ticket; 25 percent discount for a round trip made within one day; 40 percent discount for children aged 4-11; 25 percent discount for holders of Young Person's Card (under 26 years of age) or Gold Card (over 60 years). Holders of Eurailpass, Eurodomino and Tarjeta Turistica (Tourist Card) were given 60 percent discount for a Club ticket, 65 percent discount for First, and 85 percent discount for Tourist.

In North America, tickets and reservations can be obtained from VE Tours (800) 222-8383.

Reservation is required for all of these AVE trains. All of them charge a higher supplement than other Spanish express trains. The AVE supplement includes a reservation fee and mandatory travel insurance. All have a restaurant car.

Dep. Madrid (Atocha AVE)	09:00	11:00	14:00	16:00	18:00	20:00
Arr. Seville (S. Justa)	11:03	13:25	16:25	18:30	20:25	22:30

Dep Seville (S. Justa)	07:00	09:00	11:00	14:00	16:00
Arr. Madrid (Atocha AVE)	09:30	11:30	13:25	16:25	18:30

Dep. Seville (S. Justa)	18:00	20:00
Arr. Madrid (Atocha AVE)	20:25	22:30

Madrid - Valencia - Madrid 660

All of these trains charge supplement and have light refreshments, unless designated otherwise.

Dep. Madrid (Atocha-Cer.)	07:15 (1)	09:15	13:15 (2)	15:15 (2)	16:45 (3)
Arr. Valencia (Nord)	10:58	12:58	16:58	18:58	20:28

Sights in **Valencia**: See the Holy Grail, the chalice used at the Last Supper, exhibited in the 13th-century cathedral. The great art collection in the Convent of Pio V. The Orange Court at the 15th-century Lonja del Mercado. The popular beaches: Arenas, Nazaret and Pinedo y Saler. The scent of the vast surrounding orange groves, perfuming the night.

Dep. Valencia (Nord)	07:00 (1)	09:00	13:30	15:00 (1)	16:30 (5)
Arr. Madrid (Atocha-Cer.)	10:48 (4)	12:48 (4)	17:30 (4)	18:48 (4)	20:18 (4)

(1) Runs Monday-Saturday. (2) Runs daily except Saturdays. (3) Plus other departures from Madrid at 18:45 and 20:15 (2), arriving Valencia at 22:28 and 23:58. (4) Arrives at Madrid P. de Atocha station. (5) Plus other departures from Valencia at 18:30 (4) and 20:00 (4), arriving Madrid 22:18 and 23:38.

LUXURY TOURIST TRAINS

Two private luxury trains call Spain home, *Al Andalus* and the *Transcantabrico*.

With *Al Andalus,* you can make a Madrid-Madrid or Seville-Seville trip. This train was recently restored. Air-conditioning was added, as well as high-tech bogies (trucks) for a smoother ride. Compartments are spacious. Standard doubles have an upper and lower berth, with a wash basin. Two standard compartments can be joined to form a large room. Club accommodations offer two lower berths and a private bathroom and shower. Other classes of service have showers and bathrooms nearby. Besides five sleeping cars, the train has two restaurant cars, two shower cars, a lounge car and a club car with a dance floor.

The five-night trip takes in Cordoba, Granada, Bobadilla, Costa del Sol, Marbella, Puerto Banus, Ronda and Jerez. Various tours are included in the package, as well as meals, hotel the first night and accommodations on the train. The train operates from late March to late October. In 1997, the per-person rate for a standard cabin was $1,875 Madrid-Madrid (included AVE fare to Seville and return), $1,625 Seville-Seville; single supplement was $933. A double superior cabin was $2,209 per person Madrid-Madrid, $1,958 Seville-Seville, Club class was $2,583 per person Madrid-Madrid and $2,333 Seville-Seville; single supplement $642. These prices do not include air fare to Spain. Contact DER Travel for 1998 prices, (800) 782-2424.

The other train, *Transcantabrico,* covers the northern and northwestern regions of Spain known as España Verde (Green Spain), from San Sebastián (País Vasco), to Santiago de Compostela. Like *El Andalus, Transcantabrico* is luxuriously appointed and has air-conditioning, showers, a bar and live music. For 1998 schedules and prices, call Conference Travel International at (800) 527-4852.

INTERNATIONAL ROUTES
FROM PORTUGAL

The two routes to France and beyond are Lisbon-Madrid and Lisbon-San Sebastian (see below).

The only practical way from Lisbon to southwestern Spain has been very indirect since 1991—via Madrid. Lisbon-Madrid schedules appear under "The Madrid Routes."

Lisbon - San Sebastian - Bordeaux - Paris   46

The two-hour stop in Hendaye is for changing the train's wheels to conform with the narrower track in France.

"Sud Express." Carries a sleeping car and restaurant car Lisbon-Irun. Has couchettes Lisbon-Paris.

Arrive in Paris four hours earlier by changing in Hendaye to a TGV.

Dep. Lisbon (S. Apol.)	17:03 (1)	
Set your watch forward one hour		
Dep. Salamanca	01:35	-0-
Dep. San Sebastian	08:22	-0-
Arr. Irun	08:45	-0-
Arr. Hendaye	08:52	-0-
Dep. Hendaye	09:37 (3)	10:09 (2)
Arr. Bordeaux	11:56	12:25
Arr. Paris (Austerlitz)	-0-	17:11
Arr. Paris (Montparnasse)	15:00	-0-

(1) "Sud Express." See headnote. (2) Light refreshments. (3) Change trains in Hendaye. TGV, supplement payable.

INTERNATIONAL ROUTES
FROM SPAIN

Spanish National Railways (RENFE) makes reservations for only four trips to other countries: Madrid–Lisbon, Madrid–Paris, Barcelona–Geneva–Zurich and Barcelona–Milan.

When traveling by train from another country to Spain, if you want to travel later from Spain back into France and/or beyond France, it is necessary to book the trip from Spain to another country *before you enter Spain*.

The Spanish gateway for rail travel to London, Paris, Brussels and Amsterdam is Madrid.

From Barcelona, there is rail service to southwestern France (via Toulouse) and to southeastern France (Avignon, Marseille and Nice), from where there are connections to Italy, Austria and Switzerland (and on to Germany and Denmark)...plus Barcelona–Zurich and Barcelona–Milan on the fabulous *Pablo Casals* (see "Barcelona–Milan").

Seville - Lisbon

The only practical way to make this trip has been very indirect since 1991: Seville–Madrid–Lisbon. See schedules previously noted under "The Madrid Routes." To speed up the trip take an AVE train from Seville to Madrid, then the overnight train from Madrid to Lisbon.

Madrid - Bordeaux - Paris 46

All arrivals in Paris are on Day 2.

Dep. Madrid (Chamartin)	10:00 (1)	15:45 (1)	19:25 (5)	23:00 (6)
Arr. Hendaye	16:50	22:00	-0-	08:00
Change trains				
Dep. Hendaye	17:28 (2+3)	22:40 (4)	-0-	09:40
Arr. Bordeaux	19:38	-0-	-0-	11:56
Arr. Paris (Austerlitz)	-0-	07:14	08:30	-0-
Arr. Paris (Montparnasse)	23:05	-0-	-0-	15:00

(1) Reservation required. Supplement charged. Light refreshments. (2) TGV. Reservation required, supplement charged. (3) Runs Monday-Saturday. (4) Carries sleeping cars and couchettes. (5) Hotel train; first- and second-class sleepers only, plus restaurant car. Special rates apply. Direct train, no change in Hendaye. (6) Reservation required. Carries sleepers and couchettes. Light refreshments.

Barcelona - Avignon - Geneva - Bern - Zurich 81

The *Pablo Casals* began in 1990 to carry one "Gran Clase" sleeping car, the most luxurious sleeping car in Europe. Each of its large single and double 'staterooms' has a private, adjoining bathroom (circular shower stall, toilet and washbasin). Two armchairs are converted into beds by the compartment attendant.

Compartments in the first-class cars also have seating that converts to beds at night and a washbasin with towels. Second-class cars contain four berths and a washbasin. The late 1997, the second-class price (Barcelona-Geveva, Barcelona-Zurich or Barcelona-Milan) was $128 per person, first class was $208 and Gran Clase $208.

Dinner is served in the restaurant car. Beverages and snacks are served in the bar car.

Substantial discounts are given to holders of Eurailpass and Eurodomino.

Dep. Barcelona (Franca)	20:15 (1)
Dep Barcelona (Sants)	-0-
Arr. Cerbere	-0-
Arr. Avignon	-0-
Arr. Geneva (Cornavin)	05:49
Arr. Bern	07:51
Arr. Zurich	09:15

(1) *Pablo Casals*. See description in headnote.

Barcelona - Torino - Milan   90

This is the route of the Euronight hotel train, *Salvadore Dali*. Reservations are required; discounts are available to Eurailpass and Eurodomino passholders. The train has a restaurant car.

Dep. Barcelona (Franca)	20:15
Arr. Torino (Porta Susa)	07:30
Arr. Milan (Centrale)	09:00

Barcelona - Paris   47

Dep. Barcelona (Sants)	08:45 (1)	11:39 (1)	17:20 (3)	20:15 (4)
Arr. Cerbere	-0-	-0-	20:00	-0-
Arr. Montpellier	13:20	16:10	-0-	-0-
Change trains				
Dep. Cerbere	-0-	-0-	20:39	-0-
Dep. Montpellier	14:03 (2)	16:55 (2)	-0-	-0-
Arr. Paris (Aus.)	-0-	21:22	07:29	08:15
Arr Paris (Lyon)	18:21	21:22	-0-	-0-

1) Supplement payable. Reservation required. Restaurant car. (2) Supplement payable. Reservation required. Light refreshments. (3) Subject to confirmation. Second class only. (4) Departs Barcelona Francia station; direct train, no changes. Hotel train, special fares apply. First- and second-class sleepers, restaurant car.

Barcelona - Rome   90

Dep. Barcelona (Sants)	19:20 (1)
Arr. Rome (Termini)	16:56 Day 2

(1) Change trains in Cerbere and Ventimiglia. First- and second-class coaches and second-class couchettes available Cerbere-Milano.

REPUBLIC OF IRELAND
AND
NORTHERN IRELAND

Getting on Track in the Republic of Ireland & Northern Ireland
• Tourist information: **Republic of Ireland:** Irish Tourist Board, 345 Park Avenue, New York, NY 10154. Telephone (212) 418-0800, toll-free in USA 800-SHAMROCK, fax (212) 371-9052. E-mail: ireland@ingress.com. On the Web: http://www.ireland.travel.ie
Northern Ireland: Northern Ireland Tourist Board, 551 Fifth Avenue, Suite 701, New York NY 10176. Telephone (212) 922-0101, fax (212) 922-0099. On the Web: http://www.ni-tourism.com/index.asp. E-mail (to main office in Belfast): general.enquiries.nitb@nics.gov.uk.
• Disabled travelers: Many hotels and guesthouses have adapted their facilities for people with disabilities. For a list of those properties, request a fact sheet from Access Department, The National Rehabilitation Board, 25 Clyde Road, Dublin 4 Ireland.
• Public holidays: January 1, March 17, 31, May 5, June 2, August 4, October 27, December 25, 26.
• Summer time: Ireland changes to summer time on the last Sunday of March and coverts back to standard time on the last Sunday of October.
• Currency: Irish punt. At press time, $1 equalled 0.5913 punt.

Overview of Republic of Ireland and Northern Ireland's Trains
Iarnrod Éireann operates the railways of the Republic of Ireland, while Northern Ireland Railways operates the trains in Northern Ireland. Both railways have helpful Web sites: Iarnrod Éireann's is http://www.clubi.ie/RailNet, Northern Ireland Railways is reachable through http://www.nics.gov.uk/transport/nir/nirctent.htm.

Ireland is not really known for its train system, but nonetheless a network sprawls from Cork in the south to Belfast in Northern Ireland with Dublin acting as the country's hub with some highly scenic lines stretching to Westport, Killarney, and Sligo.

General Rail Information
• In the Republic of Ireland, there are two basic classes of service, Standard (comparable to second class) and Super Standard (comparable to first class). On the Dublin-Cork line, a premium service called CityGold replaces Super Standard. A supplement is charged for this class of service. CityGold and Super Standard passengers may opt for a meal at their seat.
• Most trains in Northern Ireland offer only Standard class. A Super Standard class is available between Dublin and Belfast. No trains run here on December 25 and 26.
• Both railways have provisions for disabled travelers such as ramps for wheelchairs and assistance at stations. Let the railway know of your needs as far in advance of your travel date as possible, to ensure a smooth trip.
• Children under five travel free. Half-fare for children 5-15. Children 16 and older must pay full fare.
• Eurailpass Bonuses in Ireland: See introductory chapter on Eurail pass bonuses.

• Call the Irish Tourist Board for a free copy of their Irish Travel Magazine and Vacation Planner, (800) 223-6470.

REPUBLIC OF IRELAND'S TRAIN PASSES

All of these passes are sold at rail and bus stations throughout the Irish Republic and in North America at CIE Tours, (800) 243-8687, fax (800) 338-3964, 100 Hanover Avenue, P.O. Box 501, Cedar Knolls, NJ 07927-0501. Children under 12 pay half-fare. For general information about Irish rail and bus schedules, call (800) 243-7687 (09:00-17:00 Eastern Time); they'll give you point-to-point information over the phone, but cannot mail schedules. They can, however, send you a rail map.

Good news for travelers, prices for these passes and tickets have remained at 1997 levels for 1998.

Irish Explorer Rail (Republic of Ireland) Adult rate: $100. Valid for any five days of train travel within 15 consecutive days. Offers unlimited standard-class rail travel through the Republic of Ireland, and on DART and suburban services in Dublin.

Irish Explorer Rail/Bus (Republic of Ireland) Adult rate: $150. Valid for any eight days within 15 consecutive days for unlimited travel on Irish trains and buses, local services in Dublin and city bus services in Cork, Limerick, Galway and Waterford.

Irish Rover Rail (Republic of Ireland and Northern Ireland) Adult rate: $124. Valid any five days within 15 consecutive days on Iarnrod Éireann trains, Northern Ireland Railways, DART and suburban services in Dublin and suburban services in Northern Ireland.

Emerald Card Rail/Bus (Republic of Ireland and Northern Ireland) Adult rate: $174 eight days, $300, 15 days. The eight-day card is valid for use within 15 consecutive days, the 15-day card is valid for use within 30 consecutive days. Use the Emerald Card on any of these services: Iarnrod Éireann trains, Northern Ireland Railways, Irish Bus, Ulsterbus, DART, Dublin Suburban Rail, city buses in Dublin, Belfast, Cork, Limerick, Galway and Waterford.

NORTHERN IRELAND'S TRAIN PASSES

Both of these passes are sold in Belfast at: Tourist Information Centre, 59 North Street; NIR Travel Ltd., 28-30 Wellington Place; and Central Station.

Freedom of Ireland Provides seven consecutive days of unlimited bus & train travel in Northern Ireland. Prices for 1998 were unavailable at press time. In 1997 the passes cost:

1-day pass	£9
7 consecutive travel days	£30
Children 5-15 half-price	

ONE-DAY EXCURSIONS AND
CITY-SIGHTSEEING

Dublin

Capital of the Irish Republic. See the outstanding Bronze Age gold ornaments, the 9th-century Derrynaflan Chalice and the 12th-century Cross of Cong, in the National Museum, open Tuesday-Saturday 10:00–17:00 and Sunday 14:00–17:00. The collection of paintings (Rubens, Rembrandt, Goya. Reynolds, Gainsborough) at the National Gallery of Art, open Monday–Saturday 10:00–18:00 and Sunday 14:00–17:00.

The 8th-century Book of Kells, a richly illuminated bible regarded as one of the most beautiful books ever made, on view in the Old Library of Trinity College. The Hugh Lane Municipal Gallery of Modern Art.

The pulpit from which Jonathan Swift preached, at the 12th-century St. Patrick's Cathedral, and a performance of the young boys' choir there. The collection of oriental manuscripts at Chester Beatty Library. The zoo, in the 1,760-acre Phoenix Park. The 13th-century Dublin Castle. Leinster House. The restored 12th-century Christ Church Cathedral.

The 18th-century mansions on St. Stephen's Green. Window-shop on Grafton Street. Stroll on O'Connell Street. See the historic General Post Office, site of the 1916 uprising. The Georgian houses on Parnell Square. The house where George Bernard Shaw was born. Take a tour of the facilities of the Irish Sweepstakes. A tour of Guinness's Brewery.

Belfast

This is the capital of Northern Ireland. A major port. See the elegant Queen's University. The richly marbled interior of the 19th-century City Hall. The beautiful Grand Opera House. Across the street, the decorative interior of the Crown Bar. Palm House and the collection of modern Irish paintings, silver and glass and exhibits of the history, geology and botany in Ulster Museum, both at the botanic gardens. Tour the Harland and Wolff Shipyard, location of the world's largest dry dock and where many of the world's great ocean liners were built.

See the display of everything produced in Ulster factories (old farm implements, stagecoaches, a schooner, the collection of antique locomotives and train cars, modern aircraft) at the 180-acre open-air Ulster Folk and Transport Museum, a complex of 18 exhibit buildings. It also has cottages in styles spanning several centuries (some with original furniture), water-powered mills, and demonstrations of such traditional crafts as spinning and thatching. (Belfast-Bangor trains stop at Cultra Halt, by the museum.)

Genealogical research can be done at the Public Record Office, 66 Balmoral Avenue as well as by mail with the Irish Genealogical Association, 164 Kingsway, Dunmurry, Belfast BT17 9AD.

Birth and death records since 1864 and copies of marriage registrations since 1922 can be obtained at General Register Office, Oxford House, 49-55 Chichester Street, Belfast BT1 4HL.

Here are six one-day rail trips that can be made comfortably from Belfast, Cork, Dublin, Galway and Limerick, returning to them in most cases before dinnertime. Notes are provided on what to see and do at each destination. The number after the name of each route is the *Cook Timetable* reference.

Dublin - Belfast - Dublin   230

The ongoing political situation in Northern Ireland may cause these trains to be delayed or cancelled. Additionally, a new Dublin-Belfast service was to be launched in 1997. Information, however was not available at press time. Contact the Irish Tourist Board for the latest details.

Dep. Dublin (Con.)	07:55 (1)	10:15 (5)	11:00 (1)	13:00 (2)	15:00 (1+3)
Arr. Belfast (Cen.)	10:20	13:02	13:35	15:38	17:24

| | | • | • | | |

Dep. Belfast (Cen.)	08:00 (1)	10:00 (5)	09:30 (2)	11:00 (1)	15:00 (1+4)
Arr. Dublin Con.)	10:05	12:24	12:03	13:19	17:20

(1) Runs daily, except Sundays. Restaurant car. (2) Runs daily, except Sundays. Light refreshments. (3) Plus other Dublin departures at 18:20 (1) and 20:15 (2), arriving Belfast 20:27 and 22:47. (4) Plus other Belfast departures at 17:00 (2) and 18:00 (1) arriving Dublin at 19:25 and 20:25. (5) Runs Sunday only. Second class. Light refreshments.

Dublin - Cork - Dublin   245

This train travels through Ireland's lush southern area.

Dep. Dublin (Heu.)	07:30 (1)	10:15 (2)	10:35 (3)	11:25 (1)	13:20 (1+4)
Arr. Cork (Kent)	10:05	13:30	13:05	14:02	16:15

Sights in **Cork:** Parnell Bridge. The Customs House, the finest building in Cork. The collection of 19th and 20th-century works by leading Irish and English painters, in the Crawford Gallery on Emmet Place. Visit the shops on Paul Street and Patrick Street. The perpetual flea market and vegetable stands on Corn Market Street.

Dep. Cork (Kent)	05:20 (5)	07:35 (1)	09:00 (1)	11:00 (1)	14:45 (1+6)
Arr. Dublin (Heu.)	08:40	10:05	12:10	14:06	17:35

(1) Runs Monday–Friday. Restaurant car. (2) Runs Sunday only. Restaurant car. (3) Runs Friday only. Second class. Light refreshments. (4) Plus other Dublin departures at 15:25 (1), 17:20 (1), 19:05 (1) arriving Cork 17:50, 19:25, 22:10. (5) Runs Monday-Friday only. Second class. Light refreshments. (6) Plus other Cork departures at 16:30 (7), 17:30 (1) and 19:00 (1) arriving Dublin 19:10, 20:05 and 22:00. (7) Runs Sunday only. Second class.

Cork - Killarney - Tralee - Cork   245

There is much beautiful scenery throughout this fertile area.

These second-class trains run daily, except Sundays, unless designated otherwise.

Dep. Cork	09:10	11:55	12:20 (1)	15:15
Dep. Killarney	10:44	14:39	14:00	16:52
Arr. Tralee	11:25	15:25	14:50	17:35

• • •

Dep. Tralee	09:20	11:45	17:40 (1)	17:45
Dep. Killarney	09:59	12:28	18:19	18:21
Arr. Cork	12:00	14:15	20:00	19:55

(1) Runs Sunday only.

Sights in **Killarney**: It is 85 miles from Shannon Airport. See the sculpture by Seamus Murphy, called The Shy Woman of Kerry. The marvelous garden and the exhibit of early crafts and housing at Muckross House, a 19th-century mansion on the outskirts of Killarney. Shop here for linens, glassware and crocheted women's clothing.

Take the 112-mile, all-day "Ring of Kerry" bus sightseeing trip, a popular excursion. You will see many lakes and mountains.

Dublin - Galway - Dublin   240

The are many beautiful lakes in this area.

All of these trains run daily except Sundays, are second-class and have light refreshments, unless designated otherwise.

Dep. Dublin (Heu.)	07:20 (1)	09:10 (2)	11:00	14:15 (2)	18:55 (1)	20:40 (2)
Arr. Galway	10:00	11:55	13:50	17:00	21:32	23:15

Sights in **Galway:** The 14th-century St. Nicholas Collegiate Church. The ruins of a 13th-century Franciscan friary. The 13th-century town walls. Shopping at Eyre Square Centre off Eyre Square.

Dep. Galway	07:45 (1)	08:35 (2)	11:30 (3)	14:50 (2)	15:25	18:05 (4)
Arr. Dublin (Heu.)	10:18	11:15	14:07	17:30	18:13	21:05

(1) First and second class. Restaurant car. (2) Runs Sunday only. (3) Runs Friday only. (4) First and second class. Light refreshments.

Dublin - Kilkenny - Dublin   249

Dep. Dublin						
(Heuston)	07:40 (1)	09:50 (2)	11:40 (1)	14:50 (2)	15:05 (1)	18:15 (3+4)
Arr. Kilkenny	09:26	11:33	13:22	16:38	16:55	19:55

• • •

Dep. Kilkenny	08:18 (3)	10:23 (5)	11:42 (1)	15:28 (2)	15:42	18:48 (2+6)
Arr. Dublin						
(Heuston)	09:55	12:10	13:27	17:10	17:23	20:37

(1) Runs daily, except Sundays. Light refreshments. (2) Runs Sunday only. Second class. (3) Runs daily, except Sundays. Restaurant car. (4) Plus another Dublin departure at 18:20 (5), arriving Kilkenny at 20:00. (5) Runs Sundays only. Second class. Light refreshments. (6) Plus other Kilkenny departures at 19:12 (1) and 20:42 (7), arriving Dublin at 20:58 and 22:26. (7) Runs Friday only. Second class.

Sights in **Kilkenny:** The formal gardens and the 150-foot-long hall at Kilkenny Castle. The 13th-century Saint Canice Cathedral, one of the loveliest in Ireland from that era. The 13th-century Kytler's Inn, now a restaurant. The 19th-century Saint Mary's Cathedral.

Dublin - Limerick - Dublin   245

There is bus service between Limerick and Shannon Airport.

Dep. Dublin (Heuston)	08:55 (1)	17:40 (3)		
Arr. Ballybrophy	10:05	18:50		
Change trains				
Dep. Ballybrophy	10:08 (2)	18:55 (2)		
Arr. Limerick	11:31	20:20		

• • •

Dep. Limerick	07:00 (2+4)	08:25 (1+4)	14:45 (2+5)	18:28 (1+4)
Arr. Ballybrophy	-0-	-0-	-0-	-0-
Change trains				
Dep. Ballybrophy	-0-	-0-	-0-	-0-
Arr. Dublin (Heuston)	09:20	10:30	16:42	20:05

(1) Runs daily, except Sundays. Restaurant car. (2) Runs daily, except Sundays and holidays. Second class. (3) Second class. Light refreshments. (4) Direct train. No train change in Ballybrophy. (5) Runs Monday-Saturday. Second class. Light refreshments.

THE FERRY-CROSSING TO FRANCE

Rosslare - Le Havre - Paris and Rosslare - Cherbourg - Paris
269, 270 (Train), 2010, 2060 (Ferry)

Operated by Irish Ferries Company. Passage *only* (without a seat or a berth) is free all year with a Eurailpass; passengers are responsible for port taxes, which are payable in the local currency. Reservations are required for cabin space, and in July and August for all types of accommodation.

Fares for 1998 were unavailable at press time. In 1997, peak season ran from June 21-August 31. The standard single one-way fare for ferry passage only, Rosslare-Le Havre or Rosslare-Cherbourg was $160. With a first-class rail ticket, the Cherbourg-Paris portion of the trip cost an additional $69, or an additional $50 for a second-class rail ticket. A first-class Le Havre-Paris ticket cost an additional $49, second class $39. Another $7 was added for a seat on the ferry. Six-berth cabins were $10 per person, four-berth cabins $12-26 per person, three-berth cabins, $28 per person, two-berth cabins $32-44 per person, deluxe suites $75 per person.

In 1997, off-season was May 1-June 20 and September 1-September 30. Passage only, Rosslare-Le Havre or Rosslare-Cherbourg was $110. With first-class rail Le Havre-Paris, it was $159, $146 second-class rail; Cherbourg-Paris $179 with first-class rail, $160 second-class rail. Student and senior fares are also available.

There is no winter ferry service from early November to early March. There are sailings to and from Cork, Ireland during June, July and August. Days of operation and departure times vary during five different periods of the year.

For 1998 schedules, prices and reservations, contact the North American agent: Scots-American Travel Advisors, (201) 768-1187, fax (201) 768-3825, 26 Rugen Drive, Harrington Park, NJ 07640.

RAIL CONNECTIONS WITH ENGLAND
See Chapter 7.

ITALY

Getting on Track in Italy

• Tourist information: Italian Government Tourist Board, New York office, 630 Fifth Avenue, New York NY 10111. Telephone (212) 245-4822, fax (212) 586-9249. The New York office will take phone inquiries only between 09:00 and 15:00. Los Angeles office, 12400 Wilshire Blvd., Los Angeles, CA 90025. Telephone (310) 820-0098, fax (310) 820-6357. Italian Railway offices in the U.S.: CIT (Italian State Railways), Los Angeles office, 6033 W. Century Blvd., Suite 980, Los Angeles, CA 90045. Telephone (800) CIT-RAIL, (310) 338-8616, fax (310) 670-4269. New York office, 342 Madison Ave., Suite 207, New York, NY 10173. Telephone (800) 223-7987, (212) 697-2100, fax (212) 697-1394.

• Public holidays: A list of holidays is helpful because some trains will be noted later in this section as *not* running on holidays. Also, those trains which operate on holidays are filled, and it is necessary to make reservations for them long in advance. January 1,New Year's Day, January 6, Epiphany, Easter, Easter Monday, April 25, Liberation Day, May 1, Labor Day, Proclamation of the Republic (First Monday in June), August 15, Assumption Day, Victory Day (World War I) (First Monday in November), December 8, Immaculate Conception, December 25, Christmas Day, December 26, St. Stephen's Day.

• Summer time: Italy changes to Summer Time on the last Sunday of March and converts back to Standard Time on the last Sunday of September. Many Italian trains and international trains originating or terminating in Italy have different schedules during Summer Time than they do the balance of the year.

• Currency: Lira (L). At press time, $1 equalled L1777.

Overview of Italy's Trains

Ferrovie del Stato (FS) operates most of Italy's trains. The railway has had its ups and downs in recent years as it went from a government department to a state-owned corporation and in 1992, a joint-stock company. Jobs were cut and many small rail lines were converted to bus lines. More job and route cuts are expected in the next few years. The railway wants to improve service levels and to bring the company in line with the rest of Europe's railroads. In 1997, Italy's transport minister announced a plan that would pump millions of lire into the FS system. Still, Italy is hardly third-worldly when it comes to riding the rails there. After all, the Italians were responsible for designing the fabulous Pendolino tilting train! Some of those Pendolini run under the banner *Eurostar Italia*. The Italians claimed they'd registered their Eurostar first and for a time, it was thought the Channel Tunnel Eurostars might have to pick a new name. Don't quote us, but the story goes that all was hunky-dory when FS agreed to do business under the name Eurostar Italia.

Italian train travel belongs to several centuries at once, depending where you are and how you are traveling. Trains south of Rome can be snaillike whereas Rapidos live up to their name and the Pendolinos have been the most chic trains in Europe since 1990. To accommodate curves at very high speeds, the train tilts—using the motion of a pendulum.

In 1997 FS initiated hourly high-speed Pendolino service between Rome and Milan. Also new in 1997 was the introduction of new air-conditioned sleeping cars to its interna-

tional fleet. The MUn sleepers each hold 23 passengers in one to three bunks (*Gran Luxe*) and one suite (*Super Luxe*) with a double bed. Each compartment has a toilet, sink and shower. *Gran Luxe* passengers have such perks as alarm clocks and intercoms to call the car attendant. *Super Luxe* passengers have, besides the above, in-cabin remote-controlled video and music players. Older cars are being refurbished for two new classes of service, *Gran Comfort*, four-bed compartments and *Turismo*, couchette-style compartments with six berths. New first-class lounges are also in the works for selected stations.

General Rail Information

• Generally, Italy's trains have two classes of service, first and second.

• Except for EuroCity trains: children under four travel free. Half-fare for children 4-11. Children 12 and over must pay full fare.

• Italy has five types of express trains: InterCity (internal express trains, supplement payable), Eurostar Italia (high-speed Pendolino, premium fare charged), Cisalpino (Pendolino trains to and from Switzerland, premium fare charged), EuroCity (international express trains, supplement payable), EuroNight (higher standard of overnight train, premium fares charged). Other trains are classified as Interregionale (cross-country internal trains), Diretto (semi-fast trains within Italy) and Espresso, semi-fast or international trains. Passengers using individual tickets (not traveling with first-class Italian passes or one of the first-class Eurailpasses) must pay a supplemental charge when riding the express trains listed above. The supplement usually includes a seat reservation and a meal. Reservations are recommended on all express trains and are required on all Eurostar Italia, Cisalpino and on many EuroCity most InterCity trains.

• Overnight services consist of the new sleeping cars mentioned above, as well as conventional sleepers and couchettes. Not all overnight trains carry seating accommodations. All sleeper reservations should be made in advance.

The signs you will see at rail stations in Italy are:

ARRIVI	ARRIVAL
BINARIO	TRACK
CARROZZA LETTI	SLEEPING CAR
CARROZZA RISTORANTE	RESTAURANT CAR
DONNE	WOMEN
ENTRATA	ENTRANCE
ORARIO FERROVIARIO	TIMETABLE
PARTENZE	DEPARTURE
PIATTAFORMA	PLATFORM
PRENOTAZIONE POSTI	SEAT RESERVATION
SCOMPARTIMENTO PER FUMATORI	SMOKING COMPARTMENT
STAZIONE FERROVIARIO	RAIL STATION
UFFICIO BAGAGLI	BAGGAGE CHECKROOM
UFFICIO BIGLIETTO	TICKET OFFICE
UOMINI	MEN
USCITA	EXIT

EURAILPASS BONUSES IN ITALY

In 1997, Eurailpasses and Eurail Youthpasses were valid for travel on ferries from Civitavecchia to Golfo Aranci (Sardinia) and v.v. and from Villa S. Giovanni to Messina (Sicily).

Also in 1997, Eurailpasses and Eurail Youthpasses were valid on Adriatica di Navigazione or Hellenic Mediterranean lines between Italy and Greece (Brindisi-Corfu-Igoumenitsa-Patras). Both of these trips will likely remain as bonuses in 1998.

Between Italy and Greece, port taxes and cabins were extra. A $15 high season surcharge was collected from June 10 to September 30. Year-round, reservations cost $3 for Eurailpass holders. Rail Europe continues to recommend making a reservation for this trip.

The trains from northern Italy to Brindisi, timed to connect with the ferry departures, are frequently late. For that reason, it is *advisable* to arrive Brindisi the day before a ferry departure to Patras.

WARNING: The employees of other lines intimate that their ships honor the two passes and then charge fees after the boat leaves the pier.

With or without a Eurailpass or Eurail Youthpass, a reservation theoretically can be made on day of departure or day before departure but it is very unlikely that space will be available (particularly during July and August) unless a reservation is made many weeks in advance of departure date.

Those gambling on making a reservation after arriving in Patras can make application January 1 to June 9 and October 1 to December 31 only at the Adriatica di Navagazione or Hellenic Mediterranean embarkation offices in Brindisi at the Maritime Station, about a 15-minute walk from Brindisi Central station. From June 10 to September 30, those without advance reservations can apply also to any Brindisi travel displaying in its window the green badge "Eurail Information—Eurailpass." Before boarding, all passengers must check with the shipping line office at the pier to have their tickets checked, settle port taxes due and obtain the required Embarkation Ticket.

Another fee is charged for aircraft type seats, Pullman berths and cabins. Port taxes are not covered by the Eurailpass and must be paid in lire. Passengers without advance reservations must obtain the Embarkation Ticket at least two hours prior to the ship's departure time. The ferry companies reserve the right to cancel a reservation when that is not done and to give the space to a standby passenger.

Readers reported to us in 1997 that Adriatica and Hellenic ships are often older, slower and more crowded then the ferries of other lines. They also report that these ships are often not as clean as those of other lines. *Greece by Rail's* author, Zane Katsikis, highly recommends the ferry companies that sail to/from Ancona because they offer the newest ships and more convenient and frequent schedules than the Brindisi route. The extra money is worth it, he says.

In the past, we have listed a travel agency in Florida where you could make reservations for these ferries before leaving the States. That company, however, no longer provides this service. Until we find another U.S. contact, check with the Italian tourist office noted at the beginning of the chapter, for the latest information, or, in Italy, consult with a licensed travel agent or local tourist office. The number for the Italian Adriatica Lines in Brindisi is 0831 523 825. The number for the Greek Hellenic Mediterranean Lines in Brindisi is 0831 528 531.

Brindisi - Patras - Athens   For sailing dates, see *Cook's* Table
1450, 2770

Dep. Brindisi Harbor   20:00   22:30
Arr. Patras   13:00   18:00

It is a 20-minute walk from Patras' dock to its rail station.

Change to train 1450

For a view of the Corinthian Gulf and then the Corinthian Canal, sit on the left side of the train.

Dep. Patras   16:35 (1+2)   18:38 (1+2)   19:59 (1)
Arr. Athens   20:01   22:04   00:16

(1) Light refreshments. (2) Supplement payable.

ITALIAN TRAIN PASSES

When ordering any number of train tickets or any train pass *except Eurailpass* from the Italian State Railways, there is a $20 processing fee per order for ordinary tickets and a $15 fee per pass on all Italian train passes.

Anyone who purchases an Italian train pass may obtain a 10 percent discount on city sightseeing and excursion tours by presenting the pass at any Compagnia Italiana Turismo (CIT) office in Florence, Milan, Naples, Rome and Venice.

Both the Italian Train Pass and Italy Flexi Railcard offer unlimited travel on all Italian trains (including InterCity and EuroCity trains), including free seat reservations *(which can be made only in Italy) on trains for which reservations are compulsory. If you choose to make a reservation on a train for which reservations are not compulsory, you must pay an additional reservation fee.* Sleeper and couchette services are *not* included. Both passes are available at travel agencies worldwide *outside* Italy and at all offices worldwide of CIT, including those in Italy. Beginning in 1997, the supplement to ride ETR trains was $8 for Eurailpass, Europass, Eurailticket, Italy Railcard and Italy Flexi Railcard holders.

Prices for 1998 for the following tickets were unavailable; prices listed are for 1997. CIT Tours, representing Italian Rail, expects a five percent across-the-board price hike for 1998.

Italy Railcard   The 1997 prices were: First class, eight days $254, 15 days $320, 21 days $371, 30 days $447. Second class, eight days $172, 15 days $213, 21 days $248, 30 days $297. The 15, 21 and 30-day tickets can be extended to double their initial period. Half-fare for children 4–12 years old. Children under four travel free.

Italy Flexi Railcard   The 1997 prices were: First class, four days in one month $199, eight days in one month $291, 12 days in one month $365. Second class, four days in one month $135, eight days in one month $189, 12 days in one month $244.

Kilometric Ticket Permits travel up to a maximum of 20 single trips totaling 3,000 kms (1,875 miles) within two months. When used on a train that charges a supplement, the passengers using the Ticket must pay the supplement. Can be used by more than one person at a time, to a maximum of five persons. When a child 4–12 years old travels on this ticket, only half the mileage used is counted. Children under four travel free. Available before you leave home at both Italian State Railways and from travel agents worldwide. Also available in Italy at all rail stations and from Italian travel agencies.

The 1997 prices were: $264 for *first* class, $156 for *second* class. Checking FS's Web site (http://www.fs-on-line.com/), we found the Kilometric Ticket selling for L338,000, or just under $200 at the most recent exchange rate of L1777 per $1. The second-class pass was selling for L200,000. If the exchange rate is favorable, it might be a better deal (no postage or handling fees) to purchase the Kilometric Ticket, Rail Card and Flexi Rail Card in Italy. The Web site is in Italian, but easy to figure out.

ONE-DAY EXCURSIONS AND CITY-SIGHTSEEING

Pick up a comprehensive map of an area's attractions from offices marked "Azienda Autonoma di Turismo" or "Ente Provinciale di Turismo. These offices are found in most Italian cities.

Here are 68 one-day rail trips that can be made comfortably from Agrigento, Bologna, Catania, Florence (Firenze), Genoa, Messina, Milan, Naples (Napoli), Palermo, Rome and Torino (Turin), returning to those cities in most cases before dinnertime. Notes are provided on what to see and do at each destination. The number after the name of each route is the *Cook's* timetable.

Bologna

See the dissection theater in the ancient medical school. The fantastic inlaid wood panels in the Chorus at San Domenico Church. (Be sure to turn on the electric lights there in order to get a good look at the marvelous woodwork.) The Church of San Petronio. The Art Gallery. Neptune's Fountain, where Piazza Maggiore and Piazza Nettuno connect.

The two leaning towers in Piazza di Port Ravegnana: 165-foot-tall Garisenda and the 330-foot-high Asinelli. Climb the 486 steps of the Asinelli for the splendid view from the top of the tower. Visit the churches on Santo Stefano. The Municipal Archeological Museum. The Communale, Podesta, Mercanzia, Re Anzio and Bevilacqua palaces. Try the marvelous Bolognese food.

Don't miss La Piazzola market on Fridays and Saturdays, 07:00 to just before sunset, on Piazza 8 Agosto. From the train station, walk along Via dell'Indipendenza to Via dei Mille. Because it's off the tourist beat, prices aren't through the roof. Snap up embroidered tablecloths for $10-$15, sweaters, $12 and fun stuff like fancy buttons, for pennies. Another market takes over the park across the street; it's the '60s revisited, complete with flower-children, poetry readings and incense. Pick out a psychedelic bauble for your favorite baby boomer.

Florence (Firenze)

The 14th-century Cathedral of Santa Maria del Fiore (open daily 07:00–12:00 and 14:30–18:00) is where most visitors begin sightseeing in Florence. Ascend its 292-foot-high bell tower for a great view of the city. Across from the cathedral, see the magnificent sculptured bronze Ghiberti doors ("Gates of Paradise" was Michelangelo's description) on the octagonal Baptistry of San Giovanni (open 09:30–12:30 and 14:30–17:30).

See the 14th–19th-century furniture and utensils representing domestic life in those eras, in the Davanzati Palace.

There is much more to see. We've split up the sightseeing in two different directions from the cathedral-baptistry complex. Facing the baptistry, proceed north on Via Ricasoli to visit Area #1. Go South, toward the Arno River, for sightseeing in Area #2.

Area #1: See the Michelangelo sculptures and breathtaking marble floors, walls and crypts at the Medici Chapel. The street behind the Chapel is lined with vendors. On the other side of the street is an enormous food market where game with colorful furs and feathers make an unusual display.

An easy walk from the Chapel is the Academia (closed Monday), housing the stupendous statue of David. Nearby is the Fra Angelico Museum in the Church of San Marco, with its interesting frescoes and monk's cells.

Across the street from the Academia, you can board a city bus for the 20-minute ride uphill to the village of Fiesole, where there are Etruscan ruins, a Roman amphitheater, a 13th-century cathedral, the Convent of St. Francis, and a splendid view of Florence.

Area #2: The Piazza della Signoria and, next to it, the thousands of great art treasures in the 29 exhibit rooms of the Palazzo degli Uffizi (open Tuesday–Saturday 09:00–19:00, Sunday 09:00–13:00). Nearby is the Franciscan Church of Santa Croce, where Michelangelo, Machiavelli, Rossini and Galileo are buried. Also see the sculptures (Donatello's bronze David and the della Robbia glazed terra cottas) at the Bargello Palace and Museum, in a 13th-century palace. Next, cross to the other side of the Arno River, over the Ponte Vecchio (lined with tiny jewelry shops) to visit the outstanding paintings, statues, tapestries and furniture in the 28 exhibit rooms and galleries of the Palazzo Pitti (closed Monday).

The Pitti is a complex of five different museums. The palace itself contains the Palatine Gallery (noted for its Raphaels), the Modern Art Gallery, and the Silver Museum. Two other museums are located in the Boboli Gardens behind the palace: the Costume Museum and the Porcelain Museum, both of which are open only on Tuesday, Thursday and Saturday (hours during May and June are 09:00–19:00).

The Medici Chapel, Academia, Bargello, Uffizi and Pitti are open Tuesdays–Saturdays 09:00–14:00 and Sundays and feast days from 09:00–13:00.

Shopaholics won't want to miss Florence's two best markets, Mercato San Lorenzo and the Straw Market. Head to Mercato San Lorenzo for quality leather goods, from handbags to jackets. It's open daily except Sunday 09:00-20:00. From the train station take Via Nazionale, turn right on Via dell'Ariento.

The Straw Market is off Piazza della Repubblica. Besides straw items, it also sells leather goods (more expensive than San Lorenzo), scarves and knickknacks. From the piazza, walk toward the Arno River on Via Calimala for two blocks. This and the smaller market fronting the river are open daily 09:00 to 19:00. Closed Sunday in winter.

Florence is the gelato capital of Italy with gelaterias on every corner. Festival del Gelato at Via del Corso 75 offers a whopping 90 flavors. Open Tuesday-Sunday, winter 11:00 -01:00, summer 08:00-01:00.

Genoa

Italy's largest port. See the house where Columbus is said to have been born, at Piazza Dante. St. Lawrence Cathedral. *Do not fail* to walk down the 15th-century streets near the waterfront, too narrow for a tour bus and unfortunately not seen by many visitors to Genoa. The incredible Monumental Cemetery, with its vast number of dramatic statues of many of the people buried there. The landscaped hillside with colorful plants painting a flowering tapestry of Columbus' fleet: the Nina, the Pinta and the Santa Maria.

The 16th-century palaces on Via Garibaldi. The 17th-century palaces on Via Balbi. The Cathedral of San Lorenzo, constructed from 1099 to 1250.

Milan

Construction began on the Duomo cathedral in 1386 and took five centuries to complete. This marvelous building holds more than 20, 000 people and has more than 3,000 statues on its exterior. After visiting the Duomo, go through the incredibly beautiful shopping arcade, the Galleria Vittorio Emanuele, to La Scala Opera House. La Scala is one of the world's greatest theaters. It accommodates 3,600 people and was first constructed in 1776. Its opera museum is open Tuesdays–Saturdays 09:00–12:00 and 14:00–18:00. Exhibited in the museum are old paintings and engravings of the opera house before its destruction by bombs in 1943 and its reconstruction in 1946, portraits of many famous singers, several of Verdi's pianos and such other Verdi memorabilia as his manuscripts and death mask.

Opposite La Scala, behind a statue of da Vinci, is the 16th-century Palazzo Marino, now the City Hall. Just past the gate (Porta Nuova) at the end of Via Manzoni are the Museum of Natural History, the zoo and the planetarium.

See da Vinci's "Last Supper" at Santa Maria delle Grazie. It can be viewed daily 09:00–13:15 and 14:00–18:15. *Do not fail to see* the enormous and elaborate crypts at the Monumental Cemetery. Visit the Palazzo Dugnani, on Via Manin, to see the Tiepolo ceiling fresco there.

It is a short taxi ride from the Dugnani to the enormous Castello Sforzesco, which has a vast collection of paintings (including Michelangelo's last work, the Rondanini Pieta) and exhibits of harpsichords, wrought iron, tapestries and ceramics. The castle is open daily except Monday 09:30–12:00 and 14:30–17:00.

See the sculptures, Flemish and Persian tapestries, paintings, scientific instruments, glass and armor at Museo Poldi-Pezzoli, at 12 Via Manzoni, open Tuesday-Sunday 09:30–12:30 and 14:30–17:30. Many great paintings (Raphael, Tiepolo, Canaletto) are exhibited in the Accademia di Brera on Via Brera, open Tuesday–Saturday 09:00–14:00, and on Sunday 09:00–13:00.

Both the Modern Art Gallery (16 Via Palestra) and the Archaeological Museum (15 Corso Magenta) are open Wednesday–Saturday 09:30–12:30 and 14:30–17:30; on Sunday 09:30–13:00. There are marvelous paintings by Raphael, Caravaggi and Botticelli in the

Ambrosian Library, open Mondays–Fridays except holidays 10:00–12:00 and 15:00–17:00 and Saturdays, Sundays and holidays 15:00–17:00.

Gourmets will want to visit the fantastic food store called Peck's, at No. 9 Via Spadari, opened in 1892 by a Czechoslovak named Frank Peck (there's another location at Via Cesare Cantu 11). It is the Italian equivalent of Hediard, described under "Paris" in the section of this chapter on France. What you will see at Peck's are: large wedges of parmigiano and reggiano cheese, Italian wines, roasts, loins, saddles and breasts of white veal, caviar, numerous cold seafood salads, mussels, langouste, squid, lobster, celery remoulade, pates, head cheese, scampi, sturgeon, hot vegetable dishes (baked fennel, baby zucchini, asparagus Milanese), roasted quail skewered with sausages and wrapped in bacon, tripe in tomato sauce, a wide range of pasta (green ravioli al forno, tortellini, ravioli alla contadina), paella with saffron rice, white mushrooms in oil, many sausages and many fish (herring, smoked salmon, smoked eels, smoked trout).

If that is not enough, across the street from Peck's is a famous pork store, La Bottega del Maiale, with an enormous display of whole baby pigs, pork parts (loins, ears, fillets, tongue, liver) and such sausages as sopresa Calabra, salame Toscana, coppa, cacciatorini, stagionata, capocolla and finocchiona.

Next door to the pork store is Peschere Spadari, a great fish store, selling nearly everything that swims: scampi, Channel sole, mackerel, scampi, squid, mussels. A short distance down the street, at No. 1 Via Speroni, is a large cheese store.

Naples

Most museums in Naples are closed on Monday. See the view from Certosa di San Martino monastery and, inside, its San Martino National Museum. The 13th-century Castel Nuovo. The National Library. The National Archaeological Museum, with its great Grecian and Roman sculptures. The Capodimonte Park and nearby palace and art gallery. The Teatro San Carlo, home of Neapolitan opera. The Royal Palace. The botanical garden. There are good views of Naples Bay from the gardens of the Duca di Martina Museum of Ceramics at the Villa Floridiana. Splendid views of Mount Vesuvius from the quay at Santa Lucia. Nearby **Herculaneum** (now called **Ercolano**) is as interesting as Pompeii.

Rome

A special nonstop train service is operated by FS with Alitalia between Rome's da Vinci airport and Florence. This service is only for passengers with international tickets booked on Alitalia. Trains run twice per day. Schedules can vary based on flight times. The trip takes about two and a half hours. Contact Alitalia for details. Regular trains operate hourly from Roma Termini to the airport from 07:22 until 21:22, and from the airport, 08:08 until 22:08. The trip takes about 30 minutes. Second class service operates from the airport to Rome's Ostiense station from 06:58, running runs hourly until 22:58. Trains depart Ostiense from 06:52 and run hourly until 22:52. The ride is about 25 minutes. Eurailpasses and Italian passes are valid on both of these trains.

Visit St. Peter's, the most wonderful work by man in all the world. Take an elevator to the dome for views of Vatican City and Rome. Tour the Vatican to see the Sistine Chapel, Raphael Rooms, Pio-Clementino Museum, Picture Gallery, Tapestry Gallery, Map Gallery and Candelabra Gallery (all of them closed on Sunday, except the last Sunday of each month).

See Capitoline Hill. The Roman Forum. Palatine Hill. The Imperial Fora.

Marcellus Theatre. The Jewish Synagogue. The Temple of Avesta. Aventine Hill. St. Paul's Gate. The view of Rome from the Villa Borghese Park. The Protestant cemetery, with the graves of Keats and Shelley. The Colosseum. The Arch of Constantine. The Basilica of St. Paul Outside the Walls. Michelangelo's statue of Moses in the Church of St. Peter in Chains. The Pantheon. The mosaics at the Baths of Caracalla.

Castel Sant'Angelo (closed Monday). Trevi Fountain. The zoo. The Etruscan Museum (closed Monday). The Napoleon Museum (closed Monday). The Spanish Square, Steps and Fountain. The National Modern Art Gallery (closed Monday). Diocletian's Baths.

The House of the Vestal Virgins. Marvelous views of Rome from Janiculum Hill. The Monument to Vittorio Emanuele. The Bernini sculptures in the Borghese Gallery (Villa Borghese), open daily 09:00–13:30. The magnificent Velazquez portrait of Pope Innocent X in the Doria Gallery (Piazza del Collegio Romano), open Tuesday, Friday, Saturday and Sunday 10:00–13:00.

Displays of Etruscan art at the National Museum of Villa Giulia (Piazza di Villa Giulia), open daily except Monday 09:00–19:00, holidays 09:00–13:00. Exhibits of ancient Rome at the National Museum of Rome (in the Baths of Diocletian), open Tuesday–Saturday 09:00–14:00, Sunday 09:00–13:00. The Museum of Folklore (Piazza Sant' Egidio, in Trastevere), open Tuesday–Sunday 09:00–13:00, also Thursday evenings 17:00–19:30.

In the following timetables, where a city has more than one rail station, we have designated the particular station after the name of the city (in parentheses).

Bologna - Florence - Bologna   620

Exceptional mountain scenery on this easy one-day round-trip.

The train goes through the 11.5-mile-long Apennine Tunnel, Italy's longest tunnel. Some trains stop almost midpoint in the tunnel at an underground station called **Precendenze**. Residents of a small village at the crest of the mountain, in order to return home, must climb 1,863 steps inside a diagonal shaft that was used for constructing the tunnel.

All of these trains are Pendolinos, require reservation, charge a supplement and have a restaurant car, unless designated otherwise.

Dep. Bologna	07:47	08:47	10:47	12:47	16:47
Arr. Florence (SMN)	08:41	09:41	11:41	13:41	17:41

	•	•	•		
Dep. Florence (SMN)	14:19	16:19	18:05 (1)	20:19	20:46
Arr. Bologna	15:15	17:13	19:21	21:13	21:37

(1) InterCity Express. Supplement charged. Food service unavailable.

Bologna - Milan - Bologna   611

Dep. Bologna	08:00	09:20	10:30	
Arr. Milan (Cen.)	10:15	11:45	12:55	

• • •

Dep. Milan (Cen.)	14:05	16:06	17:05 (1)	18:00 (2)
Arr. Bologna	16:30	18:30	19:12	20:05

(1) Supplement charged. Restaurant car. (2) Plus other departures from Milan at 18:50, 20:05, 20:55 and 21:55, arriving Bologna 21:30, 22:30, 23:05 and 00:38.

Bologna - Parma - Bologna   611

Dep. Bologna	Frequent times from 02:10 to 20:56
Arr. Parma	50-65 minutes later

• • •

Dep. Parma	Frequent times from 02:23 to 23:46
Arr. Bologna	50-65 minutes later

Sights in **Parma:** The 19th-century Teatro Reggio opera house. Nearby, the Lombardi Museum in the Palazzo di Riserva. The restored Palazzo della Pilotta, which houses the Farnese Theater, National Gallery, Palatina Library and the National Museum of Antiquities. The latter, Italy's most modern museum, has an outstanding collection of Etruscan, Roman, medieval and Renaissance works of art, including larger-than-life-size statues of members of the Julian-Claudian family (Britannicus, the two Drussii, Livia and Claudius) that are familiar to viewers of the "I Claudius" television program.

More than 40,000 rare books are displayed in the Library (Biblioteca). Particularly interesting are the De Rossi collection of Oriental manuscripts and the Bodoni Museum, a complete collection of all the volumes of the great 19th-century typographer for whom it is named.

Visit the cathedral to view the marvelous Assumption of the Virgin fresco by Correggio in the dome. Also the Camera di Corregio, a room near the cathedral he frescoed in 1518. The 12th-century sculptures by Benedetto Antelami, in the five-story red marble baptistry, one of Italy's finest buildings. See the early 19th-century sculpture by Lorenzo Bartolini in the Madonna della Steccata church. Toscanini's room at the conservatory.

Bologna - Pisa - Bologna   614, 620

All of the Florence–Pisa (and v.v.) trains shown here are second class only.

620

Dep. Bologna	07:47 (1)	09:47 (1)	10:47 (1)	12:38 (1)	16:47 (1)
Arr. Florence (SMN)	08:41 (3)	10:41	11:41	13:32	17:41

Change trains 614

Dep. Florence (SMN)	09:35	11:00	12:35	13:35	18:35
Arr. Pisa	10:35	12:00	13:35	14:35	19:30

The #1 Bus takes you from the Pisa rail station to the Piazza del Duomo in 10 minutes.

• • •

614

Dep. Pisa	13:21	14:21	15:21	16:21	17:21
Arr. Florence (SMN)	14:19	15:19	16:19	17:19	18:19

Change trains 620

Dep. Florence (SMN)	14:34 (1)	16:28 (2)	17:19 (1)	18:19 (1)	20:19 (1)
Arr. Bologna	15:38	17:22	18:13	19:13	21:13

(1) Reservation *required*. Supplement charged. Restaurant car. (2) Reservation *required*. Supplement charged. Light refreshments.

Sights in **Pisa**: The Piazza del Duomo, with four major attractions. Walk up the spiral stairs of the Leaning Tower to its roof and see the view from there. A few feet from the base of the tower is the majestic 11th-century striped marble cathedral. Key features of it are the magnificent bronze entrance doors and, inside, paintings, statues, mosaics, a fantastic pulpit, and Galileo's lamp. While watching the lamp swing, Galileo timed each arc by his pulse and observed that every swing, long or short, took the same time span. By that, he postulated "the isochronism of the pendular movement."

Next, walk the short distance from the cathedral to the beautiful, enormous 11th-century circular marble baptistry to see its font and its six columns of porphyry, marble and oriental granite. Three of the columns rest on carved lions. Biblical scenes are carved on each panel.

A very short walk from the baptistry is a large building with a cemetery in its central court. Each section of the building exhibits many frescoes. See the 50-foot-by-19-foot "Triumph of Death" in the North Gallery.

Before the train from Florence reaches Pisa, it stops two minutes in **Campiglia Marittima**, which has a large statue of a mongrel dog at its rail station. The dog (named Lampo) appears to watch the procession of arriving and departing trains.

Lampo ("flash of lightning") liked train travel as much as we do. He learned the train schedules and took a trip every day—more than 3,000 train trips in his lifetime.

Owned by the assistant stationmaster, Lampo escorted his master's daughter to school every morning. For that reason, he made short rail trips on school days, longer journeys on weekends. Always, he would go only such distances and make the necessary connections so as to return home every day before dawn.

Prior to Lampo's death in 1961 (under a freight train), he had become known not only by every trainman in Italy but by the Italian public as well, through reports of his love of train travel that appeared on Italian television and in Italy's newspapers.

Local railway workers say only a person with a printed timetable could have equaled the dog's feat, when he once went past his stop on a certain trip and then managed to return home by taking a complex series of connecting trains to get back to Campiglia Marittia.

Bologna - Ravenna - Bologna   621

Dep. Bologna	06:08	08:17	09:43
Arr. Ravenna	07:31	09:33	10:48

Sights in **Ravenna**: The marvelous 5th-century monuments, the Mausoleum of Galla Placidia and the Orthodox Baptistry. Just behind the mausoleum, see the mosaics at the Church of San Vitale. Great mosaics also in Sant'Appollinare Nuovo Church, where it is helpful to use binoculars or even an opera glass in order to see those mosaics that are at the top of the walls. There are more dazzling mosaics in the Archiepiscopal Chapel.

See the ivory pulpit in the Archbishop's palace. Dante's Tomb. The Museum of Antiquities. The exhibits at the Academy of Fine Arts.

Dep. Ravenna	13:02	14:31	17:30	20:00
Arr. Bologna	14:32	15:44	18:46	21:12

Bologna - Rome   620

Dep. Bologna	07:47 (1)	08:47 (1)	10:47 (2)		
Arr. Rome (Ter.)	10:25	11:25	13:25		

• • •

Dep. Rome (Ter.)	14:05 (2)	16:05 (3)	18:05 (1)	19:05 (4)	19:35 (1)
Arr. Bologna	17:42	19:38	20:38	21:37	23:13

(1) Pendolino. Reservation *required.* Supplement charged. Restaurant car. (2) Supplement charged. Restaurant car. (3) Supplement charged. (4) Pendolino. Reservation *required.* Supplement charged. Light refreshments.

Bologna - Siena - Bologna   616. 620

620			*616*		
Dep. Bologna	07:21	07:56 (2)	Dep. Siena	15:35 (1)	16:35 (1+3)
Arr. Florence (SMN.)	08:21	08:51	Arr. Florence (SMN)	17:08	18:13
Change trains 616			*Change trains 620*		
Dep. Florence (SMN)	08:25 (1)	09:20 (1)	Dep. Florence (SMN)	17:19 (2)	18:19 (1)
Arr. Siena	10:04	10:50	Arr. Bologna	18:13	19:13

(1) Second class. (2) Reservation required. Supplement charged. Restaurant car. (3) Plus other departures from Siena at 18:37 (1) and 19:57 (1), departing Florence 20:19 (2) and 21:45, arriving Bologna 21:13 and 22:55.

Sights in **Siena:** The pervasive color, named for Siena, that dominates this hill town. The view of Italy's most unique square, Piazza del Campo, from the top of the Mangia Tower of the Palazzo Publico (with its marvelous 14th-century murals) or from a window of the Palazzo Publico (open daily except Sunday 9:00–13:00), where records in unbelievably beautiful calligraphy going back to the 12th century are exhibited with 15th-century costumes and fine frescoes. The Pisano sculpture and mosaic floors at the cathedral, on Piazza del Duomo. The paneled Duccio Crucifixion in cathedral's museum. Climb from there to the top of Facciatone, the skeleton for a new cathedral whose construction ceased when the Black Death of 1348 ravished Siena.

Pinacoteca, the art museum, on a street near the cathedral. Fontebranda, the old fountain with three arches. The ancient houses along Via degli Archi, Vicolo della Fortuna, and Vicolo delle Scotto, all of these streets radiating out from the Piazza del Campo.

Bologna - Venice - Bologna   620

| Dep. Bologna | 06:05 (1) | 07:45 | 08:26 | 10:38 (2) | 11:45 | |
| Arr. Venice (SL) | 08:10 | 09:42 | 10:17 | 12:22 | 13:42 | |

•   •   •

| Dep. Venice (SL) | 13:20 | 14:20 | 15:20 | 16:20 | 17:20 | 18:20 (3) |
| Arr. Bologna | 15:15 | 16:15 | 17:17 | 18:15 | 19:15 | 20:15 |

(1) Runs Monday-Saturday except holidays. (2) Supplement charged. Restaurant car. (3) Plus other departures from Venice at 19:20, 20:20 and 21:45, arriving Bologna 21:15, 22:15 and 00:10.

Sights in **Venice**: After the obligatory gondola ride, stand at either end of Piazza San Marco and try to cope with the enormity and beauty of the most impressive square in the world. Next visit St. Mark's Cathedral, the most wonderful Byzantine structure in Europe. Next door, see the Doge's Palace. Then relax at one of the outdoor cafes on St. Mark's Square and take in the wonder of it all while waiting for the figures on the enormous 15th-century clock to emerge and strike the bell.

For another view of St. Mark's Square and the entire Lagoon, go to the top of the bell tower. Walk through the colorful, narrow streets of shops to the 16th-century Rialto Bridge and, standing there, watch the canal traffic. The Rialto is lined with stores selling jewelry, linens, hand-blown glass, clothing, gloves and fabrics. After crossing over the bridge, walk a short distance to the extraordinary fish market. It's at its liveliest 07:00–11:00 and particularly on Friday.

Among the score of churches to see in Venice are: San Giuliano, Santa Maria Formosa, Santa Maria dei Miracoli, San Giovanni e Paolo, San Francesco della Vigna, San Zaccaria, Santo Stefano, Santa Maria Gloriosa dei Frari, Santa Maria del Carmine, San Sebastiano, Madonna dell'Orto and Santi Apostoli. There are also five synagogues here: the German (oldest), Spanish (most beautiful), Levantine, Italian and Canton.

See the many beautiful palaces on the Grand Canal. The exquisite 18th-century decor of the most beautiful small opera house in the world, the Gran Teatro La Fenice.

A 15-minute boat ride takes you to the **Lido**, Venice's beach resort and site of its largest gambling casino and a 14th-century Jewish cemetery. It is only a three-minute boat ride to the beautiful, white Church of Santa Maria della Salute, built on more than one million wood pilings.

It is a 15-minute boat ride to the island of **Murano** to watch glass-blowing and visit the Glassworks Museum (closed Tuesday) in Palazzo Giustiniani. Boats for Murano leave from the Fondamenta Nuove vaporetto dock. We recommend getting off the boat at the second stop, touring the Glassworks Museum, then walking past many interesting shops to the first landing for the return ride to Venice. The Glassworks Museum displays ancient Roman work and many excellent glass pieces from the Middle Ages

To see lacemaking (tablecloths, handkerchiefs, bedspreads, dresses) and buy fine lace, take a 30-minute boat ride to **Burano**. It is only a few minutes by boat from Burano to **Torcelo**, a small island of orchards, vineyards and artichoke farms. The 11th-century basilica there has splendid mosaics. Another sight on Torcello that interests some tourists is the display of the small skeleton of the martyr Santa Fosca in a glass coffin at the church there that is named for her.

Bologna - Verona - Bologna   595

| Dep. Bologna | 06:25 | 09:35 (1) | 11:31 (2) | 11:38 | 13:50 |
| Arr. Verona | 08:05 | 11:16 | 12:50 | 13:16 | 15:25 |

Sights in **Verona:** See the large and excellently preserved 1st-century arena. Then take Via Mazzini (Verona's main shopping street) to Piazza della Herbe (Herb Square), where you will find a marvelous display of fruits, vegetables, live pet birds, and dead game birds. Only a few minutes walk from there, the Veronese marble lobby of the Hotel Due Torri is worth seeing.

At Piazza dei Signori are the tombs of the Della Scala Family, once rulers of Verona. La Scala Opera House in Milan is named after them. See the paintings in the Church of Sant'Anastasia. Visit the cathedral and the Museum of Art in Castelvecchio, on Corso Cavour.

The main attraction in Verona, since Shakespeare, has always been Juliet's balcony, at Via Cappelo 17–25 (Shakespeare's "Capulet.")

| Dep. Verona | 11:25 | 13:18 (3) | 15:15 (2) | 16:40 | 18:40 | 20:06 (4) |
| Arr. Bologna | 13:25 | 15:22 | 16:34 | 18:20 | 20:20 | 22:00 |

(1) Runs Saturdays, Sundays and holidays. (2) Supplement payable. Restaurant car. (3) Second class (4) Plus other departures from Verona at 20:40 and 22:23, arriving Bologna 22:00 and 00:19.

Florence - Arezzo - Florence   615

| Dep. Florence (SMN) | 06:45 | 08:55 | 10:22 | 11:15 | 14:15 |
| Arr. Arezzo | 07:53 | 09:26 | 11:18 | 11:55 | 15:13 |

Sights in **Arezzo:** The 15th-century Piero frescoes of the Legend of the True Cross that can be seen 12:00–14:30 and 19:00–21:30 in the Church of San Francesco. The carvings on the facade of the 11th-century Church of Santa Maria della Pieve. Behind Pieve, the marvelous Piazza Grande, with its medieval palaces. There are many other fine palaces on Corso Italia.

The musical scale and staff of four lines was invented in the 10th century by Guido Monaco of Arezzo. The Piazza Guido Monaco is named for him.

See the 16th-century stained glass and the great Renaissance organ in the cathedral. Walk across the park to the enormous fortress, Medicea, built in the 16th century by the Medici family. See the collection of Etruscan and Roman artwork in the Archaeological Museum at the Convent, including the ancient Corallini vases. The remains of a Roman amphitheater can be seen in the park next to the museum. A library and museum is maintained in the home where Petrarch was born.

The collection of ivories, goldsmith work, coins, furniture, weapons, ceramics and 13th–20th-century sculptures and paintings (including Vasari's huge fresco "Feast in the House of Ahasuerus") in the Galleria e Museo Medievale e Moderno at the Bruni-Ciocchi Palace.

Other frescoes by Vasari are exhibited in the Casa del Vasari, on Via 20 Settembre.

See the 17th-century frescoed dome of the Badia Church.

Dep. Arezzo	12:47	14:47	16:06	17:21	18:47	19:56	20:47 (1)
Arr. Florence (SMN)	13:45	15:45	16:45	17:56	19:50	20:52	21:45

(1) Plus other departures from Arezzo at 22:00 and 22:49, arriving Florence 22:45 and 23:50.

Florence - Assisi - Florence　615

Dep. Florence (SMN)	06:50	10:22	Dep. Assisi	14:34	17:09
Arr. Terontola	08:19	11:43	Arr. Terontola	15:38	18:16
Change trains			*Change trains*		
Dep. Terontola	08:30	12:25	Dep. Terontola	16:21	18:21
Arr. Assisi	09:52	13:23	Arr. Florence (SMN)	17:45	19:50

Sights in **Assisi**: St. Francis' tomb in the 13th-century basilica on the Hill of Paradise, and the many outstanding paintings there, considered to be the greatest museum of Italian Renaissance mural painting. St. Claire's Church. The medieval castle. Piazza del Commune. The upper and lower churches at the Convent of St. Francis, with their many frescos. Prison Hermitage. The 16th-century Church of Santa Maria degli Angeli. The 12th-century Cathedral of St. Ruffino. The 14th-century La Rocca Maggiore fortress. The Temple of Minerva.

Florence - Bologna - Florence　620

See Bologna schedules.

Florence - Livorno - Florence 614

On the departures from Livorno, there is time to taxi 10 minutes from Pisa's station to the Leaning Tower and return to the station for a later departure to Florence.

All of these trains are second class, unless designated otherwise.

Dep. Florence (SMN)	07:02	11:35	Dep. Livorno	13:05	15:05 (1)
Arr. Pisa	-0-	-0-	Arr. Pisa	-0-	-0-
Dep. Pisa	08:03	12:35	Dep. Pisa	13:21	15:21
Arr. Livorno	08:18	12:49	Arr. Florence (SMN)	14:19	16:19

(1) Plus other Livorno departures at 16:05, 18:05, and 20:05 departing Pisa 16:21, 18:21, and 20:21, arriving Florence 17:19, 19:19, and 21:29.

Sights in **Livorno**: The old and new forts, both from the 16th century. The marble statue of Ferdinand. Tacca's 17th-century bronze statues of "The Four Moors." Villas once occupied by Shelley and Byron. Italy's Naval Academy. The paintings and the Communal Library, both in the Civic Museum.

Florence - Milan - Florence 620

Dep. Florence (SMN)	07:13 (1)	08:12	08:33	09:19 (1)	10:19 (1)
Arr. Milan (Centrale)	10:00	12:45	11:50	12:00	13:00
		•	•	•	
Dep. Milan (Centrale)	15:00 (1)	16:00 (1)	17:00 (1)	17:55 (2)	20:00 (1)
Arr. Florence (SMN)	17:41	18:41	19:41	21:20	22:48

(1) Pendolino. Reservation *required.* Supplement charged. Restaurant car. (2) Light refreshments.

Florence - Padua - Florence 620

Dep. Florence (SMN)	07:18	11:07 (1)	Dep. Padua	16:49 (2)	18:43 (3+4)
Arr. Padua	09:42	13:28	Arr. Florence (SMN)	18:59	21:03

(1) Plus another departure from Florence at 15:28 (2), arriving Padua at 17:43. (2) Supplement payable. Restaurant car. (3) Light refreshments. (4) Plus another departure from Padua at 20:19, arriving Florence 22:42.

Sights in **Padua:** The 13th-century university where Petrarch lectured and Galileo taught (on the Via 8 Febraio) has guided tours on each hour, 09:00-12:00 and 15:00-17:00. It is open daily, except Saturday afternoon and all day Sunday.

Scrovegni Chapel, noted for its Giotto frescoes, is open April-September 09:00-12:30 and 14:30-17:30. From October through March, it is open 09:00-12:30 and 13:30-16:30 daily, except Sunday afternoon, Christmas, New Year's Day and Easter.

The Church of Eremitani.

The Basilica of Sant'Antonio, a major Roman Catholic shrine with several statues by Donatello, is open daily 06:30-19:45. The cathedral is open daily 08:00-12:00 and 16:00-19:00. The Art Gallery (Pinacoteca) is open daily except Sunday, 09:00-13:30;.

The Oratorio di San Giorgio and the Scuola di San Antonio are open daily except Monday, Easter and Christmas. April-September: 09:00-12:00 and 14:30-18:30. October-March: closes at 18:00. Santa Giustina is open daily 07:30-12:00 and 15:30-19:30.

Florence - Parma - Florence   611, 620

620

Dep. Florence (SMN)	07:13 (1)	08:33	09:12
Arr. Bologna	08:13	09:40	10:45
Change trains 611			
Dep. Bologna	08:30	09:44	10:30
Arr. Parma	09:23	10:33	11:23

Sights in **Parma:** See notes about Parma under "Bologna–Parma"

611

Dep. Parma	15:33	16:36 (2)	17:33	19:21
Arr. Bologna	16:30	17:30	18:30	20:17
Change trains 620				
Dep. Bologna	16:38 (3)	17:47 (1)	18:47 (1)	20:47 (1)
Arr. Florence (SMN)	17:49	18:41	19:41	21:41

(1) Pendolino. Reservation required. Supplement payable. Restaurant car. (2) Light refreshments. (3) Supplement payable. Restaurant car.

Florence - Perugia - Florence   615

Dep. Florence (SMN)	11:15 (1)	13:15 (1)		Dep. Perugia	17:00 (1)	18:40 (2+3)
Arr. Terontola	-0-	-0-		Arr. Terontola	-0-	19:21
Change trains				*Change trains*		
Dep. Terontola	-0-	-0-		Dep. Terontola	-0-	19:35
Arr. Perugia	12:58	14:58		Arr. Florence (SMN)	19:00	20:52

(1) Direct train. No train change in Terontola. (2) Second class. (3) Plus another Perugia departure at 21:21 (2) , arriving Florence 23:50 (change trains in Arezzo).

Sights in **Perugia:** Take a bus from the rail station rather than walk the steep climb uphill to the town. Visit the Municipal Palace, to see the magnificent carved and inlaid wood panels in the library, the chapel of the Stock Exchange, and the great paintings in the National Gallery (Pinacoteca). On display to the left of the main door of the Stock Exchange chapel is the white onyx ring with which the Virgin Mary was married.

Also visit the 13th-century Church of San Ercolano. Galleng Palace, with its Foreign University. The Pisano sculptures at the Fontana Maggiore in beautiful Piazza 4 Novembre. The fine collection of Tuscan paintings in the museum of the 13th-century Palazzo dei Priori. Stroll along Maesta della Volte, Via dei Priori (to the Oratory of San Bernardino), Via Bagliona and Corso Vannucci, the main street.

Florence - Pisa - Florence   614

Dep Florence (SMN)	Frequent times from 04:40 to 22:52
Arr. Pisa	60–70 minutes later

Sights in **Pisa**: See notes about Pisa under "Bologna–Pisa"

Dep. Pisa	Frequent times from 05:49 to 22:55
Arr. Florence (SMN)	60–70 minutes later

Florence - Ravenna - Florence   620, 621

620			*621*		
Dep. Florence (SMN)	07:13 (1)	08:38 (1)	Dep. Ravenna	13:02 (3)	14:31 (4)
Arr. Bologna	08:13	09:30	Arr. Bologna	14:32	15:44
Change trains 621			*Change trains 620*		
Dep. Bologna	08:17 (2)	09:43 (2)	Dep. Bologna	14:47 (1)	15:47 (1)
Arr. Ravenna	09:33	10:48	Arr. Florence (SMN)	15:41	16:41

(1) Pendolino. Reservation required. Supplement payable. Restaurant car. (2) Second class. (3) Runs Monday-Saturday except holidays. (4) Plus another departure from Ravenna at 17:30, departing Bologna 18:56, arriving Florence 19:55.

Florence - Rome - Florence   620

Dep. Florence (SMN)	06:57	08:35	10:40 (1)	12:30 (2)	14:30 (2)
Arr. Rome (Ter.)	09:28	11:15	12:15	14:55	16:55

Dep. Rome (Ter.)	16:05	18:35 (1)	19:05 (3)	20:35 (1)
Arr. Florence (SMN)	18:27	20:11	20:38	22:11

(1) Pendolino. Reservation required. Supplement payable. Restaurant car. (2) Restaurant car. (3) Pendolino. Reservation required. Supplement payable. Light refreshments.

Florence - Siena - Florence   616

All of these trains are second class only.

Dep. Florence (SMN)	06:33	08:25	09:20	11:20	13:25	14:13
Arr. Siena	07:57	10:04	10:50	13:05	15:06	15:33

• • •

Dep. Siena	13:30	15:35	16:35	17:40 (1)	18:37	19:57 (2)
Arr. Florence (SMN)	15:08	17:08	18:13	19:33	20:01	21:38

(1) Change trains in Empoli. (2) Plus another Siena departure at 21:24 arriving Florence 22:44.

Florence - Verona - Florence   595, 620

620

Dep. Florence (SMN)	07:13 (1)	09:12	10:06 (1)	12:19 (1)
Arr. Bologna	08:13	10:45	11:03	13:13
Change trains 595				
Dep. Bologna	09:35 (2)	11:31 (1)	11:38	13:50
Arr. Verona (PN)	11:16	12:40	13:16	15:25

• • •

595

Dep. Verona (PN)	15:15 (1)	16:40	18:40
Arr. Bologna	-0-	18:20	20:20
Change trains 620			
Dep. Bologna	-0-	18:47 (1)	20:47 (1)
Arr. Florence (SMN)	17:49	19:41	21:41

(1) Reservation *required*. Supplement charged. Restaurant car. (2) Runs Saturdays, Sundays and holidays.

Genoa - Bologna - Genoa   611

Dep. Genoa (Piazza Principe (PP))	07:04	16:23	17:41
Arr. Bologna	10:15	19:30	20:58

• • •

Dep. Bologna	07:40	13:30	17:30
Arr. Genoa (PP)	10:52	16:52	20:52

Genoa - Cremona - Genoa 609, 610

610

Dep. Genoa (PP)	05:48	09:21	11:21
Arr. Milan (Centrale)	07:40	10:50	12:50
Change trains 609			
Dep. Milan (Centrale)	08:20	12:20	14:20
Arr. Cremona	09:31	13:32	15:26

Sights in **Cremona**: One of Italy's most impressive squares, the Piazza del Commune, with its octagonal baptistry, 12th-century Duomo Cathedral, Loggia de Militi, and the Gothic Torrazzo (tallest bell tower in Italy).

Cremona is where the art of violin-making reached its apex, with the works of Amati, Stradivari and Guarneri. It is possible to watch young violin makers following that great tradition by visiting La Scuola Internazionale de Liuteria, in a renovated 16th-century palace.

At the City Museum every day at 11:00, an outstanding violin made by Stradivari is played by the museum curator. Located near the Liuteria are many shops which will make a special violin to order. On view at the City Hall are two original Stradivari, two Amatis and a Sacconi.

600

Dep. Cremona	12:30	15:39	19:32
Arr. Milan (Centrale)	13:40	16:45	20:45
Change trains 610			
Dep. Milan (Centrale)	14:15	17:10	21:10
Arr. Genoa (PP)	16:05	18:42	22:40

Genoa - Milan - Genoa 610

Genoa (PP)	07:21	07:54	09:21 (1)	11:54	13:21 (1)
Arr. Milan (Cent.)	08:50	09:45	10:50	13:45	14:50

• • •

Dep. Milan (Cent.)	14:15 (1)	15:10 (1)	16:15	17:10	18:15 (2)
Arr. Genoa (PP)	16:05	16:40	18:20	18:42	20:05

(1) Reservation *required*. Supplement charged. Light refreshments. (2) Plus other departures from Milan at 19:10 (1), and 20:15 , arriving Genoa 20:40 and 22:05.

Genoa - Nice 90

Dep. Genoa (PP)	08:52	16:52 (1)	Dep. Nice (Ville)	18:26 (2)	20:35
Arr. Nice (Ville)	11:46	19:56	Arr. Genoa (PP)	21:19	00:28

(1) Reservation *required*. Supplement charged. Restaurant car. (2) Restaurant car.

Sights in **Nice**: See notes about Nice under France.

Genoa - Pisa - Genoa   610

There is exceptional mountain and Mediterranean coastline scenery on this ride.

Dep. Genoa (PP)	06:25 (1)	12:50 (2)	14:15 (2)
Arr. Pisa (Cen.)	08:21	14:49	16:40

Sights in **Pisa:** See notes about Pisa under "Bologna–Pisa"

If you have time for a side-trip, the area known as **Cinque Terre** along Italy's Riviera di Levante is well worth exploring. Cinque Terre, or Five Lands, is a string of five towns on the rail line between Sestre Levante and La Spezia, which is part of the Genoa-Pisa line (about two hours east of Genoa). If you're riding a fast train from Genoa, you'll never know what you've missed as you speed through tunnels broken only by snippets of ocean flying by. But on the other side of the tunnels are these five little towns plopped along a crinkled coastline where autos are practically nonexistent, where vineyards dominate steep hillsides and reach, seemingly, to the heavens. Some towns are stacked into hillsides like books on a shelf, while others cling to jaw-dropping cliffs.

The five towns are Montorosso (Cinque Terre's only real beach), Vernazza (see the rustic seaside piazza; great restaurants; beautiful circa-1318 Gothic-Ligurian church), Corniglia (see the remains of an old fort built in 1556 to thwart pirate raids; this is the hardest town to reach, lots of stairs to climb to get to town), Manarola (hike to the vineyards from a path near Piazza Castello) and Riomaggiore (not many tourists here; lots of local color, fishermen bringing in their catches, townspeople gossiping at cafes).

You can buy a local one-day rail pass at Cinque Terre stations as well as in Sestre Levante or La Spezia (La Spezia makes a good base if there's no room in Cinque Terre). You also can hike your way between towns. Some trails are really steep (Corniglia is not for acrophobics!). Hikes can take anywhere from 45 minutes to three or four hours, depending on the trail. Take along snacks and plenty of water.

There aren't many hotels in these towns. Most visitors rent a private room or apartment; they start at about $50 per night and some have kitchen facilities. Find a room by going to the local tavern and asking the bartender. Your editor met a charming man on the train who had a wonderful room to let in Vernazza, with a kitchenette and fantastic ocean view, for $50 per night in 1996. Vernazza has lots of cozy restaurants, Gambero Roso on the town's square, was excellent. If you go, try the Cinque Terra Bianco or Coste Selezionale, two mellow and smooth, locally produced white wines. Sciacchetra is a deliciously-fruity but not overpowering dessert wine.

Dep. Pisa (Cen.)	15:13 (2)	15:25	21:11 (1)
Arr. Genoa (PP)	17:14	17:47	23:05

(1) Reservation *required*. Supplement charged. Restaurant car. (2) Light refreshments.

Genoa - Rome   610

Dep. Genoa (PP)	06:25 (1)	12:50 (2)	14:50 (2)	23:56 (3)
Arr. Rome (Ter.)	10:45	17:50	19:50	08:13

• • •

Dep. Rome (Ter.)	08:10 (2)	10:20 (2)	13:05 (2)	16:10 (2)
Arr. Genoa (PP)	13:11	15:11	18:11	21:11

((1) Reservation *required.* Supplement charged. Restaurant car. (2) Light refreshments. (3) First- and second-class sleepers, second-class couchettes.

Genoa - Torino - Genoa   610

Dep. Genoa (PP)	06:38	09:03	11:14	11:47
Arr. Torino (PN)	08:45	10:45	12:50	13:35

Sights in **Torino**: The marvelous facade of the Porta Nuova rail station, built in the 1860s. The beautiful Piazza Carlo Felice park, near the rail station.

Piazza San Carlo (considered second only to St. Mark's in Venice), dominated by a large statue (called "the bronze horse") of Emanuele Filiberto, hero king of the mid-16th century. In Piazza dello Statuto, the large monument dedicated to the completion of the Frejus rail tunnel between Italy and France in the late 19th century.

The imposing Palazzo Madama, with its enormous marble staircase and Royal Armory, in Piazza Castello, which is the heart of the city. (It is a museum.) The Museo Egizio in Palazzo Carignano, the third most important (after London and Cairo) Egyptian collection in the world. The university in Piazzo Carlo, where Erasmus of Rotterdam earned his doctorate in 1506. The view from the top of Mole Antonelliani, on Via Montebello. Parco del Valentino, with its splendid gardens and buildings.

The frescos in the Castello del Valentino. It is an easy walk from the castle to Borgo Medievale, a village built in 1884 to depict the lifestyle of this area in the year 1400. The Church of the Great Mother of God, patterned after Rome's Pantheon.

The 17th-century Royal Palace. Near it, the black and white marble Chapel of the Holy Shroud in the Church of San Lorenzo. An urn holding what is believed to be the shroud placed on Jesus when he was taken from the cross is the major attraction there. The Auto Museum on Corso Unita d'Italia, with models going back to 1893.

Dep. Torino (PN)	12:25	13:10	14:25	16:25	17:10	18:25 (1)
Arr. Genoa (PP)	14:11	14:47	16:11	18:11	18:47	20:11

(3) Plus other departures from Torino at 19:10, 20:25, 22:00 and 23:00, arriving Genoa 20:47, 22:11, 00:19 and 00:54.

Milan - Bologna - Milan   611

Most of these trains charge a supplement and have either a restaurant car or buffet.

Dep. Milan (Cen.)	07:05 (1)	07:20	08:30	10:00 (2)	12:05) (3)
Arr. Bologna	08:58	10:00	11:24	12:30	14:30

•   •   •

Dep. Bologna	12:30	14:30 (4)	16:30 (4)	18:30	20:02 (1+5)
Arr. Milan (Cen.)	14:55	16:55	18:55	20:55	21:55

(1) Supplement charged. Restaurant car. (2) Runs Monday-Saturdays except holidays. (3) Plus other departures from Milan at 13:20 and 14:05, arriving Bologna 15:17 and 16:30. (4) Light refreshments. (5) Plus other departures from Bologna at 20:30 and 20:56 arriving Milan 22:55 and 23:35.

Milan - Como - Milan   550

Reservation is required or advisable on most of these trains. All of them charge a supplement.

Milan (Cen.)	Frequent times from 07:35 to 23:10
Arr. Como (SG)	35–45 minutes later

Sights in **Como**: Take Bus #4, marked "Piazza Cavour," from the rail station to reach both the lakeshore and the cable car which ascends the 2,300-foot-high **Mount Brunate** in seven minutes. At the peak, there is a wonderful view of **Lake Como** and the Alps.

Dep. Como (SG)	Frequent times from 06:07 to 22:44
Arr. Milan (Cen.)	35–45 minutes later

Milan - Faenza - Milan   630

Dep. Milan (Cen.)	08:05	10:05 (1)
Arr. Faenza	11:12	13:11

Sights in **Faenza**: This has been Italy's city of ceramics since 1100. See the collection in the Ceramics Museum.

Many of the factories have showrooms: Mazzotti (Via Firenze 240), Gatti (Pompignoli 4), Navarra (Via XX Septembre 42A) and Morigi (Via Barbavara 7). A wide selection of ceramics is sold at the Coopertiva Artigiana Ceramisti Faentini.

| Dep. Faenza | 13:45 | 15:38 | 17:38 (2) | 19:38 |
| Arr. Milan (Cen.) | 16:55 | 18:55 | 20:55 | 22:55 |

(1) Runs Monday-Saturday only. (2) Light refreshments.

Milan - Cremona - Milan   609

| Dep. Milan (Cen.) | 08:20 | 12:20 | | Dep. Cremona | 12:30 | 15:39 | 19:32 |
| Arr. Cremona | 09:31 | 13:32 | | Arr. Milan (Cen.) | 13:40 | 16:45 | 20:45 |

Sights in **Cremona**: See "Genoa–Cremona."

Milan - Florence - Milan   620

| Dep. Milan (Cen.) | 07:00 (1) | 08:00 (1) | 09:00 (1) | 10:00 (1) | 11:00 (1) |
| Arr. Florence (SMN) | 09:41 | 10:41 | 11:41 | 12:41 | 13:41 |

• • •

| Dep. Florence (SMN) | 14:34 (2) | 15:19 (1) | 16:19 (1) | 17:19 (1) | 18:19 (1+3) |
| Arr. Milan (Cen.) | 17:40 | 18:00 | 19:00 | 20:00 | 21:00 |

(1) Pendolino. Supplement payable. Reservation required. Restaurant car. (2) InterCity train. Supplement charged. Restaurant car. (3) Plus other departures from Florence at 19:19 (1) and 20:19 (1), arriving Milan 22:50 and 23:00.

Milan - Genoa - Milan   610

See schedule under "Genoa-Milan."

Milan - Locarno - Milan   549. 590

The Camedo–Locarno portion of this trip is one of the five most scenic rail trips in Europe, with outstanding mountain, canyon and river scenery.

590

| Dep. Milan (Cen.) | 07:15 (1) | 08:15 (2) | 09:25 | 11:15 (1) | 13:25 | 17:15 (1) |
| Arr. Domodossola | 08:26 | 09:42 | 11:05 | 12:26 | 15:05 | 18:26 |

Change trains 549

Walk outside the Domodossola rail station and go to the underground track, to board the
Centovalli narrow-gauge local railway.

Dep. Domodossola	08:45 (3)	09:45 (3)	11:11 (3)	12:32 (3)	15:45 (3)	18:45 (3)
Dep. Camedo	09:52	10:52	12:14	13:37	16:52	19:52
Arr. Locarno	10:25	11:25	12:48	14:10	17:25	20:25

Sights in **Locarno**: Stroll the gardens along the shore of **Lake Maggiore** and take the funicular ride to **Orselin** to see the art treasures in the Madonna del Sasso (Madonna of the
Rock) church high above the village and, from there, the fine view of Locarno and Lake
Maggiore. From Orselin, ride the cable-car to 4,400-foot-high **Cardada**. Then take the
chair-lift from **Cardada** to **Cimetta**, more than a mile high.

　　In nearby **Ascona,** see the frescoes depicting scenes of the Old and New Testament in the
14th-century church of Santa Maria Misericordia and the adjoining cloisters of Collegio Papio.

549

Dep. Locarno	12:13 (3)	13:35 (3)	15:20 (3)	16:35 (3)	17:35 (3)	19:20 (3)
Dep. Camedo	12:48	14:09	15:54	16:09	18:09	19:53
Arr. Domodossola	13:49	15:12	17:02	18:14	19:14	21:00

Change trains 590

Walk from the underground Centovailli track, up to the main Domodossola rail station.

Dep. Domodossola	14:34 (1)	15:20 (2)	17:59 (2)	18:34 (1)	19:34 (1)	21:38 (2)
Arr. Milan (Cen.)	15:45	16:45	19:25	19:45	20:45	23:10

(1) Reservation *required.* Supplement charged. Restaurant car. (2) Supplement charged. Light refreshments. (3) Light refreshments.

CRUISING THE BORROMEAN ISLANDS
ON LAKE MAGGIORE

An overnight stay in Locarno is worthwhile, in order to have a complete day for touring the
Borromean Islands on Lake Maggiore.

　　Isola Madre is a fantastic garden island. See the 18th-century palace and stroll through
the lush gardens there (palm trees, orange and grapefruit trees, magnolias, roses, camelias,
azaleas, and many gold and silver Chinese pheasants).

　　On **Isola Bella**, visit the fascinating and very unique 17th-century palace where European
leaders met in 1925 to sign the Locarno Pact. You will be enchanted by the palace's six-room
Neptune Grotto, decorated with enormous plaster seashells, walls that simulate white coral, and
floors that are mosaics of small pebbles. Stroll through the lavish 10-terrace garden.

　　The only schedule which allows visiting both islands in one day is to take the 10:30 hydrofoil (reservation required) from Locarno Pier. Arrive Isola Madre 11:45. Depart Isola
Madre 13:00, arriving Isola Bella 13:20. Lunch there. Depart Isola Bella 16:35. Arrive back
in Locarno at 18:30.

Milan - Lugano - Milan 84

Dep. Milan (Cen.)	07:35 (1)	08:25 (2)	09:25 (2)	10:25 (1)	11:25 (2)	12:25 (1)
Arr. Lugano	09:04	09:54	10:54	11:54	12:54	13:54

Sights in **Lugano:** Take the cable car from the rail station to Piazza Cioccaro. Walk down-hill from there to the city center, Piazza Riforma. See the view of the city from the Cathedral of San Lorenzo. The collection of over 700 masterpieces (Rubens, Goya, Durer, Raphael, Tiepolo, Tintoretto, and some Americans) in the Thyssen Art Gallery of La Villa Favorita, open only from Easter to October.

Stroll the shore of lovely **Lake Lugano**.

It is 15 minutes by boat, bus, taxi or private car to **Campione** on the eastern shore of Lake Lugano, where a small gambling casino has operated since 1933. People under 18 years old are not admitted. Men must wear neckties and jackets. The Casino is open daily from 15:15 until dawn the next day.

Although Campione is located in Italian territory, no passport or any other identity document is required, and there is no customs checking.

Other sights in Campione are the frescoes in the church called Sanctuary of the Madonna dei Ghirli (Our Lady of the Swallows), first built in the Middle Ages and then rebuilt in the 18th century.

Another of the many boat trips on the lake is to the ceramic, clothing and craft shops in **Gandria**.

Dep. Lugano	14:06 (2)	15:06 (2)	16:06 (1)	17:06 (2)	18:06 (1+3)
Arr. Milan (Cen.)	15:35	16:35	17:35	18:35	19:35

(1) Reservation *required.* Supplement charged. Light refreshments. (2) Reservation *required.* Supplement charged. Restaurant car. (3) Plus other departures from Lugano at 19:06 (2), 20:06 (1), 21:06 (2) and 21:48 (2), arriving Milan 20:35, 21:35, 22:35 and 22:45.

Milan - Rome and Rome - Milan 620

Dep. Milan (Cen.)	07:00 (1)	08:00 (1)	09:00 (1)	10:00 (1)	11:00 (1)
Arr. Rome (Ter.)	11:25	12:25	13:25	14:25	15:25

Dep. Milan (Cen.)	13:00 (1)	14:00 (1)	15:00 (1)	16:00 (1)	17:00 (1+3)
Arr. Rome (Ter.)	17:25	18:25	19:25	20:25	21:25

Dep. Rome (Ter.)	06:55 (1)	08:05 (2)	09:35 (4)	11:35 (2)	12:05
Arr. Milan (Cen.)	11:20	13:05	14:00	16:00	17:40

Dep. Rome (Ter.)	13:35 (1)	14:35 (1)	15:35 (1)	16:05	17:35 (1+5)
Arr Milan (Cen.)	18:00	19:00	20:00	21:40	22:15

(1) *Pendolino.* Reservation *required.* Supplement includes reservation fee and meal. First class only. (2) Reservation *required.* Supplement charged. Restaurant car. (3) Plus other Milan departures at 18:00 (1), 19:00 (1), 19:40 (1). (4) Reservation *required.* Supplement charged. Light refreshments. (5) Plus other Rome departures at 19:35 (1), 22:40 (5) and 23:25 (6). (6) Has couchettes.

Milan - Torino - Milan   585

| Dep. Milan (Cen.) | 07:20 | 08:20 | 09:10 | 11:20 | 12:20 |
| Arr. Torino (PN) | 09:05 | 10:05 | 10:32 (1) | 13:05 | 14:05 |

Sights in **Torino**: See notes under "Genoa–Torino"

| Dep. Torino (PN) | 12:50 | 13:50 | 15:15 | 15:50 | 16:50 (2) |
| Arr. Milan (Cen.) | 14:40 | 15:40 | 16:50 | 17:40 | 18:40 |

(1) Arrives at Torino Porta Susa station. (2) Plus other Torino departures at 17:50, 19:15, 19:50, 20:50, 21:50 and 22:50, arriving Milan 19:40, 20:50, 21:40, 22:40, 23:40 and 00:40.

Milan - Venice - Milan   600

| Dep. Milan (Cen.) | 06:05 | 07:05 | 08:05 | 11:05 | 11:15 | 12:05 |
| Arr. Venice (SL) | 08:55 | 09:55 | 10:55 | 13:55 | 14:37 | 14:55 |

Sights in **Venice**: See notes under "Bologna–Venice"

| Dep. Venice (SL) | Frequent times from 05:14 to 21:18 |
| Arr. Milan (Cen.) | 3 hours later |

Milan - Verona - Milan   600

| Dep. Milan (Cen.) | 06:15 | 07:05 (1) | 08:05 (2) | 09:05 (1) | 11:05 (1+3) | 12:05 |
| Arr. Verona (PN) | 08:05 | 08:30 | 09:30 | 10:30 | 12:30 | 13:30 |

Sights in **Verona**: See notes about Verona under "Bologna–Verona"

| Dep. Verona (PN) | Frequent times from 05:55 to 22:58 |
| Arr. Milan (Cen.) | 1½ hours later |

(1) Supplement charged. (2) Reservation required. Supplement charged. Restaurant car. (3) Light refreshments.

Naples - Bari - Naples 626

Dep. Naples (P. Garibaldi)	08:20	Dep. Bari	17:46 (1)
Arr. Caserta	09:04	Arr. Caserta	21:05
Change trains		*Change trains*	
Dep. Caserta	09:20 (1)	Dep. Caserta	21:35
Arr. Bari	12:36	Arr. Naples (P. Gar.)	21:19

(1) Reservation required.

Naples - Pompeii - Naples 635

The standard-gauge trains that depart from Naples' Centrale rail station, (shown below) *are* covered by Eurailpass.

The narrow-gauge trains that leave from Naples' FS rail station are operated by Circumvesuviana Railway and are *not* covered by Eurailpass.

Salerno is as convenient a base for visiting Pompeii as Naples is.

Dep. Naples (Cen.)	07:20	09:20	11:20	13:20	15:20	17:30
Arr. Pompeii	25 minutes later					

Sights in **Pompeii:** See where 20,000 people were living and how they lived 1900 years ago when this city was buried within a few minutes under a volcanic rain of ashes from nearby (still active) Vesuvius, when it was young and strong.

Dep. Pompeii	12:09	14:13	16:13	18:13	20:13	22:16
Arr. Naples (Cen.)	25 minutes later					

Naples - Rome - Naples 620

Dep. Naples (Cen.)	07:00 (1)	07:06	08:06	09:30 (2)	10:30 (2)
Arr. Rome (Ter.)	08:50	09:45	10:45	11:20	12:20

• • •

Dep. Rome (Ter.)	13:10	14:10 (3)	15:15	16:15	17:10 (4+5)
Arr. Naples (Cen.)	15:01	16:52	17:54	18:54	19:00

(1) Supplement charged. Light refreshments. (2) Reservation *required*. Supplement charged. Restaurant car. (3) Runs daily, except Sundays and holidays. (4) Reservation *required*. Supplement charge Light refreshment. (5) Plus other departures from Rome Termini at frequent times from 16:10 to 21:15.

Rome - Anzio - Rome 622

All of these trains are second class only.

Dep. Rome (Ter.) 07:55 (1) 08:25 11:25(1) 12:25 (1) 13:25 (1)14:30 (1) 15:25 (2)
Arr. Anzio 60-65 minutes later

Sights in **Anzio**: Has been a beach resort since ancient times. Many Americans visit the nearby military cemeteries, holding those killed in the January 22, 1944 Allied invasion.

Dep. Anzio 13:53 (1) 13:53 15:08 (1) 16:53 (1) 18:53 19:53 (1) 21:58
Arr. Rome (Ter.) 60-65 minutes later

(1) Runs daily, except Sundays and holidays. (2) Plus other departures from Rome at 16:25 (1), 17:25, 19:25, 20:25 and 21:30.

Rome - Assisi - Rome 615

Dep. Rome (Ter.)	07:00	10:15 (1)	14:55		
Arr. Foligno	08:38	11:53	16:26		
Change trains					
Dep. Foligno	08:48	12:03	16:45		
Arr. Assisi	09:03	12:15	17:04		

Sights in **Assisi**: See notes under "Florence-Assisi"

Dep. Assisi	12:16 (2)	13:51 (2)	15:45	18:04 (5)	20:48
Arr. Foligno	12:30	14:06	15:58	19:16	21:00
Change trains					
Dep. Foligno	12:42 (3)	14:45 (2)	16:27 (4)	-0-	21:07 (1)
Arr. Rome (Ter.)	14:32	16:40	18:05	20:00	22:55

(1) Reservation *required*. Supplement charged. Light refreshments. (2) Second class. (3) Light refreshments. (4) Reservation *required*. Supplement charged. (5) Reservation *required*. Direct train.

Rome - Florence - Rome 615

Dep. Rome (Termini)	07:20 (1)	08:20	12:20	14:20
Arr. Florence (SMN)	09:50	11:45	15:45	17:45

• • •

Dep. Florence (SMN)	12:15	14:15	16:15	18:15
Arr. Rome (Termini)	15:40	17:40	19:40	21:40

(1) Reservation *required*.

Rome - Genoa 610

Dep. Rome (Ter.)	-0-	08:10 (2)	10:10 (2)	12:10 (2)
Dep. Rome (Ost.)	00:14 (1)	08:20	10:20	12:20
Arr. Genoa (Brig.)	05:57	13:11	15:06	17:06
Arr. Genoa (P. Prin.)	06:02	13:14	15:11	17:11

Dep. Rome (Ter.)	13:05 (2)	14:10 (2)	16:10 (2)	17:00 (3+4)
Dep. Rome (Ost.)	13:15	14:20	16:20	-0-
Arr. Genoa (Brig.)	18:06	19:06	21:06	21:45
Arr. Genoa (P. Prin.)	18:11	19:11	21:11	21:50

(1) Carries a sleeping car. Also has couchettes. (2) Supplement charged. Light refreshments. (3) Pendolino. Reservation required. Supplement charged. Restaurant car. (4) Plus other departures from Rome at 18:10 and 18:45 (3) arriving Genoa at 23:10 and 23:05.

Rome - Naples - Rome 620

Dep. Rome (Ter.)	06:30	07:15	08:10 (1)	09:10	10:15
Arr. Naples (Cen.)	08:58	09:54	10:00	11:15	12:54

Dep. Naples (Cen.)	13:00	13:30 (2)	14:00 (1)	15:00 (3)	16:00(1+4)
Arr. Rome (Ter.)	14:50	15:20	15:55	17:10	17:50

(1) Supplement charged. Light refreshments. (2) Pendolino. Supplement charged. Reservation required. Restaurant car. (3) Reservation required. Supplement charged. (4) Plus other departures from Naples at 16:50, 17:30 (2), 18:20, 20:00 (1) and 20:52 (2) arriving Rome 18:50, 19:20, 20:20, 21:50 and 22:50.

Rome - Pisa - Rome 610

Dep. Rome (Ter.)	06:10	07:05	10:10 (2)	11:10
Arr. Pisa	09:10 (1)	10:45 (1)	13:10 (1)	14:40 (1)

Sights in **Pisa:** See notes about Pisa under "Bologna–Pisa"

Dep. Pisa	13:15	13:49 (2)	14:49 (2)	15:15	16:49 (2)	17:15 (3)
Arr. Rome (Ter.)	16:50	16:56	17:50	18:50	19:50	20:50

(1) The Leaning Tower is only 10 minutes by bus or taxi from the rail station. (2) Supplement charged. Light refreshments. (3) Plus other departures from Pisa at 18:49 (2) and 20:49 (2) arriving Rome 21:50 and 23:50.

Rome - Naples - Pompeii - Naples Rome   635, 640

Trains departing Rome's Termini rail station at 07:10, 08:10, 09:40 and 11:40 arrive two hours later at Naples' Centrale or Piazza Garibaldi stations. Garibaldi is next to Centrale. A travelator provides transportation from Centrale to the FS station, from which it is a short walk to the Circumvesuviana station. Eurailpasses are not valid on the narrow-gauge trains from this station. Standard-gauge trains from Naples' Centrale station to Pompeii do accept the passes.

The ride from Circumvesuviana station to Pompeii is only 30 minutes, arriving there about four hours after having departed Rome.

Departures from Pompeii are at frequent times from noon to approximately 20:00, arriving Rome 4–5 hours later.

Sights in **Pompeii**: See notes under "Naples–Pompeii"

Rome - Spoleto - Rome   625

Dep. Rome (Ter.)	06:45 (1)	07:20	10:15 (1)
Arr. Spoleto	07:55	08:53	11:30

Sights in **Spoleto:** The tourist office in the Piazza della Liberta has many brochures, including a town map and offers three half-day walking tours.

Dep. Spoleto	13:03 (1)	15:08	16:55 (1)	18:39 (2)	21:39 (1)
Arr. Rome ("Ter.)	14:15	16:40	18:05	20:00	22:50

(1) Reservation *required.* Supplement charged. Light refreshments. (2) Reservation required.

Rome - Florence - Venice   620

Dep. Rome (Ter.)	07:10 (1)	09:05 (2)	11:45 (1)	13:45 (1)	
Dep. Florence (SMN)	09:37	11:07	13:28	15:28	
Arr. Venice (S. Lucia)	12:22	14:42	16:12	18:10	

Dep. Rome (Ter.)	15:05 (3)	17:45 (1)	19:05 (1)	19:10 (4)	20:05
Dep. Florence (SMN)	17:11	19:28	20:46	21:45	22:35
Arr. Venice (S. Lucia)	20:42	22:12	23:26	00:43	-0-

(1) Reservation *required.* Supplement charged. Restaurant car. (2) Arrives Venice Mestre 13:51. Change trains for Venice S. Lucia; leaves 14:12. (3) Arrives Venice Mestre 20:05. Change trains for Venice S. Lucia; leaves 20:33. (4) Reservation required. Arrives Venice Mestre station. No connection available to S. Lucia.

ROUTES TO THE TOE OF ITALY

Here is the rail route to southern Italy: along the Adriatic Sea from Pescara to Bari and the Ionian Sea from Taranto to Reggio di Calabria and also north from Reggio di Calabria to Pescara.

See following page for the route to southern Italy along the Tyrrhenian seacoast from Rome to Naples and on to Reggio di Calabria and north from Reggio to Rome.

Milan - Bologna - Pescara - Foggia - Barletta - Bari - Brindisi - Taranto - Catanzaro - Reggio di Calabria 630, 631, 642

This trip offers beautiful coastal scenery along both the Adriatic Sea (Pescara–Bari) and the Mediterranean (Taranto–Reggio di Calabria).

630

Dep. Milan (Cen.)	07:05 (1)	11:05 (1)	13:05 (1)		
Dep. Bologna	09:02	13:02	15:02		
Dep. Pescara	12:29	16:20	18:37		
Dep. Foggia	14:14	18:05	20:29		
Dep. Barletta	14:46	18:37	21:01		
Arr. Bari	15:19	19:07	21:46		
Dep. Bari	15:25	19:17	22:24		
Arr. Brindisi	16:36	20:14	00:12		
Change trains 642					
Dep. Brindisi	17:07(2)	21:45 (3)	04:35	08:33 (3)	13:27 (2)
Arr. Taranto	18:07	22:49	05:25	09:33	14:37
Change trains 631					
Dep. Taranto	-0-	23:14 (4)	05:26 (5)	15:37	17:02
Arr. Catanzaro	-0-	03:34	09:40	13:11	20:39
Arr. Reggio	-0-	06:15	13:34	15:40	22:57

(1) Supplement charged. Restaurant car. (2) Runs daily except Sundays and holidays. Second class. (3) Second class. (4) Has second-class couchettes and first- and second-class coaches. (5) Change trains in Catanzaro.

Sights in **Bari**: Much wine, olive oil and almonds in this area. Bari is actually a complex of three different cities. The "old town" is a peninsula which was the ancient port, rivaling Venice 900 years ago. Both the 11th-century St. Nicola Basilica and the 12th-century Romanesque cathedral are located there.

"New Bari," built in the 19th century, is where the Archaeological Museum, the Picture Gallery, concert halls and fine restaurants are located. Industrial Bari encircles the other two areas (factories, oil refineries, low-income apartments).

Don't fail to visit the rebuilt Norman Castle.

Sights in **Barletta**: The 13th-century church, S. Sepolcro. The Norman castle. The 12th-century Gothic cathedral.

Sights in **Brindisi:** Many Crusaders set out from here for Jerusalem. See the Roman column that marks the end of the Appian Way. The Civic Museum in the 11th-century circular S. Giovanni al Sepolcro Church. Frederick II's 13th-century castle. The rebuilt 11th-century cathedral.

Sights in **Catanzaro**: The Baroque S. Domenico church. The paintings in the museum.

Sights in **Foggia**: Much wool has been marketed here for centuries. See the ancient records of sheep tax at the library. The city has an art gallery, a museum and a cathedral.

Sights in **Pescara**: A nice beach resort on the Adriatic coast.

Sights in **Reggio di Calabria**: A very popular tourist resort. Founded by the Greeks in 720 B.C. See the fine archaeological collection in the Museo Nazionale della Magna Grecia. The 15th-century Aragonese castle. The reconstructed Romanesque-Byzantine cathedral. There are many Greek and Roman ruins in this area.

Sights in **Taranto**: A swing bridge connects the "old" city (on an island) with the new Taranto on the mainland. See the 15th-century Aragonese castle. The 14th-century S. Domenico Maggiore church. The exhibit of Greek vases and statues in the Museo Nazionale. The early 19th-century arsenal. The 11th-century cathedral.

The Northbound Trip

631

Dep. Reggio	07:00	14:45	23:35 (5)
Dep. Catanzaro	09:18	17:08	02:15
Arr. Taranto	13:05	20:54 (4)	06:31 (6)
Change trains 642			
Dep. Taranto	13:48 (1)	-0-	
Arr. Brindisi	14:55	-0-	
Change trains 630			
Dep. Brindisi	20:47 (2)	-0-	
Arr. Bari	22:06	22:05	08:16 (7)
Dep. Bari	22:10	23:59	09:51
Dep. Barletta	22:42	-0-	10:25
Arr. Foggia	22:22	01:08	10:57
Arr. Pescara	01:21	02:59	12:38
Arr. Bologna	04:42	06:40	15:58
Arr. Milan (Cen.)	07:30 (3)	09:10	17:55

(1) Second class. (2) Has second-class couchettes and second-class coaches. (3) Arrival time is for Milan's Lambrate station. (4) This train has through cars to Milan, including sleepers and couchettes. (5) Has second-class couchettes and first- and second-class coaches. (6) Change trains in Bari. (7) Supplement payable. Light refreshments.

Rome - Naples - Villa San Giovanni - Reggio di Calabria and v.v. 640

There is great Tyrrhenian coastal scenery between Rome and Reggio.

Dep. Rome (Ter.)	-0-	-0-	08:10 (1)	11:40 (1)
Dep. Rome (Tib.)	-0-	-0-	-0-	-0-
Dep. Naples (Cen.)	04:50	05:43	10:12	13:42
Dep. Salerno	05:44	06:34	10:56	14:20
Arr. V.S. Giovanni	10:34	11:32	14:36	17:56
Arr. Reggio di Cal.	10:53	11:50	14:50	18:10

Dep. Rome (Ter.)	15:10 (2)	16:10 (1)	22:30 (3)	23:10 (3)
Dep. Rome (Tib.)	-0-	-0-	-0-	-0-
Dep. Naples (Cen.)	17:22	18:10	01:01	-0-
Dep. Salerno	17:58	18:48	-0-	02:24
Arr. V.S. Giovanni	21:57	22:45	06:14	08:06
Arr. Reggio di Cal.	22:15	23:02	06:32	08:41

The Northbound Return Trip

Dep. Reggio di Cal.	07:58 (1)	12:10 (1)	
Dep. V.S. Giovanni	08:15	12:28	
Dep. Salerno	12:11	17:08	
Arr. Naples (Cen.)	12:48	17:44	
Arr. Rome (Tib.)	-0-	-0-	
Arr. Rome (Ter.)	14:50	19:50	

Dep. Reggio di Cal.	15:00 (1)	16:20 (4)	17:00
Dep. V.S. Giovanni	15:40	16:49	17:40
Dep. Salerno	19:11	20:12	22:09
Arr. Naples (Cen.)	19:48	20:48	23:01
Arr. Rome (Tib.)	-0-	-0-	-0-
Arr. Rome (Ter.)	21:50	22:50	01:11

Dep. Reggio di Cal.	19:40 (3)	20:25 (3)	22:30 (3)
Dep. V.S. Giovanni	19:58	20:42	22:48
Dep. Salerno	00:58	02:12	03:50
Arr. Naples (Cen.)	-0-	02:50	04:28
Arr. Rome (Tib.)	04:14	-0-	-0-
Arr. Rome (Ter.)	-0-	05:10	07:00

(1) Supplement payable. Light refreshments. (2) Supplement payable. Restaurant car. (3) Has sleepers and couchettes and first- and second-class coaches. (4) Reservation required. Supplement charged. Restaurant car.

THE RAIL TRIP TO SICILY

Milan, Florence, Rome and Naples to Messina and Palermo or Messina - Taormina - Catania - Siracusa   640

This trip includes a 35-minute ride on the ferry boat that runs between Villa S. Giovanni and Messina (Maritima).

There is beautiful seacoast scenery on this journey's Messina–Siracusa portion.

Dep. Milan (Cen.)	19:50	21:15	-0-	-0-
Dep. Florence (SNM)	23:38	01:11 (1)	-0-	-0-
Dep. Rome (Ter.)	-0-	-0-	04:06	08:10 (2)
Dep. Rome (Tibur.)	-0-	04:06	-0-	-0-
Dep. Naples (Cen.)	-0-	-0-	-0-	10:12
Dep. Naples (C. Fleg.)	-0-	-0-	-0-	-0-
Arr. Messina (Cen.)	10:40	12:50	12:50	16:10
Arr. Palermo	-0-	17:00	-0-	-0-
Arr. Taormina	12:40	-0-	13:58	17:10
Arr. Catania	13:30	-0-	14:50	18:00
Arr. Siracusa	14:00	-0-	-0-	19:20

Dep. Milan (Cen.)	-0-	-0-	-0-	-0-	-0-
Dep. Florence (Campo)	-0-	-0-	-0-	-0-	-0-
Dep. Rome (Ter.)	08:10 (2)	11:40 (2)	11:40 (2)	19:17	21:00 (3)
Dep. Rome (Tibur.)	-0-	-0-	-0-	-0-	-0-
Dep. Naples (Cen.)	10:12	13:42	13:42	21:48	23:28
Dep. Naples (C. Fleg.)	-0-	-0-	-0-	-0-	-0-
Arr. Messina (Cen.)	16:10	19:50	19:50	03:55	05:25
Arr. Palermo	19:40	-0-	23:00	08:25	-0-
Arr. Taormina	-0-	20:32	-0-	-0-	06:26
Arr. Catania	-0-	21:26	-0-	-0-	07:30
Arr. Siracusa	-0-	22:45	-0-	-0-	09:05

Dep. Milan (Cen.)	16:00 (4)	-0-	(4)
Dep. Florence (Campo)	19:40	-0-	
Dep. Rome (Ter.)	-0-	21:00	
Dep. Rome (Tibur.)	22:25	-0-	
Dep. Naples (Cen.)	-0-	23:28	
Dep. Naples (C. Fleg.)	-0-	-0-	
Arr. Messina (Cen.)	07:35	05:25	
Arr. Palermo	11:15	-0-	
Dep. Taormina	-0-	06:26	
Dep. Catania	-0-	07:30	
Arr. Siracusa	-0-	09:05	

The Northbound Trip

Dep. Siracusa	07:00 (5)	-0-	-0-	10:40 (2)	13:25
Dep. Catania	08:15	-0-	-0-	11:07	15:00
Dep. Taormina	09:05	-0-	-0-	12:10	15:47
Dep. Palermo	-0-	06:58 (5)	10:40 (2)	-0-	-0-
Dep. Messina (Cen.)	10:00	10:00	14:00	13:40	16:50
Arr. Naples (C. Fleg.)	-0-	-0-	-0-	-0-	-0-
Arr. Naples (Cen.)	15:48	15:48	19:48	19:48	-0-
Arr. Rome (Tibur.)	-0-	-0-	-0-	-0-	-0-
Arr. Rome (Ter.)	17:50	17:50	21:50	21:50	-0-
Arr. Florence (Campo)	-0-	-0-	-0-	-0-	-0-
Arr. Milan (Cen.)	-0-	-0-	-0-	-0-	-0-

Dep. Siracusa	-0-	-0-	15:05 (4)	-0-
Dep. Catania	-0-	-0-	16:40	-0-
Dep. Taormina	-0-	-0-	17:36	-0-
Dep. Palermo	11:20 (2)	13:25 (6)	-0-	15:40 (4)
Dep. Messina (Mari.)	15:25	16:50	18:40	19:25
Arr. Naples (C. Fleg.)	-0-	-0-	-0-	-0-
Arr. Naples (Cen.)	-0-	-0-	-0-	-0-
Arr. Rome (Tibur.)	-0-	-0-	-0-	-0-
Arr. Rome (Ter.)	00:02	-0-	-0-	-0-
Arr. Florence (Campo)	-0-	-0-	05:31	06:39
Arr. Milan (Cen.)	-0-	-0-	09:20	-0-

Dep. Siracusa	-0-	18:25 (6)
Dep. Catania	-0-	20:00
Dep. Taormina	-0-	20:52
Dep. Palermo	17:00 (4)	-0-
Dep. Messina (Mari.)	20:45	21:55
Arr. Naples (C. Fleg.)	-0-	-0-
Arr. Naples (Cen.)	-0-	-0-
Arr. Rome (Tibur.)	05:28	-0-
Arr. Rome (Ter.)	-0-	-0-
Arr. Florence (SMN)	07:31 (12)	09:02
Arr. Milan (Cen.)	11:10	13:00

(1) Florence Campo di Marte station. (2) Supplement charged. Light refreshments. (3) Has sleepers, couchettes, first- and second-class coaches. (4) Has sleeping cars and couchettes but no coach seats. (5) Supplement charged. (6) Has second-class couchettes and first- and second-class coaches.

Sights in **Messina**: The cathedral and the Annunciata dei Catalani church, both rebuilt in the 12th century by Norman occupiers. The beautiful astronomical clock in the modern bell tower, next to the cathedral. The art in the Museo Nazionale. The botanical gardens.

Sights in **Catania**: Founded 729 B.C. by Greek settlers. Now a very busy seaport and a popular winter beach resort. Whatever could happen to a city happened here in the 16th and 17th centuries: famines, civil wars, epidemics, pirate raids, earthquakes, and the eruption of Mt. Etna in 1693, after which Catania was almost completely rebuilt. The dark gray color of the city results from the use of volcanic matter in constructing buildings.

See the Greek and Roman theaters, aqueducts and baths. The excellent collection of art and archaeological relics in the Civic Museum of the 13th-century Castello Ursino. The tomb of the composer Vincenzo Bellini in the rebuilt 11th-century cathedral, also containing relics of St. Agatha. Sicily's largest church, San Nicolo. Next to it, the Benedictine San Nicolo Monastery, started in the 14th century.

The medieval manuscripts in the university's library. The royal chapel, Collegiata. The 18th-century palaces circling the Piazza del Duomo, with its Elephan Fountain. The museum at the birthplace of Bellini. The astronomical observatory.

Sights in **Siracusa**: Settled by Greeks in 734 B.C., five years after the founding of nearby Catania. An earthquake that destroyed much of Catania leveled Siracusa in 1693, after which Siracusa was rebuilt.

A comprehensive tour of Siracusa starts by visiting on the hill of Neapolis the Roman Amphitheater (which held 15,000 people attending gladiator fights), constructed during the reign of Augustus, before the birth of Christ. This structure was severely stripped in 1526 for the building of the city's defensive walls.

Above the amphitheater is the 600-foot-long altar of Hieron II, where 450 oxen were simultaneously sacrificed on pagan religious days. Nearby is the ancient Paradise Quarry in which the cave called "the ear of Dionysius" is located. Next to it is the 5th-century B.C. Greek Theater, where Plato and Aeschylus performed.

Behind the theater is the "Grotto of the Nymphs." The views are wonderful from the walkway to the Paradise Grotto and from the Viale Rizzo, looking down into the Greek theater and out toward the harbor. The archaeological area is open daily except Monday 09:00–17:00 (later in summer).

Five miles further, on the hill of Epipoli overlooking Siracusa, is the Castle of Euryalus, the mightiest and most complete fortress of Greek times.

Returning downhill, along Corso Gelone, you come to the ruins of the Roman Forum, at Piazzale Marconi. Go along Corso Umberto I and cross the Ponte Nuovo to reach the island of **Ortygia**. There, in Piazza Pancali, are the remains of the Temple of Apollo, which the conquering Arabs turned into a mosque.

Other sights in Ortygia are the 16th-century Santa Maria dei Miracoli church, the 15th-century arch (Porta Marina), the Maniace Castle, and the 13th-century Bellomo Palace, which houses a museum of medieval and modern art. The 17th-century Palazzo del Municipo (Town Hall), the 18th-century Palazzo of Benevantano del Bosco.

The National Archaeological Museum has one of the most important collections (Greek, Roman and Byzantine) of sarcophagi, pottery, coins and bronzes in Italy. Its most famous treasure is the 2nd-century B.C. Venus Landolina sculpture.

The ancient cathedral is dominated by the Doric columns of the original Temple of Minerva, where many works of art are exhibited.

Sights in **Palermo**: This city was entirely Arabic in ancient times. It is the modern capital of Sicily. It was severely damaged by bombs in July of 1943. Most museums and galleries here are closed on Monday. Their hours are 09:00 to 12:30 or 13:30. Most of them re-open from 15:00 to 18:00 on certain days. All are open Sunday 09:00 to 12:00 or 13:00.

See the exhibits of carretti (Sicilian horsecarts) and many other phases of traditional Sicilian life (bridal dresses, fishing boats, whips used for self-flagellation during Holy Week processions) at the Pitre Ethnological Museum. The fine archaeological collection in the Museo Nazionale on Via Roma. The Risorgimento Museum at Piazza San Domenico. The International Museum of Marionettes (located at Via Butera 1), open daily 10:00–13:00 and 17:00–19:00.

Watch tin, copper and iron being shaped into utensils in the stalls along Via dei Calderai, near Piazza Bellini. See tombs of important Sicilians, in the San Domenico Church.

See the 800-year-old cathedral and, next to it, the Archiepiscopal Palace, both on Vittorio Emanuele. Nearby, the marvelous Oriental garden at the Church of San Giovanni degli Eremiti, a converted mosque.

See statues of former Spanish rulers in the Quattro Canti (Four Corners), a small octagonal piazza. Near it are two very interesting street markets, Vucciria and Il Capo. Located on a small, twisting street, Vucciria offers Sicilian pastries, cheeses and many foods that are exotic to non-Mediterranean taste-buds: fried lungs and spleen, sea urchins, pork sausage encased in the skin of a pig's foot.

The great array of food at Il Capo (which starts at the intersection of Via Volturno and Via Carini) includes squash, cheese, mounds of tomato paste, grapes, melons, swordfish, eggplant as well as shirts, blouses, sweaters, leather handbags, etc.

See the antiques sold at Il Papireto, the flea market. Decorative tiles, Italian Victorian furniture, filigree jewelry, coins, religious art.

View one of the most splendid opera houses in Europe, the Teatro Massimo, built in 1897, also, the 12th-century Royal Palace, the Cuba and Zisa palaces and the catacombs under the Convent of the Capuchin Friars.

There are dazzling mosaics at the 12th-century Sala di re Roggero, open to the public on Monday, Friday and Saturday mornings if no official meetings of the Regional Assembly are taking place. This is only one of the many local churches and palaces built when Norman knights returned to Europe from the Crusades, ending Saracen rule of Sicily. Additional ancient mosaics can be seen in the Martorana Church in Piazza Bellini.

Don't fail to see other Norman mosaics in the Palace of the Norman Kings and at the 12th-century Arabic-Norman Palatine Chapel in nearby **Monreale**, a five-mile bus ride (#9) from Palermo. It is one of the most outstanding architectural achievements in Italy, open in the morning on Wednesday and Sunday, all other days 09:00–13:00 and 15:00–17:30 (hours vary in winter). Also the excellent mosaics in the 12th-century cathedral there.

Take the #14 or #77 bus to the bathing beach, Mondello. There are half-day bus excursions and local train service to **Segesta** and **Selinunte**, sites of substantial Greek ruins.

A local train leaves almost hourly for the 15-minute ride to **Bagheria**, where the eccentric 18th-century Villa Palagonia and the beautiful Villa Valguarnera are located.

There is hydrofoil service in the spring and summer to two interesting islands. The Blue Grotto on **Ustica a**ttracts many visitors. The archaeological museum on **Lipari** is worthwhile. From Lipari, there is boat service to other nearby islands: **Alicudi, Filicudi, Salina, Stromboli** (immortalized by Ingrid and Roberto with more passion off the silver screen than they invested in the motion picture) and **Vulcano**.

Passenger ships run from Palermo to Tunisia.

TRAIN ROUTES IN SICILY
(INCLUDING ONE-DAY EXCURSIONS)

Messina - Milazzo - Palermo   640

Dep. Messina	05:00	05:40	07:35	08:55	10:25
Dep. Milazzo	04:34	07:02	08:35	09:37	11:58
Arr. Palermo	09:50	10:15	11:00	12:20	14:00

Dep. Messina	11:20	13:10	16:28	18:27	19:50
Dep. Milazzo	11:52	13:50	17:00	19:00	20:23
Arr. Palermo	14:35	17:00	19:40	22:05	23:00

Sights in **Milazzo**: Founded seven centuries before Christ. An important naval victory over the Carthaginians was won by the Romans in Milazzo's bay more than 2,200 years ago. See the 13th-century Norman castle and 16th-century Spanish walls at the old town, on a hill above the modern city.

Dep. Palermo	04:05	06:58	08:30	10:40	11:20	
Dep. Milazzo	07:14	09:16	11:12	13:12	14:15	
Arr. Messina	08:00	09:50	11:55	13:45	15:10	

Dep. Palermo	13:25	14:30	15:40	17:00	18:05	20:40
Dep. Milazzo	15:50	17:15	18:26	19:33	21:00	23:30
Arr. Messina	16:35	17:50	19:10	20:25	21:35	00:05

Messina - Taormina - Catania - Siracusa   640

There is beautiful seacoast scenery on this route.

Dep. Messina (Cen.)	07:00	08:30	11:27	12:05 (1)	15:22 (1+2)
Arr. Taormina	08:06	09:06	12:08	14:20	16:10
Arr. Catania	09:03	10:05	13:05	15:03	17:05
Arr. Siracusa	10:25	11:40	14:27	15:42	18:23

Sights in **Taormina**: A year-around resort, with very mild winter weather, consisting mainly of three streets, each on a different level, connected to each other by many stairways, all on one side of Mont Venere. One funicular provides access to the beaches below the little town (4,000 population).

Stroll and shop for pottery, embroidery and carved wood figures along Corso Umberto, the main street. See the 3rd-century Roman theater, facing Mt. Etna. The medieval great halls in the 15th-century Palazzo Corvaja. The 14th-century Palace of the Duke of St. Stephen. The 13th-century cathedral.

Dep. Siracusa	05:03	07:00	09:10	10:40	13:25	15:05 (4)
Arr. Catania	06:30	08:15	10:43	12:10	15:00	16:40
Arr. Taormina	07:15	09:05	11:35	12:57	15:47	17:36
Arr. Messina (Cen.)	07:58	09:45	12:20	13:40	16:30	18:25

(1) Runs daily except Sundays and holidays. (2) Plus other departures from Messina at 16:32 and 19:55, (3) arriving Siracusa at 19:20 and 22:45. (3) Supplement payable. Light refreshments. (4) Plus other departures from Siracusa at 18:25 and 20:45, arriving Messina 21:35 and 00:05.

Palermo - Agrigento - Palermo 647

Dep. Palermo	07:30 (1)	10:00	12:05	13:30 (1)	14:20 (1)	16:30 (1+2)
Arr. Agrigento	09:30	12:05	14:20	15:30	16:25	18:35

Sights in **Agrigento**: Founded by Greeks in 581 B.C. See the extremely fine Greek ruins : seven Doric temples in the Valley of the Temples, many ancient aqueducts and cemeteries. The 14th-century cathedral. The 13th-century churches: S. Nicola, Santa Maria dei Greci and S. Spirito. Baroque palaces. There is an especially good archaeological museum here.

Dep. Agrigento	06:55	08:55	11:20	13:30	14:10 (1)	16:27 (3)
Arr. Palermo	08:45	10:55	13:23	15:30	16:15	18:23

(1) Runs daily, except Sundays and holidays. (2) Plus other departures from Palermo at 17:15, 19:00 (1) and 20:20, arriving Agrigento 19:25, 21:00 and 22:20. (3) Plus other Agrigento departures at 18:25 and 20:00, arriving Palermo 20:15 and 2150.

Palermo - Caltanissetta - Palermo 646

Dep. Palermo	06:42 (1)	09:10	12:50 (2)	14:05	17:30
Arr. Caltan. (Xirbi)	08:26	10:35	14:20	15:32	18:58

Sights in **Caltanissetta**: The Greek, Arabic and Norman ruins at the Pietrarossa Castle. The excellent archaeological collection in the Civic Museum. The baroque cathedral and Palazzo Moncada.

Dep. Caltan. (Xirbi)	08:45	10:14 (1)	11:18 (2)	15:31 (1)	18:12	20:05
Arr. Palermo	10:15	11:42	12:45	17:05	19:40	21:30

(1) Runs daily, except Sundays and holidays. (2) Runs Sundays and holidays.

Palermo - Catania - Siracusa   640, 645

645

| Dep. Palermo | 06:00 (1) | -0- | 09:00 | 12:05 | 14:20 (1) | 15:50 (1) |
| Arr. Catania | 09:18 | -0- | 12:25 | 16:00 | 17:45 | 19:45 |

Change trains 640

| Dep Catania | 10:55 | 12:03 | 13:05 | 17:05 (1) | 20:10 | 22:02 |
| Arr. Siracusa | 10:25 | 13:22 | 14:27 | 18:23 | 21:42 | 23:15 |

• • •

640

| Dep. Siracusa | -0- | 07:00 | 13:25 | 14:30 | 15:05 |
| Arr. Catania | -0- | 08:15 | 14:50 | 16:00 | 16:40 |

Change trains 645

| Dep Catania | 05:55 (1) | 09:08 (2) | 16:00 | 16:00 | 17:40 |
| Arr. Palermo | 09:15 | 11:30 | 19:25 | 19:20 | 21:05 |

(1) Runs daily, except Sundays and holidays. (2) Runs Sundays and holidays.

Palermo - Trapani - Palermo   646

| Dep. Palermo | 06:42 (1) | 09:10 | 11:45 (1) | 13:05 (1) | 14:05 (2) |
| Arr. Trapani | 09:15 | 11:30 | 13:55 | 15:05 | 16:15 |

Sights in **Trapani**: A major Carthaginian and Roman naval base in the 3rd century B.C. See the outstanding 14th-century Santuario dell'Annunziata, rebuilt in the 18th century. The 14th-century Santa Agostino Church. The excellent sculpture and paintings in the Museo Nazionale Pepoli. The 17th-century cathedral. The baroque Palazzo della Giudecca. The 15th-century Santa Maria di Gesu Church.

| Dep. Trapani | 08:00 | 09:25 (1) | 11:00 (1) | 12:40 | 17:25 (4) |
| Arr. Palermo | 10:15 | 11:42 | 13:20 | 15:05 | 19:40 |

(1) Runs daily, except Sundays and holidays. (2) Plus other departures from Palermo at 17:30, 18:55 and 20:35 (1), arriving Trapani 19:50, 21:22 and 22:52.

Agrigento - Caltanissetta - Agrigento   645

Dep. Agrigento	11:30	15:50	18:00
Arr. Caltanissetta (Cen.)	13:30	17:25	19:38
Arr. Caltanissetta (Xirbi)	10 minutes after arriving Centrale station		

Sights in **Caltanissetta:** See "Palermo–Caltanissetta"

Dep. Caltanissetta (Xirbi)	07:43 (1)	10:33	12:34	14:32	-0- (1)
Dep. Caltanissetta (Cen.)	08:15	10:43	12:45	14:45	17:28
Arr. Agrigento	09:40	12:22	14:40	16:22	19:00

(1) Runs daily, except Sundays and holidays. (3) Second class.

Catania - Caltanissetta - Catania   645

Dep. Catania	05:55 (1)	08:08	09:50 (1) 10:20 (1) 13:35 (1) 14:15 (3)
Arr. Caltanissetta (Xirbi)	07:41	10:33	11:40 12:34 15:30 (2) 15:06

Sights in **Caltanissetta:** See "Palermo–Caltanissetta"

Dep. Caltanissetta (Xirbi)	07:40 (1)	09:58	13:40	14:12	16:08 (1+4)
Arr. Catania	09:18	11:50	15:40	16:00	17:45

(1) Runs daily, except Sundays and holidays. (2) Second class. (3) Plus other departures from Catania at 16:00, 18:55, and 21:37, arriving Caltanissetta 17:49, 20:45, 23:27. (4) Plus other departures from Caltanissetta at 17:35, 19:24 and 19:49, arriving Catania 19:45, 21:05 and 21:55.

The Malta Cruise   2555

Reggio di Calabria, Catania and Siracusa are gateways for the boat trip to Malta.

2555

Dep. Reggio	08:30 (1)	Dep. Malta	05:30 (2)
Dep. Catania	11:00 (1)	Arr. Siracusa	14:00
Dep. Siracusa	16:30	Dep. Catania	17:45
Arr. Malta	21:30	Arr. Reggio	22:00

(1) Runs Tuesday + Saturday July 19-September 4. (2) Runs Tuesday + Saturday April 1-May 31; Tuesday, Friday + Saturday June 1- October 10.

FERRY ROUTES IN ITALY INCLUDED IN THE EURAILPASS

Villa S. Giovanni - Messina   2695

Trips on these ferries are a bonus for Eurailpass holders; there is no extra charge.

Dep. Villa S. Giovanni	Frequent times from 05:35 to 23:35
Arr. Messina	35 minutes later

• • •

Dep. Messina	Frequent times from 05:15 to 23:50
Arr. Villa S. Giovanni	35 minutes later

Civitavecchia - Golfo Aranci (Sardinia)   2699

This is the other ferry trip that is a Eurailpass bonus. These ferries run daily from early June to mid-September; the rest of the year, boats operate on Monday, Wednesday, Friday, Saturday and Sunday.

Dep. Civitaveccia	Consult latest *Cook's Overseas Timetable* or Corsica Ferries
Arr. Golfo Aranci	7 hours later

• • •

Dep. Golfo Aranci	Consult latest *Cook's Overseas Timetable* or Corsica Ferries
	7 hours later

SCENIC RAIL TRIPS

Arona - Brig   82

There is beautiful lake and mountain scenery on this portion of the Milan–Lausanne route.

Dep. Milan (Cen.)	07:15	10:15	13:25	15:25 (1)	18:15 (1)	19:05
Dep. Arona	-0-	-0-	-0-	-0-	-0-	-0-
Dep. Brig	09:00	12:06	16:17	17:47	20:06	21:46
Arr. Lausanne	10:20	13:20	17:56	19:22	21:30	22:25

(1) Reservation *required*. Supplement charged. Restaurant car.

Bologna - Florence   620

Excellent mountain scenery on this ride.

The train goes through the 11.5-mile-long Apennine Tunnel, Italy's longest tunnel.

Complete schedules appear under the "Bologna–Florence" and "Florence–Bologna"one-day excursions.

Bolzano - Brennero   595

Beautiful views of medieval castles and wild alpine mountain scenery on this portion of the route from Verona to Innsbruck, and on to Munich.

Sights in **Bolzano**: Has been Italian since only 1919. The language spoken here (called "Bozen" during the nearly six centuries it was ruled by the Hapsburgs, from 1363 until World War I) is German.

Take at least one of the three funiculars that climb up the Alps. See the 16th-to-18th-century houses on both Bindnergasse and Silbergasse. The vegetable and fruit market on Piazza delle Erbe. The 18th-century Neptune fountain.

The exceptional carved altar depicting the Nativity, in the Holy Virgin Chapel of the Franciscan church. The frescoes at both the cathedral and the Dominican church.

Stroll along the Talvera River first to the 13th-century Maretsch Castle and then to Runkelstein Castle, whose lovely frescoes can be seen on guided tours Tuesday–Saturday, 10:00–12:00 and 15:00–18:00.

Buses are available to make short trips of less than an hour to many vineyard villages. Traminer and Gewurztraminer are produced in this area.

Verona - Innsbruck - Munich   70

Dep. Verona (PN)	09:00 (1)	10:57 (1)	13:00 (1)	14:57 (2)
Dep. Bolzano	10:31	12:31	14:31	16:31
Arr. Fortezza	11:09 (3)	13:09 (3)	15:06 (3)	16:48 (3)
Dep. Brennero	11:59	13:59	15:59	17:59
Arr. Innsbruck	12:32	14:32	16:32	18:32
Arr. Munich	14:30	16:30	18:30	20:30

(1) Reservation *required*. Supplement charged. Restaurant car. (2) Light refreshments. (3) Estimated. Cook deleted Fortezza from this timetable in 1993.

Fortezza - Dobbiaco   70, 595, 596

Good mountain scenery on this spur off the Bolzano–Brennero route, appearing above. The following schedule shows how the Verona–Innsbruck–Munich trip can accommodate this en-route detour.

595			596	
Dep. Verona (PN)	09:00 (1)		Dep. Dobbiaco	13:29 (2)
Arr. Fortezza	10:57		Arr. Fortezza	14:38
Change trains 596			Arr. Bolzano	-0-
Dep. Fortezza	11:33		Arr. Innsbruck	16:01
Arr. Dobbiaco	12:39		*Change trains 70*	
			Dep. Innsbruck	16:37 (1)
			Arr. Munich	18:30

(1) Supplement charged. Restaurant car. (2) Runs Monday-Saturday.

Torino - Cuneo - Breil - Nice   581

There is spectacular scenery on the 74-mile-long Cuneo–Nice rail route through the Roya Valley and the Alps, a service that first became operational in 1928. Severe damage during World War II caused it to be closed in 1940, and it was not re-opened until the winter of 1979.

An outstanding feat of engineering, this line is a succession of very high viaducts, bridges and 60 tunnels that span 27 miles of this route, interspersed with sections that look down into deep valleys. This route has attracted many tourists.

Dep. Torino (PN)	08:50	-0-
Arr. Cuneo	09:56	-0-
Change trains		
Dep. Cuneo	10:00	10:52
Arr. Breil	11:20	12:21 (1)
Change trains		
Dep. Breil	11:25	12:22
Arr. Nice	12:23	13:43

(1) Change trains in Breil for Nice.

Sights in **Cuneo:** The 10th-century cathedral. The 13th-century Church of San Francesco. The marvelous viaduct over the Stura di Demonte. The museum in the 18th-century Palazzo Audiffredi. The 18th-century town hall.

The magnificent Cuneo–Breil scenery can also be seen on the following easy one-day round-trip from Torino.

Torino - Cuneo - Torino   581

All of these trips require changing trains in Cuneo.

Dep. Torino (PN)	07:30 (1)	08:45 (1)	Dep. Breil	18:08 (1)	19:04 (1)
Arr. Cuneo	08:41	09:56	Arr. Cuneo	19:28	20:33
Dep. Cuneo	08:46	10:00	Dep. Cuneo	19:29	20:34
Arr. Breil	10:05	11:20	Arr. Torino (PN)	20:42	21:50

(1) Direct train, no change in Cuneo.

Genoa-Torino-Cuneo-Ventimiglia-Genoa and v.v. 580, 581, 610

The right-hand column allows a layover in Torino for sightseeing and for dinner.

610		*580*	
Dep. Genoa (PP)	06:38	Dep. Genoa (PP)	12:05
Arr. Torino (PN)	08:45	Arr. Ventimiglia	15:20
Change trains 581		*Change trains 581*	
Dep. Torino (PN)	08:50	Dep. Ventimiglia	17:30
Arr. Cuneo	10:00	Arr. Breil	18:01
Dep. Breil	11:25	Arr. Cuneo	19:28
Arr. Ventimiglia	11:54	Arr. Torino (PN)	20:42
Change trains 580		*Change trains 610*	
Dep. Ventimiglia	13:15	Dep. Torino (PN)	21:25 (1)
Arr. Genoa (PP)	15:40	Arr. Genoa (PP)	23:50

(1) Plus other departures from Torino at 17:10, 18:05, 19:50, 20:25 and 23:00, arriving Genoa 18:47, 19:52, 21:34, 21:11 and 00:54.

Brindisi - Reggio and Reggio - Brindisi   631, 642

There is splendid coastline scenery on this trip.

642		*631*		
Dep. Brindisi	06:08	Dep. Reggio (Cen.)	07:00	-0-
Arr. Taranto	07:23	Arr. Taranto	13:05	-0-
Change trains 631		*Change trains 642*		
Dep. Taranto	09:37	Dep. Taranto	13:27	14:12
Arr. Reggio (Cen.)	15:40	Arr. Brindisi	14:42	15:46

Genoa - Pisa 610

There is exceptional mountain and Mediterranean coastline scenery on this ride. Complete schedules appear under the "Genoa–Pisa" one-day excursion.

Genoa - Nice - Cannes - Marseille 90

A close look at more than 100 miles of outstanding seashore resorts along the Mediterranean's Ligure coastline: the Savona and San Remo beaches (on the Italian Riviera) and the Monaco, Nice, Antibes, Cannes and St. Raphael beaches (on the French Riviera).

Dep. Genoa (PP)	08:52	16:52 (3)
Arr. Nice	11:46 (1)	19:56 (1)
Dep. Nice	12:04 (2)	20:25
Arr. Cannes	12:28	20:54
Arr. Marseille (St. Ch.)	14:22	23:51

(1) Change trains in Nice. (2) Light refreshments. (3) Reservation *required*. Supplement charged. Restaurant car.

Milan - Bern 82

The Brig–Bern portion of this ride is one of the five most outstanding scenic rail trips in Europe, with a fabulous array of lakes, mountains and rivers.

Dep. Milan (Cen.)	08:15 (1)	10:25 (2)	13:25 (3)	15:25 (1+5)
Dep. Brig	10:29	12:46	16:22 (4)	17:47
Arr. Bern	12:02	14:34	18:01	19:34

(1) Reservation required. Supplement charged. Light refreshments. (2) Reservation required. Supplement charged. Restaurant car. (3) Reservation required. (4) Change trains in Brig. (5) Plus another departure from Milan at 17:15, arriving Bern 20:26,

Milan - Genoa 580

Great views of marble quarries, mountains, farms and the Mediterranean coast, all in a two-hour one-way trip.

Milan - Locarno   549, 590

Great canyon, mountain and river scenery is seen from a narrow-gauge local train over the Domodossola-Locarno portion of this route. This Centovalli (one hundred valley) ride is one of the five most outstanding scenic rail trips in Europe. Complete schedules appear under the "Milan–Locarno" one-day excursion.

Milan - Zurich   84

This is one of the five most outstanding scenic rail trips in Europe.

A feast of beautiful farms, lakes, mountains, rivers and vineyards. You go through the 9.3-mile-long Gotthard Tunnel. Before it was opened to traffic in 1882, there was no direct rail route from Italy to eastern Switzerland through the Alps.

Prior to entering the Gotthard, the train goes through the beautiful Ticino Valley.

Immediately upon exiting the first of a series of nine tunnels, you first see the small, white Wassen Church on your right, 170 feet below the track. The next time the church comes into view, after exiting tunnel #4, the church is to your left and nearly level with the track.

Later, after exiting tunnel #6, you have a third view of the church, again to your left, this time nearly 230 feet above the track, but you will see it there only if you look far ahead and before being alongside the church. (The train is in the Kirchberg Tunnel when it is directly alongside the church.)

The turns inside three semi-circular tunnels in this area (Leggistein, Wattinger and Pfaffensprung) are engineered so well that there is no sensation of the curves that the train is making inside those tunnels.

Try this interesting experiment: make a pendulum of any object, holding the top of a weighted string, chain or handkerchief against the inner face of a train window (a left-hand window when inside Leggistein, and a right-hand window when inside Wattinger and Pfaffensprung). As the train goes around a curve, the weighted bottom will move away from the window.

The Mediterranean climate on the Italian end of the tunnel is usually much warmer than the Alpine temperature on the Swiss end. The train makes three gradients at 45–50 miles per hour.

Dep. Milan (Cen.)	08:25 (1)	10:25 (2)	12:25 (2)	14:25 (2)	16:25 (3+4)
Arr. Zurich	12:53	14:53	16:53	18:53	20:53
		• • •			
Dep. Zurich	13:07 (3)	15:07 (4)	17:07 (2)	19:07 (2)	-0-
Arr. Milan (Cen.)	17:40	19:35	21:35	23:35	-0-

(1) Reservation required. (2) Reservation *required.* Supplement charged. Light refreshments. (3) Reservation *required.* Supplement charged. Restaurant car. (4) Plus other Milan departures at 18:15 (3) and 19:25, arriving Zurich 21:53 and 23:34.

Milan - Tirano - St. Moritz - Chur - Zurich   520, 530, 547, 593

This is an alternate route from Milan to Zurich. Many rivers and lakes are seen between Milan and Tirano. There is great mountain scenery on the Tirano-St. Moritz narrow-gauge portion of this easy one-day excursion. The track reaches 7,405-foot altitude going through the Bernina Pass, Europe's highest main rail line. The descent from St. Moritz to Chur is spectacular.

593					
Dep. Milan (Cen.)	05:02 (1)	06:15 (2)	08:15	-0-	09:15
Arr. Tirano	08:29	08:37	10:40	-0-	11:47 (4)
Change trains 547					
Dep. Tirano	-0-	08:43	10:30	11:30	12:24
Arr. St. Moritz	-0-	10:58	13:02	13:56	14:56
Change trains 520					
Dep. St. Moritz	-0-	11:00 (3)	13:00 (3)	14:00	15:00
Arr. Chur	-0-	13:16	15:16	16:09	17:16
Change trains 530					
Dep. Chur	-0-	13:38	15:38 (3)	16:38	17:38 (3)
Arr. Zurich	-0-	15:53	18:11	18:53	19:53

(1) Runs daily, except Sundays and holidays. (2) Runs only on Sunday and holidays. ((3) Light refreshments. (4) Change trains in Sondrio.

Milan - St. Moritz - Milan   593, 547

Very good river and lake scenery Milan-Tirano. Great mountain scenery on the Tirano-St. Moritz narrow-gauge portion of this one-day round-trip. The track reaches 7,405-foot altitude going through the Bernina Pass, Europe's highest main rail line.

593						
Dep. Milan	05:02 (1)	06:15 (2)	08:15	09:15	12:15	14:15
Arr. Tirano	08:29	08:37	10:40	11:47 (3)	14:39	16:40
Change trains 547						
Dep. Tirano	-0-	08:43	11:30	13:12	15:05	17:30
Arr. St. Moritz	-0-	10:58	13:56	15:56	17:39	19:54

• • •

547			
Dep. St. Moritz	11:00	16:00	17:00
Arr. Tirano	13:28	18:28	19:28
Change trains 593			
Dep. Tirano	15:02	19:02 (1)	20:02 (2)
Arr. Milan	17:30	21:30	22:30

(1) Runs daily except Sundays and holidays. (2) Runs only Sunday and holidays. (3) Change trains in Sondrio at 11:15.

Naples - Siracusa   640

There is wonderful Mediterranean coastline scenery on this trip. See details earlier in this section, under "The Rail Trip To Sicily."

Naples - Sorrento   623

There is excellent Mediterranean coastline scenery on this ride.

Dep. Naples (Circumvesuviana) and Naples (FS) at two or three times per hour from 05:00 until 22:45 for the 55–65 minute ride to Sorrento.

• • •

Dep. Sorrento at two or three times every hour from 05:00 to 22:45 for the ride back to Naples. (There are stops in both directions at Pompeii.) A travolator provides transportation between Naples' FS station and Naples' Centrale station.

Naples - Taranto   635

There is very good mountain scenery on this route.

Dep. Naples (P. Gari.)	09:10		Dep. Taranto	15:00
Arr. Taranto	13:29		Arr. Naples (P. Gari.)	19:42

Reggio Calabria - Taranto - Brindisi   631, 642

There is excellent coastline scenery on this ride, which allows a sightseeing stopover in Taranto.

Brindisi is the gateway for the cruise to Greece.

631

Dep. Reggio Calabria (Cen.)	07:00 (1)	14:45				
Arr. Taranto	13:05	20:54				
Change trains 642						
Dep. Taranto	13:48	21:00	16:30	17:45	18:35 (2)	21:16
Arr. Brindisi	15:00	22:00	17:40	19:00	19:45	22:26

(1) Supplement charged. (2) Runs daily, except Sundays and holidays.

Rimini - Pescara - Brindisi   630

The excellent scenery on this route includes olive groves, vineyards and superb beaches on the Adriatic coastline. This can be broken into a two-day trip by *stopping in Pescara one night and then continuing on to Brindisi the next day.*

Also, this trip can be extended by continuing on from Brindisi to Reggio di Calabria, a ride that offers fine coastline scenery.

Dep. Rimini	08:19 (1)	10:08 (2)	14:08
Arr. Pescara (Cen.)	10:58	12:26	16:17
Dep. Pescara (Cen.)	11:03	12:29	16:26
Arr. Brindisi (Cen.)	16:09	16:36	20:14

(1) Operates late July to late August. (2) Reservation *required*. Supplement charged. Restaurant car.

Rome - Foligno - Terontola - Foligno - Rome   615

Between Foligno and Terontola, there are magnificent views of vineyards, olive groves, the hillside towns of **Spello** and **Assisi, Lake Trasimente**, and the city of **Perugia**.

These Schedules allow a sightseeing stopover in Foligno or Perugia.

Dep. Rome (Ter.)	10:20	14:20
Arr. Terontola-Cortona	12:21	16:21
Change trains		
Dep. Terontola-Cortona	12:25	16:25
Dep. Perugia	13:91	16:58
Arr.; Foligno	13:40	17:20
Dep. Foligno	14:20	18:05
Arr. Terontola	15:38	19:21

Sights in **Foligno**: An ancient Roman city that was badly damaged by earthquake in 1832 and then by heavy bombing during World War II. See the restored 12th-century cathedral. The archaeological museum and picture gallery, in the 14th-century Palazzo Trinci.

You can go by bus from Foligno eight miles to the mountain-top 14th-century village called **Montefalco**. Its main attraction is the vista from the top of its Communal Tower (Torre Comunale). Also see the interiors of St. Augustine's Church and St. Francis's Church.

Sights in **Perugia**: see notes under "Florence–Perugia"

Dep. Terontola	15:40	19:40
Arr. Rome (Ter.)	17:40	21:40

Udine - Trieste   601, 606

This portion of the Venice-Trieste ride has excellent scenery of the Adriatic coastline. Sit on the right side for best viewing. The schedules allow a sightseeing stopover in Udine.

601

Dep. Venice (SL)	06:52 (1)	09:54	11:54	12:37 (2)	15:54
Arr. Udine	08:34	11:34	13:34	14:04	17:34
Change trains 606					
Dep. Udine	09:27	12:27 (1)	13:37	17:37	18:27 (3+4)
Arr. Trieste (Cen.)	10:41	13:43	14:41	18:41	19:43

(1) Runs daily, except Sundays and holidays. (2) Restaurant car. (3) Runs daily except Saturday. (4) Plus other departures from Udine at 18:56, 19:37 and 20:30, arriving Trieste 20:22, 20:41 and 21:43.

Sights in **Udine**: see notes under "Trieste–Udine"

INTERNATIONAL ROUTES
FROM ITALY

The primary Italian gateway for rail travel to Switzerland, western Germany, Luxembourg, Belgium, Holland and northeastern France (Paris) is Milan. A secondary gateway for rail travel from Italy to Switzerland is from Torino, via Aosta, to either Brig or Geneva.

There is rail service to southern France (Nice, Marseille and Avignon), Paris, and to Spain from Milan and Genoa.

The gateways for travel to Austria, Germany and Denmark are Verona and Venice.

Venice is also the starting point for trips to Yugoslavia, Czechoslovakia, eastern Germany and the rest of Eastern Europe (Bulgaria, Greece, Romania, Hungary, Poland and Russia).

Milan - Genoa - Nice - Marseille - Barcelona   90

Pablo Casals (departing Milan 20:00) began in 1990 carrying one *Gran Clase* sleeping car, called by *Cook* "probably the most luxurious sleeping car in Europe." Each of its large single and double compartments has both a shower and a toilet. Substantial discounts are given to holders of Eurailpass and Eurodomino. Reservation is required. See the chapter on Spain and Portugal for more details about this luxurious Spanish train.

Dep. Milan (Cen.)	07:10 (1)	15:10 (2)	-0-	20:00 (4)
Dep. Genoa (P. Principe)	08:51	16:52	18:14 (3)	-0-
Arr. Nice	11:46	19:56	22:00	-0-
Arr. Marseille	14:22	23:01	00:56	-0-
Arr. Port Bou	21:13	-0-	-0-	-0-
Arr. Barcelona	22:20	06:16	-0-	09:13

(1) Reservation *required.* Supplement charged. Light refreshments. Change trains in Nice at 12:04. Depart Narbonne at 18:52(1). (2) Supplement payable to Nice. Sleepers and couchettes available Nice-Barcelona. (3) Change in Nice, 21:20. (4) *Pablo Casals* (see note above the timetable.). Reservation *required.* Supplement charged. Train has only sleeping cars. (No coaches.) Offers four different classes of accommodation: Gran Clase, single, double and four-berth tourist compartments. Restaurant car.

Milan - Luzern - Basel   84

Dep. Milan (Cen.)	08:25 (1)	09:25 (2)	11:25 (2)	13:25 (2)
Arr. Luzern	12:43	13:35	15:35	17:35
Arr. Basel (SBB)	14:06	14:46	16:46	18:46

Dep. Milan (Cen.)	15:25 (2)	18:25 (3)
Arr. Luzern	19:35	22:43
Arr. Basel (SBB)	20:46	00:11

(1) Change trains Arth-Goldeau at 12:13. (2) Reservation *required.* Supplement charged. Restaurant car. (3) Reservation *required.* Supplement charged. Light refreshments.

TORINO - AOSTA
GATEWAYS TO SWITZERLAND

(1) Via Le Grand St. Bernard

Torino - Aosta - Martigny - Brig or Lausanne   570, 573, 586

All of the Torino-Aosta trains are second class.

596

Dep. Torino (Porto Nuova)	06:25 (1)	11:25	13:25
Arr. Aosta	08:55	13:22	15:22

Change to a bus
573

Dep. Aosta (Place Narbonne)	08:00	16:40	16:40
Arr. Orsieres	-0-	-0-	-0-

Change to a train

Dep. Orsieres	-0-	18:17	18:17
Arr. Martigny	09:50	18:46	18:46

Change trains 570

Dep. Martigny	09:53	18:53 (2)	18:53 (2)
Arr. Brig	10:42	19:42	19:42

OR

| Dep. Martigny | 10:47 | 20:02 (2) | 20:02 (2) |
| Arr. Lausanne | 11:31 | 21:42 | 21:42 |

(1) Runs daily, except Sundays and holidays. (2) Light refreshments.

(2) Via Mt. Blanc Tunnel

Torino - Aosta - Chamonix - Geneva   366, 367, 368, 586

A layover in Chamonix (11:30–16:31) allows for sightseeing there.

586

Dep. Torino (Place Nuova)	06:25 (1)	09:25	13:25
Arr. Aosta	08:55	11:22	15:22
Change to bus 366			
Dep. Aosta	09:30 (1)	11:30 (2)	12:15 (2)
Arr. Courmayeur	10:50	12:30	14:50
Change buses			
Dep. Courmayeur	10:50	12:30	15:00
Arr. Chamonix	11:30	13:10	14:55

All of the Chamonix–Geneva train changes are "cross-platform," each taking less than one minute.

367

Dep. Chamonix	12:15	13:23	16:31 (3)
Dep. St. Gervais	12:58	14:28	17:23
Arr. La-Roche-sur-Foron	13:41	15:10	18:09
Change trains 368			
Dep. La-Roche-sur-Foron	14:00	15:23	18:12 (4)
Arr. Geneva (Eaux-Vives)	14:32	15:55	19:04

(1) Runs daily, except Sundays and holidays. (2) Operates early July to mid-September. (3) Light refreshments. (4) Change trains in Annemasse at 18:54.

ROUTES TO OTHER COUNTRIES

Rome - Milan - Genoa - Lausanne - Dijon - Avignon - Lyon - Paris   44

44

Dep. Rome (Ter.)	-0-	06:35 (4)	-0-	
Dep. Florence (SMN)	-0-	-0-	-0-	
Arr. Bologna	-0-	-0-	-0-	
Dep. Bologna	-0-	-0-	-0-	
Dep. Genoa (PP)	07:21 (1)	-0-	13:54	
Arr. Milan (Cen.)	08:50 (2)	10:35 (2)	15:45 (2)	
Dep. Milan (Cen.)	09:10 (3)	→	16:10 (3)	
Arr. Lausanne	-0-		-0-	
Dep. Lausanne	-0-		-0-	
Arr. Dijon	-0-		-0-	
Arr. Paris (Lyon)	15:51		22:52	

Dep. Rome (Ter.)	-0-	17:33	-0-	19:05 (5)
Dep. Florence (SMN)	-0-	-0-	19:43 (5)	-0-
Arr. Bologna	-0-	-0-	-0-	-0-
Dep. Bologna	-0-	-0-	21:03	-0-
Dep. Genoa (PP)	-0-	22:45	-0-	-0-
Arr. Milan (Cen.)	21:55 (5)	-0-	-0-	-0-
Dep. Milan (Cen.)	-0-	-0-	-0-	-0-
Arr. Lausanne	-0-	-0-	-0-	-0-
Dep. Lausanne	-0-	-0-	-0-	-0-
Arr. Dijon	05:39	06:02	06:17	07:20
Arr. Paris (Lyon)	08:25	08:47	09:08	09:50

(1) Supplement payable. (2) Change trains. (3) Reservation required. Supplement payable. Light refreshments. (4) Reservation required. Supplement payable. Restaurant car. (5) All-sleeping-car train.

Rome - Venice - Budapest - Kiev - Moscow 620, 94c

This train carries only sleeping cars. It does not have coach cars. Runs Monday, Wednesday and Friday.

620

Dep. Rome (Termini)	13:45 (1)	Day 1
Arr. Venice	18:12	
Change trains 94c		
Dep. Venice (Santa Lucia)	22:02 (2)	Day 2
Arr. Budapest (Keleti)	-0-	
Dep. Budapest (Keleti)	16:20	
Arr. St. Petersburg	-0-	Day 3
Arr. Kiev	18:30	Day 3
Arr. Moscow (Kievski)	10:09	Day 4

(1) Reservation required. Supplement payable. Restaurant car. (2) No train changes Venice-Moscow.

Milan - Venice - Innsbruck - Munich   70

Dep. Milan (Cen.)	-0-	09:10 (2)	-0-	15:10 (2)
Dep. Venice (SL)	06:58 (1)	-0-	13:30 (2+3)	-0-
Arr. Innsbruck	12:32	14:32	18:32	20:32
Arr. Munich (Hbf.)	14:30	16:30	20:30	22:30

(1) Change trains in Verona. (2) Supplement payable. Restaurant car. (3) Plus other Venice departures at 22:00 (4), arriving Munich 06:35. (4) Has sleeping cars and couchettes, plus second-class coaches.

Venice - Milan - Geneva   82

Dep. Venice (Santa Lucia)	11:58 (1)	13:58 (3)	14:58 (5)	22:00 (2+5)
Arr. Milan (Cen.)	-0- (2)	16:55	17:55	-0-
Change trains				
Dep. Milan (Cen.)	15:25	17:15 (4)	18:15	-0-
Arr. Geneva	19:58	21:42	21:55	06:42

(1) Reservation required. Supplement payable. Restaurant car. (2) Direct train to Geneva. No train change in Milan. (3) Supplement payable. Light refreshments. (4) Change trains Brig, departing 19:07. (5) Supplement payable. (6) Carries sleepers, couchettes and second-class coaches.

Bologna - Venice - Milan - Lausanne - Paris 44

Dep. Bologna	13:42 (1+2)	-0-	-0	-0-
Dep. Venice (SL)	-0-	12:58 (1+2)	-0-	20:05 (4)
Arr. Padua	-0-	-0-	-0-	-0-
Change trains				
Dep. Padua	-0-	13:32	-0-	-0-
Arr. Milan (Cen.)	15:40	15:45	-0-	-0-
Change trains				
Dep. Milan (Cen.)	16:10 (2)	16:10 (2)	21:55 (3)	-0-
Arr. Lausanne	-0-	-0-	-0-	-0-
Change trains				
Dep. Lausanne	-0-	-0-	-0-	-0-
Arr. Paris (Lyon)	22:52	22:52	08:38	08:25

(1) Direct train to Milan. No train change in Padua. (2) Reservation *required*. Supplement charged. Restaurant car. (3) Direct train to Paris, no changes. Sleeping cars, couchettes and second-class coaches. (4) All-sleeping-car train. Light refreshments.

Venice - Salzburg 88

Dep. Venice (S. Lucia)	07:55	12:37 (2)
Arr. Villach (Hbf.)	11:52	-0-
Change trains		
Dep. Villach (Hbf.)	12:00 (1)	-0-
Arr. Salzburg	14:46	18:46

(1) Restaurant car. (2) Direct train to Salzburg, no changes. Supplement payable. Restaurant car.

Venice - Vienna 88

Dep. Venice (S. Lucia)	07:55	12:37 (1)	20:35 (2)	00:10 (3)
Dep. Venice (Mestre)	08:06	12:48	20:46	00:22
Arr. Vienna (Sud.)	17:05	20:32	06:22	08:42

(1) Supplement payable. (2) Supplement payable. Carries sleepers, couchettes and second-class coaches. (3) Runs Friday, Saturday and Sunday early June to late September. Carries sleepers, couchettes and second-class coaches.

SCANDINAVIA
(DENMARK, FINLAND, NORWAY, AND SWEDEN)

Getting on Track in Scandinavia

• Tourist information: Obtain general information for all of Scandinavia through Scandinavian Tourism, P.O. Box 4649, Grand Central Station, New York, NY 10163-4649. Telephone (212) 949-2333, fax (212) 983-5260. Additional contact numbers appear under each country's listing.

• Public holidays: Information about holidays appears under each country's listing.

• Currency: Currency information appears under each country's listing.

• Summer time: Denmark, Finland, Norway and Sweden change to Summer Time on the last Sunday of March and convert back to Standard Time on the last Sunday of September. Finland is one hour ahead of Denmark, Norway and Sweden all year.

• Sun calendar: An average June day has over 17 hours of daylight in Copenhagen and almost 19 in Helsinki, Oslo and Stockholm. Above the Arctic Circle, the whole disc of the sun remains visible throughout the night for periods of 30 to 120 days, depending how far north a city is. We thought you'd find this list of the best vantage points a useful reference.

MIDNIGHT SUN CALENDAR

NORWAY				
Green Harbor	April	21	– Aug	23
North Cape	May	14	– July	30
Hammerfest	May	17	– July	28
Tromso	May	21	– July	23
Harstad	May	26	– July	19
Narvik	May	26	– July	19
Svolvaer	May	26	– July	19
Bodo	June	5	– July	9
Trondheim	June	8	– July	6
Andalsnes	June	5	– July	3

SWEDEN				
Bjorkliden	May	26	– July	19
Abisko	May	31	– July	14
Kiruna	May	31	– July	14
Gallivare	June	2	– July	12
Boden	June	4	– July	10

FINLAND				
Utsjoki	May	22	– July	24
Kilpisjarvi	May	27	– July	18
Pallastunturi	May	30	– July	15

Gallivare, Kiruna and Abisko are on the rail route from Boden to Narvik. Andalsnes, Trondheim and Bodo can be reached by train service from Oslo. Trondheim also can be reached by rail from Stockholm.

Overview of Scandinavia's Trains

The trains of Denmark, Finland, Norway and Sweden are comfortable (even second class), clean and efficient, and they travel through a range of scenery that's really candy for the

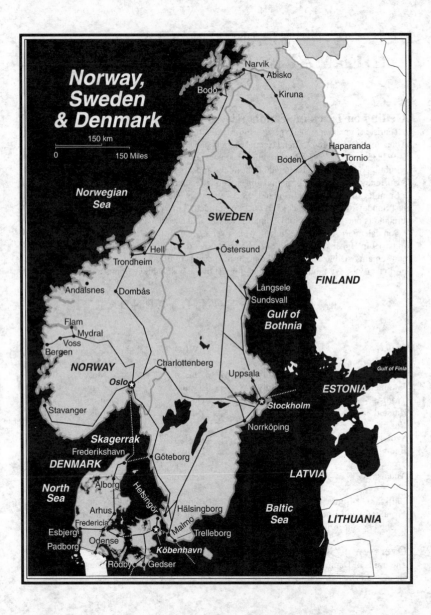

eyes. The variety is endless, from beautiful fjords and glaciers to the stark treeless arctic tundra to the cosmopolitan and chic cities of Copenhagen or Stockholm

Scandinavia is home to the Swedish X2000. This tilting train travels at speeds of up to 125 mph in commercial service. An X2000 trainset was shipped to the U.S., so Amtrak could give it a whirl as part of its testing program in advance of launching its fast train service on the busy Northeast Corridor in the eastern U.S.

In recent years, the various countries have been sprucing up their equipment, refurbishing older coaches for use on short-haul routes. New and refurbished sleeping cars are appearing on the scene here, too. Some trains have amenities like showers, audio entertainment, even mini-libraries.

Details about each country's railway appear in the individual country section.

SCANRAIL PASS

The Scanrail Pass offers unlimited travel on all trains and several ferries throughout Denmark, Finland, Norway and Sweden such as Stockholm–Turku, Rodby–Puttgarden and Trelleborg–Sassnitz. Also allows 50 percent discount on such ferries as Copenhagen–Malmo, Stockholm–Helsinki and Bergen–Flam.

Both Scanrail Pass and Scanrail 'n Drive (below) are sold worldwide (except Scandinavia) by travel agencies, tour operators, and Rail Europe and DER Travel.

	Adult		Senior*		Youth**	
	1st Cl.	2nd Cl.	1st Cl.	2nd Cl.	1st Cl.	2nd Cl.
5 days in 15	$228	$182	$203	$162	$171	$137
10 days in 1 month	$364	$292	$324	$260	$273	$219
21 days	$422	$338	$376	$301	$317	$254
1 month	$532	$426	$473	$379	$399	$320

*Senior fares apply to the Scanrail Pass 55+ and are for 55 or over. Proof of age may be required.
**Youth pass is available only to those who are under 26 on the first date of travel.
Children 4-11 pay half the adult fare. Under four, free.

SCANRAIL 'N DRIVE

The Scanrail 'n Drive Pass offers five days of rail travel and a three-day Avis car rental in Denmark, Norway and/or Sweden within 15 days.

	2 Adults*		1 Adult		Extra Days
Car Categories	1st Cl.	2nd Cl.	1st Cl.	2nd Cl.	Car
A Economy	$300	$265	$385	$345	$58
B Compact	$330	$285	$445	$395	$78
C Intermed.	$350	$305	$475	$435	$88

* Per-person price for two people traveling together. Third and fourth travelers sharing car pay only for railpass.

SCANRAIL PASS

While this pass bears the same name as passes sold by Rail Europe and DER TRAVEL, this Scanrail Pass is only available at railway stations in Scandinavia. The Scanrail Pass does not cover the surcharge on high-speed X2000 trains. In 1997, the pass included free or discounted fares (20-50 percent) on selected buses and ferries. The prices below were in effect in late 1997 and based on purchase in Scandinavia using local currency.

	Adults		Seniors*		Youth**	
	1st Cl.	2nd Cl.	1st Cl.	2nd Cl.	1st Cl.	2nd Cl.
5 days in 15	$250	$200	$220	$180	$185	$150
21 days unlimited	$390	$305	$350	$275	$295	$230

Children aged four through eleven receive a 50 percent discount.
*Adults 59 years and older. Proof of age may be required.
**Young people between the ages of 12 and 25 years old. Proof of age may be required.

DENMARK

Getting on Track in Denmark

• Tourist information: Danish Tourist Board, P.O. Box 4649, Grand Central Station, New York, NY 10163-4649. Telephone (212) 949-2333, fax (212) 983-5260. On the Web: http://www.deninfo.com/ or http://www.denmark.dt.dk/dtr.html.
• Public holidays: A list of holidays is helpful because some trains will be noted later in this section as *not* running on holidays. Also, those trains which operate on holidays are filled, and it is necessary to make reservations for them long in advance. Danish holidays include: January 1, New Year's day, Maundy Thursday, Good Friday, Easter, Easter Monday, Prayer Day (fourth Friday after Easter), Ascension Day, June 5, Constitution Day (from noon), Whit Sunday, Whit Monday, December 24 (from noon), December 25, Christmas and December 26 (Boxing Day)..
• Currency: Danish krone (Dkr). At press time, $1 equalled 6.93 Dkr.

Overview of Denmark's Trains

Danske Statsbaner (DSB) operates Denmark's trains. Generally, two classes of service are offered, first and second. Some InterCity trains have business-class accommodations, special areas called "quiet" seats (Hvilepladser) and family accommodations. DSB trains no longer carry sleeping cars.

Be advised that many InterCity trains travel in two sections, then split at a designated station to go off to different destinations. Make sure you're in the right car or you might end up taking a detour.

General Rail Information

• Denmark's two categories of fast trains are IC (InterCity) and EC (EuroCity) trains. Reservations are required on InterCity trains traveling these routes: Copenhagen-Frediricia-Aalburg, Copenhagen-Fredericia-Herning and Copenhagen-Fredericia-Esbjerg. Ferry service to England operates from Esbjerg.

• Lyntog is another category of train found in Denmark. These trains offer first- and second-class coaches and Business Plus and Business class. Reservations are required on all Lyntog trains, except between Arhus and Aalborg.

• Supplements are payable on EC trains that travel between Denmark and Germany and on EC trains for trips Copenhagen-Hoje Taastrup-Naestved and v.v.

• Children under four travel free. Half-fare for children 4-11. Children 12 and over must pay full fare.

The signs you will see at rail stations in Denmark:

AFGANG	DEPARTURE
ANKOMST	ARRIVAL
BANEGARDEN	RAIL STATION
BILLETKONTORET	TICKET OFFICE
DAMER	WOMEN
GARDEROBEN	CHECKROOM
HERRER	MEN
INDGANG	ENTRANCE
KOREPLAN	TIMETABLE
LYNTOG	FAST INTERCITY TRAIN
OPLYSNING	INFORMATION
PLADSBESTILLINGEN	RESERVATIONS
PERRON	TRACK
RYGEKUPES	MOKING COMPARTMENT
SOVEVOGN	SLEEPING CAR
SPISEVOGN	RESTAURANT CAR
TIL PERRONERNE TO	THE PLATFORMS
TOG AFGAR	DEPARTURE TIMETABLE
TOG ANKOMMER	ARRIVAL TIMETABLE
UDGANG	EXIT

DENMARK'S TRAIN PASSES

All of Denmark's passes must be purchased in Denmark.

10-RIDE PASSES These tickets provide trips for specific distances in first and second class for approximately a 20 percent discount.

Child's Discount Children aged four through eleven pay half-fare. Children under four travel free, unless they occupy a seat.

65-Ticket Discount tickets are offered to senior citizens over 65. Further discounts are offered on second-class tickets Mondays, Thursdays and Saturdays ("inexpensive days").

Group Ticket Discounts of 20 percent and more on tickets. The group must be a minimum of three adults traveling together in second class.

Copenhagen Sightseeing Pass Provides rail travel from any German border crossing to Copenhagen and back to the German border. Valid for seven days. Between April 15 and October 15, a free canal sightseeing tour is included. The 1997 prices were:

	First class	Second class
Adult	$100	$70
Youth	$ 75	$50
Child	$ 50	$35

ONE-DAY EXCURSIONS AND CITY-SIGHTSEEING

Here are 11 one-day rail trips that can be made comfortably from Copenhagen and Odense, returning to them in most cases before dinnertime. Notes are provided on what to see and do at each destination.

Copenhagen

Travel on commuter trains is covered by train passes. Trains depart every 20 minutes to most commuter stations.

City tours start from Town Hall Square, in front of the Palace Hotel. To get to the Mermaid or Amalienborg Castle (changing of the guard daily at 12:00) on your own, take bus #1 or #6. For brewery visits, take bus #6 to Carlsberg, or take bus #1 to Tuborg.

Tivoli Gardens, one of the world's most famous amusement parks, is open early April to mid-September. Fireworks are presented several nights each week.

Also see Thorvaldsen Museum, with his sculptures and tomb. Christiansborg Palace, where the Danish Parliament meets. The Danish Resistance Museum. The zoo. Window-shop in the walking area, Stroget.

View the vast collection in the National Museum (12 Frederiksholms Kanal) reflecting Danish life from the Ice Age to the late 17th century plus Danish sculptures and paintings by European artists, open daily except Monday. From mid-June to mid-September: 10:00–16:00. From mid-September to mid-June: 11:00–15:00 Tuesday–Friday and 12:00–16:00 on Saturday and Sunday.

Danish and European paintings (an excellent Matisse collection) are displayed at the Royal Museum of Fine Arts, on Solvgade, open daily 10:00–17:00. See an exhibit of superb French Impressionists and also Egyptian, Greek, Roman and French sculptures at Carlsberg Glypotek (behind Tivoli Gardens), open daily except Monday. From May through September: 10:00–16:00. From October through April: 12:00–15:00 (10:00–16:00 on Sunday).

The Toy Museum is open all year Wednesday-Sunday 10:00–16:00. There is a good collection of weapons and uniforms in the Royal Arsenal. From May through September: 13:00–16:00 on weekdays, 10:00–16:00 on Sunday. From October through April: 13:00–15:00 on weekdays, 11:00–16:00 on Sunday.

Visit the City Museum, at 59 Vesterbrogade or take in the view from the top of Town Hall's 350-foot-high tower. Borsen, the oldest stock exchange in the world, still functioning, is worth a visit.

Take the gilded spiral staircase of the Old Saviour's Church (Vor Frelsers Kirke) to the tower; the view is wonderful. Other places of interest include Regensen, a residential university since 1623 and Thorvaldsen's marble statues of Christ and the Apostles in Our Lady's Church (Vor Frue Kirke). Stroll along Nyhavn Canal and see the line of foreign naval ships along Langelinie Promenade.

The crown jewels and other possessions of Danish monarchs in the museum at Rosenborg Palace (open daily in summer, only on Tuesday, Friday and Sunday the rest of the year), particularly the pearl-encrusted saddle of Christian IV. Nearby, the 25-acre botanical garden and the National Art Gallery.

The Frilandsmuseet open-air museum of Danish houses and farms in suburban **Sorgenfri** is open daily except Monday 10:00–17:00. mid-March to the end of September and 10:00–15:00 the first half of October. The excellent English-language guidebook sold at the ticket counter is essential for understanding the exhibits. Allow at least two hours here to stroll the two miles of paths.

The farms here are complete with livestock. You will see sheep being sheared, the carding of wool and the spinning of cloth. There are folk dances on Saturday and Sunday.

Commuter trains run three times every hour during the day for the 30-minute ride.

In the following timetables, where a city has more than one rail station we have designated the particular station after the name of the city (in parentheses).

Copenhagen - Alborg - Copenhagen   700

All of these trains require reservation and have light refreshments.

Dep. Copenhagen	06:52	07:52	08:52
Arr. Alborg	11:46	12:46	13:46

Sights in **Alborg**: This thousand-year-old town is the most important in the north Jutland area. You will find many medieval houses, down the lanes that wind off the modern boulevards. The early 15th-century Monastery of the Holy Ghost. The early 16th-century Aalborghus Castle.

The basement Duus Wine Cellar in the outstanding ornate, five-story, 17th-century Jens Bang House. The 16th-century paintings, depicting the Ten Commandments, in the 12th-century Budolphi Cathedral.

The oak-paneled room from 1602 in the Historical Museum, open daily June through August 10:00–19:00 (48 Algade). Works by Scandinavian modern artists in the North Jutland Museum of Modern and Contemporary Art, open daily except Monday 10:00–17:00 (50 Kong Christians Alle).

The more than 300 restaurants (Greek, Italian, Lebanese, Danish) on Jomfru Ane Gade.

The Shipping and Naval Museum, open daily 10:00–19:00 (75 Vestre Fjordvej). Lindholm Hoje, a museum devoted to Viking archaeology, open daily 10:00–19:00 (11 Vendilavej).

| Dep. Alborg | 15:51 | 16:51 | 17:51 | 18:51 |
| Arr. Copenhagen | 20:51 | 21:51 | 22:51 | 23:51 |

Copenhagen - Aarhus - Copenhagen 700, 725

There are two ways to make this trip. The first is by train between Copenhagen and Kalundborg, then by boat between Kalundborg and Aarhus. The boat has a smorgasbord cafeteria, and the scenery on the cruise is good.

The second way to Aarhus, entirely by train, is via Fredericia.

It makes an interesting day to go to Aarhus by the combination of train and boat via Kalundborg and return to Copenhagen by train via Fredericia.

Boat - via Kalundborg 725
Reservations are required for all trains. Tickets for the ferry must be purchased before boarding the train.

Train			Boat		
Dep. Copenhagen (H.)	06:38 (1)	12:48 (2)	Dep. Aarhus (Pier)	06:30 (1)	12:30 (2+3)
Arr. Kalundborg	08:12	14:12	Arr. Kalundborg	08:00	14:00
Change to boat			*Change to train*		
Dep. Kalundborg	08:30	14:30	Dep. Kalundborg	08:20	14:22
Arr. Aarhus (Pier)	10:00	16:00	Arr. Copenhagen (H.)	09:42	15:42

(1) Runs daily, except Sundays and holidays. (2) Runs Saturdays, Sundays and holidays. (3) Plus other Aarhus departures at 16:30 (2) and 18:30 (4), arriving Copenhagen at 19:42 and 21:42. (4) Operates Friday only.

Sights in **Aarhus**: Board the train at the Aarhus pier and take it to Aarhus' rail station. Don't fail to visit the 17th-century Clausholm Castle and its Italian garden. The magnificent decor, paintings, tapestries and furnishings of the castle are worth going to Aarhus.

It is a one-hour drive from the city to the castle, which is open only Easter to October 15. In spring and autumn, it is open only on Saturday and Sunday. From June 1 to August 15, Clausholm is open daily 11:00–17:00.

See the 60 completely furnished medieval houses and the 400-year-old mayor's residence at the Old Town open-air museum (Den Gamle By) in the botanical gardens. The 15th-century cathedral, noted for the magnificent tones of its twin organs and for the altar's woodcarvings. The ancient university. The Tivoli Friheden amusement park in Marselisborg Woods.

Take bus #6 from the rail station for the five-mile drive to see the great collection of primitive relics (Stone Age to Viking Era) in the Prehistoric Museum at **Moesgaard**, open daily in summer 10:00–17:00. It is closed Mondays the rest of the year.

Train - via Fredericia 700

All of these trains require reservation and have light refreshments.

Dep. Copenhagen (H.)	05:52 (1)	06:52	07:52	08:52	09:52
Arr. Aarhus	09:13	10:13	11:13	12:13	13:13

• • •

Dep. Aarhus	13:26	14:26	15:26	16:26	17:26 (2)
Arr. Copenhagen (H.)	16:51	17:51	18:51	19:51	20:51

(1) Runs daily, except Sundays and holidays. (2) Plus other departures from Aarhus at 18:26, 19:26 and 20:26, arriving Copenhagen 21:51, 22:51 and 23:51

THE TRIP TO LEGOLAND

Copenhagen - Billund - Copenhagen 700

All of these trains require reservation and have light refreshments.

Train 700

Dep. Copenhagen	06:52	07:52	08:22 (1)	08:52	09:52 (2)
Arr. Vejle	09:27	10:27	10:30	11:27	13:27

Change to bus

Dep. Vejle	Frequent times from 10:00 to 24:00
Arr. Billund	55 minutes later

Sights in **Billund**: Although the visit to Legoland can be made as a one-day excursion, an overnight stay in or near Billund is recommended so as to have adequate time to see everything at this 21-acre park that features the world's most popular toy.

The outdoor exhibit of buildings, monuments, cities and villages modeled after sites from all over the world (including the Statue of Liberty and Mount Rushmore sculptures in the U.S.A., the Rhine River and an African wildlife scene) is constructed from more than 33 million plastic interlocking pieces. It is open May 1 to mid-September, 10:00–20:00.

Both a monorail and a small train provide overviews of the park to see details one might miss while walking. Children can make projects at several large playrooms on tables equipped with Legos kits.

Bus

Dep. Billund	Frequent times from 05:00 to 24:00
Arr. Vejle	55 minutes later

Change to train

Dep. Vejle	18:13	19:13	20:13	21:13	22:13 (3)
Arr. Copenhagen	20:51	21:51	22:51	23:51	00:51

(1) Runs daily, except Sundays and holidays. (2) Plus other departures from Copenhagen every hour 10:52 to 19:52. (3) Runs daily except Saturday.

Copenhagen - Frederickshavn and Frederickshavn - Copenhagen 700

Most of these trains require reservation and have light refreshments.

Dep. Copenhagen (H.)	05:52 (1)	06:52	07:52	08:52	09:52 (3)
Dep. Odense	07:29	08:35	09:35	10:35	11:35
Dep. Fredericia	08:12	09:12	10:12	11:12	12:12
Arr. Arhus	09:13	10:13	11:13	12:13	13:13
Arr. Alborg	10:46	11:46 (2)	12:46	13:46 (2)	14:46
Arr. Frederickshavn	11:53	13:00	13:53	15:00	15:53

Signts in **Frederickshavn**: The military museum at the 17th-century fort. The museum in the 18th-century manor house called Bangsbo.

Dep. Frederickshavn	04:47 (4)	05:39 (1)	06:36 (5)	07:16	08:45 (6)
Dep. Alborg	05:51	06:51	07:51	08:51 (2)	09:51
Dep. Arhus	07:26	08:26	09:26	10:26	11:26
Dep. Fredericia	08:33	09:33	10:33	11:33	12:33
Dep. Odense	09:08	10:08	11:08	12:08	13:08
Arr. Copenhagen (H.)	10:51	11:51	12:51	13:51	14:51

(1) Runs daily, except Sundays and holidays. (2) Change trains in Alborg. (3) Plus other departures from Copenhagen every hour from 10:52 to 18:52 and 00:33. (4) Runs Monday-Friday, except holidays. (5) Runs Saturdays, Sundays and holidays. (6) Plus other Frederickshavn departures at 09:39, 10:47, 11:36, 12:47, 14:47, 15:02 (7), 16:47, 17:36 (8), 18:46 (9) and 22:07 (10) (7) Second class to Alborg. Runs Monday-Frudat except holidays. Change trains Alborg. (8) Runs Monday-Thursday and Sundays. (9) Runs daily except Saturdays. (10) Second class to Arhus; change trains there.

Copenhagen - Helsingborg - Copenhagen 702, 2345

Train 702

Dep. Copenhagen (H.)	Trains depart every 20 minutes from 05:29 to 00:29, with additional departures during peak times
Arr. Helsingor	55 minutes later

Change to ferry 2345

Dep. Helsingor	Ferries depart about every 20 minutes from 06:10 to 21:10
Arr. Helsingborg	20 minutes later

The ferry trip noted above and below is a bonus for Eurailpass holders.

Sights in **Helsingborg:** Stained-glass windows, depicting the city's 900 years of history, in the Radhuset (Town Hall). Karnan, the 14th-century fort with walls up to 15 feet thick, one of the best preserved medieval buildings in Scandinavia. To reach it, take the elevator at the left of the terrace, from the main square.

See the view of the sound from Rosengarden, and the beautiful roses there. The municipal museum. The magnificent pulpit in the 15th-century Mariakyrkan (Church of St. Mary). The handsome concert hall in Stadsbiblioteket (Town Library). The bronze statue in Hamntoget (Harbor Square).

Ferry 2345

Dep. Helsingborg	Ferries depart about every 20 minutes from 05:40 until 21:40
Arr. Helsingor	20 minutes later
Change to train 702	
Dep. Helsingor	Trains depart every 20 minutes from 04:59 to 23:39 with additional departures during peak times
Arr. Copenhagen (H.)	55 minutes later

Copenhagen - Helsingor - Copenhagen   702

Dep. Copenhagen (H.)	Trains depart every 20 minutes from 05:09 to 00:29 with additional departures during peak times
Arr. Helsingor	55 minutes later

Sights in **Helsingor**: Kronborg Castle (of Shakespeare's Hamlet). The stained-glass, depicting the town's history, in the Council Chamber of the Radhus (Town Hall). If time allows you to visit only Helsingor or Hillerod (described in the next listing), do *not* choose Helsingor. Fredericksborg Castle at Hillerod is by far the more interesting of the two.

Dep. Helsingor	Trains depart every 20 minutes from 04:59 to 23:39 with additional departures during peak times
Arr. Copenhagen (H.)	55 minutes later

Copenhagen - Hillerod - Copenhagen   STB (Local Timetable)

This is an excellent one-day trip by local commuter train on which Eurailpass is valid. We recommend leaving Copenhagen (Central) between 08:00 or 09:00 for the 50-minute ride. (There is service three times every hour during the day.) It is a 25-minute walk from the **Hillerod** rail station, through the village, past the lake and market square, to the 17th-century Fredericksborg Castle and its National Historic Museum of both worldwide art and Danish history. One of the most beautiful castles in Europe, it is located on an island in a small lake, reached by walking over a short bridge. You could spend many days enjoying its contents. A full morning will fly by.

The castle is open 10:00–17:00 May through September, 10:00–16:00 April and October, and 10:00–15:00 November through March.

Market days in Hillerod are Monday, Thursday and Saturday (09:00–13:00).

You can eat lunch at the castle's restaurant or in the village on your walk back to the rail station.

By leaving Copenhagen early in the day, it is easy to combine a visit to both Hillerod and **Gilleleje**, a colorful fishing port that is 40 minutes beyond Hillerod. The attractions in Gilleleje are the daily fish auction and the famous Adamsens Fiske-Udsalgr take-out stand which sells fish salads and sandwiches made of fresh-caught crab, shrimp, cod and tuna. It is only a five-minute walk from Gilleleje's rail station to its port. Trains for Gilleleje leave Hillerod hourly Monday–Friday and every 90 minutes on Saturday and Sunday.

Copenhagen - Humlebaek - Copenhagen   STB (Local Timetable)

Dep. Copenhagen	Frequent times from 05:25 to 00:55
Arr. Humlebaek	30 minutes later

Sights in **Humlebaek**: Exhibits of Giacometti sculptures, painters of the "Cobra" group, and post-1950 art (Warhol, Picasso, Lichtenstein, Calder) in the Louisiana Museum of Modern Art, open daily except Wednesday 10:00–17:00, on Wednesday 10:00–22:00. It is a 15-minute walk from the rail station to the museum.

Dep. Humlebaek	Frequent times from 05:05 to 00:05
Arr. Copenhagen	30 minutes later

Copenhagen - Malmo - Copenhagen   2362

In 1997, Eurailpass holders received a 25 percent discount on the hydrofoil trip to Sweden's West Coast. There are 16–22 sailings daily from Copenhagen (Havnegade) and Malmo for this 45-minute cruise.

Sights in **Malmo**: The Art, Archaeology, Military, Technical and Carriage Museums, all in the castle. Town Hall. St. Peter's Church. The Sailor's House (3 Fiskehamnsgatan). The 17th and 18th-century houses on Lilla Torg (Small Square). Malmo is the gateway to Skane, the beautiful chateau country of Sweden.

Copenhagen - Odense - Copenhagen   700

This trip was once made by train and ferry, but a new tunnel has made it a straight shot by train, cutting travel time considerably.

All of these trains require reservation and have light refreshments.

Dep. Copenhagen (H.)   Every hour from 05:52 to 23:33
Arr. Odense   110 minutes later

Sights in **Odense**: The home of Hans Christian Andersen, now a museum, on Hans Jensen-straede. You can visit another Andersen Museum at Munkemollestraede 3. Also see the National railway museum in the Dannebrogsgade. The 13th-century Cathedral of St. Knud.

Dep. Odense   Every hour from 05:13 to 23:15
Arr. Copenhagen (H.)   110 minutes later

Copenhagen - Roskilde - Copenhagen   700

All of these trains require reservation and have light refreshments.

Dep. Copenhagen (H.)   Frequent times from 05:33 to 00:57
Arr. Roskilde   18-21 minutes later

Sights in **Roskilde:** The 40 tombs of Denmark's kings and queens, a 500-year-old clock, and the post on which such royalty as Peter the Great and the 20th-century Duke of Windsor marked their heights (some of them with humorous exaggeration), all in the red brick cathedral. Open for tours weekdays April–September 09:00–17:45 and October–March 10:00–15:45. Also on Sundays and holidays 12:30–17:45 June–August and 12:30–15:45 September–May.

    Also see the exhibits of five ancient boats (39-to-59-feet-long) in the Viking Ship Museum. Open daily 09:00–17:00 April-October, 10:00–16:00 November-March. It is a 20-minute walk from the town center.

    The town center and the cathedral are a short walk from the rail station. The tourist office (near the cathedral) supplies an excellent English-language brochure, a city map, and a printed description of a walking tour that includes the town's most important sights.

Dep. Roskilde   Frequent times from 05:20 to 00:29
Arr. Copenhagen (H)   18-21 minutes later

SCENIC RAIL TRIPS

Copenhagen-Jaegersborg-Naerum-Copenhagen 700, Local Timetable

Called "Denmark's most scenic train ride" by Danish State Railways, this trip begins at Copenhagen's Central rail station. Change trains 30 minutes after departing Copenhagen, at Jaegersborg.

    The 30-minute rail trip Jaersborg–Naerum (frequent departures) is along meadows, forests and small lakes. It is covered by train passes. **Naerum** is a modern town.

Odense - Fredericia - Odense   700

There is fine coastline scenery on this easy one-day round trip. This can also be seen as a portion of the Copenhagen–Frederickshavn route.

All of these trains require reservation and have light refreshments..

Dep. Odense	35 minutes after each hour, from 07:35 to 23:35
Arr. Fredericia	35 minutes later

• • •

Dep. Fredericia	33 minutes after each hour, from 05:33 to 21:33 (1)
Arr. Odense	39 minutes later

(1) Plus another departure from Fredericia at 23:29 daily except Saturday.

Struer - Thisted   716

More great coastal scenery along this route.

Dep. Struer	07:53	09:48	12:21	13:57	15:22	17:24 (1)
Arr. Thisted	75-85 minutes later					

• • •

Dep. Thisted	08:00	09:57	11:52	13:58	15:38	16:06 (3)
Arr. Struer	75-85 minutes later					

(1) Plus another Struer departure at 19:37 and 21:33 (2). (2) Operates Saturday only. (3) Plus other Thisted departures at 16:57, 19:00, 22:28 (3) and 22:54 (2). (3) Operates daily except Saturdays.

INTERNATIONAL ROUTES
FROM DENMARK

Copenhagen is the gateway for travel from Denmark, Norway and Sweden to Western Europe, starting with its connections to Berlin and Hamburg, and then on from those cities to the rest of Western Europe.

Copenhagen - Berlin - Prague - Budapest   50, 60

Through trains also operate from Copenhagen (Table 715) to Struer and Thisted. There are departures from Copenhagen to Struer every two hours beginning at 06:52 until 18:52; the trip takes about four and a half hours. Connect here for Thisted. Trains leave Struer every two hours from 09:23 to 17:23.

The trains are carried Rodby–Puttgarden (a 65-minute trip) by ferries that have a restaurant.

Dep. Copenhagen (Hovedbanegard)	07:30 (1)	12:30 (1)	15:00 (5)
Dep. Rodby Ferry	09:25	14:25	-0-
Arr. Hamburg	12:23 (2)	17:22	-0-
Arr. Malmo	-0-	-0-	15:45
Dep. Malmo	-0-	-0-	16:52 (6)
Arr. Berlin (Zoo)	15:32	21:07	-0-
Change trains 60			
Dep. Berlin (Lichtenberg)	16:46 (3+4)	-0-	-0-
Arr. Prague (Holesovice)	21:30	-0-	07:09
Arr. Budapest	-0-	-0-	15:12

(1) Supplement payable. Light refreshments. (2) Change trains in Hamburg for Berlin. Supplement charged. Restaurant car. (3) Supplement payable. Restaurant car. (4) **NOTE:** The departure station is different from arrival station. There is ample time to catch a cab to the departure station.. (5) Copenhagen-Malmo is by catamaran. (6) Carries first- and second-class sleepers and second-class couchettes Malmo-Budapest; no coaches with seats.

Copenhagen - Hamburg 50

The trains are carried Rodby–Puttgarden (a 65-minute trip) by ferries that have a restaurant.

Dep. Copenhagen (H.)	07:30 (1)	09:20 (1)	12:30 (1)	15:20 (1)
Dep. Rodby Ferry	09:25	11:30	14:25	17:30
Arr. Hamburg (Hbf.)	12:23	14:26	17:22	20:26

Dep. Copenhagen	17:30 (1)	19:05	21:05
Dep. Rodby Ferry	19:25	21:30	23:30
Arr. Hamburg (Hbf.)	22:15	00:40	03:00

(1) Reservation advisable. Supplement charged. Light refreshments.

Copenhagen - Oslo 735

Dep. Copenhagen (1.)	10:01	21:45 (2)
Arr. Oslo (Sen.)	19:52	07:07

(1) Reservation required. Restaurant car. (2) Reservation required. Carries a sleeping car. Also has couchettes. Coach is second-class.

Copenhagen - Stockholm   730

All of these trains require reservation.

Dep. Copenhagen (H.)	11:25 (1)	23:15 (2)
Arr. Stockholm (Cen.)	19:17	07:53

(1) Reservation required. (2) Reservation required. Carries a sleeping car. Also has couchettes. Coach is second-class.

FINLAND

Getting on Track in Finland
• Tourist information: Finnish Tourist Board, 655 Third Avenue, New York, NY 10017. Telephone (212) 885-9737, fax (212) 885-9710. Telephone toll-free in North America: 800-FIN-INFO (346-4636). E mail: (Helsinki, main office): mek@mek.fi. On the Web (these sites are from the UK office) : http://www.finland-tourism.com or http://www.mek.fi
• Public holidays: A list of holidays is helpful because some trains will be noted later in this section as *not* running on holidays. Also, those trains which operate on holidays are filled, and it is necessary to make reservations for them long in advance. Finland's holidays include January 1, New Year's Day, Epiphany, Good Friday, Easter, Easter Monday, May 1, May Day, Ascension Day, Whit Saturday, Whit Sunday, Midsummer Eve, Midsummer's Day (June), All Saint's Day, December 6, Independence Day, December 25, C h r i s t m a s Day, December 26, Boxing Day.
• Currency: Finnish markka (Fmk). At press time, $1 equalled 5.44 Fmk.

Overview of Finland's Trains
Finland's trains are operated by VR Oy (VR Ltd.). There are two classes of service, first and second. Sleeping compartments have one berth in first class, two or three in second class.

The tilting Pendolino S 220 has made its way to Finland. The first route in Finland to offer the Pendolino is the coastal line between Turku and Helsinki.

Finland's Pendolini have a comfortable 1+2 layout, affording extra room over most other trains. The air-conditioned train is equipped with electronic doors, a service for the disabled, info monitors, public telephones, audio entertainment and a separate smoking area. These trains also have an office compartment equipped with a telephone, fax, overhead projector and other technical aids.

Top speed for the Pendolino is 220 km/h; conventional trains travel at 160 km/h. Each car has two places for travelers in wheelchairs.

Many Eurailpass holders arrive in Finland via the country's ancient capital of Turku and connect with the train immediately to the contemporary capital of Helsinki. Finland's national timetable is called Suomen Kulkuneuvot.

The northern line is dependable and mostly tree-lined.

General Rail Information

• Travel on Finnish Express (EP), InterCity (IC) or Pendolino (S 220) trains requires payment of a supplement. In 1997, supplements were based on the distance traveled. For journeys of under 76 km, the Pendolino supplement was 70 Kmk with breakfast or a snack, and 35 Kmk without breakfast or a snack; second class was 20 Kmk. For trips between 76-200 km, the supplement was 75, 40 and 25 Kmk. Supplements were the same for IC trains; on IC trains, an extra 5 Kmk was added to each category for travel over 200 km. Supplements for EP trains were comparable to second-class IC supplements.

• In 1997, per person prices (in addition to fare) for sleepers was 60-90 Kmk in a three-bed compartment, 100-150 Kmk for a two-bed compartment and 200-300 Kmk for a one-bed compartment. The high-end price reflects peak-season travel.

• The tracks in Finland are constructed with the wide Russian gauge of 50". This makes for spacious cars. The rail service extends as far north as Lapland. Service is maintained during severe winter weather. All major Finnish Express trains are equipped with radiotelephones for passenger use.

• Children under six travel free on Finland's trains.

• Contact the railway at these offices in Finland: Helsinki (09) 707 4376, Pasila (09) 707 4243, Espoo (09) 707 5404, Karjaa (019) 276 800, Salo (02) 731 3298, Turku 9600-5000 (there is a charge of 4.65mk/min+ppm for this call).

The signs you will see at rail stations in Finland are:

AIKATAULUT	TIMETABLE
LAHTO	DEPARTURE
LAITURILTA	TRACK
LIPPULUUKKU	TICKET OFFICE
MAKUUVAUNU	SLEEPING CAR
MATKALIPPUJEN MYYNTI	RESERVATIONS
MIEHILLE	MEN
NAISILLE	WOMEN
NEUVONTA (TOIMISTO)	INFORMATION
ODOTUSSALI	CHECKROOM
RAUTATIEASEMALLE	RAIL STATION
RAVINTOLAVAUNU	RESTAURANT CAR
SAAPUMINEN	ARRIVAL
SISAAN	ENTRANCE
TUPAKOITSEVILLE	SMOKING COMPARTMENT
ULOS	EXIT

FINLAND'S TRAIN PASSES

Finnrail Pass The pass offers unlimited rail travel and can be purchased worldwide and at rail stations and ports of arrival in Finland. Besides Rail Europe, these North American sales agents also sell the pass

Scantours, Inc.
3439 Wade Street
Los Angeles, CA 90066-1533
Phone: (800) 223-7226
          (310) 636-4656
Fax: (310) 390-0493
E-mail: scantours@earthlink.net

Norvista
228 E. 45th Street
New York, NY 10017
Phone: (800) 526-4927
Fax: (212) 818-0585

Scanam World Tours
933 Highway Twenty-Three
Pompton Plains, NJ 07444
Phone: (800) 545-2204
Fax: (973) 835-3030

Marketing Challenges International
10 East 21st Street, Suite 600
New York, NY 10010
Phone: (800) 869-8184
Phone: (212) 529-9069
Fax: (212) 529-4838

First-class prices for a 1998 Finnrail Pass are:

	Adults	
	First Cl.	Second Cl.
3 days in one month	$185	$123
5 days in one month	$248	$166
10 days in one month	$340	$226

Children between 6-16 pay half price. Under six, free. **NOTE:** Only the three-day pass is sold in North America.

Senior Citizens Card Travelers over age 65 may buy regular one-way or round-trip rail tickets for half-price, by showing their passport as proof of age.

Group Reduction Group tickets are sold for parties of at least three persons. The members of groups of 3-10 persons receive a 20 percent discount on single tickets, those of groups of at least 11 persons 25 percent. Round-trip tickets are sold at twice the price of a single ticket. Single tickets are valid for eight days and return tickets for one month.

Child Reduction Up to four children under six may travel free of charge in the company of a passenger who is at least 17 years old. Children's tickets for those between 6-16 years cost half the adult fare. A half fare is also charged for children under six if a separate seat is reserved for them.

Holiday Pass This pass is good for unlimited travel throughout Finland and provides a second-class compartment on the train, plus a two-night-stay at a SOKOS hotel. Purchase in North America through Rahim Tours or from Finnish Railways in Finland. The Holiday Pass is valid between June 1 and August 31. Call the tourist office or North American agents Norvista or Scanam World Tours for 1998 prices.

ONE-DAY EXCURSIONS AND CITY-SIGHTSEEING

Here are eight one-day rail trips that can be made comfortably from Helsinki, returning there in most cases before dinnertime. Notes are provided on what to see and do at each destination. The number after the name of each route is the *Cook's Timetable* reference.

Helsinki

Helsinki's single most inspiring sight is Temppeliaukio Church, known since its 1969 dedication as the "Rock Church." This fantastic structure was quarried on its site, out of the bedrock in the middle of one of the oldest residential districts of Helsinki. Because the area occupied by worshipers is below the street level, all that can be seen as you walk toward the church is a low rock wall and the massive (70-foot diameter) copper dome.

Also see the large tubular steel sculpture, symbolizing music, in Sibelius Park. Tapiola, the model "new town." Finlandia Hall. The National Museum (closed Mondays September through May). The floral cemetery. The onion towers on the Greek Orthodox Uspenski Cathedral.

It is best to visit Market Square before Noon, to see the flowers, fish and mountains of berries. Also see the Helsinki Town Hall. The Empress Stone obelisk. (Ferries from a pier near the obelisk go every hour to the island Suomenlinna Fortress.) See the impressive columns of Parliament House. The University Library and the cathedral, in Senate Square.

The paintings and sculptures in the National Art Gallery. The National Theater. The Elaintarhantie shopping complex, opposite the rail station. The rail station itself should be on your visitation list, more than just a place to hop a train. According to a travel writer just back from Helsinki, the station was noted in a *Michlen* guide as worthy of special trip. Designed by Eliel Saarinen, the U-shaped cluster of granite-walled copper-topped buildings, complete with a 179-foot-high clock tower, have withstood political ups and downs (it took forever–years–to approve final designs), wars and fires; today it is a major Helsinki landmark. Have a relaxing meal in the spacious restaurant, Eliel's, named after the designer, or Mathilda's, a first-class restaurant upstairs, and contemplate the history that's passes through these halls since the station's official March 1919 opening.

Other places to visit include the botanical gardens, in Elaintarha Park, the Linnanmaki amusement center (closed Mondays) and the collection of Finnish wood houses at the open-air Museum of Seurasaari.

These museums and attractions are also worth a visit: Ateneum Art Gallery, Gallen-Kallela Museum, the art and furniture at the Helsinki Municipal Museum, the old-fashioned and modern farm tools and implements in the agricultural museum and the Military Museum (Maurinkatu 1.) There are good views of the South Harbor and the waterfront from Observatory Hill (Tahtitornin Vuori). See the displays in the Architectural Museum of Finland (Puistokatu 4).

Take the #6 tram to Arabia and see the original site of Helsinki, Old Town. Take the ferry from North Harbor to the Korkeasaari Island Zoo.

Helsinki - Hameenlinna - Helsinki   790

All of these trains have light refreshments, unless designated otherwise.

Dep. Helsinki	06:58	07:58 (1)	08:58	09:58 (2)	10:58	11:58 (3)
Arr. Hameenlinna	65-75 minutes later					

Sights in **Hameenlinna**: The medieval castle. Ahvenisto Tower. The art museum and municipal museum.

Dep. Hameenlinna	11:47	12:46 (1)	13:50	14:50	15:47 (2)	17:49 (1+4)
Arr. Helsinki	65-75 minutes later					

(1) Supplement payable. Restaurant car. (2) Restaurant car. (3) Plus additional Helsinki departures at frequent times until 23:02. (4) Plus other Hameenlinna departures at frequent times until 22:58.

Helsinki - Hanko - Helsinki   791 + Finnish timetable

A beautiful ride through woods and along lakes.

All of the trains Helsinki–Karjaa and v.v. have light refreshments.

Dep. Helsinki	06:34	09:06 (1)	11:06
Arr. Karjaa	07:34	10:01	12:05
Change to local train			
Dep. Karjaa	07:44	10:08	12:18
Arr. Hanko	08:28	10:52	13:02

Sights in **Hanko**: The southernmost town in Finland. The tourist office is open all year Monday–Friday, 09:00–16:00 and in summer also on Saturday 09:00–16:00, Sunday 11:00–15:00. Take a two-hour cruise, leaving from the eastern harbor, operating June through mid-August. There is good fishing here. See the statue dedicated to the many Finns who disembarked from here to migrate to the United States between 1880 and 1930. Dance or try your luck at the casino.

Dep. Hanko	14:25	16:12	21:06
Arr. Karjaa	15:25	16:56	21:50
Change to a standard train			
Dep. Karjaa	15:22	17:05	22:02
Arr. Helsinki	16:30	18:02	23:10

(1) Pendolino. Reservation required. Supplement charged. Light refreshments.

Helsinki - Lahti - Helsinki   795

All of these trains have light refreshments, unless designated otherwise.

| Dep. Helsinki | 07:02 | 08:02 | 09:08 (1) | 10:26 | 11:22 | 12:25 (2) |
| Arr. Lahti | 08:28 | 09:29 | 11:00 | 11:56 | 12:49 | 13:51 |

Sights in **Lahti**: A winter sports center. The tourist office (closed Sunday) is in the rear of the Lahti Town Hall (intersection of Vesijarvenkatu and Aleksanterinkatu). See the view from the top of the 90-meter-high ski jump, its elevators operating June through September, 10:00–19:30. It is only a 10-minute walk from the Town Hall.

Visit the art gallery. The Ethnographic Museum. The Radio Museum, open Sundays 13:00–15:00. In summer, there are open-air concerts at the Mukkula Tourist Center. Shop here for marvelous Finnish glassware.

| Dep. Lahti | 12:07 | 14:05 (1) | 14:58 | 16:34 (2) | 17:36 | 18:30 (3) |
| Arr. Helsinki | 13:32 | 15:50 | 16:28 | 18:06 | 19:06 | 19:56 |

(1) Second class. No light refreshments. (2) Runs daily, except Saturday. No light refreshments. (3) Plus other Lahti departures at 19:27 (1), 19:57 (4), 20:41 and 21:31. (4) Runs Sunday only. Reservation *required*.

Helsinki - Riihimaki - Helsinki   795

| Dep. Helsinki | Frequent times from 06:00 to 23:12 |
| Arr. Riihimaki | 50-70 minutes later |

Sights in **Riihimaki**: The woodworking mills of H.G. Paloheimo. The glass factories of Riihimaen Lasi Oy. The Museum Peltosaari. The Riihimaki Municipal Museum.

| Dep. Riihimaki | Frequent times from 05:55 to 22:06 |
| Arr. Helsinki | 50 minutes later |

Helsinki - Rovaniemi   790

A trip to Lapland.

Dep. Helsinki	06:58 (1)	09:58 (2)	19:24 (1+3)	22:30 (4)
Arr. Rovaniemi	16:44	20:05	07:42	11:09

Dep. Rovaniemi	07:00 (3)	13:00 (1)	18:05 (1+3)	20:10 (1+5)	21:05 (1+3)
Arr. Helsinki	17:02	23:02	07:08	08:15	08:30

(1) Light refreshments. (2) Restaurant car. (3) Carries first- and second-class sleeping cars and second-class coaches. (4) Runs from early August. Carries first- and second-class sleepers and second-class coaches. (5) Runs Fridays and Sundays. Carries first- and second-class sleepers and second-class coaches.

Helsinki - Savonlinna   795

Dep. Helsinki	07:02 (1)	10:26 (1)	17:02 (2)
Arr. Parikkala	10:52	14:36	21:05
Change trains			
Dep. Parikkala	10:55	15:00 (3)	21:05
Arr. Savonlinna	11:46	16:15	21:56

Sights in **Savonlinna**: A charming town in the lake region, near the Russian border. The tourist office (Olavinkatu 35) is open in summer daily 07:15–22:00. There is an English-language guided tour at Olavinlinna, a medieval castle. Shop for food at the open-air market.

Dep. Savonlinna	06:15	13:38 (3)	17:00 (4)
Arr. Parikkala	07:06	14:31	17:51
Change trains			
Dep. Parikkala	07:11 (2)	15:00 (1)	18:02 (1)
Arr. Helsinki	10:58	19:06	22:04

(1) Light refreshments. (2) Reservation *required*. Restaurant car. (3) Runs through August. (4) Runs daily except Sundays and holidays.

Helsinki - Tampere - Helsinki   790

All of these trains have light refreshments, unless designated otherwise.

Dep. Helsinki	06:58	07:58 (1)	08:58	09:58 (1)	10:58	11:58
Arr. Tampere	2 hours later					

Sights in **Tampere**: The aquarium, planetarium, children's zoo, amusement park, observation tower and planetarium at the Sarkanniemi Recreation Center. The more than 30,000 objects exhibited in the Hame Museum, particularly the handwoven rugs and tapestries. Many excellent artworks, frescoes and the altarpiece in the cathedral, completed in 1907. The fine modern architecture of Kaleva Church. The National History Museum. The Haihara Doll Museum. The largest church bells in Finland, at the Orthodox church.

See a performance at Tampere's Summer Theater in Pyynikki Park, from a seat in the unique bowl-shaped auditorium that rotates 360 degrees. Everyone sitting in the last row at the beginning of a performance also has a front-row seat during the show.

Dep. Tampere	12:00 (1)	13:02	14:02	15:00 (1)	15:58	17:06 (2+3)
Arr. Helsinki	2 hours later					

(1) Restaurant car. (2) Supplement payable. Restaurant car. (3) Plus other departures from Tampere at 18:00 (1), 18:34, 19:54, 20:14 (4), 21:02 and 22:10 (1). (4) Reservation *required.* Runs Friday and Sunday.

Helsinki - Turku - Helsinki　791

All of these trains have light refreshments.

Dep. Helsinki	06:34	09:06	11:06
Arr. Turku (Stn.)	08:34	10:56	13:06

Sights in **Turku:** A "Turku Card," good for city buses, museum admissions and discounts in restaurants and shops is sold at the City Tourist Office, near Market Square, at Kasityolaiskatu 4.

See the Provincial Museum and the marvelous Banquet Hall in the 13th-century castle, a short walk from the Silja Lane rail station, only a few minutes ride past the main rail station. The castle is open 10:00–18:00 May–September, 11:00–15:00 the rest of the year. There's a great organ (6,057 pipes) in the 13th-century cathedral.

The composer's instruments and personal possessions in the Sibelius Museum. The cobbled marketplace (fruits, flowers, fish and produce), Monday Saturday 08:00–14:00

Dep. Turku (Stn.)	13:08	15:50	17:32	19:58	21:20
Helsinki	14:58	18:02	19:34	22:02	23:34

INTERNATIONAL ROUTES
FROM FINLAND

Helsinki is the gateway both to Russia (Leningrad, and on to Moscow) and Western Scandinavia (Stockholm, and on to Oslo and Copenhagen). Oulu is the starting point for trips to northern Sweden (Boden) and northern Norway (Narvik).

Helsinki - St. Petersburg 1910

Finland is the gateway to the East. It's easy to purchase tickets for this trip at the rail station in Helsinki or at a travel agency. In 1997, a one-way second-class adult ticket to St. Petersburg (included seat reservation), cost 288 Fmk. A one-way first-class ticket with a berth was 522 Fmk. Don't forget, though, if you're traveling with a Eurailpass or Scanrail Pass, you can use those passes to the Russian border and save yourself some money.

These trains require reservation and have a restaurant car.

Dep. Helsinki	06:30	15:34
Arr. St. Petersburg (Fin.)	13:30	22:50

Helsinki - Moscow 1910

As with the trip to St. Petersburg, you can buy tickets to Moscow in Finland as well. In 1997, a one-way second-class adult ticket to Moscow that included a berth, cost 523 Fmk. A one-way first-class ticket with a berth was 781 Fmk.

This train carries a sleeping car and a restaurant car.

Dep. Helsinki	17:26	Arr. Moscow	08:38

Helsinki - Stockholm 791, 2480

The price for the cruise across the Gulf of Bothnia (Turku-Stockholm) on the comfortable and pleasant Silja Line ships *is* covered by Eurailpass. The fare for a sleeping cabin is *not* covered by Eurailpass—but only for those who reserve and pay for a bed. Food on the ship is varied and delicious.

We recommend the daytime sailing in order to see the thousands of tiny islands on the ride through this extremely interesting archipelago. During the daytime cruise, there is a good smorgasbord for both lunch and dinner. On the night cruise, a live band plays music in the ship's nightclub. On both day and night cruises, the major activity is duty-free shopping.

490 Train			*2480 Ship*		
Dep. Helsinki	06:34 (1)	17:34 (1)	Dep. Turku (Abo)	09:15	21:15
Arr. Turku (Harbor)	08:50	19:42	*Set watch back one hour*		
Walk to Abo Pier			Arr. Stockholm (Var.) 19:00		07:00

(1) Light refreshments.

Helsinki - Oulu - Haparanda - Boden - Narvik   765, 769, 790, 795

790

Dep. Helsinki	06:58 (1)	12:58 (2)	19:24 (3)	22:30 (3)
Arr. Oulu	13:52	20:03	04:16	07:32

Sights in **Oulu:** Interesting art and zoological museum here. See the cathedral. The water tower, on top of Puolivalinkangas is open May-October. Picturesque, ancient waterfront warehouses. Visit the open-air museum and Kastelli Church.

790

Dep. Oulu	14:05	20:18	04:40	08:00
Arr. Kemi	15:13	21:23	05:55	09:19
Change to bus 769				
Dep. Kemi	15:20	-0-	06:42 (5)	09:23 (5)
Arr. Tornio	15:50	-0-	07:10	09:55
Walk to Haparanda bus station (about 800 meters)				
Dep Tornio	-0-	-0-	-0-	-0-
Set your watch back one hour				
Arr. Haparanda	-0-	-0-	-0-	-0-
Change buses 769				
Dep. Haparanda	16:05 (4)	-0-	07:40	10:00 (6)
Arr. Boden	18:15	-0-	09:55	12:55

We recommend stopping-over in Boden for the night so as to travel Boden–Narvik during the daylight hours in order to see the fine mountain scenery on that route. You cross the Arctic Circle going from Boden to Narvik.

Change to train 765					
Dep. Boden	07:50 (7)	10:40	-0-	-0-	-0-
Arr. Kiruna	11:07	14:02	-0-	-0-	-0-
Dep Kiruna	11:22	14:12	-0-	-0-	-0-
Arr. Narvik	14:05	17:25	-0-	-0-	-0-

(1) Light refreshments. (2) Restaurant car. (3) Carries sleeping cars and second-class coaches. (4) Runs Sundays only. The next departure is at 17:40 arriving Boden 20:00; this bus runs daily. (5) Runs daily, except Sundays and holidays. (6) Runs Monday-Friday except holidays. (7) Reservation *required.* Restaurant car.

NORWAY

Getting on Track in Norway

• Tourist information: Norwegian Information Service, 825 Third Avenue, New York, NY 10022. Telephone (212) 421-7333, fax (212) 688-0554. On the Web (this site is based out of the Oslo office): http://www.unginfo.oslo.no/index.htm.

• Public holidays: A list of holidays is helpful because some trains will be noted later in this section as *not* running on holidays. Also, those trains which operate on holidays are filled, and it is necessary to make reservations for them long in advance. These holidays are celebrated in Norway: January 1, New Year's Day, Maundy Thursday, Good Friday, Easter, Easter Monday, May 1, Labor Day, Ascension Day, May 17, Constitution Day, Whit Monday, December 25, Christmas Day and December 26, Boxing Day.

• Currency: Norwegian kroner (Nkr). At press time, $1 equalled 7.58 Nkr.

Overview of Norway's Trains

Trains in Norway are run by Norges Statsbaner (NSB). All trains carry second-class coaches and certain trains carry first-class coaches as well. Sleeping compartments have one, two or three berths. Couchettes are available on international routes and some trains have coaches with fully reclining seats. Norway's second-class cars are better than many first-class coaches in other countries. And, if you're taking an overnight train, it is often possible to gain access to your compartment up to two hours before departure (if you're leaving from a terminal station) and then stay in your compartment for some extra shut-eye or breakfast, until 08:00 on the morning of your arrival, even if the train pulled into the station at 06:00.

Norway's train service extends to the very top of the country in the Land of the Midnight Sun and to the western port of Bergen. Rail is a delightful way of touring the country, and Norway can rightfully boast that it has the most number of scenic rail trips of any Scandinavian country. Norway is among the most glorious places in which to experience the wonder of the Midnight Sun.

General Rail Information

• Norway has five varieties of fast and express trains: Ekspresstog (Et), InterCity (EC), InterCity Express (IC), InterNord (IN) and InterNordNight (INN). Reservations are required on Et, ICE, IN and INN trains except for certain local services.

• There are three types of supplements charged for travel on ICE trains: Economy, Business without a meal and Business with a meal. In 1997, they ranged from 20 Nkr for Economy to 120 Nkr for service with a meal. Seat reservations are required on many ICE departures. Check individual schedules for this information.

• The following per-person supplements were in effect for overnight trains in 1997: Seat, 20 Nkr, fully reclining seat 50 Nkr (Oslo - Trondheim - Bodø), couchette 50 Nkr (Only Oslo-Kristiansand-Stavanger), bed in a three-bed compartment 100 Nkr (except Oslo - Trondheim via Dombås), bed in a two-bed compartment 200-250 Nkr (depending on equipment), bed in a one-bed compartment 400 to 500 Nkr. Breakfast is included for passengers travelling in a one-bed or two-bed compartment.

• Children under four travel free. Half-fare for children 4-15. Children 16 and over must pay full fare.

• Norwegian State Railways have one coach on the Oslo-Bergen and Bergen-Oslo runs (and similar service on other long-distance routes) designed for conveying disabled persons and other passengers requiring special care, such as mothers traveling with young children. These special cars have a compartment accommodating two wheelchairs that are lifted aboard. An eight-seat compartment in these cars, equipped for mothers and their infants, is provided with a baby-chair, bottle heater, and other equipment helpful when caring for small children. This compartment is adjacent to a space with fitted toilets and a diaper-changing table. The car also has oxygen tanks, a stretcher and a small wheelchair for disabled persons to use in moving about inside the train.

• From Dombås and on north, you are in the land of the Midnight Sun. (See Midnight Sun Calendar.)

The signs you will see at rail stations in Norway are:

ANKOMIST	ARRIVAL
AVGANG	DEPARTURE
BANESTASJONEN	RAIL STATION
BILLETLUKEN	TICKET OFFICE
DAMER	WOMEN
GARDEROBEN	CHECKROOM
HERRER	MEN
INFORMASJON	INFORMATION
INGANG	ENTRANCE
RESERVASJONSLUKEN	RESERVATIONS
ROKERE	SMOKING COMPARTMENT
SOVEVOGN	SLEEPING CAR
SPISEVOGN	RESTAURANT CAR
SPOR	TRACK
TIL PLATTFORMENTE	TO THE PLATFORMS
TOGTABELL	TIMETABLE
UTGANG	EXIT
VEKSLIGSKONTOR	CURRENCY EXCHANGE
VINDUSPLASS	WINDOW SEAT

EURAILPASS BONUSES

In 1997, Eurailpass holders received a 30 percent reduction on the normal fares of the Color Line Steamship Company for the cruise between Kristiansand and Hirtshals (Denmark) and a 20 percent discount on the normal fares on trips via the steamship company Scandinavian Seaways between Oslo and Copenhagen.

NORWAY'S TRAIN PASSES

Norway Rail Pass This pass offers unlimited train travel in Norway. In 1998, a first-class pass for any three days in one month is $175, second class $135. A pass that's good for seven consecutive days of travel is $250 first class, $195 second class. The 14 consecutive-day pass is $335 first class, $255 second class. Children under 16 pay half fare and children under four are free (up to two children per adult provided seat reservations, or sleeper supplements are not required). Rail Europe and DER Travel sell the pass as do travel agencies and Scanam World tours, 933 Highway Twenty-Three, Pompton Plains, NJ 07444. Telephone: (800) 545-2204, fax (201) 835-3030.

Few trains offer first class in Norway, so it might be more cost-effective to purchase second-class pass and pay a small supplement for upgrading to standard class. Trains Et61/Et601/Et602/Et63/Et603/Et64 between Oslo and Bergen offer extra value for first-class passholders.

All of the following train passes can be purchased only at Norwegian rail stations.

"Green Departures" are at times when traffic volume is low. All of the following discounts are restricted to "Green Departures," marked with a green dot in Norwegian timetables.

Senior Citizen Discount Persons over 67 years old are allowed a 50 percent discount on both first-class and second-class tickets. Must obtain an ID card, available at rail stations.

Mini-Price Tickets These tickets are for trips longer than 150 km on "green" departure days. You must order the ticket no later than the day before traveling. Children under 16 years get a 50 percent discount. Mini-Price seats are limited and may not always be available. Great savings are often available by purchasing two Mini-Price tickets instead of a regular round-trip ticket. For example, the special one-way point-to-point price Oslo to Bergen, Trondheim, Kristiansand or Andalsnes would cost between between $57 and $77.

Joker Ticket The Joker is a special discount one-way-travel ticket between the largest cities. In 1997, a Joker cost 270 Nkr, and was valid in second class with seat reservation included. Seats allocated for Joker tickets are limited and may not be available.

Customer Card The holder of this card receives a 50 percent discount on green departures and 30 percent off regular second-class fares. In 1998, it will sell for $60 and is valid for one year.

Children An adult can bring two children under 12 years old free of charge on green departures. There's no charge for children under four.

ONE-DAY EXCURSIONS AND CITY-SIGHTSEEING

Here are 15 one-day rail trips that can be made comfortably from Bergen, Oslo and Stavanger, returning to them at or shortly after dinnertime. Notes are provided on what to see and do at each destination. The number after the name of each route is the *Cook's Timetable*.

In the following timetables, where a city has more than one rail station, we have designated the particular station after the name of the city (in parentheses).

Oslo

Pick up an "Oslo Card" for free admission to most Oslo museums and the Tusen Fryd amusement park, rides on public city boats, buses, trams, subways and commuter trains. Discounts of up to 50 percent are offered on sightseeing tours, theaters and the opera. The card is sold in one- two- and three-day increments and is available at most Oslo hotels, the Tourist Offices, Norway Information Center, and Oslo's Central rail station.

Walk from the rail station, up Karl Johansgate, to the Royal Palace. En route, you will pass the National Theater. Behind it is the underground suburban train station. See the massive mural, in the post World War II City Hall, commemorating the Nazi occupation of Norway.

From the pier behind City Hall, take the four-minute boat ride to Bygdoy (or take Bus #30 from the center of town) to see the interesting museums there: Viking Ship Museum (daily 09:00–18:00); Kon Tiki Museum for a look at reed Ra II rafts used by Thor Heyerdahl to recreate ancient voyages (daily 09:00–18:00); Polarship Fram, for Roald Amunden's polar exploration ship Fram; the Norwegian Maritime Museum (daily 09:00–17:45); and the outdoor collection of 170 historical buildings brought to Oslo from all over Norway along with more than 80,000 items exhibited in the Norwegian Folk Museum (daily 10:00-18:00). It's about a 20-minute walk from the Maritime Museum to the Viking ships and the Folk Museum.

Later, see the bronze and granite sculptures of Gustav Vigeland in Frogner Park. Its highlight is a 55-foot-high monolith that has 121 intertwined figures. The Vigeland Museum at Nobelsgate 32. The collection of 1,100 Munch paintings and 18,000 Munch prints in the Edvard Munch Museum (53 Toyengata). The Historical Museum. Norway's largest art collection, at the National Gallery (13 Univesitetsgaten), open Monday and Wednesday-Saturday 10:00-16:00, Sunday 11:00-14:00. Oslo Cathedral.

Visit Aker Brygge (pier), a huge entertainment, shopping and residential project. The Museum of Applied Art. The 12th-century stone Gamle Aker Church (open Tuesday and Thursday in summer).

The Resistance Museum and Defense Museum (commemorating the German occupation of Norway during World War II) in the Hjemmefront, at the 14th-century Akershus Castle and Fortress, only a five-minute walk from City Hall.

The Sonja Henie-Nils Onstad collection of modern paintings at Henie-Onstad Art Center (Monday-Saturday 09:00–22:00, Sunday 11:00–22:00). The Museum of Contemporary Art, opened in 1991. Marvelous views of Oslo and the Fjord from the Ski Jump and Ski Museum at Holmenkollen. Take the trolley to the Merchant Marine Academy at Sjomannsskolen. Take Bus #36 from Town Hall Square for a one-hour ride to **Sundvollen**. Beautiful Tyri Fjord scenery.

Oslo - Goteborg - Oslo 770

All of these trains require reservation and have a restaurant car.

| Dep. Oslo (Sen.) | 07:37 | | Dep. Goteborg | 15:00 | 18:00 |
| Arr. Goteborg | 12:03 | | Arr. Oslo (Sen.) | 19:52 | 22:18 |

Oslo - Hamar - Oslo   785

Be sure to sit on the left side for the best view of the fantastic scenery along the western shore of **Lake Mjosa**. Norway's largest lake (75 miles long).

All of these trains have light refreshments and are second-class, unless designated otherwise.

Dep. Oslo (Sen.)	08:05 (1)	09:00	10:35	13:05	15:02
Arr. Hamar	09:41	10:45	12:23	14:46	16:50

Sights in **Hamar**: The enormous outdoor Hedmark Museum complex of more than 40 buildings, most of them from the 18th and 19th century, brought here from other places. One of the buildings is a house built in 1871 in North Dakota, U.S.A., by a Norwegian emigrant.

Also visit the 7½-acre Railway Museum, open May–September, to see many early coaches and locomotives as well as Norway's first rail station.

Dep. Hamar	13:00 (2)	15:07	17:09	19:13	20:28 (2+3)
Arr. Oslo (Sen.)	14:55	16:56	18:55	20:56	22:10

(1) Reservation *required*. Has first-class coach seats. Restaurant car. (2) Runs Sunday only. (3) Plus another Hamar departure at 20:53 (1), arriving Oslo 22:25.

Oslo - Lillehammer - Oslo   785

All of these trains have light refreshments and are second-class, unless designated otherwise.

Dep. Oslo (Sen.)	08:05 (1)	09:00	10:35
Arr. Lillehammer	10:21	11:35	13:13

Sights in **Lillehammer**: Site of the 1994 Winter Olympic Games. Visit the Sandvig collection of more than 100 old buildings and craftwork demonstrations at the 100-acre open-air Maihaugen Museum, open daily 11:00–19:00 from late June to early August and 11:00–14:00 the rest of the year. See the "White Swan" paddle-wheel steamboat, Skibladner, at the city's dock.

Dep. Lillehammer	12:40 (1)	14:19	16:20	18:21	20:11 (1)
Arr. Oslo (Sen.)	14:55	16:56	18:55	20:56	22:25

(1) Reservation *required*. Has first-class coach. Restaurant car.

Oslo - Vinstra - Oslo   785

All of these trains have light refreshments and are second class, unless designated otherwise

Dep. Oslo (Sen.)	08:05 (1)	10:35
Arr. Vinstra	11:20	14:21

Sights in Vinstra: A mountain resort. Home of the legendary Peer Gynt. See the memorial over his grave in the village church. Cross-country skiing is popular here.

Dep. Vinstra	11:39 (1)	17:10	18:21 (2)	19:04 (1)
Arr. Oslo (Sen.)	14:55	20:56	22:10	22:25

(1) Reservation *required.* Has first-class coach. (2) Runs Sunday only.

THE FJORD TRAIN ROUTE

Oslo - Drammen - Tonsberg - Sandefjord - Larvik - Skien - Nordagutu - Oslo 778, 779

This one-day excursion offers great views of several fjords (starting with the Oslofjord), wooded countryside, and lovely lakes. As the schedules indicate, stops can be made for sightseeing in several of the towns on this route.

All of these trains are second class and have light refreshments Oslo-Skien (and v.v.), unless designated otherwise.
   A train change in Skien (Table 779) is necessary in both directions.

Oslo (Sen.)	06:21 (1)	09:09	11:09	13:09	14:18 (3+4)
Dep. Drammen	07:07	09:50	11:50	13:50	15:00
Dep. Tonsberg	08:05	10:43	12:42	14:42	16:01
Dep. Sandefjord	08:23	11:02	13:02	15:07	16:22
Dep. Larvik	08:40	11:18	13:18	15:22	16:44
Arr. Skien	09:24	12:06	14:04	16:12	17:28
Dep. Skien	10:10	12:15	14:10 (2)	-0-	18:33 (3)
Arr. Nordagutu	10:43	12:46	14:42	-0-	19:06

• • •

Dep. Nordagutu	09:06 (2)	10:56	12:58	14:18 (2)	16:45 (5)
Arr. Skien	09:38	11:31	13:30	14:56	17:28
Dep. Skien	09:53	11:54	13:40	15:40	17:48
Dep. Larvik	10:41	12:41	14:29	16:28	18:40
Dep. Sandefjord	11:00	12:59	14:46	16:51	18:55
Dep. Tonsberg	11:19	13:18	15:09	17:12	19:14
Dep. Drammen	12:10	14:10	16:10	18:10	20:10
Arr. Oslo (Sen.)	12:51	14:51	16:51	18:43	20:54

(1) Runs Mondays-Saturdays except holidays. No light refreshments. (2) Runs Monday-Friday except holidays. Does not run from late June to early August. (3) Runs Monday-Friday except holidays. (4) Plus other departures from Oslo at 15:09, arriving Nordagutu 19:06 (3). (5) Plus another departure from Nordagutu at 19:40, arriving Oslo 22:50.

Sights in **Drammen**: The activity along the busy docks. Many attractive old buildings. Watching the Drommensfjorden meet the Drammen River.

Sights in **Tonsberg**: Norway's oldest town. See today's whaling ships and the ruins of an ancient Viking castle, Tonsberghus. Also, the Vestfold Museum, the 12th-century St. Michael's Church, the 12th-century Sem Church, and the 13th-century Royal Castle.

Sights in **Sandefjord**: The main port for Norway's whaling ships. See the whaling monument in the square. The Whaling Museum. Nearby are the mouth of the Oslofjorden and the head of the Sandefjorden.

Sights in **Larvik**: Visit the town's museum; enjoy the sights along the fjord.

Sights in **Skien**: The large sawmill operations. The meeting of Skien River and Lake Hjelle.

"NORWAY IN A NUTSHELL"

The easiest way to take the Myrdal-Flam scenic train ride is to buy either one of the one-day "Norway in a Nutshell" packages. The Bergen round trip includes the train Bergen–Myrdal, the Flam Line cogwheel train Myrdal–Flam, the fjord boat trip Flam–Gudvangen, the bus Gudvangen–Voss, and the train from Voss back to Bergen. Total trip time: 7 to 9 hours.

The Oslo round trip includes the train Oslo–Myrdal, the "Flam Line" cogwheel train Myrdal–Flam, the fjord boat trip Flam–Gudvangen, the bus Gudvangen–Voss, and the train from Voss back to Oslo. Total trip time: 15 hours.

These companies can arrange the Norway in a Nutshell package for you before leaving the States.

Passage Tours of Scandinavia	Nordique Tours
239 Commercial Boulevard	5250 West Century Boulevard, Suite 626
Ft. Lauderdale, FL 33308	Los Angeles, CA 90045
Tel. (800) 548-5960	Tel. (800) 995-7997
Fax (954) 776-7188	Fax (310) 645-1071

When these packages are purchased in Norway, either a Eurailpass or a Scanrailpass can be used for all of the train rides, reducing the prices above substantially. Note that Eurailpass holders must now pay a supplement to ride the Flam. Check with NSB for current charges.

Sights in **Bergen**: Free admission to most Bergen museums, rides on the funicular to the top of Mt. Flojen, and discounts at cinemas, theaters, concerts, sightseeing, boat excursions, parking and car rental with "Bergen Card." Sold at Bergen hotels, Tourist Information and the bus station.

Visit Torget, a fish market that has been operating for nine centuries (weekdays: 08:30–15:00). See Bergenhus Fortress, with its 13th-century Hakon Hall. The 12th-century Maria-kirken (St. Mary's Church). Europe's most modern aquarium and the collection of 19th-century houses in Gamle Bergen (Old Bergen). Edvard Grieg's home in **Troldhaugen**.

Take the five-minute funicular ride to the top of 2,000-foot-high **Mt. Floien**. See the

Hanseatic Museum. The Maritime Museum. The Arts and Crafts Museum. The Bryggen Museum. The Leprosy Museum. Take the cable car to the top of **Mt. Ulriken**.

It is only 22 minutes for the bus ride and short walk to see the 13th-century Fana Church and Fantoft, the 12th-century Stave Church.

SCENIC RAIL TRIPS

Bergen to Oslo...and The Stalheim-Flam Detour   780

Indisputably, the most scenic rail route in Europe. There are several ways to make the detour, either in a single day or by adding one or two days to the Bergen-Oslo trip.

The most carefree way to make the detour in a single day is to check baggage direct from Bergen to Oslo, rather than be bothered with it all day.

The complete Bergen–Oslo line was opened in 1909 as the only year-round land transportation between Norway's two largest cities. It was electrified in 1964. Terrain and climate both caused construction problems which prior to then had never been encountered in building a railway line. The 300-mile length of track must pass through 200 tunnels and 18 miles of snow sheds in addition to crossing more than 300 bridges.

The first 40 minutes after leaving Bergen is along the lovely Sorfjorden. Travelers are frustrated by the interruptions of viewing the scenery caused by the many snow sheds.

However, it would be impossible for the trains to operate daily year round on this route and stick to a strict timetable if it were not for these structures.

When taking the Voss-Stalheim–Flam–Myrdal detour we have been recommending since 1971, you omit the 63-minute Voss–Myrdal portion of the main Bergen–Oslo line.

Voss - Stalheim - Flam - Myrdal Detour   780, 781

The Gudvangen-Flam cruise on the Sognefjord (called "King of the Fjords:") is the most scenic fjord trips in Norway.

780		780	
Dep. Bergen	07:33 (1)	Dep. Oslo (Sen.)	07:42 (1)
Arr. Flam	08:38	Arr. Myrdal	12:25
Change to bus		*Change to narrow-gauge train 781*	
Dep. Voss	09:50	Dep. Myrdal	12:32
Arr. Stalheim	10:25	Arr. Flam	13:30
Dep. Stalheim	10:35	*Change to fjord boat*	
Arr. Gudvangen		Dep. Flam	14:30
Change to fjord boat		Arr. Gudvangen	16:35

Dep. Gudvangen	11:30		*Change to bus*	
Arr. Flam	13:30		Dep. Gudvangen	16:55
Change to narrow-gauge train 781			Arr. Stalheim	17:40
Dep. Flam	13:45		Dep. Stalheim	17:50
Arr. Myrdal	14:38		Arr. Voss	18:10
Change trains 780			*Change to train 780*	
Dep. Myrdal	16:58 (1)		Dep Voss	19:00
Arr. Oslo (Sen.)	21:55		Arr. Bergen	20:19

(1) Reservation *required.* Restaurant car.

Sights in **Voss**: The 13th-century church. The restored farmhouses and other buildings in the outdoor folk museum.

NOTE: On the Oslo-Bergen route (right-hand column above), there are only seven minutes to change trains in Myrdal. *In mid-summer, hundreds of people compete for the few seats on the Flam Line train.* Bus tour groups which board the Flam Line in Vatnahalsen (three minutes after Myrdal) have to stand, which is very difficult on this route.

En route Bergen-Oslo, the one-hour bus ride from Voss to **Stalheim** passes (on your left) the spectacular Tvinde waterfall. At Stalheim there is only a Norwegian village museum and a hotel—which we recommended with high praise for 23 years.

Sadly, we have received reports from readers that the hotel is concentrating its services on tour groups. Its management is discouraging individual travelers.

Those traveling independently were told there were no porters to help with luggage and that they could not be seated in the dining room until groups were finished with lunch, by which time the fabled smorgasbord had been decimated.

The journey via Stalheim is still recommended. The change is withdrawing our recommendation about staying or dining at the hotel. For the same reason, we also no longer recommend staying at the Fretheim Hotel in Flam.

If you do decide to stay at the hotel anyway, you'll see is a view here of such magnificence that Kaiser Wilhelm II came to Stalheim annually for 25 years to look at it.

The land here has been farmed since 400 A.D. Some facility for food and lodging has existed here since 1647 when mail was carried by Norway's "pony express" from Bergen to Oslo, and Stalheim was one of the stations for changing horses and riders, right up until 1900.

An inn was operated at Stalheim before 1700. The first hotel here, constructed in 1885, burned in 1900. A second hotel, built in 1901, met the same fate in 1902. Another hotel, constructed and used first in Voss, was moved to Stalheim in 1906, enlarged in 1912, and burned down in 1959.

The present Stalheim Hotel was built in the winter of 1959–60 and enlarged in 1967 to its present capacity of 130 units, ranging from single rooms to doubles and then suites consisting of a double room plus sitting-room with fireplace. Stalheim can accommodate 219 guests, and it is filled nearly every day in its April-September operation with tour groups.

The terrace of the hotel provides a view over the Naro, Brekke and Jordal valleys, the Sivle and Stalheim waterfalls, and the conical peak of Mt. Jordal.

Two mounds on the right-hand side of the hotel's terrace date from 800 A.D. These were opened in 1890, revealing the remains of a woman who had been buried with her frying-pan, loom, bronze brooches and bracelets and the remains of a man, with his sword, axes and other utensils. These relics were given to the museum in Bergen. The mounds have been reconstructed, and photos of the relics are displayed in the hotel's entrance hall.

The hotel will arrange (for guests) a tour of its open air Ancient Village Museum. A commentary is on the old log buildings, the lives that were led in them, the white mansion of the landowner who built it in 1726, and the contents of all the structures. These objects dramatize the contrasting life-style between the rich and the poor of that era. Among the contents are antique Norwegian furniture, arms, glass, silver, pewter and brass, some of which are also displayed in the hotel lobby.

If your schedule does not allow staying overnight at Stalheim, from mid-June to mid-August a boat leaves Gudvangen (only a 30-minute bus ride from Stalheim) at 16:50 and 19:50 for a cruise along the Sognefjord, all in Midnight Sun daylight, arriving Aurland at 18:15 and 21:20.

You can leave Stalheim by bus on Day 2 at 10:35 to connect with the Gudvangen–Flam boat ride on the **Sognefjord**, starting at 11:35 for arrival in Flam at 13:30. Snacks and beverages are available on the boat, or you can have lunch after you reach **Flam**.

On the morning of the following day, start the 12½-mile Flam Line railway ride to Myrdal (Table 781) late May to mid-September at 10:00 or mid-September to late May at 10:40, arriving Myrdal 10:55 or 11:35, changing to the 12:25 departure for Oslo, and arrive Oslo 18:10.

The 41-minute Flam-Myrdal trip is one of the five most beautiful train rides in Europe.

The Flam Line goes along the **Aurlandsfjord**, a branch of the Sognefjord. Watch for sturdy, wild mountain goats that often cluster on huge granite boulders only a few feet from the track. There is an ascent of 2,845 feet from sea level in the first 12 miles. This railway has the greatest incline of any Norwegian track, 5.5 percent at one stretch.

The descent is so steep that the train takes a longer time to go downhill than it does to go up. It has five different braking systems, any one of which is sufficient to stop the train.

The mountainside is so steep along one stretch that the train has to go through reverse tunnels. In one particular short distance, the track must go on three different levels on one side of Kjosfossen Gorge and on two levels on the other side of the gorge. There are 20 tunnels with a combined length of 3.7 miles in the 12½-mile route.

The train proceeds slowly or stops completely at the finest scenic sections in order for passengers to have the best possible views of magnificent scenery and of a road that was built in 1895 to supply materials for building the railway. This road has 21 hairpin bends. Along another stretch, the train crosses a 110-yard-long embankment and stops there for several minutes so that passengers can get off and walk closer to the enormous raging Kjos waterfall that cascades close to the train. Its force is marvellous to see and hear.

The first stop en route from Myrdal to Oslo is at **Finse**, highest elevation (4,267 feet) of the entire Bergen–Oslo line. Workers are stationed permanently at Finse to fight snow on the tracks nine months out of the year and repair the snow sheds during the three-month spring-summer-autumn there.

Between Finse and Oslo, the scenery changes from glacier to ski resorts, waterfalls, and then beautiful valley farms and fast-moving rivers.

If time does not permit going to Stalheim, you can leave Bergen (late May to mid-September) at 08:45, terminating in Myrdal at 11:00. Depart Myrdal 11:45 on the Flam Line, arriving Flam 12:45. Depart Flam 15:00 for the ride back to Myrdal, arriving Myrdal 15:55 and connecting with the train that departed Bergan at 15:30. Depart Myrdal on that train at 17:21 (reservation required). Arrive Oslo at 22:12. Despite the late arrival, you will see all of the interesting scenery between Myrdal and Oslo in daylight if you are taking this trip in summer.

Oslo to Bergen with Myrdal-Flam Detour   790, 781

Depart Oslo (Sentral) for Bergen at 07:42, 10:48, 14:55 or 16:09, arriving there 14:20, 18:33, 21:43 and 22:38. All trains require a reservation and have a restaurant car.

To take the Myrdal–Flam–Myrdal round-trip detour, leave Oslo 07:42 or 10:48, arriving Bergen 14:20 or 18:33. The 14:55 and 16:09 Oslo departures reach Myrdal too late for making the detour.

For a two-day Oslo-Bergen trip, overnight in Flam. Then, on the morning of Day 2, leave Flam Pier 08:45 for the boat trip on Sognefjord to Gudvangen, take the bus Gudvangen-Stalheim-Voss, and then by train Voss to Bergen.

All of these trains are second class, unless designated otherwise.

Dep. Voss	06:33 (1)	08:45 (1)	10:45	13:13 (2)	14:55 (3)
Arr. Bergen	07:49	09:58	12:03	14:20	16:16

(1) Runs Monday-Friday except holidays. (2) Reservation required. Restaurant car, first- and second-class coaches. (3) Plus other departures from Voss at 16:00, 17:20 (2), 19:00, and 21:32 (2), arriving Bergen 17:14, 18:33, 20:18 and 22:38.

If time does not permit going to Stalheim on Day 2, you can depart Flam by fjord boat [table 782] at 15:40 (early June to mid-September), arriving Bergen at 20:40 the same day.

Oslo - Dombas - Andalsnes   785

This 71-mile "Rauma Line" detour off the "Dovre Line" (Oslo to Trondheim) is, mile for mile, one of the five greatest scenic rides in Europe.

Even for one who is not going further north than Dombas, the two-day round-trip is well worth the time involved. There is no question that the route is worth seeing twice, and from two perspectives.

Be sure to obtain a free brochure at Oslo's Central rail station before beginning the trip. Depart Oslo (Sentral) at 08:05 or 16:05; there's a train change in Dombas. Arrive Andalsnes 13:51 or 21:55. In the summer, you can read a newspaper there by sunlight at midnight.

Soon after the train leaves Dombas it crosses the granite Jora Bridge, which spans a 120-foot-deep gorge. At **Bjorli,** the Romsdal Valley comes into view, and you will see (at least in late spring and early summer) unmatched foaming torrents of thawed- glacier water, rushing at 80 miles an hour down vertical mountain slopes and through the boulder-strewn Rauma River bed.

The descent from Bjorli involves a double spiral through two circular mountain tunnels, first the 1,550-yard-long Stavem Tunnel, then through the 500-yard-long Kylling Tunnel.

Between these two tunnels, at **Verma** rail station, there is a monument that commemorates the opening of the Rauma Line by King Haakon in 1924. Along the opposite side of the Rauma River are small, well-kept farms, lush from the benefit of the warmth of the Gulf Stream, which keeps temperatures moderate along most of the coast of Norway.

The train next crosses Kylling Bridge, 200 feet above a thundering run of the Rauma River through a steep, narrow gorge. You are now approaching the valley floor.

Near **Flatmark,** you cross Foss Bridge and see Bridal Veil, best known of the numerous waterfalls on this route. At **Marstein** rail station, the sun is visible only seven months of the year due to the combination of the tall surrounding mountains and the arc of the sun at this latitude.

After passing along the glaciated foot of the majestic Romsdalshorn Mountain, whose peak rivals the Matterhorn as a climber's challenge, one can see on the left the highest vertical rock face in northern Europe, the "Troll's Wall" (Trollveggen), which is 3,000 feet high.

The "Rauma Line" reaches sea level in the Romsdall Valley before ending at **Andalsnes** (population 2,500) on the shore of Isfjord, at the head of the Romsdallfjord.

There is a bus connection between Andalsnes and **Alesund.** At Alesund, one can make flights to Oslo, Bergen or Trondheim, or make coastal express boat trips to Bergen or Trondheim.

The Rauma River is fished by sportsmen for salmon and trout.

To return to Oslo, depart Andalsnes 09:05. Depart Dombas 11:44. Arrive Oslo 14:55. Or, depart Andalsnes 16:30. Depart Dombas at 18:08, arrive Oslo 22:25. Both Dombas-Oslo trains require reservation and have a restaurant car.

The Oslo-Andalsnes-Oslo round trip can be made without stopping overnight in Andalsnes. There is a night departure from Andalsnes at 23:40 that operates daily except Saturday, arriving Oslo the next morning at 06:55. What a shame, to take this ride at night!

The only overnight lodging we know of in **Andalsnes** is at the 65-room Grand Hotel Bellevue. Advance room reservations are recommended.

There is a two-hour bus/ferry connection [785] from Andalsnes to **Molde**, Norway's "town of roses" located on a fjord and surrounded by 87 beautiful snowcapped peaks. In Molde, see the many ancient wood buildings from the 11th century. The Romsdal Museum, largest Norwegian provincial museum. The floral decorations in the modern concrete and glass Town Hall. The view of the Norwegian Sea and the countryside from the Varden Restaurant, 1300 feet above the town. An international jazz festival (music, art, poetry and theatrical events) has been held in Molde the first week of August every year since 1960.

Take the Eide bus 18 miles to visit the grottos and caves at the Troll's Church and the waterfall that tumbles against a marble mountain.

Oslo - Andalsnes - Trondheim - Bodo - Narvik   785, 786

This is a marvelous five-day rail trip up Norway's Gulfstream-warmed coastline. There is very good mountain and lake scenery Oslo–Trondheim, and excellent mountain, lake and seacoast scenery Trondheim-Bodo.

Keep in mind when reading the timetables that there is constant daylight on this route during June and July.

A transplanted herd of gigantic musk oxen live along the Dombas–Trondheim route, Day 2 of this journey. It's not unusual to see a mother and baby grazing late at night on a grassy slope near the train track.

The scenery of forests, rich valleys, waterfalls, rivers and farms is lovely almost all the way to the crossing of the Arctic Circle, on the ride from Trondheim to **Bodo**.

Passengers are given a brochure with details about the Arctic Circle trip. Announcements during the ride over a public address system alert passengers to approaching points of interest. A steward or hostess is on board to provide information.

Upon reaching the stone monument that marks the Arctic Circle, the train stops there for five minutes, allowing passengers adequate time to take photographs.

Don't be surprised if you see snow when crossing the Arctic Circle in June; it'll really give you the feeling of a polar environment. And don't be surprised, either, if a few hours later, as the train comes close to the coastline, and is considerably north of the Arctic Circle, that the weather is sunny and warm!

The northernmost rail service from Oslo is to Bodo. Passage from Bodo to Narvik is via an all-day bus trip through beautiful countryside interspersed by three ferryboat crossings.

The following schedules are for a recommended rail trip from Oslo to Narvik, and then from Narvik across northern Norway to northern Sweden and then south to Stockholm. On the trip from Narvik to Sweden (Boden), you cross the Arctic Circle north-to-south, although without the interesting ceremony that is presented on the south-to-north Trondheim–Bodo ride.

Day 1 (Table 785)		*Day 3 in Trondheim*	
Dep. Oslo (Sen.)	08:05 (1+2)		
Arr. Andalsnes	13:51	*Day 4 (Table 786)*	
		Dep. Trondheim	08:32 (1)
Day 2 (Table 785)		*Cross the Arctic Circle*	16:12
Dep. Andalsnes	16:30	Arr. Bodo	18:35
Arr. Dombas	17:59		
Change trains		*Day 5 Bus*	
Dep. Dombas	20:14 (1)	Dep. Bodo	07:30 (3)
Arr. Trondheim	22:48	Arr. Narvik	14:20

(1) Reservation required. Restaurant car. (2) Change trains Dombas. (3) Food is available at occasional stops.

Keep in mind that during late June, all of July and most of August, the Midnight Sun allows you to see the scenery all the way to Trondheim, despite the 22:48 arrival time there. The light is not blinding, but you can read a newspaper by it straight through the night.

Deleting Overnight in Andalsnes and Trondheim

Here are schedules for those wishing to continue on from Andalsnes to Narvik without spending 21 hours in Andalsnes or a night in either Trondheim or Bodo and who don't mind missing a daytime view of the Andalsnes–Dombas "Rauma Line." The bus Fauske–Narvik is *not* covered by Eurailpass.

785		
Dep. Oslo (Sen.)	08:05 (1)	16:05 (1)
Arr. Dombas	12:19	20:14
Arr. Andalsnes	13:51	21:55
Return to Dombas		
Dep. Andalsnes	16:30	23:40 (2)
Arr. Dombas	17:59	01:20

Change trains 785		
Dep. Dombas	20:14 (1)	04:30 (3)
Arr. Trondheim	22:48	07:35
Change trains 786		
Dep. Trondheim	23:05 (3)	08:32 (1)
Cross the Arctic Circle		
Arr. Fauske	09:05	17:48
Change to a bus		
Dep. Fauske	09:30	18:15
Arr. Narvik	14:20	23:00

(1) Reservation *required*. Restaurant car. (2) Runs daily except Saturday. (3) Reservation *required*. Carries a sleeping car. Coach is second class only.

Sights in **Trondheim**: This is the gateway for northern cruises. See the old Nidaros Cathedral, the largest medieval structure in Scandinavia. The 18th-century rococo Strift-sgarden royal residence. The Bishop's Palace. The open-air folk museum, open daily 10:00–18:00. The dazzling array of unusual musical instruments in the Ringve Museum of Musical History (including an Eskimo drum made from a walrus stomach, a Tibetan trumpet, a violin made of matches).

Sights in **Narvik:** The second (after Murmansk) most northern rail passenger terminus in the world.

Founded in 1901 at the western tip of **Ofot Fjord** to provide an ice-free port for the mid-winter export of iron ore from Swedish mines which cannot ship via the frozen Bay of Bothnia during winter.

For the most breathtaking view of Midnight Sun sky, fjords, mountains and the town of Narvik, take the 10-minute walk from Grand Hotel Royal to the base of the cable that lifts you 2,000 feet in 13 minutes to the top of **Mt. Fagernesfjell**.

Food and beverages are sold in the Fjellsheimen restaurant on the peak, an ideal site for taking spectacular photos and watching the sun revolve clockwise around the horizon.

A crucial British-German naval battle (commemorated at a small museum in the center of town) was fought in Narvik's fjords during World War II. Destroyed in 1940, Narvik was completely rebuilt after the war.

The Direct Trip

Oslo - Trondheim and Trondheim - Oslo 785

Dep. Oslo (Sen.)	08:05 (1)	10:35 (2)	15:02 (2)	16:05 (1)	23:00 (3)
Arr. Trondheim	14:53	18:34	22:46	22:48	07:16

• • •

Dep. Trondheim	08:15 (1)	12:55 (4)	14:11 (5)	15:40 (1)	22:28 (3)
Arr. Oslo (Sen.)	14:55	18:28	22:10	22:25	06:55

(1) Reservation *required.* Restaurant car or light refreshments. (2) Second class. Light refreshments. (3) Reservation required. Carries sleepers and second-class coaches. Restaurant car, (4) Runs Friday and Sunday only. Light refreshments. (5) Runs Sunday only. Light refreshments.

Narvik - Boden - Stockholm   760

There is fine mountain scenery Narvik–Kiruna.

Day 6

Dep. Narvik	13:40 (1)	Day 6 of the Oslo–Narvik–Stockholm trip.
Arr. Kiruna	17:05	
Dep. Kiruna	17:05	
Arr. Boden	20:48	
Arr. Stockholm (Cen.)	10:15	Day 7 of the Oslo–Narvik–Stockholm trip.

(1) Reservation *required.* Carries first- and second-class sleeping cars, second-class couchettes and second-class coaches. Restaurant car.

Oslo - Kritiansand - Stavanger   775

There is excellent mountain scenery between Kristiansand and Stavanger.

Dep. Oslo (Sen.)	08:48 (1)	14:48 (2)	22:48 (3)
Dep. Kristiansand	14:10	19:40	04:33
Arr. Stavanger	17:16	22:37	07:48

Sights in **Stavanger**: Many old streets and houses in this 1100-year-old town. See the market of fruits, vegetables, flowers and fish. The 11th-century cathedral. Outside the city, see the prehistoric Viste Cave. Try a deep-sea fishing trip.

Dep. Stavanger	07:06(2)	12:50 (1)	22:00 (3+4)
Arr. Kristiansand	09:58	16:10	01:20
Arr. Oslo (Sen.)	14:42	21:39	07:12

(1) Light refreshments. Reservation from starting station and other selected stations. (2) Reservation *required.* Restaurant car. (3) Carries a sleeping car. Coach is second class. (4) Runs daily, except Saturday.

Stavanger - Kristiansand - Stavanger   775

From Stavanger, it is an easy one-day round trip to see the fine mountain scenery en route to Kristiansand.

All of these trains require reservation and have light refreshments, unless designated otherwise.

Dep. Stavanger	07:05 (1)	12:50	Dep. Kristiansand	14:10	19:40 (1)
Arr. Kristiansand	09:58	16:10	Arr. Stavanger	17:16	22:37

(1) Restaurant car.

Voss - Ulvik   777, 780

This spur off the Bergen–Oslo route affords great farm, mountain and river scenery. It is an easy one-day round trip.

481 Train

Dep. Bergen	10:20 (1)	13:10	15:44(1)
Arr. Voss	11:30	14:25	16:46
Change to bus 777			
Dep. Voss	11:35 (2)	15:35	17:30 (3)
Arr. Ulvik	12:45	16:40	18:35

• • •

Dep. Ulvik	13:55	15:10 (3)	18:50 (3)
Ar. Voss	15:00	16:10	19:50
Change to train 780			
Dep. Voss	16:00 (2)	19:00	21:32 (1)
Arr. Bergen	17:14	20:18	23:38

(1) Reservation *required.* Restaurant car. (2) Runs daily, except Sundays and holidays. (3) Runs daily except Saturday.

INTERNATIONAL ROUTES
FROM NORWAY

Bergen is Norway's starting point for *cruises* to England. Oslo is the gateway for *rail* trips to Sweden (Stockholm, and on to Finland) and Denmark (Copenhagen, and on to Germany and the rest of Western Europe).

Bergen - Newcastle   2215 (Ship)

The arrivals in Newcastle are on Day 2 after departing Bergen.

Dep. Bergen	11:00 (1)	11:00 (2)	17:15(3)	17:00 (4)
Dep. Stavanger	18:00	17:15	00:15	23:59
Arr. Newcastle (Tyne)	12:00	09:30	16:30	19:00

(1) Operates late Monday only mid-January-early May and September-late December. Runs Monday only. (2) Runs Friday only mid-May-early September. (3) Operates mid-May-early September. Runs Tuesday only. (4) Runs Thursday only. Operates early March to mid-May and early September to mid-December.

Narvik - Boden - Haparanda - Kemi - Oulu - Helsinki   760, 769

The schedule below indicates that it is necessary to layover one night in Boden when going from Narvik to Helsinki. In order to see the entire Boden–Oulu portion during daylight, take the 08:00 departure from Boden. To see the entire Oulu–Helsinki portion during daylight, layover one or more nights in Oulu and on Day 3 or later depart Oulu 09:56.

760 Train

Dep. Narvik	10:30 (1)	13:40 (1)			
Arr. Boden	17:15	20:48			
Change to bus 769					
Dep. Boden	08:05	11:15	14:05		
Arr. Haparanda	10:15	13:15	16:20		
Walk 800 meters to Tornio bus station; change buses 769					
Dep. Tornio	13:30 (2)	13:40 (4)	17:15		
Set your watch forward one hour					
Arr. Kemi	14:00	14:08	19:15		
Change to a train 790					
Dep. Kemi	14:25 (3)	14:25 (3)	20:10 (3+4)	22:43 (2+4)	08:32 (5)
Dep. Oulu	16:05	16:05	22:10	00:15	09:56
Arr. Helsinki	23:02	23:02	07:08	08:30	17:02

(1)) Reservation *required*. Second class. (2) Runs daily except Saturdays. (3) Light refreshments. (4) Carries sleeping cars and second-class coach. (5) Restaurant car.

Oslo - Stockholm   750

Dep. Oslo (Sen.)	09:35 (1)	22:50 (2)
Arr. Stockholm	15:23	06:11

(1) Change trains in Karlstad. Karlstad-Stockholm X2000. Supplement payable. Reservation *required.* Restaurant car. (2) Carries sleeping cars, couchettes, second-class coaches.

Oslo - Copenhagen   735

All of these trains require reservation.

Dep. Oslo (Sen.)	07:37 (1)	22:43 (2)
Arr. Helsingborg	15:05	05:25
Arr. Copenhagen (H.)	16:58	07:42

(1) Restaurant car. (2) Reservation required. Carries sleeping cars, couchettes second-class coaches.

SWEDEN

Getting on Track in Sweden
• Tourist information: Swedish Travel and Tourism Council, P.O. Box 4649 Grand Central Station, New York, NY 10163-4649. Telephone (212) 885-9700, fax (212) 885-9710. E-mail: info@gosweden.org. On the Web: http://www.gosweden.org.
• Public holidays: A list of holidays is helpful because some trains will be noted later in this section as *not* running on holidays. Also, those trains which operate on holidays are filled, and it is necessary to make reservations for them long in advance. These holidays are celebrated in Sweden: January 1, New Year's Day, Epiphany, Good Friday, Easter, Easter Monday, May 1, Labor Day, Ascension Day, Whit Monday, Midsummer Day, All Saint's Day, December 25, Christmas, December 26, Boxing Day.
• Currency: Swedish Krona (Skr). At press time, $1 equalled 7.95 Skr.

Overview of Sweden's Trains
Statens Jarnvager (SJ) operates Sweden's trains. Two classes of service are offered, first and second.
    Most train travelers coming into Sweden cross over on one of the quick ferries from Denmark (Helsingborg-Helsingor) which connects to the Stockholm line.

General Rail Information
• These classifications are used for Swedish trains: X2000, Sweden's fastest train, InterCity (IC) and InterRegio (IR). Sleepers come in two varieties: Older cars have one berth in first class, two or three in second class. Newer cars have two configurations, a compartment with a shower and toilet and one or two berths in first class or compartments with the shower and toilet down the hall, with one or two berths in first class, two berths second class. Couchettes are also found on Swedish trains. Supplements are charged for these accommodations.

• Reservations are required for all X2000 trips and for night trains. Reservations are also required for trips of over 150 km on other trains. A supplement is charged for travel on X2000 trains.
• Children under 12 travel free when accompanied by an adult (to a maximum of two children for each adult). Half-fare for children 12-15. Children 16 and over must pay full fare.

The signs you will see at rail stations in Sweden are:

ANKOMST	ARRIVAL
AVGANG	DEPARTURE
BILJETTLUCKAN	TICKET OFFICE
DAMER	WOMEN
GARDEROBEN	CHECKROOM
HERRAR	MEN
JARNVAGSTATION	RAILWAY STATION
INGANG	ENTRANCE
INFORMATIONSDISKEN	INFORMATION
LIGGPLATSVAGN	COUCHETTE CAR
PLATSBILJETTER	RESERVATIONS
RESTAURANGVAGN	RESTAURANT CAR
SOVVAGN	SLEEPING CAR
SPAR	TRACK
TILL SPAREN	TO THE PLATFORMS
UTGANG	EXIT
VAXELKONTORET	CURRENCY EXCHANGE

EURAILPASS BONUSES IN SWEDEN

These boat trips were Eurailpass bonuses in 1997: Helsingborg-Helsingør (Denmark) operated by the Swedish and Danish State Railways; Trelleborg-Sassnitz (Germany); and, Umeå-Vaasa (Finland) and Sundsvall-Vaasa on the Silja Line, Helsingborg–Helsingor, Stockholm–Turku. Pass holders also received 50 percent off regular fares for crossings on TT Line's Trelleborg-Travemünde ferries, 50 percent off regular fares for crossings on TR Line's Trelleborg-Rostock ferries, 50 percent off on Stena Line ferries between Göteborg-Frederikshaven (Denmark), 50 percent reduction on the Inlands Banan between Mora and Gällivare and 25 percent off Flyvebådne Company hydrofoils between Malmö and Copenhagen.

SWEDEN'S TRAIN PASSES

All of Sweden's passes are sold *only* in Sweden, at main rail stations and travel agencies.

Reslust Card Entitles the holder to 25 percent discount on *all* trains on Tuesday, Wednesday, Thursday and Saturday — plus other advantages such as restaurant car discounts and special summer rates. In 1997, the price was $20 (only $7 for persons over 67). The card gives travelers a 25 percent discount on all journeys over 50 miles.

Red Departure Discount Ticket The holder is allowed 50 percent discount for trains marked in red on Finnish timetables on *second*-class tickets that are valid for 36 hours. No stopovers. The minimum ticket must be $14, or $10 for persons holding the "Reslust Card" (see above). If the station's ticket office is closed when the train departs, "Red Departure" can be purchased on the train. Seat reservation, at $3 each, is required for InterCity trains and for many long distance trains.

ONE-DAY EXCURSIONS AND CITY-SIGHTSEEING

Here are eight one-day rail trips that can be made comfortably from Stockholm and Goteborg, returning to them in most cases before dinnertime. Notes are provided on what to see and do at each destination. The number after the name of each route is the *Cook's Timetable*.

Goteborg

A great seaport. The one-hour sightseeing bus tour leaves from Stora Teatern. There are one-hour boat trips covering the seven-mile harbor and its canals, leaving from Kungsportsbron. See the view of the harbor and city from the Sailor's Tower near the Maritime Museum at Gamla Varvsparken. The Liseberg amusement park. The magnificent City Theater, Concert House and Art Museum, all in the large square, Gotaplatsen. Antikhallarna, Scandinavia's largest permanent antiques and collectors market.

The view from Ramberget, highest point on the Hisingen side of Goteborg. The botanical garden. The 07:00 fish auction, weekdays, at Scandinavia's largest fish market. The 17th-century Elfsborg Fortress. The historical and archaeological collections at the Goteborg Museum, located in the city's oldest (1643) building. Art from all over the world, at the Rohss Museum. Slottsskogen Zoo. The view of the harbor and city from the top of Sjomanjtornet, a 193-foot-high tower. Stroll down the broad Kungsportsavenyn, hub of the city.

Stockholm

Maps, literature and advice can be obtained at the Stockholm Tourist Association in Sweden House (Hamngatan 27), in the central business-shopping district (open Monday–Friday 08:30–18:00, Saturday and Sunday 08:00–17:00).

Bus connections to the city's airport are available at a terminal across the street from the Central rail station. Stockholm's subways depart from the same level as the Tourist Information Office in Central rail station. Buy a Tourist Ticket, either for one day or three days. It's good for rides on both buses and subways, and is sold at the Tourist Information Office in Central rail station.

Take bus #47, across the street from Central rail station, to the 75-acre Skansen amusement park, open 08:00–23:30 June through August. Its prime attraction is the Vasa Museum (open daily 09:30–19:00 June through mid-August, 10:00–17:00 the rest of the year), where a 17th-century battleship is on exhibit. This ancient ship sank in Stockholm harbor at the moment she set forth on her first voyage as flagship of the Swedish Navy and rested in 100 feet of water from 1628 until it was raised in 1956, restored and turned into a museum.

Located near the Nordic Museum in the Galarvarv area of Djurgarden Island, the Vasa Museum can be reached by bus or by ferries that leave continuously from Nybroplan and from the end of Gamla Stan. It is an easy five-minute walk from the ferry docks at the island to the Vasa Museum.

Also popular are Skansen's Zoo and its outdoor museum of life in early Stockholm (more than 150 buildings from the 18th and 19th centuries).

At the Royal Palace, the treasury and Armory are open in summer 10:00–16:00. The king's silver throne in the Hall of State can be seen 12:00–15:00. Also see the Bernadotte and Festival suites. The historic and art treasures in the Royal Chapel. The Changing of the Guard in the courtyard takes place daily at 12:10.

Other sights: the 15th-century Storkyrkan Cathedral, with its sculpture of St. George and the Dragon, is a short walk from the palace. The tall old houses and Stock Exchange on Stortorget, the city's oldest square. The modern architecture in Skarholmen, a suburb

The collection of Carl Milles statues at Millesgarden sculpture park. Fine views of the city and the archipelago from the 504-foot-high Kaknas television tower, open May through August 09:00–24:00. The exhibit of 16th through 19th-century paintings by European masters at the National Museum of Fine Arts, open daily 10:00–16:00 (see the 9 Rembrandts on the second floor). Rosendal Palace, closed Monday. The Chinese Pavilion, Court Theater and Museum, all at Drottingholm Palace, open April through October.

Do not miss seeing the Golden Hall, Blue Hall, Prince's Gallery, Terrace and the view from the tower, all at Town Hall (1 Hantverkgatan), one of Europe's most famous buildings, where guided tours are offered daily at 10:00 (plus 12:00 on Sundays and holidays). The Nobel festivities take place there.

Goteborg - Kalmar - Goteborg   746

| Dep. Goteborg | 06:40 (1) | Dep. Kalmar | 17:45 (2) |
| Arr. Kalmar | 11:05 | Arr. Goteborg | 21:44 |

(1) Runs daily except Sundays and holidays. Light refreshments. (2) Runs Daily except Saturdays. Light refreshments.

Sights in **Kalmar**: The moat, courts and towers of the castle. A bus trip to the nearby glassworks.

Stockholm - Eskilstuna - Stockholm 754, 757 Bus

757 Bus

Dep. Stockholm	07:35	10:25	13:35	15:35
Arr. Vasteras	08:55	11:55	14:55	16:55

Change to train 754

Dep. Vasteras	09:00(1)	13:00 (1)	15:00 (1)	17:00 (1)
Arr. Eskilstuna	09:30	13:00	14:15 (2)	17:00

• • •

754 Train

Dep. Eskilstuna	12:30 (1)	14:30 (1)	16:30 (1)
Arr. Vasteras	13:00	15:00	17:00

Change to bus 757

Dep. Vasteras	14:08	15:08	17:08
Arr. Stockholm	15:35	17:50	19:35

(1) Light refreshments. (2) Runs daily except Saturday.

Sights in **Eskilstuna:** The six Rademacher Forges that are more than 300 years old, on display in the center of town. Eskilstuna is the capital of Sweden's steel industry. Also see the wooden Fors Church and the statue of the 10th-century English missionary, Saint Eskil, for whom the town was named in 1659, one year after Reinhold Rademacher built the forges which launched the local industry.

See the zoo and amusement park. The 12th-century church. The wonderful collection of Scandinavian art in the art museum. Take a local bus eight miles to Sundbyholm Castle. Shop for gold, iron and copper souvenirs.

Stockholm - Gavle - Stockholm 760

All of these trains require reservation.

Dep. Stockholm (Cen.)	06:05 (1)	08:23 (2)	10:23 (2)	12:23	14:23(2)
Arr. Gavle	07:51	10:07	12:07	14:07	16:07

Sights in **Gavle:** The Swedish Railway Museum.

Dep. Gavle	10:00 (3)	12:00 (2)	16:00 (2)	16:55 (1)	20:00 (2)
Arr. Stockholm (Cen.)	11:43	13:43	17:45	18:43	21:43

(1) Runs Monday–Friday, except holidays. Restaurant car. (2) Restaurant car. (3) Runs daily except Saturday. Light refreshments.

Stockholm - Goteborg - Stockholm 740

All of these trains require reservation and have a restaurant car, unless designated otherwise.

Dep. Stockholm (Cen.)	07:00 (1+2)	08:00 (1)	10:00 (1)	12:00 (1)
Arr. Goteborg (Cen.)	10:11	11:14	13:20	15:15

• • •

Dep. Goteborg (Cen.)	14:00 (1)	16:05 (1)	17:10 (1)	18:05 (1+3)
Arr. Stockholm (Cen.)	17:17	18:59	21:29	21:11

(1) X2000 high-speed train. Supplement charged includes reservation fee and meal. (2) Operates Monday-Friday except holidays. (3) Plus another Goteburg departure at 20:10 (4), arriving Stockholm 23:41. (4) Runs daily except Saturday.

Stockholm - Malmo - Stockholm 730

This trip is impractical as a one-day Stockholm excursion.

All of these trains require reservation and have a restaurant car., unless designated otherwise.

Dep. Stockholm (Cen.)	06:12 (1)	07:30	10:06 (1)	11:30	14:18 (1)	16:18 (1+2)
Arr. Malmo (Cen.)	10:47	13:47	14:33	16:18	18:47	20:43

• • •

Dep. Malmo (Cen.)	05:44 (1)	07:13 (1)	09:18 (1)	11:25 (1)	13:07 (1)	15:13 (1+3)
Arr. Stockholm (Cen.)	09:53	11:47	13:53	15:59	17:41	19:41

(1) X2000 high-speed train. Supplement charged includes reservation fee and meal. (2) Runs daily except Saturday. (3) Plus other departures from Malmo 17:22 and 23:00 (4), arriving Stockholm 23:25 and 06:23. (4) Carries sleepers, couchettes and second-class coaches.

Stockholm - Borlange - Mora - Stockholm 761

There is excellent lake and mountain scenery Borlange-Mora.

All of these trains require reservation and have light refreshments, unless designated otherwise.

Dep. Stockholm (Cen.)	06:47	09:42 (1)	Dep. Mora	12:24	13:43 (1+2)
Arr. Borlange	09:24	12:12	Arr. Borlange	13:47	14:52
Arr. Mora	10:47	13:11	Arr. Stockholm (Cen.)	16:18	17:04

(1) X2000 high-speed train. Supplement includes seat reservation and meal. Runs Monday-Friday except holidays. (2) Plus other departures from Mora at 16:13 (3) and 18:22 (4) arriving Stockholm 20:18 and 22:18. (3) Runs Saturdays, Sundays and holidays. (4) Runs daily except Saturday.

Sights in **Mora**: The outdoor museum of 40 timber buildings, some 600 years old. The collection of Anders Zorn, Sweden's most famous painter.

Stockholm - Norrkoping - Stockholm   730

All of these trains require reservation and have a restaurant car, unless designated otherwise.

Dep. Stockholm (Cen.)	06:12 (1)	08:06 (1)	10:06 (1)	12:06 (1)
Arr. Norrkoping	07:31	09:21	11:23	13:20

Sights in **Norrkoping**: The amazing collection of more than 25,000 cactus plants in beautiful Karl Johans Park. Take the short sightseeing trip by boat, from the pier at the end of this park.

See the 3,000-year-old Bronze Age carvings and also the display of roses in Himmel-stalund Park, to the right of the rail station. On the other (east) side of the rail station, visit the ruins of the star-shaped Johannisborg Fort. See the Lindo Canal. Hear the bell-chiming at 13:00 in front of the Radhuset (Council House). See Hedvigs Kyrka, the German church.

See the demonstration of antique textiles (from rugs to doilies) and textile machinery in the museum of old factory buildings and tour the restored residence of the factory owner, the Stadsmuseet, a short walk from the rail station. Also exhibited there are interesting scale models of the city as it was in various past centuries.

Dep. Norrkoping	12:35 (1)	14:40 (1)	15:17 (1)	16:53	18:20 (1+3)
Arr. Stockholm (Cen.)	13:53	15:59	16:35 (2)	18:47	19:41

(1) X2000 high-speed train. Supplement payable. (2) Runs Fridays only. (3) Plus another departure from Norrkoping at 20:25 arriving Stockholm 21:47.

Stockholm - Uppsala - Stockholm   761

All of these trains require reservation, unless designated otherwise.

Dep. Stockholm (Cen.)	06:47 (1)	09:42 (2)	11:47 (3)	13:47
Arr. Uppsala	40–50 minutes later			

Sights in **Uppsala:** The cathedral, near the rail station, is the largest church in Scandinavia.
England's Princess Louise (after whom Lake Louise in Canada is named) visited it in 1929. An anecdote about that occasion has been passed on to generations of Britons:
The Swedish bishop whose command of the English language was imperfect, led the Princess on a tour of the church. After having shown her many priceless religious objects in several

areas of the cathedral, he led her into the sacristy where he conducted her to a large cabinet of several drawers and began to open one of them. In halting English, he announced to her: "I will now open these trousers and show your Royal Highness even more precious treasures."

Also visit Sweden's largest library, Carolina Rediviva, with more than 20,000 hand-illuminated medieval manuscripts, including the only book in existence that is written in pure Gothic, the famous Codex Argentus, the 5th-century Silver Bible. The Great Hall of State in the old red castle, open 11:00–18:00 from mid-May to mid-September.

The 18th-century Linnaeus Garden at 27 Svartsbacksgatan (open May–December 09:00–21:00) was created for the study of plant species by Karl von Linne, Sweden's "Prince of Botanists." The present collection numbers 1,300 plants. It was Linne who originated the system of sexual plant classification and the dual nomenclature for natural science.

Take a bus marked "Gamla Uppsala" for a two-mile ride to see relics of heathen worship going back to the 5th century.

Dep. Uppsala	14:26 (2)	15:37	16:26 (2)	18:03 (3+4)
Arr. Stockholm (Cen.)	40–50 minutes later			

(1) Runs Monday-Saturday except holidays. (2) X2000 high-speed train. Supplement payable. (3) Runs Monday–Friday, except holidays. (4) Plus other Uppsala departures at 18:37, 19:37 and 21:37.

INTERNATIONAL ROUTES
FROM SWEDEN

Stockholm is the gateway for rail trips to northern Norway (Trondheim and Narvik) and to northern Finland (Oulu), as well as by boat to Helsinki, and on to Leningrad. It is also the gateway for travel to southern Norway (Oslo, and on to Bergen or Stavanger). Malmo is the starting point for rail travel to Denmark, (Copenhagen, and on to Germany and the rest of Western Europe).

There is fine lake scenery on the Ostersund–Storlien portion of this route.

Stockholm - Trondheim   760

476

Dep. Stockholm (Cen.)	10:23 (1)	22:30 (2)
Dep. Ostersund	16:22	06:45
Arr. Storlien	18:46	09:40
Arr. Trondheim	20:51	13:00

(1) Reservation *required.* Restaurant car. (2) Carries sleeping cars, couchettes and second-class coaches.

Stockholm - Copenhagen 730

All of these trains require reservation and have a restaurant car, unless designated otherwise.

Dep. Stockholm (Cen.)	06:12	10:36	22:30
Arr. Copenhagen (Hoved.)	13:14	18:23	07:00

Stockholm - Helsinki 791, 2480 Boat and Train

This is the short route to Helsinki, *across* the Gulf of Bothnia.

Passage is free on day sailings of the Silja Line ferry for Eurailpass holders for the cruise across the Gulf of Bothnia on the comfortable and pleasant Silja Line ships. The fare for a sleeping cabin is *not* covered by Eurailpass. Food on the ship is varied and delicious.

We recommended the 08:00 sailing in order to see the thousands of tiny islands on the ride through this extremely interesting archipelago. During the daytime cruise, there is a good smorgasbord for both lunch and dinner.

A small band plays music in a delightful bar area. Movies are shown in a small theater. There is a duty-free shop on board. The ships also ferry autos.

All of the Turku–Helsinki trains have light refreshments.
2480 Boat

Dep. Stockholm (Var.)	08:00	20:00
Arr. Turku (Harbor)	19:00	08:00

Walk to either rail station
791

Dep. Turku (Harbor)	-0-	08:35
Dep. Turku (Stn.)	19:58	09:00
Arr. Helsinki	22:02	11:02

Stockholm - Narvik 760

There is good mountain scenery on the Kiruna–Narvik portion of this trip.

Both of these trains require reservation. Coach cars on both trains are second class.

Dep. Stockholm (Central)	18:00 (1)
Arr. Boden	07:22
Arr. Kiruna	11:07
Arr. Narvik	14:05

(1) Carries sleeping cars, couchettes, second-class coaches, also a restaurant and cinema/bistro car.

Stockholm - Oslo   750

Dep. Stockholm (Cen.)	07:18 (1)	23:42 (2)
Arr. Oslo (Sen.)	13:25	07:32

(1) Light refreshments.   (2) Reservation *required.*. Carries sleeping cars, couchettes and second-class coaches.

Stockholm - Oulu - Helsinki   760

By stopping-over one night in Oulu, the Oulu-Helsinki trip can be made the next day in daylight by departing Oulu 07:15, 09:56 or 12:52.

760

Dep. Stockholm (Cen.)	18:00 (1)	20:20 (1)	-0-	
Arr. Boden	07:22	09:50	-0-	
Change to bus 769				
Dep. Boden	08:05	11:05 (3)	14:05	
Arr. Haparanda	10:15	13:15	16:20	
Walk 900 meters to Tornio station and change buses				
Dep. Tornio	13:30 (2)	13:30 (3)	19:25	
Set your watch forward one hour				
Arr. Kemi	14:00	14:00	19:58	
Change to a trains 790				
Dep. Kemi	14:25	14:25	20:10 (4)	-0-
Arr. Oulu	15:42	15:42	21:27	-0-
Dep. Oulu	16:05	16:05	22:10	07:15 (5+6)
Arr. Helsinki	23:02	23:02	07:08	13:58

(1) Reservation *required.* Carries sleeping cars, couchettes and a cinema/bistro car. Coach is second class. (2) Runs daily, except Saturdays. (3) Runs Mon.-Fri., except holidays. (4) Carries sleeping cars, and second-class coaches. (5) Restaurant car. (6) Plus other Oulu departures at 9:56 (5), 12:52 (5) and 16:05 (7), arriving Helsinki 17:02, 20:02 and 23:02. (7) Light refreshments.

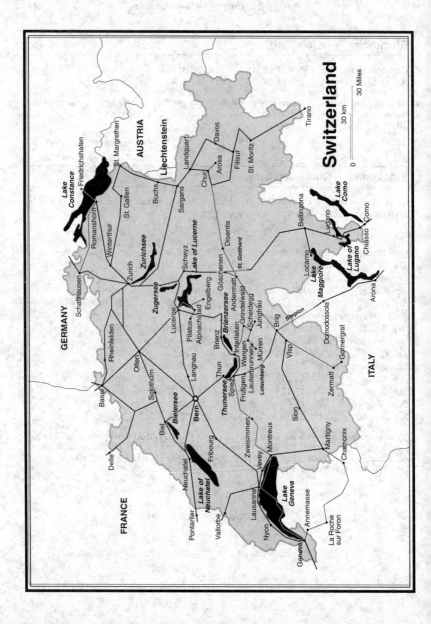

Switzerland

30 km

30 Miles

0

SWITZERLAND

Getting on Track in Switzerland
• Tourist information: Switzerland Tourism, 608 Fifth Avenue, New York, NY 10020. Telephone (212) 757-5944, fax (212) 262-6116 E-mail: stnewyork@switzerlandtourism.com. Los Angeles office, 222 No. Sepulveda Boulevard, Suite 1570, El Segundo, CA 90245-5982. Telephone (310) 335-5985, fax (310) 335-5982. On the Web: http://www.switzerlandtourism.ch/.
• Public holidays: A list of holidays is helpful because some trains will be noted later in this section as not running on holidays. Also, those trains which operate on holidays are filled, and it is necessary to make reservations for some Inter-City, Euro City and TGV trains. The following holidays are celebrated in Switzerland: January 1, New Year's Day, January 2, Good Friday, Easter Monday, Ascension Day, Whit Monday, December 25, C h r i s t m a s Day, December 26, Boxing Day.
• Currency: Swiss franc (Sfr). At press time, $1 equalled Sfr1.50.

Overview of Switzerland's Trains
Switzerland has a plethora of rail operators, but the companies providing most of the main-line services are Schweizerische Bundesbahnen (SBB), Chemins de fer Federaux (CFF) and Ferrovie Federali Svizzere (FFS). Eurailpasses are valid on these trains. Many of those little lines operating over some of Switzerland's most scenic routes, however, do not accept Eurailpasses, although discounts are offered on selected lines. To take the mystery out of where your Eurailpass is or isn't usable, tale a look at the reference list later in the chapter.

Switzerland is the scenic treasure that it is made out to be, although its people and their traditions are relatively little known outside of the country. Train travel here is easy and predictably efficient, with a range of modern and rather traditional train services available to Eurailpass holders. Switzerland is one country where the train can get you places that the automobile could not.

General Rail Information
• There's an alphabet-soup of trains running in Switzerland. Among the speedsters: German InterCityExpress (ICE), Italian Cisalpino (CIS; Pendolino), French TGV and EuroCity (EC). More conventional trains include: InterCity (IC), express service within Switzerland, EuroNight (EN) quality international overnight service, InterRegio (IR), inter-fast regional trains and RegioExpress (RX), slower than IR trains.
• Some international trains carry sleepers or couchettes.
• Supplements are charged for travel aboard TGV trains and for travel on first-class observation cars (these cars are popular, so it's best to reserve space as soon as possible). If you travel aboard a CIS or ICE train solely within Switzerland, no supplement is charged.
• See "Swiss Family Card" for children's free fares.

• The signs you will see at rail stations in Switzerland are those you would see in France, Germany or Italy depending on the section of the country you are in.
• French is the language south and southwest of Bern. Italian is dominant in the southeast corner of Switzerland. Elsewhere, the prevailing language is German.
• Free timetables distributed at most rail stations.
• Seat reservations are advised for most EuroCity and Intercity trains.
• A traveler with a confirmed flight reservation for a departure from Zurich or Geneva airport can check bags at a special counter in the rail station at nearly 100 Swiss cities.
• Unencumbered with luggage, the passenger using "Fly Luggage Service" rides a train from places such as Bern, Locarno, and Luzern directly to the airport, checks-in at the airport's "Express" counter, boards the airplane and claims the luggage at the end of the flight. The time required for baggage deposit in advance of train departure varies from one Swiss rail station to another. Be sure to obtain that information before departure day. Because of USA security procedures, "Fly Luggage Service" is not available to passengers who are departing on a US airline.
• Log on to SBB's official Web site for lots of excellent rail-travel information, including links to private Swiss railways: http://www.sbb.ch/.

EURAILPASS BONUSES IN SWITZERLAND

For no extra charge, Eurailpass holders can ride the steamers plying the waters of these lakes: Geneva, Lucern, Thun, Brienz, Zurich, Neuchatel, Biel, Murten. You're also entitled to ride down the Rhine between Schaffhausen and Kreuzlingen and on the Aare between Biel and Solothurn. A 50 percent reduction is available on Lake Constance boats and a 35 percent reduction on Mt. Pilatus funicular/Kriens cable car fares and entry to the Lucern Transport Museum, hailed as the largest transport museum in Europe. There's also a 35 percent reduction on steamer service on Lake Constance between Rorschach and Romanshorn, a 50 percent reduction on Bürgenstock funicular and a 25 percent discount on the Jungfrau Region Railway and the Vitznau/Rigi Railways.

OTHER SWISS RAILWAYS OFFERING
FREE TRAVEL TO EURAILPASS HOLDERS

Nyon-St. Cergue-Morez (NStCM)
Biere-Apples-Morges (BAM)
Compagnie Generale de Navigation
    Lac Leman (CGN)
Chemins de fer Fribourgeois
    Guere-Fribourg-Morat (GFM)
Regionalverkehr Bern-Solothurn (RBS)
Emmental-Burgdorf-Thun (EBT)

Ferrovie Autolinee Regionali Ticinesi (FART)
Schiffahrtsgesellschaft des Vierwaldstattersees
    (SGV) (Lake Lucern)
Bern-Lotschberg-Simplon Bahn (BLS)
    (includes ships)
Spiez-Erlenbach-Zweisimmen (SEZ)
Montreaux-Oberland-Bernois (MOB)
Chemin de fer Aigle-Leysin (AL)

Schweizerische Sudostbahn (SOB)
Bodensee Toggenberg Bahn (BT)
Appenzeller Bahnen (AB)
Mittelthurgau Bahn (MThB)
Rhatische Bahn (RhB)
Luzern-Stans-Engleberg Bahn (LSE)

Chemin de fer Aigle-Le Sepey-Les Diablerets (ASD)
Chemin de fer Aigle-Ollon-Monthey-Champery (AOMC)
Chemin de fer Bex-Villars-Bretaye (BVB)
Chemin de fer Martigny-Chatelard (MC)
Martigny-Orsieres (MO) (includes buses)

SWITZERLAND'S TRAIN PASSES

These passes are good for unlimited travel on all trains covered by Eurailpass, *plus* many expensive trains that do *not* honor Eurailpass, and on lake steamers and postal buses *not* covered by Eurailpass, plus local subways, buses and trams in 25 major Swiss cities.

Swiss Pass Sold worldwide, including in Switzerland. In addition to the services described above, also provides either free travel or discounts up to 50 percent on many extremely scenic and very expensive privately-owned mountain railroad and aerial cable car routes that are *not* covered by a Eurailpass. It's not unusual to save 50-60 Sfr or more, per person, on rail trips with this pass. Valid for consecutive days. New for 1998 is a 21-day Swiss Pass. Also, the companion discount is now available all year.

	2 Adults*		1 Adult	
	1st Cl.	2nd Cl.	1st Cl.	2nd Cl.
4 days	$211	$150	$264	$188
8 days	$253	$190	$316	$238
15 days	$294	$230	$368	$288
21 days	$322	$256	$403	$320
1 month	$406	$320	$508	$400

*Price per person based on two people traveling together. Includes 40 percent companion discount. Children under 16 free with parent. Children 6-15, half price, under six free.

Swiss Flexipass Swiss Flexipass changes in 1998 include a longer validity period, 21 days, up from 15 days, the option of purchasing up to six additional rail days and companion fares available all year.

	2 Adults*		1 Adult	
	1st Cl.	2nd Cl.	1st Cl.	2nd Cl.
3 days in 15	$211	$141	$264	$176
Extra rail days (6 max.)	$24	$19	$30	$24

*Price per person based on two people traveling together. Includes 40 percent companion discount. Children under 16 free with parent. Children 6-15, half price, under six free.

Swiss Card The Swiss Card is good for a one-day trip from any entry point (airport or border station) to any single destination in Switzerland and a one-day trip from any place in Switzerland to any departure point. In addition, the holder can purchase an unlimited number of both round-trip and one-way tickets for Swiss trains postal buses and lake steamers at 50 percent discount (25 percent discount on some mountain railroads). Valid for one month, the 1998 prices are: *first* class $166, *second* class $128. Children under 16 free with parent. Children 6-15 receive 50 percent discount off second class, 40 percent discount off first class, under six, free.

Swiss Family Card Children under 16 travel free if accompanied by at least one parent and holder of a Swiss Pass, Swiss Flexi Pass or Swiss Card. If the Swiss Family Card is purchased in Switzerland (sold at rail stations), it costs 20 Swiss francs. There is no charge for this card when it is obtained from Rail Europe in conjunction with the purchase of a Swiss train ticket or a Swiss train pass.

Regional Passes Sold only in Switzerland. For details on eight separate passes, obtain a brochure from any Switzerland Tourism office (see beginning of chapter).

ONE-DAY EXCURSIONS AND CITY-SIGHTSEEING

Here are 129 one-day rail trips that can be made comfortably from cities in Switzerland, returning to them in most cases before dinnertime. Notes are provided on what to see at each destination. The number after the name of each route is the *Cook's Timetable* reference. The 13 base cities are: Basel, Bern, Brig, Chur, Geneva, Interlaken, Lausanne, Locarno, Luzern, St. Moritz, Spiez, Zermatt and Zurich. When no station is designated for cities in Austria, Switzerland and West Germany, the station is "Hauptbahnhof."

Basel (Appears as *Bale* in French timetables)

The superb Picasso, Holbein, Delacroix, Gauguin, Matisse, Ingres, Courbet and Van Gogh paintings in the Kunstmuseum. The Historical Museum in the Franciscan Church in Barfusserplatz. The Municipal Casino. The collection of 18th-century clothing, ceramics and watches in the Kirschgarten mansion. Shop on Freiestrasse. See the 16th-century Town Hall. The fish market. The 15th-century New University.

The beautiful Munsterplatz. Fifteenth-century tapestries in the 14th-century Barfuserkirche. The tombs of Queen Anne and Erasmus of Rotterdam at Munster, the 13th-century cathedral. Nearby, the Folk Art Museum.

The more than 100,000 rarities from every continent (particularly those from New Guinea and the South Seas) in the Ethnological Museum at Augustinerstrasse 2. In the same complex, the extraordinary geological section at the Museum of Natural History.

The Jewish Museum of Switzerland, at Kornhausgasse 18, where Theodore Herzl presided over the first Zionist Congress, in 1897. One of the world's greatest collection of animals, at the zoo (Binningerstrasse 40), open 08:00–18:30 in summer, 08:00–17:30 in winter. Switzerland's largest, it is a short stroll from the SNCF and SBB rail stations. Or, take tram #4 or #7 from the stations.

Take a boat excursion from the pier in the back of the Hotel Three Kings. See the view of the city from the Wettstein Bridge.

Bern

The capital of Switzerland. See the comic antics of the denizens of the Bear Pit. How they love figs! The rose gardens, north of the Bear Pit. The performance of the 16th-century clock tower, the Zytglockenturm, at 11:57. The nearby old arcaded streets. Lunch on the terrace of the Casino restaurant and enjoy the view from there of the River Aare. The Art Museum, with the largest Klee collection in the world.

Climb the 254 steps to the top of one of the towers of the cathedral for a marvelous view. Play chess with people-size chessmen on the huge slate chessboard near the cathedral. The elaborate statue honoring the world postal system, without which it would be impossible to have one country handle and deliver to an addressee a mailing for which another country had been paid the postage by the addressor.

One of the world's largest stamp collections, at the Swiss PTT Museum. The view of the Alps from the terrace of the Federal Palace, and the nearby open-air flower and produce market (Tuesday and Saturday mornings). The Swiss Alpine Museum. The Natural History Museum. Prison Tower. Holy Ghost Church. The botanical gardens. The many window-boxes with flowering geraniums throughout the streets in the city center.

Geneva

The six-minute train ride [Table 505] *from* the airport to the center of Geneva runs 05:34 to 23:44. From the center of Geneva *to* the airport, it runs 05:19 to 23:37.

Walk from the rail station, down Rue du Mont Blanc, to the shore of Lake Leman. See the enormous Jet d'Eau (water fountain). Walk on the bridge across the lake to the Jardin Anglais. It has a fabulous clock of living flowers and plants and a monument to international Protestantism. It is on that side of the lake you will find the city's old narrow streets and, in St. Peter's Cathedral, the pulpit from which Calvin preached. See the view of Geneva and Lake Leman from the top of the cathedral's north tower, a climb of 153 steps.

In modern Geneva: Palais des Nations, today the European headquarters of the United Nations Organization. The chinaware collection in the Ariana Museum, open daily except Monday during summer. The Far East art (Japanese jade, Chinese porcelain, many pieces from Sri Lanka) at the Baur Collection. The botanical garden. The Museum of Historic Musical Instruments, open Tuesday, Thursday and Friday. The Ethnographic Museum, closed Monday.

The Art and History Museum, 2 Rue Charles-Galland (bus #1 from the rail station) has an archaeological collection, paintings, decorative art and sculptures, open daily except Monday 10:00–17:00. The National History Museum, 11 route de Malagnou (bus #5 from the rail station), one of the most modern museums in Europe, open Tuesday–Sunday 10:00–12:00 and 14:00–18:00, on Monday 14:00–18:00.

The Voltaire Museum, 25 rue des Delices (bus #6 from the rail station), open Monday-Friday 14:00–17:00. The world-famous Davidoff's Cigar Store at Rue de Rive 2, open Monday-Friday 08:30–18:45 and Saturday 08:00–17:00. Davidoff's has the world's biggest choice of cigars and enormous ebony and mahogany humidors.

Luzern

Walk across the 14th and 15th-century bridges spanning the Reuss River and see the 120 paintings on the ceiling of Kappelbrucke depicting Luzern's history and the 45 "Dance of Death" paintings inside the Spreuerbrucke.

See the immense 30-foot-high, 42-foot-long Lion of Luzern, carved in 1821 into a sandstone cliff which became in 1872 the entrance to the Glacier Gardens outdoor museum. The lion commemorates the bravery of those Swiss soldiers who defended Marie Antoinette during the French Revolution.

You will see at the Glacier Museum, open 08:00–18:00, the absolute proof that palm trees grew here 20,000,000 years ago when this area was tropical. A bank manager, planning to augment his income by turning a meadow into a vineyard, blasted this area so as to make a wine cellar in the rock. A geologist friend spotted a bowl-like recess in the sandstone and convinced the banker to cease the blasting. The 32 round holes found there were made by the erosion from ice-age waterfalls.

The old railway cars, locomotives, trolley cars, buses, autos, many scale models, and the simulated ride in an engine cab at the Swiss National Transport Museum at Lidostrasse 5, largest museum of its kind in Europe. There is also a very interesting model of the Gotthard Tunnel (see "Zurich–Lugano"). The museum is open 09:00–18:00 March-October, 10:00–16:00 November–February. Next door is a planetarium. Visit the art museum, near the rail station.

The giant (12,000 square foot) canvas Grand Panorama, depicting the winter campaign of the 1870–71 Franco-Prussian War.

Zurich

There is 12-minute rail service [Table 500] *from* the airport to Zurich's Hauptbahnhof (main rail station) from 06:11 to 23:41. From Zurich's Hauptbahnhof *to* the airport, it runs 06:54 to 23:34. A cruise on Lake Zurich is covered by Eurailpass. Board the boat at the lake end of Bahnhofstrasse.

Here is a great two-hour walk: Upon arriving at the main Zurich rail station, take the escalator down one level and enjoy a snack or meal in Shopville, the enormous underground shopping center beneath Bahnhof Platz, the square in front of the station. Come up from Shopville on the other side of Bahnhof Platz. Walk one mile down one side of Bahnhofstrasse, lined with smart stores. When this city's Fifth Avenue ends at the shore of Lake Zurich, take in the lakeside promenade before returning to the rail station by walking along the opposite side of Bahnhofstrasse that you walked earlier.

Upon returning to the station, go all the way through it, cross Museumstrasse, and visit the National Museum to see its collection of medieval and Renaissance art, prehistoric artifacts, elaborately carved ancient peasant furniture and much more. Open Tuesday-Friday and Sunday 10:00–12:00 and 14:00–17:00, on Saturday 14:00–16:00.

Other sights: The Bellevue Platz amusement center. The paintings and sculptures at the Kunsthaus. African and Asian art at the Rietberg Museum. Kunstgewerbemuseum (The Museum of Applied Arts): handicrafts, architecture and industrial design. The zoo. The botanical garden. The five Chagall stained-glass windows (red, blue and green) in the 13th-century Fraumunsterkirche, open Monday–Saturday 10:00–16:00, Sunday 14:00–16:00.

Basel - Baden Baden - Basel   945

Reservation is advisable for all of these trains and all of them have a restaurant car, unless designated otherwise.

Dep. Basel (SBB)	-0-	07:05 (1)	08:14 (2)	09:14	11:14
Dep. Basel (Bad. Bf.)	06:18	07:12	08:21	09:21	11:21
Arr. Baden-Baden	07:40	09:18	10:58	10:41	12:41

Sights in **Baden-Baden:** Praised for its hot salt springs since the Romans discovered the curative water in this area nearly 2,000 years ago. The illnesses treated here include rheumatism, abnormal blood pressure, metabolic disturbances, respiratory ailments, and problems caused by lack of physical exercise.

Nearly 300 prominent European families once had their permanent homes here. Fantastic landscape. The Oos Valley has been called the most beautiful valley in the world. Exotic trees include the Japanese maple, American tulip, East Asian ginkgo, Chinese trumpet, magnolia and fig. The colors of many deciduous trees make autumn glorious here.

See the Louis XIII and Louis XIV decor of the halls in the casino. The fancy boutique shops. Exhibitions of international art in the Staatliche Kunsthalle (City Art Gallery).

Motorized vehicles are not permitted in the central area of Baden-Baden. There is a constant schedule of balls, fashion shows and concerts. Food specialties here are Grunkernsuppe (a vegetable soup), game pate, pike dumplings, Blaufelchen (a kind of whitefish, from Lake Constance), raspberry schnapps and kirsch with smoked bacon, bread baked by charcoal, and pate of truffled goose-liver from nearby Strasbourg.

Dep. Baden-Baden	11:14	13:14	13:34 (3)	15:34 (3+4)
Arr. Basel (Bad Bf.)	12:38	14:38	15:37	17:38
Arr. Basel (SBB)	8 minutes later			

(1) Change trains in Offenburg. Supplement charged Basel-Offenburg. Restaurant car. (2) Change trains in Offenburg. Restaurant car to Offenburg, light refreshments to Baden-Baden. (3) Change trains in Offenburg. Light refreshments to Offenburg. (4) Plus other Baden-Baden departures at 17:34 (3), 19:14, and 21:27.

Basel - Bern - Basel 500

Reservation is advisable for most of these trains.

Dep. Basel (SBB)	07:03 (1)	07:26 (2)	08:03 (1)	08:10	09:03 (2+3)
Arr. Bern	08:12	08:35	09:12	09:31	10:12

• • •

Dep. Bern	11:48 (1)	12:48 (1)	13:48 (1)	14:48 (1)	15:48 (2+4)
Arr. Basel (SBB)	12:57	13:57	14:57	15:57	16:52

(1) Restaurant car. (2) Light refreshments. (3) Plus other departures from Basel at 10:03 (2), 11:03 (1) and 12:03 (1), arriving Bern 11:12, 12:12 and 13:12. (4) Plus other departures from Bern at 16:48 (1), 17:48 (2), 18:48 (1), 19:48, 20:48 (1), 21:48 (1) and 22:19 (2), arriving Basel at 17:57, 18:57, 19:57, 20:57, 21:57, 22:57 and 23:38.

Basel - Interlaken - Basel 560

Reservation is advisable for most of these trains, and most of them have light refreshments, unless designated otherwise.

Dep. Basel (SBB)	07:03 (1)	08:03	09:03	10:03 (2)	11:03 (1+3)
Arr. Interlaken (West)	09:12	10:12	12:12	13:12	14:12
Arr. Interlaken (Ost)	3 minutes later				

Sights in **Interlaken**: A fine summer resort and health spa. Take the funicular to **Heimwehfluh** for a marvelous view of the mountains.

Dep. Interlaken (Ost)	12:45	13:45 (2)	14:45 (1+3)	16:45	17:56 (4)
Dep. Interlaken (West)	5 minutes later				
Arr. Basel (SBB)	14:57	16:57	17:57	18:57	20:57

(1) Restaurant car. Change trains in Spiez. (2) Change trains in Spiez. (3) Plus another departure from Basel at 12:03, arriving Interlaken (West) 14:12. (4) Plus other departures from Interlaken (Ost) at 18:47 (1+3) and 20:45 (1) arriving Basel 21:57, and 22:57 .

Basel - Luxembourg - Basel 385

Dep. Basel (SNCF)	08:32 (1)	Dep. Luxembourg	14:59	19:01	22:01
Arr. Luxembourg	12:00	Arr. Basel (SNCF)	18:25	22:39	01:40

(1) Restaurant car.

Basel - Luzern - Basel 550

Dep. Basel (SBB)	05:59	07:11 (1)	07:53 (1)	09:14 (2)	09:53 (1+3)
Arr. Luzern	70 minutes later				

• • •

Dep. Luzern	09:56	10:56 (1)	11:42 (2)	12:56 (1)	13:42 (3)
Arr. Basel (SBB)	70 minutes later (6)				

(1) Light refreshments. (2) Restaurant car. (3) Plus other departures from Basel at 11:53 (1), 12:53 and 13:53 (1).

Basel - Rheinfelden - Basel 510

Dep. Basel (SBB)	Every hour from 07:51 to 21:51 + 23:35
Arr. Rheinfelden	12-17 minutes later

Sights in **Rheinfelden**: This has been a world-famed health spa since 1844. There are tours of the Cardinal and Feldschlosschen breweries. Visit the island park on the Rhine River.

Dep. Rheinfelden	07:19 + every hour from 07:56 to 22:57 and 00:30
Arr. Basel (SBB)	12-17 minutes later

Basel - Strasbourg - Basel 385

Dep. Basel (SNCF)	07:04 (1)	08:32 (2)	09:37 (3)	11:45 (1)	12:33 (3)
Arr. Strasbourg	08:38	09:55	10:53	13:00	13:50

• • •

Dep. Strasbourg	14:03 (4)	16:17 (1)	17:08 (5)	17:39	19:22 (6)
Arr. Basel (SNCF)	16:12	17:35	18:25	18:58	20:30

(1) Runs Monday-Friday, except holidays. (2) Restaurant car. (3) Runs daily, except Sundays and holidays. (4) Change trains in Mulhouse. Runs Monday-Friday, except holidays. (5) Reservation advisable. Supplement charged. Restaurant car. (6) Runs daily, except Saturday.

Basel - Zurich - Basel 510

Dep. Basel (SBB)	Frequent times from 05:55 to 21:48
Arr. Zurich	60 minutes later

• • •

Dep. Zurich	Freuant times from 06:13 to 23:00
Arr. Basel (SBB)	60 minutes later

Bern - Basel - Bern   500

Dep. Bern	Frequent times from 06:24 to 22:19
Arr. Basel (SBB)	70–80 minutes later

• • •

Dep. Basel (SBB)	Frequent times from 05:49 to 21:53
Arr. Bern	70–80 minutes later

Bern - Geneva - Bern   500

Dep. Bern	05:57 (1)	06:49 (2)	07:49 (2)	08:21 (1)	08:49 (2+3)
Arr. Geneva	07:50	08:34	09:34	10:20	10:34

• • •

Dep. Geneva	11:31 (1)	13:26 (2)	13:40 (1)	14:17 (2)	15:17 (2+4)
Arr. Bern	13:16	13:11	15:39	16:11	17:11

(1) Light refreshments. (2) Restaurant car. (3) Plus other Bern departures at frequent times from 09:49 to 23:24 .(4) Plus other Geneva departures at frequent times from 15:31 to 23:31.

Bern - Interlaken - Bern   560

Dep. Bern	06:59 (1)	07:22 (2)	08:22 (1)	09:22 (2)	10:22 (2+3)
Arr. Interlaken (West)	07:48	08:12	09:12	10:12	11:12
Arr. Interlaken (Ost)	3 minutes later				

• • •

Dep. Interlaken (Ost)	Frequent times from 05:30 to 21:43
Dep. Interlaken (West)	4 minutes after departing Ost rail station
Arr. Bern	45-55 minutes after departing Interlaken (Ost)

(1) Restaurant car. (2) Light refreshments. (3) Plus other departures from Bern at frequent times from 11:22 to 22:26.

Bern - Lausanne - Bern   500

Dep. Bern	Frequent departures from 06:34 to 23:24
Arr. Lausanne	70 minutes later

Sights in **Lausanne:** The cathedral. The Castle of St. Maire. City Hall. The Federal Palace of Justice. There are 13 museums here, including the collection of photographs at Musee Cantonal de l'Elysee (18 Avenue de l'Elysee), and the Pipe Museum (7 Rue de l'Academie).

| Dep. Lausanne | Frequent departures from 05:20 to 22:02 |
| Arr. Bern | 70 minutes later |

Bern - Fribourg - Lausanne - Bern   500

It is possible to stop and sightsee in both Fribourg and Lausanne on the same one-day excursion.

| Dep. Bern | 08:21 | 08:49 | 09:21 | 10:21 | 10:49 | 11:21 | 12:21 |
| Arr. Fribourg | 08:44 | 09:11 | 09:42 | 10:44 | 11:11 | 11:42 | 12:44 |

Sights in **Fribourg**: The 17th-century altar in the Church of the Augustines. Farmers and their wives in traditional local dress, at the Wednesday and Saturday markets. The many stone fountains in the winding streets that lead to the 16th-century Town Hall.

| Dep. Fribourg | 10:11 | 10:44 | 11:11 | 12:44 | 13:11 | 14:11 | 14:44 |
| Arr. Lausanne | 10:58 | 11:35 | 11:58 | 13:35 | 13:58 | 14:58 | 15:35 |

| Dep. Lausanne | Frequent times from 05:20 to 23:25 |
| Arr. Bern | 70 minutes later |

Bern - Fribourg - Bern   500

Here are the schedules for a one-day excursion involving only Fribourg.

| Dep. Bern | Frequent times from 05:57 to 23:24 |
| Arr. Fribourg | 20-22 minutes later |

Sights in **Fribourg**: See notes in preceding listing.

| Dep. Fribourg | Frequent times from 06:13 to 2:48 |
| Arr. Bern | 20-22 minutes later |

Bern - Luzern - Bern   515

Outstanding farm and forest scenery as you travel through Switzerland's beautiful Emmental (valley of the Emme River).

All of these trains have light refreshments.

| Dep. Bern | 06:30 | 07:30 | 08:50 | 09:30 | 10:50 | 11:30 | 12:50 (1) |
| Arr. Luzern | 07:47 | 08:47 | 10:19 | 10:47 | 12:19 | 12:47 | 14:19 |

• • •

Dep. Luzern	11:12	11:41	13:12	13:41	15:12	15:41	17:12 (2)
Arr. Bern	12:30	13:09	14:30	15:09	16:30	17:09	18:30

(1) Plus frequent other Bern departures from 13:30 to 21:44. (2) Plus frequent other Luzern departures from 17:41 to 23:13.

Bern - Langnau - Luzern - Bern 515

It is possible to stop and sightsee in both Langnau and Luzern on the same one-day excursion.

All of these trains have light refreshments, unless designated otherwise.

Dep. Bern	07:30	09:30	11:30	13:30
Arr. Langnau	25 minutes later

Sights in **Langnau:** The antique household utensils and local industry products (linen-weaving, tanning embroidery) in the museum housed in a 16th-century wood building.

Dep. Langnau	10:00	12:00	14:00	16:00	17:00
Arr. Luzern	10:47	12:47	14:47	16:47	17:47

Dep. Luzern	13:12	13:41	15:42	17:12	18:12	19:12 (1)
Arr. Bern	14:30	15:09	16:30	18:30	19:30	20:30

(1) Plus other departures from Luzern at 19:41, 20:56, 21:56, 22:54, arriving Bern 21:09, 22:15, 23:23, 00:31.

Bern - Langnau - Bern 515

Here are the schedules for a one-day excursion involving only Langnau.

All of these trains have light refreshments, unless designated otherwise.

Dep. Bern	07:30	09:30	11:30	13:30
Arr. Langnau	30 minutes later

• • •

Dep. Langnau	10:01	12:01	14:01	16:01	18:01	19:01	20:01
Arr. Bern	30 minutes later

Bern - Neuchatel - Bern   511

Dep. Bern   Frequent times from 06:04 to 23:52
Arr. Neuchatel   40–60 minutes later

Sights in **Neuchatel:** The 16th and 17th-century houses, fountains and towers. Painted, carved 16th-century statues. The exhibit of androids, a seated draftsman, scribe and musician, that have been performing since 1774 and attracting tourists from all over the world since then.

After many years of recommending a visit to the Suchard chocolate factory, we received a letter from the Suchard people telling us it *does not offer tours during July and August* when its employees take vacations and it slows down production during those months. At any time of year, Suchard requires advance notice "of at least a couple of days" before it can provide a factory tour. For chocolate maniacs, if a tour of Suchard is imperative try phoning them at (038) 21-11-55.

Failing the Suchard tour, see the city's museum of mechanical dolls and music boxes. Take a stroll up winding streets, past elegant renaissance and 17th-century houses, to the hilltop castle. Visit the Fine Art Museum. Take the funicular to the top (3,839 feet) of Chaumont for a view of the Alps.

Boat rides on the two nearby lakes (Biel and Neuchatel) *are* covered by Eurailpass.

Try the great Fondue Neuchatelois, made from white wine and kirsch schnapps. On the first Sunday of October, the local grape harvest is celebrated with a colorful parade and "Battle of Flowers." On this day, wine flows from the city's outdoor fountains instead of water.

Dep. Neuchatel   Frequent times from 05:40 to 23:16
Arr. Bern   40–60 minutes later

Bern - Zurich - Bern   500

Most of these trains have a restaurant car or light refreshments.

Dep. Bern   Frequent times from 04:50 to 23:50
Arr. Zurich   60–90 minutes later

• • •

Dep. Zurich   Frequent times from 04:46 to 0:03
Arr. Bern   60–90 minutes later

Chur - Andermatt - Chur 575

Not covered by Eurailpass. Free *with* a Swiss Pass:

Dep. Chur	05:25 (1)	06:50	07:57	08:57 (2)	09:57	10:57 (2)
Arr. Disentis	07:15	08:15	09:15	-0-	11:15	-0-
Change trains						
Dep. Disentis	07:17	08:17	09:17	-0-	11:31	-0-
Arr. Andermatt	08:24	09:24	10:45	11:23	12:45	13:21

Sights in **Andermatt:** A great ski resort. See the rock crystal altar crucifix and other treasures in the baroque St. Peter and St. Paul Church.

Dep. Andermatt	08:28	10:16	11:58 (2)	12:16	13:30 (2)	14:16 (3)
Arr. Disentis	09:38	11:26	-0-	13:33	-0-	15:33
Change trains						
Dep. Disentis	09:52	11:52	-0-	13:52	-0-	15:52
Arr. Chur	11:11	13:11	14:31	15:11	16:10	17:11

(1) Runs daily except Sundays and holidays. (2) *Glacier Express.* Runs Early June to mid-October. Reservation required (tel. 081-252-1425). Supplement charged. Direct train to and from Anermatt. No train change in Disentis. Restaurant car. (3) Plus other departures from Andermatt at 16:28, and 18:28 (4), arriving Chur 19:11, and 21:11. (4) Runs from early June to mid-October.

Chur - Arosa - Chur 541

These are cogwheel trains that leave from the front of the Chur rail station. A very scenic ride.

Dep. Chur	06:15	07:50	09:00	10:00	10:50	11:50	12:50 (1)
Arr. Arosa	58-65 minutes later						

Sights in **Arosa**: Great summer and winter sports. Fantastic mountain scenery.

Dep. Arosa	07:34	09:00	10:00	11:00	12:00	13:00	14:00 (2)
Arr. Chur	58-65 minutes later						

(1) Plus other departures from Chur every hour 13:50–16:50, then hourly from 18:00-22:00 (last departure is a bus). (2) Plus other departures from Arosa every hour 15:00–22:00; another departure at 23:10 is by bus.

Chur - Filisur - St. Moritz - Chur 540

Dep. Chur	06:42 (1)	07:52 (1)	08:55 (1)	09:55 (1)	10:52	11:52 (2+3)
Arr. Filisur	07:57	09:00	10:00	11:00	12:00	13:00
Arr. St. Moritz	08:53	09:53	10:53	11:53	12:53	13:53

• • •

Dep. St. Moritz	10:00 (2)	11:00 (1)	12:00 (1)	13:00 (1)	14:00 (1)	15:00 (1+4)
Arr. Filisur	11:02	12:02	13:02	14:02	15:02	16:02
Arr. Chur	12:05	13:05	14:05	15:05	16:05	17:05

(1) Light refreshments. (2) Restaurant car. (3) Plus other departures from Chur at 12:52 (1), 13:52 (1), 14:52 (1), 15:52 (1), 16:52, 17:55 (1), 18:52, 19:55 and 20:52. (4) Plus other departures from St. Moritz at 05:50, 07:00 (1), 08:00, 09:00 (1), 16:00 (1), 17:00 (1), 18:00 (2), 19:00 and 20:00

Sights in **Filisur:** Near a very high railway bridge, Filisur is located in a narrow valley. The Hotel Grischuna, close to the rail station, has some rooms with a view of the village and the valley. Train fans might prefer other rooms that face the rail line.

It is only a 30-minute walk to the edge of the roaring **Landwasser River**, where you can look up at the trains going over the bridge.

Chur - Zurich - Chur 520

Dep. Chur	06:16 (1)	07:16 (1)	08:16 (1)	09:16 (1)	10:16 (2)	11:16 (2)
Arr. Zurich	07:50	08:50	09:50	10:50	11:50	12:50

• • •

Dep. Zurich	11:10 (1)	12:10 (1)	13:10 (1)	14:10 (1)	15:10 (1)	16:10 (1+3)
Arr. Chur	12:44	13:45	14:45	15:45	16:45	17:45

(1) Restaurant car. (2) Reservation advisable. Restaurant car. (3) Plus other departures from Zurich at 17:10 (1), 18:10 (4), 19:10 (1), 20:10 (1), 21:10 (1) and 22:10. (4) Light refreshments.

Geneva - Annecy - Geneva 368

Dep. Geneva (Eaux-Vives)	08:13	11:10 (1)	13:14
Arr. Annecy	09:52	12:27	14:25

Sights in **Annecy**: Pronounced "Ahn–see." This is a beautiful lake resort. See the 12th-century Island Palace. The shops in the old quarter.

Dep. Annecy	09:09 (1)	12:32 (2)	14:44	17:30 (3)
Arr. Geneva (Eaux-Vives)	10:40	13:42	15:55	19:04

(1) Runs Saturdays, Sundays and holidays. (2) Runs daily, except Sundays and holidays. (3) Change trains in Annemasse (arr. 18:40-dep. 18:54).

Geneva - Basel - Geneva   500

Dep. Geneva (Corn.)	07:46 (1)	08:26 (2)	09:46 (3)	10:26 (2)	11:46 (3)
Arr. Basel (SBB)	10:38	11:38	12:38	13:38	14:38

• • •

Dep. Basel (SBB)	13:22 (3)	14:22 (2)	15:22 (3)	16:22 (2)	17:22 (3+4)
Arr. Geneva (Corn.)	16:14	17:34	18:14	19:34	20:14

(1) Reservation advisable. Restaurant car. (2) Change trains in Lausanne. (3) Light refreshments. (4) Plus other departures from Basel at 18:22 (2), 19:22 (5), 20:23 and 21:22 (6), arriving Geneva 21:20, 22:43, 22:37, 23:37 and 00:42. (5) Change trains in Biel and Lausanne. (6) Change trains in Biel.

Geneva - Bern - Geneva   500

All of these trains have a restaurant car, unless designated otherwise.

Dep. Geneva (Corn.)	06:26	06:40 (1)	07:26	08:26	09:26 (2)
Arr. Bern	08:11	08:39	09:11	10:11	11:11

• • •

Dep. Bern	12:49	14:21 (1)	14:49	15:49	16:21 (1+3)
Arr. Geneva (Corn.)	14:34	16:20	16:34	17:34	18:22

(1) Light refreshments. (2) Plus other departures from Geneva at 09:40 (1) and 10:26. (3) Plus other frequent departures from Bern from 16:49-23:24.

Geneva - Dijon - Geneva   375, 505

505
Dep. Geneva (Corn.)	06:40 (1)	08:40 (1)	11:49
Arr. Lausanne	07:21	09:21	12:21

Change trains 375
Dep. Lausanne	07:31 (3)	10:26 (3)	12:46 (3)
Arr. Dijon	09:42	12:28	14:44

• • •

505

Dep. Dijon	14:02 (3)	17:32 (3)	19:47 (3)
Arr. Lausanne	16:10	19:38	21:47

Change trains 375

Dep. Lausanne	16:39	20:00 (2)	22:39
Arr. Geneva	35-50 minutes later		

(1) Light refreshments. (2) Restaurant car. (3) TGV. Reservation advisable.

Geneva - Grenoble - Geneva   363

Dep. Geneva (Corn.)	09:30	15:32	18:38
Arr. Grenoble	11:41	17:45	20:50
	•	•	•
Dep. Grenoble	15:10	20:11	04:53
Arr. Geneva (Corn.)	17:15	22:20	07:18

Geneva - Lausanne - Montreux - Geneva   570

As these schedules indicate, a stopover in Lausanne en route to Montreux is possible.

Dep. Geneva (Corn.)	07:14	08:31	09:18	10:18	11:18	12:18 (1)
Arr. Lausanne	08:04	09:29	10:04	11:04	12:04	13:04
Arr. Montreux	20-23 minutes later					

Sights in **Montreux:** The casino offers gambling, a cabaret and a disco. The 13th-century Chillon Castle, about 1½ miles from Montreux, was immortalized by Byron. Its dungeon, used as a model for many movies, is the attraction. Board the bus to Chillon across from the Montreux rail station. Montreux is also home to the famous international jazz festival.

Dep. Montreux	11:35	12:10	13:35	14:10	15:35	16:10 (2)
Arr. Lausanne	11:56	12:31	14:42	14:31	15:56	16:31
Arr. Geneva (Corn.)	50 minutes later					

(1) Plus frequent departures from Geneva from 12:40 to 23:45. (2) Plus frequent Montreaux departures from 16:35 to 23:10.

Montreux - Gstaad - Zweisimmen - Montreux   566

This is the scenic route of both the *Panoramic Express* and *Crystal Panoramic Express*. See details about these special Observation Trains as well as the scenery and interesting places on this line under "Geneva–Montreux–Zweisimmen–Geneva"

Reservations for *Crystal Panoramic Express* are accepted only for groups, but individuals may ride if there are any vacant seats.

Dep. Montreux	09:00 (1)	10:30 (2)	11:00	12:30 (3)
Dep. Gstaad	10:12	11:48	12:30	13:29
Arr. Zweisimmen	10:34	12:15	12:58	14:05

Sight in **Gstaad:** A *very* expensive ski village.

Dep. Zweisimmen	10:44 (1)	10:50	12:00	12:44	14:00 (4)
Dep. Gstaad	11:10	11:20	12:31	13:10	14:31
Arr. Montreux	12:28	12:40	14:00	14:28	16:00

(1) Reservation required. Supplement charged. *Crystal Panoramic Express*. First class only. Runs Saturdays, Sundays and holidays. (2) Reservation required for first-class, advisable for second class. Supplement charged. *Golden Panoramic Express*. Runs daily. (3) Plus other Montreux departures at 14:00 (1), 14:30 (2) and 15:00. (4) Plus other Zweisimmen departures at 14:44 (2), 16:00, 16:50, 18:00 and 20:00, arriving Montreux at 16:28, 18:00, 18:40, 20:00 and 21:48.

Geneva - Lyon - Geneva   372

The first 90 minutes from Geneva is noted for scenic canyons. Occasionally, two trains depart from the same track at Lyon's Perrache rail station, heading in opposite directions. Be sure to stand at the correct end (North or South) of the track in order to board the train you want to ride. Check the departure signs at the underground passageway. Do not rely merely on a track number when departing from Perrache rail station!

Next to the north passageway of Track "A" is a take-out restaurant, handy for provisioning your trip.

Dep. Geneva (Corn.)	07:08	10:22	12:55 (1)
Arr. Lyon (Part-Dieu)	08:56	12:13	14:42
Arr. Lyon (Per.)	9 minutes later		

•   •   •

Dep. Lyon (Per.)	12:16 (1)	17:10	19:21 (1)
Dep. Lyon (Part-Dieu)	9 minutes later		
Arr. Geneva (Corn.)	14:14	19:06	21:29

(1) Light refreshments.

Geneva - Neuchatel - Geneva 500

Dep. Geneva (Corn.)	07:26 (1)	09:26 (1)	10:46	11:26 (1+2)
Arr. Neuchatel	09:00	11:00	12:06	13:00

Sights in **Neuchatel:** See notes under "Bern–Neuchatel"

Dep. Neuchatel	12:54 (3)	13:00 (1)	13:54 (3)	14:54 (3)	15:54 (3+4)
Arr. Geneva (Corn.)	14:14	14:34	15:14	16:14	17:14

(1) Change trains in Lausanne. Restaurant car or light refreshments. (2) Plus other frequent Geneva departures from 12:26 to 22:18. (3) Light refreshments. (4) Plus other frequent Neuchatel departures from 16:00 to 23:00.

Geneva - Zurich - Geneva 500

Reservation is advisable for all of these trains and all of them have a restaurant car or light refreshments.

Dep. Geneva (Cor.)	Frequent times from 04:34 to 21:17
Arr. Zurich (Hbf.)	3 hours later

• • •

Dep. Zurich (Hbf.)	Every hour from 06:11 to 20:39
Arr. Geneva (Cor.)	3 hours later

Interlaken - Bern - Interlaken 560

Dep. Interlaken (Ost)	Every hour from 05:30 to 21:43
Dep. Interlaken (West)	5 minutes after departing Ost rail station
Arr. Bern	53 minutes after departing Interlaken (Ost)

• • •

Dep. Bern	Every hour from 06:59 to 23:26
Arr. Interlaken (West)	48 minutes after departing Bern
Arr. Interlaken (Ost)	5 minutes later

Interlaken - Lausanne - Interlaken   500, 560

560

Dep. Interlaken (Ost)	07:08	07:45 (2)	08:45 (1)	09:45 (1)	10:45 (1)
Dep. Interlaken (West)	5 minutes later				
Arr. Bern	08:05	08:38	09:38	10:38	11:38
Change trains 500					
Dep. Bern	08:21 (2)	08:49 (1)	09:49 (1)	10:49 (1)	10:49 (1)
Arr. Lausanne	09:35	09:58	10:58	11:58	11:58

•   •   •

500

Dep. Lausanne	13:02 (1)	14:02 (1)	14:25 (2)	15:26 (1)	16:25 (2+3)
Arr. Bern	13:48	15:11	15:39	17:14	17:39
Change trains 560					
Dep. Bern	14:22 (2)	15:22 (1)	16:22 (1)	17:28 (1)`	17:56
Arr. Interlaken (West)	15:12	16:12	17:12	18:16	18:50
Arr. Interlaken (Ost)	5 minutes later				

(1) Reservation advisable. Restaurant car. (2) Light refreshments. (3) Plus other Lausanne departures at 17:02 (1), 17:25 (2), 19:02 and 22:02, arriving Bern (West) 18:11, 18:39, 20:11 and 23:11.

Interlaken - Murren - Jungfraujoch - Interlaken   564

This one-day trip covers the heart of the Bernese Oberland area. *It is not covered by Eurail-pass.* The Swiss Pass provides a discount.

All of the train changes shown here take less than one minute.

Hiking and trout fishing are summer activities in **Murren**. Both it and **Wengen** are postcard Alpine villages. There have been top ski resorts in this area since 1906. **Jung-fraujoch** is the highest (11,333 feet) rail station in Europe. From there, you can see the Jungfrau, Eiger and Monch peaks. The highest waterfall in Europe (2,000-foot drop) is spectacular there in late spring and early summer.

The following schedule is just one example of the many schedule combinations available for this trip. For instance, you can pick a later departure time from Interlaken (from 09:02 to 12:32), make the circle trip and still get back in time for your choice of dinner times. Service is frequent in the summer, with trains running every 15 to 30 minutes.

Dep. Interlaken (Ost)	08:32	*Change trains*	
Arr. Lauterbrunnen	08:54	Dep. Scheidegg	11:30
Change to funicular		Arr. Jungfraujoch	12:22
Dep. Lauterbrunnen	09:02	*Change trains*	
Arr. Murren	09:32	Dep. Jungfraujoch	13:00
Return to Lauterbrunnen		Arr. Scheidegg	13:49
Dep. Murren	10:00	*Change trains*	
Arr. Lauterbrunnen	10:30	Dep. Scheidegg	13:59
Change to a train		Arr. Grindelwald	14:44
Dep. Lauterbrunnen	10:35	*Change trains*	
Dep. Wengen	10:55	Dep Grindelwald	14:50
Arr. Scheidegg	11:20	Arr. Interlaken (Ost)	15:27

Interlaken - Luzern - Interlaken   561

There is a very scenic 48-mile panorama of the Alps on this trip along the shore of Lake Brienz.

Dep. Interlaken (Ost)	07:13	07:56	09:19	10:19 (1)	11:00 (1)
Arr. Luzern	09:05	10:05	11:05	12:05	13:05
		•	•	•	
Dep. Luzern	11:54	12:54 (1)	13:54	14:54	15:54 (2)
Arr. Interlaken (Ost)	14:00	14:40	15:59	16:40	17:59

(1) Restaurant car. (2) Plus other departures from Luzern at 16:54, 17:54, 18:54 and 20:24, arriving Interlaken 18:40, 20:02, 20:40, 21:21 and 22:22.

Lausanne - Sion - Lausanne   570

Dep. Lausanne	08:04	08:29 (1)	08:53 (2)	09:29	09:53	10:29 (3)
Arr. Sion	09:0	09:50	09:47	10:38	11:00	11:40

Sights in **Sion**: Ruins of the 13th-century Valere Castle and the 4th–11th-century religious art in the museum there. The world's oldest operable pipe organ (built in 1390), carved and painted wood chests and 15th-century frescoes in the Church of Our Lady of Valere, open daily except Monday, 9:00–12:00 and 14:00–18:00.

The collection of Roman antiquities in the Cantonal Archaeological Museum on rue des Chateaux. Paintings by artists of this area in the Majorie Fine Arts Museum. Both museums are open daily except Monday 9:00–12:00 and 14:00–18:00.

The astronomical clock and carved doors of the 17th-century City Hall. The ancient Tour de Sorciers (Tower of the Wizards). The 9th-century Romanesque bell-tower of the

Cathedral. Supersaxo, the 16th-century mansion of a Renaissance nobleman.

| Dep. Sion | 13:23 | 14:17 | 15:17 | 15:52 | 16:17 (2+5) |
| Arr. Lausanne | 14:27 | 15:27 | 16:27 | 17:03 | 17:27 |

(1) Light refreshments. (2) Supplement payable. Restaurant car. (3) Plus other departures from Lausanne at 11:04 (1), 11:29, 12:04 (1) and 13:04 (1).

Luzern - Andermatt - Luzern   550, 577

The Goschenen-Andermatt-Goschenen portion of this one-day excursion (a thrilling ride in the Schollenen Canyon) is by rack railway and is *not* covered by Eurailpass. *There is no extra charge with* a Swiss Pass.

550

Dep. Luzern	07:16	10:24 (1)	12:24 (2)	13:16 (3)
Arr. Goschenen	08:50	11:50	13:50	14:50
Change trains 577				
Dep. Goschenen	09:15	11:51	13:57	16:11
Arr. Andermatt	09:25	12:06	14:06	16:25

Sights in **Andermatt**: A great ski resort.

577

Dep. Andermatt	12:50	15:30	17:30
Arr. Goschenen	13:05	15:45	17:45
Change trains 550			
Dep. Goschenen	13:10 (3)	16:10 (2)	18:10 (1)
Arr. Luzern	14:43	17:34	19:35

(1) Reservation advisable. Restaurant car. Change trains in Arth-Goldau. (2) Supplement charged. Restaurant car. Change trains in Arth Goldau. (3) Light refreshments.

Luzern - Basel - Luzern   550

| Dep. Luzern | 06:43 (1) | 07:54 (1) | 08:54 (1) | 09:54 (1) | 10:54 |
| Arr. Basel (SBB) | 07:55 | 09:06 | 10:06 | 11:06 | 12:06 |

•   •   •

| Dep. Basel (SBB) | 11:14 (2) | 11:53 (1) | 13:14 (2) | 13:53 (1) | 15:14 (2+3) |
| Arr. Luzern | 12:19 | 13:05 | 14:19 | 15:05 | 16:19 |

(1) Light refreshments. (2) Reservation advisable. Supplement charged. Restaurant car. (3) Plus other departures from Basel at frequent times from 15:53 to 23:10.

Luzern - Bern - Luzern   515

Most of these trains have light refreshments.

Dep. Luzern	06:43	07:12 (1)	07:41	09:12 (1)	09:41	11:12 (1)	11:41
Arr. Olten	07:23	-0-	08:18	-0-	10:18	-0-	12:18
Change trains							
Dep. Olten	07:31	-0-	08:22	-0-	10:22	-0-	12:22
Arr. Bern	08:12	08:30	09:09	10:30	11:09	12:30	13:09

•   •   •

Dep. Bern	13:30 (1)	14:50	15:30 (1)	16:30 (1)	17:30 (1)	18:30 (1+2)
Arr. Olten	-0-	15:38	-0-	-0-	-0-	-0-
Change trains						
Dep. Olten	-0-	15:42	-0-	-0-	-0-	-0-
Arr. Luzern	14:47	16:19	16:47	17:47	19:47	19:47

(1) Direct train. No train change in Olten. (2) Plus other frequent Bern departures from 18:50 to 22:19.

Luzern - Interlaken - Luzern   561

Dep. Luzern	06:30	07:54 (1)	08:54	09:10	10:54 (2)
Arr. Interlaken (Ost)	08:40	09:40	10:40	10:55	12:40

•   •   •

Dep. Interlaken (Ost)	10:19 (1)	11:00	12:19 (3)	13:00	14:19 (4)
Arr. Luzern	12:05	13:05	13:05	15:05	16:05

(1) Restaurant car. (2) Plus other departures from Luzern at frequent times from 11:24 to 20:24. (3) Light refreshments. (4) Plus other departures from Interlaken at frequent times from 15:00 to 19:35.

Luzern - Neuchatel - Luzern   511, 515

515

Dep. Luzern	06:43 (1)	07:12 (2)	08:12 (1)	09:41 (2)	11:12 (1)	11:31 (1)
Arr. Bern	08:12	08:30	09:30	11:09	12:30	13:09
Change trains 511						
Dep. Bern	08:23	05:54	09:54	11:23	12:54	14:22
Arr. Neuchatel	08:56	09:43	10:43	11:56	12:43	14:57

•   •   •

511

Dep. Neuchatel	14:04	15:04	16:04	17:04	18:04	19:04 (3)
Arr. Bern	14:49	15:49	16:49	17:49	18:49	19:49

Change trains 515

Dep. Bern	14:50 (1)	16:30	16:50 (1)	18:30	18:50 (1)	19:30
Arr. Luzern	16:19	17:47	18:19	19:47	20:19	20:47

(1) Change trains in Olten. Light refreshments. (2) Light refreshments. (3) Plus other departures from Neuchatel at 21:13 and 22:06, arriving Bern 22:08 and 23:18.

Luzern - Schwyz - Luzern 550

Dep. Luzern	07:16	08:24 (1)	09:16 (2)	10:24 (1)	11:16 (2)	12:24 (3)
Arr. Schwyz	50 minutes later					

Sights in **Schwyz:** Visit the Staatsarcivmuseum (National Archives Museum), to see the 13th-century Oath of Eternal Alliance, the document which marks the founding of Switzerland. This village's name became the name of the country (Schweiz). The museum is one mile (uphill) from the rail station. A bus meets every train. There are also nicely restored 17th and 18th-century patrician homes here.

Dep. Schwyz	11:57 (2)	12:57 (2)	13:57 (2)	14:57 (1)	15:57 (2)	16:57 (1+4)
Arr. Luzern	50 minutes later					

(1) Change trains in Arth Goldau. (2) Light refreshments. (3) Reservation advisable. Restaurant car. Change trains in Arth Goldau. (4) Plus other departures from Schwyz at 17:57 (2), 18:57 (1), 19:57, 20:57.

Luzern - Zurich - Luzern 555

Most of these trains have light refreshments.

Dep. Luzern	Frequent times from 06:04 to 23:10
Arr. Zurich	50-65 minutes later

• • •

Dep. Zurich	Frequent times from 06:01 to 00:13
Arr. Luzern	50-65 minutes later

Zurich - Andermatt - Zurich   550, 574

The Goschenen–Andermatt–Goschenen portion of this one-day excursion (a thrilling ride down the **Schollenen Canyon**) is by rack railway. It is not covered by Eurailpass. *With* a Swiss Pass there is no extra charge.

All of the trains **Zurich–Gochenen** *and vice-versa, have light refreshments, unless designated otherwise.*

550

Dep. Zurich	08:07 (1)	10:07 (1)	12:07 (1)
Arr. Goschenen	09:45	11:45	13:45
Change trains 577			
Dep. Goschenen	09:57	11:51	13:57
Arr.. Andermatt	15 minutes later		

Sights in **Andermatt**: A great ski resort.

577

Dep. Andermatt	11:30	14:30	16:30	18:30
Arr. Goschenen	10:45	14:45	16:45	19:45
Change trains 550				
Dep. Goschenen	11:10 (2)	15:10 (2)	17:10 (2)	20:10 (3)
Arr. Zurich	12:53	16:53	18:53	21:53

(1) Light refreshments. (2) Change trains in Arth Goldau.

Zurich - Arosa - Zurich   520, 541

520

| Dep. Zurich | 06:10 (1) | 07:10 (1) | 08:10 (2) | 09:10 (1) | 10:10 (3) | 11:10 (4) |
| Arr. Chur | 07:45 | 08:44 | 09:44 | 10:44 | 11:44 | 12:44 |

The Chur–Arosa cogwheel train leaves from the front of the Chur rail station. This is a very scenic ride.

Change trains 541

| Dep. Chur | 07:50 | 08:50 | 09:50 | 10:50 | 11:50 | 12:50 |
| Arr. Arosa | one hour later | | | | | |

Sights in **Arosa**: Great summer and winter sports. Fantastic mountain scenery.

541

Dep. Arosa	10:00	11:05	12:00	13:00	14:00	15:00 (5)
Arr. Chur	11:07	12:07	13:07	14:07	15:07	16:07

Change trains 520

Dep. Chur	11:16 (4)	12:16 (4)	13:16 (4)	14:16 (4)	15:16 (1)	16:15 (4)
Arr. Zurich	12:50	13:50	14:50	15:50	16:50	17:50

(1) Light refreshments. (2) Reservation advisable. Restaurant car. (3) Reservation advisable. Light refreshments. (4) Restaurant car. (5) Plus other departures from Arosa (parenthesis designate Chur–Arosa service) at 16:00, 17:00, 18:00, 19:00 and 20:00, arriving Chur 1 hour later.

Zurich - Basel - Zurich   510

Many of these trains have a restaurant car or light refreshments.

Dep. Zurich	Frequent times from 04:46 to 23:30
Arr. Basel (SBB)	60–70 minutes later

Dep. Basel (SBB)	Frequent times from 05:21 to 23:31
Arr. Zurich	60–70 minutes later

Zurich - Bern - Zurich   500

Many of these trains have a restaurant car or light refreshments.

Dep. Zurich	Frequent times from 04:46 to 22:03
Arr. Bern	90 minutes later

Dep. Bern	Frequent times from 04:50 to 23:11
Arr. Zurich	90 minutes later

Zurich - Chur - Zurich   520

Many of these trains have a restaurant car or light refreshments.

Dep. Zurich	Frequent times from 06:10 to 23:10
Arr. Chur	90 minutes later

Sights in **Chur:** This 2,100-year-old village is located at what has been a strategic pass in the Alps since Roman times. Walk from the station up through the small business area to a hilltop church and see the unusual cemetery there. The modern portion of it has rows of graves that are solidly decorated with living, blossoming plants.

Also see the fine stained-glass and the 12th-century carved altar in the 15th-century cathedral. The Bishop's Palace. A one-hour walking tour of Chur is made easy by following red and green footprints painted on the sidewalks. The footprints are matched to a map available at the city's tourist office.

Dep. Chur   Frequent times from 04:54 to 22:16
Arr. Zurich   90 minutes later

Zurich - Landquart - Davos - Zurich 520, 545

520

Dep. Zurich	07:10	08:10	09:10	10:10	11:10
Arr. Landquart	08:34	09:34	10:34	11:34	12:34
Change trains 545					
Dep. Landquart	08:45	09:45	10:45	11:45	12:45
Arr. Klosters	09:29	10:29	11:20	12:20	13:20
Arr. Davos (Platz)	28 minutes after arriving Klosters.				

Sights in **Davos**: One of the world's most popular ski resorts. Also popular for its skating rinks, hiking trails, a sled run, horse-drawn sleigh rides, indoor swimming, hang-gliding, horseback riding and ice hockey.

Take the 22-minute ride on the Parsenn cable railway, once described by Vogue Magazine as "the Rolls Royce of mountain railways," to the ridge of **Weissfluh**. A cable car ascends from there to the summit, the start of the different ski runs to **Serneus**, **Sass** and **Klosters**.

A general-fare ticket allows unlimited use of the entire network of funicular railways, ski lifts and cable cars for six days. It also covers the buses that run every 15 minutes from one end of Davos to the other.

545

Dep. Davos (Platz)	12:02	13:02	14:02	15:02	16:02 (1)
Dep. Klosters	29 minutes after departing Davos				
Arr. Landquart	13:10	14:10	15:10	16:10	17:10
Change trains 520					
Dep. Landquart	13:26	14:26	15:26	16:26	17:26
Arr. Zurich	14:50	15:50	16:50	17:50	18:50

(1) Plus other departures from Davos at 17:05, 18:05, 19:05, 20:00 and 21:00, arriving Zurich 19:50, 20:50, 21:50, 22:50 and 23:50.

Zurich - Frankfurt - Zurich   73

Both of these trains charge a supplement that includes reservation fee and have a restaurant car.

Dep. Zurich	05:57	07:57	Dep. Frankfurt	16:05	18:05
Arr. Frankfurt	09:53	11:53	Arr. Zurich	20:03	20:03

Zurich - Geneva - Zurich   500

Most of these trains have a restaurant car or light refreshments. Reservations are advisable

Dep. Zurich	Frequent times from 04:46 to 21:06
Arr. Geneva (Corn.)	3 hours later

• • •

Dep. Geneva (Corn.)	Frequent times from 04:34 to 22:02
Arr Zurich	3 hours later

Zurich - Interlaken - Zurich   560

All of these trains have light refreshments, unless designated otherwise.

Dep. Zurich	06:00	08:03 (1)	10:03 (1)	11:03 (2)	12:03 (2)	13:03 (2)
Arr. Interlaken (Ost)	08:15	10:15	12:15	13:15	14:16	15:15

Sights in **Interlaken**: See notes about sightseeing in Interlaken under "Basel–Interlaken"

Dep. Interlaken (Ost)	13:35 (2)	14:45 (2)	15:45 (2)	17:45 (1)	18:45 (1)	20:45 (1)
Arr. Zurich	15:67	16:57	17:57	19:57	20:57	20:57

(1) Restaurant car. (2) Light refreshments.

Zurich - Lugano - Zurich   550

Dep. Zurich	06:33 (1)	07:04 (2)	08:33 (1)	09:07 (2)	10:07 (1)	11:07 (2)
Arr. Lugano	09:50	09:45	11:22	12:03	13:23	14:06

• • •

Dep. Lugano	12:37 (1)	13:57 (1)	14:37 (1)	15:57 (2)	16:37 (1)	17:57 (2+3)
Arr. Zurich	15:53	16:53	17:53	18:53	19:53	20:53

(1) Light refreshments. (2) Reservation advisable. Supplement charged. Restaurant car. (3) Plus other Lugano departures at 19:12 (2), 20:41 (1) arriving Zurich, 21:53 and 23:24.

Zurich - Luzern - Zurich   555

Most of these trains have light refreshments.

Dep. Zurich	Frequent times from 06:01 to 00:13
Arr. Luzern	50 minutes later

• • •

Dep. Luzern	Frequent times from 06:04 to 23:10
Arr. Zurich	50 minutes later

Zurich - Milan - Zurich   84

See the description of this very scenic trip under either "Zurich–Bellinzona–Lugano"

Reservation is advisable for all of these trains, and all of them have a restaurant car.

Dep. Zurich	07:04	08:43 (1)	Dep. Milan (Cen.)	16:25	18:15 (1)
Arr. Milan (Cen.)	10:45	12:45	Arr. Zurich	20:53	21:53

(1) Supplement charged.

Zurich - Munich - Zurich   75

Reservation is advisable for all of these trains, and all of them have a restaurant car.

Dep. Zurich	07:33 (1)	09:33 (1)	Dep. Munich	14:02 (1)	18:15 (1)
Arr. Munich	11:52	13:57	Arr. Zurich	18:26	22:23

(1) Supplement payable.

Zurich - Neuchatel - Zurich   500

Dep. Zurich	07:06 (1)	08:06 (1)	09:06 (1)	10:06 (2)	11:06 (1+3)
Arr. Neuchatel	00:90	09:54	11:00	11:54	13:00

Dep. Neuchatel	12:06 (2)	13:01 (1)	14:06 (1)	15:01 (1)	16:06 (1+4)
Arr. Zurich	13:54	14:54	15:54	16:54	17:53

(1) Light refreshments. (2) Reservation advisable. Restaurant car. (3) Plus another Zurich departure at 12:06 (1), arriving Neuchatel 13:54. (4) Plus other Neuchatel departures at 17:01 (2), 18:06 (1), 19:01 (1), 20:06 (1) and 21:01 (1), arriving Zurich 18:54, 19:54, 20:54, 21:54 and 22:54.

Zurich - Rheinfelden - Zurich   510

Dep. Zurich	06:13 (1)	07:00 (1)	08:00 (1)	09:00 (2)	10:00 (2+3)
Dep. Brugg	06:45	07:25	08:25	09:25	10:31
Arr. Rheinfelden	07:19	07:56	08:56	09:56	11:08

Sights in **Rheinfelden**: A world-famed health spa since 1844. There are tours of the Cardinal and Feldschlosschen breweries. Visit the island park on the Rhine River.

Dep. Rheinfelden	13:03 (2)	15:03 (2)	17:03 (2)	18:03 (1)	19:03 (2+4)
Arr. Zurich	65 minutes later				

(1) Restaurant car. (2) Light refreshments. (3) Plus other departures from Zurich at 11:00 (2), 12:00 (1) and 14:00 (2). (4) Plus other departures from Rheinfelden at 20:03 (1), 21:03 (2), 22:03 (2) and 23:48 (2).

Zurich - St. Moritz - Zurich   520

Dep. Zurich	07:10 (1)	08:10 (2)	Dep. St. Moritz	12:00 (2)	13:00 (1+3)
Arr. Chur	08:44	09:44	Arr. Chur	-0-	-0-
Change trains			*Change trains*		
Dep. Chur	08:51 (2)	09:51	Dep. Chur	-0-	-0-
Arr. St. Moritz	10:53	11:53	Arr. Zurich	15:50	16:50

(1) Light refreshments. (2) Restaurant car. (3) Plus other departures from St. Moritz at 14:00, 15:00, 16:00 (2), 17:00 (2), 18:00 (1), 19:00 and 20:00, departing Chur 16:09 (1), 17:10 (2), 18:09, 19:10 (2), 20:16, 21:16 and 22:16, arriving Zurich 17:26, 18:28, 19:26, 20:28, 21:50, 22:50 and 23:50.

Sights in **St. Moritz:** The lovely scenery of the Alps, reflected on the Lake of St. Moritz. The curative waters. Great summer sports (swimming, sailing, fishing, golf, mountain climbing) as well as winter sports. The creme de la creme of the international jet set is here December to April.

See the collection of porcelain stoves, furniture and carved woodwork in the Engadine Museum, open Monday–Saturday 09:30–12:00 and 14:00–17:00, also on Sunday 10:00–12:00. Many paintings of this beautiful area by Giovanni Segantini in the Segantini Museum, open Monday–Saturday 09:30–12:00 and 14:00–16:00, on Sunday 14:30–16:00.

Zurich - Schwyz - Zurich   550

Dep. Zurich   06:33 (1) 08:07 (1) 09:07 (2) 10:07 (1) 11:07 (2) 12:07 (1)
Arr. Schwyz   one hour later

• • •

Dep. Schwyz   10:57   11:57 (2) 12:57 (2) 13:57 (2) 14:57 (2) 15:57 (2) 16:57(2+3)
Arr. Zurich   one hour later

(1) Light refreshments. (2) Change trains in Arth Goldau. Plus other departures from Schwyz at 17:57
(2), 18:57 (1) and 19:57 (2).

Zurich - Solothurn - Zurich   500

All of these trains have a restaurant car or light refreshments.

Dep. Zurich   Frequent times from 06:06 to 22:06
Arr. Solothurn   60-70 minutes later

Sights in **Solothurn**: Switzerland's oldest town. (It and Trier, in Germany, are the two oldest towns north of the Alps.) This is the best preserved Baroque town in Switzerland, located in the **Aare Valley**, at the foot of the **Jura Mountains**. Everything worth seeing here
can be reached by walking the town's narrow streets: the town's many fine statues, 11
churches and chapels, 11 ornamental fountains, and the 11 steps leading to the entrance of
the Cathedral of St. Ours which has 11 bells, 11 towers and 11 altars.

Solothurn became in 1481 the *eleventh* canton to join the Swiss Federation!

See the outstanding ancient art here. Holbein's Madonna in the museum. Traces of the 4th-cen-
tury Roman wall. Farmers selling flowers, fruits and vegetables in the town center every Wednesday
and Saturday. The marvelous Assumption over the high altar in the Jesuit church.

The bulb domes on the twin towers of the Town Hall. The comprehensive collection of arms and
armor in the Old Arsenal Museum, said to be the second largest collection of weapons in Europe. It
has 400 suits of armor among its exhibits. The Italian belltower of the cathedral.

Dep. Solothurn   Frequent times from 05:41 to 21:02
Arr. Zurich   60-70 minutes later

Zurich - Stuttgart - Zurich   84

Dep. Zurich	06:13	09:13	10:33	
Arr. Stuttgart	09:13	12:17	14:17	

• • •

Dep. Stuttgart	13:46	15:46	16:46	18:46
Arr. Zurich	16:47	18:47	19:47	21:47

Zurich - Winterthur - Zurich   530

Dep. Zurich	Frequent times from 06:01 to 23:45
Arr. Winterthur	22-27 minutes later

Sights in **Winterthur**: More art treasures than any other place in Switzerland, at the country's National Gallery in the Am Roemerholz mansion. Great Austrian, German and Swiss paintings.

Dep. Winterthur	Frequent times from 05:56 to 23:51
Arr. Zurich	22-27 minutes later

Zurich - Zug - Zurich   550

Dep. Zurich	Frequent times from 06:33 to 23:07
Arr. Zug	26-29 minutes later

Sights in **Zug**: This village is located on the northeast shore of the 14-mile-long Lake Zug. See the spires and massive towers of the 15th-century Church of St. Oswald. The stained-glass for which this area is noted and also gold and silver work, embroidery and wood carvings in the Museum at the 16th-century Town Hall.

See the narrow, ancient houses (most of them with overlapping second and upper floors) on Ober-Alstadt and Unter-Alstadt. The elaborately-carved choir stalls in the 15th-century St. Oswald's Church.

To reach the top floor of the 3,255-foot-high **Zugerberg**, either take the 20-minute bus ride from the rail station to the **Schoenegg** suburb and then a cable railway from there, or make the two-hour climb by foot. The splendid view at the top is of **Lake Zug** and parts of **Lake Luzern**, framed by the Alpine giants Mount Pilatus, Mount Rigi, Jungfrau, Eiger and Finsterahorn.

Visit the seven-story Glass House, facing the rail station. Its shopping center has stores that offer fine shoes, gourmet food, wine, jewelry and flowers.

There are short boat trips, to **Walchwil** and to **Arth**.

Try the local specialties: *rotel* (a tasty salmon-like fish from the lake), the local cherries that are used for producing the liqueur kirsch, and the local cake, kirsch-torte, laced with the cherry liqueur.

Dep. Zug	Frequent times from 06:28 to 23:09
Arr. Zurich	26-29 minutes later

SCENIC RAIL TRIPS IN SWITZERLAND

Basel - Schaffhausen - Basel 939

An easy one-day round-trip, to see the marvelous Rhine Falls.

Dep. Basel (Bad Bf.)	08:18	10:18	12:18	14:18	16:18
Arr. Schaffhausen	09:33	11:33	13:33	15:33	17:3
		•	•	•	
Dep. Schaffhausen	10:28	12:28	14:28	16:28	18:38
Arr. Basel (Bad Bf.)	11:45	13:45	15:46	17:45	19:46

Bern - Brig - Bern 560

An easy one-day round-trip that affords a view of **Rhone Valley** and **Lonza Valley** canyons, lakes and mountains plus the Lake Thun scenery at Spiez about which we enthuse in the "Geneva–Spiez" trip .and going through the nine-mile Lotschberg Tunnel and over the Bietschtal Bridge. This structure takes the train 255 feet above the ravine it crosses.

Dep. Bern	06:20	07:26 (1)	08:11	08:50	09:25 (1+2)
Arr. Spiez	06:50	07:56	08:31	09:20	09:55
Dep. Spiez	06:52	07:58	08:41	09:21	09:57
Arr. Brig	07:56	09:03	09:48	10:19	11:02

Sights in **Brig**: Switzerland's largest private residence, the 17th-century Stockalper Castle, built by a very successful businessman.

Dep. Brig	07:58 (3)	08:58 (3)	09:58 (3)	10:58 (1)	11:58 (3)	12:58 (3+4)
Arr. Spiez	09:02	10:02	11:02	12:02	13:02	14:02
Dep. Spiez	09:03	10:03	11:03	12:03	12:03	14:03
Arr. Bern	31 minutes after departing Spiez.					

(1) Light refreshments. (2) Plus other departures from Bern at frequent times from 10:26 to 23:26. (3) Restaurant car. (4)) Plus other departures from Brig at frequent times from 13:50 to 21:50.

Bern - Brig - Domodossola - Bern 560

To see all of the scenery and Lotschberg Tunnel noted above under "Bern–Brig" plus having the experience of going through the 11.9-mile Simplon (Europe's longest rail tunnel), make the Bern–Domodossola portion of the Bern–Milan trip.

The Simplon is actually two tunnels, one southbound and a 65-foot longer bore for the separate northbound tunnel.

280

Dep. Bern	07:34 (1)	08:50 (1)	12:58 (1)	
Arr. Brig	-0-	-0-	-0-	
Change trains				
Dep. Brig	08:56	10:19	14:28	
Arr. Domodossola	09:32	11:02	15:05	

• • •

Dep. Domodossola	09:56 (1)	12:12 (1)	17:13 (1)	18:28 (1)
Arr. Brig	10:31	12:58	17:58	19:02
Change trains				
Dep. Brig	-0-	-0-	-0-	-0-
Arr. Bern	12:02	15:57	19:34	20:26

(1) Reservation advisable. Direct train. No train change in Brig. Restaurant car or light refreshments.

Bern - Interlaken - Brienz - Interlaken - Bern   560, 561

There is fine canyon, lake and mountain scenery on this easy one-day round-trip.

Most of the trains Bern–Interlaken and v.v. have light refreshments.

560

Dep. Bern	07:22	08:22 (1)	09:22	10:22	11:22 (1+2)
Arr. Interlaken (Ost)	08:15	09:15	10:15	11:15	12:15
Change trains 561					
Dep. Interlaken (Ost)	09:19	09:40	10:19 (1)	11:32	12:19
Arr. Brienz	09:39	10:02	10:39	11:55	12:38

• • •

561

Dep. Brienz	09:02	10:22	11:04	12:22	13:03
Arr. Interlaken (Ost)	09:26	10:40	11:26	12:40	13:27
Change trains 560					
Dep. Interlaken (Ost)	09:45 (1)	10:45	11:45	12:45	13:45
Arr. Bern	10:38	11:28	12:28	13:28	14:28

(1) Restaurant car. (2) Plus other departures from Bern (that allow the same round-trip) at 12:22, 13:22 (1), 14:22, 15:22, 16:22 and 17:22 (1), arriving back in Bern 15:28, 16:28, 17:28, 18:28, 19:28 and 20:28.

Bern - Interlaken - Wengen - Jungfrau - Grindelwald - Interlaken - Bern   560, 564

This easy one-day trip covers the heart of the Bernese Oberland area and offers very good gorge, lake and mountain scenery. There have been popular ski resorts in this area since 1906.

The Interlaken-Jungfraujoch-Interlaken portion of this excursion is *not* covered by Eurailpass. *With* a Swiss Pass there was a discount.

At **Jungfraujoch**, passengers alight to look down on the great Jungfrau glacier and stroll in the "Ice Palace" carved inside the glacier. Jungfraujoch is the highest (11,333 feet) rail station in Europe. Fabulous views of the Jungfrau, Eiger and Monch peaks can be seen from the revolving restaurant, which rotates completely every 50 minutes. The highest waterfall in Europe (2,000-foot drop) is spectacular in late spring and early summer.

We suggest, for variety, you go from Interlaken to Jungfraujoch *via Wengen* and then return to Interlaken *via Grindelwald*.

560		
Dep. Bern	07:22	08:22 (1)
Arr. Interlaken (Ost)	08:15	09:15
Change trains 564		
Dep. Interlaken (Ost)	08:32	09:32
Arr. Wengen	09:14	10:24
Arr. Scheidegg	09:45	10:55
Change trains		
Dep. Scheidegg	10:02	11:02
Arr. Jungfraujoch	10:53	11:53
Sightsee in Jungfraujoch		

564		
Dep. Jungfraujoch	12:00	13:00
Arr. Scheidegg	12:49	13:49
Change trains		
Dep. Scheidegg	13:02	14:02
Arr. Grindelwald	13:45	14:45
Change trains		
Dep. Grindelwald	13:50	14:50
Arr. Interlaken (Ost)	14:27	15:27
Change trains 560		
Dep. Interlaken (Ost)	14:45	15:45 (1)
Arr. Bern	15:38	16:38

(1) Light refreshments.

Bern - Lausanne - Brig - Spiez - Bern   500, 560, 570

Excellent canyon, lake and mountain scenery on this easy one-day circle trip. There is time for a stopover in Lausanne and/or Spiez. You go through the nine-mile Lotschberg Tunnel after leaving Brig.

500

Dep. Bern	06:49 (1)	07:21 (2)	08:21 (3)	09:21 (4)	10:21 (3+5)
Arr. Lausanne	07:58	08:26	09:35	10:35	11:35
Change trains 570					
Dep. Lausanne	08:04	08:53 (1)	09:53	10:32	12:04
Arr. Brig	09:53	10:17	11:38	12:23	13:42
Change trains 560					
Dep. Brig	09:58 (1)	10:58	11:58 (1)	13:01 (2)	14:58 (3)
Arr. Spiez	11:02	12:02	13:02	14:05	15:02
Dep. Spiez	11:03	12:03	13:03	14:07	15:03
Arr. Bern	11:33	13:57	13:34	14:40	15:34

(1) Restaurant car. (2) Runs Monday-Friday except holidays. (3) Light refreshments. (4) Runs Saturdays, Sundays and holidays. (5) The same circle trip can be made in daylight by leaving Bern at 10:49 (1), 11:49 (1), 12:49 (1), 13:49 (1) and 14:21 (3).

Bern - Locarno - Bern   549, 560, 590

Complete notes on the Domodossola–Locarno portion of this easy one-day round-trip, one of the five most scenic rail journeys in Europe, appear under "Brig–Domodossola–Locarno."

590

Dep. Bern	07:34 (1)	08:50 (1)	12:42 (2)
Arr. Brig	-0-	10:27	-0-
Dep. Brig	-0-	10:29	-0-
Arr. Domodossola	09:32	11:02	14:00
Change trains 549			
Walk from the Domodossola station and go to the underground Centovalli track. Hurry!			
Dep. Domodossola	09:45	11:11	14:44
Arr. Locarno	11:25	12:48	17:25
Dep. Locarno	12:13	13:35	17:35
Arr. Domodossola	13:49	15:12	19:40
Change trains 590			
Walk from the underground Centovalli track, up to the main Domodossola station. Hurry!			
Dep. Domodossola	15:22 (1)	17:13 (1)	21:13
Arr. Brig	15:55:	-0-	21:46

Change trains 560

Dep. Brig	15:58	-0-	21:50
Arr. Bern	17:34	19:34	23:25

(1) Reservation advisable. Restaurant car. (2) Supplement payable. Restaurant car.

Bern - Luzern - Alpnachstad - Pilatus   515, 551, 558

Very nice canyon, lake and mountain scenery on this easy one-day round-trip that can include a stopover in Luzern. There are good views and several restaurants at the peak of **Pilatus.**

Note that the Pilatus Rack Railway trip (Alpnachstad–Pilatus–Alpnachstad) operates *only* May through November. Eurailpass and Swiss Pass holders receive a discount on this trip.

515				*551*		
Dep. Bern	07:30	09:30 (1+2)		Dep. Pilatus Kulm	10:45	12:05 (3)
Arr. Luzern	08:47	10:47		Arr. Alpachstad	11:15	12:35
Change trains 558				*Change to ordinary train 558*		
Dep. Luzern	09:15	11:20		Dep. Alpachstad	11:57	13:10
Arr. Alpnachstad	09:45	13:05		Arr. Luzern	13:25	14:44
Change to rack railway 551				*Change trains 515*		
Dep. Alpnachstad	10:50	11:30		Dep. Luzern	13:41 (1)	15:12 (1)
Arr. Pilatus Kulm	11:20	12:00		Arr. Bern	15:09	16:30

(1) Light refreshments. (2) Plus other departures from Bern at 11:30 (1) and 12:50, arriving Pilatus Kulm 14:30 and 15:10. (3) Plus other departures from Pilatus Kulm at 15:45 and 16:25, arriving Bern 18:30 and 19:30.

Bern - Spiez - Bern   560

Great canyon, lake and mountain scenery on this easy one-day round-trip. This is a portion of the "Geneva–Spiez–Geneva" trip listed earlier. Plenty of time to stroll in Spiez and enjoy the beauty of Lake Thun and the mountains above it.

Dep. Bern	Frequent times from 06:20 to 23:26
Arr. Spiez	30 minutes later
Dep. Spiez	Frequent times from 05:59 to 22:54
Arr. Bern	30 minutes later

Bern - Spiez - Brig - Lausanne - Bern   500, 560, 570

Marvelous canyon, lake, mountain and river scenery on this easy one-day circle trip. This is the reverse of the "Bern–Lausanne–Spiez–Bern" ride listed earlier. A stroll in Spiez is a nice way to break the journey. You go through the 10-mile Lotschberg Tunnel after leaving Spiez.

All of these trains have light refreshments, unless designated otherwise.

560

Dep. Bern	07:26 (1)	08:11 (1)	08:50 (2)	09:25	10:26 (1)	11:26 (2+4)
Arr. Spiez	08:02	08:40	09:20	09:55	10:56	11:56
Dep. Spiez	08:04	08:41	09:21	09:57	10:58	11:58
Arr. Brig	09:03	09:48	10:19	11:02	12:02	13:03
Change trains 570						
Dep. Brig	09:03	10:18	10:36	11:18 (2)	12:07	13:18 (3)
Arr. Lausanne	10:20	11:56	12:31	12:56	14:03	14:56
Change trains 500						
Dep. Lausanne	11:02 (1)	12:02 (1)	13:02 (1)	13:03 (1)	14:10 (3)	15:02 (1+5)
Arr. Bern	12:11	13:14	14:11	14:11	15:22	16:11

(1) Reservation advisable. Restaurant car. (2) Reservation advisable. Light refreshments. (3) Light refreshments. (4) Plus others Bern departure at 12:26 (1) and 13:26 (1), arriving back in Bern 17:39 and 18:14. (5) Plus other departures from Lausanne at frequent times from 16:25 to 22:02.

Brienz - Rothorn - Brienz   551

This is a cogwheel line. It goes through forests, mountains and meadows to the magnificent view from the 7,714-foot-high peak of **Rothorn**, from which there is an excellent four-hour walk on a good mountain path to **Brunig**. There is a superb network of well-maintained hiking trails in this area. Extra trains run at busy times. No trains operate from late October to early June.

Not covered by Eurailpass. Swiss Pass holders receive a discount.

Dep. Brienz	08:30 (1)	09:15	09:45	10:15 (1)	10:55
Arr. Rothorn	55-60 minutes later				

Dep. Brienz	12:55	14:00	15:00	16:00
Arr. Rothorn	55-60 minutes later			

• • •

Dep. Rothorn	09:45	10:15	11:25 (1)	12:40	13:30
Arr. Brienz	55-60 minutes later				

Dep. Rothorn	14:30	15:30	16:30	17:25
Arr. Brienz	55-60 minutes later			

(1) Operates early July—late August.

Brig - Andermatt - Disentis - Brig 575

Fine canyon and mountain scenery on this easy one-day round-trip. A stopover can be made in Andermatt, a great ski resort.

This trip is a portion of the *Glacier Express* route. See details about reservations and prices under "St. Moritz–Zermatt and Zermatt–St. Moritz"

Sit on the right side for best views from Brig, on the left side from Disentis.

This trip is *not* covered by Eurailpass. No extra charge with a Swiss Pass.

Dep. Brig	06:21	08:29 (3)	09:54 (1)	10:30 (1)	11:30 (1)
Arr. Andermatt	08:22	10:09	11:27 (2)	11:57 (2)	13:20 (2)
Arr. Disentis	09:38	11:26	12:37	13:00	14:33

Sights in **Disentis**: The stained glass in the cathedral

Dep. Disentis	10:22 (1)	12:20 (1)	13:45 (1)	16:17 (3)	17:17 (3)
Dep. Andermatt	11:25 (2)	13:29 (2)	14:50 (2)	17:24	18:28
Arr. Brig	13:11	15:10	16:14	19:51	20:54

(1) *Glacier Express*. For details see "St. Moritz–Zermatt" section. Plus another *Glacier Express* at 13:45, arriving Disentis 16:31. (2) Operates late May to late October. (3) Change trains in Andermatt.

Brig - Arona - Brig 82, 590

Beautiful lake and mountain scenery on this easy one-day round-trip, which can also be seen as a portion of the Lausanne–Milan route. This ride takes you through Europe's longest (19.8 km or 11.9 miles) tunnel, the Simplon.

It is the third longest tunnel in the world, after Japan's Seikan Tunnel (33.4 miles, between Tappi and Yoshioka) and Japan's Daishimizu Tunnel (13.4 miles, between Tokyo and Niigata).

Dep. Brig	08:22 (1)	09:34 (2)	10:31 (3)	14:28 (1)	15:17 (2)	
Arr. Arona	09:54	11:01	11:58	15:57	16:50	

• • •

Dep. Arona	09:45 (4)	11:16 (2)	13:16 (2)	14:43 (2)	16:16 (2)	17:16 (6)
Arr. Brig	11:10 (5)	12:43	14:40	16:13	17:43	18:40

(1) Reservation advisable. (2) Reservation advisable. Light refreshments. (3) Reservation advisable. Supplement charged. Restaurant car or light refreshments. (4) Reservation advisable. Supplement charged. (5) Light refreshments. (6) Plus other departures from Arona at 17:41 (7) and 18:15 (3) arriving Brig 19:23 and 19:43. (7) Runs Saturdays and Sundays June 5-September 24.

Here is the daytime schedule for the Lausanne–Milan route.

82

Dep. Lausanne	08:53 (1)	10:04 (2)	12:42 (3)	15:04 (4)
Arr. Brig	-0-	-0-	14:23	16:40
Dep. Brig	10:31	11:44	14:00	17:04
Arr. Milan (Cen.)	12:45	14:20	17:00	19:25

(1) Supplement payable in Italy. Restaurant car. (2) Light refreshments. (3) Reservation required. Includes supplement for international journeys. Restaurant car. (4) Change trains in Brig.

Brig - Bern - Brig 560

An easy one-day round-trip that affords a view of Rhone Valley and Lonza Valley farms, canyons, lakes and mountains plus the Lake Thun scenery at Spiez about which we enthuse in the "Geneva–Spiez" trip and going through the 10-mile-long Lotschberg Tunnel and over the Bietschtal Bridge. This structure takes the train 255 feet above the ravine it crosses.

We recommend a stop in Spiez and a stroll there on either the outbound or homebound leg of this trip.

For best views, sit on the right side Brig to Spiez, on the left side Spiez to Brig.

Dep. Brig	06:58 (1)	07:58 (1)	08:58 (1)	09:58 (2)	10:58 (2+3)
Arr. Spiez	08:03	09:02	10:02	11:02	12:02
Dep. Spiez	08:03	09:03	10:03	11:03	12:03
Arr. Bern	30 minutes after departing Spiez.				

• • •

Dep. Bern	09:55 (2)	10:26 (1)	11:26 (2)	12:26 (1)	13:26 (1+4)
Arr. Spiez	09:55	10:56	11:56	12:56	13:56
Dep. Spiez	09:57	10:58	11:58	12:58	13:58
Arr. Brig	66 minutes after departing Spiez.				

(1) Restaurant car. (2) Light refreshments. (3) Plus other departures from Brig that allow daylight viewing in summer months at frequent times from 11:58 to 21:35. (4)) Plus other departures from Bern at frequent times from 14:26 to 22:26.

Brig - Domodossola - Locarno - Domodossola - Brig 549, 560

We call the Domodossola–Locarno portion of this one-day round-trip one of the five most scenic rail trips in Europe. It is a spectacular narrow-gauge local train ride offering great gorge, mountain and river scenery on the Centovalli (one hundred valleys) route.

Be sure to have your passport with you. On this trip, you go from Switzerland to Italy, then Switzerland, back to Italy, and then again to Switzerland.

This ride takes you through Europe's longest (19.8 km or 11.9 miles) tunnel, the Simplon (between Brig and Domodossola). It is the third longest tunnel in the world, after Japan's Seikan (33.4 miles, between Tappi and Yoshioka) and Japan's Daishimizu Tunnel (13.4 miles, between Tokyo and Niigata).

When departing Locarno, look for the "Ferrovia Centovalli" sign that directs you to stairs descending to an underground track. Stops en route from Locarno include **Intragna**, with its many churches; **Verdasio,** which has a train connection to the mountain town of **Rasa; Palagnedra,** which has a lake; **Camedo**; and **Druogno**, the highest point on this scenic route.

See detailed notes about Locarno under "Milan–Locarno–Milan."

When changing trains in Domodossola, keep in mind that trains to and from Brig are located at street level. Trains to and from Locarno are on an underground track, connected by a walkway to the street level.

560
Dep. Brig	08:56 (1)	09:34 (2)	10:31 (3)	12:31 (3)	14:28 (1)
Arr. Domodossola	09:32	10:07	11:07	13:04	15:01
Change trains 549					
Dep. Domodossola	09:45	10:16	11:20	13:15	15:20
Arr. Locarno	11:25	11:50	13:00	14:50	17:00

• • •

549
Dep. Locarno	12:13	13:35	16:22	17:22	19:10
Arr. Domodossola	13:49	15:12	18:00	19:00	20:46
Change trains 560					
Dep. Domodossola	14:08 (1)	15:41 (3)	18:13	19:13 (3)	21:00 (2)
Arr. Brig	30 minutes later				

(1) Reservation advisable. Supplement charged. Restaurant car or light refreshments. (2) Reservation advisable. Light refreshments. (3) Reservation advisable. Supplement charged. Restaurant car or light refreshments.

Brig - Spiez - Interlaken - Brienz - Interlaken - Brig   560, 561

Very good canyon, lake and mountain scenery on this easy one-day round-trip.

For best views, sit on the right side Brig to Spiez, on the left side Spiez to Brig. Between Brig and Spiez, the train goes through the 10-mile-long Lotschberg Tunnel and over the Bietschtal Bridge. This structure takes the train 255 feet above the ravine it crosses.

Most of the trains Brig–Spiez (and v.v.) and Spiez-Interlaken (and v.v.) below have light refreshments.

560			561		
Dep. Brig	08:58	09:58	Dep. Brienz	12:22	13:03
Arr. Spiez	10:02	11:02	Arr. Interlaken (Ost)	12:40	13:27
Change trains			*Change trains 560*		
Dep. Spiez	10:54	11:54	Dep. Interlaken (Ost)	12:45	13:45
Arr. Interlaken (Ost)	11:15	12:15	Arr. Spiez	13:05	14:05
Change trains 561			*Change trains*		
Dep. Interlaken (Ost)	11:32	12:19	Dep. Spiez	13:58	14:58
Arr. Brienz	11:55	12:38	Arr. Brig	15:03	16:03

Brig - Interlaken - Wengen - Jungfrau - Grindelwald - Brig   560, 564

There is excellent canyon, lake and mountain scenery on this easy one-day round-trip. See "Bern–Interlaken–Wengen–Jungfrau."

It is for variety that we suggest you go from Interlaken to Jungfraujoch via Wengen and then return to Interlaken via Grindelwald.

Most of the trains Brig–Spiez (and v.v.) below have light refreshments or a restaurant car.

560			564		
Dep. Brig	07:58	09:58	Dep. Jungfraujoch	14:00	15:00
Arr. Spiez	10:02	11:02	Arr. Scheidegg	14:49	15:45
Change trains 564			*Change trains*		
Dep. Spiez	10:54	11:54	Dep. Scheidegg	15:00	15:55
Arr. Interlaken (Ost)	11:15	12:15	Arr. Grindelwald	-0-	-0-
Change trains 564			*Change trains*		
Dep. Interlaken (Ost)	11:32	12:32	Dep. Grindelwald	-0-	-0-
Arr. Wengen	12:30	13:20	Arr. Interlaken (Ost)	16:27	17:27
Arr. Scheidegg	12:55	13:48	*Change trains 560*		
Change trains			Dep. Interlaken (Ost)	16:45	17:45
Dep. Scheidegg	13:02	14:02	Arr. Spiez	17:05	18:07
Arr. Jungfraujoch	13:53	14:53	*Change trains*		
Sightsee in Jungfraujoch			Dep. Spiez	17:58	18:58
			Arr. Brig	19:03	20:03

Brig - Zermatt - Gornergrat - Zermatt - Brig 576, 578

Great canyon and mountain scenery on this easy one-day round-trip that includes an outstanding 5½–mile narrow-gauge cogwheel train ride to Gornergrat (10,200 feet) for a close view of the **Gorner Glacier**, the **Matterhorn** (14,692 feet) and more than 50 other peaks.
 This trip is *not* covered by Eurailpass.

576

Dep. Brig	Frequent times from 05:10 to 19:18
Arr. Zermatt	80-90 minutes later
Change trains 578	
Dep. Zermatt	Frequent times from 07:05 to 18:00
Arr. Gornergrat	45 minutes later

• • •

578

Dep. Gornergrat	Frequent times from 07:55 to 19:07
Arr. Zermatt	45 minutes later
Change trains 576	
Dep. Zermatt	Frequent times from 06:00 to 20:05
Arr. Brig	80-90 minutes later

Lausanne - Zermatt - Gornergrat - Lausanne 570, 576, 578

Nice canyon, lake, mountain and river scenery on this easy one-day round-trip. Eurailpass holders receive a 25 percent discount on the Visp–Zermatt–Gornergrat trip.

570

Dep. Lausanne	06:29	08:04 (1)	09:29 (1)	11:29
Arr. Visp	08:15	09:46	11:17	13:17
Change trains 576				
Dep. Visp	08:31	10:31	11:31	13:31
Arr. Zermatt	09:42	11:42	12:42	14:42
Change trains 578				
Dep. Zermatt	10:00	12:00	12:48	14:48
Arr. Gornergrat	10:45	12:45	13:33	15:33

• • •

578

Dep. Gornergrat	11:07	12:19	13:55	15:55
Arr. Zermatt	11:45	13:04	13:50	16:50
Change trains 576				
Dep. Zermatt	12:05	13:05	14:10	17:15
Arr. Visp	13:31	14:31	15:22	18:31
Change trains 570				
Dep. Visp	13:43 (1)	14:43	15:28	19:14 (1)
Arr. Lausanne	15:31	16:31	17:07	20:56

(1) Light refreshments.

Chur - Brig - Zermatt - Gornergrat - Zermatt   575, 578

There is fabulous Rhone Valley scenery on this ride plus crossing Oberalp Pass (6,700 feet) and going through the eight-mile long Furka Tunnel on the Chur–Brig portion. This trip crosses the highest bridges in Europe and includes the outstanding cogwheel train ride to Gornergrat (10,200 feet) for a close view of the Matterhorn (14,692 feet) and more than 50 other Alpine peaks.

575
Dep. Chur   08:57 (1+2)
Arr. Zermatt   14:42
Change to a narrow-gauge train 578
Dep. Zermatt   15:12   15:36 (3)   16:00   17:12   18:00
Arr. Gornergrat 15:57   16:21   16:45   17:57   18:45
                                   •   •   •
Dep. Gornergrat 16:19 (3)   16:43 (3)   17:07   17:55   19:07
Arr. Zermatt   45 minutes later

(1) *Glacier Express*. Restaurant car or light refreshments. See details about reservations and prices under "St. Moritz–Zermatt" (2) Runs late May to mid-October. (3) Runs daily except late May to mid-June.

Chur - St. Moritz - Chur   540

Marvelous canyon, lake and mountain scenery on this easy one-day round-trip. It is a very scenic ride involving going through double spiral tunnels and across the amazing Landwasser Viaduct. Ask at the Chur rail station which trains have open-air cars. The views from them are even more thrilling than from the closed cars.

All of these trains have light refreshments, unless designated otherwise.

Dep. Chur   06:42   07:52   08:55   09:55   10:52   11:52 (1+2)
Arr. St. Moritz   08:53   09:53   10:53   11:53   12:53   13:53
                                  •   •   •
Dep. St. Moritz   10:00 (1) 11:00   12:00   13:00   14:00   15:00 (3)
Arr. Chur   12:05   13:05   14:05   15:05   16:05   17:05

(1) Restaurant car. (2) Plus frequent other departures from Chur 12:52 to 20:52. (3) Plus other departures from St. Moritz 16:00, 17:00, 18:00 (1), 19:00 and 20:00.

Geneva - Lausanne - Brig - Spiez - Bern - Lausanne - Geneva
500, 560, 563, 570

One of the five most scenic rail trips in Europe.

The succession of beautiful scenes defy verbal description: 15 miles of terraced vineyards and Lake Geneva shoreline between Geneva and Lausanne. Great river scenery en route from Martigny to Brig. Upon leaving Brig, take a seat on the side of the train that faces the Brig rail station. In the 52 miles between Brig and Thun, the train goes through 37 tunnels (including the 10-mile Lotschberg) and crosses the top of 25 bridges and viaducts. The 866-foot-long **Kander Viaduct** is 92-feet-high.

Upon emerging from the Lotschberg Tunnel, there is such beautiful farm and mountain scenery around tiny **Kandersteg** and **Fruitigen** that you want to get off the train and spend the rest of your life there. It is only a 15-minute downhill walk from the Spiez rail station to the castle overlooking Lake Thun, the most beautiful lake scene on this planet. If the view of Lake Thun and the mountains reflected on its surface does not thrill you, pack up and go home because you will not find any landscape more beautiful in this world. From here, you can see the peaks of Jungfrau, Eiger, Monch and Finsteraarhorn.

You can return to Geneva (via Bern) either by boarding a train in Spiez or by first taking the 45-minute boat ride (covered by Eurailpass) from Spiez to **Thun** village and then boarding the train in Thun. It is a 10-minute downhill walk from the Spiez rail station to the Spiez pier. The lake steamer ties up 100 feet from Thun's rail station.

On the way back to Geneva from Bern, you pass through the same lake and vineyard scenery you saw between Lausanne and Geneva that morning, at the start of this fabulous one-day trip.

The schedules shown below allow a stopover in Bern.

570

Dep. Geneva (Corn.)	08:14 (1)	08:18	08:40 (1)	10:18 (1)	10:40 (1+4)
Dep. Lausanne	08:53	09:04	09:29	11:04	11:29
Dep. Martigny	-0-	09:53	10:22	11:53	12:53
Arr. Brig	10:17	10:42	11:24	12:42	13:24
Change trains 560					
Dep. Brig	10:31	10:58 (1)	11:58 (1)	12:58	13:58 (1)
Arr. Spiez	11:29	12:02	13:02	14:02	15:02
Dep. Spiez	11:31	12:03	13:03	14:03	15:07
Dep. Thun	11:42	12:14	13:14	14:14	15:14
Arr. Bern	12:02	12:34	13:34	14:34	15:34
Change trains 500					
Dep. Bern	12:09 (1)	12:49 (2)	14:18 (3)	14:49 (3)	15:49 (3+5)
Arr. Lausanne	13:35	13:50	15:26	15:58	16:58
Arr. Geneva (Corn.)	14:20	14:34	16:02	16:34	17:34

(1) Light refreshments. (2) Reservation advisable. Supplement charged. Restaurant car. (3) Restaurant car. (4) Plus other frequent Geneva departures from 10:48 to 13:48. (5) Plus other frequent Bern departures from 16:18 to 23:26.

Here are the Lake Thun (Spiez–Thun) boat schedules (covered by Eurailpass) to combine with departures from Thun village for Bern.

563 Boat

Dep. Spiez	13:22 (1)	13:49 (2)	14:54 (1)	15:18 (1)	16:13 (1)	17:13 (3+4)
Arr. Thun (Pier)	14:08	14:55	15:40	16:04	16:59	18:02

It is a two-minute walk from the boat pier to the train.

560 Train

Dep. Thun (Stn.)	14:34	15:14	15:18	16:18	17:18 (3)	17:41
Arr. Bern	20 minutes later					

(1) Has restaurant. (2) Late May to mid-June: light refreshments. Mid-June to late September: restaurant car. (3) Light refreshments. (4) Plus other boat departures from Spiez at 18:17 (1), 19:16 (1) and 20:02.

Geneva - Chamonix (Mt. Blanc) - Geneva   368

Be sure to have your passport with you on this trip filled with fantastic mountain scenery, as you will be going from Switzerland to France. From Chamonix, take the two-mile-high cable-car ride that goes nearly to the top of the tallest mountain in Europe, the 15,771-foot Mt. Blanc, towering almost 10,000 feet above Chamonix, for a view of Alpine peaks extending 80 miles.

After descending, there is just time to also take the narrow-gauge train to see the "Sea of Ice" glacier bed (which does not operate in winter). The tombstones in the small cemetery, a five-minute walk from the rail station, are fascinating. Nearly one-fourth of the headstones read "died on the mountain" (climbers and their rescuers).

All of these connections are easy cross-platform train changes, each taking less than one minute.

Dep. Geneva			Dep. Chamonix	12:15	16:31
(Eaux Vives)	07:07 (1)		Arr. St. Gervais	-0-	17:22
Arr. La Roche	07:41		*Change trains*		
Change trains.			Dep. St. Gervais	-0-	17:23
Dep. La Roche	08:07		Arr. La Roche	13:41	18:09
Arr. St. Gervais	-0-		*Change trains*		
Change trains			Dep. La Roche	14:00	-0-
Dep. St. Gervais	09:09		Arr. Geneva		
Arr. Chamonix	09:44		(Eaux Vives)	14:32	-0-

(1) Runs daily, except Sundays and holidays.

Geneva - Martigny - Chamonix - Geneva   368, 570, 572

This one-day circle trip avoids the repetition involved in the Geneva–Annemasse–Chamonix–Geneva round-trip described in the previous listing and also allows time for the activities in Chamonix described above. The scenery Martigny–Vallorcine–Chamonix is fantastic!

All of the Chamonix–Geneva connections are easy cross-platform train changes, each taking less than one minute.

570			368		
Dep. Geneva (Corn.)	06:18 (1)	07:14 (1)	Dep. Chamonix	13:23	16:31
Arr. Martigny	07:57	08:57	Arr. St. Gervais	-0-	17:23
Change trains 572			*Change trains*		
Dep. Martigny	08:35	09:38	Dep. St. Gervais	-0-	17:30
Arr. Le Chatelard	09:24 (2)	10:26 (2)	Arr. La Roche	15:10	18:20
Dep. Le Chatelard	09:29	10:32	*Change trains*		
Arr. Vallorcine	09:34	10:38	Dep. La Roche	15:17	-0-
Arr. Chamonix	10:06	12:09	Arr. Geneva		
			(Eaux-Vives)	15:55	-0-

(1) Light refreshments. (2) Change trains in Le Chatelard-Frontiere.

Geneva - Lausanne - Geneva   505

Here is a short trip packed with fine scenery of 15 miles of terraced vineyards, nearly the entire route following the lovely shoreline of Lake Geneva. Complete schedules are listed under the "Geneva–Lausanne" one-day excursion.

Geneva - Lyon - Geneva   372

The first 1½ hours from Geneva is noted for scenic canyons.

Geneva - Martigny - Geneva   570

This is a scenic trip of intermediate length, longer than the Geneva–Lausanne ride and shorter than the Geneva–Brig–Bern–Geneva circle trip. Very good canyon, lake, mountain and vineyard scenery.

Dep. Geneva (Corn.)	06:18 (1)	07:18 (1)	08:18 (1)	09:18	10:18 (1+2)
Arr. Martigny	07:53	08:53	10:53	11:53	12:53

• • •

Dep. Martigny	08:07 (1)	09:07 (1)	10:07 (1)	11:07 (1)	12:07 (1+3)
Arr. Geneva (Corn.)	09:42	10:42	11:42	12:42	13:42

(1) Light refreshments. (2) Plus other departures from Geneva at frequent times from 11:18 to 23:02. (3) Plus other departures from Martigny at frequent times from 13:07 to 22:02.

Geneva - Montreux - Zweisimmen - Spiez - Bern - Geneva
500, 560, 565, 566, 570

This narrow-gauge variation on the scenic trip described earlier (Geneva–Brig–Bern-Geneva) runs parallel and north of the Martigny–Brig route. You miss going through the Lotschberg Tunnel, but you are able to see all of the Geneva–Lausanne vineyard and Lake Geneva scenery plus Lake Thun (Spiez) and a possible stopover in Bern, en route back to Geneva.

Before traveling the normal-gauge Zweisimmen–Spiez leg, there is time to take the very scenic narrow-gauge 13 km (9 miles) detour from Zweisimmen to Lenk (and back to Zweisimmen).

There is time to leave the train in Spiez, take the lake boat from Spiez to Thun, and then take the train from Thun to Bern. See notes under the "Geneva–Brig–Bern–Geneva" scenic trip.

The narrow-gauge ascent from Montreux to Zweisimmen is very scenic as the train climbs from the shore of Lac Leman to Les Avants in a series of hairpin bends. The funicular ride from **Les Avants** to **Sonloup** is worth stopping over in Les Avants and rejoining the Montreux–Zweisimmen route later in the day. **Gstaad** is a very expensive ski resort.

We recommend departing Montreux on *Panoramic Express* or *Crystal Panoramic Express*. The comfortable coaches of these special narrow-gauge Observation Trains have glass domes and large side windows for viewing the marvelous scenery. Refreshments are available from vending machines in their bar car.

For "Crystal Panoramic," reservations are accepted only for groups. Individuals may ride it if there are any vacant seats.

There are seats in the front car, which has an elevated cab for the engineer. The next car is a bar car which seats 45 passengers. The third and last car is the locomotive.

Regardless which train you ride, sit on the right side Montreux-Zweisimmen for best views.

570

Dep. Geneva (Corn.)	08:40 (1)	09:18 (1)	10:18 (1)	11:18 (1)	12:18 (1)
Arr. Montreux	09:50	10:25	11:25	12:25	13:25
Change trains 566					
Dep. Montreux	10:30 (2)	11:00	12:30	13:00	14:00 (3)
Arr. Les Avants	10:53	11:24	12:53	13:24	– 0 –
Dep. Gstaad	11:48	12:30	13:49	14:30	15:12
Arr. Zweisimmen	12:15	12:58	14:05	14:58	15:34
Change trains 565					
Dep. Zweisimmen	12:21	13:05	14:21	15:05	16:05
Arr. Spiez	12:18	13:51	14:58	15:51	16:51

Spiez: See notes under "Geneva-Brig-Bern-Geneva." For marvelous views of mountains and lakes, walk to the Burg Woods and Burg Hill. Spiez is an ideal base for one-day rail trips to Bern, Interlaken, Luzern, Gstaad, Montreux, Zermatt, Grindelwald, Stresa, Jungfraujoch and Solothurn.

Change trains 560					
Dep. Spiez	13:04 (1)	14:02 (4)	15:03 (1)	16:03 (4)	17:03 (4)
Dep. Thun	13:18	14:14	15:14	16:14	17:14
Arr. Bern	13:38	14:34	15:34	16:34	17:34
Change trains 500					
Dep. Bern	14:21 (1)	15:49 (4)	16:21 (1)	16:49 (1)	18:21 (1+5)
Arr. Geneva (Corn.)	16:20	17:34	18:22	18:34	20:20

(1) Light refreshments. (2) *Panoramic Express*. See details in text on previous page. (3) *Crystal Panoramic*. See details in text on previous page. (4) Restaurant car. (5) Plus other departures from Bern at 18:40 (1), 19:21, 20:21, 20:49, 21:49 and 22:21, arriving Geneva 20:34, 21:20, 22:20, 22:34, 23:34 and 00:20.

Geneva - Nyon - Geneva 505

See the magnificent views of **Lac Leman** (the Lake of Geneva) and the Alps, particularly of Mont Blanc, from **Nyon**, a medieval hilltop village on the shore of Lac Leman.

Dep. Geneva (Corn.)	Frequent times from 06:15 to 22:59
Arr. Nyon	14-17 minutes later

Sights in **Nyon**: Sailing is popular here.

Dep. Nyon	Frequent times from 06:05 to 23:05
Arr. Geneva (Corn.)	14-18 minutes later

Interlaken - Mt. Pilatus - Interlaken   551, 561

Great canyon and mountain scenery on this easy one-day narrow-gauge round-trip. There are good views and several restaurants at the peak of Pilatus.

A round-trip ticket is available in Luzern covering train or boat Luzern-Alpnachstad, rack railway Alpnachstad-Pilatus Kulm, cablecar and gondolas Pilatus-Kriens, and trolley-bus Kriens-Luzern.

The Alpnachstad–Pilatus–Alpnachstad rack railway portion operates only May-November.

561

Dep. Interlaken (Ost)	07:46	09:19	10:19 (1)	11:00	12:19 (2)	13:00
Arr. Sarnen	-0-	10:44	11:41	-0-	13:37	-0-
Change trains						
Dep. Sarnen	-0-	11:03	12:07	-0-	14:03	-0-
Arr. Alpnachstad	09:49	11:13	12:17	12:44	14:17	14:44

Change to rack railway for the ride to the top of Mt. Pilatus 551

Dep. Alpnachstad	10:50	11:30	13:10	13:50	14:30	15:10
Arr. Pilatus Kulm	11:20	12:00	13:40	14:20	15:00	15:40

• • •

551

Dep. Pilatus Kulm	12:05	13:05	14:25	15:45	16:25
Arr. Alpnachstad	12:45	13:45	15:05	16:25	17:05

Change to a standard train 561

Dep. Alpnachstad	13:40	14:11	15:40	16:11	18:11
Arr. Sarnen	13:52	-0-	15:53	-0-	-0-
Change trains					
Dep. Sarnen	14:23 (1)	-0-	16:23	-0-	-0-
Arr. Interlaken (Ost)	15:59	15:59	17:59	17:59	20:02

(1) Restaurant car. (2) Light refreshments.

Interlaken - Luzern - Interlaken   561

A very scenic 48-mile panorama of the Alps on this trip along Lake Brienz, an easy one-day excursion. Schedules appear under "Interlaken–Luzern."

Interlaken - Spiez - Bern - Spiez - Interlaken   560

Excellent canyon, lake and mountain scenery on this easy one-day round-trip that includes visiting Lake Thun and a possible stopover in Bern. See earlier notes about Spiez and taking a boat on Lake Thun from Spiez to Thun village, under "Geneva–Brig–Bern–Geneva."

Dep. Interlaken (Ost)	07:45	08:45	09:45	10:45	11:45
Dep. Interlaken (West)	5 minutes later
Dep. Spiez	08:07	09:07	10:07	11:07	12:07
Dep. Thun	08:18	09:18	10:18	11:18	12:18
Arr. Bern	20 minutes later

Dep. Bern	Frequent times from 06:59 to 21:28
Arr. Interlaken (West)	45–60 minutes later
Arr. Interlaken (Ost)	5 minutes after arriving West station

Interlaken - Spiez - Brig - Spiez - Interlaken   560

Nice canyon, lake and mountain scenery on this easy one-day round-trip which includes visiting Lake Thun and going through the 10-mile Lotschberg Tunnel.
    The schedules below allow time to stopover in Spiez.

Most of the trains Spiez–Brig and v.v. have light refreshments.

Dep. Interlaken (Ost)	06:40 (1)	07:08		08:45 (1)	09:45 (1)	10:45 (1)	11:45 (2+3)
Dep. Interlaken (West)	5 minutes later
Arr. Spiez	07:05	07:28		09:05	10:05	11:05	12:05
Change trains
Dep. Spiez	07:58 (2)	08:41		09:21(2)	10:58 (2)	11:58 (1)	12:58 (2)
Arr. Brig	09:03	09:48		10:19	12:03	13:03	14:03

• • •

Dep. Brig	Frequent times from 04:42 to 21:36
Arr. Spiez	70 minutes later
Change trains.
Dep. Spiez	Frequent times from 07:31 to 21:58
Arr. Interlaken (West)	15 minutes later
Arr. Interlaken (Ost)	5 minutes after arriving West station

(1) Restaurant car. (2) Light refreshments. (3) Plus other Interlaken departures from 12:45 to 20:45.

Interlaken - Jungfraujoch - Interlaken   564

Great canyon and mountain scenery on this easy one-day round-trip. This spectacular route ends at Europe's highest (11,333 feet) rail station. It includes two stops in the tunnel through Mount Eiger, for viewing through "windows" which the railroad's builders cut in the face of the cliff.

At Jungfraujoch, passengers alight to look down on the great Jungfrau glacier and stroll in the "Ice Palace" carved inside the glacier. Fabulous views can be seen from the revolving restaurant, which rotates completely every 50 minutes. For variety, we show how to go from Interlaken to Jungfraujoch via Wengen, and then return to Interlaken via Grindelwald.

Grindelwald sits at 3,400-feet altitude. The majestic peaks that rise around this village are: **Jungfrau** (13,642 feet), **Eiger** (13,026), **Wetterhorn** (12,142), **Breithorn** (12,409), **Monch** (13,449), **Schreckhorn** (13,380), **Gspaltenhorn** (11,277) and **Tschingelhorn** (11,736).

Eurailpass holders receive a 25 percent discount on these trains.

(Via Wengen)

Dep. Interlaken (Ost)	07:38	08:05 (1)	08:32	09:02 (1)	09:32	10:02 (1)	10:32 (2)
Arr. Scheidegg	08:55	09:20	09:45	10:24	10:55	11:24	11:45

Change trains

Dep. Scheidegg	09:02	09:30 (1)	10:02	10:30 (1)	11:02	11:30 (1)	12:02
Arr. Jungfraujoch	09:53	10:22	10:53	11:22	11:53	12:22	12:53

• • •

Dep. Jungfraujoch	11:00 (1)	12:00	13:00	14:00	14:30 (1)	15:00 (3)
Arr. Scheidegg	11:49	12:49	13:49	14:49	15:19	15:45

Change trains (*via Grindelwald*)

Dep. Scheidegg	12:00	13:02	13:59	15:00	15:32 (1)	16:00
Arr. Grindelwald	12:45	13:45	14:45	15:45	16:15	16:45

Change trains

Dep. Grindelwald	12:50	13:50	14:50	15:50	16:20 (1)	16:50
Arr. Interlaken (Ost)	13:27	14:27	15:27	16:27	16:57	17:27

(1) Does not operate May 29-June 3. (2) Plus other frequent Interlaken departures from 11:32 to 15:32. (3) Plus other frequent Jungfraujoch departures from 14:00 to 18:00.

Lausanne - Brig - Lausanne   570

Enjoy the fine canyon, lake, mountain and river scenery on this easy one-day round-trip.

Dep. Lausanne	Frequent times from 06:42 to 23:45
Arr. Brig	1½–2 hours later

Sight in **Brig**: Switzerland's largest private residence, the 17th-century Stockalper Castle, built by a very successful businessman.

Dep. Brig	Frequent times from 04:16 to 22:02
Arr. Lausanne	1½–2 hours later

Lausanne - Brig - Spiez - Bern - Lausanne   560, 570

Marvelous canyon, lake, mountain and river scenery on this easy one-day round-trip, a portion of the "Geneva–Lausanne–Spiez–Bern–Geneva" scenic trip.

Locarno - Camedo - Locarno   549

One of the five most scenic rail trips in Europe. Fantastic canyon, river and mountain scenery. Hillside farms that are nearly vertical. The ride is called "Centovalli," and you will see a hundred valleys. This trip can be made either as an easy one-day round-trip or as a portion of these routes: Milan–Locarno, Bern–Locarno, Brig–Locarno, Luzern–Locarno, and Locarno–Brig.

Please note that this trip does not start from the Locarno rail station. You catch what looks like a trolley car at the central bus stop, across from the train station.

At Camedo, a small hotel (Osteria Grutly) is only a five-minute walk from the rail station. The granite slab roofs on the houses in this area are unique.

Dep. Locarno	08:35	10:35	12:13	13:35	15:20	16:35	17:35
Arr. Camedo	09:10	11:09	12:48	14:09	15:54	17:09	18:09

• • •

Dep. Camedo	10:52	12:14	13:37	15:53	16:52	19:11	19:52
Arr. Locarno	35 minutes later						

Locarno - Domodossola - Brig - Domodossola - Locarno   549, 590

Very good canyon, mountain and river scenery on this one-day round-trip that includes the wonderful **Centovalli** ride described in the previous trip plus going through the 12-mile Simplon, longest main line rail tunnel in the world. Be sure to take your passport on this trip from Switzerland to Italy, Switzerland, back to Italy and then again to Switzerland.

Follow the "Ferrovia Centovalli" sign down a flight of stairs to the underground portion of Locarno's rail station. Stops en route include **Intragna**, with its many churches; **Verdasio**, which has a train connection to the mountain town of **Rasa**; **Palagnedra**, which has a lake; **Camedo** ; and **Druogno**, highest point on this scenic route.

The Domodossola–Brig (and v.v.) portion of this route takes you through Europe's longest (19.8 km - 11.9 miles) tunnel, the Simplon. It is the world's second-longest tunnel, after Japan's Daishimizu Tunnel between Tokyo and Niigata (22.3 km - 13.4 miles).

549		
Dep. Locarno	08:35	10:35 (1)
Arr. Domo.	10:16	12:14

Change trains 590. Walk from the underground Centovalli track, up to the main Domodossola station

Dep. Domo.	11:28 (2)	12:26 (2)
Arr. Brig	12:00	13:00

590		
Dep. Brig	14:00 (1)	17:04 (1)
Arr. Domo.	14:32	17:44

Change trains 549. Walk outside the Domodossola station and go to the underground Centovalli track.

Dep. Domo.	14:44 (1)	18:04
Arr. Locarno	16:25	19:46

(1) Reservation advisable. Light refreshments. (2) Restaurant car. Reservation required.

Luzern - Brunnen - Fluelen - Luzern   557

Here is an excellent one-day round-trip boat ride on Lake Luzern, that is covered by Eurailpass.

All of these boats have a restaurant, unless designated otherwise.

Dep. Luzern (Stn. Quay)	09:00 (1)	09:25	10:26	11:15 (2)	11:25 (1+3)
Arr. Brunnen	11:04	11:50	12:40	13:00	13:57
Arr. Fluelen	11:50	12:37	13:37	13:45	14:52

• • •

Dep. Fluelen	12:00 (1)	12:48	13:50	14:20 (2)	15:00 (1+5)
Dep. Brunnen	12:50	13:42	14:45	15:33	16:00
Arr. Luzern (Stn. Quay)	15:00	16:20	16:44	17:40	18:35

(1) Paddle steamer. Runs daily. (2) Paddle steamer. Runs Sunday only. No restaurant. (4) Runs Sunday only. (3) Plus other departures from Luzern at 13:15, 14:26 (4) and 16:30 (4). (4) Light refreshments. (5) Plus other departures from Fluelen at 16:20 (1) and 17:46 (4).

Luzern - Interlaken - Luzern   560

Great canyon and mountain scenery on this easy one-day round trip. Complete schedules are listed under "Luzern–Interlaken–Luzern."

Luzern - Interlaken - Brig - Domodossola - Locarno - Luzern 548, 549, 561, 590
This circle route includes going through the nine-mile Lotschberg Tunnel, the 12-mile
Simplon and the nine-mile St. Gotthard, as well as seeing the beautiful Centovalli scenery
between Domodossola and Locarno.

561		*549*	
Dep. Luzern	07:00	Dep. Domodossola	15:45
Arr. Interlaken (Ost)	09:26	Arr. Locarno	17:25
Change trains 560		*Change trains 548*	
Dep. Interlaken (Ost)	09:45 (1)	Dep. Locarno	17:30 (3)
Arr. Spiez	10:05	Arr. Bellinzona	17:53
Change trains 560		*Change trains 550*	
Dep. Spiez	10:58 (1)	Dep. Bellinzona	18:06
Arr. Brig	12:03	Arr. Luzern	20:43
Change trains 590			
Dep. Brig	14:00 (2)		
Arr. Domodossola	14:32		

(1) Restaurant car. (2) Supplement payable. Reservation required. Restaurant car. (3) Plus other departures from Locarno at 17:59 and 18:30, arriving Luzern 20:54 and 21:43.

Luzern - Interlaken - Jungfraujoch - Interlaken - Luzern 561, 564

There is marvelous canyon, lake and mountain scenery on this easy one-day round-trip. See
details about Jungfraujoch under "Interlaken–Jungfraujoch."

For variety, go from Interlaken to Jungfraujoch via Wengen, and then return to Interlaken via
Grindelwald. The Interlaken–Jungfraujoch–Interlaken portion is not covered by Eurailpass.

For the best views, sit on the right-hand side Luzern–Meiringen, on the left side Meringen–
Interlaken. For the return ride, sit on the right Interlaken–Meiringen and on the left Meiringen–Luzern.

561		*564*		
Dep. Luzern	08:54 (1)	Dep. Jungfraujoch	14:00	15:00
Arr. Meiringen	09:48	Arr. Scheidegg	14:49	15:45
Arr. Interlaken (Ost)	10:40	*Change trains*		
Change trains 564		Dep. Scheidegg		
Dep. Interlaken (Ost)		(*via Grindelwald*)	15:00	16:00
(*via Wengen*)	11:32	Arr. Interlaken (Ost)	16:27	17:27
Arr. Scheidegg	-0-	*Change trains 561*		
Change trains		Dep. Interlaken (Ost)	17:20	18:19 (1)
Dep. Scheidegg	-0-	Arr. Meiringen	17:38	18:30
Arr. Jungfraujoch	13:53	Arr. Luzern	19:05	20:05

(1) Restaurant car.

Luzern - Interlaken - Spiez - Brig - Andermatt - Goschenen - Luzern   560, 561, 575

Here is a marvelous one-day circle trip, crammed with outstanding scenery. Although this schedule allows only 50 minutes in Spiez, if you take a packed lunch from Luzern there are benches outside the Spiez rail station where you can sit and eat and have a fabulous view of the village, Lake Thun and the mountains reflected on its surface.

From Spiez to Brig, there is a good view of the Matterhorn from the right side of the train. Walk to the front of the Brig rail station to board the train to Andermatt.

En route from Brig to Andermatt, you see the beautiful Rhone Valley and go through the eight-mile long Furka Tunnel. The Brig–Andermatt–Goschenen portion of this trip is *not* covered by Eurailpass.

561			*Change trains 575*	
Dep. Luzern	08:54	09:24	Dep. Brig	14:26
Arr. Interlaken (Ost)	10:40	11:26	Arr. Andermatt	16:21
Change trains 560			Dep. Andermatt	16:30
Dep. Interlaken (Ost)	10:45	11:45	Arr. Goschenen	16:45
Arr. Spiez	11:25	12:05	*Change trains 550*	
Change trains 560			Dep. Goschenen	17:10 (2)
Dep. Spiez	11:58 (1)	12:58 (2)	Arr. Luzern	18:43
Arr. Brig	13:03	14:03		

(1) Light refreshments. (2) Restaurant car.

Luzern - Mt. Pilatus - Luzern   551, 561

See the fine canyon and mountain scenery on this easy one-day round trip. The Alpnachstad–Pilatus–Alpnachstad rack railway portion operates only from May to the end of November. Eurailpass users receive a 35 percent discount on this ride. There are good views and several restaurants at the peak of Pilatus.

561							
Dep. Luzern	08:24	09:24	10:24	11:24	12:24	13:24	14:24 (1)
Arr. Alpnachstad	08:40	09:40	10:40	11:40	12:39	13:40	14:39
Change to rack railway (551) for the ride to the top of Mt. Pilatus.							
Dep. Alpnachstad	08:50	09:30	10:50	11:30	13:10	13:50	14:30
Arr. Pilatus Kulm	09:20	10:00	11:20	12:00	13:40	14:20	15:00

•   •   •

551

Dep. Pilatus Kulm	09:25	10:45	11:25	12:05	13:45	14:25	15:05 (2)
Arr. Alpnachstad	10:05	10:25	12:05	12:45	14:25	15:05	15:45

Change to a standard train 561

Dep. Alpnachstad	11:13	-0-	12:17	13:13	14:44	15:13	16:17
Arr. Luzern	18-20 minutes later

(1) Plus another departure from Luzern at 15:24 arriving Pilatus Kulm 16:20. (2) Plus another departure from Pilatus Kulm at 15:45 and 16:25.

Luzern - Engelberg - Mt. Titlis - Luzern   552

There is very good canyon and mountain scenery on this easy one-day round trip. The Engelberg–Titlis–Engelberg rack railway is *not* covered by Eurailpass and does not operate late October to early December.

Engelberg is a popular ski resort. It also has more than 20 miles of level walking and hiking paths, toboggan runs, a gambling casino and indoor swimming pools.

There are great views from the restaurant on the top of **Mt. Titlis**. See the 11th-century illuminated manuscripts in the Benedictine monastery.

Dep. Luzern	07:35	08:13	09:13	10:13	11:13	12:13	13:13 (1)
Arr. Engelberg	08:35	09:12	10:12	11:12	12:12	13:12	14:12

Change to the funicular

Dep. Engelberg	Frequent times
Arr. Mt. Titlis	60 minutes later

• • •

Dep. Mt. Titlis	Frequent times
Arr. Engelberg	60 minutes later

Change to the train

Dep. Engelberg	10:45	11:45	12:45	13:45	14:45	15:45	16:45 (2)
Arr. Luzern	60–65 minutes later

(1) Plus other departures from Luzern at frequent times from 14:13 to 19:13 for Luzern round-trip. (2) Plus other departures from Engelberg at 17:45, 18:45, 19:45 and 20:40.

Luzern-Engelberg-Mt. Titlis-Luzern-Mt. Pilatus-Luzern   552, 561

From May through October, *all three* mountains can be ascended in one day by following this schedule.

Neither the Engelberg-Titlis nor Alpnachstad-Pilatus one-class round trips are covered by Eurailpass.

552	
Dep. Luzern	08:13 (1)
Arr. Engelberg	09:12
Change to the funicular	
Dep. Engelberg	09:30 (2)
Arr. Mt. Titlis	10:30

• • •

Dep. Mt. Titlis	11:00 (2)
Arr. Engelberg	12:00
Change to the train 552	
Dep. Engelberg	12:45 (3)
Arr. Luzern	13:45

561	
Dep. Luzern	13:54 (4)
Arr. Alpnachstad	14:11
Change to rack railway 551	
Dep. Alpnachstad	14:30
Arr. Pilatus Kulm	15:00

• • •

Dep. Pilatus Kulm	15:05 (5)
Arr. Alpnachstad	15:05
Change to the train 561	
Dep. Alpnachstad	15:13
Arr. Luzern	15:35

(1) Plus hourly Luzern departures from 09:13 to 20:13. (2) Estimated. Thomas Cook Timetables does not publish Engleberg-Titlis schedules. (3) Plus other Engleberg departures. See above table. (4) Plus another Luzern departure at 14:24. (5) Plus other Pilatus Kulm departures at 15:45 and 16:25, arriving Luzern 16:50 and 17:50.

Luzern - Mt. Rigi (via Arth-Goldau) - Luzern   550, 551

The excellent canyon and mountain scenery on this route (unlike the route via Vitznau that follows) is entirely by train. This is an easy one-day round trip.

 The Arth-Goldau to Regi Kulm (and v.v.) trains operate late May to mid-October. Times shown below are for the period early July to mid-October.

550

Dep. Luzern	09:14	10:23 (3)	12:23	14:23	15:14 (1)
Arr. Arth Goldau	09:40	10:48	12:48	14:48	15:40
Change to rack railway 551					
Dep. Arth Goldau	10:10	11:10	13:10	15:10	16:10
Arr. Rigi Kulm	10:47	11:47	13:47	15:47	16:47

• • •

Dep Rigi Kulm	11:04	12:04	14:04	16:04	17:04 (2)
Arr Arth Goldau	11:48	12:48	14:48	16:48	17:48
Change to standard train 550					
Dep. Arth Goldau	12:18	13:10 (4)	15:10 (4)	17:10 (4)	18:18
Arr. Luzern	25 minutes later				

(1) Plus another Luzern departure at 16:19 (4), arriving Rigi Kulm 17:30. (2) Plus another Rigi Kulm departure at 19:04, arriving Luzern 20:46. (3) Reservation recommended. (4) Reservation required. Supplement charged.

Luzern - Mt. Rigi (via Vitznau) - Luzern 551, 557

There is very nice canyon, lake and mountain scenery on this easy one-day round trip that includes a boat ride (*covered by Eurailpass*) on Lake Luzern. From Vitznau to Mt. Rigi, the train climbs 4,000 feet in 4¼ miles. Over 450,000 passengers take this ride every year. There is good skiing at **Rigi** in the winter. This line was constructed in 1871.

The Vitznau–Rigi ride is *not* covered by Eurailpass. *All of the boats have a restaurant or light refreshments.*

557 Boat

Dep. Luzern						
(Bahnhof.)	09:00 (1)	09:25	10:26	11:25 (1)	12:03	13:15 (1+2)
Arr. Vitznau (Pier)	09:59	10:22	11:40	12:36	12:51	14:17

Change to rack railway adjacent to the quay 551

Dep. Vitznau	10:10	10:45	11:45	13:00	13:50	16:10
Arr. Rigi Kulm	10:40	11:15	12:15	13:30	14:20	16:40

•   •   •

551

Dep. Rigi Kulm	10:45	11:40	12:35	14:25	15:05	15:55
Arr. Vitznau	11:25	12:20	13:15	15:05	15:50	16:55

Change to boat adjacent to the rail station 557

Dep. Vitznau (Pier)	11:27	12:52	13:50 (1)	15:08	15:50	17:30 (1)
Arr. Luzern						
(Bahnhof.)	55–70 minutes later					

(1) Paddle steamer. (2) Plus another departure from Luzern at 14:25, arriving Rigi Kulm 15:50.

St. Moritz - Tirano - St. Moritz 547

Great mountain scenery on this easy one-day narrow-gauge round-trip into Italy. (Take your passport!) It is absolutely breathtaking. The track goes through the Bernina Pass, making this Europe's highest main rail line, reaching 7,400 feet at Bernina Hospiz. Buy a lunch in St. Moritz to eat on the train.

Dep. St. Moritz	07:20	09:05	09:30	10:03	11:00
Arr. Tirano	09:53	11:28	11:46	12:24	13:28

•   •   •

Dep. Tirano	10:30	11:30	12:24	13:12	14:05 (1+2+3)
Arr. St. Moritz	13:02	13:56	14:56	15:56	16:22

(1) Special tourist train. Reservation required. Supplement charged. (2) *Heideland Bernina Express.* Operates mid-May to late October. (3) Plus other Tirano departures at 14:40 (1+2),15:05, 15:30, 16:30 and 17:30, arriving St. Moritz 16:50, 17:39, 17:56, 18:53 and 19:54.

St. Moritz - Zermatt and Zermat - St. Moritz   575

Many ordinary trains which do not require reservation, are not packed, and have seats that are as comfortable as those of "Glacier Express" run every day. Their only disadvantage is that they require changing trains *four* times: in Chur, Disentis, Andermatt and Brig.

All of the schedules below are for the direct-ride, luxury, "Glacier Express," for which a reservation is required. During the summer, seats in its elegant 34-seat restaurant car are usually reserved several months in advance. Reservations both for assigned seats and also for lunch in the elegant 34-seat paneled restaurant car can be made as much as two months in advance of travel date through a travel agency—and must be made 14 or more days prior to departure from the U.S. Passengers may also have food served at their seats from a minibar that is rolled down the aisle.

St. Moritz–Zermatt, sit on the left for the best views, on the right Zermatt– St. Moritz. There is marvelous canyon, mountain and Rhone Valley scenery on this ride, which crosses 291 bridges (including Europe's highest ones) and goes through 91 tunnels, including the nine-mile-long Furka, as the train traverses the 6,700-foot Oberalp Pass. This "Albula Line" is one of the world's greatest feats of railroad engineering. Its **Landwasser Viaduct** towers over a rampaging Alpine stream. Some of its tunnels are spirals inside the mountains, tunnels that you exit traveling in the same direction as you entered them, but at either a higher or lower level.

On *Glacier Express*, the entire route is free with Swiss Pass and Swiss Flexipass. There is no discount for Eurailpass. The 1997 charges for the Disentis–Brig or v.v. portion was $71 for first class, $48 for second class, one way. The Brig–Zermatt–Brig portion was $108 and $68.

575

Dep. St. Moritz	07:00 (1+2)	09:00	10:00 (2)
Dep. Chur	08:57	10:57	12:20
320			
Dep. Disentis	10:10	12:20	13:45
Dep. Andermatt	11:25	13:21	14:48
Dep. Brig	13:11	15:10	16:14
Arr. Zermatt	14:42	16:42	17:53

•   •   •

Dep. Zermatt	08:49 (2)	09:49 (2+3)	10:15
Dep. Brig	10:30	11:30	11:51
Dep. Andermatt	11:58	13:20	13:30
Dep. Disentis	13:15	14:43	15:00
Arr. Chur	14:31	16:10	16:10
Dep. Chur	14:40	16:52	16:52
Arr. St. Moritz	16:53	18:11	18:11

(1) Change trains to *Glacier Express* in Reichenau-Tamins. (2) Runs early June to mid-October. (3) Change to ordinary train in Reichenau-Tamins.

Sights in **Zermatt**: Access to the Matterhorn. Great skiing in woods, pastures and hills. Displays of the challenges that mountaineers face are exhibited at the Alpine Museum. There are many hiking trails here, so easy that neither special shoes nor gear is necessary. Although each trail climbs about 2,000 feet, they are effortless because the incline is spread over many miles. Because autos have to park several miles away, the air here is pristine.

Sights in **Disentis**: The stained glass in the cathedral.

Zermatt - Gornergrat - Zermatt 578

This is a great cogwheel train ride to the 10,200-foot-high Gornergrat for a close view of the Matterhorn (14,692 feet) and more than 50 other Alpine peaks.
    This ride is not covered by Eurailpass.

Dep. Zermatt 07:05, 08:00, 08:24, 08:48, 09:12, 09:36, 10:00, 10:24, 10:48, 11:12, 11:36, 12:00, 12:24, 12:48, 13:12, 13:36, 14:00, 14:24, 14:48, 15:12, 15:36, 16:00, 16:24, 17:12, 18:00.

Arr. Gornergrat 43-45 minutes later

• • •

Dep. Gornergrat 07:55, 08:43, 09:07, 09:31, 09:55, 10:19, 10:43, 11:07, 11:31, 11:55, 12:19, 12:43, 13:07, 13:31, 13:55, 14:19, 14:43, 15:07, 15:31, 15:55, 16:19, 16:43, 17:07, 17:55, 19:07.

Arr. Zermatt 43-45 minutes later

Zurich - Sargans - Vaduz - Zurich   (The Trip To Liechtenstein) 520, 530

There is fine scenery along the shores of **Lake Zurich** and **Lake Walen** on this easy one-day round trip.
    It is only a 30-minute *bus ride* from Sargans to **Vaduz**, in the tiny country of Liechtenstein. Buses leave Sargans' rail station every 20 minutes for the 27-minute ride to Vaduz.

520

Dep. Zurich	07:10 (1)	08:10 (2)	09:10 (1)	09:33 (2)	10:10 (1)	11:10 (2+3)
Arr. Sargans	08:11	09:21	10:18	10:31	11:21	12:19
Change to bus 530						
Dep. Sargans	08:29	09:29	10:29	10:49	11:29	12:29
Arr. Vaduz	05:58	09:58	11:58	11:18	11:57	12:58

530

| Dep. Vaduz | 13:00 | 14:00 | 15:00 | 16:00 | 17:00 | 18:00 (4) |
| Arr. Sargans | 13:34 | 14:34 | 15:34 | 16:34 | 17:34 | 18:34 |

Change to train 520

| Dep. Sargans | 13:39 (2) | 14:40 (2) | 15:40 (1) | 16:40 (1) | 17:40 (1) | 18:40 (2) |
| Arr. Zurich | 14:50 | 16:50 | 16:50 | 17:50 | 18:50 | 19:50 |

(1) Light refreshments. (2) Restaurant car. (3) Plus frequent Zurich departures hourly from 12:10 to 22:10. (4) Plus other frequent Vaduz departures from 19:00 to 21:00 and 22:10.

Sights in **Vaduz**: Capital of the principality of Liechtenstein, a country that is 16 miles long by 4 miles wide, nestled between Switzerland and Austria. The extensive network of walking paths is very popular. Many excellent restaurants here.

See the collection of paintings by Rubens and other old masters at the National Art Gallery, open daily (April–October: 10:00–12:00 and 13:30–17:30. November–March: 10:00–12:00 and 14:00–17:30.) The exhibits of prehistoric and Roman articles: ancient weapons, coins, wood carvings, folk art and handicrafts, items from the area's medieval castles and other historical artifacts in the National Museum, open May–September daily 10:00–12:00 and 13:30–17:30. October–April: daily except Monday, 14:00–17:30.

The Postage Stamp Museum is open daily all year 10:00–12:00 and 14:00–18:00.

Zurich - Chur - Arosa - Chur - Zurich   520, 841

See the good canyon, lake and mountain scenery on this easy one-day round trip. There is time for a stopover in Chur, as shown by the schedules below.

Most of the Zurich–Chur and Chur–Zurich trains have a restaurant car or light refreshments.

520

| Dep. Zurich | 07:10 | | 08:10 (1) | 09:10 | 10:10 (1) | 11:10 | 12:10 (1+2) |
| Arr. Chur | 08:44 | | 09:44 | 10:44 | 11:44 | 12:44 | 13:44 |

Change trains 841

| Dep. Chur | 09:00 | 10:00 | 10:50 | 11:50 | 12:50 | 13:50 |
| Arr. Arosa | 58-65 minutes later | | | | | |

Sights in **Arosa**: Great summer and winter sports. Fantastic mountain scenery.

841

Dep. Arosa	10:00	11:00	12:00	13:00	14:00	15:00
Arr. Chur	60 minutes later					

Change trains 520

Dep. Chur	11:16	12:16 (1)	13:16	14:16 (1)	15:16	16:16 (1+3)
Arr. Zurich	12:50	13:50	14:50	15:50	16:50	17:50

(1) Reservation advisable. (2) Plus another Zurich departure at 13:10, arriving back in Zurich 18:50. (3) Plus other departures from Chur at 17:16, 18:16 (1), 19:16, 20:16, 21:16 and 22:16, arriving Zurich 18:50, 19:50, 20:50, 21:50, 22:50 and 23:50.

Zurich - Chur - Zermatt - Gornergrat - Zermatt   520, 575, 578

There is fabulous Rhone Valley scenery on this ride plus crossing Oberalp Pass (6,700 feet) and going through the eight-mile long Furka Tunnel on the Chur–Brig portion.

This trip includes going over the highest bridges in Europe and, by departing Zurich at 07:10 or 09:10, you can include the outstanding cogwheel train ride to Gornergrat (10,200 feet) for a close view of the Matterhorn (14,692 feet) and more than 50 other Alpine peaks.

The Chur–Zermatt, Zermatt–Gornergrat and Gornergrat–Zermatt portions of this trip are not covered by Eurailpass.

All of the Chur–Zermatt trains in this timetable are *Glacier Express*, for which reservation is required. For services, prices and reservations, see "St. Moritz–Zermatt."

Do not let this timetable discourage you. This trip is easier to make than it was to prepare the table!

520				*Change trains 578*		
Dep. Zurich	07:10 (1)	09:10 (1)		Dep. Zermatt	14:48	17:12
Arr. Chur	08:44	10:45		Arr. Gornergrat	15:29	17:55
Change trains 575				• • •		
Dep. Chur	08:57 (2)	10:57 (2)		Dep. Gornergrat	15:31	17:55 (4)
Arr. Zermatt	14:42 (3)	16:42 (3)		Arr. Zermatt	16:15	18:37

(1) Light refreshments. (2) *Glacier Express*. See details about reservations and prices under "St. Moritz–Zermatt" (3) Operates early June to mid-October. (4) Plus other departures from Gornergrat at 15:55, 16:19, 16:43, 17:07 (all year), 17:55 and 19:07, arriving Zermatt 16:39, 17:03, 17:27, 17:51, 18:38 and 19:49.

Zurich - Davos - Filisur - Thusis - Zurich   520, 540, 545

In order to make a scenic *circle-trip* that avoids repeating the Landquart–Filisur route in the Zurich–Davos round trip, return to Zurich from Filisur via Thusis.

The Davos–Filisur portion of this trip is *not* covered by Eurailpass.

520

Dep. Zurich	07:10 (1)	08:10 (2)	09:10 (1)	10:10 (1)	11:10 (3+6)
Arr. Landquart	08:34	09:34	10:34	11:34	12:34
Change trains 545					
Dep. Landquart	08:45	09:45	10:45	11:45	12:45
Dep. Klosters	09:29	10:29	11:29	12:20	13:20
Arr. Davos Platz	09:54 (4)	10:54	11:46	12:46	14:46
Arr. Filisur	10:55	11:55	12:55	13:55	14:55
Change trains 540					
Dep. Filisur	11:02 (3)	12:02 (1)	13:02 (1)	14:02	15:02 (1)
Dep Thusis	11:35	12:35	13:35	14:35	15:35
Arr. Chur	12:05	13:07	14:05	15:05	16:05
Change trains 520					
Dep. Chur	12:15 (5)	13:16 (3)	14:16 (5)	15:16 (1)	16:16 (3)
Arr. Zurich	13:50	14:50	15:50	16:50	17:50

(1) Light refreshments. (2) Reservation advisable. Light refreshments. (3) Restaurant car. (4) Change trains. (5) Reservation advisable. Restaurant car. (6) Plus other departures from Zurich at 12:10 (2) and 13:10 (3), arriving back in Zurich 18:50 and 19:50.

Zurich - Landquart - Davos - Landquart - Zurich   520, 545

Excellent canyon, lake and mountain scenery may be viewed on this easy one-day round trip.

Zurich - Bellinzona - Lugano   550

The Zurich – Lugano portion of the Zurich-Milan route (one of the five most scenic rail trips in Europe) can be seen on a one-day round-trip from Zurich. A feast of beautiful farms, lakes, mountains, rivers and vineyards. You go through the 9.3-mile-long Gotthard Tunnel.

Before the Gotthard was opened to traffic in 1882, there was no direct rail route from eastern Switzerland through the Alps to Italy. For seven years and five months, 2,500 men worked in three shifts day and night to build this engineering marvel. Immediately after exiting the third of a series of nine tunnels, the train passes the small, white Wassen Church to your right, and about 230 feet above the track. The next time the church comes into view, after leaving Wassen Station, it is also to your right, and nearly level with the track. Later, after exiting tunnel #7, you have a third view of the church, this time to your left and 170 feet above the track.

The turns inside three semi-circular tunnels in this area (Pfaffensprung, Wattinger and Leggistein) are engineered so well that there is no sensation of the curves that the train is making inside those tunnels.

Try this interesting experiment: make a pendulum of any object, holding the top of a weighted string, chain or handkerchief against the inner face of a train window (a left-hand window when inside Pfaffensprung and Wattinger, a right-hand window when inside Leggistein).

As the train goes around a curve, the weighted bottom will move away from the window.

Climate on the Swiss side of the tunnel is usually much cooler than the Mediterranean temperature on the Italian end. There is a beautiful descent from the Italian end of the tunnel down the Ticino Valley. The train makes 3 percent gradients at 45–50 miles per hour.

At Bellinzona, the line forks. One branch goes to Locarno, the other to Lugano and Milan.

Dep. Zurich	07:04 (1)	08:33 (2)	09:07 (1)	10:07 (2)	11:07 (1)
Arr. Bellinzona	09:21	10:56 (3)	11:33 (3)	12:54	13:33
Arr. Lugano	09:45	11:22	12:03	13:23	14:03

Sights in **Bellinzona**: The Museum of Costumes and Prints, located in Castello di Sasso Corbaro, 320 feet above the town. Open daily except Monday 09:00–12:00 and 14:00–17:00, there are great views from it of the Alps, the Ticino River Valley and Lago (Lake) Maggiore.

The outdoor Saturday market: peasant sausages, breads, mountain cheeses, kitchenware, clothing. The 4th-century Castello Grande, sitting on a 150-foot-high hill in the center of the town.

The Post Office on Viale della Stazione is the newest (1990) tourist attraction because of its post-modernism architecture.

One can take a passageway under the railroad tracks (starting at a point between the rail station and the Post Office) to begin walking up a hillside to the 15th-century Castel Piccolo (small castle) for good views of the area.

See the views of the Ticino River Valley and the collection of medieval art, ancient coins and old weapons at the Civic Museum in the former dungeons of Castle Piccolo, open daily except Monday June–September 09:30–12:00 and 14:00–17:30: October–May 09:30–12:00 and 14:00–17:00.

The frescoed and arcaded old houses with wrought-iron balconies and marble portals, particularly Ca Rossa, called "Red House" because of the terra cotta ornaments on its facade.

The elegant clock tower on the ancient Town Hall, at Piazza Nosetto. Nearby the large rose window on the Collegiate Church and the beautiful sculptured 15th-century font there. A 10-minute walk from it is the interesting frescoed wall at Santa Maria delle Grazie Church.

Dep. Lugano	10:37 (2)	11:57 (2)	12:37 (2)	13:57 (2)	14:37 (2+4)
Dep. Bellinzona	11:06	12:26	13:06	14:26	15:06
Arr. Zurich	13:53	14:53	15:53	16:53	17:53

(1) Reservation advisable. Restaurant car. (2) Light refreshments. (3) Supplement payable. (4) Plus other frequent Lugano departures from 15:57 to 20:41.

Zurich - Mt. Rigi - Zurich   550. 551

The Arth Goldau–Mt. Rigi-Arth Goldau round-trip portion of this trip is not covered by Eurailpass.

The Arth Goldau–Rigi Kulm (and v.v.) schedules shown here are for the period early April to mid-October. Arth Goldau-Rigi (and v.v.) trains additional to those shown below operate early July to mid-October.

550

| Dep. Zurich | 09:07 (1) | 10:07 (2) | 12:07 (2) | 14:07 | 15:07 (3) |
| Arr. Arth Goldau | 09:48 (4) | 10:48 | 12:48 | 14:48 | 15:48 (4) |

Change to rack railway 551

| Dep. Arth Goldau | 10:10 | 11:10 | 13:10 | 15:10 | 16:10 |
| Arr. Rigi Kulm | 10:47 | 11:47 | 13:47 | 15:47 | 16:47 |

• • •

551

| Dep. Rigi Kulm | 11:04 | 12:04 | 14:04 | 16:04 | 17:04 | 19:04 |
| Arr. Arth Goldau | 11:48 | 12:48 | 14:8 | 16:48 | 17:48 | 19:48 |

Change from rack railway to a standard train 550

| Dep. Arth Goldau | 12:12 (1) | 13:12 (2) | 15:12 (2) | 17:12 (2) | 18:12 (1) | 20:12 (1) |
| Arr. Zurich | 12:53 (4) | 13:53 | 15:53 | 17:53 | 18:53 (4) | 20:53 (4) |

(1) Reservation advisable. Restaurant car. (2) Light refreshments. (3) Reservation advisable. Light refreshments. (4) Supplement payable.

Zurich - Luzern - Mt. Pilatus - Luzern - Zurich 555, 551, 561

There is fine canyon and mountain scenery on this easy one-day round trip.

The Alpnachstad–Pilatus–Alpnachstad rack railway portion operates only from May to the end of November.

There are good views and several restaurants at the top of Pilatus.

Most of the trains Zurich-Luzern (and v.v.) have light refreshments.

555

| Dep. Zurich | 07:01 | 08:01 | 09:01 | 10:01 | 11:01 | 12:01 | 13:01 (1) |
| Arr. Luzern | 07:49 | 08:49 | 09:50 | 10:50 | 11:50 | 12:50 | 13:50 |

Change trains 561

| Dep. Luzern | 08:24 | 09:24 | 10:21 | 11:24 | 12:24 | 13:24 | 14:24 |
| Arr. Alpnachstad | 08:40 | 09:40 | 10:39 | 11:40 | 12:39 | 13:40 | 14:39 |

Change to rack railway 551

| Dep. Alpnachstad | 08:50 | 09:30 | 10:50 | 11:30 | 13:10 | 13:50 | 14:30 |
| Arr. Pilatus Kulm | 09:20 | 10:00 | 11:20 | 12:00 | 13:40 | 14:20 | 15:00 |

• • •

551

| Dep. Pilatus Kulm | 09:25 | 10:45 | 11:25 | 12:05 | 13:45 | 14:25 | 15:05 (2) |
| Arr. Alpnachstad | 10:05 | 11:25 | 12:05 | 12:45 | 14:25 | 15:05 | 15:45 |

Change to standard train 561

| Dep. Alpnachstad | 11:13 | 12:17 | 12:41 | 13:13 | 14:44 | 15:13 | 16:17 |
| Arr. Luzern | 11:35 | 12:35 | 13:05 | 13:35 | 15:05 | 15:35 | 16:35 |

Change trains 555

| Dep. Luzern | Frequent times from 06:04 to 23:10 |
| Arr. Zurich | 50 minutes later |

(1) Plus another departure from Zurich at 14:01, arriving Pilatus Kulm 16:20. (2) Plus other Pilatus departures at 15:45 and 16:25, arriving Zurich 17:35 and 19:05.

Zurich - Romanshorn - St. Gallen (St. Gall) - Zurich   525, 550, 535

There is excellent lake and mountain scenery on this easy one-day circle round-trip that visits **Lake Constance** (**Konstanz** in German). One hundred miles of the lake's shore are in Germany, 16 in Austria, 43 in Switzerland. The microclimate here is so balmy that even palm trees grow in this area.

Sights in **St. Gallen:** The history of lacemaking and embroidery from the 16th century to the present, and lacework worn by European nobility, at the Gewerbemuseum (Embroidery Museum). The paintings in the Historisches Museum. The 100,000 volumes (including illuminated manuscripts), more than 1,000 years old, in the rebuilt rococo library of the ancient abbey. The twin-towered baroque 18th-century cathedral. Near it, many old houses decorated with frescoes and oriel windows, in the city's old quarter.

535

| Dep. Zurich | 08:10 (1) | 09:10 (1) | 10:10 (2) | 11:10 | 12:10 (1+3) |
| Arr. Romanshorn | 09:22 | 10:22 | 11:22 | 12:22 | 13:22 |

Take time for a boat ride on Lake Konstanz
(09:36–11:24, 10:36–12:24 or 11:36–13:24 — 50% discount with Eurailpass)

525

| Dep. Romanshorn | 09:34 | 11:34 | 12:34 (1) | 13:34 | 14:34 |
| Arr. St. Gallen | 09:59 | 11:59 | 12:59 | 13:59 | 14:59 |

Change trains 530

| Dep. St. Gallen | Frequent times from 05:09 to 22:41 |
| Arr. Zurich | 70 minutes later |

(1) Light refreshments. (2) Restaurant car. (3) Plus other departures from Zurich at 13:10, 14:10 and 15:10, arriving back in Zurich 16:43, 17:43 and 18:16.

Romanshorn - Friedrichshafen   536

This is the ferry service between Romanshorn and Friedrichshafen (50% discount with Eurailpass).

All of these boats have a restaurant.

Dep. Romanshorn	09:36	10:36	11:36	12:36	13:36	14:36 (1)
Arr. Friedrichshafen	40–45 minutes later					

Sights in **Friedrichschafen**: The first rigid airship, the Zeppelin, was built here in 1900, and this town became the principal European terminal for regularly scheduled trans-Atlantic airship service to New York and Rio de Janeiro. See the models, documents, photographs and collection of engines and other parts at the Zeppelin Museum.

Many of the towns on the German shore of Lake Constance (or Konstanz) have attractions. The local wine, pleasant inns and cozy taverns along their steep, winding cobblestoned streets bring crowds of visitors to them.

At **Unteruhldingen,** the open air museum of Stone Age and Bronze Age villages features reconstructed thatch-roofed, adobe houses built on wood piles between 4,000 and 1,000 B.C.

For devotees of Baroque and roccoco decor, there are the 18th-century church at **Birnau** and the banquet hall, reception rooms, library and private chambers of the palace and the interior of the 12th-century abbey at **Salem**.

See **Ueberlingen**, a living page from the Middle Ages and the Renaissance: massive walls, 15th and 16th-century house, a lavish Town Hall.

Konstanz is the largest city on the lake (70,000). Because it is surrounded by Switzerland, it was spared from air raids in World War II. Founded about 300 A.D., it is the best base for visiting the lake's most popular islands: **Mainau** and **Reichenau**. The sights on Mainau are its tropical orchards (bananas, lemon, orange and mandarin trees) and profusion of flowers. It also has a Baroque castle.

The Benedictine abbeys and three churches on Reichenau provide a view of monastic life in the Middle Ages. See the Byzantine, Baroque and Gothic art at the treasury in St. Mary's Church.

The 18th-century Montfort Palace in **Tettnang** is one of the most richly decorated and lavishly furnished chateaus in southern Germany.

Dep. Friedrichshafen	10:431	11:41	12:41	13:41	14:41	15:41 (2)
Arr. Romanshorn	40–45 minutes later					

(1) Plus other departures from Romanshorn at 15:36, 16:36, 17:36, 18:36 and 19:36. (2) Plus other departures from Friedrichshafen at 16:41, 17:41, 18:41 and 19:41.

Zurich - Schaffhausen - Zurich   940

A trip to see the marvelous **Rhine Falls**.

Dep. Zurich	Frequent times from 07:13 to 22:13
Arr. Schaffhausen	38-41 minutes later

Sights in **Schaffhausen**: A bus takes you in 10 minutes from the rail station to the cataracts below the tumultuous seven-story-high Rhine Falls (less than a one-hour walk from the town's waterfront). The most impressive sight is usually in early July, when the snow in the Swiss and Austrian Alps is melting. For a great view of the Rhine River, climb to the 16th-century Munot Fortress.

Visit the gold and silver room in the Allerheiligen Museum. The Thursday market.

Take the uphill path, through vineyards, a 15-minute walk to the hilltop castle, for the view from there. Ride the cable car to the summit of 8,215-foot-high **Mt. Santis** for a spectacular view of many Alpine peaks, including Germany's Zugspitze.

Take the 90 minute river boat to **Stein am Rhein** to see the 11th-century Hohenklingen Castle. See the depiction of 11th-century life in the museum at the 11th-century St. George Monastery, the ruins of Tasgetium (a Roman fort), and the stained glass, wood walls and medieval firearms on the top floor of the 16th-century Town Hall.

Dep. Schaffhausen   Frequent times from 06:07 to 23:09
Arr. Zurich   38-41 minutes later

A GLORIOUS WEEK IN SWITZERLAND

Here is a great seven-day circle itinerary of Switzerland that gives you, in the span of one week, a visit to most of the country's major cities plus a view of much of Switzerland's great scenery. (Eurailpass holders are entitled to a 25 percent discount on rides to Jungfraujoch and Mt. Rigi.)

Day 1   Geneva, Montreux, Zweisimmen, Spiez (Lunch). Lake Thun boat to Interlaken.
Day 2   Interlaken, Jungfraujoch, Grindelwald (lunch), Interlaken.
Day 3   Interlaken, Luzern.
Day 4   Luzern, Vitznau, Mt. Rigi (lunch), Arth-Goldau, Lugano.
Day 5   Lugano, Bellinzona, Locarno.
Day 6   Locarno, Domodossola, Bern.
Day 7   Bern to Geneva or Zurich.

A MAGNIFICENT ONE-DAY TRIP

Here are several of the most scenic rail trips in Europe, combined in a single day.

All of these rides are covered by Eurailpass.

Table 560	Dep. Spiez	07:54 (1)	Arr. Brig	09:03
590	Dep. Brig	10:11	Arr. Domodossola	10:45
549	Dep. Domodossola	11:11	Arr. Locarno	12:48
549	Dep. Locarno	14:10	Arr. Bellinzona	14:53
550	Dep. Bellinzona	15:26 (2)	Arr. Luzern	17:41
561	Dep. Luzern	17:54	Arr. Interlaken (Ost)	20:02
560	Dep. Interlaken (Ost)	20:45 (3)	Arr. Spiez	21:05

(1) Light refreshments. (2) Reservation advisable. Restaurant car. Supplement charged. (3) Reservation advisable. Restaurant car.

THE "GOLDEN PASS" ROUTE

Luzern - Interlaken - Spiez - Zweisimmen - Montreux - Lausanne   560, 561, 565, 566, 569

There are snow-capped Alpine peaks, flowering meadows, and sparkling mountain streams on this marvelous one-day trip. As the timetables show, a layover in Spiez is possible.

561			*Change trains 565*		
Dep. Luzern	08:54		Dep. Spiez	12:02	13:08 (2)
Arr. Interlaken (Ost)	10:40		Arr. Zweisimmen	12:39	13:55
Change trains 560			*Change trains 566*		
Dep. Interlaken (Ost)	10:54 (1)		Dep. Zweisimmen	14:00	14:44 (3)
Arr. Spiez	11:15		Arr. Montreux	16:00	16:28
			Change trains 569		
			Dep. Montreux	16:52	17:52
			Arr. Lausanne	17:26	18:26

(1) Restaurant car. (2) Plus other departures from Spiez at 14:08, 15:08. (3) Reservation required. Light refreshments.

INTERNATIONAL ROUTES
FROM SWITZERLAND

The Swiss gateways for travel to West Germany are Basel (to Cologne), Geneva (to Frankfurt), and Zurich (to Munich). Zurich is also the starting point for the train trip to Austria (Innsbruck, and on to Vienna and East Europe) and for train travel to Italy (Milan and beyond).

Basel is also a starting point for trips to Belgium, Holland and France (Paris, and on to London or Madrid).

Geneva (via Aosta, and on to Torino) as well as Bern and Brig (via Domodossola) are also departure cities for rail rides to Italy (Milan, and beyond).

There is also rail service from Geneva to Paris, and from Geneva to southern France (Avignon) and on to Spain (Barcelona).

Basel - Amsterdam   73

Dep. Basel (SBB)	13:14 (1)	14:14 (1)	23:25 (2)
Arr. Amsterdam	20:52	21:52	08:54

(1) Reservation advisable. Supplement charged. Restaurant car. (2) Has couchettes.

Basel - Cologne   910

Sit on the right side of the train for best views of the marvelous Rhine River scenery.

Reservation is advisable for all of the Basel–Cologne day trains. All of them have a restaurant car.

Dep. Basel (SBB)	Every hour 08:14 to 18:14
Dep. Basel (Bad.)	7 minutes after departing SBB rail station
Arr. Cologne	13:00 to 23:08

Basel - Hamburg - Copenhagen - Oslo - Stockholm   50, 910

910

Dep. Basel (SBB)	07:05 (1)	13:05 (1)	-0-	17:46 (4+5)
Arr. Hamburg (Hbf.)	13:22	19:22	-0-	03:52 (5)
Change trains 50				
Dep. Hamburg	15:12 (2)	18:27(4)	07:30	-0-
Arr. Copenhagen	20:31	22:59	11:59	-0-
Change trains				
Dep. Copenhagen	21:45 (3)	23:15	09:45 (6)	13:01 (6)
Arr. Oslo (Sen.)	07:07	07:53	19:52	-0-
Arr. Stockholm (Cen.)	-0-	-0-	-0-	20:05

(1) Reservation advisable. Supplement charged. Restaurant car. (2) Reservation advisable. Supplement charged. Light refreshments. (3) Reservation *required*. Carries a sleeping car. Also has couchettes. Coach is second class. (4) Train has only sleeping cars and couchettes. No coaches. (5) Direct train to Copenhagen. No train change in Hamburg. (6) Reservation *required*. Restaurant car.

Zurich - Munich   75

Reservation is advisable for all of these trains. All of them charge a supplement and have restaurant car.

Dep. Zurich	07:33	09:33	13:33	17:33
Arr. Munich	11:52	13:57	17:48	21:54

Zurich - Innsbruck - Salzburg - Vienna   86

About 2½ hours out of Zurich, the train passes through one of Europe's largest tunnels, the 6.3-mile-long Arlberg. There is a very beautiful view of Alpine scenery as the train comes out of the tunnel.

Dep. Zurich	09:33 (1)	13:33 (1)	22:33
Arr. Innsbruck	13:19	17:19	-0-
Arr. Salzburg	15:29	19:29	-0-
Arr. Vienna (West.)	18:45	22:45	08:05

(1) Reservation advisable. Supplement charged. Restaurant car.

Bern - Brig - Milan   82

This trip takes you on the marvelous scenic route via Spiez (see "Geneva–Spiez") and through both the 10-mile-long Lotschberg Tunnel Bern–Brig) and the 11.9-mile-long Simplon (Brig–Milan), longest tunnel in Europe and world's third longest, after Japan's Seikan Tunnel (33.4 miles, between Tappi and Yoshioka) and Japan's Daishimizu Tunnel (13.4 miles, between Tokyo and Niigata).

Reservation is advisable for all of these trains.

Dep. Bern	07:34 (1)	08:50 (2)	12:58 (2)	15:26 (1)	17:34 (1)
Arr. Brig	08:19	10:29	14:32	17:04	19:00
Arr. Milan (Cen.)	10:45	12:45	16:45	19:25	20:45

(1) Restaurant car. (2) Light refreshments.

Zurich - Milan   84

See detailed notes about the wonderful scenery on this route (one of the five most scenic rail trips in Europe) under "Zurich–Lugano"

Reservation is advisable for all of these trains.

Dep. Zurich	07:04 (1)	08:33 (2)	09:07 (1)	11:07 (1)	13:07 (2+4)
Arr. Milan (Cen.)	10:45	12:45 (3)	13:35 (3)	15:35 (3)	17:35

(1) Restaurant car. (2) Light refreshments. (3) Supplement charged. (4) Plus other Zurich departures at 15:07,17:07 and 19:07, arriving Milan 19:35, 21:35 and 23:45.

Basel - Luxembourg - Brussels   40

Dep. Basel (SBB)	08:32	13:30 (1)	16:23 (1)
Arr. Luxembourg	12:00	16:49	19:56
Arr. Brussels (Q.L.)	14:22	19:10	22:18
Arr. Brussels (Nord)	14:32	19:20	22:28
Arr. Brussels (Midi)	8 minutes after arriving Nord rail station.		

(1) Reservation advisable. Supplement charged. Restaurant car.

Geneva - Milan - Venice   82

Dep. Geneva (Corn.)	08:14 (1)	09:18 (2)	12:05 (1+3)	23:02 (4)
Arr. Milan (Cen.)	12:30	14:17	15:45 (2)	-0-
Dep. Milan (Cen.)	12:45	15:05 (3)	16:05	-0-
Arr. Venice (S.L.)	15:55	17:57	18:55	06:58

(1) Reservation advisable. Restaurant car. (2) Change trains. (3) Supplement payable. (4) Carries sleepers, second-class couchettes and second-class coaches.

Bern - Paris   42

Dep. Bern	06:56 (1)	09:05	17:05
Dep. Frasne	-0-	10:58	18:35
Dep. Frasne	08:33	11:19 (1+2)	18:47 (1+2)
Arr. Paris (Lyon)	11:32	14:12	21:42

(1) TGV. Reservation required. Supplement charged. Restaurant car. (2) Change trains in Frasne.

Geneva - Paris   372

Reservation is advisable for these trains. All are TGV, run daily and have light refreshments, unless designated otherwise.

Dep. Geneva (Corn.)	05:40 (1)	07:34	10:00	12:30	16:38	19:08
Arr. Paris (Lyon)	09:22	11:11	13:38	16:13	20:17	22:46

(1) Restaurant car.

Zurich - Bern (or Basel) - Geneva - Avignon - Barcelona   81

The *Pablo Casals* (19:53 departure from Zurich) began in 1990 to carry one "Gran Clase" sleeping car, the most luxurious sleeping car in Europe. Each of its large single and double compartments has a shower and toilet. The train also has ordinary sleeping compartments and four-berth tourist compartments. There are no coach seats. The train has a restaurant car. Travel is not covered by any rail passes. A supplement is charged. This is a direct train. No train change in Port Bou.

Dep. Zurich	-0-	-0-	19:33 (4)
Dep. Bern	-0-	-0-	21:22
Dep. Basel (SBB)	-0-	-0-	-0-
Dep. Geneva (Cor.)	10:45 (1)	21:54	23:29
Dep. Avignon	14:10 (2)	01:57	-0-
Arr. Port Bou	17:20	05:36 (3)	-0-
Arr. Barcelona (Sants)	19:16	09:04	-0-
Arr. Barcelona (Franca)	-0-	-0-	09:30

(1) TGV. Supplement charged. Reservation required. Restaurant car. (2) Change trains in Montpellier. Supplement charged. Reservation required. Restaurant car. (3) Has couchettes. Change trains in Port Bou at 05:25. (4) *Pablo Casals*. See description above.

AOSTA-TORINO GATEWAYS TO ITALY

(1) Via San Bernardo Tunnel

Lausanne or Brig to Martigny and **Martigny - Aosta - Torino**
570, 573, 586

Train 570			*Train* 570		
Dep. Lausanne	07:04 (1)	15:29	Dep. Brig	06:43 (1)	15:36 (1)
Arr. Martigny	07:57	16:22	Arr. Martigny	07:37	16:37

• • •

Bus 573				
Dep. Martigny (Stn.)	08:10	-0-	16:30	-0-
Arr. Aosta (P. Narbonne)	10:00	-0-	18:30	-0-
Change to train 586				
Dep. Aosta	10:40	12:40	19:40	20:40
Arr. Torino (Porta Nuova)	12:35	14:35	21:35	22:35

(1) Light refreshments.

(2) Via Mt. Blanc Tunnel

Geneva - Chamonix - Aosta - Torino   361, 366, 367. 586

All of the train changes Geneva–Chamonix are cross-platform, taking less than one minute.

368

Dep. Geneva (Eaux-Vives)	07:07 (1)	08:13	11:10 (2)	14:36
Arr. La Roche-sur-Foron	07:41	08:44	11:47	15:09
Change trains 367				
Dep. La Roche-sur-Foron	08:07	10:15	12:02	15:18
Arr. St. Gervais	08:57	11:10	12:46	16:13
Change trains 367				
Dep. St. Gervais	08:57	11:15	13:04	16:17
Arr. Chamonix	09:44	11:56	13:42	16:59
Change to bus 366				
Dep. Chamonix	10:05 (3)	13:30 (3)	16:15 (3)	17:45
Arr. Aosta	11:40	16:00	18:00	19:30

(1) Runs daily, except Sundays and holidays. (2) Runs Saturdays, Sundays and holidays. (3) Operates late June to mid-September.

Change to a train 586

Dep. Aosta (P. Narbonne)	14:40	18:33 (1)	-0-	19:40	20:40
Arr. Torino (P. S.)	16:35	20:37	-0-	21:35	22:35

A good break in this journey is to spend the night in Aosta and continue on to Torino the next day. Here are the schedules for the other departures from Aosta:

Dep. Aosta (P. Narbonne)	07:40	08:40
Arr. Torino (P. S.)	09:35	10:32

(1) Runs Sundays and holidays.

CHAPTER 7

BRITAIN
ENGLAND, WALES AND SCOTLAND

Getting on Track in Britain

• Tourist information: UK/British Tourist Authority, New York office, 551 Fifth Avenue, Suite 701, New York, NY 10176-0799. Telephone (800) GO 2 BRITAIN or (212) 986-2200. Canada office, 111 Avenue Road, Suite 450, Toronto, ON M5R 3J8, Canada. Telephone (416) 925-6326, fax (416) 961-2175. Toll-free phone in Canada (888) VISIT UK. On the Web: http://www.visitbritain.com/.

• Public holidays: **Nearly all train, bus and subway services are reduced on holidays. The main holidays on which to avoid travel are all "Bank" holidays (whose dates vary) and the period from December 25 through January 1. If you cannot avoid intra-city travel on a holiday, it is advisable to reserve a taxi by telephone the day prior.** The following holidays are celebrated in Britain: January 1, January 2 (Bank Holiday in Scotland), Good Friday, Easter Monday (not in Scotland), May Day Bank Holiday (first Monday in May), Spring Bank Holiday (last Monday in May, Summer Bank Holiday (first Monday in August (Scotland), last Monday in August rest of Britain), December 25, Christmas Day and Boxing Day, December 26.

Summer time: Britain changes to Summer Time on the last Sunday of March and converts back to Standard Time on the last Sunday of October.

• Currency: British pound (£). At press time, $1 equalled £0.62

Overview of Britain's Trains

It's been an interesting time for railroading in Britain, since the breakup of the mighty British Rail began in the mid-1990s. Privatizing has resulted in the creation of 25 different railways franchised to private operators. Coordinating all these railways–fares, schedules, etc.–has been a challenge, to say the least. It's proven a lot more confusing for Brits than for railpass-carrying Americans on holiday. All the more reason to buy a BritRail pass before leaving the States.

General Rail Information

• First and Standard are the classes of service offered on British trains. Some trains also may offer Pullman service, where first-class passengers have light refreshments or an at-seat meal included in the ticket price. Many trains have buffet or restaurant cars or serve light refreshments from a cart that's rolled through the train. Most trains are air-conditioned.

• First-class sleeping compartments have one berth, Standard-class, two berths. Generally, overnight passengers may remain in sleeping cars at destinations the next morning until 07:30. Pullman trains, for which reservation is advisable, offer full meals to first-class passengers at their seats.

• Children under five travel free. Half-fare for children 5–15. Children 16 and over must pay full fare.

• Britain's 750 "InterCity" trains, linking more than 200 towns each weekday, average 98 to 140 miles per hour on some routes.

• Reservations are required on the fast day trains. If there are vacant spaces, the conductor at the departure platform can allocate available places.

• Railtrack (they are responsible for railway infrastructure–tracks signals, stations, etc.– usually makes repairs to train lines from late Saturday through Sunday afternoon. If you plan to travel by train during those times, telephone the rail station or 0345 48 49 40 and confirm the time for routes you intend to use.

• Cycles can be taken on many trains, but there are some restrictions due to lack of space. Reservations may be required, and full details are available at major stations. Some railways charge from £3 for each complete trip. Motorcycles, mopeds, motorized cycles and scooters cannot be taken on any train.

• Travelers with disabilities can get free information about wheelchair-accessible hotels, restaurants and transportation providers by contacting Holiday Care Service, 2nd Floor, Imperial Buildings, Victoria Road, Horley RH6 7PZ. Telephone 011 44 (01293) 774535, fax 011 44 (01293) 784647.

• Get the latest fares and news from BritRail Travel International's Web site: http://www.britrail.com/us/ushome.htm. See Appendix B for more interesting UK sites.

BRITAIN'S TRAIN PASSES AND DISCOUNT TICKETS

See Chapter 2 for BritRail Pass prices. Unless noted otherwise, the passes listed here can be purchased through BritRail Travel International and, now, also through Rail Europe and BritRail's joint effort, Eurostar USA; call (800) EUROSTAR.

BritRail Southeast Railpass This pass offers unlimited train travel in southeast England. Because many of the trains in this region have only second-class accommodations, first-class pass prices have been adjusted to reflect this. With the Southeast Railpass, you can visit many cities such as Oxford, Salisbury, Cambridge and Brighton. The pass is not valid for trips to Bath, however, or other services vis Reading, such as to Exeter. The 1998 prices are:

	Adult		Child*	
	1st Cl.	Standard	1st Cl.	Standard
Any 3 days in 8	$94	$69	$27	$18
Any 4 days in 8	$126	$94	$27	$18
Any 7 days in 15	$166	$126	$27	$18

*Children 5-15 years; under five, free.

London Visitor Travelcard Can be purchased worldwide. Valid for unlimited travel on London's buses and subways, plus discounts on the admission prices at such attractions as London Transport Museum, London Zoo, Madame Tussaud's, Kensington Palace, Tower Bridge and the Cabinet War Rooms. (A version sold in Britain does not include discounts at historical sites.) The 1998 adult prices are: $29 for 3 days, $39 for 4 days, $59 for 7 days. Children age 5–15: $12, $14 and $22.

BritRail Family Pass Buy one adult or senior pass and one accompanying child (5-15) gets a pass of the same type and duration, free. Additional children purchase the appropriate pass at half off the adult pass price. Children under five ride free. The Family Pass is available with BritRail Classic Pass, BritRail Flexipass, BritRail Senior Pass, BritRail Pass + Car, BritRail Pass + Ireland.

BritRail + Eurostar 1998 information was unavailable at press time. Check with BritRail Travel or Rail Europe to see if this combination is still offered. In 1997, travelers could combine a first- or standard-class BritRail Flexipass with a standard-class Eurostar trip through the Channel Tunnel. The pass was valid for travel around Britain for either four or eight days out of a three-month period. Eurostar reservations had to be made before departure. A Eurostar ticket voucher was issued and then exchanged for the ticket. Children's discounts weren't available in 1997. Prices listed here are from 1997.

	One-way Eurostar		Round-trip Eurostar	
	First Cl.	Standard Cl.	First Cl.	Standard Cl.
4 days in 3 months	$422	$262	$557	$319
8 days in 3 months	$553	$354	$693	$413

The following tickets will make your London sightseeing hassle-free. The cards are sold at London Transport Travel Centres, underground stations and authorized agents throughout London.

One-Day Travelcard This card is the no-frills version of the London Visitors Travelcard mentioned earlier. With this card, there are no discount vouchers for local attractions. It does offer, though, unlimited travel after 09:30 Monday-Friday and all day Saturday and Sunday on London Transport buses, underground trains, Docklands Light Railway and any rail service within the travel zones on your ticket (it is not valid for travel on night buses or tour buses). Buy it at underground and bus stations. In late 1997 it cost £3.00 (central zones 1 and 2), £3.50 (4 zones) and £3.90 (all 6 zones). For longer stays, you can buy a weekly, monthly or even yearly Travelcard. You'll need a passport-sized photo. For more information about these passes, contact any London Transport Travel Centre.

Weekend Travelcard The Weekend Travelcard is just like a One-Day Travelcard but is valid for the two days of the weekend. It is also valid for travel on any two consecutive days during public holidays. The card is valid for use on all the same transport services as the one-day version. In late 1997, it cost £4.80 (central zones 1 and 2), £5.40 (4 zones) and £6.00 (all 6 zones), about a 25 percent savings as the one-day card.

Carnet While the "carnet," or book, of tickets has been a popular Paris metro item for years, the idea didn't catch on with London Transport until 1996. Tickets are sold in books of 10 for £10.00, a saving of £2.00 over the cost of 10 separate single tickets. Carnet tickets are good for travel only within Zone 1, and are not valid on London Transport buses. Tickets must be validated on the day of travel. Usually this is done by passing through the entry ticket gate. Buying a carnet will save money over a pass, for those who plan to take only a trip or two per day.

SCOTLAND'S TRAIN PASSES

Scottish Area Rover passes are sold at main rail stations and Travel Centres in the area of the "ticket." All of these allow 33 percent discount for children 5–15. Children under five travel free.

The two passes described below are sold at main British rail stations and in the U.S.A. by BritRail Travel International and by Scots-American Travel Advisors, 26 Rugen Drive, Harrington Park, NJ 07640, (201) 768-1187. They do not have discounts for children.

Freedom of Scotland Travelpass Unlimited *standard*-class train travel on rail lines north of Berwick and Carlisle, also on ferries to many scenic islands, plus discounts on ferries to Orkney and Shetland islands, and travel on some local bus services. Prices for 1998 were unavailable at press time. Prices listed here (in British currency) are from 1997: £99 for eight consecutive days and £139 for 15 consecutive days.

Freedom of Scotland Flexipass Unlimited *standard*-class travel on the same train, ferry and bus services as the pass above for consecutive days. The 1998 prices are $110 for any four days of travel within 15 days, $160 for any eight days within 15 and $210 for any 12 days within 15 days. No children's discounts.

NORTHERN IRELAND'S TRAIN PASSES

Both of these passes are sold in Belfast at: Tourist Information Centre, 59 North Street; NIR Travel Ltd., 28-30 Wellington Place; and Central Station.

Freedom of Ireland Provides seven consecutive days of unlimited bus & train travel in Northern Ireland. Prices for 1998 were unavailable at press time. In 1997, the passes cost:

1 day pass	£9
7 consecutive travel days	£30
Children 5-15 half-price	

COMBINING BRITAIN AND
THE CONTINENT

When planning to travel both in Britain and on the European Continent, keep in mind that the maximum value of combining a British train pass with a Eurailpass is achieved by scheduling Britain for either the start or end of a tour (see also "Eurostar" for Channel Tunnel connections). For example, to start a tour in Amsterdam and have one's itinerary then go to Paris, London, and then return to the continent for additional Eurailpass traveling would require a longer (and more expensive) Eurailpass because of consuming Eurailpass days while in Britain.

Conversely, to start a tour in London, followed by travel on the Continent, and then concluding with more travel in Britain will require a longer and more expensive British pass since the days spent on the Continent will consume British pass days.

We present in this chapter descriptions of four categories of rail service. First, the train connection services between London and the Continent (Paris, Brussels and Amsterdam). Next, 41 one-day rail trips that can be made comfortably out of London, with departure and arrival times, on-board-services, and what to see and do at each destination before returning to London, in most cases at dinnertime. See Appendix A for single-ticket price examples.

Third are itineraries for trips to Cork, Ireland and to Edinburgh, Scotland. The chapter concludes with details about rail trips in Scotland from Aberdeen, Edinburgh, Glasgow and Inverness. Several of those routes are very scenic.

The extensive notes in this book about train times are intended to both help you *plan* your itinerary and are also useful after your trip begins (if you bring the *Guide* along!) for making impromptu last-minute travel plans.

Before commencing any journey, always — without exception — double-check the times in this book or in any published timetable, as they are subject to change without prior notice. We have made every effort possible to publish correct departure and arrival times, but schedules are subject to constant change.

WARNING: Many cities have two or more rail stations. London has eight rail stations. We take pains to tell you for every trip in this book the name of the rail station from which your train departs, by noting the station in parenthesis immediately after the name of the city, such as: London (King's Cross).

All of London's rail stations are interconnected by subway (underground or "tube") service, providing far easier and quicker transfers than by surface streets. For example, when entering England by rail from France, at Dover, you will come into Victoria station. To continue on to Edinburgh, it is necessary to first transfer by subway (Circle line) from Victoria (along to Thames River) to King's Cross station, on the opposite side of London from Victoria station.

A brief description of the areas served by London's eight major rail stations:

CHARING CROSS STATION This station services suburban commuters between London and Folkestone, and between London and Hastings. It connects at Dover (Priory station) with Hovercraft service to and from France.

EUSTON STATION A part of Central England and the northwestern area of Britain are reached from Euston station, starting with Coventry and Birmingham, and then running through Stafford, Chester, Liverpool, Manchester and Blackpool, on into Glasgow. Also, Holyhead, gateway to Dublin.

KING'S CROSS STATION Northeastern England (Leeds, York, Hull, Newcastle) and Edinburgh are reached by trains from King's Cross station. Newcastle is the gateway to Norway. Hull is a gateway to Denmark, Germany and Holland.

LIVERPOOL STREET STATION This station services the area immediately northeast of London: Colchester, Cambridge, Ipswich, Harwich (gateway to Holland, Germany, Austria, Yugoslavia and Norway), Norwich and King's Lynn.

PADDINGTON STATION The area in southern England, west from Weymouth (Exeter, Plymouth and Penzance), is reached out of Paddington station as is also that portion of southwestern England running north to Bristol, Swansea, Fishguard (gateway to Rosslare, at the southeastern tip of the Republic of Ireland), Gloucester, Worcester, Hereford and Oxford.

ST. PANCRAS STATION Trains going due north from London to Leicester, Derby, Nottingham and Sheffield leave from St. Pancras station.

VICTORIA STATION Gatwick Airport, once a Mecca for charter flights has, in recent years become attractive to major carriers that can't get slots at Heathrow and to domestic airlines serving the region. Rail service is fast (30 minutes) and frequent (every 15 minutes during peak times) to the airport from Victoria. Catch a train every 15 minutes from 05:00 to 00:00. After that, trains depart at 00:30, 01:30, 02:30, 03:30 and 04:30. The transfer from airplane to train, or vice versa, is entirely indoor as the rail station at Gatwick is a part of the airport. Some airlines offer check-in at the station. Porters are also available, at no charge, to help with luggage. Purchase tickets on the train or at the Gatwick Express ticket office on Platform 14 or on the Plaza. In 1997, a one-way first-class fare was $23, standard class, $17.

Victoria station services the small area of Southern England just East of but not including Portsmouth: Worthing, Brighton, Newhaven, Eastbourne, Hastings and Dover (gateway to France, Spain, Belgium, Switzerland, Italy, Austria and Yugoslavia).

WATERLOO STATION Services South Central England: Southampton, Bournemouth and Weymouth. Eurostar trains serve Paris and Brussels from Waterloo International.

HEATHROW – LONDON UNDERGROUND CONNECTION

The train service is between Heathrow airport and every subway station on Piccadilly Line between Heathrow and Kings Cross rail station. Trains depart both terminals every 4–10 minutes 05:30–23:00 daily except Sundays and holidays, and 07:30–23:30 on Sundays. Journey time is 50–58 minutes.

GATWICK – LONDON
TRAIN CONNECTION

See above under "Victoria Station" for details about Gatwick trains. Trains leave Gatwick every 15 minutes from 05:20 to 00:50. Thereafter, trains leave at 01:35, 02:35, 03:35 and 04:35.

Two other companies also serve Gatwick, Connex South Central and Thameslink. Connex claims they've got the cheapest rail fare from Gatwick to Victoria, at £7.50 one way. Both South Central and Thameslink trains make a stop or two along their routes.

DAYS OF THE WEEK VARIANCES

For the time schedules given in this book, "daily" means Monday through Sunday. Where Sunday departure and arrival times are specified in conjunction with a list of daily schedules, this refers to *additional* service on Sunday, not to substitute service.

In other words, if a daily schedule lists departures at 10:00 and 11:12, and the Sunday schedule indicates a departure at 13:05, there are three departures on Sunday: at 10:00, 11:12 and 13:05.

Conversely, if Monday-Friday or Monday-Saturday schedules show departures at 10:00 and 11:12, and there is a listing of a Sunday departure at 13:05, then the only departure on Sunday for that trip is 13:05.

The same treatment applies to "Saturday only" schedules in connection with times given as "Monday–Friday" or as "daily."

SUMMER AND WINTER SCHEDULES

In most European countries, winter schedules usually start on the Sunday following the last Saturday of September and runs through the Saturday preceding the last Sunday in May of the following year.

British timetables differ from the Continental pattern. Summer timetables for British rail service begin on the second Monday in May. There are two changes in winter schedules, occurring on the first Monday in October and on the first Monday in January.

Unless designated otherwise, the departure and arrival times given in this chapter are for the summer season and apply to trips that are made from early May to early October.

London

The capital of England. See the changing of the guard at Buckingham Palace. Downing Street, official residence of the Prime Minister. The Tower of London. London Bridge. The Houses of Parliament. The Wellington Museum (Aiseley House) and Wellington Arch. Hyde Park. Tate Gallery.

Don't miss the London Transport Museum, in the former Covent Garden Flower Market. In 1993, the museum was closed for nine months for a complete overhaul to provide a better showcase for its buses, trams and trains. Try your hand at the throttle of a London Underground train or at one of the other interactive exhibits. Pick up reproductions of those famous London Transport posters (also postcard size) in the museum's gift shop. Lots of other goodies here from excellent rail-oriented books to trinkets for the kids. The Museum is open every day (except 24th, 25th and 26th December) from 10.00 (Fridays 11.00) until 18.00, with the last admission at 17.15. Adults £4.95, seniors and children (5-15) £2.95. Learn more about the museum and getting around on London Transports buses and trains by logging on to their Web site: http://www.londontransport.co.uk/. (See Appendix B for more British Web sites.)

Visit the Kensington Gardens complex of Royal Albert Hall, the Science Museum, Geological Museum, Natural History Museum, and the Victoria and Albert Museum (closed on Fridays). Piccadilly Circus. The National Gallery and National Portrait Gallery.

The British Museum. Dickens' House (closed Sunday). St. Paul's Cathedral. Gray's Inn. The Imperial War Museum. The Royal Botanic Gardens (Kew). Regent's Park. Westminster Abbey. Nelson's Monument in Trafalgar Square. St. James's Palace. St. James's Park. The 53-acre Green Park.

Admiralty Arch. The Museum of London. The Royal Academy. The Museum of Mankind. The Sunday orators at Speaker's Corner. Marble Arch. Lambeth Palace, the residence of the Archbishop of Canterbury.

The dragon at Temple Bar Memorial. Mansion House, the residence of the Lord Mayor of London. Tower Bridge. The South Bank Arts Centre complex of National Theatre, Queen Elizabeth Hall, Royal Festival Hall, and Hayward Gallery. The Victoria Tower. Whitehall, the compound of government offices.

One of the world's greatest food stores, in Harrods Department Store, presents a spectacle of more than 500 cheeses, 120 different breads, 21 kinds of butter, produce from California, and a meat hall 90 feet long by 60 feet wide containing hams, pork, sausages, beef and lamb. There is also venison, shellfish, poultry, salmon (smoked and fresh), tinned foods from all over the world, eggs, teas from everywhere, caviar, wine, and the list goes on forever.

Another great London food store is Fortnum and Mason (also a complete department store). Operating since 1707, it's on Picadilly Circus. Open 09:30–18:00, daily except Sunday. 'Fortnums', as Londoners call it, has three restaurants. "The Fountain," in the basement, has an American-style soda fountain. It is open 09:30–24:00, very popular for after-theater snacks. "The Patio," on a mezzanine, offers the same light menu as "The Fountain" but also has grilled meats. It is open 09:30–16:30. The elegant fourth-floor "St. James" offers more extensive and more expensive food, open 11:30–18:00.

For a different view of food, visit Smithfield Meat Market, England's largest meat and poultry market, covering over 10 acres and employing almost 3,000 people. On a busy day, it sells in 19 hours more than 4,000 tons of meat, poultry and game: grouse, ducks, partridges, rabbits, pheasant, hams, green bacon, Danish bacon, smoked bacon, Irish bacon, lamb, beef and many exotic imported meats. Open Monday-Friday 05:00–12:00.

Near Smithfield is the very interesting 12th-century St. Bartholomew the Great Church. Stroll the entire area: St. John's Lane, Charterhouse Street and many narrow alleys for a look at the London of 300 years ago.

For a different view of London, explore the city on a Sunday, by foot. Walk along Whitechapel Road to see the (still working) foundry where the Liberty Bell was cast. From Whitechapel, it's an easy walk to the Tower of London and the St. Katherine marina.

Explore London attractions to the east, from the tower of London, through Docklands to Greenwich, aboard the elevated Docklands Light Railway (DLR). The automated trains seem to fly through the air, between buildings and across water, as they make their way to the Docklands, once the greatest port in the world. After World War II and later, politics, doomed the area, it fell into disrepair. A comeback was launched in the 1980s, and now the area is "the place to be," with chic riverside condos, cozy pubs and restaurants and ultra-modern structures like the huge Canary Wharf, melding with historic landmarks. From Island Gardens station, take the foot tunnel under the Thames to Greenwich. Or make a day of it with a "Sail and Rail" pass. The pass is valid from 09:30 and lets you roam the area at leisure, starting from DLR's Tower Gateway station or Westminster pier. Explore the Docklands historic wharves and preserved warehouses, then take a cruise on a riverboat to Greenwich. In late 1997, an adult pass cost £7.20; a child's pass was £3.80. Prices included 20 percent discount off National Maritime Museum, Royal Observatory and Queens House at Greenwich. Passes are sold at Information Centres at Island Gardens, Tower Gateway, Westminster and Greenwich. For more information on boat times, call Westminster Pier, 0171 930 4097 or Greenwich Pier 0181 858 3996.

Travalcards are also valid on DLR trains (Zone 1 and 2). Check out the DLR Web site at http://www.dlr.co.uk/index.htm.

Another enjoyable way to spend an afternoon is to cruise the Camden Locks on a canal boat. The London Waterbus Company operates 90-minute trips between Little Venice and Camden. You'll see a different side of bustling London as you float beneath towering trees, past the vast grounds of Regent's Park and a stone's throw from the residents of the London Zoo. When you get to Camden you can forage through the chaos of the Camden Canal Market. This is a great place for people-watching, but also for pickpockets, so watch your wallet. You'll find everything here from antique glassware to oriental rugs and just plain junk. Most of the stalls are open from Thursday or Friday and through the weekend. Stores are open all week.

For all the latest London happenings, pick up a copy of *Time Out* at any newsstand.

CONNECTIONS WITH THE CONTINENT

Aside from the Channel Tunnel route, the shortest route from England to the Continent is Dover to Calais or Boulogne, by ferry.

The validity of one's BritRail Pass stops or starts, as the case may be, at the British shore. Similarly, the validity of one's Eurailpass stops or starts at the Continental port where your boat ride begins or ends. In all cases, the channel boat fare is *not covered* by either pass, and with the arrival of Eurostar, passes that once included a Hovercraft round-trip have been discontinued. With all the competition between the ferries, airlines, Eurostar and Le Shuttle, though, it shouldn't be too hard to locate discount ferry tickets.

Regular ferries run the following routes: Dover–Calais, Ramsgate–Oostende, Folkestone–Boulogne, Portsmouth-Cherbourg, Portsmouth-Le Havre, Harwich–Hoek van Holland and Newhaven–Dieppe.

Hovercraft service, faster and more expensive, is provided Dover–Boulogne, Dover–Calais,

Ramsgate–Oostende, Newhaven–Dieppe and Ramsgate–Dunkerque.

Both regular ferries and hovercraft carry autos. *All of the regular ferries have a restaurant.*
Eurostar schedules for Paris and Brussels follow the ferry schedules.

London - Paris via Newhaven and Dieppe and v.v. 109, 269, 2125

109			*269*		
Dep. London (Vic.)	06:10	18:31	Dep. Paris (St. Laz.)	12:40	20:36
Arr. Newhaven Harbour	07:35	20:10	Dep. Rouen (Rive Dr.)	13:47	21:52
Change to a ferry 2125			Arr. Dieppe	14:43	22:34
Dep. Newhaven Harbour	08:45	20:45	*Change to a ferry 2125*		
Set your watch forward one hour,			Dep. Dieppe	15:45	03:45
except late Sept. to late Oct.			Arr. Newhaven	19:45	07:45
Arr. Dieppe	12:45	00:45	*Set your watch back one hour,*		
Change to train 269			*except late Sept. to late Oct.*		
Dep. Dieppe	13:00	06:01	*Change to train 109*		
Arr. Rouen (Rive Dr.)	13:59	07:04	Dep. Newhaven (Har.)	20:54	08:00
Arr. Paris (St. Laz.)	15:42	08:30	Arr. London (Vic.)	22:56	09:58

London - Paris via Portsmouth and Le Havre (regular ferry) and v.v. 132, 269, 2165

Frequent trains make the 83–108 minute ride London (Waterloo) to Portsmouth and v.v.

2165 Ferry			
Dep. Portsmouth	08:00 (1)	14:45 (2)	22:30 (3)
Set your watch forward one hour, except late September to late October			
Arr. Le Havre	14:30	21:15	07:00
Change to train 269			
Dep. Le Havre	17:05 (4)	21:24 (5)	07:57
Arr. Paris (St. Laz.)	19:07	23:49	09:56

• • •

269		
Dep. Paris (St. Laz.)	12:40 (6)	17:58
Arr. Le Havre	14:39	20:05

Change to a ferry 2165
Dep. Le Havre   16:00 (7)   23:00 (8)
Set your watch back one hour, except late September to late October.
Arr. Portsmouth   20:30   06:00

(1) Doesn't run December 24-26. (2) Doesn't run September 21 or December 24-31. (2) Doesn't run September 21 or December 25, 26. (4) Supplement charged. Light refreshments. (5) Runs Sundays and holidays only. (6) Runs daily, except Sundays and holidays. (7) Doesn't run September 20 or December 24-31. (8) Doesn't run September 21 or December 24-26.

OTHER CHANNEL-CROSSING SCHEDULES

London - Paris via Calais or Boulogne   and v.v. 10

Schedules shown here are for early June to late September.

All of the trains from French ports to Paris and v.v. have light refreshments, unless desig-nated otherwise.

Train
Dep. London (Char. X)	07:00 (1)	08:30 (1)	08:55	11:30 (1)
Arr. Folkestone	-0-	-0-	19:53	-0-
Arr. Dover (Priory)	08:58	10:27	-0-	13:29
Change to ferry				
Dep. Folkestone	-0-	11:15	11:15 (2)	-0-
Dep. Dover (East.)	09:45	-0-	-0-	14:15
Set your watch forward one hour				
Arr. Boulogne	-0-	-0-	13:19	-0-
Arr. Calais	12:15	13:45	-0-	16:45
Change to train				
Dep. Boulogne	-0-	-0-	14:42	-0-
Dep. Calais	14:14	13:50	-0-	18:11
Arr. Paris (Nord)	17:17	19:29	17:17	21:11

•   •   •

Train
Dep. Paris (Nord)	09:25	09:25	14:19
Arr. Calais	-0-	12:58	17:24

Arr. Boulogne	12:16 (2)	-0-	-0-
Change to ferry			
Dep. Calais	14:00	14:30	19:00
Dep. Boulogne	-0-	-0-	-0-
Set your watch back one hour			
Arr. Dover (East.)	-0-	15:00	19:30
Arr. Folkestone	13:55	-0-	-0-
Change to train			
Dep. Dover (Priory)	-0-	16:22	20:50
Dep. Folkestone	14:40	-0-	-0-
Arr. London (Char. X)	16:35	17:38	22:25

(1) Runs Monday-Saturday. (2) Hoverspeed catamaran. Reservation required. Supplement charged.

London - Brussels via Oostende (Jetfoil)   12, 2190

Reservation is required on all of the London–Ramsgate trains. Reservation is required and supplement charged for the one-class jetfoil, which has light refreshments.

Passengers from London *must* check-in at the Jetfoil Lounge in Victoria rail station and obtain the Jetfoil boarding card at least 60 minutes before train departs.

Change to jetfoil in Ramsgate				
Dep. London (Vict.)	08:05	11:05	13:05	16:05
Set your watch forward one hour				
Arr. Oostende	13:25	16:30	18:55	22:00
Change to train				
Dep. Oostende	14:34	16:57	19:34	22:34
Set your watch back one hour				
Arr. Brussels (Midi)	15:43	18:04	20:43	23:45
Arr. Brussels (Nord)	12 minutes later			

London - Brussels via Oostende (regular ferry)   12, 2190

Reservation is required for all the London–Ramsgate trains and these ferries.
    Times shown below are for summer service (early June to late September). Change to a ferry in Ramsgate. All of the ferries have a restaurant.

15

Dep. London (Vict.)	11:05	22:05
Set your watch forward one hour		
Arr. Oostende	16:30	06:00
Change to train		
Dep. Oostende	16:57	06:34
Arr. Brussels (Midi)	18:04	07:43
Arr. Brussels (Nord)	12 minutes later	

London - Amsterdam via Hoek van Holland (regular ferry)
and v.v. 15

Change to ferry in Harwich Parkeston Quay (en route to Amsterdam) and in Hoek van Holland (en route to London).

Dep. London (Liverpool Street)	08:55 (1)	17:25 (1)
Dep. Harwich	10:50 (2)	19:30 (1)
Set your watch forward one hour, except from late Sept. to late Oct.		
Dep. Hoek van Holland	16:06 (2)	00:35 (2)
Arr. Amsterdam (Cen.)	17:28	02:14

• • •

Dep. Amsterdam (Cen.)	05:53 (1)	13:52
Arr. Hoek van Holland	-0- (3)	15:07
Dep. Hoek van Holland	07:15	16:10 (1)
Set your watch back one hour, except from late Sept. to late Oct.		
Dep. Harwich	10:35 (2)	19:35 (2)
Arr. London (Liverpool Street)	11:48	20:46

(1) Ferry reservation required. (2) Change trains. (3) Change trains in Schiedam-Rotterdam West for Hoek van Holland; arrive Hoek can Holland 06:47.

London - Paris - London (Eurostar) 10

All Eurostar trains require a reservation; check in a minimum of 20 minutes before departure. All trains have meal and buffet service. When traveling London-Paris, set your watch back one hour; Paris-London, ahead one hour. Schedules reflect the time change.

Dep. London (Waterloo)	05:08 (1)	06:19 (1)	07:23	07:53 (1)	08:23
Dep. Ashford	06:16	07:19	08:24	-0-	09:23
Dep. Calais	-0-	08:56	-0-	-0-	-0-
Arr. Paris (Nord)	09:23	10:23	11:23	11:47	12:23

Dep. London (Waterloo)	08:53	09:53	10:23	11:57	12:53
Dep. Ashford	-0-	10:53	-0-	-0-	13:53
Dep. Calais	-0-	-0-	-0-	14:29	-0-
Arr. Paris (Nord)	12:53	13:52	14:17	15:56	16:53

Dep. London (Waterloo)	13:57	15:23	15:53 (2)	16:23	17:15 (3)
Dep. Ashford	-0-	-0-	-0-	17:24	-0-
Dep. Calais	-0-	17:56	-0-	-0-	-0-
Arr. Paris (Nord)	17:56	19:23	19:53	20:29	21:17

Dep. London (Waterloo)	17:23 (4)	17:48 (3)	17:57 (5)	18:23 (4)	18:53 (4)
Dep. Ashford	-0-	-0-	-0-	19:23	-0-
Dep. Calais	-0-	20:26	20:29	-0-	-0-
Arr. Paris (Nord)	21:17	21:53	21:56	22:23	22:47

Dep. London (Waterloo)	18:53 (1)	19:23 (2)	19:53
Dep. Ashford	19:54	20:23	-0-
Depart Calais	-0-	-0-	-0-
Arr. Paris (Nord)	22:53	23:23	23:47

• • •

Dep. Paris (Nord)	06:37 (1)	07:16 (1)	08:13 (1)	08:07 (4)	09:10 (1)
Dep. Calais	08:04	-0-	-0-	09:34	-0-
Dep. Ashford	-0-	-0-	09:11	09:11	-0-
Arr. London (Waterloo)	08:46	09:09	10:13	12:30	11:09

Dep. Paris (Nord)	09:10 (4)	09:43	10:19 (1)	11:43	12:19
Dep. Calais	-0-	-0-	-0-	-0-	-0-
Dep. Ashford	-0-	10:41	-0-	-0-	-0-
Arr. London (Waterloo)	11:26	11:43	12:13	13:43	14:13

Dep. Paris (Nord)	12:19 (4)	13:04	14:16 (2)	14:49 (6)	15:19
Dep. Calais	-0-	14:31	-0-	-0-	-0-
Dep. Ashford	-0-	14:08	-0-	-0-	-0-
Arr. London (Waterloo)	14:30	15:09	16:09	16:43	17:13

Dep. Paris (Nord)	16:07	17:10	18:19	19:19	20:07
Dep. Calais	17:34	-0-	-0-	-0-	-0-
Dep. Ashford	17:11	18:11	-0-	20:14	21:11
Arr. London (Waterloo)	18:13	19:13	20:13	21:13	22:13

Dep. Paris (Nord)	20:49 (2)	21:13
Dep. Calais	-0-	-0-
Dep. Ashford	-0-	22:11
Arr. London (Waterloo)	22:43	23:16

(1) Operates Monday-Saturday. (2) Runs Fridays and Sundays. (3) Runs Monday-Friday. (4) Runs Sundays only. (5) Runs Saturdays and Sunday. (6) Runs daily except Saturdays.

London - Brussels - London　(Eurostar) 12

All Eurostar trains require a reservation; check in a minimum of 20 minutes before departure. All trains have meal and buffet service. When traveling London-Paris, set your watch back one hour; Paris-London, ahead one hour. Schedules reflect the time change.

Dep. London (Waterloo)	06:53 (1)	08:27	09:27 (2)	10:27	12:27
Dep. Ashford	07:53	09:27	10:27	-0-	13:27
Dep. Lille Europe	09:59	11;32	-0-	13:27	15:32
Arr. Brussels	11:10	14:44	13:44	14:38	16:44
Dep. London (Waterloo)	14:23	17:19 (3)	17:23 (4)	18:27	19:27 (5)
Dep. Ashford	-0-	-0-	18:23	19:27	20:27
Dep. Lille Europe	17:23	-0-	-0-	21:34	-0-
Arr. Brussels	18:34	21:38	21:38	22:45	23:43

•　•　•

Dep. Brussels	07:31 (1)	08:27	10:31	12:31	15:28
Dep. Lille Europe	08:42	09:37	11:42	13:41	16:39
Dep. Ashford	-0-	09:41	-0-	-0-	16:41
Arr. London	09:39	10:43	12:43	14:43	17:43
Dep. Brussels	17:22	18:27 (3)	19:27 (2)	19:52 (6)	
Dep. Lille Europe	18:33	19:37	20:37	-0-	
Dep. Ashford	18:37	19:42	20:41	21:07	
Arr. London	19:39	20:43	21:43	22:09	

(1) Runs Monday-Saturday. (2) Runs Monday-Friday. (3) Runs daily except Saturdays. (4) Runs Saturdays. (5) Runs Sundays. (6) Runs Saturdays and Sundays.

ONE-DAY EXCURSIONS FROM LONDON

Here are 41 one-day rail trips that can be made comfortably, returning to London in most cases at dinnertime. Notes are provided on what to see and do at each destination.

The notation "frequent times" in these schedules means at least one departure (and usually more) every hour. Some schedules are not in the *Cook Timetable* and have been obtained from Railtrack, the entity responsible for Britain's railway infrastructure.

London - Bath - London   130

Dep. London (Pad.)	07:15	08:15	08:45	09:15	09:45 (1)
Arr. Bath	08:37	09:42	09:55	10:36	11:12

Sights in **Bath**: For interesting walking tours here, go to the Tourist Information Centre and purchase "Official Guidebook" and "Walks Around Bath." During summer, guided 1½-hour tours on foot (at no charge) start at the churchyard of the abbey.

See the Roman baths. Buy a glass of curative mineral water in the 18th-century Pump Room, above the baths. Visit antique shops around Abbey Green. The Circus, a group of three-story, classical 18th-century houses constructed of honey-colored Bath Stone, located on Gay Street. Nearby, the Museum of Costume in the Assembly Rooms. The Royal Crescent row of town houses. Queen Square. The shops on Pulteney Bridge.

The American Museum at Claverton Manor, open daily except Monday 14:00–17:00. The collection of Eltonware and Nailsea glass in the 14th-century Clevedon Court manor house, open Wednesday, Thursday and Sunday 14:30–17:30. There is much elegant 18th-century architecture here.

Bath is a great base for seeing many of the best sights in England. Several good, inexpensive motorcoach tours go to Gloucester, Salisbury, Stonehenge and Cheddar Gorge. These buses stop for photo-taking along the way.

Dep. Bath	11:26	12:26	13:26	14:26 (2)
Arr. London (Pad.)	12:50	13:50	14:50	15:55

(1) Plus other departures from London at frequent times from 10:00 to 23:30. (2) Plus other departures from Bath at frequent times from 15:26 to 21:31.

London - Birmingham -London   140

Dep. London (Eus.)	07:15	07:45	08:15	08:45	09:15 (2)
Arr. Birmingham (New St.)	08:55	09:25	10:25	10:25	11:25

Sights in **Birmingham**: The Tourist Information Centre has brochures on walking tours. The Cadbury Company's "World Chocolate Experience" museum at its factory here features an exhibit on the history of chocolate. Visitors can sample a chocolate drink made from an ancient Aztec recipe, see chocolate being made, and sample chocolate at the factory's restaurant, ice cream parlor and souvenir shop.

See the restored 18th-century water mill, Sarehole Mill. The 17th-century house furnished as it was in its era, Blakesley Hall. The first (1734) English locomotive can be seen at the Science Museum.

Dep. Birmingham (New St.)	12:15	12:45	13:15	13:45	14:15 (2)
Arr. London (Eus.)	13:55	14:25	14:55	15:25	15:55

(1) Plus other departures from London at frequent times from 09:44 to 23:45. (2) Plus other Birmingham departures at frequent times from 14:46 to 22:50.

London - Bournemouth - London   105

Most of these trains have buffet.

Dep. London (Wat.)   Frequent times Monday–Saturday: 05:35–23:53
                      Sunday: 07:55–22:55
Arr. Bournemouth   Monday–Saturday: 1½ -2 hours later
                      Sunday: 2½ hours later

Sights in **Bournemouth**: A large seaside resort. Stroll through Pavillion Rock Garden. There are three gambling casinos. Many lovely parks and gardens.

Dep. Bournemouth   Frequent times Monday–Saturday: 05:24–23:32
                     Sunday: 07:22–22:00
Arr. London (Wat.)   Monday–Saturday: 1½ -2 hours later
                     Sunday: 2½ hours later

London - Brighton - London   102

Dep. London (Vic.)   Frequent times Monday–Saturday: 04:00–01:00
                     Sunday: 05:47–23:32
Arr. Brighton   55–70 minutes later

Sights in **Brighton**: Walk from the rail station down Queen Street to the seashore and the Aquarium at Palace Pier. See the antique shops in the many alleys, called "The Lanes." The Regency style of architecture is prevalent here. See the Royal Pavillion and the ornate chandelier in Banquet Hall.

This is one of Britain's leading antique centers. An outdoor antique market is held on Saturdays starting at 07:00, on Upper Gerdner Street, near the rail station. See the collection of Art Nouveau and Art Deco furniture and furnishings in the City Museum.

Dep. Brighton   Frequent times Monday–Saturday: 04:00–23:30
                     Sunday: 04:00–23:02
Arr. London (Vict.) 55–70 minutes later

London - Bristol - London   130

Dep. London (Paddington)   Frequent times 05:50 to 23:20 (from 07:55 on Sunday)
Arr. Bristol (Temple Meads)   90 minutes later

• • •

Dep. Bristol (Temple Meads)   Frequent times 05:40 to 21:30 (from 07:35 on Sunday)
Arr. London (Paddington)   90 minutes later

Sights in **Bristol**: A famous seaport. Everything here is either a short walk or can be reached by bus. The city operates 1½-hour guided walking tours June, July and August from the Exchange on Corn Street. Check with them for tour times. Some of Bristol can be seen from a tour boat at the harbor. That tour operates daily at 12:00, 14:00, 15:00 and 16:00.

See the many excellent Georgian buildings on Royal York Crescent, Cornwallis Crescent, Windsor Terrace, West Mall, Caledonia Place, Queen Square and Berkeley Square. The Christmas Steps, built in 1669. The 12th-century St. James' Church.

The John Wesley Chapel, world's first Methodist preaching house, with a bronze statue of Wesley in the courtyard. The 11th-century St. Mary-le-Port Church. St. John's Church. The 13th-century St. Mary Redcliffe, one of England's largest churches. The 12th-century cathedral.

The exhibit of period furniture in the 18th-century Georgian House. The view from the top of Cabot Tower, on Brandon Hill. The collection of porcelain, models of early sailing ships and paintings of the waterfront in the Bristol Museum and Art Gallery, open every day 10:00–17:00. See the beautiful gardens and the rare animals (including the Okapi and the white tigers) at the zoo. Brunel's Clifton Suspension Bridge, built in 1864, straddling Avon Gorge, 245 feet above the water. Tour Brunel's iron steamship, The *Great Britain* (the first ocean screw steamship, launched in 1843), returned to Bristol in 1970 from the Falkland Islands. It is open 10:00–18:00.

London - Cardiff - London   130

Dep. London (Paddington)   Frequent times from 07:00 to 23:30 from 09:00 on Sunday)
Arr. Cardiff (Central)   2 hours later

Sights in **Cardiff**: Llandaff Cathedral. Cardiff Castle. The National Museum of Wales, featuring Welsh handicraft and art. It is a short train ride from Cardiff's Queen Street rail station to **Caerphilly**, whose castle is nearly as large as Windsor Castle and has many interesting exhibits.

Dep. Cardiff (Central)   Frequent times from 04:25 to 21:25 (from 08:00 on Sunday)
Arr. London (Paddington)   2 hours later

London - Bristol - Cardiff - London 130

As these schedules indicate, it is easy to visit both Cardiff and Bristol in one day.

These schedules are for travel daily, except Sundays and holidays.

Dep. London (Pad.)	08:15		Dep. Cardiff (Cen.)	16:25 (1)
Arr. Bristol (T.M.)	09:55		Arr. London (Pad.)	18:35
Sightsee in Bristol				
Dep. Bristol (T.M.)	12:27			
Arr. Cardiff (Cen.)	13:11			

(1) Plus other departures from Cardiff at 17:25, 18:25, 19:25 and 21:30.

Sights in **Bristol:** The Temple Meads rail station, completed in 1841, is one of the most beautiful in England.

In summer, open-top buses make a circle tour that includes Temple Meads, Clifton Bridge, the zoo, downtown, the harbor and the 13th-century Church of St. Mary Redcliffe (one of England's largest churches). Queen Elizabeth I described it as "the fairest, goodliest and most famous parish church in England."

London - Cambridge - London 176

Dep. London (Kings X)	06:51	07:45	08:45	09:45	10:45 (1)
Arr. Cambridge	49–88 minutes later				

• • •

Dep. Cambridge	Monday–Saturday: frequent times from 06:00 to 23:15
	Sundays: frequent times from 06:00 to 21:15
Arr. London (Kings X)	49–88 minutes later

(1) Plus other London every 30 minutes from 11:15 to 23:15.

Sights in **Cambridge**: To see buildings that have housed great colleges for more than 700 years, take bus #101 to Market Street. See King's College Chapel and Queen's College. Visit the Wren Library at Trinity College. The medieval and renaissance armor, weapons, tapestries and manuscripts in the Fitzwilliam Museum on Trumpington Street.

Visit the botanical gardens. On Castle Street, see the Folk Museum and the modern paintings and sculpture at Kettles Yard Art Gallery. Hire a boat at Mill Bridge or Anchor Inn, and paddle along the idyllic Cam River. Four miles away is the American Cemetery.

London - Canterbury - London 100 and Railtrack Timetable

For this two-hour ride, there are frequent departures both from London's Waterloo and Charing Cross rail stations to Canterbury's West rail station. There are also frequent departures from London's Victoria station to Canterbury's East station. The walk from Canterbury's *West* station to the famous cathedral allows you to view interesting buildings.

Canterbury's *East* rail station is nearer the cathedral and therefore more convenient than the West station to use for returning to London, after visiting the cathedral. A departure from Canterbury's East station will take you to London's Victoria station. Or, you can depart from Canterbury's West station, arriving London's Waterloo or Charing Cross stations.

Sights in **Canterbury**: Guided tours (Monday–Friday) start at 14:15 at a kiosk in Longmarket, a pedestrian area next to Christ Church Gate.

See the great cathedral, housing the tomb of Thomas a Becket. Medieval inns (Falstaff, Beverlie, Olive Branch). The cemetery, where Christopher Marlowe and Joseph Conrad are buried. The Old Weaver's House, built in 1500. Excavated Roman ruins. Plays, ballet, cricket.

London - Sevenoaks - Chartwell - London 101

There are many departures daily from London's Charing Cross rail station for the 45-minute ride to Sevenoaks. Take a taxi for the seven-mile trip from Sevenoaks to Chartwell.

Sights in **Chartwell:** The country house that Winston Churchill bought in 1922, where he painted and wrote his books during the years he was out of power. You will see here the best collection of Churchilliana in the world: his collection of eccentric hats, his World War II "jump suit," Knight of the Garter uniform, many of his paintings, and a model of the Invasion Day harbor at Arromanches. Also the brick wall and cottage he built with his own hands on a small part of the 79 acres there. The main house is open Wednesday, Thursday, Saturday and Sunday from April to mid-October.

London - Chester - London 155

| Dep. London (Euston) | 09:50 | Dep. Chester | 15:30 | 17:31 |
| Arr. Chester | 12:10 | Arr. London (Euston) | 18:18 | 20:23 |

Sights in **Chester**: The two-mile-long Roman Wall. The excellent collection of Roman artifacts (glass, tools, coins, weapons, tombstones) at Grosvenor Museum. The "Rows," long, covered balconies (to protect shoppers from rain) that are full-length streets above the streets of Chester. These are lined with shops. Also see St. Werburgh's Cathedral. The castle overlooking the **River Dee**. The marvelous carving of animals and historic scenes on the front of the 17th-century Bishop Lloyd's House on Watergate Street. The antique shops on Lower Bridge Street and Watergate Street. The 16th-century mansion, Stanley Palace.

The 30-minute slide show of Chester's history, in the British Heritage Centre.

Sightseeing bus tours start in Market Square, opposite the tourist office at the Victorian Gothic Town Hall. Or, ask the folks at the tourist office about guided walking tours.

The 130-acre open-space zoo, just north of the city, attracts nearly 1,000,000 people a year.

London - Chichester - London   108

This service is daily. Most of these trains have light refreshments Monday–Saturday.

Dep. London (Vic.)	Frequent times 08:17 – 19:17
Arr. Chichester	About 100 minutes later

Sights in **Chichester**: The Marc Chagall stained glass window and the John Piper Holy Trinity tapestry in the 12th-century Norman Cathedral. The 2nd-century Roman wall. The 16th-century arcaded Market Cross. The 200-year-old "stately homes" on streets called East, West, North and South Pallant.

Go two miles west to see the museum and mosaic floors in the 3rd-century palace at Fishbourne, the largest Roman residence in Britain, open daily, March through October. See the attractive mosaic floors in the 1st-century Roman villa at **Bignor**, two miles east; open daily except Monday, March through October.

There is extraordinary filigree woodcarving in the 17th-century Petworth House, 13 miles northeast. It is open April through October on Wednesday, Thursday, Saturday and Sunday 14:00–18:00.

A few miles west of Chichester is an 11th-century Saxon church and a marvelous yacht harbor at **Bosham**, a beautiful seashore village.

Dep. Chichester	Frequent times 06509 to 21:20
Arr. London (Vic.)	About 100 minutes later

London - Coventry - London   140

Dep. London (Eus.)	07:15	07:45	08:15	08:45	09:15	09:45 (1)
Arr. Coventry	08:27	08:57	09:27	09:57	10:27	10:57

Sights in **Coventry**: Completely rebuilt since the Nazi air attacks, Coventry was the site of Lady Godiva's notorious horseback ride. See the Graham Sutherland tapestry, the abstract stained-glass windows and the enormous engraved glass wall at the new (1962) cathedral.

Dep. Coventry	12:07	12:37	13:07	13:37	14:07	14:37 (2)
Arr. London (Eus.)	13:25	13:55	14:25	14:55	15:29	15:55

(1) Plus other frequent London departures from 10:15 to 23:45 (2) Plus other frequent Coventry departures from 15:07 to 23:12.

London - Dover - London 101

Dep. London (Char. X)	08:55 (1)	09:30 (2)	10:00 (1+3)
Arr. Dover (Priory)	10:40	11:27	11:40

Sights in **Dover**: It is a short walk downhill from the Priory rail station to the village. Or, you can ride a bus. See the legendary white cliffs. The mighty castle. The busy harbor. The museum in the 4th-century Roman painted house.

Dep. Dover (Priory)	15:08 (2)	15:51 (1)	16:03 (2)	16:53 (2+3)
Arr. London (Char. X)	17:06	17:38	18:06	18:35

(1) Runs Monday-Friday except holidays. Light refreshments. (2) Runs daily, except Sundays and holidays. (3)Light refreshments. (3) Plus other Dover departures at 17:05 (1), 17:49, 18:50 (2), 19:50 (2) and 20:49 (2).

London - Exeter - London (main line via Reading) 110

Dep. London (Pad.)	07:46	09:35	09:45	10:30
Arr. Exeter (St. David's)	10:16	12:03	12:35	12:40

Dep. London (Pad.)	10:45	11:35	11:45 (1)	12:35
Arr. Exeter (St. David's)	12:44	13:53	14:06	14:49

Sights in **Exeter**: The 11th-century cathedral, with its 300-foot nave and row of statutes. Rougemont Castle. The Mint. The underground water channel at Princesshay. The paintings and oak paneling in Exeter Guildhall.

The exhibit of boats from all parts of the world at the very interesting maritime museum.

Dep. Exeter (St. David's)	14:12	14:59	15:32	15:46 (2)	16:32
Arr. London (Pad.)	16:40	17:10	17:45	18:49	19:05

Dep. Exeter (St. David's)	16:55 (2)	17:26	17:37 (2)	18:15 (1)	18:49 (2+3)
Arr. London (Pad.)	19:26	19:45	20:14	20:50	21:19

(1) Runs Saturdays only. (2) Runs Sundays only. (3) Plus other Exeter departures 19:32, 19:45 (1) and 20:17 (2).

OR

London - Exeter - London (via Salisbury) 117

Most of these trains have light refreshments.

Dep. London (Waterloo)	07:09 (1)	08:35 (2)	08:57 (3)	10:35	13:35
Arr. Exeter (Central)	10:23	11:36	12:09	13:36	15:37
Arr. Exeter (St. David's)	5 minutes later				

• • •

Dep. Exeter (St. David's)	15:45 (2)	16:20 (2)	17:45 (1)	18:22 (2)	19:15 (3)
Dep. Exeter (Central)	5 minutes later				
Arr. London (Waterloo)	18:50	19:47	21:19	22:25	22:36

(1) Runs Monday–Friday, except holidays. (2) Runs daily, except Sundays and holidays. (3) Runs Sunday only.

London - Greenwich - London   Docklands Light Railway

See the entry under "London" about buying ticket to ride these trains.

Sights in **Greenwich**: Take the Docklands Light Railway, opposite the Tower of London, for the 20-minute ride to the "Island Gardens" terminus. Walk from it through the pedestrian tunnel that goes under the Thames River, ending next to the famous 1870 clipper ship Cutty Sark. Near the Cutty Sark, see the 53-foot Gypsy Moth sailboat which Chichester sailed solo around the world in 1966–67. Both Cutty Sark and Gypsy Moth are open May–September 14:30–18:00 daily; October–April 11:00–17:00 Monday–Saturday and 14:30–17:00 Sunday.

Visit the Royal Observatory's museum of navigation, astronomy and chronometry (astrolabes, hourglasses, clockwork planetariums, quadrants, chronometers). See the Meridian Building's brass strip which marks the division of the eastern and western hemispheres. All distances and time worldwide are measured from this, the prime meridian.

See the marvelous exhibits (ship models, scientific instruments, marine paintings, chronometers, naval uniforms) in the National Maritime Museum.

Both the Royal Observatory and the Maritime Museum are open Monday–Saturday 10:00–17:00, Sunday 14:00–17:00 (October–April) and 14:00–18:00 (May–September).

See the enormous Painted Hall in the Royal Naval College, open daily except Thursday 14:30–17:00. Lunch in one of the good "pubs" at the riverside.

For the return to London, a boat ride on the Thames is an enjoyable alternative to the train.

London - Hampton Court - London   Railtrack Timetable

Dep. London (Waterloo)	Monday–Saturday: Frequent times from 06:29 to 23:24
	Sunday: Frequent times from 07:13 to 23:13
Arr. Hampton Court	35 minutes later

Sights in **Hampton Court**: This is the riverside palace built by Cardinal Wolsey and then given to Henry VIII, after he expressed his desire to have it. Walk through the ancient maze.

Dep. Hampton Court	Monday–Saturday:	Frequent times from 06:09 to 23:25
	Sunday:	Frequent times from 08:09 to 23:09
Arr. London (Waterloo)	35 minutes later	

London - Hastings - London   101, Railtrack Timetable

All of these trains have light refreshments.

| Dep. London (Char. X) | 07:43 (1) | 09:40 | 10:40 (2) | 11:40 (2) | 12:40 (2) |
| Arr. Hastings | 09:30 | 11:18 | 12:18 | 13:18 | 14:18 |

Sights in **Hastings**: This is where William became the Conqueror, of the Saxons. Take buses #5, #252, #485 or #486 to see the ancient battlefield. Visit the old fishing harbor and stroll the three-mile promenade along the beach. Obtain a printed description of the castle at the Tourist Information Center, 4 Robertson Terrace.

See the 243-foot-long tapestry in Town Hall, illustrating the 81 greatest events of British history since 1066: the battle of Hastings, the Boston Tea Party, the first television broadcast, etc.

| Dep. Hastings | 13:52 (3) | 14:52 (2) | 15:11 (2) | 15:52 (3) | 16:52 (3+4) |
| Arr. London (Char. X) | 15:21 | 16:19 | 17:04 | 17:21 | 18:22 |

(1) Runs Monday-Friday, except holidays. (2) Runs daily, except holidays. (3) Runs daily, except Sundays and holidays. (4) Plus other departures from Hastings at frequent times from 17:40 to 20:41.

London - Isle of Wight (Yarmouth) - London   (via Lymington) Railtrack Timetable

There are 148 miles of well-posted footpaths on Wight, including a 60-mile path along the entire coastline of this island that measures 13 miles at its widest, by 23 miles at its longest. Also several bus lines. Many quiet beaches. Good fishing.

Twenty-two orchid species grow here. See the dinosaur bones in the Museum of Wight Geology over the public library. Carisbrooke Castle. Quarr Abbey, near Ryde. Take the boat trip that starts at Alum Bar.

Train			*Ferry*		
Dep. London (Wat.)	08:30 (1)	09:30 (1)	Dep. Yarmouth	14:00 (1)	15:00 (1+2)
Arr. Brockenhurst	09:56	10:54	Arr. Lym. Pier	14:30	15:30
Change trains			*Change to train*		
Dep. Brockenhurst	09:59	11:00	Dep. Lym. Pier	14:43	15:43
Arr. Lym. Pier	10:08	11:09	Arr. Brockenhurst	14:52	15:52
Change to ferry			*Change trains*		
Dep. Lym. Pier	10:15	11:15	Dep. Brockenhurst	15:00	16:00
Arr. Yarmouth	10:45	11:45	Arr. London (Wat.)	16:28	17:28

(1) Runs Monday–Saturday. (2) Plus other Yarmouth departures every 30 minutes from 15:00 to 18:30, plus 19:30, 20:30 and 21:00.

London - Kings Lynn - London   175

Dep. London (Kings X)	08:45 (1)	09:45 (1)	10:45 (1)	11:45 (1)
Arr. Kings Lynn	10:19	11:19	12:19	13:19

Sights in **Kings Lynn**: The "Town Trail" brochure, available at the City Information Center, is very helpful for touring the winding, twisting streets here in one of England's most historic towns.

See the attractive merchants' houses on Queen Street. The King John Cup and one of the oldest paper books in the world (the Red Register), at the Treasury in the 15th-century Town Hall. The country market, every Tuesday near Duke's Head Hotel and every Saturday opposite Town Hall.

Dep. Kings Lynn	14:28 (1)	15:28	16:05 (1)	16:24 (2)
Arr. London (Kings X)	16:06	17:06	17:48	18:28

(1) Runs Monday–Saturday, except holidays. (2) Plus other frequent Kings Lynn departures from 17:28 to 22:16.

London - Leicester - London   160

Dep. London (St. Pan.)	07:00	07:30	08:00	08:30 (1)
Arr. Leicester	08:25	08:43	09:26	09:48

Sights in **Leicester**: The Jewry Wall, to see outstanding Roman ruins. The Church of St. Mary de Castro.

Dep. Leicester	12:30	13:00	13:30	14:00 (2)
Arr. London (St. Pan.)	13:48	14:17	14:49	15:23

(1) Plus other frequent London departures from 09:00 to 22:00. (2) Plus other frequent Leicester departures from 14:30 to 22:00.

London - Lincoln - London   170, 171

170

Dep. London (Kings X)	07:00	08:20	09:10	11:10
Arr. Newark (Northgate)	08:21	09:41	10:26	12:27

Change trains. 171

| Dep. Newark | 10:03 | 12:00 | 14:35 |
| Arr. Lincoln (Cen.) | 10:35 | 12:32 | 15:01 |

Sights in **Lincoln**: The wonderful cathedral. Newport Arch. Roman relics in the City and County Museums. The houses on High Bridge.

171

Dep. Lincoln (Cen.)	12:38	14:55	17:05	20:33
Arr. Newark	13:16	15:26	17:35	21:10
Change trains 170				
Dep Newark	14:00	15:59	18:39	21:14
Arr. London (Kings X)	15:31	17:31	20:09	21:44

London - Norwich - London   180

| Dep. London (L'pool) | 07:30 (1) | 08:00 (2) | 08:30 (3) | 09:30 | 10:30 (4) |
| Arr. Norwich | 09:24 | 09:40 | 10:23 | 11:23 | 12:23 |

Sights in **Norwich**: Norwich Grammar School. (Its alumni include Lord Nelson.) The cathedral. The collection of lace, pottery, teapots, paintings and coins at the Museum in the Castle, built in 1068 by William the Conqueror.

Walk down the Elm Hill alley. See the view of Norwich from the Castle. Assembly House. The Strangers Hall. The 16th-century house on the 12th-century High Bridge.

| Dep. Norwich | 13:05 | 14:05 | 15:05 | 16:05 | 17:05 (5) |
| Arr. London (L'pool) | 14:53 | 15:53 | 16:53 | 17:58 | 18:54 |

(1) Runs Saturday only. (2) Runs Monday–Friday, except holidays. (3) Runs daily, except Sundays and holidays. (4) Plus other frequent London departures from 11:30 to 23:30. (5) Plus other frequent Norwich departures from 18:05 to 23:00,

London - Nottingham - London   160

| Dep. London (St. Pan.) | 08:00 (1) | 09:00 (1) | 09:15 (2) | 10:00 | 12:00 (3) |
| Arr. Nottingham | 09:53 | 10:49 | 11:04 | 11:45 | 13:48 |

Sights in **Nottingham**: The Duke of Newcastle's castle, which was a new Newcastle castle in 1679; it has an excellent art collection. The great council house. The Natural History Museum in Wollaton Hall.

| Dep. Nottingham | 12:33 (2) | 13:33 | 14:24 (4) | 14:33 | 15:33 (5) |
| Arr. London (St. Pan.) | 14:17 | 15:23 | 16:14 | 16:25 | 17:25 |

(1) Runs daily, except Sundays and holidays. (2) Runs Saturdays only. (3) Plus another London departure at 13:30 arriving Nottingham 14:51. (4) Runs Sundays only. (5) Plus other departures from Nottingham at 16:33, 17:33, 17:59 (4), 19:03 (2) and 19:32 (4), arriving London 18:21, 19:28, 20:00, 21:01, and 21:32.

London - Oxford - London 144

| Dep. London (Pad.) | Frequent times from 07:20 to 23:48 |
| Arr. Oxford | 65–80 minutes later |

Sights in **Oxford**: Daily guided tours by open-top, double-decker bus depart the rail station every 15 minutes 09:30–17:30 (until 18:30 in July and August).

This is the home of one of the greatest universities in the world, comprising 23 different colleges. Start your stroll at the center of Oxford (Carfax Tower), where the Information Center is located. There is bus service from the rail station to Carfax Tower.

Begin by walking south from Carfax Tower, down St. Aldates Street to Folly Bridge, the cathedral and the numerous portraits (John Wesley, William Penn, Lewis Carroll, William Gladstone) at Christ Church College. Founded by Cardinal Wolsey and Henry VIII, it is the largest and most splendid of all the colleges here.

Later, see Merton College and Corpus Christi before continuing on to Oriel and then into High Street. See Bodleian Library, which has a copy of every book published in England. See the decorative bookcases in the library of Queen's College. Most popular among visitors is Magdalen College, with its beautiful main quadrangle.

At 20:55, hear "Great Tom's" 101 strokes every night as the heavy bell calls the original number of Osney Abbey's students to return to their rooms before the nightly closing of its gates.

Stroll the lane behind Holywell Street to see attractive Tudor and Elizabethan houses. There are many late 18th-century houses on Beaumont Street.

| Dep. Oxford | Frequent times from 07:10 to 22:38 |
| Arr. London (Pad.) | 65–80 minutes later |

Nearby: Blenheim Palace (Churchill's Birthplace)

To see lovely Blenheim Palace, take a bus in Oxford from Gloucester Green bus station for the eight-mile trip to **Woodstock**. This magnificent 18th-century structure was the birthplace of Winston Churchill in 1874.

A gift from Britain to the Duke of Marlborough after this ancestor of Churchill defeated the French in 1704 at Blenheim in Bavaria, the beautiful 300-room mansion is open daily March–October, with guided tours 11:30–17:00.

Letters, documents, photos, even a lock of Churchill's hair (at the age of five) are exhibited in the tiny room where he was born prematurely and unexpectedly on November 30, 1874, in his mother's seventh month of pregnancy.

Other rooms throughout the palace have more memorabilia: some of Churchill's paintings (see "London–Chartwell"), recordings of his speeches, his letters, etc. A visit here is worthwhile if only to see the 180-foot-long library, with its marvelous Willis pipe organ.

There is time in the same day to visit nearby Bladon Churchyard. A simple tombstone there that reads merely "Winston Leonard Spencer Churchill 1874/1965" marks the burial place (alongside his American mother Jenny Spencer) of the greatest Englishman of the last 1,000 years.

London - Penzance - London 110

Reservation is advisable for all of these trains, especially for sleeping cars and Pullman service

| Dep. Lon. (Pad.) | 07:35 (1) | 07:46 (2) | 08:45 (2) | 10:45 (2) | 12:35 (2) | |
| Arr. Penzance | 12:50 | 13:20 | 14:41 | 15:40 | 17:55 | |

| Dep. Lon. (Pad.) | 13:15 (3) | 14:15 (3) | 15:35 (2) | 17:35 (2) | 17:50 (1+4) | |
| Arr. Penzance | 19:22 | 19:52 | 21:00 | 22:30 | 23:00 | |

• • •

| Dep. Penzance | 05:15 (2) | 06:45 (1) | 08:33 (3) | 09:45 (1) | 10:33 (3) | 11:27 (3) |
| Arr. Lon. (Pad.) | 09:56 | 11:46 | 14:06 | 15:00 | 16:05 | 17:00 |

| Dep. Penzance | 12:35 (3) | 14:40 (2) | 15:50 (3) | 16:40 (1) | 17:20 (3) | 22:15 (5) |
| Arr. Lon. (Pad.) | 18:01 | 19:45 | 21:19 | 22:21 | 22:42 | 05:05 |

(1) Runs Saturday only. (2) Runs Monday–Friday except holidays. (3) Runs Sunday only. (4) Plus other London departures at 18:15 (3) and 23:50 (5), arriving Penzance 23:50 and 08:20. (5) Carries sleepers and standard-class coaches.

Penzance and the rest of Cornwall deserve a stay of several days, although Penzance can be visited on a one-day train excursion from London. Sights in **Penzance**: Take the walk described in the free brochure called "A day in Chapel Street, Abbey Street and Quay Street" and visit the Egyptian Shop, the Admiral Benbow Inn, the Nautical Museum and Morrab Gardens. See the view of Mount's Bay from Bolitho Gardens.

It is only a 10-mile bus trip to **Land's End**, the westernmost edge of England and a beautiful seascape of waves crashing against the granite cliffs. In another direction, it is also only a 10-mile bus ride to **St. Ives**, a quaint fishing village and the location of The Hepworth Gallery, containing the work of Britain's best-known sculptress. (Both buses leave from the terminal next to the rail station.)

Go three miles by city bus to **Marazion** and then by small motorboat to visit **St. Michael's Mount,** a tiny island only a half-mile offshore. There has been a church at the summit since 1135. The castle has been occupied by the St. Aubyn family from 1659 to the present day. Visitors are allowed to enter most of the rooms of the castle and are provided a brochure describing its history and the many interesting contents: furniture, costumes, guns, maps, portraits, banners.

Penzance is also the gateway to the more than 100 **Isles of Scilly**. The largest island is the 3-miles-by-2-miles St. Mary's. For information, about the 2½-hour ferryboat ride to the island, contact Isles of Scilly Steamship Company, Quay St., Penzance, Cornwall TR18 4BD, United Kingdom.

There is 20-minute helicopter service from Penzance to both St. Mary's Island and Tresco Island. For current schedules, write to: British International Helicopters, Heliport, Eastern Green, Cornwall, England.

The northern half of **Tresco**, dominated by the ruins of the 16th-century King Charles Castle and the 17th-century Cromwell's Castle, is windswept and treeless. Its southern half, lush and semitropical, has wide beaches, a roofless 16th-century stone fort from which there are beautiful views, and the marvelous Abbey Gardens with its collection of restored figureheads salvaged from ships that were wrecked in this area.

There is boat service from Tresco to **St. Mary's**, the commercial center of the archipelago, where the main attractions are a 16th-century Star Castle and a museum open every day except rainless Sundays 09:30–12:30, 13:30–16:30 and 19:30–21:00 (old rowboats, Roman pottery, stone tools).

St. Mary's also offers sandy beaches (washed by frigid water), many beautiful gardens of sub-tropical plants, coastal walks, nature trails, and a nine-hole golf course along the seacoast. Small launches serve the other inhabited islands: **Bryher**, **St. Agnes** and **St. Martin's**.

London - Portsmouth - London   104

See Cook's Table 107 for service to Portsmouth from London's Victoria rail station and Gatwick Airport.

Dep. London (Waterloo)	07:20 (1)	07:22 (2)	08:15 (3)	08:45 (3)	09:15 (3+4)
Arr. Portsmouth (Hbr.)	09:07	08:48	09:53	10:41	10:53

Sights in **Portsmouth**: England's great naval base. See Lord Nelson's flagship H.M.S. Victory, which won the battle of Trafalgar over the combined Spanish and French fleets. The nearby Victory Museum (Nelson relics, good marine paintings, ship models) at the Naval Yard. Nearby is Henry VIII's man-of-war, "Mary Rose," raised in 1982 from the seabed where it had lain since it sank in 1545.

The Dickens Museum at the house where the author was born, 393 Commercial Road. Many fine 17th and 18th-century houses on Lombard Street and High Street.

Dep. Portsmouth (Hbr.)	14:12 (1)	14:50 (1)	15:20 (3)	15:50 (1)	16:20 (2)	16:50 (2+5)
Arr. London (Waterloo)	15:25	16:23	16:53	17:23	18:10	18:23

(1) Runs Saturday only. (2) Runs Monday-Friday except holidays. (3) Runs Sundays. (4) Plus additional London departures every 20 to 30 minutes until 23:45 Monday-Saturday and 23:15 Sundays.

London - Isle of Wight (Shanklin) - London   (via Portsmouth)
Railtrack Timetable

As these schedules indicate, it is easy to visit both Portsmouth and the Isle of Wight in one day by stopping-over in Portsmouth at 08:48 or 10:07 until 11:30, 12:00 or 12:30. Light refreshments are served on these trains.

Dep. London (Wat.)	07:22	08:20	08:15 (1)	09:15 (1)	09:20 (2+3)
Arr. Portsmouth (Hbr.)	08:48	10:07	10:00	11:00	11:02
Change to ferry					
Dep. Portsmouth (Hbr.)	09:20	10:20	10:20	11:20	11:30
Arr. Ryde Pier Head	09:35	10:35	10:35	11:35	11:48
Change to train					
Dep. Ryde Pier Head	09:42	10:42	10:42	11:42	12:00
Arr. Shanklin	10:06	11:06	11:05	12:05	12:25

There are full-day and half-day bus tours of the island, starting from Ryde Esplanade.

Sights in **Ryde**: Six miles of pretty beaches and many nice gardens. Take the nine-mile island train from Ryde Pier to Shanklin. En route is Ryde Esplanade, a working-class resort. A three-mile steam railway round-trip from there offers pretty views.

Sights in **Shanklin**: One of Britain's loveliest towns. Ten minutes' walk from the rail station there are views of the sea and farms from East Cliff Promenade. On the way back to Shanklin, walk through the Chine (deep ravine) to the mile-long beach and see the lovely Old Village. Buses (on Carter Avenue, two blocks from the rail station) go to Cowes on the north coast. Near Cowes is Osborne House, queen Victoria's summer mansion, which can be toured from the day after Easter through early October.

Dep. Shanklin	13:54	15:15	15:35	16:35 (4)
Arr. Ryde Pier Head	14:16	15:39	16:00	16:59
Change to ferry				
Dep. Ryde Pier Head	14:30	15:50	16:10	17:10
Arr. Portsmouth (Hbr.)	14:46	16:05	16:25	17:25
Change to train				
Dep. Portsmouth (Hbr.)	14:54	16:12	16:50 (2)	17:50 (1)
Arr. London (Wat.)	16:23	17:45	18:27	19:25

(1) Runs Sunday only. (2) Runs daily except holidays. (3) Plus another London departure at 10:20 arriving Shanklin 13:06. (4) Plus additional frequent Shanklin departures from 17:15 to 22:32.

London - Rochester - London   Railtrack Timetable

Dep. London   Frequent times from 05:02 to 00:21 (07:35 to 00:21 on Sunday)
  (Victoria)
Arr. Rochester   60 minutes later

Sights in **Rochester**: The 17th-century Bull Hotel, where Charles Dickens' characters, Pickwick and his friends, spent the first night of their long and memorable trip

See the little house at 11 Ordinance Terrace, where Dickens lived from the time he was four until he was nine years old. Visit the red brick mansion where he lived his last 10 years and died. The cemetery here has many markers from which Dickens took the names for the people he cast in his stories.

Visit the City Museum in Eastgate House, open daily except Friday 14:00-17:30.

Dep. Rochester   Frequent times from 05:56 to 22:29 (06:46 to 21:20 on Sunday)
Arr. London (Victoria)   60 minutes later

London - Rye - London   Railtrack Timetable

Dep. London (Lon. Bridge)   Frequent times from 05:18 to 21:07
                              (08:17 to 21:07 on Sunday)
Change from suburban train 90 minutes later, in Ashford
Arr. Rye   2 hours after departing London

Sights in **Rye**: This delightful little hilltop town was once an important seaport, but it is now two miles from the sea. See the 14th-century city walls. The 14th-century wood Monastery, now housing one of the town's six potteries.

It is a 10-minute walk up Conduit Hill to the 12th-century Norman church and then to the oldest structure in Rye, the 13th-century Ypres Tower, now the city's museum; open from Easter to the end of September, Monday-Saturday 10:30–12:30 and 14:15–17:30, Sunday 11:15–12:30.

Dep. Rye   Frequent times from 06:10 to 21:46
                              (10:47 to 20:47 on Sunday)
Change to Suburban train 30 minutes later, in Ashford.
Arr. London (Lon. Bridge)   2 hours after departing Rye

London - Salisbury - Stonehenge - London   117

Most of these trains have light refreshments.

Dep. London (Wat.)	07:09 (1)	08:35 (1)	09:35 (2)	10:35 (2)	10:57 (3+4)
Arr. Salisbury	08:37	09:55	11:16	11:56	12:38

Sights in **Salisbury**: The cathedral, with its tombs of Crusaders and one of the four existing copies of the Magna Carta.

Buses operate between the Salisbury rail station and Stonehenge to view the mysterious oval of 50-ton stones there, about 4,000 years old. This is the most important prehistoric relic in Britain. How were these stupendous weights moved 20 miles from their quarry…and why?

The nearly two-hour round-trip departs Salisbury Monday–Friday at 10:15, 11:15, 12:15, 13:15, 14:15 and 16:15 (different but similar times on Saturday and Sunday).

Dep. Salisbury	13:17 (2)	13:51 (3)	14:25 (5)	14:29 (3)	15:23 (2)	16:35 (5+6)
Arr. London (Wat.)	14:42	15:40	15:56	16:18	16:47	18:11

(1) Runs Monday-Saturday except holidays. (2) Runs Monday-Friday except holidays. (3) Runs Sundays. (4) Plus frequent London departures from 12:35 to 22:35. (5) Runs Saturdays. (6) Plus other frequent Salisbury departures from 16:52 to 22:40.

London - Stratford-upon-Avon - London   126

In addition to the schedules below, there is an escorted "Shakespeare Connection" service between London's *Euston* rail station, Coventry and (by bus) Stratford. Details are available from British Travel Centre, 12 Regent Street, London. The special bus that transfers passengers between Coventry and Stratford has a guide and stops near the Stratford office that books various local tours.

There's still another option for making this trip. The luxurious British Pullman also schedules trips to Stratford-upon-Avon as well as to other destinations such as Bath, Windsor, Canterbury and Edinburgh. Day trips, weekenders and longer trips are offered. In 1997, daytrips started at $240 per person, weekend trips from $550, double occupancy. The British Pullman also is the London-Folkestone link for passengers taking the Venice Simplon Orient Express (VSOE) on the Continent. For a brochure with the latest British Pullman or VSOE travel dates and prices, call Orient Express Reservations, (800) 524-2420 or visit the Orient Express Web site: http://www.orient-expresstrains.com/.

Dep. London (Pad.)	09:18 (1)	11:18 (2)	13:45 (2+3)
Arr. Stratford	11:10	13:24	16:00

•   •   •

Dep. Stratford	17:31 (2)	17:55 (4)	23:15 (1)
Arr. London (Pad.)	19:42	20:11	01:24

(1) Runs Monday–Friday except holidays. (2) Runs Monday-Saturday except holidays. (3) Plus two Sunday departures leaving London at 08:45 and 11:45 arriving Stratford 12:07 and 14:00. (4) Sunday only.

Those wishing to attend a performance at the Royal Shakespeare Theater *cannot* purchase tickets for that night's performance until arriving at the theater and chance the possibility that all tickets have been sold. There are afternoon performances at the Royal Shakespeare Theater on some Thursdays and Saturdays.

There are many restaurants and pubs in Stratford, and visitors may picnic either by the theater or in the garden along the river.

See the house of Mary Arden, Shakespeare's mother. The cottage of Anne Hathaway, his wife, and Shakespeare's tomb in Trinity Church. Stratford also was the home of John Harvard, founder of America's great university.

London - Torquay - Paignton - London   112

Dep. London (Pad.)	07:45 (1)	08:35 (2)	09:35 (2)	10:30 (2)	12:35 (4)
Dep. Exeter (St. Davids)	10:19	11:44	12:20 (3)	12:52	14:52
Arr. Torquay	10:59	12:20	12:55	13:27	15:33
Arr. Paignton	6–10 minutes later				

Sights in **Torquay:** An 11-mile coastline that resembles a Mediterranean resort, palm trees and all. The British "Riviera." Pronounced "tor-kee." Stroll the walk along the formal gardens at the waterfront to the park, where concerts and dances are held in the summer. Visit the model railroad and house miniatures in the Victoria Arcade at the harbor.

See the collection of 17th-century silver and 18th-century glass at the Municipal Art Gallery and Museum in the 18th-century building next to the ruins of the 12th-century Torre Abbey. Nearby is the Model Village, open in summer 09:00-22:00, in winter 09:00 to dusk. The exhibits of archaeology, natural history and Devon folk life in the Museum of Natural History, open daily except Sunday from March through October 10:00–16:45, and Monday-Friday from November through February.

Paignton has many bed-and-breakfast inns. Sights there include the restored 14th-century Great Hall of Compton Castle, open May through October on Monday, Wednesday and Thursday 10:00–17:00. The ballroom filled with silver mirrors at Oldway House, called "a miniature Versailles," open Monday-Saturday 09:00–13:00 and 14:15–17:00, Sundays 14:00–17:00.

Dep. Paignton	14:57 (5)	15:14 (6)	16:07 (5)	17:24 (7+8)
Dep. Torquay	6 minutes after departing Paignton			
Arr. Exeter (St. Davids)	15:43	16:04 (2)	16:52	18:12
Arr. London (Pad.)	18:42	19:05	19:26	20:50

(1) Runs Monday–Saturday, except holidays. Restaurant car. (2) Runs Monday-Friday except holidays. Light refreshments. (3) Change trains in Exeter. (4) Runs Monday-Friday except holidays. Restaurant car. (5) Runs Sundays. Light refreshments. (6) Standard class only. Operates Monday-Friday except holidays. Light refreshments. (7) Runs Saturdays. (8) Plus another Paignton departure at 18:26, arriving London 22:0

London - Winchester - London   105

All of these trains run daily.

Dep. London (Wat.)	Frequent times from 05:35 to 23:55 (07:55 to 22:55 on Sunday)
Arr. Winchester	60 minutes later (80 minutes later on Sunday)

Sights in **Winchester**: King Arthur's roundtable in the Great Hall at the castle. The 11th-century cathedral, with the tombs of King Alfred, Jane Austen and Izaak Walton.

Dep. Winchester	Frequent times from 05:27 to 23:15 (08:03 to 23:15 on Sunday)
Arr. London (Wat.)	60 minutes later (80 minutes later on Sunday)

London - Windsor - London   Railtrack Timetable

Dep. London (Waterloo)	Monday–Saturday: Frequent times from 06:15 to 23:21
	Sunday: Frequent times from 07:53 to 22:53
Arr. Windsor (Riverside)	40–60 minutes later

Sights in **Windsor**: Windsor Castle with its collection of Da Vinci drawings and, occasionally, members of the Royal Family. See the Changing of the Guard there, at 11:00 Monday-Saturday. Also visit Queen Mary's Doll House and St. George's Chapel.

In the town, stroll down the three-mile "Long Walk." See Eton College, where once it did not matter if you won or lost, in the days when observing niceties was more important than the final score.

Dep. Windsor (Riverside)	Monday–Saturday: Frequent times from 06:11 to 22:45
	Sunday: Frequent times from 07:02 to 23:02
Arr. London (Waterloo)	40–60 minutes later

London - York - London   170

Dep. London (Kings X)	06:15 (1)	07:00 (2)	07:30 (3)	08:00 (1)	09:00 (3)
Arr. York	08:30	09:07	09:27	09:52 (3)	11:00

Dep. London (Kings X)	09:30 (3)	10:00 (3)	10:30 (3)	11:00 (3)	11:30 (3)
Arr. York	11:34	11:53	12:26	13:00	13:33

•   •   •

Dep. York	14:37 (1)	14:52 (2)	15:32 (1)	15:54 (2)	16:32 (1)
Arr. London (Kings X)	16:45	16:51	17:40	17:57	18:39

Dep. York	16:55 (1)	17:17 (4)	17:30 (2)	17:51 (1)	18:28 (2+5)
Arr. London (Kings X)	19:07	19:24	19:36	20:09	20:35

(1) Runs Monday-Friday except holidays. (2) Runs Saturday only. (3) Pullman service and meals available in first class. (4) Runs Sunday only. (5) Plus other York departures at 19:42 (2), 19:58 (4) and 20:45 (4).

Sights in **York**: Ask at the tourist office (Exhibition Square) about the free walking tours offered in summer.

York was founded by Romans in A.D. 71. Very crowded with tourists in July and August. Most of the interesting places are located within the one square mile that is encircled by three miles of ancient walls.

York Minister, the largest Gothic cathedral in Britain (open daily 07:30 to dusk) has fantastic stained glass. Its Great East Window is the size of a tennis court. Use binoculars to study the detail on both the windows and the plaster work on the ceilings.

See the 14th and 15th-century stained glass in All Saints Church, on North Street. The brass rubbings center at St. Williams College (outside the cathedral's Great East Window). Stroll along the top of the city walls for a great view of the ancient buildings that surround the cathedral.

Walk down "The Shambles." Visit the restored Guildhall on St. Helen's Square to see its modern stained glass and timbered roof. Castle Museum, Britain's largest folk museum, off Tower Street is open daily 09:30–18:30. The shrine commemorating the 12th-century massacre of Jews at Clifford Tower, in the center of York.

You'll find exhibits of Bronze Age, Iron Age and Roman-era remains, in the Yorkshire Museum on Museum Street (open Monday–Saturday 10:00–17:00, Sunday 13:00–17:00). View 25 vintage locomotives and many train cars (including Queen Victoria's ornate coach) at the National Railway Museum on Leeman Road.

There are special excursion trains from London, to the railway museum, for a few days in August, September, October and November each year. The all-day excursions include round-trip train service from London and four hours touring the museum.

SCENIC TRAIN TRIPS

There is much fine scenery on nearly every rail route in England. The next four train rides offer exceptional scenic views, as do several rail trips in Scotland.

London - Pwllheli - London   Railtrack Timetable

There is excellent coastal scenery on this ride plus a splendid view of Harlech Castle.

This trip is too long as a one-day London round-trip.
All of these departures require changing trains at one or two rail stations among five different stations—in Birmingham for most trips. The ticket office at London (Euston) will advise where to make a train change.
A layover in Birmingham should be considered.

Dep. London (Euston)	08:14	12:35	16:45	18:45 (1)
Arr. Pwllheli	14:51	19:04	23:07	09:26

Sights in **Pwllheli**: This summer seaside resort is on the southern side of the Lleyn Peninsula. The major attraction here is boating in **Tremadog Bay**.

Dep. Pwllheli	08:02	09:42	11:28	13:53 (2)	14:58 (3)
Arr. London (Euston)	14:25	16:25	18:25	20:41	22:15

(1) Sleepers available. (2) Runs on Sundays. (3) Plus another Pwllheli departure at 19:09 (1), arriving London 10:40.

Leeds - Settle - Carlisle   162

The 62-mile Settle–Carlisle portion of this route is considered by many to be the most scenic train route in England. It goes through the **Pennine Hills** and the **Yorkshire Dales National Park**, close to the Lake district. This line has 14 tunnels and 21 viaducts, including the 104-foot-high Ribblehead Viaduct.

All of these trains have light refreshments, unless designated otherwise.

Dep. Leeds	08:47 (1)	09:47 (1)	10:47 (1)	12:47 (1)	13:27 (2)	14:47 (1)
Dep. Settle	09:45	10:49	11:45	13:45	14:23	15:44
Arr. Carlisle	11:26	12:30	13:27	15:25	16:06	17:25

Sights in **Settle**: A pretty town. Since 1429, a market has been held here every Tuesday.

Dep. Carlisle	14:25 (1)	15:19 (1)	16:25 (1)	16:30 (2)	17:57 (1)
Dep. Settle	16:03	16:57	18:03	18:11	19:33
Arr. Leeds	17:04	18:09	19:04	19:08	20:38

(1) Runs daily, except Sundays and holidays. (2) Runs Sunday only.

London - Windermere - London   149, 150

The breathtaking scenery of England's "Lake country."

The Oxenholme–Windermere (and v.v.) trains are second class only.
150

Dep. London (Euston)	08:25 (1)	12:25 (1)
Arr. Oxenholme	11:48	15:41
Change trains 149		
Dep. Oxenholme	12:37	16:38
Arr. Windermere	12:57	17:01

• • •

149

Dep. Windermere	15:11 (1)	16:05 (1+2)	17:14 (1)
Arr. Oxenholme	15:31	16:24	17:34
Change trains 150			
Dep. Oxenholme	15:40 (1)	16:24 (1+2)	17:40 (1)
Arr. London (Euston)	19:15	20:16	21:20

(1) Runs daily, except Sundays and holidays. (2) Change trains in Preston.

A DAY THROUGH WALES

There is a marvelous one-day circle train trip from London that takes you through the incredibly beautiful rural scenery in the heart of Wales, between Swansea and Shrewsbury. As shown below, this trip can be made either clockwise or counter-clockwise.

London - Swansea - Shrewsbury - London   130, 134, 140, 142

130		*140*	
Dep. London (Pad.)	09:00 (1)	Dep. London (Euston)	07:15 (1)
Arr. Swansea	11:55	Arr Birmingham (New St.)	08:55
Change trains 134		*Change trains 142*	
Dep. Swansea	13:23 (2)	Dep. Birmingham (New St.)	09:17 (2)
Arr. Shrewsbury	17:08	Arr. Shrewsbury	10:16
Change trains 142		*Change trains 134*	
Dep. Shrewsbury	17:24 (2)	Dep. Shrewsbury	13:27 (2)
Arr. Birmingham (New St.)	18:21	Arr. Swansea	16:58
Change trains 140		*Change trains 130*	
Dep. Birmingham	18:36	Dep. Swansea	17:32 (1)
Arr. London (Euston)	20:51	Arr. London (Pad.)	20:25

(1) Runs Monday-Friday except holidays. (2) Runs Monday-Saturday except holidays.

Sights in **Shrewsbury**: The 1,000-year-old castle. In **Wroxeter**, a short bus ride from here, are the reconstructed ruins of Roman baths built there 2,000 years ago.

If you have a few extra days to explore Wales, don't miss riding at least one or two of the "Great Little Trains of Wales." The "Great Little Trains of Wales" is a consortium of eight independent narrow-gauge steam railways that take in some of the best scenery in Britain. Most railways operate from late March or early April to September or October. Some have weekend trains or special excursions throughout the year. Here's a rundown of where the lines go and how long a round trip lasts. A closer look at three of the railways follows the list.

- Bala Lake Railway: Llanuwchllyn-Bala. Round trip: 1 hour.
- Brecon Mountain Railway: Pant-Dolygaer. Round trip 50 minutes.
- Ffestiniog Railway: Porthmadog Harbour-Blaenau Ffestiniog. Round trip: 2 hours 20 mins.
- Llanberis Lake Railway: Llanberis Padarn Park-Penllyn. Round trip: 40 minutes.
- Talyllyn Railway: Tywyn-Abergynolwyn-Nant Gwernol. Round trip: 2 hours 20 mins.
- Veil of Rheidol Railway: Aberystwyth-Devil's Bridge. Round trip: 3 hours.
- Welsh Highland Railway: Porthmadog-Pen-y-Mount. Round trip: 30 minutes.
- Welshpool and Llanfair Railway: Llanfair Caereinion-Welshpool. Round trip: 2 hours 20 mins.

While trains are usually steam-hauled, it is possible diesels could be substituted.

Engine No. 14 on the Welshpool and Llanfair, a coal-fired steamer, was originally built in Leeds in 1954. It ended up in Sierra Leone, though, and was about to be sold for scrap with the railway intervened. On its route between Llanfair Caereinion and Welshpool, the train climbs one of steepest inclines on a preserved railway, the Golfa incline. Sparks and cinders fly as the train chugs past meadows and wildflowers.

In 1989, the Veil of Rheidol line became British Rail's last steam line to be privatized. On the three-hour round trip from Aberystwyth, the train goes from 16 feet above sea level to over 600 feet at the Devil's Bridge terminal. Along the way, it negotiates sharp curves, hugging the green mountainside. The deep gorges and distant waterfalls are spectacular. At Devil's Bridge, there are actually three bridges, one built atop another. If time permits, hike down to Mynach Falls.

The most touristy of Wales' little trains is the Ffestiniog Railway. It travels from Porthmadog Harbour to Blaenau Ffestiniog. These trains are very crowded in summer, despite operating every 30 minutes. To avoid the crowds go early in the morning or in late afternoon. After passing green meadows full of sheep, the train starts its ascent to Ffestiniog. You can reach out the open window and touch the slate rock walls of the mountainside. A spiral, built to help the train gain height, and the Moelwyn Tunnel that the train passes through are probably the largest European civil engineering work project completed by a volunteer force.

To find out more about these and the other narrow-gauge lines, write: The Secretary, The Great Little Trains of Wales, FREEPOST, The Station, Llanfair Caereinion, Powys SY21 OBR, Wales, United Kingdom. Rail passes are available that include travel on these trains. For about $55, buy a Mid-Wales Rover Ticket from any train station. It covers travel on all trains north of Aberystwyth, English connecting trains, the Ffestiniog Railway and Welsh buses. If you plan to do lots of riding, consider buying a Great Little Trains of

Wales Wanderer Ticket. In late 1997, a pass good for eight days of travel within 15 days, sold for $50. A pass valid for four days of travel within seven days sold for $30. These tickets are available at stations of the participating railways.

RAIL CONNECTION WITH IRELAND
VIA WALES

There is bus service between Swansea's rail station and its ferryport.

London - Swansea - Cork   Cork - Swansea - London   130, 2075

130 Train			*2075 Ferry*		
Dep. London (Pad.)	17:00 (1)		Dep. Cork	09:00 (2)	21:00 (2)
Arr. Swansea	19:45		Arr. Swansea	19:00	07:00
Change to ferry 2075			*Change to train 130*		
Dep. Swansea	21:00 (2)		Dep. Swansea	20:32 (1)	08:32 (1)
Arr. Cork	07:00		Arr. London (Pad.)	23:25	11:30

(1) Runs Monday-Friday, except holidays. (2) Runs Monday, Wednesday, Thursday, Friday and Sunday June 23-September 18; Runs Tuesday, Thursday, Friday and Sunday September 20-December 23.

RAIL CONNECTIONS WITH SCOTLAND

These are the schedules for rail travel between London (*Kings Cross* rail station) and the capital of Scotland.

London - Edinburgh   and   Edinburgh - London   170

Seat reservation is advisable for all of these trains, particularly for Pullman service—which is more comfortable and provides at-seat meals and refreshments. Unless noted otherwise, these trains have meals service or light refreshments.

Dep. London	06:15 (1)	07:00 (2)	08:00 (1)	09:00 (1)	10:00 (1)
Arr. Edinburgh	11:06	11:36	12:15	13:40	14:12

Dep. London	10:30 (1)	11:00 (1)	11:30 (1)	12:00 (1)	13:00 (1)
Arr. Edinburgh	14:50	15:29	16:00	16:25	17:25

Dep. London	13:30 (1)	14:00 (1)	15:00 (1+3)	16:00 (1)	17:00 (1)
Arr. Edinburgh	18:08	18:20	20:08	20:24	21:13 (3)

| Dep. London | 18:00 (1+3) | | | | |
| Arr. Edinburgh | 22:47 | | | | |

• • •

Dep. Edinburgh	06:00 (1)	07:00 (1)	08:00 (1)	08:35 (2)	09:00 (2)
Arr. London	09:59	11:36	12:36	13:14	13:36

Dep. Edinburgh	09:30 (2)	10:00 (1)	10:30 (1)	11:00 (1)	11:30 (1)
Arr. London	13:56	14:41	14:55	15:40	15:57

Dep. Edinburgh	12:00 (1)	12:30 (1)	13:00 (1)	13:30 (2)	14:10 (1)
Arr. London	16:45	16:51	17:40	17:57	18:39

Dep. Edinburgh	15:00 (1+3)	15:00 (2)	16:00 (1)	16:30 (2)	17:00 (1)
Arr. London	19:10	19:35	20:38	21:50	21:58

| Dep. Edinburgh | 18:00 (1+3) | | | | |
| Arr. London | 23:30 | | | | |

(1) Runs Monday–Friday except holidays. (2) Runs Monday-Saturday except holidays. (3) Pullman service available in first class. (3) Runs Sundays.

SCOTLAND

The two rail trips north from Edinburgh (to Dundee–Aberdeen and to Perth–Inverness) are very scenic. There is also train service between Aberdeen and Inverness.

From Inverness, there is a rail route to Wick in northernmost Scotland, and to Kyle of Lochalsh on the west coast of Scotland. Other train routes to the same coastal area are from Glasgow to both Oban and to Mallaig. The other principal rail service in Scotland is between Edinburgh and Glasgow.

See the "Freedom of Scotland Travelpass and Flexipass" sections earlier in the chapter for details about buying Scottish rail passes.

Edinburgh

Edinburgh is the capital of Scotland. Most of the 25-acre rail station there is under glass. Visit Edinburgh Castle, sitting on a cliff 270 feet above the city, on a site where there have been forts since the 6th century. A cannon has been fired from there every day since 1858. The castle is open every day in the summer: 09:30–18:00 Monday-Saturday, 11:00–18:00 on Sundays. The panoramic view of Edinburgh from the castle is breathtaking.

At the castle, see the hammer-beamed timbered ceiling in the Great Hall of James IV, the Scottish Crown Jewels, the small St. Margaret's Chapel, and the State Apartments, including the rooms once occupied by Mary Queen of Scots.

Below the Castle is the 37-acre Princess Street Gardens, with the city's main rail tracks running through it, at a lower level than the surface of the park.

Also visit the 17th-century Palace of Holyrood House to see the Throne Room and also the portraits of 110 Scottish kings (painted by the same artist) in the gallery. You will notice that all 110 noses are the same! Stroll through 648-acre Holyrood Park, which has three lakes.

Other interesting sights in Edinburgh: the paintings at both the National Gallery of Scotland and in the National Portrait Gallery. The National Museum of Antiquities. The collection of technology, art, archaeology, geology and natural history in the Royal Scottish Museum. The Museum of Childhood (historic books, toys and materials about child rearing), closed on Sundays. The adaptation of Athens' Temple of Theseus. The month-long International Festival of Music and Drama.

The pottery, hand-crafted glass, textiles and woodwork at the Scottish Craft Center, in Acheson House, open daily except Sunday 10:00–17:00. The collection of Robert Burns, Sir Walter Scott and Robert Louis Stevenson manuscripts and memorabilia in the 17th-century Lady Stair's House.

The exhibit (Picasso, Hockney, etc.) at the Scottish National Gallery of Modern Art on Belford Road, open Monday–Saturday 10:00–17:00, Sunday 14:00–17:00. Henry Moore sculptures decorate the grounds. A sign behind this museum directs you to a path that goes to Dean Village, once a grain-milling center. Nearby is St. Bernard's Well, a Doric temple built at a mineral spring in 1789.

Then stroll to Stockbridge (once an industrial village) on St. Stephen Street, where many interesting antique shops are located. Stockbridge is next to New Town, notable for its Georgian houses and elegant crescents.

Edinburgh - Dundee - Aberdeen 200

This is a very scenic rail trip.

Dep. Edinburgh	07:05 (1)	08:10 (1)	09:10 (1)	10:25 (1)	11:10 (1)
Arr. Dundee	08:27	09:26	10:26	11:45	12:26
Arr. Aberdeen	09:42	10:45	11:38	12:56	13:40
		•	•	•	
Dep. Aberdeen	13:10 (1)	13:50 (2)	14:20 (1)	14:55 (1+3)	
Arr. Dundee	14:27	14:32	15:30	16:06	
Arr. Edinburgh	15:48	16:18	16:48	17:20	

(1) Runs daily, except Sundays and holidays. Light refreshments. (2) Runs Sundays only. (3) Plus other departures from Aberdeen at 15:25 (1), 16:15 (1), 17:15 (1), 18:15 (1), 19:00 (2), 20:00 (1), 20:50 (2) and 21:14 (1).

Sights in **Dundee**: A very ancient city, predating Roman occupation. Mountains of jam and preserves are processed here. Visit the Spalding Golf Museum in nearby Camperdown Park, and the frigate "Unicorn," launched in 1824, now tied at Victoria Dock. Dundee has four castles: Dudhope, Claypotts, Broughty and Mains.

Sights in **Aberdeen:** A very popular tourist center and busy seaport that straddles two rivers, Aberdeen is the center of Scotland's fishing industry (see the 07:00 fish market). See the 15th-century Cathedral of St. Machar and streets that were laid out in the 13th and 14th centuries. The local history museum in the 17th-century Provost Skene's House.

The 16th-century Provost Ross's House. The 18th-century St. Nicholas Church. Two very old bridges: the 14th-century Brig o'Balgownie and the 16th-century Old Bridge of Dee. The 19th-century Music Hall. The 19th-century Marischal College, considered the world's largest and finest granite building.

Edinburgh - Perth - Inverness   195

A very scenic train ride through the heart of the **Grampian Mountains**. Winter sports, including skiing, are the attraction at the **Aviemore** vacation resort.

Dep. Edinburgh	06:48 (1)	09:35 (2)	13:40 (3)	15:40 (3)
Dep. Perth	08:05	10:49	14:55	17:00
Dep. Aviemore	09:49	12:29	16:30	18:36
Arr. Inverness	10:35	13:10	17:18	19:15

* * *

Dep. Inverness	12:13 (1)	14:37 (3)	18:30
Dep. Aviemore	13:01	15:22	19:15
Dep. Perth	14:49	16:55	20:51
Arr. Edinburgh	16:10	18:14	22:10

(1) Runs Monday-Saturday except holidays. Change trains in Perth. Light refreshments Perth–Inverness (and v.v). (2) Runs Sundays only. (3) Runs Monday-Saturday except holidays.

Sights in **Perth**: A popular tourist center. There is much whiskey distilling and weaving of tartans here. Good winter sports. Sailing and water skiing in the summer. See the 360-degree panoramic color slide-show and hear the stereophonic presentation at the Round House waterworks. Also of interest, St. John's Kirk and the Perth Art Gallery and Museum, on George Street. A short distance from there, at North Post, visit the Fair Maid's House, an important locale in Sir Walter Scott's novel, "The Fair Maid of Perth."

Sights in **Inverness**: Located in the mountainous Highlands. Very cold winters and cool summers here. A popular tourist resort for hunting of grouse and deer, hiking, fishing, sailing, camping and winter sports. Many whiskey distillers in this area. Visit the castle. Stroll the garden paths along the River Ness. Nearby is Great Britain's highest mountain, Ben Nevis (4,406 feet).

Take a cruise on **Loch Ness,** and see if you can spot the "monster." Boats go from the lake through the **Caledonian Canal** and return to Inverness on cruises that take 2½ hours in the morning, 3½ hours in the afternoon, and 2½ hours in the evening.

Aberdeen - Inverness   201

Dep. Aberdeen	06:28 (1)	07:30 (1)	09:22 (1)	10:00 (2)	11:35 (1+3)	
Arr. Inverness	08:47	09:46	11:46	12:14	13:48	

•   •   •

Dep. Inverness	05:00 (2)	05:58 (2)	08:07 (2)	09:55 (3)	10:43 (2)	12:17
Arr. Aberdeen	07:14	08:16	10:36	12:10	12:56	14:36

(1) Runs daily, except Sundays and holidays. (2) Runs Sundays and holidays. (3) Plus other Aberdeen departures at 13:10 (1), 15:22 (1), 17:14, 18:18 (1), 20:06 (1) and 21:45 (1), arriving Inverness 15:23, 17:53, 19:35, 20:32, 22:24, and 23:56.

Inverness - Kyle of Lochalsh - Inverness   202

This is one of the most scenic train trips in Britain. The track climbs and descends, turns and twists through the **Wester Ross Mountains** as it goes along the shoreline of lovely lakes through the heart of the Highlands. Spring brings fields of red and orange rhododendron; see fields of purple heather all year.

In the high **Luib Summit** area there are forests and snow-capped mountains. It is only an eight-minute ferryboat ride from Kyle to the **Isle of Skye**.

Dep. Inverness	08:10 (1)	10:45 (2)	12:35 (1)	18:00 (3)	
Arr. Kyle	10:41	13:15	15:06	20:30	

•   •   •

Dep. Kyle	07:20 (1)	09:52 (4)	11:45 (1)	15:20 (1)	17:05 (1+5)
Arr. Inverness	09:49	12:25	14:23	17:48	19:38

(1) Runs daily, except Sundays and holidays. Light refreshments. (2) Light refreshments. (3) Operates late June to early September. (4) Sundays only. (5) Late June to mid-September: runs daily except holidays; from mid-September runs Sunday only. Light refreshments all year.

Edinburgh - Dunbar - Edinburgh   Railtrack Timetable

Dep. Edinburgh   09:00 (1)   14:00 (1)   17:00 (1)
Arr. Dunbar   20-25 minutes later

Sights in **Dunbar**: A small fishing port, the birthplace of naturalist John Muir (128 High Street). See the castle ruins at the harbor.

Take a 45-minute walk and visit the Old Harbor with its Lifeboat Museum, the roost for domesticated pigeons in Friar's Croft, and the Georgian houses (Castellau and Lauderdale). This walk is detailed in a guidebook available at the town's tourist information center in the 17th-century Town House on High Street, open during summer Monday-Saturday 09:00–19:00, Sunday 11:00–13:00.

Also visit the 1,667-acre John Muir Country Park, containing a wide variety of birds and plants. Near it are the restored 17th-century Preston watermill and many old towns and villages: **Gifford**, **Haddington**, **Dirleton** and **North Berwick**. A list of hotels, guest houses and bed-and-breakfast places can be obtained by writing to the Dunbar Tourist Information Centre, if sufficient international reply coupons are enclosed.

Dep. Dunbar   07:47 (1)   09:47 (1)   13:12 (1)   16:53 (1)
Arr. Edinburgh   20-25 minutes later

(1) Runs Monday–Friday, except holidays.

Edinburgh - Glasgow - Edinburgh   196

Dep. Edinburgh   Monday–Saturday: Frequent times from 05:50 to 23:30
                                      Sunday: Frequent times from 08:30 to 23:30
Arr. Glasgow (Queen St.)   50–70 minutes later

•   •   •

Dep. Glasgow (Queen St.)   Monday–Saturday: Frequent times from 05:55 to 23:30
                                      Sunday: Frequent times from 08:00 to 22:30
Arr. Edinburgh   50–70 minutes later

Sights in **Glasgow**: Glasgow is a major seaport and Scotland's largest city. See the great shipyards on the River Clyde.

View dozens of antique streetcars, motorcycles and trains (including King George VI's 72-foot-long railway coach, built in 1941 with wartime armor-plated shutters) in the Museum of Transport at Kelvin Hall on Albert Drive. Nearby, a fine collection of weapons, paintings (Rembrandt, Monet), Mackintosh furniture and natural history exhibits is displayed at the Kelvingrove Art Galleries and Museum.

A vast collection of paintings by James Abbott McNeil Whistler—the world's best collection—is in the Hunterian Art Gallery at Glasgow University. The Gallery also features a reconstruction of three floors of the home of the great architect Charles Mackintosh.

Also of interest is the Glasgow Art Gallery and the botanic gardens. Find your Scottish roots in the genealogy section at the Mitchell Library on North Street. It's Europe's largest municipal reference library with over 1,250,000 books, some 40 newspapers and more than 200 periodicals. It has a helpful, knowledgeable staff and modern studying facilities.

See the more than 8,000 treasures of the Burrell Collection, in Pollok House: over 700 stained glass items (one of the world's best collections). Paintings by Rembrandt, Bellini, Memling, Degas, Manet. Excellent Chou Dynasty pieces. Neolithic burial urns. The more than eight-ton marble Warwick Vase, discovered in Rome in 1771. Also on view: jade, carpets, porcelain, silver, furniture, glass and gold. Open Monday-Saturday 10:00–17:00, Sunday 14:00–17:00.

Glasgow - Oban - Glasgow   193

There is marvelous Highland scenery on this route.

Dep. Glasgow (Queen St.)	08:42 (1)	12:40	18:10
Arr. Oban	11:40	15:39	21:15

Sights in **Oban**: This has been a holiday resort for nearly a century, and a fishing port for even longer.

Dep. Oban	08:05 (1)	12:35 (2)	18:10
Arr. Glasgow (Queen St.)	11:14	15:44	21:14

(1) Runs daily, except Sundays & holidays. (2) Runs Sunday only.

Glasgow - Fort William - Mallaig - Glasgow   193

The Fort William–Mallaig portion, the train ride with the most beautiful scenery in Britain, offers better views than an alternative auto route does of many lochs (lakes), glens (valleys) and bens (mountains).

These trains provide a guide who tells about the sights on this route: the 4,406-foot-high Ben Nevis (highest peak in Britain), the Caledonian Canal built in 1822, fabled Loch Lomond, the heather-encrusted wild Rannoch Moor, the man-made Loch Trieg, the forested Loch Eil, Bonnie Prince Charlie's monument, and the 1,000-foot-long Glenfinnan Viaduct. The highest altitude on Britsh rails is 347 feet, at Corrour Summit, between Glasgow and Fort William

During the summer, a steam train operates between Fort William and Mallaig (from mid-June to late September). In 1997, the train departed Fort William at 10:35, arriving in Mallaig 12:35; the return trip left Mallaig at 14:10 arriving Fort William 16:10. For information about this trip, contact the West Coast Railway Company in Scotland at 01397 70391.

Dep. Glasgow (Queen St.)	08:12	12:40	18:10
Arr. Crianlarich	09:59	14:27	20:03
Dep. Crianlarich	10:05	14:33	20:15
Arr. Fort William	11:49	16:22	22:05
Dep. Fort William	12:00	16:27	22:10
Arr. Mallaig	13:22	17:49	23:30

Sights in **Mallaig:** There is a two-hour ferryboat ride from this little fishing village to Kyle of Lochalsh.

Dep. Mallaig	06:00	10:30	16:10
Arr. Fort William	07:20	11:52	17:37
Dep. Fort William	07:30	12:03	17:42
Arr. Crianlarich	09:19	13:49	19:23
Dep. Crianlarich	09:25	13:53	19:29
Arr. Glasgow (Queen St.)	11:14	15:44	21:14

CHAPTER 8

CENTRAL AND EASTERN EUROPE

Getting on Track in Central and Eastern Europe
• Tourist information: Tourist information numbers appear under each country's listing.
• Public holidays: Information about holidays appears under each country's listing.
• Currency: Information about currency appears under each country's listing.

Overview of Central and Eastern Europe's Trains
Generally, trains in Central and Eastern Europe are, while not as flashy as the TGV, Pendolino and Eurostar trains found in the rest of Europe, comfortable and clean. Expect to find less-than-stellar accommodations, though, in the Balkans. Trains are often in a state of disrepair and extremely crowded.

As the world of politics in the region changes, railways are finding that they must change too, if they want to stay in business. While under the wing of Communist rule, they cared less about marketing their services or worrying about bottom lines. Everything was guaranteed. Now, new railpasses are popping up and railways are actually seeking business from U.S. travelers. For instance, for several years now, Russia's railroad has had a deal with Rail Europe to market its services. Reservations can be next to impossible to arrange in Russia, and your patience will be put to the test at every turn if you decide to tackle this task yourself. Between arrangements like this one and the new crop of railpasses, travel in this interesting area will continue to become easier in the future.

As we told you last year, travel conditions have been changing in central and eastern Europe at such a turbulent pace that guidebooks cannot possibly keep up. This is still true today. Travel in general has grown phenomenally in eastern Europe, and so more people need more and better information in order to experience the region in an interesting and rewarding way. With that in mind, we have investigated numerous new sources of up-to-date information and surfed through the region's offerings on the Internet. We also interviewed seasoned train travelers with recent eastern European experience and local residents in the countries represented here.

A few areas of consensus emerged. Because eastern Europe is in a state of social, economic, and political flux, it is absolutely necessary that travelers confirm and reconfirm travel information. So, remember to check information and then reconfirm newly acquired information with still other people. Then check again. A train connection time printed on a schedule at the time you purchased your ticket may very well change the morning of your trip. The three-hour layover in Warsaw you were informed of may be reduced to an hour and half at the last minute. Track 8 may not even exist. And on and on. Jim Haynes, Paris's most famous American expatriate and author of the *People to People* guides to eastern Europe, maintains that local people "know the current situation better than any up-to-date guidebook." People who live in the countries you are about to visit are your greatest source of "real info, friendship, and security," Jim acknowledges.

Although train travel in the region is quickly coming into greater homogeny with train travel in Western Europe, train travel east of Poland remains highly exotic, often disorienting, and at times less than reassuring for western travelers. Many experienced travelers love those exciting trips through the Ukraine, Russia, and the Baltic States and are the first to advise neophyte travelers to proceed with great caution and informed intelligence. Urban train stations in the Commonwealth of Independent States and the former Yugoslavia can range from confusing and seedy to outright dangerous. Try to sort out the myth from the truth. Horror stories of theft on night trains, rowdy gangs, sleeping gas, sordid violence, and roaming pirates in the East abound, but much is lore. As the economies of the region evolve, the public relationship to money responds. In that western travelers bring cash, care must be taken in how one travels and how one handles ambiguous situations. Bring one-dollar bills and take them out sparingly and one at a time—they buy a lot and they don't require change. Jody Jenkins, an American writer who lives on a barge in Burgundy and has recently completed *The Low Lights of Winter*, a collection of stories about life in contemporary eastern Europe, contends that travelers in the East must be able to "flow with the tide." Ghengis Khan–type characters were habitually harassing Jody and his girlfriend Gwen as they trained from Moscow to Tashkent in Uzbekistan. First-class tickets cost them $5 each, but it was the on-board bribes of $10 each and a pack of chewing gum that allowed them to win over the conductor and to feel secure in an otherwise alienating environment.

Jim Haynes strongly advises western travelers to be met and dropped off at train stations in the East. And don't hang out at stations; you will invite unwelcome experiences. It's always better to hail a taxi or private car a few hundred meters from the station than to subject yourself to being ripped off by a taxi waiting at the station.

Another shared point. In the more exotic places and for the overnight and long hauls, always bring your own food. Bring an extra supply for your neighbors, conductors, and compartment mates, for whom a small act of generosity and openness will buy solidarity. Cigarettes, gum, and trinkets work wonders in gaining instant companions and bodyguards. Also think ahead in terms of your travel needs. Toilet paper, for one, is a must, as Catrinel Plescu from Bucharest reported on her recent trip from the Romanian capital to Vienna, Austria. Bottles of water, flashlights, and matches are all good ideas.

Lastly, there are now scores of general travel guides to eastern Europe. Pick up at least one or two to accompany your Eurail guide. Select editions that are as recent as possible. The travel information included here will serve as a good start, but for more detailed descriptions and commentary you'll need a more general source of data. Pick up brochures along the way and share them with other travelers. Of course, we're open to receiving your comments, suggestions, and experiences in order to better report on the region in each successive update.

TRAIN PASSES AND INFORMATION

European East Pass The European East Pass, sold exclusively through Rail Europe, offers unlimited first-class travel in Poland, Hungary, Czech Republic, Slovakia and Austria for 5-10 days within a one-month period. The 1998 prices are:

5 days in 1 month*	$199
add'l rail day (5 max.)	$ 22

* Children 4-11, half-off, under four free.

In 1997, Rail Europe started offering car rentals in Eastern Europe that included pick-up and drop-off of Avis cars in Germany for use in Poland, Czech Republic, Hungary, Slovenia and 10 other Eastern European countries. Called "Germany East," two categories of car were available in 1997 and prices started at $395 for a seven-day compact car rental. Rail Europe also offered Hertz rentals in individual countries, including Czech Republic, Hungary, Poland and Slovenia. Prices ranged from $117 to $273 for a three-day rental. Call Rail Europe for the latest prices, (800) 4EURAIL.

Balkan Flexipass Rail Europe also sells the Balkan Flexipass for first-class travel in Bulgaria, Greece, Macedonia, Romania, Turkey and Yugoslavia (Serbia and Montenegro).

	Adult	Junior*
Any 5 days in 1 month	$152	$90
Any 10 days in 1 month	$264	$156
Any 15 days in 1 month	$317	$190

Children 4-11 pay half the adult fare.
*Junior pass is available to those who are under the age of 26 on their first date of travel.

Baltic Pass This pass is available to ISIC, ITIC and GO 25 card holders and their accompanying spouses and children (See Chapter 2 "Student, Teacher, Youth Discount Cards" for ISIC information), for unlimited rail travel in Estonia, Latvia and Lithuania. Passes cost $38 for 7 days, $56 for 14 days and $75 for 21 days. For details, check with Campus Travel in England. From U.S. dial (011 44 171) 730 3402; in Britain and Europe dial 0171 730 3402. Visit Campus Travel's Web site at: http://www.campustravel.co.uk/. At the site, you'll find various E-mail addresses to direct queries for information. They will usually answer within 24 hours.

ALBANIA

Getting on Track in Albania
• Tourist information: Embassy of the Republic of Albania, 1511 K St. NW, Suite 1010, Washington, DC 20005. Telephone (202) 223-4942, fax (202) 628-7342.
• Currency: Albanian lek. At press time, $1 equalled 155.00 lek.

Overview of Albania's Trains
Albania's trains are operated by Herkurudhe e Shqipense. The railway offers only one class of service. Tickets cannot be purchased in advance, only on the day of departure. Due to the ongoing civil unrest in Albania, trains are subject to suspension. All services were suspended in March 1997 for this reason, but have gradually returned. Still, embassies are recommending extreme caution when traveling in Albania, and avoiding travel there entirely, if possible, until the conflicts have been resolved.

Currently there is only one international rail connection in and out of Albania—it consists of the passenger link with Mali izi, Montenegro to the north via Lezhe and Shkoder. The longest train journey in the country runs a total of 96 miles between the capital, Tirana, and the southern port of Vlorë, and it takes approximately five hours. Otherwise, boat connections from Vlorë to Brindisi, Italy, which is only 80 miles away, and from Sarande to Corfu, just 16 miles south, exist, although travel details are difficult to confirm in advance. The train system runs east-west also between Durrës on the Adriatic Coast and Pogradec on the eastern lake frontier with Greek Macedonia. Some of the most interesting mountain villages are off the train route and must be visited by bus or car.

Train travel within the country requires tolerance and time. One seasoned traveler, John Hodgson, recently back from Albania, writes: "I have traveled by train in all the countries of Eastern Europe, and the best train journey is in Albania, from Tirana to Pogradec. The line is 147 kilometers, the journey takes seven hours, and it costs $1.50 U.S. All the railways in Albania were built by 'volunteer' young people under communism, and their technical standards are very low. Poor maintenance has also meant that speed limits are down to a crawl. Albanian railways have Czech-built diesels, and used to have Chinese carriages, but most of these were reduced to bits in the 1991 revolution and have been replaced by cast-off carriages donated by Italian railways."

Tirana-Pogradec trains pass through most of central Albania, via Durrës, Rrogozhine, Elbasan, and Librazhd. The later part of the journey, up the Shkumbin valley, is exceptionally beautiful, with many tunnels and bridges. After a final tunnel the line emerges on lovely Lake Ohrid, which forms the border with Macedonia.

These trains can be very dirty, crowded and smoky. Take your own food, and take some to share around. According to Hodgson, though, despite the less-than-perfect surroundings, the trip is worth it.

EXCURSIONS AND CITY-SIGHTSEEING

Tirana

The predominance of indestructible and ubiquitous concrete bunkers, or "pillboxes," sprinkled throughout the countryside perpetually remind visitors of the past and this country's century-long trail of invasions. Tirana's inroads into Western Europe were best heard via its notorious attacks on capitalism on Radio Tirana broadcasts in English. Although intrigue still lurks in contemporary Tirana and tourism remains greatly undeveloped, a new atmosphere of possibility pervades daily life. There is little traffic, and at times an unsettling calm cloaks the city. Air connections to and from Rinas Airport exist with Istanbul, Athens, Sophia, Rome, Budapest, Vienna, Lubliana, and Zurich.

The Albanian capital with its 400,000 inhabitants hosts some 170 museums. The Museum of Natural History houses a worthwhile yet limited collection of prehistoric and Illyrian objects and folk art from the region as well as an imposing mosaic mural depicting examples of warriors through the ages struggling for "freedom." A large room dedicated to the communist period has been roped off but not yet removed or reorganized, a detail that indicates the conflict of the national debate on the treatment of history.

Crowning the highest hill in the city is a mammoth statue commemorating "The Heroes," which guards the cemetery below. The major buildings around the main square capture the nation's history. There is the old Byzantine church, which long ago was converted into a mosque with the addition of a tall and narrow minaret. The government buildings date from World War II, when Mussolini's troops occupied the city (1939–1944).

As the Albanian-born New York writer Fron Nazi states, contemporary Albanian life transpires in the coffee shops, where right- and left-wing politicians, corrupt intellectuals, charming criminals, ideologue artists, spies and double agents, and sleazy businesspeople all congregate and swap stories, rumors, dreams, plots, and plans for deals, articles, government reforms, and revolutionary projects.

Durrës

Albania's Adriatic port, Durrës, built on the ruins of Greek and Roman towns, offers excellent sand beaches. This city has served as the nation's resort area, offering functional hotels built for "the people." The city also has a Roman amphitheater, several interesting bazaars, and a variety of Moslem mosques, the largest located in the main square. A curiosity: a beached boat now serves as a popular coffee shop. Durrës is a good starting point for exploration to nearby villages. All train trips in Albania pass through Durrës. Each day seven trains make the 36-kilometer haul in 90 minutes between Durrës and Tirana.

Kruje

Kruje is a mountainside city north of Tirane. An interesting citadel/museum is dedicated to Skanderbeg, the national hero who led a revolt against the Turks in the middle 1400s, resulting in a brief period of independence. There is a quaint marketplace street that offers folkloric items.

Berat

Crowning the isolated steep hill is a walled citadel overlooking the broad valley below. Inside is an ancient Byzantine church which had been converted into an icon museum during the decades when religious practices were prohibited. The old part of Berat, along the riverbanks, has been preserved and restored as a museum town. The hilltop 16th-century Ardenitza Monastery has been converted into an inn.

Vlorë

This ancient seaport is surrounded by hills of olive trees which serve the local olive oil refinery. Popular lore has it that the city takes its name from the "Turk" who declared Albania's independence in 1912, Ismail Kemal Bey Vlorë. This is not so—the name dates to Roman times. The Tirana-Vlorë train makes the 155-kilometer trek in five hours.

Sarande

Sarande is the southernmost city on the Adriatic coast, almost on the border with Greece and across a narrow body of water from the island of Corfu. The town is on a curved shoreline, making it most attractive. The walls and houses are ablaze with bougainvillea and the streets are shaded with palms. A few miles farther south are the ruins of Butrint, a city founded in pre-Greek times by Illyrians and perhaps exiled Trojans, followed by the civilizations of Greece, Rome, and Byzantium. The layers of stone ruins are clearly visible. Foundations, walls, heroic gates, colorful mosaics, fallen columns, and the citadel atop the hill all combine to make this a most interesting site.

Gjirokaster

The small mountainside city of Gjirokaster, crowned by a citadel that was used by the Italians, Nazis, and communists as a prison, is now a war museum. The monumental statue of the deceased dictator recently had been removed from this prominent spot.

Other villages worth visiting include Apollonia, Fiera, Shkodra, and Butrinti.

For information about Albanian tours, contact Kutrubes Travel Agency, 328 Tremont Street, Boston, MA 02116. Telephone (800) 878-8566, fax (617) 426-3196.

Tirane - Durres - Vlore and v.v. 1390

Dep. Tirane	07:50	12:05	Dep. Vlore	06:10	13:15
Dep. Durres	09:29	13:35	Dep. Durres	10:20	17:15
Arr. Vlore	12:50	17:35	Arr. Tirane	11:30	18:24

BULGARIA

Getting on Track in Bulgaria

• Tourist information: Bulgarisches Fremdenverkehrsverband, Stephanstraße 1-3, 60313 Frankfurt, Germany. Telephone 011 49 69 295284, fax 011 49 69 295286.

• Public holidays: January 1, New Year's Day, May 1, 2, Labor Day, May 24, Education Day, June 2, Memorial Day, September 9, 10, Liberation Day, November 11, Revolution Day.

• Currency: Bulgarian lev. At press time, $1 equalled 1806.00 lek.

Overview of Bulgaria's Trains

Bulgarski Durzhavni Zheleznitzi (BDZ) operates Bulgaria's trains. Trains have two classes of service, first and second. It is possible to reserve seats on most express trains. Some Bulgarian trains carry sleeping cars and couchettes.

The BDZ Bulgarian State Railway has an extensive system of more than 4,000 kilometers of track, and the trains come in three speeds: express, fast, or slow (putnichki). The popular Sofia-Burgas route passes by either Karlovo or Plovdiv, and travelers often opt to break up this stint with a stopover. Similarly, the Sofia-Ruse route passes by Pleven or Gorna Oryahovitsa. Book a seat and/or sleeper reservations in a Rila tourist office well in advance for the express trains to the Black Sea.

The most significant travel destinations in Bulgaria are the capital city of Sofia, the ancient trading center of Plovdiv, and the Black Sea resort towns of Varna and Burgas.

Train travel into Bulgaria is dominated by its routes from Bucharest, Romania; Nis, Yugoslavia; Thessaloniki, Greece; and Edirne, Turkey; with major connections to Athens, Berlin, Budapest, Warsaw, Kiev, Moscow, Vilnius, and St. Petersburg. As elsewhere in Eastern Europe, buses are often cheaper and more reliable than trains, and this is especially true when traveling between Bulgaria and Romania. The Romanian train into Bulgaria originates in Russia, and travelers often report being told they were not allowed on these trains despite their purchased tickets. A $10 "tip" in almost all cases will resolve any potential conflict. Don't get too righteous about these things—have small bills, cigarettes, and chewing gum conveniently ready. The 11-hour Bucharest-Sofia jaunt can only be taken on an overnight and unreserved basis. Be ready for horrible crowding and arrive at the station well in advance of the departure time.

The famous *Orient Express* from the late 1800s ran through Sofia on its way from Paris to Istanbul, and the legacy is carried forward in the form of the *Istanbul Express* coming from Munich and the *Balkan Express* coming from Warsaw. Some cost-sensitive travelers recommend buying westbound tickets up to the Turkish frontier town of Kapikule and then paying for the additional fare into Bulgaria on the train.

Traveling to Bulgaria from Greece has been reported as difficult and painful, especially at the border. The bus is preferable. However, train travel in the other direction seems less problematic. The overnight *Transbalkan Express* links Sofia and Athens in 18 hours. Other Greek-Bulgarian connections include the *Plovdiv* and *Alexandroupolis* run.

The *Meridian Express* is a daily linking Berlin and Sofia by way of Prague, Budapest, and Belgrade. The *Istanbul Express* runs four days a week from Munich to Istanbul via Salzburg, Belgrade, and Sofia. Since the war in former Yugoslavia, these train routes to

Belgrade and beyond host all sorts of unsavory characters. Caution should be used in making this journey. No one will understand why you are heading to Belgrade and it is not certain that you'll be allowed to carry on.

As elsewhere in Eastern Europe, train stations in Bulgaria are not always clearly marked and it is easy to miss your stop, especially when the name is written in cyrillic script! Pay attention and ask locals on the train to announce when you've arrived.

Many seasoned travelers agree that Bulgaria's most spectacular train trip is the Sofia-Mezdra climb up the Iskar Gorge on the line to Vidin and Pleven. This can be accomplished as a day trip, but two days are preferable. The Central Railway Station in Sofia is located at Maria Luiza Blvd. Call for train information or have a Bulgarian person call for you. The telephone number is 3-11-11 to 3-11-20. For international train ticket information, call 87-59-35 or stop in at 5 Gurko Street. The official train ticket offices are called Rila and are located in all Bulgarian towns served by rail.

BULGARIAN FLEXIPASS

Bulgarians will often advise you not to take their trains—they'll tell you that they are dirty and unreliable. However, there still is no better way to see the "Jewel of the Balkans" than by rail, and the highly useful Bulgarian Flexipass is a great asset.

The Bulgaria Flexipass offers unlimited first-class train travel in Bulgaria for three days in one month for $70. Buy the pass through Rail Europe.

EXCURSIONS AND CITY-SIGHTSEEING

Sofia

Sofia's central train station has little charm and can be a bit disorienting. Platforms are called *peron* and are numbered in Roman type while the tracks or *kolovoz* are marked with Arabic numbers. Don't panic, just keep asking. There is a waiting room that is slightly more comfortable than elsewhere in the station but there is a small fee to gain access.

Ticket windows are separated by floors depending on national or international destinations. Same-day, Bulgarian train tickets are sold on the lower level. But these things change so keep asking.

Although daily life in Sofia has been transformed since the end of communist rule, the Bulgarian capital remains oppressively sedate, well behaved, and rather uneventful. The former Communist Party, under a new name, still holds the most seats in the national government, and change comes begrudgingly. The cyrillic alphabet and the Turkish mosques are clear reminders of this nation's eastern roots. Sophia hosts some of the most memorable icons in Europe, notably those found at Alexander Nevsky Memorial Church and the Byzantine 6th-century Sancta Sophia church. The Archaeological Museum in Bouyouk, the largest mosque in Sophia, requires a visit, as do the early renaissance frescos in the brick Rotunda of the St. Georgi Church, the city's oldest standing building. Art enthusiasts should also plan to visit the medieval Boyanna Church just outside the city and the Rila Monastery, an hour and a half from the capital.

Sofia is noted for its remarkable churches. The official religion in Bulgaria is Christian Orthodox, and most of the churches in Sofia perform Orthodox services. A few key sites not to miss include the following:

• Alexander Nevsky Cathedral. This central landmark shines from every part of the city.

• The Rotunda of St. George. This red brick rotunda church dating from the 4th century is considered the oldest structure in Sofia.

• St. Sophia Church. St. George is the oldest church, but St. Sofia is the oldest Eastern Orthodox church in Sofia.

• Banya Bashi Mosque. This Islamic shrine was built in 1576.

• Church of St. Cyril and St. Methodius and Their Five Disciples. Bearing the name Sveti Sedmochislenitsi, this church dates to 1528.

The art scene is focused on the National Art Gallery, located at 1 Alexander Batenberg Square. It's open Tuesday through Sunday 10:00 to 17:30 and is closed on Mondays. Standing exhibitions feature Bulgarian and foreign art from the Middle Ages to the present day. Extention in a crypt of the Alexander Nevsky Cathedral displays one of the largest original icon collections in Bulgaria. In addition, a surprising number of private art galleries have been appearing in downtown Sofia.

Sofia also hosts a number of restaurants, where traditional national dishes can be sampled. Try *gyuvech,* a meat and mixed vegetables dish, or *sarmi,* vine leaves filled with spicy mince meat. *Palneni chushki* (dolmas) are peppers stuffed with spicy minced meat. *Tarator* is a cold yogurt soup with chopped cucumbers and garlic, ideal in the summer. The traditional drink is what the Bulgarians consider their world famous and cheap Bulgarian wine, both red and white, and *rakiya,* a strong brandy distilled from grapes and plums. In both cases, be prepared for a headache the next morning.

The Rila Mountains

The Rila Mountains are an absolute must for travelers to Bulgaria, offering exquisite hiking possibilities. A trip across these mountainous wonders, a visit to the Complex Malyovitsa and the Rila Monastery, 74 miles from Sofia, are unforgettable. The monastery, founded in 927 as a colony of hermetic monks by Ivan Rilski, is best visited by bus. Other important sites include the 14th-century Cherepish Monastery, found in the Iskar Gorge on the way from Sofia to Vidin close to the Lakatnik rocks, approximately 35 kilometers from the capital city. Legend links the monastery with the battles of the last Bulgarian medieval tsar, Ivan Shishman, who clashed with the Turks.

Plovdiv

An ancient strategic trading hub on the Maritsa River serving early caravans that moved between Europe, Asia Minor, and Africa, Plovdiv today is Bulgaria's second largest city. The train station is an easy 10-minute walk from the Central Square and the historic old town. A visit to the Roman Forum and amphitheater is recommended, as are visits to the Djoumaya and Imaret Mosques. The Archeological Museum houses excellent exhibits of Tracian gold utensils, although some of the most famous pieces have been moved to Sofia.

Varna

Bulgaria's largest Black Sea port dominates summer life in the country. Dating back to the days of ancient Rome and Greece, this lively seaside resort city enjoys a colorful past. When the train connecting Varna to Ruse was completed in the 1860s, a direct trade route from the Danube to the Black Sea was created. Today the city offers excellent beaches, parks, street life, and restaurants. The center of the city can be reached on foot from the train station, and a convenient luggage storage office is located across the street. The celebrated summer hydrofoil service from Varna to Nesebar, Burgas, and Sozopol was shut down in 1993 for economic reasons, although a hydrobus still runs from Varna to Balchik.

Train travel to the coast is recommended, but bus travel up and down the coast between Varna and Burgas is the most convenient form of transportation. Nesebar, which can be reached by bus or taxi, hosts the ruins of thirteen churches dating back as early as the 9th century.

Burgas

Burgas, a beach resort on the Black Sea, is less crowded than Varna. The city's connection to the national train system via Plovdiv at the turn of the century accounts greatly for its growth. A bit too industrial for many vacationers' taste, Burgas still serves as a good seaside base for Black Sea exploration. The art gallery in the former synagogue is worth a visit. The old opera house, however, has been rented out as a car showroom, an indication of the realities of post-communist Bulgaria. Thirty-six kilometers north of Burgas is Bulgaria's largest tourist resort, Sunny Beach, which offers beaches, sailing, family restaurants, and baby-sitting services—perhaps a relaxing destination for families.

Ruse

Ruse is Bulgaria's leading port on the Danube River and a prime stopover for Russian river traffic, despite the air pollution. A daily train from Bucharest also arrives in Ruse, bringing with it hoards of Romanians and other visitors. Ruse is only a few kilometers from the longest steel bridge in Europe, ironically named the Friendship Bridge, which carries both car and train traffic and links Bulgaria and Romania. Train-lovers should plan on a visit to the Transportation Museum near the Danube—it was here that Bulgaria inaugurated its first train station, which was built in 1866.

Gorna Oryathovitsa

This town is important as a train junction and transit point that travelers often pass through on their Bulgarian journeys. Connection times often require long waits here despite your impression that you had a through ticket. Some smart travelers opt for a bus from Gorna to save time. The Sofia-Varna and Ruse–Veliko Tarnovo routes meet at Gorna.

Pleven

Famous for its battles between Turkish pashas and Russo-Romanian armies, Pleven is located between Ruse and Sofia and offers an authentic Bulgarian experience. Osman Pasha surrendered his sword to Tsar Alexandrer II of Russia here, and you can see the sword at the National Revival Park. The greatest advantages to Pleven are that it is less visited by travelers than other towns are and that its location is on the train route that follows the stunning Iskar Gorge. From Pleven, many spirited train travelers with an open ticket jump on the unreserved eight-hour Bucharest train in the middle of the night.

ONE-DAY EXCURSIONS

Sofia - Burgas - Sofia   1520

Dep. Sofia	06:30 (1)	07:05 (2)	10:15 (3)	12:30 (4)	14:15 (3)	16:00 (1)	22:45 (5)
Arr. Burgas	12:30	13:35	16:55	18:50	20:55	21:45	06:00

Sights in **Burgas**: A good beach resort.

Dep. Burgas	05:30 (1)	06:30 (3)	10:30 (4)	11:45 (3)	14:10 (4)	16:05 (1)	22:55 (5)
Arr. Sofia	09:45	13:21	16:57	18:21	21:03	22:03	06:10

(1) Reservation required. Restaurant car. (2) Reservation required. Light refreshments. (3) Restaurant car (4) Light refreshments. (5) Carries a sleeping cars and couchettes. Light refreshments.

Sofia - Plovdiv - Sofia   1540

Dep. Sofia	06:30 (1)	10:15 (2)	12:15 (3)	14:15 (3)	17:15 (4)
Arr. Plovdiv	08:32	12:31	14:31	16:31	19:19

Sights in **Plovdiv:** This city has been a commercial center for more than 2,000 years, serving the early caravans that moved between Europe, Asia and Africa. There are excellent exhibits of Thracian gold utensils in the Archaeological Museum. See the Bachkovo Monastery and, near it, the ruins of Tsar Ivan Asen II's fort. The Roman ruins. The Church of Constantine and Helena. The Turkish Imaret Djamiya.

Dep. Plovdiv	07:40 (4)	11:00 (2)	14:00 (3)	16:00 (2)	20:00 (1)
Arr. Sofia	09:40	13:21	16:21	18:21	22:03

(1) Reservation required. Restaurant car. (2) Restaurant car. (3) Light refreshments. (4) Reservation required. Light refreshments.

Sofia - Varna - Sofia   1520

Dep. Sofia	06:30 (1)	10:00 (2)	12:15 (3)	14:15 (1)	21:32 (4+5)
Arr. Varna	13:47	17:40	20:30	21:31	05:46

Sights in **Varna:** An ancient, lively and important seaport and a very popular beach resort.

See the relics of Greek, Roman, Byzantine, Turkish and Bulgarian eras in the Museum of Art and History (41 Boulevard Dimitar Blagoev), open daily except Monday 09:00–17:00 in summer, 10:00–17:00 in winter. Many museums and art galleries. The oldest gold ever found (from 3,500 years B.C.) is displayed there: jewelry and decorations from a burial site.

The Roman Bath. The cells and the chapel carved into the side of a chalk cliff at the 13th-century Aladzha Monastery in **Druzhba**, a few miles to the north. It is open daily except Monday 10:00–17:00.

During the summer, a hydrofoil service goes from Varna to Nesebar, Burgas and Sozopol. In **Nesebar** (a $7-U.S. taxi ride from Burgas), there are ruins of 13 churches dating back as early as the 9th century on this small islet at the end of a causeway. See the Church of John Aliturgetus and the 16th-century St. Stephen's Church.

Dep. Varna	06:00 (1)	08:10 (3)	10:45(2)	14:15 (1)	21:32 (6)
Arr. Sofia	13:12	16:21	18:25	21:35	05:46

(1) Reservation *required*. Restaurant car. (2) Restaurant car. (3) Light refreshments. (4) Carries a sleeping car. Light refreshments. (5) Plus another Sofia departure at 23:00 (6), arriving Varna 07:07. (5) Carries sleeping cars, couchettes and first- and second-class coaches.

INTERNATIONAL ROUTES
FROM BULGARIA

Sofia is the gateway for train travel to Yugoslavia (and on to Western Europe), Romania and Greece (and on to Turkey).

Sofia - Belgrade   1380

There is great mountain scenery on the Dragomagoman-Crveni Krst portion of this route.

Dep. Sofia	11:10 (1)	15:20 (2)	22:45 (3)
Set your watch back one hour			
Arr. Belgrade (Belgrade)	18:42	22:21	06:37

(1) Supplement charged. (2) Reservation required. Supplement charged. Restaurant car. (3) Supplement charged. Carries sleeping cars, couchettes and, first- and second-class coaches.

Sofia - Bucharest - **Kiev** or **St. Petersburg** or **Moscow**   94d

All of these trains have only sleeping cars. No coaches.

Dep. Sofia	21:25
Arr. Bucharest (Nord)	08:13 (1+2+3)
Arr. Kiev	14:42
Arr. St. Petersburg	-0-
Arr. Moscow (Kievski)	06:22

(1) Day 2. (2) Departs from Bucharest Baneasa. (3) Transfer in Bucharest for St. Petersburg; arrival 15:25 Day 3.

Sofia - **Athens** or **Istanbul**   97, 1550

Dep. Sofia	20:40	22:00	
Dep. Belgrade		19:15: (1)	Day 2
Arr. Athens	-0-	16:51	
Arr. Istanbul	08:30	-0-	

(1) Change trains in Belgrade and Thessaloniki.

COMMONWEALTH OF INDEPENDENT STATES

Getting on Track in the Commonwealth of Independent States

• Summer time: The Commonwealth changes to Summer Time the last Sunday of March and converts back to Standard Time on the last Sunday of September.

Overview of Commonwealth of Independent States' Trains

The CIS, the catch phrase replacing the former Soviet Union (FSU), has come to suggest many unclear notions in the minds of travelers. Few Westerners can name more than a few of the fifteen states, and travel beyond Moscow and St. Petersburg is still complicated and at times even surrealist. Train travel in Russia and the Ukraine as well as the Baltic States of Estonia, Latvia, and Lituania, however, has generally become far more accessible to western travelers since 1990. For political and cultural reasons, each country in this section of this guide has been listed separately, although in many cases the rail infrastructure of one small country is connected to that of another.

Most seasoned travelers agree that Russia and its related states present some of the most exciting train trips available today. Most also agree that the sensibilities of travelers never cease to be shocked when traveling in that region, and that mental preparation for the journey is required. One highly experienced world traveler reports that he could not remember even one moment of relaxation during his month-long trek from Paris to Tashkent via Moscow. Be ready for some wonderful experiences mixed with some trying and tiring moments of international survival.

As soon as you reach the eastern border of Poland, you are confronted with a major shift in aesthetics and functionality. When the train pulls into the station at Brest in Belarussia, it is lifted into the air and its wheels are changed to adapt to the wider Russian tracks. Walking underneath the train is a strange experience. At one border crossing, passengers are instructed to disembark while the train pulls onto a siding for a wheel change. Stay close by: it is often difficult to find the train again or to find the access to that siding. A garbled announcement shouts that the train will be leaving shortly, and hoards of panicked travelers push and scramble, jump onto the tracks to get to another platform, pass battered suitcases over their heads, and so on. Then, after surviving this pandemonium on the quai, you may find yourself in an Old World dining car drinking Bulgarian champagne and downing spoonfuls of red caviar for a whopping $2! Such is the charm of Russian train travel.

Lastly, one cannot generalize about trains in the CIS. They are all different, and they depend on everything from time of year, available equipment, mood of the conductor, exchange rates, weather, destination, application of laws, and luck.

General Rail Information

Children under five travel free. Half-fare for children between the ages five and nine. Reservations are usually required for all trains. In the case you do not have reservations but need to get on a train, it's up to you to negotiate with the conductor. Don't be too passive or quick to pay a lot, but definitely be sensitive to the fact that an extra $5 or $10 may represent a month's salary to the conductor.

There are two classes of train cars in the CIS. Soft Class is the upholstered seats which convert to bunks in four-berth compartments and Hard Class are plastic or fake leather seats which sometimes convert into bunks and sometimes do not. Bedding is available at an extra charge.

Sleeping cars are also available in two-berth compartments equipped with folding tables, a closet, and a speaker over which music and announcements come. Conductors on these trains serve tea from large samovars, one of the few features you can always count on.

Because the tracks in the CIS are five feet wide, passenger cars are roomy. Of course the change of wheels at the Polish border represents a delay, but you can't have everything.

One border crossing through the north of Poland on the way to the Baltic States is organized differently and instead of changing the wheels, passengers walk across the border and board an awaiting Lithuanian train.

Although the CIS has nine different time zones, all timetables indicate Moscow time only.

The topography of Uzbekistan is highly diverse. The southeast portion contains the foothills and valleys of the Tian Shan (Tien Shan) mountain range. The north central lowland portion is occupied by desert.

ARMENIA

The good news is that Armenia is a fantastically interesting country with a rich and diverse cultural heritage. The bad news is that Armenia is enduring a transportation and natural gas embargo that is causing severe food and medical shortages, frequent interruptions in electrical power, and shortages of transportation fuel. Internal travel, especially by air, may be disrupted by fuel shortages and other problems. Tourist facilities are not highly developed, and many of the goods and services taken for granted in other countries are not yet available, according to the United States State Department.

If you do go, remember that a visa is required. Without a visa, travelers cannot register at hotels and may be required to leave the country immediately via the route by which they entered.

Yerevan is the capital of Armenia. Since 1988, armed conflict has taken place in and around the enclave of Nagorno-Karabakh (located within Azerbaijan), and there is frequent shelling along many areas of the Armenian-Azerbaijani border. A cease-fire has been in effect since May 1994, though there have been some reports of minor violations.

Train transportation may be unreliable and uncomfortable. Train service to neighboring Georgia is subject to frequent disruptions and delays, and crime on board is an increasing problem.

AZERBAIJAN

• Tourist information: Embassy of the Republic of Azerbaijan, 917 15th Street, NW, Suite 700, Washington, DC 20005. Telephone (202) 842-0001, fax (202) 842-0004. E-mail: azerbaijan@mcimail.com. On the Web: http://ourworld.compuserve.com/homepages/azerbaijan.

Azerbaijan is located in southwestern Asia, between Armenia and Turkmenistan, bordering the Caspian Sea. With its capital in Baku, it is slightly larger than the state of Maine including the Nakhichevan Autonomous Republic and Nagorno-Karabakh, whose autonomy was abolished by the Azerbaijani Supreme Soviet in 1991. Azerbaijan borders with Armenia to the west, Georgia and Iran to the south, and Russia, Turkey, and the Caspian Sea to the east.

The country is ethnically dominated by Azeris and is predominantly Muslim. Its violent and long-standing disputes with ethnic Armenians of Nagorno-Karabakh and with the ethnic Azeri portion of Iran have not been resolved. Additionally, severe pollution problems have not helped encourage visitors to the region.

Azerbaijan is less developed industrially than either Armenia or Georgia, the other Transcaucasian states. It resembles the other Central Asian states in its majority Muslim population, high unemployment, and low standard of living. The country has more than 2,000 kilometers of railroad track, but connections with Europe are long and tiring.

BELARUS

• Tourist information: Embassy of Belarus, 1619 New Hampshire Ave NW, Washington, DC 20009. Telephone (202) 986-1606, fax (202) 986-1805. Or, Consulate General of Belarus, 708 3rd Avenue, Suite 1802, New York, NY 10017. Telephone (212) 682-5392, fax (212) 682-5491.

Located east of Poland, Belarus with its 10 million people is slightly smaller than the state of Kansas. It borders with Latvia, Lithuania, Poland, Russia, and the Ukraine, with Minsk as its capital. Its people speak primarily Byelorussian and belong to the Eastern Orthodox church.

Known for its cold winters, Belarus is flat and marshy. On April 26, 1986, Belarus was severely hit by the fallout of radioactive dust from the Chernobyl nuclear power plant. In December of 1991, with Russia and the Ukraine, Belarus formed the core of the CIS.

More modernized than other CIS states, Belarus has always served as a transport link for Russian oil exports to the Baltic states and eastern and western Europe. Train travelers to Moscow undoubtedly pass through Belarus and thus get a good glimpse of the state.

GEORGIA

• Tourist information: Embassy of Georgia, 1511 K St., Suite 424, Washington, DC 20005. Telephone (202) 393-5959, fax (202) 393-6060.
• Currency: Rouble (SUR). At press time, $1 equalled SUR 5811.00.

Located in southwestern Asia between Turkey and Russia, bordering the Black Sea, Georgia is slightly larger than the state of South Carolina. It borders Armenia, Azerbaijan, Russia, and Turkey. Georgia is a nation undergoing profound political and economic change. A newly independent nation, it is in the process of stabilizing its relations with neighboring countries.

Tourist facilities outside of the capital are not highly developed, and many of the goods and services taken for granted in other countries are not yet available. Travel, especially by air, may be disrupted by fuel shortages and other problems. The recent assassination attempt of Georgian speaker of parliament Eduard Shevardnadze hasn't helped to reassure tourists, who are eager to experience the otherwise calm Mediterranean-like Crimea.

Visitors who enter at the Tbilisi airport receive a temporary passport stamp and are instructed to obtain a visa from the Consular Division of the Ministry of Foreign Affairs. Travelers who have a valid multiple-entry visa from Armenia or Azerbaijan are not required to obtain a Georgian visa. Those arriving from or departing to other countries, including other former Soviet states, must obtain a Georgian visa in order to leave the country. On an exceptional basis, the Georgian Ministry of Foreign Affairs can assist travelers in obtaining visas at the checkpoint at Sarpi (on the border with Turkey) and at the port of Batumi on the Black Sea. Arrangements must be made *in advance* to issue a visa at one of these entry points.

Travel in the separatist-controlled Georgian autonomous Republic of Abkhazia remains hazardous. Since March 1995, there has been increased Abkhaz terrorist activity in southern Abkhazia and attacks on United Nations personnel in the Sukhumi and Gali districts of Abkhazia. In addition, land mines pose a threat to all travelers in Abkhazia. This should tell you enough about the prospects of enjoyable travel in the region. Also, the U.S. government does not recognize an independent republic of Abkhazia separate from the Republic of Georgia. For the time being, it is recommended that you choose other countries in which to rail around.

Another warning: high crime rates in south Ossetia make unofficial and unescorted travel there risky. All train and vehicular traffic is vulnerable to robbery. Please note that terrorist incidents have occurred in the country in connection with regional conflicts. Passenger trains traveling between Georgia and Armenia have been the targets of bombings.

Georgia currently has a cash-only economy, with the use of Russian ruble being banned in July 1993.

KAZAKHSTAN

• Tourist information: Embassy of Kazakhstan, 3421 Massachusetts Avenue, NW, Washington, DC 20007. Telephone (202) 333-4507, fax (202) 333-4509.
• Currency: Kazakhstan tenge (KTE). At press time, $1 equalled KTE 75.49.

Located in Central Asia, northwest of China, Kazakhstan is immense, nearly four times the size of Texas. It borders China, Kyrgyzstan, Russia, Turkmenistan, and Uzbekistan, as well as the Aral Sea and the Caspian Sea, whose international borders are not yet determined. The country has a population of more than 17 million, of which most are ethnically Kazakh and Russian, and equally split between Muslim and Russian Orthodox religions.

The capital is Almaty. Kazakhstan is so far from Moscow by train that, other than foreign travelers on their way to Beijing, the country is seldom a selected destination.

KYRGYZSTAN

Kyrgyzstan is a newly independent nation in a state of dramatic change. Do not take anything for granted if traveling to or through this region. The capital is Bishkek (formerly Frunze). Visas from Russia and neighboring Commonwealth of Independent States, except Georgia and Tajikistan, allow for temporary stays in Kyrgyzstan for up to three days.

With the breakup of Aeroflot into many small airlines, air travel in the former Soviet Union is often unreliable. Travelers must often cope with unpredictable schedules and difficult conditions, including poor quality of service and overloading. At present, no airline provides dependable, regularly scheduled international air service into Bishkek. Most international air travelers fly to Almaty and then travel overland (approximately three hours) to Bishkek.

Train travel in Central Asia is irregular and arduous. About four-fifths of Kyrgyzstan is mountainous. The mountains include the Tian Shan (Tien Shan) range, extending into the

Xinjiang (Sinkiang) region of northwestern China, the Kirghiz Mountains of north Kyrgyzstan, and the Alai range in the southwest. The highest elevation is Pobeda (Victory) Peak on the Chinese border (7,437 meters/24,400 feet).

Kyrgyzstan, like the other Central Asian countries, is a cash-only economy.

MOLDOVA

Moldova, according to the U.S. State Department Travelers Warning, is "a nation undergoing profound political and economic change. It is a newly independent nation still in the process of stabilizing its relations with neighboring countries. Tourist facilities are not highly developed, and many of the goods and services taken for granted in other countries are not yet available. Internal travel, especially by air, may be disrupted by fuel shortages and other problems."

Visas for travel to other former Soviet states are necessary and difficult to obtain in Moldova. The U.S. Embassy in Chisinau advises that only essential travel should be undertaken into or through the Transnistria region. There are frequent checkpoints in Transnistria that are manned by armed, young, inexperienced paramilitary units who are not under the control of the Moldovan government and whose members rarely understand English. Tourists and truckers may be subject to extortion or robbery at checkpoints.

Only Air Moldova and Tarom (Romania's national airline) regularly fly to Moldova. Air Moldova service is well below Western standards. Aircraft appear to be old and cabin areas are in poor condition. Train service is also below Western standards, and an increasing number of Americans have been victimized while traveling on international trains to and from Moldova.

Mumansk

The largest city in the world north of the Arctic Circle, Mumansk was founded in 1915 as a supply post in World War I. Used in World War II as Russia's principal port for receiving supplies from Britain and the United States, the city exudes historic exoticism beneath its current commercial fishing and ship repair industries.

RUSSIA

• Tourist information: Russian National Tourist Office, 800 Third Avenue, Suite 3101, New York, NY 10022. Telephone (212) 758-1162, fax (212) 758-0933. On the Web: http://www.russia-travel.com/.

• Public holidays: January 1, 7, March 8, May 1, 2, 9, June 12.

• Currency: Rouble (SUR). At press time, $1 equalled SUR 5811.00.

Russia has for many years been a land of mystery and intrigue to the people of the West. For hundreds of years it has been an enigma, friend, or enemy, as the political climate has shifted time and again. Since the dissolution of the Soviet Union, Russia has bounded in diverse and often contradictory directions socially, politically, culturally, and economically, making travel hard to predict yet extremely interesting.

Traveling to Russia by train has been an experience that more and more Westerners have indulged in, and most come back with fantastic stories and a will to return or venture deeper into this vast land. Most also come back with words of caution. Jody Jenkins and Gwen Strauss tell of a horrific journey by train from Moscow to Tashkent: a band of drunken nuclear submarine captains took over one compartment while Ghengis Khan look-alikes proceeded to shake down the most vulnerable travelers. American expatriate Jim Haynes, who has traveled throughout eastern Europe and has written five books, admits that the train south through Ukraine to Odessa and the Black Sea is the route that has peaked his imagination the most.

For first-time visitors to Russia, the train to Moscow and the Moscow–St. Petersburg route are wonderful initiations.

Due to the extraordinary political changes in Russia and changing attitudes in the United States, most sources of local information confirm loudly that it is now possible for individuals and companies to do business in Russia. Runaway inflation, however, is causing contact with local travelers to be tainted by an air of mercantilism. While there is relatively little inflation in dollar terms, inflation in ruble terms is terrifying. This situation has caused local hardship and is affecting the security of travel.

Russia is technically located in northern Asia between Europe and the North Pacific Ocean, although the area west of the Urals is sometimes considered to be Europe. Russia is the world's largest country and borders Azerbaijan, Belarus, China, Estonia, Finland, Georgia, Kazakhstan, North Korea, Latvia, Lithuania, Mongolia, Norway, Poland, and the Ukraine.

Pricilla Sharp is an experienced travel writer whose comments on trains appear regularly on-line in the Train Forum on Compuserve. She has traveled extensively on trains in Russia, Belarus, and a bit of Ukraine, specifically from Moscow to St. Petersburg, St. Petersburg to Minsk, Minsk to Gomel, Gomel to Kiev, Kiev to Moscow, and St. Petersburg to Archangel. She swears that the overnight trips are the best: "You must travel first class, and it is preferable to buy all four tickets in the compartment to ensure privacy, especially on the 'overnighters.' The trains are well-worn, creaky monstrosities. For example, on the Kiev–Moscow train, our compartment was directly over the wheels, which groaned, clanked, crunched, and made various other loud noises all night long! There is no air conditioning in summer, but the only time I was uncomfortable was on the 'local' three-hour Minsk to Gomel. There were forest fires all the way (thus, unfortunately, stirring up the radioactivity which had settled in the area from Chernobyl) and the heat was unbearable. The windows in the compartments rarely open, but the windows in the hallways do."

Pricilla also states that the bathrooms are uniformly filthy. There is nothing you can do about it except do *not* sit down. Russians will very often stand on the toilet seat and squat, thus, in her words, adding boot mud to the mixture. "Whenever I travel in Russia I always bring my own toilet paper—at least one and a half rolls per week! And, don't laugh, but I always wear long skirts when riding on trains. It's much cleaner and easier to pull something *up* around my neck than *down* toward that filthy floor!" Successful train travel in difficult places relies on the sharing of practical information like Pricilla's.

"Edible food is almost nonexistent. I always pack my own: sausages, bread, cheese, hard-boiled eggs, peanut butter, etc. We always bring our own single-pack coffee bags and just ask for hot water, which is provided by the train attendant from a huge samovar that's constantly kept boiling hot in each car. Actually, the tea is always very good, if you prefer tea. Whenever the train stops, there are usually vendors at the stations who come and offer vegetables, pirogis (little popovers of meat and bread), cookies, and the like. On the overnight trains, such as one from Moscow to St. Petersburg, you won't need any food because the train arrives at about 07:00 in St. Petersburg."

When in Moscow and in need of reliable train or other travel information, try contacting the Travelers Guest House at 50 Bolshaya Pereyaslavskaya, 10th Floor, Moscow, Russia 129401; Tel. (7095) 971-4059, 280-8562; Fax (7095) 280-7686. The Travelers Guest House is very close to the downtown area, including Red Square and the Kremlin. It would take approximately 20 minutes to get there from the closest metro station and only a few stops on the metro.

IRO Travel, an American owned and managed agency, can help in issuing train tickets, visas, and invitation letters when needed.

The Europe Library of The Travel Forum on Compuserve stores a healthy supply of relevant rail information. Here is more on the various Trans-Siberian options.

Scantours, Inc. can arrange point-to-point rail travel in Russia. Contact them at 3439 Wade Street, Los Angeles, CA 90066-1533, (800) 223-7226, (310) 636-4656, fax (310) 390-0493 or E-mail: scantours@earthlink.net.

For more information about traveling in Russia, call Intourist, (212) 757-3884.

Moscow

Start at the Kremlin, the Grand Kremlin Palace, or Red Square, and satisfy the great mythical draw of this international landmark. Closed on Thursdays. Red Square, with Lenin's Mausoleum, is open daily except Monday and Friday.

The Cathedral of Saint Basil the Blessed has become a symbol of Russia to those in the West. This colorful 16th-century church sits on the north side of the Kremlin. Interestingly, Red Square is not named for the red bricks which pave it, but for the Russian word meaning beautiful, literally "Beautiful Square."

On a sunny fall afternoon Red Square is crowded with families, tourists, and vendors selling stacking dolls, shish kebab, and other small goods. The prices here, as in any area in the world frequented by tourists, will be higher than elsewhere. If you have the time, the best place to do your souvenir shopping is at Izmailovsky Park. Here there is a large flea market with hundreds of vendors selling everything under the sun. It is open on weekends only.

The south side of Red Square is bounded by Lenin's tomb (now closed to the public) and the wall of the Kremlin. The church above has beautiful bells which are rung on weekends and other times. It is well worth the time to soak in the sites and sounds of Red Square on a sunny day. Weekends are best as there are few official events. Remember that the Kremlin is the seat of government, so during the week Red Square may be closed when officials or visiting dignitaries are arriving and leaving. Try to visit at night. The buildings are caught in strong spotlights and the scene is filled with magic.

The south side of Red Square is the north side of the Kremlin, a 13th-century fortress that's surrounded by a high brick wall and many towers. Most of the towers are still crowned with illuminated red stars. It is not impossible to visit the inside of the Kremlin during some days and hours, but you should ask your Russian hosts to help set this up.

Americans and others who visit Russia for the first time will be amazed at how expensive it is. A quality hotel room will cost from $100 to $300 per night. Restaurant meals are on par with those in New York in cost, but not necessarily in quality. A taxi ride is similar in cost to those in any major city. While there are dispatched taxis, most any private car headed in your direction will give you a ride for a small fee. Hailing a taxi in Moscow rarely takes more than 30 seconds on a busy street, which is far from the reality of St. Petersburg! Agree on the fee ahead of time, and if at all possible have a Russian do the talking and negotiate the price.

Moscow has the world's busiest metro (subway) system. It carries nearly four billion people each year. There are many English newspapers and maps available—most of them are free and will have a metro map in them.

Russian cultural performances and exhibitions are truly world class. Pick up a copy of the *Moscow Times* for listings. Tickets for most events are very reasonable.

In Moscow, don't miss the Tretyakov Gallery, which just reopened after several years of renovations. Another important cultural insight is the Orthodox church. Try to stop by a functioning church. If a service is going on, don't be intimidated—services are long and most Russians don't stay for the whole thing. Orthodox church music is unbelievably beautiful.

Also see the Uspensky, Blagoveshchensky, and Archangelsky cathedrals, which date to the 15th century. The priceless jewelry, costumes, gold and silver objects, Fabergé eggs, and weapons located in the Armory Museum will impress you. Don't miss the 16th-century 38-ton canon, Czar Pushka. The weekend bird market on Kalitnikovskaya Street is highly original. The Bolshoi Theater should be attended if possible, as well as the Lenin State Library and Lenin Museum. For public art deco, make sure you pass through the Komsololskaya, Ploshchad, Revutsi, Kropotkinskay, and Mayakovskaya metro stations.

In Moscow, there are culinary alternatives to the bland hotel food, the incredibly expensive western hotel food, and McDonald's and Pizza Hut. Georgian food comes highly recommended. Watch out the beautiful bowl of fruit on your table trick. If you want a reasonably priced meal, *don't eat the fruit*—your pocketbook will regret it.

Fun weekend things to do in Moscow include the Ismailovsky Park flea market. Russian handicrafts, souvenirs, etc., for cheap prices. Haggle. Good stuff, much cheaper than in shops. If you buy lacquered boxes, make sure they're painted, not decoupaged—a common trick.

Note that Moscow has *nine* major railroad stations:

> Byelorussia—trips to Warsaw and on to western Europe
> Kazanski—trips to Tashkent and Samarkand
> Kievski—trips to Kiev and Eastern Europe
> Kurski—trips to Sochi and the Caspian Sea
> Leningradski—trips to St. Petersburg and on to Helsinki
> Paveletski—check *Thomas Cook* timetables
> Riga—trips to Riga and the Baltic States
> Savelovski—check *Thomas Cook* timetables
> Yaroslavski—trips to Siberia, Central Asia, and Beijing

LONG-DISTANCE TRIPS
FROM MOSCOW

Here are schedules for rail trips from Moscow to nine interesting cities, with notes on what to see at each destination.

Moscow - Kiev   and v.v. 1740

The following trains are ones we recommend.

Dep. Moscow (Kiev.)	09:17 (1)	10:01 (1)	12:16 (1)	13:32 (1)	15:14 (1)	16:15 (2)
Arr. Kiev	01:50	01:12	03:05	03:49	06:12	06:55

Sights in **Kiev:** See notes about sightseeing in Kiev under "St. Petersburg–Kiev"

Dep. Kiev	04:38 (2)	11:22 (1)	11:42 (1)	12:15 (1)	17:00 (1)	18:49 (1)
Arr. Moscow (Kiev.)	20:06	04:47	04:20	05:39	09:05	10:09

(1) Restaurant car. (2) Light refreshments.

Moscow - St. Petersburg   and v.v. 1900

Dep. Moscow (St. P.)	01:00	01:52	12:27	17:20	20:35
Arr. St. Petersburg (Mos.)	10:07	11:10	20:50	23:09	04:50

Dep. St. Petersburg (Mos)	12:15	15:58	20:20	21:55	23:59
Arr. Moscow (St. P)	07:06	21:43	05:15	06:00	08:30

Moscow - Riga   and v.v. 1830

Dep. Moscow (Riga)	20:00	21:16
Arr. Riga	10:53	12:25

Sights in **Riga:** An important Baltic seaport. See the great pipe organ at the 13th–15th-century cathedral. The 14th-century Riga Castle.

Dep. Riga	16:30	18:40
Arr. Moscow (Riga)	09:03	12:01

Moscow - Sochi - Sukhumi and v.v. 5025 (Cook Overseas Timetable)

Dep. Moscow (Kurski)	14:09 (1)	23:32 (2)
Arr. Sochi	05:30 (3)	13:42 (3)

• • •

Dep Sochi	02:36	08:06	16:36 (1)
Arr. Moscow (Kurski)	15:50 (3)	23:53 (3)	08:53 (3)

(1) Carries first-class sleepers and first- and second-class coaches. Restaurant car. (2) Second class only. (3) Day 2.

Sights in **Sochi:** A popular Black Sea resort. Over 800 species of trees at the Dendrarium. Scenic Lake Ritsa is a five-hour bus trip away.

    Sights in **Sukhumi**: This is the heart of Russia's subtropical area: citrus fruits, tobacco, etc. See the monkey farm used by Russian scientists in their program of studying human behavior.

Moscow - Tashkent - Samarkand and v.v. 5031, 5133 (Cook Overseas Timetable)

5031

Dep. Moscow (Kaz.)	23:54 (1)	01:04 (1)
Arr. Tashkent	11:45 (2)	17:40 (2)
Change trains 5133		
Dep. Tashkent	16:50 (1)	18:00 (3)
Arr. Samarkand	22:38	00:03

• • •

5133

Dep. Samarkand	16:16 (3)	01:26 (1)
Arr. Tashkent	22:10	07:10
Change trains 5031		
Dep. Tashkent	06:50	02:03 (1)
Arr. Moscow (Kaz)	09:05	03:15

(1) Has first- and second-class coaches. Restaurant car. (2) Day 4 from Moscow. (3) Has first-class sleepers and second-class coaches. Restaurant car.

Sights in **Tashkent**: This has been an important center of trade and handicraft on the major caravan route (the "silk road") between Europe and China and India for nearly 2,000 years. There are many 15th and 16th-century churches. Heavy Muslim cultural influence here.

See: The Academy of Sciences. The Navoi Public Library. The Navoi Theater of Opera and Ballet.

Sights in **Samarkand:** One of the oldest cities in Central Asia. Alexander the Great captured Samarkand 2300 years ago. Heavy Turkish cultural influence here since the 6th century. Uninhabited from 1720 to 1770 due to an economic decline at that time caused by constant attacks by nomad tribes. The inception of train service in 1896 revived the city. See the enormous colored domes of the 14th-century mausoleums, decorated in marble and gold. The 14th-century mosque. The ruins of a 16th-century aqueduct.

Moscow - Volgograd - Rostov　— 　Rostov - Moscow　5030, 5085 (Cook Overseas Timetable)

Here is a great combination train and boat trip: a circle, from Moscow to Volgograd by train, and from Volgograd to Rostov by ship on the Volga–Don Canal. Then, return to Moscow by train.

5030

Dep. Moscow (Pav.)	14:10 (1)	18:47 (2)	23:47 (3)	02:05 (3)
Arr. Volgograd	09:56	15:00	23:59	06:35

(1) Carries first-class sleepers and second-class coaches. Restaurant car. (2) First- and second-class coaches. Restaurant car. (3) Second-class coaches. Restaurant car.

Change to a ship for the Volgograd–Rostov cruise. Check Intourist for current Volga–Don Canal cruise timetables. The complete 2,000-mile ship trip runs from Moscow to Rostov. Change to a train in Rostov.

5085

Dep. Rostov	Frequent times from 04:02 to 20:18
Arr. Moscow (Kur.)	22 hours later

Sights in **Volgograd:** Renamed (from Stalingrad) after being destroyed during a seven-month battle in 1942–43. See: The enormous 63-mile canal. The huge industrial complex, particularly the Tractor Factory. But, most of all, the Soviet Union's Eternal Flame, memorial to their millions of World War II dead, in the Hall of Valor. All of those names are carved in its walls.

Sights in **Rostov:** Another post-World War II metropolis based on heavy industrial manufacturing. See the enormous theater on Teatralnaya Square. Window-shop Engels St.

Here is the reverse route for this circle trip:

5085

Dep. Moscow (Kur.)	Frequent times from 00:25 to 23:32
Arr. Rostov	22 hours later

Change to a ship for the Rostov-Volgograd cruise. Check Intourist for current Don Canal-Volga cruise timetables. Change to a train in Volgograd.

5030

Dep. Volgograd	14:30 (1)	18:25 (2)	19:40 (3)
Arr. Moscow (Pav.)	10:30	14:30	18:15

Trans-Siberian Express   (Cook's Table 1990)

1. The *Trans-Mongolian* (Chinese train #4) leaves Moscow every Tuesday at 19:53. This train takes you via Ulan Bator, Mongolia, and after 7,885 kilometers you arrive in Beijing on Monday at 15:33 on the seventh day.

2. The *Trans-Manchurian* (Russian train #20) leaves Moscow every Friday at 20:15. This train takes you through Manzhouli and Harbin, and after 9,001 kilometers and eight days you arrive in Beijing on Friday at 06:32.

3. The *Trans-Siberian to Vladivostok (train #2: The Russia Express)* leaves Moscow every odd day at 14:15. This train travels straight through Siberia, and after 9296 kilometers and eight days, you arrive at Vladivostok at 02:40 local time.

Here are some options for breaking up the trip to Beijing. These trips can be arranged through most travel agencies.

1. To *Beijing with stop in Irkutsk for four days and Mongolia for four days (3/3 days in winter)*. This highly popular trip allows you to see and enjoy both Irkutsk and Mongolia to their fullest. You will stop in Irkutsk and Lake Baykal (often spelled Baikal) for a total of four days and three nights.

2. *To Beijing with 1 day/1 night stop in Irkutsk and Ulan Bator.* This quick stopover option lets you get a feel for Irkutsk with maximum freedom to do it on your own.

3. *To Beijing with stop in Irkutsk for 4 days/4 nights.* You will stay in both Irkutsk and in the village of Listvyanka, right on the shores of Lake Baykal. At least one full day is spent sightseeing in Irkutsk and visiting two or three museums and churches throughout the city. Part of the tour is spent at Lake Baykal, where you will be shown the Lymnological Institute and Museum of Wooden Architecture. You'll have plenty of free time to enjoy an exciting view of Baykal Lake and its shores. Packages are available that include all meals, guides, and transfers. You will stay in either a hotel or with a family (one to two people in a room) in Irkutsk. Accommodation in Listvyanka is a typical Siberian wooden house for at least one night.

4. *Stop in Mongolia for 3 days/3 nights or 5 days/5 nights.* Minimum two nights will be spent in a traditional Mongolian Ger (*yurt*) in a camp at Terelj (70 kilometers outside of Ulan Bator) in the beautiful Mongolian countryside, which features vast grasslands, rugged hills, and horses running free. On the remaining nights you will stay at a hotel in Ulan Bator (either the Negdelchin or Zul).

Safety Tips on Traveling in Russia

One travel writer, Kathryn Coombs, offers these practical tips that all train travelers should take to heart.

If you take the train from St. Petersburg to Moscow, take a bicycle lock and one of those flexible wire "chain" things that you wind through the spokes of your bike. There have been a lot of robberies/attacks on the trains. If you loop this through the door handle of your compartment, then attach it to the luggage rack, the bad guys can't get in. When you leave the compartment for any reason during the day, chain your luggage to the luggage rack with this. And lock the luggage. Bring train munchies (all the Russians do), it's a long trip and all they offer you is endless tea. There is a big samovar (hot water boiler) on the train, so pot noodles are a good idea.

Do not drink the water in St. Petersburg. It is contaminated with an intestinal parasite that you'll have trouble getting rid of. Drink bottled water and brush your teeth in bottled water. If you take baths instead of showers, bring water purification tablets with you and drop a few in the bath and wait about 10 minutes (follow directions on package) before you get in. These parasites can enter you through either end (yuck!). This happened to a friend of mine.

Moscow water is generally safe to drink if boiled first, unlike St. Pete's, but do use water purification tablets there as well. It's all right to shower. The way to avoid getting mugged is to avoid looking obviously foreign or rich. Leave your fancy jewelry at home.

Don't wear clothes that scream out "I am an American tourist" (if you're not American, sorry for presuming). This means no plaid trousers or bright preppy greens. Do not sling your camera around your neck. Most Russians carry some kind of shoulder bag with them—as they tend to do shopping on the way home from work. Find a camera bag that doesn't look like a camera bag, and you'll blend in.

Hang around with a Russian guide whenever you can. There are good people you can hire for the whole day, or your whole stay in a city, who are cheap. They will add to your enjoyment and understanding and increase your safety, helping you blend in.

Regarding arrival at Sheremetyevo Airport, make sure your travel agent arranges your airport transport in advance. The taxi drivers that congregate in the international terminal are real sharks (will charge you as much as $100 to get to town, whereas you can book a cab in advance for about $40). Most of these sharks are safe at least, but some are not, and you never know.

Watch out for "gypsy" kids—there have been some recent problems. An elderly Canadian gentleman was mugged in front of the Moskva Hotel and beaten by eight-year-old kids. They tend to hang around the less expensive tourist hotels. Often they will pretend to be begging, or trying to sell you something (postcards, usually) with the idea that when you open your wallet, ZAP! Sadly, the best policy is to avoid giving to begging children, many of whom have been put up to it by their parents. However, the metros are full of begging grannies and disabled veterans. *Always* give to them if you can—consider it reparations for winning the cold war. These pensioners are trying to live on $9 a month and are some of the nicest people you'll meet. Grannies (babuski) are the victims of crimes, not the perpetrators, so you're safe here.

Try to keep your spending money (for ice cream, beggars, small purchases, etc.) separate from your main stash of cash, to avoid flashing large wads of bills around. Sensible advice in any big city.

You will be less conspicuous if you are not in a huge group of foreigners. If you stray off the beaten track, keep to small groups of, say, four people, and have your Russian guide with you.

Watch your property when you're in restaurants—a new trick is "kidnapping" property. If they think you're a foreign businessperson, they might take your papers—worthless to anyone but you—and then send a representative to negotiate your payment to get them back. This happened when I had escorted a group to dinner at the Minsk Restaurant on Tverskaya Street, where an Azeri gang hangs out. When I had checked out the restaurant the night before, everything was OK, but I was with a group of Russians and they thought I was Russian.

Get cholera and diptheria shots before you go, just to make sure. Outbreaks in Moscow/St. Petersburg have been only a few cases, and the risk is minimal, but its best to make sure, just in case, particularly if you are older. If you have any medical problems while you are there, the place to go is the American Medical Center (takes credit cards)—all hotels know how to find number. Also, State Department travel advisory bulletins are worth getting for any country you're visiting. You can access these via Compuserve.

Trans-Siberian Express: Moscow to Vladivostok

Nothing excites the imagination more than a train ride for six days across the former Soviet Union. Six days on a train. Thoughts of Pasternak's *Doctor Zhivago* rush to mind. Heading west, the train leaves Vladivostock station at midnight. Vladivostock, rich in natural resources and labeled the Seattle of Russia, has emerged in the mid-1990s as a wild town of gangsters and street warfare. Most people get on in Moscow, but the few who manage to take the train in the other direction have a particularly pure experience, especially for the first half of the trip, when very few foreigners are on board. The problem many have with the Moscow-Vladivostock run is getting back. It's easier to continue east to Japan and fly from there. One American couple recently shared their westbound journey on Compuserve's Train Forum and some of their impressions have been incorporated here.

The Trans-Siberian Express across the nation is the longest single train ride in the world. Curiously, the entire journey is quoted in Moscow time—stops, meals, everything —even though the capital can be as much as six days away.

As is true on all long voyages in the CIS, it is advised that you bring your own food, and plenty of it. Food in varying degrees of quantity and quality is always attainable, but the negotiations and "backshish" needed to come by it is too unreliable and tiring to make the effort worth it.

The route traveled covers just under 6,000 miles: from the Pacific coast along the Amur River, across the Siberian taiga, by Lake Baykal (the biggest freshwater lake in the world), through industrial towns such as Sverdlovsk (now renamed Ekaterinberg), past enormous coal fields, over the Urals (the great Europe/Asia divide) and between huge wheat fields.

"Over the six days of the journey, we must have spent more than forty hours propped in the corridor staring out of the window. And the views? Well, interesting, but not spectacular. Or rather, we expected more. But the memories will be of the people, not the views. We had come prepared with a library of books to stave off boredom. We read Eric Newby's *Big Red Train Ride*—his account of the Trans-Siberian Railway from Moscow to the east—which was excellent read backwards. Apart from that we hardly dipped into any of the books. Time—perhaps not the train itself—certainly flew by.

Surprisingly, some of the most attractive scenery on the whole journey was on the outskirts of Moscow. As we came into the area called the Golden Triangle, we could see in the distance golden spires glowing in the sunset; we were passing through green fields and forests and then suddenly we were in Moscow. After six days, across seven time zones, in a country that seemed to be falling apart at the seams, the train pulled into Yaroslavl Station ten minutes late."

The Moscow-Khabarovsk-Yokohama route of the Trans-Siberian Express is much like the above the journey, except it is advisable to stop over in Novosibirsk and Irkutsk on the 5300 mile trip.

Czar Nicholas officiated at the ceremony in Vladivostock when construction of the line began in 1891. Six separate sections were developed independently. Prisoners sent to Siberia were offered reduced sentences for working on the construction; eight months of work reduced a sentence by one year. By 1900 two unconnected sections had been completed: Moscow–Sretensk (east of Lake Baykal) and Khabarovsk–Vladivostock. Passengers traveled from Sretensk to Khabarovsk by river boat.

A line from Lake Baykal to Khabarovsk (the Chinese Eastern Railway, via Manchuria) was completed in 1903 and was much shorter than the present line. Russia lost it one year later, after the 1904 Russo-Japanese War, and had to begin building the present line from Baykal to Khabarovsk. Twelve years later the present Moscow–Vladivostock line, entirely on Russian territory, was completed and Russia began to develop Siberia.

Moscow - Khabarovsk - Yokohama and v.v. 1990, 5020, 5050
Cook Overseas Timetable

It is necessary to check 1998 sailing dates of the Nakhodka–Yokohama (and v.v.) ships before determining dates on which to reserve Moscow or Nakhodka train departures.

1990 (*Train*)		
Dep. Moscow		
(Yar.)	14:15 (1)	
Arr. Novosibirsk	16:56	Day 3
Arr. Irkutsk	01:38	Day 5
Arr. Khabarovsk	13:12	Day 7
Change trains 5020		
Dep. Khabarovsk	08:10 (2)	
Arr. Nakhodka	04:00 (3)	Day 8
Change to boat 5050		
Dep. Nakhodka	12:00 (4)	Day 8
Arr. Yokohama	15:00	Day 10

5050 (*Boat*)		
Dep. Yokohama	12:00 (4)	
Arr. Nakhodka	17:00	Day 3
Change to train 5020		
Dep. Nakhodka	12:50 (2+3)	Day 3
Arr. Khabarovsk	05:12 (2)	Day 4
Change trains 1990		
Dep. Khabarovsk	07:48 (1+2)	Day 4
Arr. Irkutsk	20:03	Day 6
Arr. Novosibirsk	04:12 (2)	Day 7
Arr. Moscow (Yar.)	06:30	Day 10

(1) Carries a first-class sleeping car. Also has second-class coaches with seats that convert to berths. Restaurant car. (2) Local time (7 hours later than Moscow). Runs only on days prior to sailings from Nakhodka to Yokohama. Carries a sleeping car. Also has second-class coaches that convert to berths. Restaurant (3) Estimate. Schedule information unavailable at press time. (4) For specific sailing dates, check Far Eastern Shipping Co.

Sights in **Novosibirsk**: The Theater of Opera and Ballet, which is larger than Moscow's Bolshoi Theater. Take the 18-mile bus ride to **Akademgorodok**, the "Science Town," located along the Ob Sea, a man-made reservoir. There, top Soviet scientists and technicians live, work and shop in the USSR's most modern apartments, office buildings and stores.

Sights in **Irkutsk**: A large industrial city with no major tourist attraction. However, Irkutsk is the gateway for visiting the most unique place in the Soviet Union: **Lake Baykal**. Buses take tourists through a virgin forest to the shore of the world's deepest (6,365 feet) lake, 380 miles long and 12 to 50 miles wide, containing one-fifth of the fresh water on the earth's surface (four-fifths of the fresh water in Russia). Its waves sometimes measure over 15 feet.

Formed nearly 30,000,000 years ago by a rupture in the earth's crust, it is fed by 336 rivers and streams. There are 1,800 species of animals and plants in the lake. About three-quarters of them are found nowhere else in the world.

The day-trip includes a stop at the Limnological Museum, where hundreds of local flora and fauna are exhibited. The excursion to Baykal ends with a 90-minute hydrofoil ride from the Museum, up the **Angara River**, to Irkutsk.

Sights in **Khabarovsk**: Named after Yerofei Khabarov, a Slavak Daniel Boone who led a Cossack expedition to explore this area in the 17th century. Khabarovsk was first settled in 1858 by a handful of people living in tents along the banks of the **Amur River.**

When the Bolsheviks came into power in 1917, Khabarovsk was too far from Moscow for the embryonic Soviet regime to defend it, and the city was grabbed by Manchuria. Soviet rule here was re-established in 1922. By then, the old Khabarovsk had been reduced to ruins by the Manchurians. The city that exists today was started from scratch in 1922.

Its commercial air connections with Japan make Khabarovsk the eastern gateway to the Soviet Union. Japanese tourism to Moscow and Leningrad begins and ends in Khabarovsk. The city is so geared to Japanese tourism and has so little tourism from elsewhere that several of its tourist brochures are printed only in the Japanese language.

There is a good museum here, with exhibits on the natural and political history of this area. The many 19th-century wood and brick buildings are interesting. River boat excursions depart hourly from a dock that is across the park from the Intourist Hotel (one of the best hotels in Russia). **Vladivostok**, a major naval and long-range missile base, was opened to tourists in 1991 for the first time since the 1917 revolution.

Moscow - Khabarovsk - Yokohama   and v.v.   1990

This is the eastward route of the Trans-Siberian Express.

It is advisable to stopover in Novosibirsk (population 1,500,000) and Irkutsk on the

7½-day 5,301-mile-long Moscow–Khabarovsk trip. The Hotel Novosibirsk used to have better accommodations than were available in either Irkutsk or Khabarovsk. It is always recommended to bring toilet paper and soap when traveling on Soviet trains, including the Trans-Siberian Express.

The times shown here are Moscow Time, considerably different than actual arrival and departure times as this 5,777-mile route covers eight time zones.

For example, the real arrival time in Khabarovsk and Vladivostock is seven hours *later* than the Moscow Time listed. Also the real departure time from Vladivostock and Khabarovsk (for the westward trip to Moscow) is seven hours *earlier* than indicated.

The number of travel days is represented by capital letters: B = Day 2, C = Day 3 etc.

Moscow - Khabarovsk - Vladivostock and v.v. 5020 (Overseas Timetable)

Dep. Moscow (Yar.)	09:40 (1)	14:15 (1)
Dep. Kirov	01:55 B	05:36 B
Dep. Ekaterinberg	16:58	19:56
Dep. Omsk	05:26 C	08:09 C
Dep. Novosibirsk	15:25	17:10
Dep. Krasnoyarsk	04:58 D	06:19 D
Dep. Irkutsk	00:42 E	01:19 E
Dep. Ulan Ude	08:30	09:00
Dep. Chita	18:06	18:32
Dep. Skovorodino	17:21 F	16:26 F
Arr. Khabarovsk	15:42	13:35
Arr. Vladivostock	05:57 H	02:40 H
	• • •	
Dep. Vladivostock	05:35 (1)	17:55 (1)
Dep. Khabarovsk	22:26	07:48 B
Dep. Belogorsk	06:09 B	19:00
Dep. Skovorodino	10:08	03:48 C
Dep. Chita	17:27 D	02:19 D
Dep. Ulan Ude	02:53	11:55
Dep. Irkutsk	10:40 E	20:04 E
Dep. Krasnoyarsk	03:10 F	15:03
Dep. Novosibirsk	18:09	04:12
Dep. Omsk	03:12 G	13:12 F
Dep. Ekaterinberg	15:42	01:47 G
Dep. Kirov	05:42 H	15:18
Arr. Moscow (Yar.)	21:05	06:30 H

---

(1) Has second-class coaches with seats that convert to berths.

St. Petersburg

Many travelers consider St. Petersburg, formerly Leningrad, the most beautiful and stimulating city in the CIS. The Hermitage Museum, alone, with its 2.5 million works of art could keep you hostage for days. Don't miss the Summer Palace, and of course the 112 columns and gold cupolas at St. Isaac's Cathedral. The 600-ton Alexandrovskaya Column marking Russia's victory over Napoleon, the Summer Gardens of Peter the Great, and the Monument to the Heroes of the Revolution should not be overlooked. Nor should the excursion to the magnificent Yekaterinsky Palace in Pushkin be forgotten. In the summer, take a hydrofoil cruise on the River Neva.

Do not miss Tsarskoye Selo, just outside of town. A former Royal Palace turned into a school, there are entire rooms of malachite walls and columns. It is breathtaking.

The St. Petersburg metro operates from 05:30 to 00:30. Unless you really want massive intimate contact with the Russian people, try to avoid traveling during the peak commuter hours. Note that the doors in the stations weigh a ton and swing back and forth with the force of a wrecking ball.

Tickets for the two trains to Helsinki from St. Petersburg can be bought right in St. Petersburg.

LONG-DISTANCE TRIPS FROM ST. PETERSBURG

Here are schedules for rail trips from St. Petersburg to five other interesting cities, with notes on what to see at each destination.

St. Petersburg (Leningrad)

The Commonwealth's most interesting city. The Hermitage Museum (closed Monday) has the world's largest exhibition of fine arts, over 2,500,000 articles. Visit the Summer Palace (open daily except Tuesday, May through November). See the 112 columns, gold cupola and priceless paintings and mosaics at St. Isaac's Cathedral (closed Tuesday, Wednesday and the last Monday of each month).

The park and palace at Petrodvorets. The Winter Palace. The 600-ton, 154-foot-high Alexandrovskaya Column, marking Russia's victory over Napoleon. The Peter-Paul Fortress and cathedral. The summer gardens of Peter the Great. The Museum of the History of Religion and Atheism, in Kazansky Cathedral (closed Wednesday).

The Monument to the Heroes of the Revolution, in the Field of Mars. The Central Museum, at the Marble Palace. The State Museum of the History of St. Petersburg (closed Wednesday). The State Museum of Russian Art, in Mikhailovsky Palace (closed Tuesday). The Arctic and Antarctic Museum (closed Monday and Tuesday).

In the Kunstkammer, the Peter the Great Museum of Anthropology and Ethnography and the Lomonosov Museum (closed Friday and Saturday). Visit the botanical garden and nearby museum (the museum open only Wed., Sat. and Sun.). There's also a railway museum in the area.

Take an excursion to **Pushkin** to see the magnificent Yekaterinsky Palace (closed Tuesday and the last Monday of each month). In the summer, hydrofoils cruise the **River Neva.**

St. Petersburg - Kiev   and v.v. 1920

Dep. St. P. (Viteb.)	13:30 (1)	17:53 (1)	Dep. Kiev	08:00 (1)	23:00 (1)
Arr. Kiev	19:47 (2)	18:42 (2)	Arr. St. P. (Viteb.)	11:30 (2)	08:48 (3)

(1) Restaurant car. (2) Day 2. (3) Day 3.

Sights in **Kiev:** The 11th-century catacombs at the Pecherskaya Lavra Monastery. The frescos and mosaics at the 11th-century St. Sophia Cathedral. The Golden Gate (Zolotiya Vorota) at the intersection of Sverlovskaya and Vladimirskaya. The Museum of Russian Art. The Museum of Western and Oriental Art.

Below are schedules for continuing on from Kiev to Odessa:

Kiev - Odessa   and v.v.   1750

The coaches on all of these trains are second-class only.

Dep. Kiev	03:20 (1)	11:08 (1+3)	Dep. Odessa	11:22 (1)	21:00 (4)
Arr. Odessa	14:35	22:30	Arr. Kiev	23:03	09:19 (2)

(1) Restaurant car. (2) Light refreshments. (3) Plus another Kiev departure at 19:52, arriving Odessa 08:08. (4) Plus another Odessa departure at 22:31 (1), arriving Kiev 11:06.

Sights in **Odessa**: A sea resort and Russia's largest port. See the beautiful Opera and Ballet Theater. The Potemkin Stairway, descending 455 feet from Primorsky Boulevard to the waterfront.

St. Petersburg - Moscow   1900

Dep. St. Petersburg (Mos.)	00:35	13:05	15:58	20:20	21:55
Arr. Moscow (Len.)	10:03	21:55	21:43	05:15	06:00
Dep. St. Petersburg (Mos.)	22:30	22:45	23:10	23:33	23:55
Arr. Moscow (Len.)	06:45	07:10	07:15	07:45	08:25

St. Petersburg - Murmansk   and v.v. 1915

Murmansk is the world's northernmost passenger rail terminus.

All of these trains have a restaurant car and arrive on Day 2, unless designated otherwise.

Dep. St. Petersburg (Moskovski)	14:25	17:35
Arr. Murmansk	19:20	22:20

Sights in **Murmansk**: The largest city in the world north of the Arctic Circle. Founded in 1915 as a supply post in the First World War. Valuable in World War II as Russia's principal port for receiving war supplies from Britain and the U.S. Its ice-free harbor has made Murmansk a major ship repair center and commercial fishing base.

Dep. Murmansk	08:40	00:44
Arr. St. Petersburg (Moskovski)	13:10	14:13

St. Petersburg - Tallinn   and v.v. 1800

Dep. St. Petersburg (Varshavski)	23:10 (1)
Arr. Tallinn	08:16

Sights in **Tallinn**: A fortified town for more than 2,000 years. The capital of Estonia from 1918 until that country was annexed in 1940 by the former Soviet Union, Tallinn became the capital again when Estonia left Russia in 1991. In the walled Lower Town, see the 13th century Toom Church. Also visit the 13th-century Great Guildhall, 14th-century Town Hall, ruins of the 13th-century fort built by invading Danes on Toompea Hill, the Gothic churches, Niguliste and Oleviste and the old castle.

Dep. Tallinn	20:10 (1)
Arr. St. Petersburg (Varshavski)	06:54

(1) Reservation *required*. Carries first-class and second-class sleeping cars. Coach is second class. Light refreshments.

INTERNATIONAL ROUTES
FROM RUSSIA

Here are the schedules for rail trips from St. Petersburg to Helsinki (and the rest of Scandinavia) and to Warsaw (and Western Europe).

Other schedules show the route from Moscow to Bucharest (and the rest of Eastern Europe as well as to Athens and Istanbul), Khabarovsk (and Nakhodka, Yokohama and Hong Kong), Beijing, Tehran and Warsaw (and Western Europe).

St. Petersburg - Helsinki and Moscow-Helsinki   1910

All of these trains have a restaurant car.

Dep. St. Petersburg (Finlandski)	-0-	07:00 (2)	16:15 (2)
Dep. Moscow (St. Petersburg)	22:17 (1)	-0-	-0-
Set your watch back one hour			
Arr. Helsinki	11:30	12:30	21:34

(1) Carries only first and second-class sleeping cars and a restaurant car. No coaches. (2) Reservation required. Has first-class and second-class coach cars.

St. Petersburg - Warsaw   93

Dep. St. Petersburg (Varshavski)	12:20 (1)	22:45 (1)
Arr. Grodno	08:28 (2)	14:41 (2)
Set your watch back one hour		
Arr. Warsaw (Gdanska)	14:36	21:13

(1) Carries only first and second-class sleeping cars. No coaches. (2) Day 2.

Moscow - Warsaw - Berlin   56

A 2½-hour layover in Brest is for changing train wheels to conform with Western Europe's narrower tracks.

Dep. Moscow (Smol.)	23:21 (1)	23:59 (1)
Dep. Brest	15:15 (2)	17:00 (2)
Set your watch back one hour		
Arr. Warsaw (Cen.)	19:10	21:55
Arr. Berlin (Licht.)	-0-	06:05

(1) Carries only first-class and second-class sleeping cars. No coaches. (2) Day 2 from Moscow.

Moscow - Beijing   5000 Thomas Cook Overseas Timetable

Both of these trains carry a first-class sleeping car. They also have first and second-class coaches that convert at night to berths and bunks, and a restaurant car.

Dep. Moscow (Yar.)	19:55 (1)	20:15
Dep. Irkutsk	04:04 (2)	04:55 (2)
Arr. Beijing	15:33 (8)	06:32 (3)

(1) Runs Tuesdays. Has first-class sleepers and first- and second-class coaches. Restaurant car. (2) Day 5. (3) Day 8.

Moscow - Bucharest   94d

All of these trains carry only sleeping cars.

Dep. Moscow (Kievski)	00:21 (1)
Arr. Bucharest (Nord)	19:15 (2+3)

(1) Light refreshments. (2) Day 3. (3) Arrives at Bucharest's Baneasa Rail station.

Moscow - Warsaw - Frankfurt - Berlin - Cologne - Geneva - Paris - Madrid   24, 46. 55, 56, 94a

	94a	55	56	24	56
Dep. Moscow (Smol.)	15:35 (1)	15:35 (3)	23:59 (5)	23:21 (1)	23:21 (1)
Dep. Brest	06:35	06:35	17:00 (2)	15:15 (2)	15:15 (2)
Set your watch back one hour					
Arr. Warsaw (Wsch.)	09:05 (2)	12:48 (2)	21:55	19:10	19:10
Arr. Warsaw (Cen.)	09:25	13:04	22:12	19:25	19:25
Arr. Frankfurt/Main	-0-	06:09 (4)	-0-	-0-	01:27 (8)
Arr. Berlin (Licht.)	-0-	-0-	06:05	-0-	-0-
Arr. Cologne	-0-	-0-	-0-	-0-	10:02
Arr. Geneva	-0-	-0-	-0-	-0-	-0-
Arr. Paris (Nord)	-0-	-0-	-0-	16:05 (6)	-0-
Dep. Paris (Aust.)	-0-	-0-	-0-	20:00 (7)	-0-
Arr. Madrid (Cham.)	-0-	-0-	-0-	08:48	-0-

(1) Carries first- and second-class sleeping cars; no coaches. (2) Day 2. (3) Carries first- and second-class sleeping cars, second-class couchettes and first- and second-class coaches. (4) Day 3. (5) Carries first- and second-class sleepers; no coaches. Restaurant car. (6) Change trains in Brussels for Paris. (7) Change trains and stations (Table 46). Supplement charged for Trenhotel. Carries first- and second-class sleepers and restaurant car. (8) Frankfurt Oder station.

Moscow - Pyongyang	5000 Thomas	Cook Overseas	Timetable

Dep. Moscow (Yar.)	14:15 (1)	20:15 (5)
Dep. Irutsk	20:04 (2)	04:55 (2)
Dep. Khabarovsk	07:35 (3)	-0-
Dep. Shenyang	-0-	03:45 (6)
Arr. Pyongyang	10:10 (4)	10:41 (6)

(1) This train runs once per week, day of departure can vary. Carries a first-class sleeping car. Coach is second class. (2) Day 5. (3) Day 7. (4) Day 9. (5) Runs Friday only. Carries a first-class sleeping car. Has first and second-class coaches. Restaurant car. (6) Day 8.

TAJIKISTAN

• Tourist information: Permanent Mission of Tajikistan, 136 East 67th Street, New York, NY 10021. Telephone (212) 472-7645.
• Public holidays: January 1, March 8, May 1, 2, 9, October 7, November 7, 8.
• Currency: Rouble (SUR). At press time, $1 equalled SUR5811.00.

Tajikistan is a Central Asian country bounded on the south by Afghanistan, on the west by Uzbekistan, on the north by Uzbekistan and Kyrgyzstan, and on the east by the Xinjiang (Sinkiang) region of northwestern China. Its capital city is Dushanbe. The Russian military continues to play a major role in the region.

More than 90 percent of Tajikistan is mountainous; all of its eastern territory is in the high Pamirs, known as "the roof of the world." The highest elevation was named Communism Peak (7,495 meters).

The Tajik people, who form over half of the population, are Sunnite Muslims. Unlike their Turkic neighbors, they are of Iranian origin, descended from the Persian-speaking peoples that occupied the Trans-Oxus region long before the coming of the Uzbeks and other conquerors.

Tajikistan is a poor country. Its per capita income usually ranks among the lowest of all the Soviet republics. Sheep breeding remain the leading activity, and the reality is that most Westerner travelers don't spend much time in Tajikistan.

TURKMENISTAN

Turkmenistan, with its capital in Ashkabad, is a country in Central Asia bounded on the west by the Caspian Sea, on the north by Kazakhstan and Uzbekistan, on the east by Uzbekistan, and on the south by Afghanistan and Iran.

More than 80 percent of Turkmenistan consists of the Kara Kum Desert. Along the border with Iran is the Kopet Dagh, a dramatic mountain range that rises to nearly 3,000 meters.

The population is concentrated in oases in the east, along the foot of the Kopet Dagh, and along the Murgab and Tedzhen rivers. The Turkmen population, Sunnite Muslims, speak a Turkic language.

Passenger train travel is limited, although since independence, travel has increased, mostly American and European businesses negotiating agreements to develop the country's natural gas reserves, and a rail line has been started to connect Ashkhabad with the Persian Gulf via Iran. Still too exotic for the casual backpacker!

UKRAINE

• Tourist information: Embassy of Ukraine, 3350 M Street NW, Washington, DC 20007. Telephone (202) 333-7507, fax (202) 333-7510.
• Public holidays: January 1, March 8, May 1, 2, 9, October 7, November 7, 8.
• Currency: Ukranian hryvna. At press time, $1 equalled 1.76 hryvna.

Kiev

Kiev, the capital of Ukraine and the country's largest city with more than 2.5 million people, is located on the banks of the Dnepr River, at the halfway point of its 2,255-kilometer (1,400-mile) route from northwest Russia to the Black Sea. Originally founded on the river's right bank, on terrain marked by steep hills, Kiev sprawls onto both sides of the Dnepr.

As the country's capital, Kiev is Ukraine's political, industrial, and cultural center and a major transportation hub and river port. Kiev is also the Ukraine's most important educational and research center. It is the seat of the Ukrainian Academy of Sciences and a number of other research institutions. The city boasts of excellent and numerous theaters and concert halls, including the Ivan Franko Ukrainian Drama Theater, the Taras Shevchenko Opera, the Ballet Theater, and the Philharmonic Concert Hall.

Most of the city's historic monuments are in Old Kiev, on the right bank of the Dnepr. The city's oldest surviving church, St. Sophia's (Holy Wisdom) Cathedral, dates from 1037 and contains the tomb of Yaroslav the Wise, the 11th-century ruler of Kiev. Other architectural monuments include the 11th-century Golden Gate, one of the city's original gates, and St. Andrew's Church (1747–53), a fine example of the Russian baroque style. Kiev's most celebrated historic site is the Pechersky Lavra, or Monastery of the Caves. Dating from 1051, the monastery covers a sprawling campus and comprises many churches, cathedrals, bell towers, and monastic cells. Two separate networks of underground caves beneath the monastery contain the mummified bodies of more than 100 monks and six subterranean churches. Of utmost importance is the Babi Yar monument (1976) marking the site where thousands of Jews and Soviet prisoners of war were massacred by the Germans during World War II, an event that the Russian poet Yevgeny Yevtuskenko immortalized in his 1961 poem "Babi Yar."

See the 11th-centruy catacombs at the Pecherskaya Lavra Monastery in Kiev. The frescos and mosaics at the 11th-century St. Sophia Cathedral is definitely worth a visit. The Golden Gate at the intersection of Sverlovskaya and Vladimirskaya and the Museum of Russian Art should be included in Kiev town visits.

L'viv

L'viv, located exactly 600 kilometers from both the Baltic and the Black Sea, was founded as a fort in the mid-13th century by Prince Danylo Halitski of Galicia, a former principality of Kyivan Rus. The first mention of L'viv in early chronicles is from 1256, although archeological excavation in 1993 revealed that the first settlements appeared in the 6th century.

The city's favorable location on the crossroads of trade routes led to its rapid economic development. Galicia was taken over by Poland in the 14th century. Its nobility eventually adopted the Polish language and Roman Catholicism but the vast majority of people remained Ukrainian Orthodox and later joined the Greek Catholic Church, which acknowledged the Pope's spiritual supremacy but adhered to the area's Orthodox forms of worship. Thus, you begin to understand the cultural complexity of the city.

L'viv was occupied by the Nazis from 1941 to 1944. Almost the entire Jewish population was murdered in concentration camps in and around L'viv. Under Soviet rule, L'viv became an important center of activities of Ukrainian dissidents. Since the late 1980s the city has emerged as a leading force in Ukraine's movement toward sovereignty.

On the square next to the town hall the buildings captivate visitors with their beauty. Nearby is L'viv's world-famous theatre, the I. Franko Theatre. This is not to be missed.

Odessa

This major seaport of the Black Sea has inspired tourists, world travelers, and immigrants for centuries. Russia's leading seaport, maritime traffic is impressive heading through the Bosporus at Istanbul. The Opera House and Ballet Theater are particularly worth seeing, as is the famous Potemkin Stairway, which descends 455 feet from Primorsky Boulevard to the waterfront. This is where you want to send your postcards from.

UZBEKISTAN

Uzbekistan is a country in Central Asia, bordered by Kazakhstan on the north and west, Turkmenistan on the southwest, Afghanistan on the south, and Tajikistan and Kyrgyzstan on the east with its capital in Tashkent. It has the largest population of the Central Asian states; among the former Soviet republics it is exceeded in population only by Russia and Ukraine. Uzbekistan is also the main heir to the rich Islamic civilization of Central Asia, containing within its borders the historic Muslim cities of Samarkand, Bukhara, and Khiva.

Tashkent

Tashkent, the capital, with a population of more than two million, is the largest single city in Central Asia and has been a center of Islamic civilization in that area since medieval times. Situated in the foothills of the Tian Shan mountains in an oasis irrigated by the Chirchik River, Tashkent today is a major manufacturing and transport center and cotton-textile mill, based on its cotton-fiber production. To its credit, the urban area is served by a subway system.

An opera and ballet theater and both Uzbek and Russian drama theaters are based in Tashkent six museums including a Uzbekistan history museum and an Uzbek arts museum grace the capital.

Annexed by Russia only in 1865, Tashkent now consists of an old Asian section, with winding narrow streets, and a modern city, dating from the mid–19th century. Rail connections with Russia were completed in 1898, and industrial development followed. The city's growth was spurred in World War II, when many industries were evacuated there from the European part of the USSR. A devastating earthquake in 1966 was followed by large-scale reconstruction.

Samarkand

Samarkand, the ancient city of southern Uzbekistan, situated in the valley of the Zeravshan River about 275 kilometers southwest of Tashkent, is one of the oldest cities of central Asia. Samarkand has many noted architectural remains from the 14th to the 17th century, when it flourished as the fabled capital of the Mongol empire of Timur. See the ruins of the mosque of Bibi Khanom (1399–1404), with its distinctive turquoise cupola, and the great open Registan Square, lined with the remains of three Muslim religious colleges.

Known in antiquity as Maracanda, Samarkand is believed to date back to the 6th century B.C., when it was the capital of ancient Sogdiana. It was destroyed in 329 B.C. by Alexander the Great. After the 8th-century Arab conquest it flourished under the Samanid dynasty of the 9th and 10th centuries before it fell to Genghis Khan in 1219.

Following completion of a railroad in 1888, the city's economy developed. Samarkand served as the capital of the Uzbekistan from 1924 until 1930, when the capital was moved to Tashkent. Access is possible by train, but adventurous travelers often opt for the small plane. Recently returning Americans explained that they paid $64 to get to Samarkand from Tashkent by plane and $1 for the return portion to Tashkent! Don't try to understand.

BALTIC STATES

Estonia

Bordering the Baltic Sea, between Sweden and Russia, Estonia, with Tellinn as its capital, is slightly larger than New Hampshire and Vermont combined including its 1,500 islands in the Baltic Sea. It borders with Latvia and Russia. Only slightly more than a million and a half people occupy this small but proud Lutheran nation, which occupies a strategic geographic position in Eastern Europe.

Bolstered by a widespread national desire to reintegrate into Western Europe, the Estonian government has pursued a program of market reforms and rough stabilization measures, which is rapidly transforming the economy. Several years after independence, and the introduction of the kroon, Estonians are beginning to reap tangible benefits; inflation is low, production declines appear to have bottomed out, and living standards are rising.

Folk culture is at the heart of Estonian spirit. The oldest Estonian religious beliefs probably reach back to the Stone Age. These included the belief that the spirit of a witch could leave the body and gain wisdom from the place of the dead (shamanism) and belief in the image of an animal as the emblem of tribal ancestor (totemism). The cosmogonic myths about the creation of the world from the egg of a miraculous bird, and the creation of the Milky Way from a giant tree have been preserved in folklore, and are just as old. Everything in nature (trees, stones, arable land, bodies of water, fire, wind, and so on) was believed to have a spirit (animism). The most important holiday in Estonian tradition was Christmas, which was endowed with fertility magic. The most original part of Estonian folklore, the runic folksong, originated in the 1st millennium BC, as a result of interaction between primitive Balto-Finnic singing (warbling, keening) and the songs of the Baltic tribes. Heroic legends have blended with legends about hills. Estonian proverbs have been researched in detail, and 82,000 have been published.

Major train routes include the *Balti Ekspress* from Warsaw and Sestokai, the Brest-Minsk connection, the *Tallinna Ekspress* between Moscow, St. Petersburg and Tallinn, the *Admiraltejets* to and from Riga. Jim Haynes's *People to People* guide on Estonia, Lativa, and Lithuania provides valuable contacts in these towns. For train information to and from Tallinn call (+372 2) 446 756, 456 851.

Estonia, located on the Baltic Sea, is considered to be one of the most progressive of the former Soviet Republics. U.S. citizens do not need an entry visa at this time. This small country is strategically located as a transportation hub. Many of you may remember the tragic loss of life from the loss of a passenger ferry in the fall of 1994. The port of Tallinn has regular links to Helsinki Finland, it was on the way to Helsinki that the ferry was lost.

Tallinn

In Tallinn, definitely plan to walk around the Lower Walled Town. Check out the 13th-century Toom Church and the fort built by the invading Danes on Toompea Hill. Visitors to Tallinn truly feel like they have rediscovered a long lost medieval Europe.

Latvia

The Republic of Latvia, with its capital in Riga, one of the "Baltic States" of northern Europe, is bordered by the Baltic Sea on the west, Russia on the east, Lithuania and Belarus on the south, and Estonia on the north. It was independent from 1918 to 1940, when it was forcibly annexed by the USSR, an event that indelibly marked the Latvians. Independence was restored in 1991. Russian intellectuals will confirm that Riga, after Moscow, is the cultural hub of the CIS. Many small publishing houses and literary journals have emerged there since independence.

Latvia's landscape with many lakes and rivers and its seaside location have strongly effected the commercial and cultural life of the country. The river estuaries provide ice-free commercial and fishing harbors, and Latvia enjoys a moderate climate, with cool summers and mild winters.

The Latvians speak a Baltic language related to Lithuanian, use Latin script, and have a mostly Lutheran background. Ethnic Russians constitute 33 percent of the population, reduced from nearly 50 since independence when many Russians were more or less forced to leave.

Riga

Riga, the capital of Latvia with nearly a million people, is situated on the Western Dvina (Daugava) River, near the river's mouth on the Gulf of Riga, an arm of the Baltic Sea.
Riga consists of an old medieval city center, with narrow, winding streets and distinctive Gothic architecture, and a newer section with a grid street plan and modern buildings. The city has a cool, maritime climate. An attractive seacoast of sand dunes to the west of the city is the site of a popular beach resort, Jurmala.

The port of Riga carries on an active commercial cargo trade with Western Europe and serves as the base for an Atlantic deep-sea fishing fleet. As the cultural center of Latvia, the city is the seat of Latvian University (1919) and of the Latvian Academy of Sciences. Founded in 1201 by the Teutonic Knights, Riga developed as a trading center between Russia and the Baltic Sea. It was a member of the Hanseatic League. It passed to Russia in 1721 and became one of that country's major seaports; manufacturing followed during the second half of the 19th century.

Lithuania

Lithuania borders the Baltic Sea between Latvia and Russia and also borders with Belarus and Poland. Interestingly, it has a dispute with Russia in that the Nemen River border is presently located on the Lithuanian bank and not in midriver as by international standards. Its nearly four million inhabitants have adjusted well to a system set on distancing itself from the old Soviet ways, and many travelers will remember the tension in Vilnius, the capital, reported in the international news in 1990.

Significant outbreaks of diphtheria have occurred during the winter of 1993-94. Street crime, including purse snatchings and muggings, occur, especially at night near major tourist hotels and restaurants. Robberies have occurred on trains, in train stations, and in hotel rooms. Be careful.

Vilnius

Vilnius, the capital of Lithuania, is located on the Neris River. With a population of over a half a million, the city is an important cultural and industrial center, accounting for about one-fourth of the manufacturing output of Lithuania.

Vilnius has the ruins of a 14th-century castle and buildings in a variety of architectural styles, ranging from Gothic to baroque. It is the seat of the Lithuanian Academy of Sciences and has a university, founded in 1579.

Settled during the 10th century, Vilnius became the capital of the Grand Duchy of Lithuania in 1323 and, despite destruction by the Teutonic Knights in 1377, developed into a major trading center. It declined after Lithuania was formally united with Poland in 1569. Vilnius passed to Russia in 1795. After World War I the city was disputed between the new governments of Lithuania and Poland; the Poles won control of it in 1920. The USSR took Vilnius from Poland in 1939 and ceded it to Lithuania, only to annex all of Lithuania the following year.

Vilnius was also an important Jewish center of Eastern Europe until the Nazi extermination of the Jews in World War II.

CZECH REPUBLIC

Getting on Track in the Czech Republic

• Tourist information: Czech Service Centre, 1511 K Street NW, Suite 1030, Washington DC 20005. Telephone 800-Y-PRAGUE (800-977-2483) toll-free in USA and Canada, fax (202) 638-5308.

• Public holidays: January 1, New Year's Day, Easter, Easter Monday, May 1, Labor Day, May 9, Liberation Day, October 7, November 7, 8, December 25, Christmas Day, December 26.

• Summer time: Czechoslovakia changes to Summer Time on the last Sunday of March and converts back to Standard Time on the last Sunday of September.

• Currency: Koruna (also krowns). At press time, $1 equalled 32.43 koruna.

Overview of Czech Republic's Trains

As most travelers know, the country Czechoslovakia is now two countries, the Czech Republic and the Slovak Republic. And although the two republics are intimately connected—they both take the same telephone country code—the languages are different, the currency is different, and ultimately the experience of traveling in the two countries is distinct. The Czech Republic is made up of two distinct regions, Bohemia and Moravia, both of which offer travelers a wealth of attractions.

After the fall of communism in Czechoslovakia, the success of the Velvet Revolution, and the election of dissident playwright Vaclav Havel, Prague opened up spiritually and materially not only to the Czechs but to the West—and at a pace that has rarely been seen before. In two years, nearly 40,000 Americans moved to Prague is search of new horizons, a Bohemian existence, and economic success. Then the prices of apartments and consumer goods shot up.

Today, among the wonders of this exquisite city, it is difficult to mill around without hearing an English twang. For Czechs, the brunt of their new ethnic jokes are Americans, their new immigrants. Upon arriving at the Prague airport or train station you are greeted by the neon sign MASTERCARD WELCOMES YOU TO THE CZECH REPUBLIC, and quickly you begin to understand who really won the cold war! Prague is particularly overrun in the summer, but don't let that dissuade you—it is still one of the most enchanting cities in Europe, where the old and the new mix and the spirit of Franz Kafka still lurks.

Travel conditions in the Czech Republic, especially in Prague, are now up to snuff with conditions in other European countries. You can buy telephone debit cards in tobacco shops for international use in telephone booths. You can reach your AT&T operator at 00-420-00101, MCI operator at 00-420-0011, and Sprint operator at 00-420-87187. There are beeper services and Internet service providers galore if you want to be accessible as you get lost in the Bohemian landscape.

Train travel within the Czech Republic is relatively easy and well developed. There is even a Prague Excursion Pass, an enhancement to holders of the Eurailpass, Germanrail pass, or Austrian Railpass. This allows you to travel from any Czech border crossing to Prague and return within a seven-day period. This pass is available through DER TRAVEL, (800) 782-2424. Regional passes are also available and come in various validity periods from a week to a month, even a year. A one-week pass runs about $20; tack on an extra $6 or so to ride InterCity and EuroCity trains.

The Czech railways distinguish themselves between the following types of trains:

• Personal train (*osobní vlak*). Local trains that stop at all stations and have only second-class seats.

• Speed train (*spesn vlak*). Usually provide longer routes over more than one track. They stop at important stations only. The importance of a station, however, depends on the particular route. For instance, a speed train from Prague to a mountain region will stop at every village in the mountains but will skip small stations on the remainder of the route. Speed trains have first- and second-class cars. In the timetables, speed train schedules are printed in bold.

• Fast train (*rychlék*). Long-distance trains that stop at certain stations only. Some of them have dining cars, some are overnight trains and have couchettes and sleepers. You can reserve your seat in a fast train, and reservations are required for some connections. In the timetables, fast train schedules are printed bold on a gray background.

• Express train (express). Only about two connections are called express today. The difference between express trains and fast trains is too insignificant to discern.

The actual speed of the Czech trains depends on the quality of the track. For example, a personal train on the main track from Prague to Ceske Trebove may be faster than a fast train from Prague to Chomutov.

Several trains have cars or sections for smokers. In general, smoking is forbidden in all trains and stations (including platforms), but be prepared for violators. Remember, this country's president smokes three packs a day.

A word on train tickets. In addition to ticket windows, there are machines at some stations that sell tickets for rides of up to 100 kilometers. You can pay with coins or with debit cards. If you arrive late, you can buy your ticket from the conductor. If you do not have a valid ticket, report to the conductor before he approaches you and pay a surcharge of only Kc 10. Otherwise, the surcharge will be Kc 100. If there is no ticket office at your departure station (or it is not open), the conductor will sell the tickets without any surcharge. Local fares in Czech krowns are reasonable. The fares for first class are 50 percent higher than second class. There are special fares for children and dogs. No special surcharge is required for fast trains if you buy a full-fare ticket. A passenger can book a seat on a fast train for which he has got a valid ticket as long as 30 days and as little as 15 minutes before the departure. It is always advisable to reserve, and a reservation costs only Kc 10.

A note: you probably will not be traveling with a canoe, but if you are, you'll be pleased to know that in the summer months it is permissible to lug such fluvial items on the train as checked luggage.

Rail travel to and from Prague mainly revolves around two international stations: Praha Hlavni nádraze and Praha Holesovice, both accessible by subway line C. Hlavni, Prague's largest station, serves the Cheb, Karlovy Vary, Kosice, and Tabor connections. Holesovice serves the Berlin and Budapest connections. Trains to Bratislava and Brno stop in both stations, usually. To be sure, recheck connections, times, and stations before heading to catch a train.

For domestic train travel there are several other important stations: Praha Masarykovo nádraze for trains to Chomutov, Zsté nad Labem and Kolén. Train and other travel reservations and services are obtainable from the Czech national tourist agency Satur, which until 1994 was the ubiquitous CEDOK.

A visa is required to enter the Czech Republic. As of October 1995, foreigners must prove that they have a minimum of $20 U.S. cash available per day for the first ten days or a fixed amount of $270 U.S. for longer visits. (The Czech Republic has just opened a second consulate in Los Angeles to serve the demand for visas.) This measure is designed to limit the flow of drifters making Prague their beat. A fascinating update on the conditions in Prague was posted recently in the Travel Forum on Compuserve: it reported that of the thousands of Americans who are now long-term residents of the Czech Republic, many wrote for their college newspaper and hoped that the experience would land them a job at the *Prague Post* or *Prognosis,* the now defunct arts weekly. They have since learned otherwise. Be prepared to bus tables, pour beer at a sports bar, or to be a night manager of a laundromat in between English tutoring gigs. Also be aware that apartment rental rates in central parts of Prague are now comparable to those in San Francisco. Unless you have a good source of income, you'll either be living on the outskirts or sharing a one-bedroom with three or four people.

We recently heard from an American, Neil Curran, living in Prague, with a rail-travel update. He reports that the nation's railway, Ceske Drahy (CD), had its ups and downs in 1997, with strikes, floods and a fare hike. Though fares were increased by one-third, they are still an incredible bargain at about three cents per mile. As the world of government subsidies comes to an end for the railway, the company is contemplating major changes, including the possibility of partial privatization. Since the early 1990s, the railway has lost money, so accounting types are looking at ways to cut expenses. A likely target is the company's 100,000 employees and money-losing routes. It's possible more strikes could be on the horizon if the railway union and CD can't agree about contract issues. Rail ridership is stable, though, and expected to rise. The equipment has seen better days and the tracks are often rough, but Curran highly recommends roaming around the Republic by train as a way to meet the people and take in some stunning scenery from woodland to lush greenery. He notes that only a handful of the Republic's routes actually appear in the *Thomas Cook*

European Timetable. No wonder, the CD has some 344 printed timetables! Curran suggests buying a copy of Cook's *New Rail Map of Europe*, if you'll be doing any serious rail-riding in Eastern Europe.

Pick up a copy of "Tips for Train Trips" at any Prague train station. The 56-page booklet is printed in English for the first time, and lists all sorts of interesting rail trips that can be made from Prague. Curran notes that three worthwhile back-country trips weren't included, though. He surmises it's probably because CD thought tourists wouldn't be interested in going off the beaten track. Here are Curran's recommendations:

• Cesky Krumlov: About 75 miles south of Prague, it's close to Austria; you won't find a listing in *Cook's* for part of this trip. Travel time from Prague is about 3 1/2 hours, a little longer if you change trains in Cesky Budejovice (*Cook's* Table 1140). Highlights in Cesky Krumlov include a large castle rising from the river and stretching along the bluffs, an historic brewery, excellent restaurants and hotels.

• Telc: About 88 miles from Prague. Because of a circuitous route, it takes about 4 1/2 hours to make this trip from Prague, with two train changes. The town is surrounded by ponds, and in the middle of it is a spectacular arched central square, or "namesti." A large well-preserved chateau is nearby. The railway station is within walking distance to most attractions, including the chateau, hotels and restaurants.

• Karlovy Vary: See additional notes under "City-Sightseeing." By train, the trip takes between three and four hours, with a ticket on a fast train costing a mere $3.20 each way (*Cook's* Table 1140). Express busses make the trip in about two hours, if you're in a hurry. Besides being a spa center, the town also hosts an annual film festival and music events throughout the year. Check out nearby hilly parks for great city views.

TRAIN PASSES

Czech Flexipass Unlimited *first*-class train travel any five days within 15 days. The 1998 price was unavailable at press time. In 1997, the pass sold for $69. Children age 4-12 paid half-fare; children under four traveled free.

EXCURSIONS AND CITY-SIGHTSEEING

Prague

Despite the rapid influx of foreigners, Prague is a delight. When those who have read Kafka's *The Castle* see Prague's Hradcany Castle complex (where the government is situated), they know it is worth the visit alone. Visit the awesome medieval Jewish cemetery and nearby synagogue, the oldest in Europe, and the majestic 14th-century Charles Bridge (Karlov Most) with its thirty statues of saints and hordes of street people. The charming back streets of Mala Strana district echo Mozart and Milos Forman's film *Amadeus*. Visit the little streets beyond the Hradcany Castle and stop in at Kafka's house, number 22, on the Golden Lane (Zlata Ulicka), now a bookshop. If you have a prerevolution guidebook, references to Kafka will be glaringly absent.

There is no lack of freshly updated travel guides to Prague, though, and you'll need one. Kakfa's grave is a few tram rides from the city center; it takes a bit of an effort to find, but it's worth it. Starímestskí namesti Square is the heartbeat of the old Prague with its ancient clock tower, its 1410 Gothic horologe, the Baroque St. Nicholas Church and Tyn Church, and the medieval Carolinum, the oldest remnant of the original Prague University.

One of the great pleasures of being in Prague is simply sitting in the café of the Hotel Europa and watching people. Waiters in polyester tuxedos rush around brusquely serving sparkling water, shots of slivovitz, and portions of strudel. You will find yourself in a quirky time warp that is indicative of today's Prague.

Getting around Prague is quick and easy: aside from walking, the public transportation system is excellent. There is an underground tram system with three lines connecting all areas of the city, a dense network of trams with Lazarská as the central change point, buses serving the outskirts, and a funicular that runs from Malá Strana to the hill of Petrín.

Prague taxi drivers don't enjoy the best of reputations due to their habit of overcharging and taking circular routes. Be vigilant and never give the impression that you don't know where you are. Insist that the driver uses the meter, watch that he doesn't change the rate on the taximeter, and always ask for a receipt.

To get to the Praha Ruzyne International Airport, in the northwestern suburbs, take the 119 bus from the subway station Dejvická on the A line.

Brno

Located in the Moravian part of the Czech Republic, often overshadowed by Bohemia, Brno is noted for its craftsmanship—fine woodcarvings, lace, pottery, and costumes, as well as its excellent art galleries.

Culturally speaking, Brno is rich, and theater buffs and art enthusiasts will love it here, especially because the over-the-top commercialism that has invaded Prague has yet to reach user-friendly Brno. A visit to the Macocha and Sloup grottoes via an underground cruise is a highlight. Don't miss the Brno Castle, Moravian Museum, and the open-air market. Brno makes for a perfect stop between Prague and Budapest. Highly recommended.

Ceske Budejovice

Home of the original Budweiser (Budvar) Brewery, this virtually unchanged medieval city and capital of southern Bohemia is filled with Old World wonder; it has a fascinating history. Halfway between Vienna and Plzen, Ceske Budejovice is where the Vltava meets the Malse River. Railroad buffs will want to know that it was here that the first horse-drawn railway arrived in 1832, coming from Linz, Austria. The brewery here does not have the same charm as the Urquell Brewery in Plzen, and is probably not worth the time. The best thing to do in Ceske Budejovice is to simply walk through the old streets off the large square and around Samson's Fountain and down by the river.

Cheb

Cheb is a medieval town on the Ohre River in the western part of the country. An easy day trip from either Karlovy Vary or Marianske Lazne, it is a Germanic town with scenic burgher houses in its old section. The area around the train station is reported to be particularly ugly, so don't judge Cheb by your first impressions.

Karlovy Vary

Formerly Carlsbad, Karlovy Vary is a scenic city that is world renown since the 1300s for its curative waters. Peter the Great, Bismarck, Goethe, Tolstoy, Beethoven, Mozart, Edward VII, and Karl Marx are among the people who have visited this spa for its water. The city is also famous worldwide for its Bohemian crystal. Visit the Moser crystal glass factory. There is an interesting porcelain factory in nearby **Slakov**.

There are express trains from Prague and Cheb to and from the Karlovy Vary station on the north side of the town. Trains to and from Marianske Lazne use the Karlovy Vary station near the bus depot.

Liberec

Noted for its 17th-centruy Reichenberg architecture, Liberec lends itself to lovely walks in the old town and in the scenic Jested Hills area on the outskirts.

Marianske Lazne

You would most likely recognize this famous spa town by its old name, Marienbad, which has been frequented by an impressive list of international celebrities. Local life revolves around the spas, walks, and the Maxim Gorky Colonnade.

Plzen

Plzen, or Pilsen, a traditional trading center halfway between Prague and Nuremberg, is the capital of West Bohemia. The 19th-century ironworks factory founded by Emile Skoda gave its name to the famous Czech car the Skoda. Beer brewing in this town is so historic that it has left its name on the process: pils. The Pilsner trademark known as Urquell internationally comes from Plzen. Go on a brewery tour and do visit the Museum of Beer Brewing, located in an original medieval malt house (but don't count on ambitious sightseeing afterwards!). Also visit the underground corridors.

Tabor

Founded in 1420 on a religious principle of communal life, contributing to the modern sense of the word *Bohemian,* Tabor is a perfect day trip from Prague. Visit the Museum of the Hussite Movement—it is all one needs to understand the history and significance of Tabor and its 14th-century reformation.

ONE-DAY EXCURSIONS

Prague - Bratislava - Prague   1160

Dep. Prague (Hole.)	00:43 (1)	07:27 (2)	-0-	11:39 (2)	15:39 (2)
Dep. Prague (Hlav.)	-0-	-0-	11:52	-0-	-0-
Arr. Bratislava	06:21	12:26	17:29	16:38	20:38

Sights in **Bratislava**: An important Danube port in ancient Roman times. See the 14th-15th- century castle. Visit the Hussite House, the old city hall, the cathedral, the palaces on Mirove Square, Michalska Street and Gottwald Square. Few of the museums here offer information in English.

Dep. Bratislava	00:48 (1)	05:50	09:15 (2)	12:02	13:15 (2)
Arr. Prague (Hlav.)	06:42	11:01	-0-	17:32	-0-
Arr. Prague (Hole.)	-0-	-0-	14:21	-0-	18:18

(1) Carries a sleeping car. Also has couchettes. (2) Supplement charged. Restaurant car.

Prague - Brno - Prague   1160

Dep. Prague (Hole.)	07:27 (1)	11:39 (1)	13:39 (1)	15:39 (1)
Arr. Brno	10:42	14:51	16:51	18:51

Sights in **Brno**: The folk-art exhibit of woodcarving, laces, pottery and costumes in the Moravian Museum. Brno Castle. Take a cruise on one of the underground rivers to see the Macocha and Sloup grottos. The outstanding 13th-century Pernstejn Castle, near Brno.

Dep. Brno	13:03 (1)	15:03 (1)	17:18 (1)	19:22 (1)	00:19
Arr. Prague (Hole.)	16:18	18:18	20:37 (2)	22:45	03:41

(1) Supplement charged. Restaurant car. (2) Arrives at Prague's Hlavni rail station.

Prague - Ceske Budejovice - Prague   1140

Dep. Prague (Hlavni)	06:13	08:52	Dep. Ceske Bude.	13:30	16:19 (1)
Arr. Ceske Bude.	08:43	11:30	Arr. Prague (Hlavni)	15:59	19:00

(1) Plus other Ceske departures at 18:07, 19:12 and 21:26, arriving Prague 20:37, 21:59 and 23:59.

Sights in **Ceske Budejovice**: This city appears the same now as it did in the Middle Ages. Visit the Budvar brewery.

Prague - Karlovy Vary - Prague   1105

Dep. Prague (Hole.)   04:30   06:39 (1) 09:14   12:17
Arr. Karlovy Vary   08:33   09:58 (2) 13:04   16:14

Sights in **Karlovy Vary:** Once called Carlsbad, famous for its curative waters since 1347. Peter the Great, Beethoven, Mozart and England's Edward VII are among the celebrities that have come here to drink the elixir and use the monumental baths in their search for improved health. An international film festival is held here every July. Visit the Moser crystal glass factory. There is an interesting porcelain factory in nearby **Slakov**.

Dep. Karlovy Vary   04:52 (2)   09:53   13:56   17:40   17:57
Arr. Prague (Hole.) 08:41 (3)   13:52   1759:   21:44 (3) 21:51

(1) Departs from Prague's Hlavni rail station. (2) Second class. (3) Arrives Prague's Hlavni rail station.

Prague - Liberec - Prague   1115

Both of these trains are second class.

| Dep. Prague (Hlavni) | 06:53 | Dep. Liberec | 17:25 |
| Arr. Liberec | 09:50 | Arr. Prague (Hlavni) | 20:16 |

Sights in **Liberec:** This town is noted for its 17th-century Reichenberg architecture. Walks in the encircling Jested Hills are recommended.

Prague - Marianske Lazne - Prague   1100

Dep. Prague
   (Hlav.)   04:25 (1)   10:31   13:09 (1)   14:28   17:53 (1)   20:58 (2)
Arr. Marianske 07:36 (3)   13:23   15:50   17:35   20:57   00:15

Sights in **Marianske Lazne**: Once called Marienbad, still a famous health spa.

Dep. Marianske 04:31   05:30   06:52   12:43 (1)   14:06 (1)   15:25   17:35 (3)
Arr. Prague
   (Hlav.)   08:06   08:12   10:03   15:51   16:46   18:12   20:39

(1) Restaurant car. (2) Plus other Prague departures at 22:00, arriving Marianske Lazne 00:48. (3) Plus another Marianske Lazne departure at 19:14, arriving Prague 22:14.

Prague - Plzen - Prague   1100

Dep. Prague (Hlavni)	07:51 (1)	08:58	10:31
Arr. Plzen		09:19 (2)	10:42	12:08

Sights in **Plzen:** Visit the enormous Urquell brewery, where more than 200 million pints of beer are bottled annually. They have been producing beer here (hence "Pilsener") for over 800 years.

Dep. Plzen	14:07 (1)	15:10 (1)	16:34	18:55	20:34 (1+3)
Arr. Prague (Hlavni)	15:51	16:46 (2)	18:12	20:39	22:14

(1) Restaurant car. (2) Supplement charged. (3) Plus another Plzen departure at 22:42, arriving Prague 00:22.

Prague - Tabor - Prague   1140

Dep. Prague (Hlv.)	07:13 (1)	09:19 (1)	Dep. Tabor	14:29	17:24 (2)
Arr. Tabor	08:45	11:50	Arr. Prague (Hlv.) 15:59	19:00

(1) Second class. (2) Plus other Tabor departures at 19:05, 20:28 and 22:33, arriving Prague 20:37, 21:59 and 23:59.

Sights in **Tabor:** A museum town, preserved to immortalize the unusual Hussite 14th-century reform movement which held that all people are brothers and equal.

SCENIC RAIL TRIPS

Bratislava - Kosice - Bratislava   1180

Very good mountain scenery, through the Low and High Tatras Mountains.

All of these trains have a restaurant car.

Dep. Bratislava	05:45 (1)	07:55 (2)	Dep. Kosice	12:15 (3)	17:25 (1+2)
Arr. Kosice	10:50	14:05	Arr. Bratislava	18:15	22:23

(1) Reservation required. (2) Supplement charged. (3) Runs daily except Saturday.

Poprad-Tatry to Stary Smokovec and Tatranska Lomnica 1180, 1189

This spur off the Bratislava-Kosice route is the most scenic rail trip in Czechoslovakia. Forty minutes of the spectacular Tatras Mountains. Then, you can continue on to the **Tatranska Lomnica** ski resort and take a funicular to the top of 8,645-foot **Lomnicky Stit**.

"Pleso" means "lake." It is a popular one-hour stroll to Poprodske Pleso, another of the more than 100 glacial lakes in this area. Strbske Pleso is the main ski resort in the 16-mile-long Tatra mountain range.

1180		*1189*	
Dep. Bratislava	08:05 (1)	Dep. Tatranska Lomnica	17:22
Arr. Poprad-Tatry	12:45 (2)	Arr. Poprad-Tatry	17:57
Change trains 1189		*Change trains 1180*	
Dep. Poprad-Tatry	14:06	Dep. Poprad-Tatry	18:34 (1)
Arr. Tatranska Lomnica	14:41	Arr. Bratislava	22:23

(1) Restaurant car. Supplement charged. (2) Change in Studeny Park.

Strba - Strbske Pleso 1180, 1189

This other spur off the Bratislava–Kosice line is a second great Tatras Mountain scenic rail trip. Winter sports are popular in the area around Strbske Pleso.

All of the Bratislava–Strba (and v.v.) trains have a restaurant car.

1180			*1189*		
Dep. Bratislava	07:55 (1)	09:55 (1)	Dep. Strbske Pleso	Frequent times	
Arr. Strba	12:28	14:28	Arr. Strba	14-18 minutes later	
Change trains 1189			*Change trains 1180*		
Dep. Strba	Frequent times		Dep. Strba	13:52 (1)	15:52 (1)
Arr. Strbske Pleso	14-18 minutes later		Arr. Bratislava	18:15 (2)	20:15

(1) Supplement charged. Restaurant car. (2) Runs daily except Saturday.

INTERNATIONAL ROUTES
FROM THE CZECH REPUBLIC

Prague is the Czech Republic's gateway to Berlin (and on to Copenhagen and all of Scandinavia), Belgrade, Budapest, Bucharest (and on to Athens), Nurnberg (and on to the rest of Western Europe), Vienna, and Warsaw (and on to Moscow).

Because the Czech Republic is not a Eurailpass country, passengers traveling from Prague to Austria, Germany (and on, to Switzerland or France) and Hungary must pay for a ticket from Prague to the border of those Eurailpass countries. None of the travel from Prague into Poland is covered by Eurailpass. Travel to Austria, Hungary and Poland is covered by European East Pass.

Prague - Berlin 60

All of these trains require reservation, unless designated otherwise. All night trains carry a sleeping car and have couchettes. All day trains have a restaurant car.

Dep. Prague (Hlavni)	-0-	08:16 (1)	12:16 (1)	-0-
Dep. Prague (Holesovice)	03:58	08:29 (2)	12:31 (2)	14:29 (1+2)
Arr. Berlin (Licht.)	09:36	13:10	17:10	19:10

Dep. Prague (Hlavni)	-0-	-0-
Dep. Prague (Holesovice)	16:29 (1)	18:29 (1)
Arr. Berlin (Licht.)	21:10 (2)	23:10 (2)

(1) Restaurant car. (2) Supplement charged.

Prague - Budapest - Belgrade or Bucharest 60, 61

Dep. Prague (Holesovice)	01:09 (1)	07:39 (3)	15:39 (3)	11:39
Arr. Budapest (Keleti)	09:47	15:12 (4)	23:22 (4)	19:22
Arr. Belgrade	-0-	-0-	08:24	08:24 (2)
Arr. Bucharest (Nord)	23:58 (2)	07:51	-0-	10:38

(1) Carries a sleeping car. Also has couchettes. Supplement charged. (2) Day 2. (3) Supplement charged. Restaurant car. (4) Change trains in Budapest.

Prague - Frankfurt - Paris 30

Dep. Prague (Hlavni)	06:29 (1+2)	18:37 (3)	21:00 (3)
Arr. Frankfurt/Main	14:35	-0-	06:43
Dep. Frankfurt/Main	14:51	-0-	07:26
Arr. Paris (Est)	21:05	09:40	13:42

(1) Departs Prague Holesovice station. (2) Reservation advisable. Supplement charged. Restaurant car. (3) Carries first-class sleeping cars, second-class couchettes and coaches.

Prague - Nurnberg or Munich and Zurich 57

Dep. Prague (Hlavni)	07:51 (1)	13:09 (1+2)	16:56 (1)	22:00(3)
Arr. Nurnberg	-0-	18:17	-0-	03:27
Arr. Munich	13:52	-0-	23:06	06:30
Arr. Zurich	18:26	-0-	-0-	10:47

(1) Supplement charged. Restaurant car. (2) For Munich, change trains in Marktredwitz at 17:49, arrival 21:01. (3) Carries a sleeping car. Also has couchettes. Light refreshments.

Prague - Vienna 96

Dep. Prague (Hole.)	-0-	01:09 (2)	13:39 (1)	17:39 (3)
Dep. Prague (Hlavni)	09:21 (1)	-0-	-0-	-0-
Arr. Vienna (F. J. Bf.)	-0-	-0-	-0-	-0-
Arr. Vienna (Sud.)	14:33	06:55	18:48	22:48

(1) Supplement payable. Restaurant car. (2) Carries sleepers, couchettes, second-class coaches. (3) *Antonin Dvorak.* Supplement payable. Restaurant car.

Prague - Warsaw 95a

Dep. Prague (Hlavni)	13:20 (1)	18:42 (2)	20:36 (2)
Arr. Warsaw (Centralna)	22:31	07:06	06:49
Arr. Warsaw (Gdanska)	22:44	07:22	07:00

(1) Reservation required. Restaurant car. (2) Carries a sleeping car. Also has couchettes.

SLOVAK REPUBLIC

Getting on Track in the Slovak Republic

• Tourist information: Slovakia Travel Service, 10 East 40th Street, Suite 3604, New York, NY 10016. Telephone (212) 725-0948, fax (212) 213-4461. E-mail: viktvl@aol.com. On the Web (if you're an America Online subscriber): http://members.aol.com/viktvl/slovakia/page01.htm.

• Public holidays: January 1, New Year's Day, January 6, Easter, Easter Monday, May 1, Labor Day, July 5, September 1, 15, November 1 December 24, 25, 26.

• Currency: Koruna. At press time, $1 equalled 33.65 loruna.

Overview of Slovak Republic's Trains

The eastern half of the former Czechoslovakia, the Slovak Republic today is tucked in below Poland to the north, Hungary to the south, the Ukraine to the east, and Austria and the Czech Republic to the west.

Europe's newest country, Slovakia managed to break away from the Czechs in 1993. The country has a tremendous amount to offer nature-lovers and sports-oriented visitors. Its Tatra mountain region is ideal for hikers and skiers; its unspoiled medieval villages are priceless for their beauty and authenticity. Visitors are received in an open and friendly manner. Travelers will experience the discovery of a long-lost part of Eastern European history and tradition at reasonable prices by including Slavakia, beyond Bratislava, in their itineraries. Bratislava, of course, the country's cultural and intellectual center, necessitates a visit on its own terms.

Our contact in the Czech Republic, Neil Curran, reports that the Slovak Republic has been rebuilding major parts of its rail network. He notes that the Slovak system is less dense than its Czech counterpart, mainly due to the rough topography. He also notes with interest that the Slovaks seem to be moving along faster with their improvements than the Czechs, despite the country's weaker economy. Improvements include more international services and additional deluxe, fast internal trains, which require payment of a supplement. Also, there are more trips through the bubble bath for rolling stock, stations are being spruced up and graffiti removed from stations and rights-of-way.

The easiest access to Slovakia is via the Vienna-Bratislava connection. Only 64 kilometers away, four direct trains make this jaunt in less than 90 minutes daily. For trains from Germany and other western European countries that pass through the Czech Republic, a transit visa may be required. Other trains to Slovakia from eastern European countries that pass through the Czech Republic may also present visa problems for travelers: if travelers do not hold Czech transit visas and the train enters the Czech Republic in the middle of the night, on-board visas will not be issued and voyagers risk being put off the train. This is not like the CIS, where a huffy conductor may be tamed at the sight of Abraham Lincoln or Queen Elizabeth. Inquire. Bratislava enjoys no less than nine direct trains from Budapest (including the *Hungaria*, *Pannonia* and *Metropol*, leaving from Keleti station), which is only three hours away. All travel via Sturovo. Many guides recommend the morning *Hungaria* and afternoon *Metropol* for getting to Bratislava; they originate in Budapest and run on time. The others connect to Budapest from Romania and are often late. Several express night trains pass through Slovakia at Trencin, but reservations are mandatory in order to board, and, again, if you don't have the Czech transit visa you may find yourself sitting in the chill of the night on the tracks at the border wondering how this happened.

The eastern Slovak city of Kosice enjoys four direct trains daily with the Hungarian towns of Miskolc and Satoraljaujhely, if that helps you. The *Rakoczi* Express makes the Budapest-Kosice run in four hours, leaving Budapest-Keleti in the morning and Kosice in the afternoon with a partial service continuing to Poprad-Tatry. And, the Polish Cracovia express train passes through Kosice between Budapest and Kracow in the middle of the night, as does the Karpaty *Express* between Krakow and Warsaw.

Reservations are required and precision planning is needed to coordinate these travel options. Jumping on an express train at whistle stop in the middle of the night excites the imagination, but also requires willpower. Crawling into a sleepy compartment of strangers is not the easiest way to make friends, but at times a late-night connection may be the most practical way of joining up segments of your trip.

Kosice also serves as a stop between Prague and Moscow (the Dukla Express) and Bratislava and Moscow (the Slovakia Express). Both trains pass through Kiev in the Ukraine.

Visitors to Slovakia are required to have at least $15 U.S. or equivalent per day of their stay in Slovakia when entering the Slovak Republic.

EXCURSIONS AND CITY-SIGHTSEEING

Bratislava

Slovakia's largest city, Bratislava, aside from being the cultural and administrative capital of this young country, sits at a strategic geographic location on the Austrian border, minutes from Hungary, on the Danube River, at the foot of the Carpathians. The geography contributes to the city's historic diversity with Hungarian influence felt in the architecture and names.

The main train station is actually located slightly north of the city and is easily reached by tram. But note that there is another train station that is on the eastern side of the city, called Stanica Bratislava-Nove. It is not as often used for major train connections, but things are always changing.

With its 450,000 inhabitants, Bratislava offers a rich cultural program and ambitious economic aspirations. Start your visit with the Bratislava Castle; built on a hill it dominates the center of Bratislava, and its four towers have become a symbol of this Danube port city. Inhabited from Neolithic Hallstadt and Roman eras, the castle was first mentioned in 907. Today, after reconstruction, it shelters the historical part of the Slovak National Museum. Bratislava Castle is also the residence of the president of the Slovak Republic, with the Slovak parliament residing in the new building nearby.

The Slovak National Museum, a key point of interest, is located opposite the hydrofoil terminal on the river. Contrasting the traditional aesthetics of this museum is the very contemporary Slavak National Gallery, which holds Bratislava's most important art collection. Add to your cultural itinerary the art nouveau Reduta Palace concert hall and the turn-of-the-century National Theater, which recently celebrated its 75th anniversary.

Walking around the city is a pleasant experience. In the evening, Bratislava excels in its choice of wine cellars. Tourists are advised not to chance money on the streets—black marketeers have been known to stick gullible visitors with wads of worthless banknotes from defunct despotic republics.

Regular train connections between Bratislava and Kosice are frequent and efficient. The night train with its couchette service is a particularly good idea, and some savvy travelers who've found it difficult to land an affordable hotel room in Bratislava have even booked a couchette to Kosice as a lodging and transportation solution.

Trencin

This town of 50,000 hosts a noted castle at one of the gateways to Slovakia. Once the most northern Roman military camp, Trencin today is a textile center. The city serves as a stop-over between Bratislava and Kosice via Zilina.

Poprad-Tatry

Industrial and of little interest to travelers, Poprad requires a mention nonetheless in that it is a train hub, north and south, and the pivot point for the electric train that climbs 13 kilometers to the Tatry mountain resort of Stary Smokovec.

Kosice

The second largest city in Slovakia with nearly 250,000 inhabitants, this formerly Hungarian town is now an industrial hub specializing in metallurgy. The old town nonetheless presents much of interest to visitors, and many have used Kosice as a base for regional travel. Trains run every day to Krakow, Poland, and Budapest, Hungary. Visit the remarkable Gothic Cathedral of St. Elizabeth.

POLAND

Getting on Track in Poland

• Tourist information: Polish National Tourist Office, 275 Madison Ave, Suite 1711, New York, NY 10016. Telephone (212) 338-9412, fax (212) 338-9283.
• Public holidays: January 1, New Year's Day, Easter, Easter Monday, May 1, Labor Day, Corpus Christi, Assumption Day, November 1, All Saints' Day, November 11, Day of Independence, December 25, Christmas Day, December 26.

• Summer time: Poland changes to Summer Time on the last Sunday of March and converts back to Standard Time on the last Sunday in September.
• Currency: Zloty. At press time, $1 equalled 3.29 zloty.

PASSPORT ALERT! We have had reports from readers that Polish customs demands passport valid for one year from the date you enter Poland. Before leaving the States, double-check with the tourist office, and make sure your passport meets these requirements. If you're traveling in summer, it could take longer to renew your passport. Forewarned is forearmed!

Overview of Poland's Trains

Polskie Koleje Panstwowe (PKP) operates Poland's trains. With over 200,000 employees, PKP is one of the larger railways of eastern or western Europe.

Like other countries in the region, Poland has had to operate with declining government subsidies. Ridership has declined in recent years as more people buy automobiles. As a result, PKP has had to reduce services, abandon lines and increase fares. Still, it's not a completely bleak picture for Poland's railway. New InterCity and EuroCity lines are being introduced, along with new rolling stock. A project also is underway to upgrade the Berlin-Poznan-Warsaw line for high-speed traffic. Unfortunately, as PKP adapts to the free-market economy, bringing on-line more deluxe and upgraded services between large and medium-sized cities, it'll probably mean the demise of those charming back-country routes.

As the *CIA World Factbook* reminds readers, Poland is slightly smaller than New Mexico and borders with Belarus, the Czech Republic, Slovakia, Germany, Lithuania, Russia, and the Ukraine. For train travelers, that comparative scale doesn't really help orient travel nor plan itineraries. The size of Poland and the placement of its national borders, however, has always been a sensitive issue in history. Poland's boundaries have responded with the elasticity of political events, and anyone with access to a chronological atlas of Europe will note that Poland, with its vulnerable flatness and lack of natural boundaries has both sprawled with expansion and retracted out of existence only to return a century later as a geographic double of its former self. In 1943, at the Teheran Conference, Churchill, Stalin, and Roosevelt decided that land east of the Oder River and Neisse River was to be returned to Poland after centuries of German control, while the eastern provinces would become part of the Soviet Union and thus postwar Poland became 20 percent of its prewar self, and yet closer to the nation it once was back in the 1200s! And this border agreement was ratified in the famous Warsaw Pact of 1955. More than a country, its the cities that have maintained a consistent cultural phenomenon, with Krakow being one of the historic intellectual capitals of Europe. An hour away by car or train, one visits Auschwitz and Birkenau, perhaps the quintessential living symbol of humanity's ability to inflict horror and cruelty. Poland is many things indeed.

Poland's Solidarnosc trade union, led by Lech Walesa, played a pioneering role in the transformation of Eastern Europe. Walesa went on to become Poland's elected president. The fact that there is a Polish Pope has not been an inconsequential factor as well in the transformation of the region. Poland, if anything, must be viewed as a vital stage on which many of the world's major issues appear and reappear. Today, despite the growing pains of converting to a market economy, Poland has a vibrant people with a furtive urge to create both art and commerce. And at this writing, Poland is by far the largest country in eastern Europe.

Poland is highly accessible by trains, and trains have played a deeply felt role in 20th-century Polish history. It is quite easy to move around the country by rail, and in general the atmosphere and openness of the Poles and their new system has removed the heaviness and oppression previously experienced when traveling in Poland.

If you have not opted for a train pass that includes Poland (the Inter-Rail pass includes Poland), you should note that train tickets purchased for Poland in the eastern countries are much cheaper than those prebought in the West. And domestic train tickets are rather reasonable. So, when planning your Polish itinerary, you can stop at the first Polish city of interest to you after crossing the border and buy the continuing tickets there. If you're planning to use a credit card to buy tickets, be advised that only Warsaw and Krakow stations currently accept plastic.

Here are some useful tips for riding Poland's trains, brought to us with some help from rail enthusiast Jeff Dobek's Web site (his Web address appears at the end of the section, before Polrail Pass information).

• Polish trains have several classes: Pociag osobowy ("person train"): These are local trains that make lots of stops They're slow and usually second class, but riding them is a good way to meet the locals, hence, the nickname "person train!" Pociag pospiersny: Faster trains that stop at most mid-sized stations. They usually run with first- and second-class cars. Pociag expresowy: Express trains that operate between major cities. Supplements of up to 33 percent more than regular trains are charged, and reservations are required to ride. Food service is usually available. Pociag InterCity/EuroCity: These are top-notch trains. Introduced in the early 90s, they feature the newest and most comfortable equipment, few stops, and high speeds. Often there will be a full-service restaurant car or at least a buffet car. A supplement is charged and a reservation required.

• Holders of rail passes do not need to hold reservations, but you can obtain them free of charge if you would like to be guaranteed a space. Pass holders still must pay extra for sleeping car charges.

• Make sure you're in the right place to board the right train! Most stations will have posters prominently posted with trains times. White posters show arrival times (marked "przyjazdy") and yellow posters departure times ("odjazdy"). On the departure poster find the time of your train, then read across to the right to find the platform number in the column marked "Peron." Follow the signs in the station to the proper platform ("peron"). Many platforms have two tracks ("tor"), so don't get on the first train you see. Look for an overhead sign showing the destination and departure time of the train. If you don't see one, look for signboards on the side of the coach showing the destination. If all else fails, ask the train conductor or a railroad employee (point to the train and ask "do (and name your destination)?") Sometimes a train will be split along the way, with some of the coaches going to one place, and the rest to somewhere else. Usually trains of this type will have signs on the side of each section showing the destination of that part of the train. First-class cars are usually red and white, and second-class cars are green and white. First-class cars also have a yellow stripe above the window. There will be a 1 or a 2 by the entry door indicating the class of the car. If you have a reservation, look at the reservation slip. It will show the car number ("wagon") and the seat number ("miejsce"). The car number will be found in red on a little white tag on the side of the car. Once inside, the seat numbers are posted outside each compartment and also above each seat in the compartment. If someone is sitting in your seat, show them the reservation slip, and likely they will move. If they don't, ask for help from the train conductor.

• Polish sleeping cars: Some Polish trains feature sleeping cars or food service cars. These cars are run by the Wars (Przedsiebiorstwo Wagonow Sypialnych i Restauracyjnych–Restaurant and Sleeping Car Company), a private company separate from the PKP.

Three types of sleeping-car accommodations are available: couchettes: Poland's couchettes ("wagon kuszetki") have the usual six-berth configuration found in Western Europe and cars. Compartments: Sleeping cars ("wagon sypialny") with compartments, offer first-class and second-class rooms with two beds in first class and three in second class. You may find yourself sharing a compartment with a perfect stranger. If you are traveling solo and like your privacy, consider buying up the remaining beds! As in many other Central and Eastern countries, at night the conductor locks the doors between the sleeping cars and the rest of the train. Note too, that it isn't unusual for the conductor to keep your tickets overnight.

When buying sleeper space, look for the ticket window marked "sprzedaz i przedsprzedazbilety w komunikacji krajowej." If that's too much to remember, there should also be a pictogram with a bed or a Wars logo.

• Eating options: Most mainline trains have a bar car ("wagon barowy"). A limited menu of snacks is usually offered along with one or two hot dishes. There are tables where you can stand and eat (although some cars are now being refurbished with sit-down tables). Wars also. Be on the lookout for a couple of experimental "video bar cars." Some long-distance and international trains feature carry a full restaurant car ("wagon restauracyjny").

• Children under four travel free. Half-fare for children 4–10. Children 11 and over must pay full fare.

To get to Poland from Western Europe, note that the celebrated Ost-West *Express* leaves Paris-Nord station everyday and arrives in Warsaw 22 hours later. This train functions like a puzzle, and cars from around northern Europe, the United Kingdom, Holland, Belgium, and so on, get coupled on along the way. Some travelers have reported that the morning train from London is a better connection than the afternoon one, which requires a change in Germany.

There are many trains between Germany and Poland, with Berlin being only an hour from the Polish border. If you're not familiar with German geography, note that Frankfurt/Oder and Frankfurt/Main are not the same place! The former is the border crossing with Poland in eastern Germany; the latter is the large city. The EuroCity *Berolina* makes the Berlin-Warsaw journey in under seven hours. The Gedania Express between Berlin and Dynia by way of Szczecin takes 10 hours and has sleeping cars. There is also an overnight train between Cologne and Warsaw and Cologne and Krakow via Leipzig, Dresden, and Wroclaw.

From the other eastern countries, Poland is accessible via numerous routes. The Prague-Warsaw train, the overnight *Bohemia*, takes 12 hours. The *Silesia Express* goes between Prague and Warsaw by way of Katowice, while the Baltic Express from Prague to

Gdansk via Wroclaw and Poznan takes 16 hours. From Vienna the *Sobieski* and Chopin express trains run both at night in the days and pass by Breclav and Katowice. Other connections may be noted in the chapters on Hungary, the Czech Republic, and Slovakia. Good deals on the Trans-Siberian Railroad can be found in Warsaw.

If you are inexperienced in international train travel in the East, the following story of an innocent traveler attempting to make two sets of reservations between Poland and Romania may be instructive: "We went to the ticket office to book our train. The woman did not speak English and there were loads of people behind us waiting (despite there being about 15 empty windows). Using a pen and paper as our only common language we were told we didn't need a reservation on that day from Warsaw to Krakow, so we just asked for one from Krakow to Bucharest for the following day. Instead of just reservations, she issued us tickets, which we didn't want, so we had a row about that until someone helped out, and we ended up with some reservations. After we'd paid, a Polish kid came up and asked if he could help us, as he spoke English. It turned out we'd been given reservations from Warsaw to Krakow for the following day. Totally useless."

The Polish national railroad takes the ubiquitous initials PKP. Express trains with reservations assure you the fastest and most comfortable way of traveling, whereas the direct trains and local trains are slower and more crowded but afford you a greater taste of local life.

The national tourist agency Orbis serves as reservation center for all train travel, and the ease and inexpensive fees are strong reasons to use this service. The express trains heading to or coming from the capital all have dining cars and comfortable seats. And the new Intercity trains between Warsaw and Krakow in under three hours are state of the art. As in France or Germany, second class is perfectly comfortable. One experienced rail user adds, "First-class accommodations are inexpensive and should be used where possible. The language problem is the largest difficulty, and missing a train in a larger station a reality." Polish rail aficionado, Jeff Dobek, enjoys answering questions and chatting with others about Poland's railways. He has launched a great Web site containing a wealth of information about riding Poland's trains. Log on at: http://walden.mo.net/~jdobek/pkptrav.html. You can contact him through his Web site. Jeff adds that travelers shouldn't leave luggage unattended in the train, even when you go to the dining car.

Others have added that travelers should be careful not to take currency that is marked in any way; only perfectly clean notes will be accepted by change bureaus or banks. Still others openly write of fearful and sleepless nights on Polish trains—one is not certain if thieves are really plotting to steal your luggage, money, passport, and travelers checks or if the ambiance of total insecurity prods the imagination into zones of paranoia.

Polrail Pass Unlimited first and second class travel (express trains included) on Poland's railways. These prices are valid through early 1998:

	Adult		Junior	
	First Cl.	Second Cl.	First Cl.	Second Cl.
8 days	$95	$65	$67	$45
15 days	$110	$75	$77	$52
21 days	$130	$85	$90	$60
1 month	$160	$110	$110	$77

Orbis Polish Travel Bureau, Inc. sells the Polrail Pass. To issue a pass, they need your name as it appears on your passport and passport number. If you know your travel dates, include them with the order, otherwise they will issue an "open" pass that must be validated at a railway station before boarding any trains. Junior passes are available to those under 26. Children under 10 pay half the adult fare. A $10 handling fee will be added to all orders. Contact Orbis at 342 Madison Avenue, Suite 1512, New York, NY 10173, (800) 223-6037, (212) 867-5011, fax (212) 682-4715, E-mail, orbisinfo@orbis-usa.com.

EXCURSIONS AND CITY-SIGHTSEEING

Warsaw

Warsaw has been the capital of Poland since the beginning of the 17th century. At present it has about two million inhabitants, which ranks it seventh in Europe both in population and area. The Main Town and Old Town are on the higher, left bank of the Vistula River, with parks and squares sloping gently down to the river. Within an easy day's travel from Berlin, Prague, Vienna, and Budapest, Warsaw is relatively accessible by train. The population of Warsaw suffered brutally under the Third Reich and the city was ultimately leveled. Some 35 percent of the Warsaw population was Jewish before the war, with the Warsaw Ghetto representing the last holdout of surviving Jews. Miraculously, the old city was reconstructed in a highly convincing way.

Most travelers arrive at the lower level of the Central Station, which has four levels. The station is well equipped with services—and pickpockets. So be warned: the thieves here are organized and efficient, working in small groups. And be wary when getting on and off trains: pairs of thieves arrange to climb on in front of and behind you, one serving to distract your attention while the other grabs the goodies.

Note that when you check your luggage at the train station, you'll be asked to assign a value to your belongings and pay a fee according to that value. This is normal.

Plac Zamkowy is at the mouth of the old city (Stare Miastro) and is a good place to start your walking tour. Visit the Barbicon Wall, Blacha Palace, the Royal Way, and the ancient market here. A visit to the reconstructed Chopin Family Drawing Room in the side wing of the former Raczynski Palace should be on your list. For a bright view of the city, climb to the top of the 37th floor of the Palace of Culture and Science. Also visit the Monument to the Heroes of the Ghetto and the Lenin Museum. For Warsaw information you can now consult the *Warsaw Voice*, Poland's only general-interest English-language weekly newspaper, now on-line on the World Wide Web.

Warsaw is also noted for its music, its art scene, and it cultural festivals.

Krakow

Undoubtedly one of Europe's most beautiful cities, Krakow was spared by the Nazis during World War II at the negotiated request of the Vatican. Krakow is the former capital of Poland, the royal residence, and a symbol of Polish culture that constantly shines with the reflection of its one-time splendor.

Krakovians see their city as the place which is said to be a mystical city: once a center of magic and astrology where Faustus began his studies; one of the seven places in the world protected by magical stones…

Start in the middle of the city at the medieval Wawel Castle. Krakow gets its name from Prince Krak, who founded a settlement on Wawel Hill. Krakow emerged as a student town in the Middle Ages, and Jagiellonian University was founded here in 1364. Spend some time walking though the Market Square or rynek Glowny and its quaint archways, and the Renaissance Cloth Hall, where crafted goods are sold. The live trumpet sounds that call out every hour from the top of the Church of Our Lady and end abruptly is a tradition dating from the 13th century, when the trumpeter was pierced in the neck by a Tatar arrow. The Kazimierz district is now silent with echoes and ghosts; it was here that the Jewish community, and later, the ghetto, was situated. Spielberg filmed much of the movie *Schindler's List* on location. Nearly all the Jews of Krakow were sent to the death camps, and Oswiecim (Auschwitz in German) is only an hour from the city. The site of the Plaszow work camp can be visited outside the city.

Krakovians will suggest that a visitor buy grain for Kracow's pigeons (this is a tradition), or give a flower from the Krakow flower sellers to a passing beauty (another tradition). Rest in the "Planty" in the shade of a 100-year-old chestnut and the 600-year-old university. Walk through Kazimierz through Wolnica between Sw. Wawrzynca, Dajwor, Miodowa and Krakowska Streets. Spend some time on a street which is a really a small, elongated square, called Szeroka Street. Here you will find the Remu'h Synagogue and cemetery. In the renaissance Old Synagogue you will see a beautiful collection of Jewish art and objects.

Check the schedule for cultural events in Krakow; the city hosts a rich selection of festivals, including the Short Film Festival and Music in Old Krakow.

Auschwitz

After this day trip from Krakow, a 60-kilometer trip, you will never be the same. Be prepared to do nothing else all day. After a tour of the concentration camp, make sure you also witness the extermination camp of Birkenau, two kilometers away. One and a half million people, mostly Eastern European Jews from nearly 30 countries, were murdered here. One traveler reminds others not to be tempted to pay 50 zloty for an organized trip to Auschwitz from Krakow. A coach from the central bus station to Oswiecim costs just four zloty each way and leaves from Stand 3. The Oswiecim rail station is two kilometers north of the Auschwitz camp, a 20-minute walk. There are six daily trains from Krakow Glowny station, 12 per day from Krakow Plaszow station, and 15 per day from Katowice.

Zakopane

Zakopane, an Alp-like mountain resort in the Tatras, has attracted visitors, hikers, skiers, and vacationers for centuries. The Tatra National Park costs 1 zloty to enter, and is highly regulated to protect the natural setting. For example, it is forbidden to pick berries, herbs, mushrooms, and so on. The guidebook *Zakopane and Its Vicinity,* by Maciej Pinkwart, available in many languages including English, is highly recommended. Should you decide to take the raft trip down the Dunajec Gorge in the Pieniny National Park, book in advance via Orbis Tourist. The queues are quite horrendous on fine days.

The train to Zakopane from Krakow took nearly five hours via Nowy Targ in the pre-war days. Today, the Kasprowy makes the run in half that time twice a day leaving from Krakow, and the Giewont leaving from Zakopane. There is also a funicular railway up Mt. Gubalowska that offers a memorable view of the mountain valley.

The Zakopane bus trip to Morskie Oko, the largest lake in the Tatras, is available via the village of Plana Palenica; the lake is a nine-kilometer walk from there.

The seasonal *Tatry Express* takes six hours from Warsaw to Zakopane. To cover the entire north-south expanse of Poland you can ride the overnight Zakopane-Gdansk train, which stops in Wroclaw, Poznan, and Warsaw.

Wroclaw

In the heart of Lower Silesia, this tongue-twister dates back to the 13th century. On the Odra, this city boasts of more than 120 canals. Cultural life and student activity are vibrant here. The pubs fill with young people nightly. St. Dorothy's Church demands a visit.

Lublin

An ancient city with the oldest private university in the country, Lublin is worth visiting because it is authentic and deeply historic. From the castle-like architecture of the main train station slightly out of town, Lublin's old town affords visitors a taste of the decadence of times gone by. Visit the castle and the Krakoski Gate as well as the many impressive old churches.

Poznan

Between Berlin and Warsaw, Poznan is famous for its Przemyslaw Castle and sculptures at the Dzialynski Castle. Walk through the old town and then visit the unique Musical Instrument Museum. The stained glass at the Church of the Holy Virgin is of particular beauty, as is the brick Gothic cathedral at Ostorw Tumski. For train travelers, Poznan is actually easy to visit—many trains pass through the city.

Torun

This Teutonic medieval city is located on the Vistula River between Gdansk and Poznan. Visit the Gothic churches. Birthplace of Copernicus (1473), travelers can visit his house and inspect the instruments he used to determine that the earth revolves around the sun. The Church of St. John contains one of the largest bells in Poland. The honey gingerbread is a local specialty.

The *Kujawiak Express* serves Torun from Warsaw every day, but requires reservations.

Czestochowa

This sacred place of pilgrimage attracts Catholic worshipers from all over the country. They come to the Luminous Mountain Monastery (Jasna Gora) to worship the image of the Black Madonna, the holiest icon in Poland. There are direct train connections from Warsaw, Krakow, and Zakopane.

Gdansk, Gdynia, and Sopot

Gdansk, Gdynia, and Sopot, known as the tri-cities, are sprawled for 30 kilometers along the Gulf of Gdansk on the Baltic Sea, with Gdansk serving as Poland's leading port and shipbuilding center. Its shipyard is the birthplace of Lech Walesa's Solidarnosc labor party. Also known as Danzig, it was declared a free city in the Treaty of Versailles after World War II. There is international ferry service to and from Finland and Sweden.

Gdynia, a leading port and fishing center, is the most northern of the three cities and the only one technically on the Baltic.

Sopot is the chic seaside resort that has attracted international bathers for centuries. Connected by electric train, Sopot offers wide white beaches, but the local pollution is so intense that swimming is no longer thinkable.

Major trains stop in all three cities, while southbound trains usually originate in Gdynia. The Warsaw-Gdansk trains *Neptun, Slupia*, and *Kaszub* take 3½-4 hours, while the Lajkonik Express between Krakow and Gdansk takes seven hours.

ONE-DAY EXCURSIONS

Warsaw - Czestochowa - Warsaw   1060

It is only a 2½-hour drive from Warsaw by taxi on Poland's best highway.

Dep. Warsaw (Wsch.)	06:35(1)	09:00 (2)	Dep. Czestochowa	06:35	19:10
Dep. Warsaw (Cen.)	06:50	09:15	Arr. Warsaw (Cen.)	09:29	21:56
Arr. Czestochowa	09:28	13:10	Arr. Warsaw (Wsch.)	09:44	22:14

(1) Restaurant car. (2) Change trains in Lodz.

Warsaw - Gdansk - Gdynia - Warsaw   1030

Dep. Warsaw (Cen.)	-0-	02:22 (1)	07:02 (2)	09:23 (3+4)
Dep. Warsaw (Wsch.)	01:44 (1)	02:48	07:12 (3)	09:28
Arr. Gdansk	05:36	06:55	10:31	12:30
Arr Gdynia	06:12	07:28	10:51	12:55

•   •   •

Dep. Gdynia	04:42 (2)	05:41 (2)	06:44 (2)	08:41 (2+5)
Dep. Gdansk	05:10	06:10 (3)	07:10	09:10
Arr. Warsaw (Wsch.)	08:36	09:23	10:32	12:37
Arr. Warsaw (Cen.)	10 minutes after arriving Wschodnia rail station			

(1) Carries a sleeping car. Also has couchettes. Light refreshments. (2) Reservation required. Light re-

freshments. (3) Runs Monday-Friday except holidays. (4) Plus other frequent Warsaw (Cent.) departures from 11:02 to 22:02. (5) Plus other frequent Gdansk departures from 11:10 to 23:06.

Warsaw - Krakow - Warsaw   1065

Dep. Warsaw (Cen.)	07:00 (1)	09:08 (1)	11:00 (2)	13:00 (2)	15:00 (1)
Arr. Krakow (Glowny)	09:38	11:44	13:35	15:35	17:37 (3)

• • •

Dep. Krakow (Glowny)	01:17(4)	02:00 (4)	06:39 (1)	07:25 (2)	10:22 (1+5)
Arr. Warsaw (Cen.)	05:56	07:18	09:15	10:00	13:00

(1) Reservation required. Light refreshments. (2) Reservation required. Restaurant car. (3) Plus other Warsaw departures at 16:00 (2), 17:00 (1), and 19:00 (1), arriving Krakow 18:35, 19:37, and 21:37. (4) Carries sleepers and couchettes. (5) Plus other Krakow frequent times from 10:10 to 23:00.

Warsaw - Lublin - Warsaw   1055

Dep. Warsaw (Centralna)	-0-	06:46	10:42 (2)	14:46 (3)
Dep. Warsaw (Wschodnia)	02:49 (1)	06:56	10:57	14:56
Arr. Lublin	05:10	09:05	12:51	17:02

• • •

Dep. Lublin	07:17 (1)	10:35	12:35	15:08 (4)
Arr. Warsaw (Wschodnia)	09:12	12:47	14:47	17:05
Arr. Warsaw (Centralna)	10 minutes after arriving Wschodnia rail station			

(1) Light refreshments. (2) Reservation required. Light refreshments. (3) Plus other Warsaw (Cen.) departures at 16:46 (1), 18:42 (2) and 20:46, arriving Lublin 19:02, 20:42 and 23:05. (4) Plus another Lublin departure at 16:35, arriving Warsaw (Cen.) 18:57.

Warsaw - Poznan - Warsaw   1000

Dep. Warsaw (Wsch.)	05:57 (1)	06:15 (1)	09:15 (1)	13:15 (1)	15:15 (1)
Dep. Warsaw (Cen.)	15 minutes after departing Wschodnia station				
Arr. Poznan (Gl.)	09:16	09:47	12:52	16:48	18:39

Dep. Warsaw (Wsch.)	16:05 (1)	17:15 (2)	19:10 (2)	21:55 (1)	23:00 (1)
Dep. Warsaw (Cen.)	15 minutes after departing Wschodnia station
Arr. Poznan (Gl.)	19:21	20:42	22:45	01:35	03:06

Dep. Poznan (Gl.)	02:00 (3)	06:26 (1)	07:08 (2)
Arr. Warsaw (Cen.)	05:45	09:35	10:35
Arr. Warsaw (Wsch.)	14 minutes after arriving Centralna station

Dep. Poznan (Gl.)	10:12 (1)	11:26 (1)	15:14 (1+4)
Arr. Warsaw (Cen.)	13:50	14:44	18:49
Arr. Warsaw (Wsch.)	14 minutes after arriving Centralna station

(1) Reservation required. Restaurant car. (2) Reservation required. Light refreshments. (3) Carries a sleeping car. Also has couchettes. (4) Plus other Poznan departures at 17:09 (1), 18:22 and 19:49 (1), arriving Warsaw (Cen.) 20:30, 21:40 and 22:55.

Warsaw - Sopot - Warsaw   1030

Dep. Warsaw (Cen.)	16:02 (1)	22:02 (2)
Dep. Warsaw (Wsch.)	10 minutes after departing Centralna station
Arr. Sopot	19:47	02:36

• • •

Dep. Sopot	06:53 (1)	01:38 (2)
Arr. Warsaw (Wsch.)	10:32	05:37
Arr. Warsaw (Cen.)	15 minutes after arriving Wschodnia station

(1) Reservation required. Light refreshments. (2) Carries a sleeping car. Also has couchettes.

Warsaw - Torun - Warsaw   1035

Dep. Warsaw (Wsch.)	06:20 (1)	16:40 (1+2)	22:30 (3)
Dep. Warsaw (Cen.)	06:40	16:55	22:45
Arr. Torun	09:42	19:51	02:24

• • •

Dep. Torun	06:59 (1+2)	18:26 (1)	04:15 (3)
Arr. Warsaw (Cen.)	09:55	21:33	07:46
Arr. Warsaw (Wsch.)	10:09	21:47	07:59

(1) Light refreshments. (2) Reservation required. (3) Carries a sleeping car.

INTERNATIONAL CONNECTIONS
FROM POLAND

Warsaw is Poland's gateway for rail travel to Berlin (and on to both Scandinavia and north-western Europe), Moscow, and Vienna (and on to Italy, southeastern Europe and south-western Europe).

Warsaw - Berlin   56

Dep. Warsaw (Wsch.)	05:57 (1)	16:05 (1)	22:00 (2)	23:20 (2)
Dep. Warsaw (Cen.)	06:12	16:17	22:20	23:35 (3)
Arr. Berlin (Licht.)	12:38	22:33	06:16	07:23
Arr. Berlin (Hbf.)	-0-	-0-	-0-	-0-
Arr. Berlin (Zoo)	-0-	-0-	-0-	-0-

(1) Supplement payable. Reservation required. Restaurant car. (2) Carries a sleeping car. Also has couchettes. (3) Reservation required.

Warsaw - Moscow   94a

Dep. Warsaw (Gdan.)	-0-	-0-
Dep. Warsaw (Cen.)	09:28 (1)	14:12 (2)
Set your watch forward one hour		
Arr. Brest	14:39	19:11

A short distance from the Brest rail station, the train is held for about 2 hours while the train's wheels are changed so as to conform to the wider Soviet track.

Dep. Brest	-0-	-0-
Arr. Moscow (Smol.)	08:30	11:58

(1) Carries only sleeping cars. (2) Carries only sleeping cars. Has restaurant car Brest–Moscow. (3) Carries a sleeping car. Also has couchettes. Coaches are second class.

Warsaw - Vienna   95a

Dep. Warsaw (Wschodnia)	08:45 (1)	20:20 (2)
Dep. Warsaw (Centralna)	09:00	20:40
Arr. Vienna (Sudbf.)	16:48	06:55

(1) Reservations required. Restaurant car. (2) Carries a sleeping car. Also has couchettes.

ROMANIA

Getting on Track in Romania

• Tourist information: Romanian National Tourist Office, 14 East 38th Street, 12th Floor, New York, NY 10016. Telephone (212) 545-8484, fax (212) 251-0429.
• Public holidays: January 1, New Year's Day, January 2, May 1, Labor Day, May 2, August 23, Liberation Day, August 24, December 25, 26, 30.
• Summer time: Romania changes to Summer Time on the last Sunday of March and converts back to Standard Time on the last Sunday in September.
• Currency: Leu. At press time, $1 equalled 7085 Leu.

Overview of Romania's Trains

Rail Europe sells the first class Romanian Pass for $60. Travel any three days within any 15 days. Children 4-11: half adult fare.

To buy a Romanian timetable, ask for "Mersul Trenurillor."

Passengers who board a train that requires reservation without obtaining a reservation are charged a penalty fee.

It has taken time, but the dark and perverse images of Romania that used to correspond to the reality of Ceausescu's Romania are fading quickly as the country, its people, and its institutions respond to a new world of possibilities. Romania today offers travelers more than they might have previously anticipated. Romania's history, language, and geographic beauty position it as a country worth the time one is willing spend to discover its treasures. Aside from its time-warped capital, Bucharest, Romania offers visitors the lush and romantic medieval mountain villages of Transylvania, the iconoclastic monasteries of proud Moldavia and intellectual Bukovina, and the Roman- and Turkish-influenced resort towns on the Black Sea. The infrastructure of material life in this least developed of the new Eastern European countries is still unpredictable and seemingly illogical, and many Romanians have a strangely ironic take on reality, having emerged from the horrors of one of the century's most twisted dictators. But give them a chance and show some sensitivity toward their history and you'll be touched by the local readiness to open up and share the best of the indigenous culture. If you are seeking an experience that is real, inexpensive, and filled with emotional challenge, a trip through Romania by train is highly recommended.

Romania is farther east and south than most Westerners imagine, with the Ukraine and Moldova to the north and east, the Black Sea to the east, Bulgaria to the south, Yugoslavia to the southwest, and Hungary to the west. Making the journey by train from western Europe requires some time and a few long stints on the tracks. Due to the very low salaries that they receive, Romanian intellectuals and artists eager to visit other cities in Europe are almost always obliged to take the train, and thus you'll often meet fascinating folks on the Bucharest-Vienna run, for example.

Catrinel Plescu, program director at the Romanian Cultural Foundation in Bucharest, shared her recent experience on the *Dacia* express train to Vienna: "We left Bucharest at 4:30 (16:30) and I was a bit nervous about the journey, fearing the old, worn-out carriages.

Having to cross three frontiers, a nightmare in itself for an Eastern European, I am worried about the rumors we hear about train attacks in the night. Surprisingly, the carriage is brand-new and cheerfully colorful, navy blue and red, not that terrible military green that reminds one of war convoys and typified Romanians trains. The sheets and the blankets are clean; the towels are threadbare but clean too. The loo is impeccable. I am almost moved. It's the Romanian human touch of gentle corruption—I notice that the toilet paper, paper towels, and liquid soap has already been stolen. The stern schoolmarm in me wants to tell the conductor that this is not civilized, that it spoils our image, that it only confirms that Romanians have no 'klo-kultur,' as the Germans would say. But he helps us with the luggage, he has a nice face with a drooping mustache, two children, a small salary…so I let it be, the tired Romanian in me says…at least he is friendly and human. I've got my own toilet paper (ancestral wisdom) anyway."

Catrinel goes on to report of an incident at the first border crossing. "I refuse to pay the compulsory tourist tax that the custom officer tells me has just been passed in parliament. I want him to show me the law, and secondly, I tell him I'm not a tourist. My fear of people in uniforms turns to anger. This has helped me many times to be brave before 1989. I control my anger and try to sound rational, feminine, and sweet. The man in uniform threatens to put me off the train. This is Hegeshalom; I don't want to spend the night in Hegeshalom. I remember my father's advice: 'Never show them you are frightened; if they feel your fear you are finished'. At the same time I wonder if this is worth the fight. I state that I am expected at a journalists' conference and if he wants an uproar, that's OK with me. He goes off to talk to a superior, and I hear him say that that woman threatened him. They glare at me and I glare back and smile sweetly. My tummy aches. The other Romanians are staring at me because I have dared to be different. This is painfully familiar. I reaffirm what I already know; they want to make the others hate you for defending your rights. I wonder what will happen. I wait. Nothing happens. What a relief; what happiness.

"I've shown them for once, for the first time, that we are stronger than they. The conductor comes back and we drink a glass to each other's health and he tells me, 'Madame, I was so frightened for you! Why did you do that? You know people in uniforms are always right!' Well, this time they weren't. The Hungarian customs officer then asked a Japanese couple to get off the train because there was something wrong with their visas. They got off in tears, not understanding what it was all about. If I could only have explained it to them! Cultural misunderstanding!"

As for domestic travel in Romania, stories vary from western tourists, but in almost all cases a deep sense of contentment seems to pervade those who have decided to commit a part of their itineraries to this still crude land of surprises. Contact with Romanians seems to outstrip the geography or landmarks as the most rewarding aspect of Romanian travels.

One of the most moving travelogues written on Romania was penned on-line on Compuserve's Travel Forum by Melissa Harris, an assistant professor of architecture on exchange in Vienna who spent two weeks exploring the Romanian landscape and mindset by train. "When we arrived in Arad, Romania, at 05:00, we couldn't decide if it was necessary to get off the train to buy our tickets onto Bucharest. When purchased in the country of travel, tickets are significantly less expensive. We decided to get off, but failed to reboard in time and the train left without us. It would be five hours before the next train departed. It was still dark in Arad as we fumbled our way about the station, looking first for a place to purchase tickets and then for baggage storage which would free us to roam the city during our layover. At the end of the waiting room, we were instructed, there was luggage storage. When I first pushed open the swinging doors, a terrible odor confronted us. Sudden darkness blinded us temporarily. The air was thick and heavy—dank, stagnant air that stank of alcohol and caused us to choke. Perhaps it, like the people who emerged from it, had not stirred for hours. If one can conceive of space as a solid, this waiting room seemed impenetrable.

"As our eyes adjusted, we saw motionless people packed densely on the floors and benches. We moved through the room like a small wave causing ripples in a tangle of arms and legs. Coughing and moaning jostled the unconscious, though daybreak was still an hour away. Time froze as the faint light signaling the end of the room never seem to get any closer. We were moving in slow motion through invisible mud, fighting the paralysis of this violent act of contrast—the 'haves' slicing through the 'have nots.' But if one believes in fate, our ignorance of the train system blessed us with the opportunity to meet our first guardian, Imre, a 23-year-old budding businessman from Brasov. For me, Romania is best summarized by the characters of three people we met, who in each individual situation framed my perceptions and actions."

Imre went on to escort her to his colorful, rural Transylvanian village of Sacele, where, aside from slaughtering a lamb, our heroine learned the routine of daily Romanian life in the countryside.

When it came to looking for more classical means of lodging, like a hotel, Melissa writes that "this is where the myth of cheap travel in Eastern Europe is exposed. Our running joke throughout the trip was the parrot-like response we got when we asked 'How much does this cost?' The answer was always another question: 'Where are you from?' 'America' insured the highest possible rate. If you are a tourist, it is almost impossible to find a hotel room for less than $80 to $100 per night. In other Eastern European countries, accommodations in private homes cost much less, but this doesn't exist yet in Romania. If you are Romanian with proper identification, the same room costs $6."

Bucharest's Gara du Nord train station is reknown for its confusion, so take your time and keep your head. "No visitor leaves without a brush against the sticky fibers of an invisible web of complications almost too bizarre to handle," Melissa recounts. "Many innocent visitors, in fact, become stunned and temporarily paralyzed. We still have no idea if some of the people we encountered were intertwined, but as the night progressed into morning, it seemed more and more likely that we were tangled in a broader net than we could imagine." Again, just be careful, be discreet, be less than trusting, and, when possible, have local Romanians meet you and send you off. It's better to start off overprotected than find your holiday ruined by a black market scam or an unfriendly shakedown.

Melissa's description of the approach to Gara du Nord is realistic, and it should help you imagine what you may head into: "The dingy yellow light of a large bonfire in front of the station cast a spooky glow over hovering bodies and lighted our path to the entrance. A man without legs, almost indistinguishable from the color of the ground, dragged himself past as we dodged the spit of a crippled Gypsy boy retaliating against another throwing sand. My desire to flee was mounting. We were about to discover the underbelly of the infamous Gara du Nord."

If there weren't so many consistent stories about conspiring groups of thieves it would be hard to believe these horrific tales as true. Undoubtedly, things have improved since 1993 but to what degree is unclear. Melissa completed her Romanian experience in style. Her train was delayed for hours; she waited huddled on the platform with her travel companions in the station, only to discover that the track number had been changed at the last minute, and then it was a mad rush to catch it at all.

"Panic swept through our small crowd. Dave ran off to reinspect the information board and the rest of us scurried, looking for anyone in a uniform. I found the closest guy and managed to communicate that we were looking for the train to Sofia. Sympathizing with our desire, our need to get out, this man knew immediately that we were in trouble. He began to run and motioned us to follow. He wanted us to make it. We ran. Rounding the corner, passing track after track, I prayed he knew where he was going. We had pinned all of our hopes on this guy. There was maybe a minute left, maybe seconds, before departure. No more room for errors. As we raced with our packs bouncing, I was running as fast as I possibly could not for the train to Sofia but from the idea of a night in the Gara du Nord."

Of course the train was packed—other people were in their reserved seats and refused obstinately to budge—and Melissa and friends tried to obtain justice. "We remained patient as the conductor pushed his way to the controversial cabin. But when he, too, returned empty handed, irritation began to rise. We paid for these seats and we wanted them. The conductor told us to wait while he conferred with his buddies in their compartment. When he emerged, he escorted us into the business compartment as the other conductors gathered their belongings. They were giving up their seats. If things weren't complicated enough already, we then had to purchase our tickets to Sofia. We only had tickets to the border, where you must get off to buy the rest. Or you can buy them from the conductor for a slightly higher price. So before we all moved in to occupy our places for the night, this guy pulls out a price book and begins to write out the prices. Dave and I were watching closely. 'Don't trust anyone,' the man at the Romania Travel Bureau in Vienna had told us. 'No one.'

"And considering the hassle we had encountered previously with the Arad conductor who was so drunk he couldn't focus and refused to give us our return tickets back, requiring that we essentially push him aside and grab them, we were on high alert. Everything looked feasible until he slapped down a 3,200-lei figure. None of our tickets had been more than 800 lei. Now he was telling us our total would be 5,200 lei each. Though it is only ten dollars, we knew it was severely escalated. Despite our questioning, the guy remained firm. He had us and he knew it. We all forked over the money. It was worth knowing that we had our places for the rest of the night and morning. We got him to write down all the seat numbers again. Who cared about a sleeper at this point? I couldn't wait to have this seat, the protection that such a bribe would provide.

"Just as we had all settled back, leaning wearily into the vinyl seats, Ted's face dropped. He pointed to the aisle window. Briefly speechless, he then gasped, 'It's him. Oh, no. It's that fat—' It was the round man who had pushed over my shoulder while I was buying the tickets. He was now pushing his way toward our compartment. When he attempted to open the door, Ted said no, and held it closed. The guy pressed his face and hands against the glass like some horror movie. Dave quickly pulled the curtains. The man said his wife was pregnant and his family needed a place to sit. Certainly it was his crew who had already occupied our original seats. It seemed as though the entire mass of people standing outside the door wanted into our compartment. They began to pull on the door, pressing their faces to the window. Ted and Dave moved swiftly. With collected belts and luggage straps and harnessed the door and secured it. Ted sat right by the door. There would be no sleeping tonight. The frustrations, the discomfort of the weary travelers outside our door could easily turn on us. They had the numbers. Each time this nightmare seemed to end, another face appeared. We rode like this for three hours. Strangely, when we got to Ruse, just over the Romanian border, the entire train emptied."

EXCURSIONS AND CITY-SIGHTSEEING

Bucharest

This city needs to be walked. Have local friends or a well-recommended guide take you around. Much of prewar Bucharest remains untouched and some of the most elegant properties are now returning to their pre-Ceausescu owners. You can even visit the streets and residences that belonged to the dictator and his wife, entire portions of the city that was off-limits to citizens. One mansion is noted as having solid gold scales in the kitchen which were used to weigh the meat fed to Ceausescu's pack of Dobermans and German shepherds.

The gargantuan Casa Poporului, the administrative office bloc that was to be Ceausescu's legacy, rose from the ruins of churches, monasteries, and other historic buildings, now looms over the city center in front of a boulevard that dwarfs Paris's Champs-Elysées. Fountains burst in obscene spurts for kilometers in the center of this avenue while the residents of Bucharest were deprived of drinking water in a harsh rationing scheme. The People's House was never finished and there is talk today among intellectuals of converting the monster into a Museum of Human Folly!

Near the Atheneum concert hall is Revolution Square, the site of the dramatic events of December 1989, flanked by the former royal palace, now housing the national art collection, and the former Communist Party headquarters, now housing the Romanian Senate. Visit all of these.

Brasov

Excellent Transylvania mountain scenery. Visit the 14th-century Black Church.

Bukovina

Northeast of Bucharest in the northern Moldavian region of Bukovina, priceless monasteries beckon your attention: Voronet, Humor, Sucevita, Moldovita, and Arbore. What makes these monasteries unique are the extraordinary frescoes.

Sighisoara

Sighisoara, with its lovely old citadel square, includes the birthplace of Vlad Tepes, the historical Count Dracula. Visit the museum of the walled town.

Sinaia

This lovely winter resort town, filled with mystique and lore, is noted for its late-19th-century extravaganza, Peles Castle, which Prince Carol of Hohenzollern built. Peles was designed as a residence with large halls, elaborate carving, and sumptuous decorations. Access to this and other gems of the Romanian patrimony were restricted during the long and harsh reign of Ceausescu.

ONE-DAY EXCURSIONS

Bucharest - Brasov - Bucharest   1600

All of these trains require reservation, unless designated otherwise.

Dep. Bucharest (Nord)	06:00 (1)	08:32	08:54 (2)	13:02 (2+3)
Arr. Brasov	08:28	11:03	12:08	15:53

Sights in **Brasov:** Excellent Transylvania Mountain scenery in this area. See the 14th-century Black Church. The Museum of History. The Art Museum. The Museum of the Romanian School. A popular winter resort, **Poiana Brasov**, is nine miles from here.

Dep. Brasov	02:09	03:18 (1)	05:34 (1)	06:05 (4)
Arr. Bucharest (Nord)	05:01	06:14	08:10	08:40

(1) Carries a sleeping car. Also has couchettes. (2) Restaurant car. (3) Plus other Bucharest departures at frequent times from 16:10 to 23:25. (4) Plus other Brasov departures at 07:34 (2), 09:20 (2), 10:42 (2), 17:02 (2), 19:57 (2), and 21:28 (2).

Bucharest - Constantza - Eforie - Mangalia   and v.v. 1670

Dep. Bucharest (Nord)	06:45 (1)	07:55 (1)	09:00 (1)	11:10 (1)	14:00 (1)
Arr. Constantza	09:05 (2)	10:15 (2)	11:05 (2)	13:29	16:42
Dep. Constantza	09:20	10:30	-0-	-0-	17:00
Arr. Eforie (Nord)	09:37	10:48	-0-	-0-	17:00
Arr. Mangalia	10:19	11:30	-0-	-0-	18:13

•   •   •

Dep. Mangalia	05:35 (1+2)	-0-	-0-	14:50 (1+2)	-0-
Dep. Eforie (Nord)	06:26	-0-	-0-	15:38 (3)	-0-
Arr. Constantza	06:45	-0-	-0-	15:27	-0-
Dep. Constantza	07:00	08:10 (2)	13:20 (2)	16:15	16:35 (1+2)
Arr. Bucharest (Nord)	09:44	10:52	15:57	18:34	18:54

(1) Restaurant car. (2) Reservations required. (3) Plus other Mangalia departures at 17:17 (2), and 19:00 (1+2), arriving Bucharest 21:30, and 22:44.

Sights: **Constantza** is a very large resort. See the Museum of Archaeology Parvan. The Open Air Museum of Archaeology. The Roman Mosaic. The Museum of the Black Sea. **Eforie** and **Mangalia** are popular Black Sea beach resorts.

Bucharest - Galati - Bucharest   1630

Dep. Bucharest (Nord)	14:50	17:49 (1+2)	19:20 (3)
Arr. Galati	18:18	20:50	22:42

Sights in **Galati**: The most splendid array of birdlife in all of Europe.

Dep. Galati	05:58 (1+2)	13:06 (3)	17:55 (3)
Arr. Bucharest (Nord)	09:00	16:30	21:20

(1) Runs daily, except Saturday. (2) Reservations required. Restaurant car. (3) Reservation required. Light refreshments.

Bucharest - Sighisoara - Bucharest   1600

All of these trains require reservation.

Dep. Bucharest (Nord)	08:32	13:02 (1)
Arr. Sighisoara	12:55	17:53

Sights in **Sighisoara**: The birthplace of Count Dracula. This is an interesting medieval fortress city. See the Museum of the Walled Town. Stroll through the old section.

Dep. Sighisoara	18:03 (1)	19:33
Arr. Bucharest (Nord)	22:46	23:58

(1) Restaurant car.

Bucharest - Sinaia - Bucharest   1600

All of these trains require reservation.

Dep. Bucharest (Nord)	06:00	08:32 (1)	09:10 (1)	13:02 (1)	16:10 (1+2)
Arr. Sinaia	07:28	10:00	10:52	14:50	17:44

Dep. Bucharest (Nord)	16:30 (1)	17:56 (1)	20:10 (1)	21:50 (3)	
Arr. Sinaia	18:02	19:27	20:42	21:13	

Sights in **Sinaia**: This is a major winter resort.

Dep. Sinaia	04:33	06:33	07:04	08:34 (1)	10:20 (1+2)
Arr. Bucharest (Nord)	06:14	08:10	08:40	10:08	12:00

Dep. Sinaia	12:01 (1)	18:03 (1)	20:38 (1)	21:04 (1)	22:26
Arr. Bucharest (Nord)	13:36	19:41	22:12	22:46	23:58

(1) Restaurant car. (2) Runs Monday-Friday, except holidays. Restaurant car. (3) Plus another Bucharest departure at 21:25.

INTERNATIONAL ROUTES
FROM ROMANIA

Bucharest is Romania's gateway for rail travel to Belgrade (and on to Yugoslavia's Adriatic cities), Budapest (and on to Western Europe), Kiev (and on to Moscow and Leningrad), and Sofia (and on to Athens and Istanbul).

Bucharest - Belgrade   1365

This train requires reservation and carries a sleeping car.

Dep. Bucharest (Nord)   21:05
Set your watch back one hour
Arr. Belgrade (Dunav)   09:23

Bucharest - Budapest   1600

All of these trains require reservation.

Dep. Bucharest (Nord)	06:00	21:35 (1)
Set your watch back one hour		
Arr. Budapest (Nyugati)	-0-	-0-
Arr. Budapest (Keleti)	18:02	09:52

(1) All-sleeping-car train.

Bucharest - Kiev - Moscow   94d

All of these trains carry only sleeping cars, unless designated otherwise.

Dep. Bucharest (Nord)	08:13
Arr. Ungeni	-0-
Arr. Vadu Siret	17:21

Ungeni and **Vadu Siret** are the Russian border stations where the wheels of the trains are changed to fit the wider Soviet rail gauge.

Dep. Ungeni	-0-
Dep. Vadu Siret	22:00
Arr. Kiev	14:42 (1)
Set your watch forward one hour	
Arr. Moscow (Kievski)	06:22

(1) Day 2.

Bucharest - Sofia - Istanbul   1550

This train runs Thursday only and carries only sleeping cars.

Dep. Bucharest (Baneasa)	12:55
Dep. Sofia	-0-
Arr. Istanbul	06:15

YUGOSLAVIA
(Serbia, Montenegro, and Kosova)

Getting on Track in Yugoslavia

• Tourist information: All overseas tourist offices were closed in 1991, but local offices still exist in Belgrade, Novi Sad and Podgorica.
• Public holidays: January 1, New Year's Day, January 2, Orthodox Christmas (early January), May 1, 2, Labor Day, May 9, Victory Day WWII, July 4, Veterans Day, November 29, 30, Republic Days.
• Summer time: Yugoslavia changes to Summer Time on the last Sunday of March and converts back to Standard Time on the last Sunday of September.
• Currency: Dinar. At press time, $1 equalled 5.71 dinar.

Technically, present-day Yugoslavia is the combined states of Serbia and Montenegro. Croatia, Macedonia, Slovenia, and Bosnia-Herzegovina are all independent countries and are treated separately.

Former Yugoslavia is the term referring to the whole nation prior to 1991. The war in the region has rendered daily life, let alone train travel, unpredictable. International train access to Belgrade is exclusively routed via Budapest, Subotica, and Novi Sad. The Meridian originates in Berlin and Sofia, the *Skopje-Istanbul* in Munich, and the Avala and *Beograd* in Vienna. Travel from Zagreb in Croatia to Belgrade in Serbia requires the circuitous route through Budapest, Hungary. Via Timisoara, the *Bucuresti* connects Bucharest and Belgrade. Other local trains connect western Romania and Yugoslavia. The *Istanbul Express* from Munich passes through Belgrade, as does the *Meridian* from Berlin to Sofia. Athens and Belgrade are linked via Skopje and Thessaloniki twice a day.

Internally, there is a very scenic route between Belgrade and the coastal town of Bar on which overnight sleeper cars are available. Inter Rail passes are honored in Yugoslavia, but Eurail passes are not. Belgrade is gray and uninspiring, was once a popular transit city in the summer months when northern European students would migrate to the beaches of the Greek islands. Today, Belgrade, aside from being grim, is prohibitively expensive. Some travelers courageous enough to make this leg of the trip spend the day in Belgrade and book a sleeper bunk on the night train out. Most have decided not to include Yugoslavia this year.

Montenegro is seated north of Albania in the southwest corner of the country. Aside from the Adriatic city of Bar, Montenegro hosts a bucolic rail line between Podorica and Kolasin. The 100-mile Tara Canyon is located beyond Kolasin. Montenegro is highly isolated now in times of war and only the port of Bar seems like a unique contact with the outside world. Budva is the best beach in the region.

Montenegro hosts a surprising variety of natural beauty. It is difficult not to be amazed by the stunning changes that occur at frequent intervals in the landscape. Hence the fantastic and inspired descriptions of Montenegro. Nature is harsh and gentle. The region hosts some of the deepest canyons in the world.

KOSOVA

Kosova, also known as Kosovo, is the region disputed over by its Albanian majority and Serbia. The Serbian government has imposed a police state in Kosova by stripping away its autonomy, closing Albanian-language schools, dismissing Albanians from their jobs, suspending Kosova's legal parliament and government—the systematic oppression and flagrant violations of basic rights of Albanians in Kosova. The 90 percent Albanian majority of Kosova have held free elections in which they have chosen their leadership, expressed their determination for the independence of Kosova in the 1992 referendum, and declared the independence of Kosova, first from Serbia, then from the Yugoslav federation. The Albanian leadership has declared that it will seek a peaceful resolution of the problem of Kosova. Prishtina is the capital of Kosova.

BOSNIA-HERZEGOVINA

The Department of State warns U.S. citizens not to travel to the Republic of Bosnia-Herzegovina because of ongoing tensions. Instability around Sarajevo severely restricts the American embassy's ability to assist U.S. citizens, even in emergencies.

The Republic of Bosnia and Herzegovina, formerly one of the Yugoslav republics, continues to be in a tortured state of war. The resulting deaths, destruction, food shortages, and travel disruptions affecting roads, airports and railways, make travel to all parts of Bosnia and Herzegovina extremely hazardous. The popular religious shrine at Medjugorje is located within Bosnia and Herzegovina's borders, but tourism in the region is virtually nonexistent and the idea of travel here at this time in history is unthinkable.

Permission to enter Bosnia and Herzegovina is currently granted at the border on a case-by-case basis. Over 70 percent of Bosnia is under the control of Bosnian Serb military forces. General lawlessness and deteriorating economic conditions have brought an increase in crime, and adequate police response in the event of an emergency is doubtful. Anti-American sentiments run high in many parts of the country, particularly in Serb-dominated areas. Roadblocks manned by local militias are numerous. These militia groups frequently confiscate relief goods and trucks, and may otherwise behave unprofessionally. Sarajevo, the beautiful city of Oriental mosques which hosted the 1984 Winter Olympics, is now characterized by its main avenue, popularly called Sniper Alley.

SLOVENIA

This small country tucked in between northeastern Italy and southern Austria enjoys the geography of the Julian Alps and the north Adriatic. In 1990 Slovenia was the first to break away from communist Yugoslavia. That sense of freedom and independence is strongly felt in Slovenian cultural production—the nation offers excellent original music and a dynamic avant art scene called Neue Slowenische Kunst which not only runs an excellent Web site on the Internet but has issued its own passports to a virtual country that is wholly peaceful.

Slovenia, even today, makes for a pleasurable and surprisingly peaceful journey. Don't think of Slovenia as former Yugoslavia. Llubljana, the capital, is filled with interesting sites and activities. The most popular train routes into Slovenia are via Vienna and Salzburg to Jesenice and Llubljana. Routes from Munich and other German cities are functioning, and five trains a day run from Trieste to Llubljana. Slovenian-Croatian connections require a change of train mid-route, and via Croatia one can connect from Llubljana to Budapest.

Aside from Llubljana with its old town, Presernov Square, and triple bridge, side trips to the chic resort lake town of Bled is a must. Marshal Tito kept his summer house on a hill above this sparkling lake.

CROATIA

Before the war, the Croatian coast on the Adriatic attracted millions of tourists with its resort towns of Split and Dubrovnik. All that has changed. The islands off the coast, curiously, have not been disrupted by the war and are lovely and safe although desolate.

Zagreb, the capital and center of cultural life, remains bright and vibrant. There are overnight intercity trains from Munich to Zagreb via Salzburg and Ljubljana. Reservations southbound are required but only recommended northbound. From Vienna to Zagreb, there is the EuroCity *Croatia* daily. Three express trains run between Venice and Zagreb via Trieste and Ljublijana. The Simplon Express offers a connecting service from Geneva and Rome; Budapest-Zagreb connections are plentiful. Note though that there are no Serbian-Croatian train connections.

Zagreb - Ljubljana - Zargreb   1320

Dep. Zagreb	05:40	07:50 (1)	12:03 (2)	14:35	18:05
Arr. Ljubljana	08:00	10:00	15:05	16:55	20:30
		•	•	•	
Dep. Ljubljana	12:10	15:05	19:58 (2)	21:05	22:05
Arr. Zagreb	14:28	17:40	22:10	23:21	00:27

(1) Restaurant car. (2) Second class.

Sights in **Ljubljana**: Several walking tours are described in "Ljubljana City Guide," a book with maps that is sold at the bookstore at Titov Cesta, near the corner of Subiceva Ulica in the new city. All of the walks begin at the square called Presernov Trg, where the 17th-century Franciscan Church of the Anunciation is located.

See the triple bridge that crosses Ljubljana River (two for pedestrians, one for vehicles). Ascend a hill to reach the castle for a view of the city from it.

There is free sampling of hundreds of different Yugoslav wines at the Autumn Wine Fair.

SCENIC RAIL TRIPS

Belgrade - Priboj - Bar   and v.v. 1370

This is the most scenic rail route in Yugoslavia. Steep canyons, turbulent rivers and mountains. The world's highest railway span, completed in 1976, is the 495-foot-high Mala Rijeka Bridge on this route.

The 325-mile line has 254 tunnels and 234 concrete and steel bridges. The trip climbs from the Danube to heights of 4,000 feet before descending to sea level on the Adriatic coast. The line from Priboj to Bar is narrow-gauge as the train descends to the valley of the **Rzav River**.

Dep. Belgrade	03:00	10:10 (1)	14:10 (2)	22:10	22:40 (3)
Dep. Priboj	08:20	14:30	18:09	02:38	02:59
Arr. Bar	15:55	18:53	22:02	06:50	07:14

* * *

Dep. Bar	10:05 (3)	14:10 (4)	19:40	22:05 (3)
Dep. Priboj	14:07	18:00	23:44	02:10
Arr. Belgrade	18:45	22:07	04:45	07:03

(1) Light refreshments. (2) Reservation required. First class only. Restaurant car. (3) Carries a sleeping car. Also has couchettes. Light refreshments.

Ljubljana - Postojna - Ljubljana   1300

The longest and most beautiful river cave of Europe is near **Postojna**, where the **Pivka River** flows through an underground passage.

Tourists, traveling through the cave on a small train, are able to see wonderful rows of stalactites and stalagmites, gigantic underground rooms, chasms and little lakes. A 16th-century castle is at the entrance to the cave. Conducted tours are offered daily, every half-hour. June 1–September 1, from 08:30–16:00, plus 17:00 and 18:00. September 2 to May 31, from 09:30–13:30.

Because the cave is not deep, visitors can go a long distance through it. It extends 19 miles! A narrow-gauge railway takes passengers more than one mile into the cave. Its terminal (Postojna Station) is larger than New York's Grand Central. English-speaking guides conduct tourists from it on a 1½-mile figure-eight walk. Great Mountain Room is more than 900-feet-high.

Dep. Ljubljana	Frequent times from 03:20 to 23:50
Arr. Postojna	55-65 minutes later

* * *

Dep. Postojna	Frequent times from 02:27 to 23:35
Arr. Ljubljana	55–65 minutes later

Ljubljana - Jesenice - Sezana - Ljublana   1300, 1305, 1320

We show the long scenic route for a daylight ride to Sezana and then the shorter route for returning to Ljubljana from Sezana at the end of the day.

1320

Dep. Ljubljana	10:03 (1)	15:31 (3)
Dep. Kranj	-0-	16:04
Dep. Lesce-Bled	10:43	16:30
Arr. Jesenice	10:56	16:47
Change trains 1305		
Dep. Jesenice	11:27 (2)	16:55 (3)
Arr. Nova Gorica	-0- (2)	18:43
Change trains 1305		
Dep. Nova Gorica	-0-	18:50 (3)
Arr. Sezana	14:17	19:47
Change trains 1300		
Dep. Sezana	19:21	01:40
Arr. Ljubljana	21:00	03:20

(1) Reservation required. Has first-class and second-class coaches. Restaurant car. (2) Direct train. No train change in Nova Gorica. (3) Second class.

INTERNATIONAL ROUTES FROM YUGOSLAVIA

There are rail connections from Belgrade to Athens (and on to Istanbul), Bucharest (and on to Kiev and Moscow), Budapest (and on to Moscow, Prague, Vienna and Warsaw), Salzburg (and on to the rest of Western Europe and to Scandinavia), Sofia (and on to Athens and Istanbul), and to Venice (and on to the rest of Italy and Southern Europe).

Belgrade - Athens   97

Dep. Belgrade	19:15 (1+2)
Set your watch forward one hour	
Arr. Athens (Larissa)	16:51

(1) Carries sleeping cars and couchettes. (2) Change trains in Thessaloniki for Athens.

Belgrade - Bucharest   1365

Dep. Belgrade (Dunav)	20:00 (1)
Set your watch forward one hour	
Arr. Timisoara (Nord)	01:59
Arr. Bucharest (Nord)	09:50

(1) Reservation required. Carries a sleeping car.

A stopover in **Timisoara** is worthwhile, to see the opulence of the Hapsburg rulers at the Dicasterial Palace. Also the Catholic and Serbian cathedrals and the Museum of Fine Arts on Piata Unirii, a picturesque square. See a show at Puppet Theater, on Piata Furtuna.

Belgrade - Budapest - Vienna   61

Dep. Belgrade	08:00 (1)	19:10 (2)
Arr. Budapest (Keleti)	15:25	02:13
Arr. Vienna (West)	18:30	05:30

(1) Restaurant car. (2) Carries a sleeping car. Also has couchettes.

Belgrade - Sofia   1380

Dep. Belgrade	05:20 (1)	10:00 (2)	22:00 (2+3)
Set your watch forward one hour			
Arr. Sofia	14:40	20:05	08:50

(1) Supplement payable. Restaurant car. (2) Supplement payable. (3) Has sleepers and couchettes.

EURAIL AND BRITISH ROUTE CHARTS

In view of the fact that there are over 100,000 miles of railroad lines in just the 17 Eurailpass countries, it would be impossible to list every conceivable trip one could make by train in Europe. We do provide you in this appendix a list of 734 trips that most people touring Europe might make, showing the travel time and one-way first-class fare for each. And for the first time, we have included sample fares for Britain to various cities in the U.K., from London.

The list of ticket prices enables our readers to (a) compute the cost of ordinary tickets for an itinerary and (b) compare that total cost with one or a combination of the train passes described in Eurail Guide.

We have condensed route descriptions by listing them only in alphabetical priority. For example, the first route is Alborg to Copenhagen. If you were looking for the trip from Copenhagen to Alborg, you would refer to the name that has alphabetical priority: Alborg. Similarly, the trip Rome-Paris will be found as Paris-Rome, etc.

The rates listed are first-class fares, in U.S. dollars. To compute second-class fares, figure 66 percent of the first-class fare shown. While this will not always be the exact second-class fare, it will be very close to it.

Also remember that European train fares, like the prices of all other European goods and services, are subject to change relative to the exchange rates for U.S. dollars and other non-European currencies.

On the other hand, once a Eurailpass, France Railpass, German Railpass, or any other train pass has been issued to you, you are protected from the devaluation of your currency increasing the cost of your train transportation — another hidden plus to having a pass.

All the fares listed in this chapter are subject to a seat reservation fee of $3 or more (U.S.) per person (if you want to be sure of having a seat). This is a charge whether traveling with a ticket or with Eurailpass. However, a Eurailpass holder does not have to pay this *supplement* when riding on some EuroCity or TGV trains (savings range from $3 to $8).

Keep in mind that on trips which involve both a Eurailpass country and also a country not covered by Eurailpass such as Vienna-Athens (via non-Euralpas Yugoslavia), the passenger holding a Eurailpass has to purchase a ticket for the non-Eurailpass portion of that trip.

Note: Because Paris and London have more than one rail station, we indicate in parenthesis the name of the Paris or London rail station at which a train is departing or arriving.

EURAIL GUIDE ROUTE CHART

1997 first-class train fares, *not* including seat reservation fee. Many thanks to the folks at Rail Europe for tracking down the really hard-to-find fares.

	Travel Time	Fare
ALBORG		
Copenhagen	6½	66.00
ALGECIRAS		
Cordoba	4½	38.00
Granada	5½	36.00
Madrid	11½	84.00
Malaga	5	34.00
Seville	6	43.00
ALICANTE		
Valencia	2	23.00
ALKMAAR		
Amsterdam	¾	15.00
AMSTERDAM		
Antwerp	2¼	47.00
Basel (via Roosendaal)	7¾	234.00
Berlin	7	175.00
Bremen	4	100.00
Brussels	3	57.00
Cologne (Koln)	3	78.00
Copenhagen (Kobenhavn)	11	242.00
Dusseldorf	2¼	65.00
Frankfurt	5	142.00
Hamburg	5	134.00
Hannover	4¼	104.00
Heidelberg	6½	147.00
Hoek Van Holland	1¼	31.00
Luxembourg (via Brussels)	6½	91.00
Milan	14¾	351.00
Munich (Munchen)	8¼	275.00
Paris (Nord)	4¾	121.00

Rome	20	452.00
Rotterdam	1	23.00
Salzburg	9¾	324.00
Utrecht	½	15.00
Vienna (Wien)		
(via Cologne)	13	337.00
Wiesbaden	6	124.00
Zurich	9	284.00

ANDALSNES

Oslo	6	119.00

ANDERMATT

Brig	2	55.00
Chur	2½	45.00
Luzern	2	55.00
Zurich	2	71 .00

ANTWERP

Brussels	¾	14.00
Paris (Nord)	2¾	94.00
Rotterdam	1¼	31.00

AOSTA

Milan	3½	35.00
Turin (Torino)	1¾	29.00

ARHUS

Copenhagen (Kobenhavn)	4¼	66.00

AROSA

Chur	1	21.00
Zurich	3	76.00

ASSISI

Florence (Firenze)	2½	32.00
Rome	2½	32.00

ATHENS

Patras	3¼	46.00
Thessaloniki	9	74.00

AVIGNON

Barcelona	6½	81.00
Cannes	3	64.00
Carcassonne	2½	54.00
Geneva	4½	85.00
Lourdes (via Toulouse)	5½	114.00
Lyon	2	54.00
Marseille	1	34.00
Nice	3½	68.00
Paris (Lyon)	3½	110.00
Port Bou	4	64.00

BADEN-BADEN

Basel	1½	57.00

BARCELONA

Bilboa	9½	77.00
Carcassonne	4½	68.00
Geneva	11	149.00
Genoa	13	171.00
Lourdes	9	121.00
Lyon	8½	135.00
Madrid	7	83.00
Marseille	8½	107.00
Nice	9½	134.00
Paris (Austerlitz)	12½	166.00
Rome	18½	237.00
Seville	12½	115.00
Toulouse (Via Port Bou)	7	73.00
Valencia	4	45.00
Vigo	18¼	118.00
Zaragoza	4½	47.00

BARI

Bologna	7½	76.00
Brindisi	1½	23.00
Messina	9	76.00
Milan	8	120.00
Naples	5	48.00
Pescara	3	45.00
Rome	4½	77.00

Taranto	1¾	23.00
Turin (Torino)	13	118.00
Venice	8½	107.00

BASEL

Bern	1¼	34.00
Brig	3	98.00
Brussels	6	110.00
Bucharest (Partly covered by Eurailpass)	29	353.00
Budapest	16	234.00
Cologne (Koln)	5	166.00
Copenhagen (Kobenhavn)	11½	389.00
Florence (Firenze)	9	171.00
Frankfurt	3	124.00
Geneva	3¾	105.00
Genoa	9	140.00
Hamburg	6½	274.00
Hannover	5½	224.00
Heidelberg	2½	73.00
Innsbruck	5	128.00
Interlaken	2¼	82.00
Lausanne	2½	87.00
Locarno	4½	110.00
Luxembourg	3½	70.00
Luzern	1	48.00
Milan	5½	127.00
Montreux	3	90.00
Paris (Est)	5¼	93.00
Rome (via Milan)	10½	216.00
Rotterdam (via Brussels)	8	136.00
Salzburg	9	152.00
Strasbourg	1½	36.00
Venice	8	161.00
Vienna (Wien)	10	228.00
Wiesbaden	3½	101.00
Zurich	1	55.00

BAYONNE

Madrid	6¾	98.00
Paris	5	122.00

BAYREUTH

Nurnberg	1	32.00

BERGEN

Bodo	26½	262.00
Flam	3½	42.00
Goteborg	12	192.00
Myrdal	2¼	43.00
Oslo	7	122.00
Trondheim	14	243.00
Voss	1¼	30.00

BERLIN

Bremen	4¾	128.00
Brussels	11	222.00
Cologne (Koln)	5¾	186.00
Copenhagen (Kobenhavn)	8	164.00
Dusseldorf	5	167.00
Frankfurt/Main (via Erfurt)	5	192.00
Hamburg	3¾	89.00
Hannover	2¾	100.00
Leipzig	2	52.00
Luxembourg	8½	278.00
Malmo	8¾	195.00
Munich (Munchen) (via Leipzig)	7½	198.00
Nurnburg	5½	141.00
Oslo	17¼	325.00
Paris (Nord)	13	270.00
Rotterdam	7½	180.00
Stockholm	15	303.00
Vienna (Wien) (Sudbf.) via Prague	10	157.00

BERN

Brig	1¾	70.00
Geneva	1¾	76.00
Interlaken	1	39.00
Lausanne	1	48.00
Lugano	5½	123.00
Luzern	1¼	50.00
Milan	4	97.00
Montreux	1¼	65.00

Paris (Lyon) via Verrieres	4½	135.00
Zurich	1½	74.00

BILBAO

Hendaye	4	36.00
Madrid	6½	66.00
Vigo	14½	89.00
Zaragoza	4½	61.00

BODEN

Haparanda (Bus)	2	54.00
Narvik (2nd class)	7	87.00
Stockholm	13½	180.00

BODO

Goteborg	24½	275.00
Oslo	19	264.00
Trondheim	10	195.00

BOLOGNA

Florence (Firenze)	1	19.00
Genoa	3	45.00
Innsbruck	5¾	72.00
Milan	1¾	35.00
Naples	5¼	89.00
Paris (Lyon)	10	205.00
Ravenna	1½	11.00
Rimini	1¾	23.00
Rome	3	64.00
Turin (Torino)	4½	51.00
Venice	2¼	29.00
Verona	1½	23.00

BONN

Cologne (Koln)	½	15.00
Frankfurt (Main)	2	59.00
Koblenz	½	23.00

BORDEAUX

Geneva	10	201.00
Hendaye	2½	52.00
Lourdes	3½	58.00

Lyon	8	168.00
Marseille	6¼	111.00
Nice	8	137.00
Paris (Austerlitz)	3	117.00
Toulouse	2	56.00
Tours	3	77.00

BREMEN

Budapest	19½	341.00
Cologne (Koln)	3	102.00
Copenhagen (Kobenhavn)	6	154.00
Dusseldorf	2	90.00
Essen	2¼	79.00
Frankfurt/Main	3¼	169.00
Hamburg	1	39.00
Hannover	1	47.00
Heidelberg	5½	182.00
Munich (Munchen)	7	252.00
Stuttgart	5	223.00
Vienna (Wien)	13	312.00

BRIG

Chur	4	107.00
Interlaken	2½	59.00
Lausanne	2	66.00
Zermatt	1¼	54.00

BRUGGE

Brussels	1	24.00

BRUSSELS

Budapest	16¾	362.00
Calais	4½	53.00
Cologne (Koln)	2¾	55.00
Copenhagen (Kobenhavn)	13½	292.00
Frankfurt	5¾	119.00
Ghent	½	26.00
Hamburg	8	184.00
Liege	1	24.00
Luxembourg	3	46.00
Munich (Munchen)	8½	254.00
Paris (Nord)	2	103.00

Rotterdam	2	40.00
Vienna (Wien) (via Nurnberg)	13½	365.00
Zurich	13	160.00

BUCHS

Innsbruck	2¼	46.00
Zurich	1¼	59.00

BUDAPEST

Cologne (Koln)	13½	358.00
Frankfurt/Main	11	243.00
Hamburg	12¼	390.00
Milan	13¾	201.00
Munich (Munchen)	8	159.00
Paris (Est)		
via Munich	20	365.00
via Basel	25	325.00
Prague	9¼	108.00
Rome	21	238.00
Sofia	16½	123.00
Trieste	16	132.00
Venice	16	155.00
Vienna (Wien)	3	62.00
Zurich	18½	210.00

CADIZ

Madrid	6	136.00
Seville	1¾	37.00

CALAIS

Paris (Nord)	1½	83.00
Strasbourg	9½	104.00

CANNES

Florence	8	73.00
Geneva	8½	132.00
Genoa	3¾	52.00
Lille	7	185.00
Lyon	5	122.00
Marseille	2	49.00
Milan	5¾	60.00

Paris (Lyon)	7	134.00
Rome	9½	103.00
San Remo	3½	23.00

CARCASSONNE
Lourdes	3	86.00
Marseille	3¼	98.00
Nice	6	97.00
Paris (Austerlitz)	7	195.00
Port Bou	2½	63.00
Toulouse	1	59.00

CHAMONIX-MONT BLANC
Geneva	2¾	38.00
Grenoble	2¼	53.00
Martigny	1½	33.00
Paris (Lyon)	7½	112.00

CHARTRES
Paris (Montparnasse)	1¼	31.00

CHERBOURG
Paris (St. Lazare)	3½	69.00

CHUR
St. Moritz	2	59.00
Zurich	1¼	63.00

COLOGNE (KOLN)
Copenhagen (Kobenhavn)	10½	245.00
Dortmund	1¼	39.00
Dusseldorf	½	18.00
Essen	1	29.00
Frankfurt	2	69.00
Hamburg	4	137.00
Hannover	3	93.00
Koblenz	1	32.00
Luxembourg (Via Koblenz)	3¼	70.00
Luzern	6½	214.00
Mainz	2	53.00
Mannheim	2½	88.00
Milan	10½	280.00

Munich (Munchen)	5½	199.00
Paris (Nord)	5	103.00
Rotterdam	3¼	81.00
Salzburg	7	240.00
Stuttgart	3¼	137.00
Vienna (Wien)	10	259.00
Wiesbaden	2	50.00
Zurich	6	218.00

COIMBRA

Lisbon	2½	35.00

COMO

Lugano	¾	19.00
Luzern	4	91.00
Milan	1	12.00
Venice	4	48.00
Zurich	5	100.00

COPENHAGEN (KOBENHAVN)

Frankfurt	11	280.00
Fredrickshavn	6	105.00
Hamburg (via Puttgarden)	5	115.00
Helsinki (Partly by Ship)	23¾	212.00
Hoek Van Holland	12	207.00
Kristiansand (Ship)	15½	(est.) 280.00
Luxembourg (via Koln)	13½	296.00
Malmo (Hydrofoil)	½	31.00
(Not covered by Eurailpass)		
Milan	20	468.00
Munich (Munchen) (via Berlin)	20	521.00
Narvik	33	217.00
Odense	2½	45.00
Oslo	9¼	161.00
Paris (Nord)	17½	340.00
Rome	22	531.00
Rotterdam	12	265.00
Stockholm (via Hassleholm)	7	139.00
Trondheim (via Goteborg)	19	266.00
Venice	22	439.00
Vienna (Wien)	18	321.00
Wiesbaden	9½	286.00

CORDOBA

Granada	4½	32.00
Madrid	1¾	54.00
Malaga	2½	31.00
Seville	¾	22.00

DAVOS

St. Moritz	1½	44.00
Zurich	3	82.00

DIJON

Lausanne	22½	63.00
Lyon	1¾	35.00
Paris	1¾	74.00
Strasbourg (via Belfort)	4½	71.00

DORTMUND

Paris (Nord)	6¼	132.00

DUSSELDORF

Essen	½	16.00
Frankfurt/Main	2½	80.00
Hamburg	3½	126.00
Hannover	3¼	86.00
Munich (Munchen)	5¼	197.00
Paris (Nord)	6	111.00

FLAM

Myrdal (2nd class fare)	1	19.00
Oslo	6½	101.00

FLORENCE (FIRENZE)

Geneva	8	158.00
Genoa	3½	39.00
Innsbruck	8	76.00
Lausanne	6¾	143.00
Livorno	1¼	23.00
Luzern	7½	142.00
Marseille	10¾	119.00
Milan	3	48.00
Munich (Munchen)	9	120.00
Naples	4	77.00

Nice	8	66.00
Paris		
(Lyon) via Iselle	15	218.00
(Lyon) via Pisa	18	179.00
(Lyon) via Turin (Torino)	18	172.00
Perugia	2	29.00
Pisa	1¼	18.00
Ravenna	3	18.00
Rome	2	48.00
Siena	1½	19.00
Turin (Torino)	5	77.00
Venice	3	42.00
Vienna (Wien)	11	139.00

FRANKFURT/MAIN

Hamburg	3¼	181.00
Hannover	2½	138.00
Heidelberg	1	43.00
Innsbruck	5¼	196.00
Luxembourg	3½	86.00
Mainz	½	16.00
Mannheim	1	41.00
Nurnberg	2½	73.00
Paris (Est)	6¼	141.00
Rotterdam	5¼	150.00
Salzburg	6	181.00
Stuttgart	1½	86.00
Vienna (Wien)	7¼	197.00
Wiesbaden	½	12.00
Zurich	4	157.00

FREDRICKSHAVN

Hamburg	7½	174.00
Oslo (Ship) (Not covered by Eurailpass)	9	(est.) 150.00
Stockholm (Ship) (Not covered by Eurailpass)	7½	(est.) 150.00

GARMISCH-PARTENKIRCHEN

Innsbruck	1¼	24.00
Munich (Munchen)	1½	35.00

GAVLE

Stockholm	2	40.00

GENEVA

Genoa		
via Milan	5½	143.00
via Turin (Torino)	7	72.00
Grenoble	2	51.00
Grindelwald	4½	114.00
Gstaad	2½	79.00
Interlaken (via Bern)	3½	96.00
Lausanne	½	39.00
Locarno	4½	124.00
Lourdes	10¼	185.00
Luzern	2¾	126.00
Lyon	2	44.00
Marseille (via Lyon)	6	91.00
Milan	4	114.00
Montreux	1	49.00
Nice (via Lyon)	8	117.00
Paris (Lyon)	3½	132.00
Rome	10	189.00
Turin (Torino)	6	108.00
Venice	7½	182.00
Zurich	3	115.00

GENOA

Lausanne	5¼	124.00
Luzern	5¾	126.00
Marseille	6	90.00
Milan	1½	29.00
Monaco-Monte Carlo	3	34.00
Munich (Munchen)	9	164.00
Naples	7¼	112.00
Nice	3¼	37.00
Paris (Lyon) (via Torino)	8½	188.00
Pisa	2	29.00
Rome	5¼	77.00
Salzburg	14	113.00
San Remo	2	26.00
Turin (Torino)	2	29.00
Venice	7½	58.00

GOTEBORG

Copenhagen (Kobenhavn)	5	75.00
Hamburg	10	190.00
Helsingborg	3	59.00
Kalmar	4½	112.00
Oslo	5	94.00
Stockholm	4½	103.00
Trondheim	21	174.00

GRANADA

Madrid	5½	57.00
Malaga	3½	26.00
Seville	4	36.00
Valencia	9½	126.00

GRAZ

Vienna (Wien)	2½	53.00

GRENOBLE

Lyon	1½	34.00
Marseille	3¼	69.00

GRINDELWALD

Interlaken (Not covered by Eurailpass)	1	18.00
Zurich (Only partially covered by Eurailpass)	3½	103.00

HAMBURG

Hannover	1¼	66.00
Heidelberg	6¼	201.00
Helsinki (Partly by Ship)	33	243.00
Luxembourg	8¼	220.00
Munich (Munchen)	6	253.00
Oslo	15	259.00
Paris (Nord)	9	232.00
Rotterdam	6	157.00
Salzburg	7½	302.00
Stockholm	12	254.00
Stuttgart	5	229.00
Vienna (Wien)	9¼	328.00

HANNOVER
Munich (Munchen)	4½	205.00
Paris (Nord)	8½	189.00
Rotterdam	5	103.00
Wurzburg	2	189.00

HAPARANDA
Helsinki	12	140.00

HEIDELBERG
Koblenz	2	58.00
Luzern	3½	121.00
Mainz	1	32.00
Munich (Munchen)	3	107.00
Nurnberg	4	100.00
Paris (Est)	6	126.00
Rothenburg ("Castle Road" Bus)	3	105.00
Stuttgart	1	38.00
Wiesbaden	1½	29.00

HELSINKI
Kuopio (Day)	4½	97.00
(Night)	6½	97:00
Oslo (Partly by Ship)	21	211.00
Oulu (Day)	5	126.00
(Night)	10½	126.00
Stockholm (Ship)	12½	73.00
Turku	2	49.00

HENDAYE
Lisbon	17	101.00
Lourdes	2½	46.00
Madrid	8	74.00
Paris (Austerlitz)	5½	139.00
Zaragoza	4¼	36.00

HOEK VAN HOLLAND
Innsbruck	13	293.00
Munich (Munchen)	12	250.00
Rotterdam	½	13.00

INNSBRUCK

Kitzbuhel	1	31.00
Luzern	4½	139.00
Milan	5½	70.00
Munich (Munchen)	2	55.00
Paris (Est)	10¼	243.00
Rome	8½	119.00
Salzburg	2	60.00
Venice	6	63.00
Verona	3½	56.00
Vienna (Wien)	5¼	99.00
Zurich	3¾	100.00

INTERLAKEN

Lausanne	2	87.00
Luzern	2	38.00
Milan	4	87.00
Montreux	3¾	79.00
Paris (Lyon) via Verrieres	6	153.00
Zurich	3	90.00

KARLSTAD

Oslo	3	64.00
Stockholm	3½	76.00

KLAGENFURT

Salzburg	3½	80.00
Venice	4½	76.00
Vienna (Wein)	4½	100.00

KLOSTERS

Zurich	2½	76.00

KOBLENZ

Luxembourg	2	48.00
Munich (Munchen)	5	175.00
Paris (via Reims)	5¾	127.00
Vienna (Wien)	9	234.00
Wiesbaden	1	26.00

KONSTANZ

Zurich (via Berg)	1¼	58.00
(via Romashorn-Schaffhausen)	1¼	54.00

KRISTIANSAND

Oslo	5	122.00
Stavanger	3	87.00

LAUSANNE

Locarno	4	106.00
Lugano	5¼	121.00
Luzern	2¼	98.00
Milan	3¾	95.00
Montreux	½	17.00
Paris (Lyon)	4	115.00
Rome	8¾	184.00
Venice	6¾	137.00
Zurich	2½	96.00

LE HAVRE

Paris (St. Lazare)	2	49.00

LIEGE

Luxembourg	1½	34.00
Paris (Nord)	3¼	67.00

LINZ

Salzburg	1¼	38.00
Vienna (Wien)	2¾	48.00

LISBON

Madrid (Atocha)	10½	73.00
Paris (Austerlitz)	19¼	228.00
Porto	3	33.00
Santiago de Compostela	18	155.00
Seville	13½	153.00
Vigo	9	42.00

LIVORNO

Pisa	¼	8.00
Rome	3½	48.00

LOCARNO

Lugano	1	28.00
Luzern	3	84.00
Milan	1	42.00
Zurich	3½	89.00

LOURDES

Madrid	14	112.00
Paris (Austerlitz)	5½	131.00
Toulouse	2	42.00

LUGANO

Luzern	3	83.00
Milan	1½	26.00
Venice	5¼	50.00
Zurich	3	90.00

LUXEMBOURG

Marseille	10	138.00
Metz	1	22.00
Munich (Munchen)	7	224.00
Nurnberg	6	159.00
Paris (Est)	4	78.00
Salzburg (via Strasbourg)	8½	273.00
Strasbourg	2	50.00
Stuttgart (via Strasbourg)	3¾	113.00
Vienna (Wien)	11	283.00
Zurich	4½	125.00

LUZERN

Milan	4¼	97.00
Montreux	2½	115.00
Munich (Munchen)	6	145.00
Paris (Est)	6½	136.00
Rigi (rail/via Arth-Goldau)	1½	73.00
Rigi Kulm (boat/via Witznau)	1½	80.00
Rome	9¾	179.00
Venice	7½	132.00
Vienna (Wein)	9¾	212.00
Zurich	1	39.00

LYON

Marseille	3	73.00
Milan	5½	83.00
Nice	6	99.00
Paris (Lyon)	2	101.00
Strasbourg	5¼	86.00
Turin (Torino)	4	64.00
Tours	5	112.00

MADRID

Malaga	4½	69.00
Pamplona	5	59.00
Paris (Austerlitz)	13	201.00
Port Bou	10	90.00
Rome	29½	320.00
San Sebastian	6½	73.00
Santiago de Compostela	7½	82.00
Seville	3	80.00
Toledo	1¼	14.00
Valencia	4	69.00
Vigo	8	71.00
Zaragoza	3	45.00

MAINZ

Munich (Munchen)	4	151.00
Paris	6¾	161.00

MALAGA

Seville	3	32.00

MALMO

Stockholm	6¾	126.00

MARSEILLE

Milan	7½	106.00
Nice	2¾	53.00
Paris (Lyon)	4¼	114.00
Port Bou	4½	72.00
Rome	11¾	156.00
Toulouse	4	81.00
Venice	12¾	144.00

MILAN
Montreux	4	86.00
Munich (Munchen)	7½	114.00
Naples	7	114.00
Nice	5	53.00
Padua	2½	55.00
Paris (Est) via Chiasso	9	212.00
Paris (Lyon) via Vallorbe	8	170.00
Rome	5	89.00
Stuttgart	8	171.00
Turin (Torino)	2	29.00
Trieste	5	64.00
Venice	3	42.00
Verona	1½	40.00
Vienna	10¾	139.00
Zurich	4½	107.00

MONTREUX
Paris (Lyon)	4¾	127.00
Zurich	3	103.00

MOSJOEN
Oslo	14	220.00

MUNICH (MUNCHEN)
Nurnberg	2	73.00
Oberammergau	2	47.00
Paris (Est)	8¾	210.00
Rome	11	163.00
Rotterdam	10½	280.00
Salzburg	1½	49.00
Stuttgart	2	73.00
Venice (via Innsbruck)	7	104.00
Vienna (Wien)	5	111.00
Wiesbaden	4	139.00
Zurich	4¼	123.00

MYRDAL
Oslo	5	91.00

NANCY
Paris (Est)	3	67.00

NAPLES

Nice	11	138.00
Paris (Lyon)		
via Rome-Florence	20¼	281.00
via Rome-Pisa	16¾	306.00
Reggio Calabria	5	98.00
Rome	2	35.00
Taranto	4½	68.00
Turin (Torino)	9	130.00
Venice	8½	107.00
Vienna (Wien)	18¼	180.00

NARVIK

Oslo	25	364.00
Stockholm	22	180.00

NICE

Paris (Lyon)	6½	137.00
Rome (via Pisa)	9	103.00
Turin (Torino)	3½	50.00
Venice	10	91.00

OSLO

Stavanger	8½	178.00
Stockholm	6	138.00
Trondheim	7	121.00
Voss	5½	103.00

PALERMO

Paris (Lyon)	32	268.00
Rome	11	126.00

PARIS

Port Bou (Austerlitz)	10₂	150.00
Reims (Est)	1½	40.00
Rome (Lyon) via Pisa	14	229.00
Rouen (St. Laz.)	1¼	36.00
Salzburg (Est)		
(via Munich)	10	225.00
San Sebastian (Austerlitz)	6½	129.00
Stockholm (Nord)	22	479.00

Strasbourg (Est)	4	86.00
Stuttgart (Est)	6	142.00
Toulouse (Austerlitz)	7	127.00
Tours (Aust.)	1	66.00
Trieste (Lyon)	12	264.00
Turin (Torino) - (Lyon)	6½	145.00
Venice (Lyon) via Vallorbe	12½	235.00
Vienna (Wein) - (Est)	13½	317.00
Zurich (Est)	6	142.00

PERUGIA

Rome	3	35.00

PISA

Rome	3¼	51.00
Siena	1½	23.00

PRAGUE

Rome	17	264.00
Vienna (Wein)	5	72.00
Warsaw	10½	83.00

RATTVIK

Stockholm	3	91.00

RAVENNA

Rimini	1	12.00
Venice	3	32.00

RIMINI

Venice	2¾	42.00

ROME

Siena	3¼	42.00
Trieste	7	101.00
Turin (Torino)	7	95.00
Venice	5	83.00
Vienna (Wien)	13	182.00
Zurich	8¼	188.00

ROTTERDAM
    Vienna (Wein)   19   309.00

SALZBURG
    Trieste   7½   57.00
    Venice   7   83.00
    Vienna (Wien)   3¼   67.00
    Villach   3   48.00
    Zurich   6½   138.00

STOCKHOLM
    Trondheim   13   259.00
    Turku (ship; one class)   12½   59.00
    Uppsala   1   23.00

STUTTGART
    Vienna (Wien)   7¾   179.00
    Zurich   3   85.00

TRIESTE
    Venice   2   29.00
    Vienna (Wien)   8½   104.00

TURIN (Torino)
    Venice   4½   64.00

VENICE
    Verona   1½   33.00
    Vienna (Wien)   9   110.00
    Zurich   8   202.00

VIENNA (WIEN)
    Zurich   9   173.00

BRITAIN ROUTE CHART

All of the following trips are based out of London. Departure stations are in parenthesis. Average travel times are followed by the first-class one-way fare.

ABERDEEN (King's Cross)	5¾	179.00
BATH (Paddington)	1¼	68.00
BIRMINGHAM (Euston/Paddington)	1¾	65.00
BRISTOL (Paddington)	1½	68.00
CARDIF (Paddington)	1¾	87.00
CARLISLE (Euston)	3¾	157.00
CHESTER (Euston)	2¾	96.00
DUNDEE (King's Cross)	6	164.00
EDINBURGH (King's Cross)	4	161.00
EXETER (Paddington)	2	95.00
GLASGOW (King's Cross/Euston)	5	161.00
INVERNESS (King's Cross)	8	179.00
LEEDS (King's Cross)	2¼	120
LIVERPOOL (Euston)	2¼	96.00
MANCHESTER (Euston)	2½	96.00
NEWCASTLE (King's Cross)	3	157.00
PENZANCE (Paddington)	5	123.00
PLYMOUTH (Paddington)	2¾	110.00
YORK (King's Cross)	2	120.00
GATWICK AIRPORT (Via Gatwick Exp.) (Victoria)	½	23.00

CYBERSPACE GUIDE TO RAIL TRAVEL

If you love to surf the Web, but don't have time to track down all the cool rail sites out there, look no further then these pages. Besides sites geared to rail travel, we've included locations to help you plan your trip, from the huge Expedia site to the State Department's travel advisory list. If a site is in a language other than English, we've noted it.

As with the schedules in this guide, the Web sites are subject to change, so don't be too upset if you go to a site and find that it has disappeared into the depths of cyberspace. More often than not, though, a forwarding address will be given. We've also found that not all Internet providers are created equal. Your pal down the block may log on with ease to a particular site, using a local provider, while you have no luck whatsoever getting where you want to go on say, America Online (AOL) or Prodigy. And of course those mega-providers like AOL or Compuserve often have their own special travel sites that are off-limits to non-subscribers.

Virtually every site listed here has links to other rail-oriented sites.

Enjoy the ride!

General Rail Sites Europe and the World

http://www.raileurope.com   Rail Europe is the grand-daddy of rail pass providers. From train schedules and fares to hotel, airline and car rental information, this site is one-stop shopping for European travel.

http://www.dertravel.com/   DER Travel Services is the other major player in the world of rail passes, after Rail Europe. Check out DER's latest deals.

http://www.eurostar.com   Plan your Eurostar trip through the Channel Tunnel with this site's timetables and fares. Also look for special fares and the latest Eurostar news.

http://www.visitbritain.com/external_links.asp?url=www.eurostar.com/eurostar
This site is linked to the British Tourist Authority's site and provides the latest information about Eurostar services.

http://www.thalys.com   Timetables, fares and information on the high speed rail system between Paris, Brussels and Amsterdam.

http://www.le-shuttle.com/car/lesuk/uk_frame.htm Official site of Le Shuttle, the car-carrying trains that run through the Channel Tunnel.

http://mercurio.iet.unipi.it/eurostar/LeShuttle.html Unofficial site of Le Shuttle, the car-carrying trains that run through the Channel Tunnel.

http://mercurio.iet.unipi.it/ Site of the European Railway Server, you can check out the latest official European railway sites, plus many sites developed by railway enthusiasts. Also good links to sites outside Europe.

http://metro.jussieu.fr:10001/english/info.html Roam the subways of major cities, worldwide.

http://www.membrane.com/~elmer/ Developed by an individual; this interesting site covers rail, air and sea topics.

http://bjr.acf.nyu.edu/railinfo/railinfo.html All sorts of rail links here, plus information about rail publications, books. Good info on New York's subway.

http://tucson.com/concor/ Explore the world's railways from this site.

http://www.mcs.net/~dsdawdy/cyberoad.html This huge site will connect you to some 1,300 other rail oriented sites all over the world

http://ds.dial.pipex.com/historian/lits.htm If you have an interest in the famous European blue sleeping cars that belong to Wagons-Lits, roll on over to the Wagons-Lits Society home page. Good links to other European rail sites. Sometimes this site disappears then resurfaces again. Just in case that happens and you can't connect, here's the Society's address: c/o Rob Heron, Secretary and Treasurer, 1 Morton Road, Great Totham, Essex CM9 8QB, Great Britain.

http://www.orient-expresstrains.com/ Check out the latest Orient Express itineraries, from the British Pullman, Venice-Simplon to the Eastern & Oriental, and more.

http://ds.dial.pipex.com/town/avenue/zh62/internat.htm If you're interested in learning where working steam trains are, head to this extensive site. Lots of pictures and other contacts. Includes news from around the world, from Cuba and China to Vietnam.

Country Rail Sites Around Europe and the World

Australia
http://www.railpage.org.au/   This is an unofficial site maintained by an individual. Lots of good info about riding Australia's rails.

http://www.aussie.net.au/pl/atc   A catchall site leading to rail information for Australia.

Belgium
http://www.win.tue.nl/cs/fm/laan/nmbs/index.html The official site for Belgium's railway.

Canada
http://www.viarail.ca/   VIA Rail Canada's official site. Describes all onboard accommodations and fares. Make reservations, too.

http://www.bcrail.com/bcr/   British Columbia's BC Rail official site.

http://www.rkymtnrail.com/   Rocky Mountaineer maintains an extensive listing of its trips around Western Canada; includes capsule descriptions, photos, schedules and fares.

China
http://severn.dmu.ac.uk/~mlp/news.html Good overview of what's going on in China rail-wise, from steam to diesel passenger trains.

Czech Republic
http://www.ms.mff.cuni.cz/acad/webik/~dzem0338/zeleznice/cdrahy.en.1.htm   Czech Railways official site. We've encountered some difficulty accessing this site through AOL, but had no problem with other providers. Get around this by going to the European Railway Server site, listed earlier.

Denmark
http://www.dsb.dk/   This official site for Denmark's railway has one drawback, it's completely in Danish.

Finland
http://www.vr.fi/   Finnish Railways official site. Lots of excellent info on riding Finland's trains.

France
http://www.sncf.fr/   Official site for SNCF, the French National Railway. Look for special train-travel deals here For instance, through September 1997, two people traveling together could buy a Paris-London round-trip ticket for about $165 second class or $250 first

class, if they stayed in Britain at least two nights. Also on the site: fares and schedules, good tips for riding the train, from advice for travelers in wheelchairs to traveling with kids and choosing accommodations on night trains.

http://www.ratp.fr/   Official site for RATP, the Paris transportation system of buses and metros. It's written in French, but you can get a good idea of what's going on; includes fares and special tickets.

Germany
http://www.bahn.de/   German Rail's official site is mostly in German. If you understand just a little German, you can get updates on fares and special tickets, as well as check schedules. If you have a specific question, you can send them an E-mail and they will get back to you either by E-mail or snail-mail.

http://rail.rz.uni-karlsruhe.de/rail/english.html   Unofficial site offering information about travel on German trains.

Greece
http://www.ose.gr/   Official site of Greek railway, lots of links to other sites, plus fares and schedules for Greek trains, including couchette and sleeper fares. There is even a section with details about scenic trips. E-mail address: ose1@ose.gr.

Hungary
http://mercurio.iet.unipi.it/list/hungary.html   This official site for Hungary's railway has been difficult to access at times through AOL.

India
http://people.clemson.edu/~nsankar/india/guide.to.india.html   Like Hungary above, this site, with information about traveling India's rails doesn't always open through AOL.

Indonesia
http://caddsys.iptek.net.id/~anto/railway.html   While this site detailing the railways of Indonesia is readily accessible through most Internet providers, once again, AOL doesn't always cooperate.

Ireland and Northern Ireland
http://www.clubi.ie/RailNet/   Official site of Iarnrod Éireann, the railway of the Republic of Ireland. Check schedules and all the latest special fares.

http://www.nics.gov.uk/transport/nir/nirctent.htm   This site will lead you to the Northern Ireland Railways pages.

Italy

http://www.fs-on-line.com The official site for FS, the Italian railway company. This fantastic site, unfortunately is mostly in Italian. It's pretty easy to figure out, though, using a little logic. Some titles are in English, like "Frequent Railers," "Italy Railcard," "Senior," etc. All current fares are listed, and you can plug in city pairs for schedules.

Netherlands

http://www.ns.nl/   Official site of Netherlands Railway. (Text in Dutch)

http://mercurio.iet.unipi.it/ns/ns.html A rail enthusiast developed this interesting site about Dutch trains.

New Zealand

http://www.waikato.ac.nz/nz/rail/timetable.html   Get all the latest information about traveling New Zealand by rail.

Norway

http://www.nsb.no/   This official site for Norway's railway is in Norwegian.

http://www.njk.no/~njk/museums/index_e.html This site, in English, put together by an individual, has links to all sorts of rail museums in Norway.

http://www.ifi.uio.no/~terjek/rail/travel/ Another unofficial site (in English). Very extensive, with lots of details about trips off the mainline, schedules, links to other Norwegian rail sites.

Poland

http://walden.mo.net/~jdobek/pkptrav.html   Rail enthusiast Jeff Dobek put together this extensive site about rail travel in Poland.

Portugal

http://www.cp.pt/   Official site for Portugal's rail system. Has prices, schedules and maps for a few lines, along with some sightseeing information.

South Africa

http://www.pix.za/iq/rovos   and   **http://www.mg.co.za/mg/classic/rovos.html**   See what this luxury South African tourist train, Rovos Rail, is all about.

Spain

http://www.renfe.es/renfe1/homglish.htm The official site of Spain's railway, RENFE, goes on for days. There are detailed explanations about every class of service offered, along with some sample fares. You can check schedules, too.

Sweden

http://www.sj.se/   This official site for Sweden's railway is in Swedish.

Switzerland
http://www.sbb.ch/ This excellent official site will make your trip around Switzerland a breeze; great links to private Swiss railways, too.

United Kingdom
http://www.britrail.com/us/ushome.htm Find the latest fares and pass information at BritRail Travel's site.

http://www.rail.co.uk/ Map out your train trips around Britain with these on-line schedules.

http://www.railtrack.co.uk/home.html Railtrack is the entity that oversees various facets of rail operations in Britain, since the demise of British Rail. See what Railtrack is up to these days. There's even a link where they'll help you find the best schedule to your destination. With all the new railways popping up in Britain since privatizing, rail travelers need all the help they can get!

http://www.gatwickexpress.co.uk Get on track to Gatwick Airport, with a visit to the Gatwick Express site.

http://www.uel.ac.uk/pers/1278/Rly-Pres/ Tourist railways of Britain, with links to sites around the world. Watch the automated train zipping across the screen!

http://www.aber.ac.uk/~rah94/talyllyn.html Take this site for a spin around British narrow-gauge railways.

http://www.londontransport.co.uk/ The official London Transport site. Everything you'll need for getting around on London's tube and bus routes. All the latest news, too, about London Transport activities.

www-mice.cs.ucl.ac.uk/misc/uk/london/tube/index.html More info on London's famous underground railway.

http://www.dlr.co.uk/ Learn about the latest happenings and special fare deals on the Docklands Light Railway.

United States
http://www.amtrak.com/ This comprehensive Amtrak site has all the tools for planning a trip around the U.S., and now you can even make reservations online for most destinations.

http://www.amtrak.com:80/amtrak/travel/west/ Amtrak West have their own site. It has lots of great tips for sightseeing in this region. Map out your trip, check out the onboard accommodations, even see what's on the *Coast Starlight's* dining-car menu.

http://trainweb.com.crocon/amtrak.html If you're interested in keeping up with news about Amtrak, stop by the Friends of Amtrak site. It was developed by a schoolteacher in Conn., Craig O'Connell. Sign up for his regular E-mail updates. There's no charge.

http://www.globalinfo.com/noncomm/SDMRM/sdmrm.html Visit the San Diegp Railroad Museum in the city's Balboa Park.

http://www.ggrm.org/ Golden Gate Museum site, with links to other Bay Area transit information.

http://www.transitinfo.org/CalTrain/ Explore California's Bay Area with a trip to the Caltrain site.

General Travel Sites

http://www.stolaf.ed u/network/travel-advisories.html or **http://www.travel.state.gov/travel_warnings** Know before you go. The U.S. State Department's travel advisories warn you of hot spots around the world.

http://www.cdc.gov/travel/blusheet.htm Find out about health conditions around the world through the Centers for Disease Control and Prevention site.

http://www.ic.gov/94fact/fb94toc/fb94toc.html This is the site for the CIA World Factbook. It includes basic geographical, economic and political information on every country in the world.

http://www.forsyth.com/splash_forsyth.html Forsyth Travel Library's site has all the information you will need to plan your rail and other travel adventures. Check often as new information appears regularly.

http://www.lonelyplanet.com Those prolific folks at Lonely Planet have mini-versions of their guidebooks on-line. Click on the "destinations" map and you'll be whisked off to the latest news and sightseeing tips about this country or that. There are links to just about everywhere you could imagine.

http://www.expedia.com This mega-site will give you capsule descriptions of destinations around the world; includes overviews of transportation options.

http://www.campustravel.co.uk/ The UK-based Campus Travel has lots of good information for students on the go, including details about Inter Rail passes, Student Identity Cards, and GO 25 cards.

http://www.ciee.org/travel/index.htm Council Travel's site offers complete information about how to obtain student/faculty discount cards. You can even apply on-line.

http://www.istc.org/   Here's another site offering information about student travel cards.

http://www.hostels.com/   If you want to take the hostelling route, log on to *The Internet Guide to Hostelling.* You'll learn all about hostels and budget travel. There's also a huge database of hostels around the world.

http://www.visitbritain.com/   The British Tourist Authority's new site is better than ever.

http://www.paris.org   Everything you've ever wanted to know about Paris, and more. Read the online monthly newsletter for a keen insight into the soul of the City of Lights, written by expatriates living in the city. Good information about museums and getting around, although some of transit information was out of date the last time we looked.

http://www.franceguide.com   Explore the rest of France through Maison de la France's online guide. Lots of links to different regions.

http://www.thomascook.com   A good general travel site, has currency conversion, etc., but doesn't have much railway information.

http://www.disabled-travel.com   AccessAbility Travel gives tips and information for travelers with special traveling needs.

http://www.timeout.co.uk   The Web version of the popular magazine outlining sights and fun things to do in major cities around the world.

www.youra.com/intlferries.html Dan Youra put together this ferry guide listing web sites sponsored by several major ferry operators in Europe.

http://www.fsz.bme,hv/hungary/homepage.html   This site will take you to Hungary's home pages and a tour of the country.

INDEX OF CITIES, RESORTS
AND SCENIC PLACES